MW01235513

Measuring Information Technology Investment Payoff:
Contemporary Approaches

Mo Adam Mahmood
University of Texas, El Paso

Edward J. Szewczak
Canisius College

IDEA GROUP PUBLISHING
Hershey, USA • London, UK

Senior Editor: Mehdi Khosrowpour
Managing Editor: Jan Travers
Copy Editor: Terry Heffelfinger
Printed at: BookCrafters

Published in the United States of America by
        Idea Group Publishing
        1331 E. Chocolate Avenue
        Hershey PA 17033-1117
        Tel: 717-533-8845
        Fax: 717-533-8661
        E-mail: jtravers@idea-group.com
        Website: http://www.idea-group.com

and in the United Kingdom by
        Idea Group Publishing
        3 Henrietta Street
        Covent Garden
        London WC2E 8LU
        Tel: 171-240 0856
        Fax: 171-379 0609

Library of Congress Cataloging-in-Publication Data

Mahmood, Mo Adam.
        Measuring information technology investment payoff: contemporary
    approaches / Mo Adam Mahmood, Edward J. Szewczak
            p.   cm. -- (Series in information technology management)
        Includes bibliographical references and index.
        ISBN 1-878289-42-X
            1. Information technology--Economic aspects. 2. Capital Investments.
    I. Szewczak, Edward J. II. Title. III. Series.
HD30.2.M344 1998
656.15'2--dc21   98-42507
                                                                   CIP

British Cataloguing in Publication Data
A Cataloguing in Publication record for this book is available from the British Library.

IDEA GROUP PUBLISHING

Hershey, PA, USA • London, UK

Series in Information Technology Management

The surge in information technology during the latter part of the 20th century has forced organizations to meet its challenges with an increased use and management of information resources. This series takes an in-depth look at trends, current practices, and problem resolution in information technology management and offers you a first-class source for expanding the reader's knowledge in this ever-growing field.

Books in this series:

- **Information Systems Innovation and Diffusion: Issues and Directions (Tor J. Larsen and Eugene McGuire)**
- **The Virtual Workplace (Magid Igbaria and Margaret Tan)**
- **Information Systems Success Measurement (Edward Garrity and G. Lawrence Sanders)**
- **Cases on Information Technology Management in Modern Organizations (Jay Liebowitz and Mehdi Khosrowpour)**
- **Collaborative Technologies and Organizational Learning (R. Neilson)**
- **Information Systems Outsourcing Decision Making: A Managerial Approach (L.A. de Looff)**
- **Information Technology and Organizations: Challenges of New Technologies (Mehdi Khosrowpour)**
- **Management Impacts of Information Technology (Edward Szewczak)**
- **Managing Information Technology Investments with Outsourcing (Mehdi Khosrowpour)**
- **Business Process Change: Reengineering Concepts, Methods and Technologies (Varun Grover and William Kettinger)**
- **Reengineering MIS: Aligning Information Technology and Business Operations (Kevin Coleman, Jim Ettwein, Clelland Johnson, Dick Pigman and Deborah Pulak)**

For more information, or to submit a proposal for a book
in this series, please contact:
Idea Group Publishing
1331 E. Chocolate Avenue
Hershey, PA 17033-1117
Tel: 1/800-345-4332 or 717/533-8845
Fax: 717/533-8661
E-mail: jtravers@idea-group.com
Website: http://www.idea-group.com

Other IDEA GROUP Publishing Books

Measuring Information Technology Investment Payoff: Contemporary Approaches
Table of Contents

Information Technology Investment and Organizational Performance: New Perspectives from Information Systems Research and Practice

> Mo Adam Mahmood, University of Texas at El Paso
> Edward J. Szewczak, Canisius College

Introduction to Part I

> Mo Adam Mahmood, University of Texas at El Paso
> Edward J. Szewczak, Canisius College

An Integrative Research Approach to Assess the Business Value of Information Technology

> James D. McKeen & Heather A. Smith, Queen's University
> Michael Parent, University of Western Ontario

A Road Map For IS/IT Evaluation

> William Wehrs, University of Wisconsin at La Crosse

The Relationship Between Firms' Information Systems Policy and Business Performance: A Multivariate Analysis

> Niv Ahituv, Stan Lipovetsky, and Asher Tishler, Tel-Aviv University

Evaluating Information Technology Investment:
A Methodology for Managing Risk

       Kurt J. Engemann, Iona College
       Holmes E. Miller, Muhlenberg College

TECHNOLOGY INVESTMENT PAYOFF

Introduction to Part III

       Mo Adam Mahmood, University of Texas at El Paso
       Edward J. Szewczak, Canisius College

An Empirical Assessment of Financial EDI Value to
Corporate Adopters

       Marielle Bergeron, Université Laval
       Albert S. Dexter, University of British Columbia

A Framework for Assessing IT Investment in
Reengineering Initiatives: A Case Study

       Tim Tatum, Virginia Commonwealth University
       Peter Aiken, Virginia Commonwealth University and
                     Defense Information Systems Agency

Achieving Information Systems Value: A Case Study Analysis

       Jack D. Callon, San Jose State University

Measuring the Success of Implementing Multimedia
CBTs in Business

       Kathryn A. Marold, Metropolitan State College of Denver

Business Use of the Internet

       Elizabeth R. Towell, Northern Illinois University

Acknowledgments

We were gratified by responses we had received on our first book in the IT investment and organizational performance area. It was our pleasure working on a much–needed second book in the area. We thank the Idea Group Publishing for providing us with an opportunity to undertake this book project. We especially thank Mehdi Khosrowpour for his encouragement to start working on a second book in the area. We also appreciate Jan Travers' efforts in managing the project and making sure that it is printed on time.

Initially, we asked for proposals for chapters on measuring IT investment payoff from prospective authors through a Call for Papers that was mailed to everyone listed in the Directory of Management Information Systems (MIS) Faculty. We also published the Call for Papers in various MIS journals. We were impressed by the responses we had received from the authors in the area. Each initial proposal was sent to two reviewers who had expertise in the area. The reviewers were given a copy of the Call for Papers and guidelines for reviewing the chapter proposal. If a proposal received two REJECTs from the reviewers, the proposal was rejected outright. If a proposal received two ACCEPTs, the author(s) were invited to develop a full–blown manuscript using the guidelines provided by the editors and reviewers. If a proposal received one ACCEPT and one REJECT, one of the editors made the final decision as to whether the author(s) should be given an opportunity to develop a full–blown manuscript. Once the complete manuscript was received it was sent, if available, to the same two reviewers. If an original reviewer was not available, a substitute reviewer was used. The same procedure was followed in accepting or rejecting the full–blown manuscripts. In other words, if a manuscript received two ACCEPTs, it was accepted; if it received two REJECTs, it was rejected; and if it received one REJECT and one ACCEPT, it was left to an editor to decide as to whether the manuscript should be accepted or rejected. All accepted manuscripts underwent at least one revision to satisfy the editors' and reviewers' concerns. Some accepted manuscripts went through two revisions. The contributors were highly responsive to reviewers' and editors' suggestions in revising their manuscripts. The authors' willingness to work with the reviewers and editors contributed, in our opinion, to the high quality of their scholarship.

We also wish to acknowledge the contributions of the people who reviewed and critiqued the original proposals, full manuscripts, and revised manuscripts. Without their help, it would have been extremely difficult for us to bring the project to fruition.

We appreciated support provided for this project by the University of Texas at El Paso and Canisius College in New York. We especially thank Ellis and Susan Mayfield for endowing the professorship that bear their name that supported this book endeavor. Jo Willems also deserves our thanks. We valued her care and attention to details that brought this project to a smooth completion. Finally, we thank our families for being understanding and offering an environment at home that was instrumental in completing the book.

Introduction

Information Technology Investment and Organizational Performance: New Perspectives from Information Systems Research and Practice

Mo Adam Mahmood, University of Texas at El Paso
Edward J. Szewczak, Canisius College

It would seem that business investment in information technology (IT) is at root no different from business investment in anything else. After a careful consideration of the costs of the investment and its anticipated benefits, a decision is made as to whether the benefits of the investment outstrip the costs and by how much. If the benefits are competitive with other investment alternatives (say, a major marketing campaign), then the business will commit financial resources to the IT proposal. Otherwise, it won't. This decision making process is at the heart of capital budgeting. As Dickson and Wetherbe (1985, p. 170) note:

> The approach taken to economically evaluate a system is the same as that applied to any capital investment. The argument is that an organization can make investments in many things, which can be one or more information systems. The task is to decide upon the set of investments to make, given constraints on the organization's financial resources in any given time period, which will maximize the overall rate of return.

Senior executives have been making IT investment decisions for well over three decades. So why is the measurement of IT investment payoff so difficult and controversial? Why do we need a book dealing with contemporary approaches to measuring IT investment payoff? Another way to state the question is: Why have earlier approaches to measuring IT investment payoff proven unsatisfactory? In what respects have earlier approaches fallen short? Do we need to scrap earlier approaches entirely or can we find important improvements to these approaches such that they can be newly applied to effectively measure IT investment payoff in ways that are convincing to senior management?

In an earlier book, Banker, Kauffman and Mahmood (1993, p. 2) observed:

Evaluating investments in information technology poses a number of problems that investing in the traditional assets does not present. The focus shifts from measuring hard and quantifiable dollar benefits that will appear on the firm's income statement to measuring indirect, diffuse, qualitative and contingent impacts that are difficult to quantify well.

But the traditional financial investment evaluation methods of net present value and discounted cash flow analysis require numbers. And delivering numbers often requires a lot more "fudging" and reliance on a "gut feel" for what is going to happen than many executives feel comfortable with on a continuing basis. That is a problem.

Much of the problem stems from the nature of IT itself. IT does not merely develop over time. IT "emerges," as from a primordial swamp. When it appears, it is often unfamiliar and threatening. Often we are not sure if it is friend or foe, a means to continued business success or a means to short-terms and perhaps lasting business failure. A cautious attitude toward emerging IT seems a natural and wise reaction on the part of senior management. However, too much caution for too long a time can also spell trouble for the senior manager. Missed opportunities may not only result in opportunity costs and lost revenue, it may also contribute to a company's competitive environment by helping to spawn new competitors.

An overdependence on quantitative analyses focusing on such measures as net present value (NPV), internal rate of return (IRR), or return on investment (ROI) may be comforting, but the success of such analyses is dependent on a number of factors. As Banker, Kaufmann and Mahmood (1993, p. 6) note:

> It depends on the level of analysis. It depends on the qualities of technology in which the investment occurs. It depends on the environment into which the technology is deployed. Perhaps most importantly, it depends on the vision and effectiveness of the senior management team in employing IT to transform the firm's business prospects...

And all of these are complicated by whether the evaluation that a senior manager wishes to accomplish involves looking into the past, the present, or the future.

One problem with numbers is that they can be misleading or, at least, confounding to senior managers trying to understand the value of IT investment. In the 1980s, U.S. industries invested more than $1 trillion in IT, yet the U.S. government reported that productivity rose less than 1% annually. Brynjolfsson (1993, p. 76) attributes this "productivity paradox" to four factors: 1) measurement error (outputs and inputs of information-using industries are not being properly measured by traditional approaches; 2) time lags (lags in IT payoffs make analysis of current costs compared to current benefits appear misleading); 3) redistribution activities (IT is used in redistribution, making it privately beneficial to firms without adding to total output); and 4) mismanagement (managers misallocate and overconsume information because there are no explicit measures of information value).

The issue of measuring IT investment payoff is critical here. Measures may be quantitative in nature but they must also be qualitative as well. Brynjolfsson (1993, p. 76) observes:

> The business transformation literature highlights how difficult and perhaps inappropriate it would be to try to translate the benefits of IT usage into quantifiable productivity measures of output. Intangibles such as better responsiveness to customers and increased coordination with suppliers do not always increase the amount or even intrinsic quality of output, but they do help make sure it arrives at the right time, at the right place, with the right attributes for each customer. Just as managers look beyond "productivity" for some of the benefits of IT, so must researchers be prepared to look beyond conventional productivity measurement techniques.

Of course, Brynjolfsson (1993) also points to management practices related to IT as well as measurement issues in measuring IT investment payoff. While much of what management accomplishes can be quantified, what it does and how it does it also falls into the realm of process. Strassmann (1990) proposed a way of measuring management quality by creating a ratio of economic value-added and cost of management. While not based on traditional measures of business performance, the ratio still attempts to provide a quantitative measure of management quality. Such an approach is useful in moving beyond traditional measures of IT investment payoff, but it does not begin to measure the process of using IT or the benefits of the process. Measuring process contributions related to the use of IT is more problematic than measuring quantitative outcomes and may involve qualitative judgments of quality.

Measuring IT investment payoff is further confounded by the fact that even when IT fails to confer benefits, it may still prove crucial for a business. In other words, based simply on strategic necessity, a business may be compelled to invest in IT. A case in point is investment in ATM networks by banks. It is too late for a bank to achieve competitive advantage through an ATM network. The bank will, however, be at a serious competitive disadvantage if it does not have an ATM network. In this case, based on strategic necessity, the bank will have no choice but to invest in an ATM network.

These observations bring us back to the rationale for this book; namely, to find improvements to existing methods for measuring IT investment payoff as well as to find new, innovative methods for addressing the value of emerging IT. In this sense, this book serves to address a proposal in the conclusions to Banker, Kaufmann and Mahmood (1993, p. 518) "that the primary goal of further research in this area should be to determine the extent to which the variety of newly available methods can be applied in different settings. Limiting ourselves to a single framework or a narrow research perspective at this time will reduce our ability to understand and discover the multiple sources of IT value." This is especially important in view of the fact that "the shortfall of IT productivity is as much due to deficiencies in our measurement and methodological tool kit as to mismanagement by developers and users of IT" (Brynjolfsson, 1993, p. 67).

This book is organized in three parts. Part I presents a theoretical background for measuring IT investment payoff and serves as the basis for much of the rest of this book.

Part II presents conceptual approaches to measuring IT investment payoff. Each of the methods and measures discussed deal with the quantitative and qualitative aspects of the problem in a unique, prescriptive fashion. Part III presents case studies of measuring IT investment payoff, i.e., actual descriptions of methods being used in manufacturing and service organizations. We conclude with a synthesis of key contributions of the approaches to measuring IT investment payoff proposed in the chapters, some suggestions for future research in this area, and guidelines for business executives who ultimately are responsible for making IT investment decisions.

Part I
Theoretical Background for Measuring Information Technology Investment Payoff

Mo Adam Mahmood, University of Texas at El Paso
Edward J. Szewczak, Canisius College

In writing about the art of empirical investigation, Julian Simon notes that:

> If there are well-established assumptions in a field, and if there is an apparatus that permits...deduction..., then there is said to be a body of theory. The theory must cover a substantial portion of the material in a field or subfield, or one should not say that there is a body of theory... (p. 36).

> The distinction between theory and hypotheses derived from casual experience is important and hard to grasp. Economics is by far the strongest of the social sciences in possessing a body of theory from which hypotheses can be deduced, but not all economic hypotheses come from theory...Experimental psychology also has a considerable body of strong theory. Sociology and political science are not so blessed, nor is anthropology. Therefore, in contrast to sociology and anthropology, the former fields generate more of their hypotheses by deduction from theory and then test them in classical fashion...(pp. 342-343) (Simon, 1969).

While there is no generally accepted "theory of IS/IT" that can be used to guide thinking about IS/IT development, use and evaluation, there is a large body of existing theory from other areas of scholarly research that is often appealed to when thinking about IS/IT investment. The first paper in this section is a case in point.

James McKeen, Heather Smith and Michael Parent perform an integration of a number of existing models of the firm in an interesting attempt to demonstrate strong linkages between IT investment and a wide variety of organizational performance measures. The resulting synthesized model includes elements of the Lucas model, the Weill model, the Markus and Soh model, the McKeen and Smith model, and the Trice and Treacy model as well as contributions from transaction cost economics, agency theory, and organizational economics. The synthesized model suggests that IT investment must undergo a chain of transformation processes (IT governance, IT investment, IT deployment, IT usage). The mix of internal managerial functions and external environmental factors dictates the extent to which each of these processes translates into organizational performance. The authors offer a number of propositions based on the synthesized model. These propositions address technology usage, longitudinal research, IT governance, IT expenditures, IT deployment and strategic plans, standardized computer system hours, and business revenue. It is the authors' hope that future empirical research will be conducted to rigorously test these propositions and the synthesized model as a whole. In the meantime, the proposed model may serve as a comprehensive, conceptual framework for thinking about the value of IT in organizations.

William Wehrs complements the first paper with a useful two-dimensional framework ("road map") for thinking about reference theories and associated methodological approaches to the economic evaluation of IS and IT. One dimension is the time frame of evaluation (*ex ante* and *ex post*). The other dimension is level of aggregation (individual, intermediate and economy). In terms of these dimensions, decision theory is located at the individual level of aggregation within both the *ex ante* and *ex post* time frames. On the other hand, production theory (based primarily on the Cobb-Douglas function) is located at the intermediate and economy levels of aggregation within the *ex post* time frame. Various methodological approaches to evaluation can be associated with the reference theories. For example, both information economics analysis and multiple information attributes analysis are associated with decision theory, although the two approaches differ fundamentally in the way they view the source of value for an IS. Wehrs' framework can also be used to examine empiricalresearch. Of particular interest to senior managers is the empirical research conducted at the economy level of aggregation of the "productivity paradox," i.e., the fact that a growth in information production from the utilization of IS and IT coincided with an apparent decline in the growth rate of average labor productivity. A lack of positive results at the economy level of organization is counteracted by a number of positive relationships found at the intermediate level (group, department, business unit, etc.) using ratio studies, business value linkage and business level aggregation evaluation approaches. Wehrs' "road map" is intended as a framework which can be used to address a wide variety of research efforts. Some efforts may be quantitative versus qualitative, formal versus informal, objective versus subjective, or unidimensional versus multidimensional. The approaches taken are often the result of a decision about what to consider as relevant variables and measures of investment quality.

Niv Ahituv, Stan Lipovetsky and Asher Tishler present the results of an empirical study of the relationship between firms' IS policy and business performance which argue against the productivity paradox. Using data collected from Fortune and Computerworld magazines, the authors perform various multivariate statistical analyses to classify 80 firms into groups with similar characteristics and to estimate the importance of different IS attributes on various economic indicators of firms' performance. The results show that, when firms are classified into four groups according to financial performance, very profitable firms exhibit the highest investment and expenditures on IS per employee, particularly in the areas of wages to professional personnel and the distribution of end user workstations.

In today's business workplace, end user workstations are often joined together in various networking configurations. Many companies are wrestling with the organizational and technical problems associated with migrating from a mainframe environment to a client/server platform. The paper by Amarnath Prakash addresses this issue using an innovation diffusion theory approach. He reports results of empirically testing various perceived innovation attributes that influence adoption (relative advantage, compatibility, complexity, observability, and trialability) in organizations. He then presents a client/server management payoff matrix which identifies client/server components (hardware, software, networking, and procedures) and addresses the key payoff areas of investing in client/server technology in the manufacturing sector (capacity utilization, inventory turnover, new products, and product quality) and in the service sector (service quality, service variety, speed, responsiveness). In addition, Prakash develops a business process framework for evaluating client/server technology investments in operational, managerial and strategic areas as well as a model of the effects (automotive, informative, and transformative) that client server technology can have on business processes leading to business value. Finally, he derives a client/server investment evaluation portfolio along the dimensions of client/server investment areas and client server technology value. Prakash believes that a unique contribution of this portfolio is a move away from financial measures toward process oriented measures of value.

Sanjay Singh reports on an empirical study involving 51 North American companies which tests various measures of Executive Information Systems (EIS) success. Direct measurement of EIS benefits is often difficult since they are generally intangible and difficult to quantify. Singh adopts two different approaches to measurement. Traditional measures include user acceptance, system usage, user satisfaction, and system impact on performance. A non-traditional GAP measure (a service quality measurement) is computed by analyzing the difference between the factors motivating development of an EIS and the actual support provided to those factors by the system. The results of hypothesis testing and GAP analysis suggest that EIS are being used to support the implementation and control aspects of the strategic management process and that improvement is needed in supporting organizational objectives, environmental scanning and strategy formulation. Singh notes that another useful aspect of the study is that the GAP measure can be used by organizations to measure the success of IS and to evaluate technology productivity payoff.

Regardless of the type of system being developed, all system development efforts require software, whether the software be developed in-house, purchased "off the shelf," or developed externally by contract. David Rine and Robert Sonnemann present the results of conducting a study of software reuse investment success factors involving 83 organizations from five different countries. They hypothesize that there is a set of success factors which are common across organizations and have predictability relationships to software reuse. Their results show that there is a strong relationship between reuse success and business strategy (e.g., design for manufacturability approach), technology transfer (e.g., corporate sponsorship advocating and supporting development of a software reuse capability), organization structure (e.g., having a domain engineering section), product-line approach (e.g., a software development approach built around a core set of reusable software components as the foundation for product development), system architecture (e.g., a common software architecture across the product line, to standardize interfaces and data formats), and availability of components (e.g., reusable components to leverage with customers, driving them to more generic requirements in trade for shorter development time). They conclude that large scale software business investment in these six factors will result in greater software reuse and will payoff in improved productivity.

Susan Garrod, based on the resource–based view of a firm, presents a contingency framework to evaluate the moderating effect of the competitive environment on the information resources of the firm. This is done based on the premise that the firm's performance is dependent on its environment and the environment is an important moderator of the value of the firm's strategic resources. The framework, as such, depicts a contingency relationship between the firm's information strategy and its competitive environment by combining prior theories from strategy, organizational theory, and information systems. Garrod uses the framework to assess the value of organizational capabilities to process and exploit information in the context of the competitive environment. She concludes by showing how the framework can be used to assess the value of organizational capabilities to process and exploit information in the context of competitive environment.

Chapter 1

An Integrative Research Approach to Assess the Business Value of Information Technology

James D. McKeen
Heather A. Smith
Queen's University, Canada

Michael Parent
University of Western Ontario, Canada

This chapter reviews and synthesizes the literature dealing with the assessment of the value of IT and then presents a model linking IT investment with IT usage and organizational performance. This model is exercised, and specific measures of investment, usage, and performance are recommended. The chapter proceeds to develop a means of evaluating the benefits of IT investments and concludes by drawing implications from these findings for both academicians and practitioners. Suggestions for further research are offered.

What is the value of information technology (IT)? How does investment in IT affect productivity? What is the impact of computerization on the bottom line? These questions and their variations have been the focus of considerable business and academic attention in recent years (Chismar, 1985; Oman and Ayers, 1988; Strassmann et al., 1988; Zimmerman, 1988; Bleakley, 1989; Kauffman and Weill, 1989; Roach, 1989; Weill, 1990a; Mahmood and Mann, 1991; Panko, 1991; Brynjolfsson, 1993a; Dos Santos and Peffers, 1993; Katz, 1993; Markus and Soh, 1993; Wilson, 1993a) because of the massive investments being made in IT by business (*Datamation*, 1987; Browning, 1990; McKeen et al., 1990; Harris and Katz, 1991b). Unfortunately, beyond a few isolated incidents (e.g., Harris and Katz, 1988b; Brynjolfsson, 1993a; Lichtenburg, 1993), research has not been able to demonstrate strong linkages between the investment in IT and a wide variety of performance measures. It remains that we still don't have many answers to these questions beyond our intuitive conviction that information technology contributes to the bottom line. Our inability to conclusively demonstrate any linkage between the investment in IT and a wide variety of performance measures (commonly referred to as the "productivity paradox") leaves the central problem of whether IT really does make a difference to an organization's performance unanswered (Baily, 1986; Roach, 1989; Attewell, 1991; Brynjolfsson, 1993b).

The relatively modest success achieved to date in assessing the value of IT arises from several shortcomings in current research models and business practices (see Attewell, 1993; Baily and Gordon, 1988; Brynjolfsson, 1993b; Krohe, 1993; McKeen and Smith, 1991; McKeen and Smith, 1993b; Popkin, 1993; Wilson, 1993b for a more complete discussion of these) which have resulted in an incomplete understanding of the value of IT in organizations. But even with an incomplete understanding, how is it possible for the value of information technology to remain so elusive? The willingness of industry to continue its investment in this technology suggests that it is convinced that its investment will be profitable. Furthermore, these investments are sacrosanct — they are maintained (or even increased) through recessionary periods that see all other budgets dramatically reduced. Is it possible that the return on industry's IT investment has been negligible (or indeed negative)? If so, it would qualify as the single largest collective financial misappropriation of funds known to modern day organizations. Is it possible for a return to exist without detection? Or is it just that we have been measuring the wrong things? Unfortunately and much to the dismay of senior management, these questions also remain unanswered.

This chapter was motivated by the challenge to find an adequate, comprehensive framework which might be used by both academics and researchers to definitively determine the value of information technology in organizations. In the following sections of the chapter, the literature is reviewed using various research models as a framework. From this review, a synthesis of these models and approaches is presented in an attempt to address some of the shortcomings of previous research. Proscriptions for future research are offered for both academicians and practitioners, as is a discussion of the possible limitations of the synthesis model. The chapter concludes that a cohesive and consistent approach to the measurement of the value of IT in organizations based not only on managerial practices, but also on existing theories of the firm will eventually lead to an unequivocal answer to these most critical questions.

Review of Previous Research Models

According to Banker, Kauffman, and Mahmood (1993), no consensus exists in information systems research on either the optimal approach, measures, or level of analysis to be used when measuring the business or strategic value of IT investments by organizations. Their suggested four-factor classification scheme can serve as the basis to begin exploring the various approaches which have emerged. Studies assessing the value of IT can be grouped according to their *Ontology, Value Type, Level of Analysis*, and *Data*. By Ontology, Banker, Kauffman and Mahmood mean whether the research is case-study (single or multiple cases) or model based. Value Type refers to whether the study is measuring the business (e.g., financial or economic returns) or strategic (extent to which IT is concordant with the firm's business strategy and contributes to the execution of this strategy) value. The Level of Analysis can vary from individual users, at the micro end of the spectrum, to impact on an economy as a whole at the macro-level, with most studies centered on either the firm, or functional/cross-functional work groups within the firm. Lastly, Data denotes whether qualitative, quantitative, or both kinds of data are used to support results. Most studies, they assert, tend to fall into a model-based, business value, firm-level, multiple-data source classification. As a first step to consolidating the knowledge in the field, this review will limit itself to these types of studies, and the models that have been developed to guide them.

A historical review by Lucas (1993) supports Banker, Kauffman, and Mahmood's conclusions, inasmuch as it also sees business value IT research as being in its infancy. His 1975 study was among the earliest to investigate the value of information technology, but since it did not include the cost of the technology, it could not draw conclusions regarding the return on the firm's technology investment. It was not until the 1980s that researchers attempted to look at financial performance and to collect data on a firm's investment in technology. These studies were based on tenets derived from many disciplines (e.g., microeconomics, economics, finance/accounting, and behav-

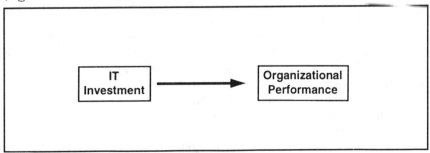

Figure 1: Basic Model

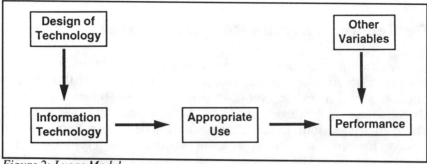

Figure 2: Lucas Model

ioral sciences), used various theories (e.g., the theory of the firm, information economics, and time value of money), and employed many dependent variables ranging from financial performance to satisfaction. The majority of the models used in this research assume a direct link between technology and some measure of performance (shown in Figure 1 and referred to as the basic model).

Researchers have enhanced this basic model in many ways by adding other variables in order to explain a greater percentage of the variation in the dependent variables used. Econometric analyses attempt to measure the contribution of IT to performance by controlling for other factors of productions such as non-computer capital, the cost of labor, and other expenses (e.g., Barua et al., 1991a; Brynjolfsson, 1993a; Loveman, 1988; Berndt and Morrison, 1992). Lucas argues for the addition of three elements to the basic model: appropriate usage of IT; design of IT; and other variables which impact organizational performance. He points out that, to demonstrate business value, the technology must be used appropriately, and that technology must be designed to fit the task. These relationships are depicted in Figure 2 and referred to as the Lucas model.[1]

Other studies have enhanced the basic model by adding other variables between IT and organizational performance. Weill (1988) has developed the concept of *conversion effectiveness* — the ability to convert IT expenditures into assets that provide value to the investing firm. Kauffman and Weill (1989), in their review of the value of IT literature, point out that researchers have neglected to consider "IT effectiveness" explicitly in their models. They argue that IT effectiveness should be an important mediating variable in the relationship between IT investment and organizational performance. This helps to explain how one company could invest heavily in a state-of-the-art system which is not especially useful and receive little or no benefit from its investment (see also Strassmann, 1985), while another could invest the same amount in another way and see the investment payoff handsomely. This may also explain the equivocal results of studies linking heavy IT investment to either high or low performance (Bender, 1986; Cron and Sobol, 1983; Harris and Katz, 1988a; Harris and Katz,

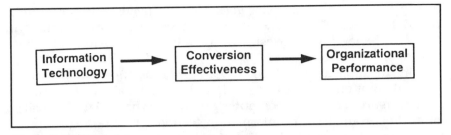

Figure 3: Weill Model

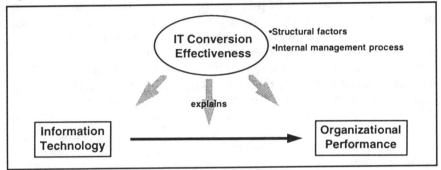

Figure 4: Markus and Soh Model

1988b). Weill concludes that it is not enough to simply identify the dollars spent on IT, one must further investigate how well or how poorly these dollars are spent. The concept of IT conversion effectiveness is included in Figure 3, referred to as the Weill model.

The notion of IT conversion effectiveness is further embellished by Markus and Soh (1993) who suggest there are two groups of moderating factors which determine whether or not IT value is realized: 1) *structural factors* (beyond the immediate control of management) that create differences among firms in their ability to derive benefits from IT spending (e.g., firm size, type of industry, competitive position within industry, and general and industry-specific economic conditions); and 2) *internal managerial processes* (under the direct control of management) including, formulating IT strategy, selecting an appropriate organizational structure for executing IT strategy, developing the right IT applications, and managing IT application development projects effectively. Markus and Soh (1993) favor a much more inclusive view of conversion effectiveness — suggesting that "conversion effectiveness is evident when there is a strong positive relationship between IT and firm performance, and when the CEO attributes firm performance to IT." This view implies an interest, not in measuring conversion effectiveness per se, but in understanding the fit between the pattern of IT assets, factors that affect the firm's ability to receive benefits from these assets, and firm performance. Reflecting this approach, we have represented the Markus and Soh model below with conversion effectiveness "explaining" the linkage between IT and firm performance. That is, conversion effectiveness is not simply boxed between IT investment and firm performance — rather, it impacts the level of IT investment as well as firm performance (see Figure 4).

In the application of these research models, McKeen and Smith (1993a) point out that IT budgets have been used almost exclusively as a measure of degree of computerization. This has led to the neglect of an important facet of information technology — its deployment. They argue that because IT is deployed to augment the work of people, it is counterproductive to attempt to consider the impact of IT on performance without taking into consideration the role of people. Only through the joint consideration of both resources — people and IT — will the value of IT be revealed. For example, in one company, computers might enable one employee to handle 50 accounts while another similar company might find that its system enables a single employee to manage 75 accounts. These two companies have opted for different deployment balances between labor and IT, with different organizational impacts. This reveals how some companies derive significantly more benefit from their IT investments than others. The authors refer to this as the *resource view* of IT. This view suggests that IT deployment consists of the ongoing managerial process of deliberate decision to selectively balance IT and labor in the pursuit of organizational value (McKeen and Smith, 1991; McKeen and Smith, 1993b). For an example of how some deployment decisions are made, see Weill

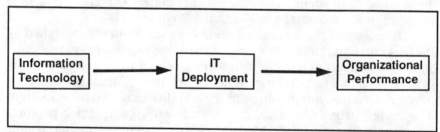

Figure 5: McKeen and Smith Model

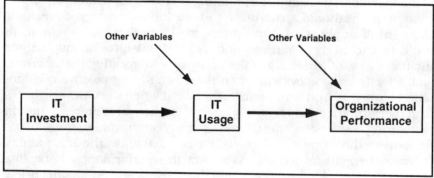

Figure 6: Trice and Treacy Model

(1993.) Because there are only two resources that must be deployed in information intensive industries — people and IT, the resource view has even greater appeal. Their model, referred to as the McKeen and Smith model, appears in Figure 5.

It is interesting to contrast the above models with a model previously proposed by Trice and Treacy (1986). Their three-construct model arose from an investigation into the measurement of system effectiveness which, as they point out, always involves measuring utilization[2] of a system. They concluded that system usage (utilization) must be an intervening variable between IT investment and organizational performance since IT cannot have an impact on performance unless it is used in some way. Although they warn that the linkages between system utilization and organizational performance are complex, they conclude that it is impossible to trace a clean theoretical path between IT and performance without including usage (see Figure 6).

There is high face validity associated with the Trice and Treacy model. There is also implicit directionality. Certainly IT investment (either purchase or development) must precede usage of the investment, and usage must exist in order that measurable benefits from its use can be derived. On the other hand, Lucas (1993) points out that there are temporal feedback mechanisms in this model, not shown explicitly. That is, over time, increased financial performance may encourage organizations to increase the usage of IT which in turn would increase the investment in IT — a case of success breeding success. Or, negative results may dampen usage and in turn decrease future investment in IT. These effects, however, can only be discerned over time due to the nature of IT investments. Because many (and certainly the majority of sizable investments) are long-lived, their usage may not always be optional, and they may be irreversible. If evidence today were to suggest that American Airlines' investment in the Sabre system was not beneficial, usage would not drop nor would investment decrease in the short run. In the long run, however, management should realize a misplaced investment and take action to correct it. This underscores the need for methods of investigation which examine IT investment, usage and their relationship to organizational performance over time.

Synthesis

In reviewing the literature, it is evident that there is a substantial degree of agreement among the models used to assess the value of IT. While it is true that no single model enjoys widespread acceptance, there is consensus that there should be a deterministic mediating factor (or factors) between IT investment and organizational performance. That is, it appears indefensible to attempt to link IT investment with organizational performance directly. At the same time, none of the models reviewed is comprehensive both in terms of the factors included, as well as in terms of the amount of time over which the investment in IT is assessed.

Recent attempts to account for this lack of robust longitudinal analysis are based on Transaction Cost Economics (TCE) theory and Agency theory to determine the optimal organizational form of a firm's "information asset" (Malone, 1987; Loh and Venkatraman, 1992; Brynjolfsson and Hitt, 1993; Brynjolfsson, 1994; Brynjolfsson, Malone, Gurbaxani, Kambil, 1994). As Brynjolfsson (1994) maintains, both theories concern themselves with allocation decisions within the firm, and the role that information and IT will play within that firm. Unlike preceding models, however, the firm is considered within the context of an economic system as a whole. As such, it is possible for an organization to define its boundaries through its ongoing decisions on whether or not to internalize key processes and systems. Combining these two approaches into an overarching theory labelled Organizational Economics (Barney and Ouchi, 1986) yields a comprehensive framework which has proven useful in assessing the value of IT.

Parent and Chan (1994) compare and contrast Organizational Economics (OE) with Agency theory and TCE to demonstrate its relevance to information systems research and decisions. The explain how Agency Theory revolves around the relationship between a principal and an agent in which the agent engages in a particular activity on behalf of the principal for some prespecified reward. The unit of analysis in agency theory is the contract, and the objective of the theory is to allow for the principal to determine the most efficient contract under which the relationship can be governed.

Like agency theory, TCE also concerns itself with the elaboration of economic contracts (Williamson 1975, 1992). Unlike agency theory, however, the unit of analysis is not the individual organization party to a contract, it is the transaction itself. Actors in this system are seen as rationally bound and opportunistic in their behavior. The extent to which such opportunism can be exercised determines the transaction costs to the firm. Hierarchical organization, or the internalization of transactions, then, is a response designed to minimize these transactional costs. TCE proposes a spectrum of organizational forms, called *governance structures*, ranging from a free and perfectly competitive market to the hierarchical form that most organizations adopt. In information terms, market transactions would govern the acquisition of non-sensitive information (e.g., reports from public databases), while hierarchical organization would be preferred for systems with strategic value (e.g., the aforementioned Sabre airline reservation system which is controlled and guarded by American Airlines).

In combining Agency Theory and TCE into OE, Barney and Ouchi (1986) offset each theory's shortcomings. Agency theory has been

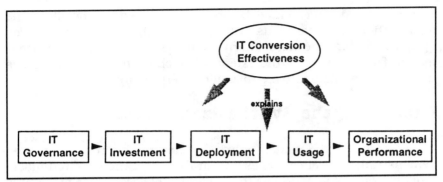

Figure 7: Synthesized Model

criticized for limiting its scope to only contractual relationships, thereby losing the context of the firm and its competitive environment. Secondly, by considering the principal dominant, and framing the contract's efficiency in terms of only this principal, the theory neglects relationships where reciprocal power might exist (e.g., knowledge workers in specialized manufacturing industries). By allowing for interaction and imbalance to exist between the principal and agent, and using the transaction as the basis of analysis, TCE can overcome these deficiencies. Similarly, by allowing for non-hierarchical control in the form of a contract, agency theory can expand the options available to the firm, its functions, and managers. As Brynjolfsson (1994) acknowledges, TCE has proven useful to researchers seeking to determine the reach of an organization, while agency theory has proven to be less flexible. This said, however, Brynjolfsson (1994) also notes that "...*it is almost too easy* [to use] *transaction cost economics.*" (p. 1646). By combining the two into a supra-framework labelled Organizational Economics, the drawbacks that each of these theories have on their own can be moderated (Barney & Ouchi, 1986).

Thus, potential mediating factors are for the most part deterministic, and not necessarily in conflict. As such, they could all arguably be included in a "synthesized model" as shown in Figure 7 which binds OE to the six other models reviewed. This synthesized model is more complete, cohesive, and can apply to all sorts of projects and organizational forms. It suggests that IT Investment must undergo a chain of transformational processes before resulting in organizational performance. Specifically, a senior management decision must be made with regards to IT, and this decision must specify the form and extent of the IT within the organization, be it internal or external to the firm, developed in-house, outsourced, or supplied through third-party vendors. Thus, the organization must decide on the form of *governance* which will be adopted on a transactional (e.g., project-by-project) or ongoing basis. This leads to a specific *investment* in IT, following which IT must be *deployed* (that is, applications and technology must be selected and implemented) before IT can be *used* beneficially by the organization to enhance its *performance*. The level of *conversion effectiveness* (i.e., the mix of internal managerial and external environmental factors) dictates the extent to which each of these variables ultimately translate into organizational performance.

Exercising the Synthesized Model

In order for the model to provide interpretable results, it must demonstrate theoretical cohesion. In this case, the research model must provide explanation as to how and why governance structures affect investment leading to usage and eventual organizational impact. The "basic model" which simply links investment to performance lacks this cohesion and granularity. In order to apply the synthesized model, a level of analysis and method of study must be established and each of the model components (IT governance, IT investment, IT deployment, IT usage, and organizational performance) must be defined. The following sections consider these issues construct by construct.

Level of Analysis

The general formulation of this model makes it theoretically applicable at different levels of analysis: to a particular system, business unit, firm, or an industry. We recommend that it be applied at the enterprise level as internal consistency between the model, its application, and its measurement can be best maintained at this level (Banker, Kauffman, and Mahmood, 1993). This decision is based on a number of factors. *First*, it has been argued persuasively by several researchers such as Attewell (1993), Crowston and Treacy (1986), Panko (1991), Powell (1994) and the U.S. National Research Council (1993) that the demonstrated lack of specificity at the macroeconomic level impairs the ability of research to successfully link the investment in IT with the operational performance of organizations comprising the economy. The high level of analysis occludes the behaviour of individually performing organizations. Part of the failure of research at this level of analysis (see Brynjolfsson, 1993b and Panko, 1991 for thorough discussions) arises directly from the fact that, as a straight percentage of the total expenses of an organization, the IT investment is small and thus limits its ability to explain a high degree of variation in overall performance. *Second*, in order to focus the research model at a lower level within an organization (at a specific system or at a business unit), measures are needed that are solely attributable to the system/business unit, its governance, usage, and performance. By way of example, Lucas (1993) suggests that if you are studying a sales information system, then measures of the sales force performance are more likely to produce meaningful results than measures of corporate profits. Furthermore, the investment in the sales analysis system must represent the complete investment even if this necessitates the proratinng of infrastructure costs. In cases where there is a standalone system or an autonomous business unit, this level of analysis is possible. In situations where there are comparable units of the organization (i.e., one with the system and one without), this level of analysis offers the researcher extra measures of control (e.g. Banker et. al., 1990). However, these situations are more the exception than the rule, making lower levels of analysis generally inappropriate for this type of research. *Third*, at the enterprise level, the perspective is broad enough to encompass all planning activities and investment decisions regarding IT, thus capturing the synergistic effects of governance structures and the entire IT portfolio (Parent & Chan, 1994; McKeen and Smith, 1993b; Markus and Robey, 1988). Lower levels of analysis miss or must ignore these effects which can of themselves bring significant benefits to an organization. This leads to our first proposition:

P1: *With the focus at the enterprise level, it should be possible to capture the effects of the total IT investment on the organization's performance provided that the performance measure is related to the usage of the technology.*

Method of Study

Typically, studies in this field have used cross-sectional analyses (e.g., Mahmood and Mann, 1993; Harris and Katz, 1991a; Weill, 1990b). In his review of the research on the business value of IT, Lucas (1993) notes that cross-sectional research designs are most popular because they are economical. However, he also points out that "because the data are collected at one point in time, it is much more difficult to argue for causal relationships..." He concludes that longitudinal designs offer the strongest evidence for a relationship between IT and business value because changes in the variables can be observed over time.

The importance of the time dimension in IT value research has been observed by other researchers as well (Markus and Soh, 1993; Smith and McKeen 1991). Markus and Soh point out that typically IT investments do not provide full benefits for several years. This is not only because systems take time to develop, but also because even after implementation, it takes time for an organization to learn to use them effectively and to modify organizational processes to accommodate the computerization of work flows. We therefore conclude that longitudinal data is critical to the assessment of the model, leading to our second proposition:

P2: *The value of IT should be reflected through its relationship with organizational performance over a period of time. This suggests it should be possible to derive the value of IT within a longitudinal research design.*

IT Governance

Williamson's (1975) breakthrough in advancing TCE as a viable theory was recognition that governance structures vary along a continuum from Market to Hierarchy. On the one end, open market transactions take place in conditions of perfect knowledge, or no uncertainty. The price mechanism communicates all that is necessary for the transaction to take place. At its opposite end, the continuum illustrates that organizations will emerge as hedges against uncertainty and opportunism, both of which increase either the overt cost of exchange, or the penalties for poor transactions. The same holds true in an agency-theoretic context. A Contractual Spectrum is said to exist, ranging once again from open market transactions (simple contracts) through to Internal Contracting (allocation of organizational resources to internal functional areas for the purpose of accomplishing strategic or operational ends) in order to minimize risk-bearing costs (see Jensen and Meckling, 1976; Mathewson and Winter, 1984; and Sappington, 1991 for a thorough discussion). Between these extremes lie contractual arrangements (one-time or long-term), joint ventures, partnerships, cooperatives and other hybrid organizational forms. Brynjolfsson (1994) describes how the Hart-Moore framework can be used to describe the degree to which a firm falls on either end of the continuum. Briefly, this framework hinges on the distribution of asset ownership within one firm, or between several firms. The more a firm (or functional area within a firm) owns or controls its assets (including information), the more it leans towards a hierarchical form of governance. Thus, our third proposition:

P3: *IT governance at the enterprise level should be determinable by establishing the level of control exercised over information assets. The greater the control, the greater the degree of hierarchy. Therefore, enterprises opting for hierarchical forms of governance will exercise greater planning and direction over IT investments than will enterprises choosing more market forms of governance.*

IT Investment

At the enterprise level, most studies have operationalized IT investment based on total IT expenditures either by organization or by industry (Bender, 1986; Banker and Kauffman, 1988; Harris and Katz, 1988a; Harris and Katz, 1988b; Loveman, 1988; Turner, 1988; Roach, 1989; Alpar and Kim, 1990b; Panko, 1991). Other researchers have used somewhat different measures of this concept: MIS dollars per office worker (Panko, 1982), amount invested in different types of systems (Weill, 1990b), a number of "substitutes for investment" such as, computer ownership, number of applications (Cron and Sobol, 1983; Alpar and Kim, 1990a), number of personal computers (Mahmood and Mann, 1991), amount spent on computer training (Mahmood and Mann, 1991), amount spent on hardware (Brynjolfsson, 1994), and type of software capabilities (Cron and Sobol, 1983). The purpose of these measures is to determine how much an organization is investing in IT so that it can be correlated with company performance. MIS budgets are the most frequently used measure of computerization since these figures are readily available and are reasonably objective.

We propose that IT investment should be operationalized as the total annual expenditure (appropriately deflated) on all IT activities including computers (of all types), software, people, and communications. This includes all purchases, lease payments, training, outsourcing contracts, payments to consultants, etc. In short, IT investment is meant to capture the entire annual investment in information technology made by each organization, and is consistent with earlier propositions which assert that the analysis should be undertaken at the enterprise level.

Because the framework is longitudinal, research should focus on the *changes* in IT investment over time as opposed to the absolute level of IT investment at any given period in time. That is, the model examines the relationship between changes in IT governance, changes in IT investment, changes in IT deployment, changes in IT usage, and changes in organizational performance. Some of the challenges to the usefulness of measures such as "revenues per employee" or "IT per revenue dollar" are aimed at the usefulness of the absolute value of these ratios and not at their relative rates of relationship and change (e.g., Strassmann, 1990).

P4: *IT investment should be accurately captured at the enterprise level by examining all IT expenditures. Furthermore, looking at changes in these figures over time and relating them to other variables in the model should be more revealing than an examination of their absolute levels.*

Conversion Effectiveness

To date, there has been only one published attempt to operationalize conversion effectiveness (Weill, 1990b). Weill aggregated existing measures of top management commitment, user information satisfaction, political turbulence, and IT experience together to form a measure of conversion effectiveness. Markus and Soh (1993) have suggested the factors that *lead to* conversion effectiveness but, have not developed a way of measuring conversion effectiveness.

IT Deployment

IT deployment, as a theoretical concept, is similar to that of conversion effectiveness. Weill (1993) has examined one aspect of deployment — that of IT infrastructure investment versus non-infrastructure investment. Grabowski and Lee (1993) have categorized IT deployment with respect to diversity, internal coordination, strategic orientation, knowledge intensitivity, and degree of integration. They propose that the deployment of different types of IT applications will have different strategic and economic impacts for organizations of different strategic orientations. That is, it is the *fit* of these five factors that will determine the impact and value of information technology. This theoretical framework, however, has not been tested empirically. Using a similar concept of "fit", Chan and Huff (1993) have examined IT deployment in terms of its alignment with business strategy. While this does not characterize IT deployment directly, it does demonstrate that there is no best strategy for deploying IT. The research into the deployment of IT is in its infancy, but holds real promise for explaining differential impacts of the investment in IT.

Both conversion effectiveness and IT deployment, though conceptually clear, remain unclear in terms of their operationalization. Both need to be developed and more thoroughly tested by future research in order that the inconsistencies noted above be clarified. Our fourth proposition takes into account their ambiguity, and simply addresses both concepts:

P5: *IT deployment, and the subsequent effectiveness with which that deployment is fitted to the organization's strategic plans should result in higher performance for the organization.*

IT Usage

Trice and Treacy (1986) have examined how researchers have operationalized computer usage. Most studies have used subjective measures, such as reported use, frequency of use, or plans to use a system. They comment that the lack of standardized measures leads to considerable error. Very few studies have used unobtrusive and objective measures, such as machine usage statistics, even though these are routinely logged and readily accessible for many computing systems. For every production system in business, the resources used by each computer transaction or access is recorded. Thus, there is a direct relationship between total production computer hours and overall system usage. Furthermore, all computer production hours (regardless of the type of mainframe computer) can be normalized for comparison purposes between organizations. Such objective measures do not fall prey to the usual challenges of psychometric validation. For these reasons, we feel that the use of standardized computer usage statistics is preferable to the use of more subjective measures.

Personal computing (end-user computing) and client/server computing present difficulties for measuring usage. Some researchers (e.g., Mahmood and Mann, 1991) have attempted to measure this by counting the number of personal computers in an organization or by asking users to subjectively assess the amount of their usage. Following arguments by Trice and Treacy (cited above), it was felt that neither of these approaches would yield an accurate assessment. The question is whether the usage of these surrogates is better than not using them. Counting computers does not measure usage and the agreement between reported and actual usage is often low. Until personal computers are equipped with monitors to measure actual usage or until personal computers are linked to network managers that monitor usage in much the same fashion as mainframe computers, accurate usage data will not likely be available. Due to the significance of end-user computing within organizations, and despite the Brynjolfsson and Hitt (1993) finding that their results did not change when they introduced personal computer data to the analysis, it is argued that failure to assess personal computing usage would represent an operational limitation of this model and could jeopardize any subsequent research into the value of IT. Thus,

P6: *at the enterprise level, the number of standardized computer system hours (be they personal computer, server, or mainframe) are the most promising surrogates for overall IT usage.*

Organizational Performance

There is no single, well-established measure of organizational performance that is used in this sort of research (Strassmann et al., 1988; Price and Mueller, 1986; Weill and Olson, 1989; Bhada, 1984; Miller and Doyle, 1987; Oman and Ayers, 1988; Strassmann, 1984; Strassmann et al., 1988; van Loggerenberg and Cucchiaro, 1981; Panko, 1991). An interesting discussion of the limitations of many organizational measures is found in Strassmann (1990). Weill and Olson (1989) note that many combinations of variables have been used: the ratio of expenses to premium income (Bender, 1986); pretax profits, return on assets, return on net worth, and five year growth rates (Cron and Sobol, 1983); return on management (Strassmann et al., 1988); and return on investment (Zimmerman, 1988). Zammuto (1982) concludes that measurement of performance really depends on what constituency the researcher is trying to address. Some of the variables that he suggests as measures of this concept include:

productivity, satisfaction, profit, quality, growth, efficiency, morale, and adaptability. Of these, the direct financial performance measures are typically favored because of the motivation to demonstrate the ability of IT to contribute to an organization's bottom line. In addition, goals such as satisfaction, morale or adaptability are important only to the extent that they eventually lead to financial performance. Unfortunately, there has yet to be a strong, demonstrable link between IT and any of these measures. Even if there were agreement that the measure of performance is financial, there are still many to choose from. (For a review of organizational performance measures, see McKeen and Smith, 1993c).

It is clear that the measures of organizational performance used can affect how the organizational value of IT is perceived. It is also clear that how one determines performance continues to be highly problematic (Weill and Olson, 1989; McKeen and Smith, 1993c). What is known, however, is that IT can affect a firm's performance in one of two ways. First, as a "process technology," IT can make the firm more productive by making labor more efficient; and second, as a "product technology," IT can generate revenues by creating a new product or service (Kriebel, 1989; Markus and Soh, 1993). Therefore, what is needed is a measure of overall performance that takes both the productivity and the revenue generation perspectives into consideration, thus capturing both forms of IT impact. It must be able to reflect not only the growth in revenues that come about due to increased sales or market share, but also cost reductions that occur through the enhancement of personnel by IT.

How should this measure of performance be operationalized? Keen (1991) has argued for "anchor measures" — operational measures of performance that can be used over time to assess the impact of IT. The advantage of appropriate anchor measures is their ability to demonstrate benefits that financial figures ignore. The example cited by Keen shows how an investment in IT looked like a financial disaster based on the traditional ROA calculation. Using the more appropriate anchor measures of sales per employee and revenue per employee, however, showed that profits per employee were actually up by 300 percent! McKeen and Smith (1993b) have proposed the adoption of a specific anchor measure derived from organizational revenues — referred to as *business revenue* — expressed as total revenue net of any revenue due to extraordinary items.[3] In a bank, for example, business revenue consists of net interest income (i.e., income from interest on loans less what they pay on deposits) plus service income. For an insurance company, business revenue represents premium income. For a retailer, business revenue represents sales. Measured this way, business revenue reflects the *volume* of business activity. Any sale or purchase, for example, triggers other activities such as payments, orders, shipments, purchases, etc. Thus increased revenues reflects increased volumes of business activity. This is where IT makes its direct impact. Business revenue expressed per capita also reflects productivity improvements in an organization since if (deflated) business revenues per capita increase over time, this indicates that employees are working more efficiently (Chakravarthy, 1986). Finally, changes in business revenue expressed per capita can be used to facilitate intra-organizational analysis.

Although business revenue can be affected by many variables (e.g., advertising, market position, pricing), few of these variables affect revenues per capita. Advertising, for example, is implemented with the express purpose of increasing revenues — it has nothing to do with productivity. Because of this, it is suggested that business revenue per capita (expressed in constant dollars) recorded over time should be used as the measure of organizational performance in order to assess the business value of IT. Unlike other measures such as dividend yields per share holder, this measure considers the specific role that IT plays and reflects the direct impact of its use. The advantage is that it captures both ways IT can affect performance — revenue growth and increased productivity. An increase in productivity or a growth in revenues (or both) will alter the ratio.

P7a: *Since business revenue reflects the volume of business activity (i.e., workload), then business revenue expressed per capita and analyzed over time should capture the effects of both revenue growth and increased productivity and therefore, constitute an appropriate indicator of organizational performance.*

Alternatively, it is possible for organizations to invest in IT as "table stakes," or simply to remain abreast of the competition. Similarly, companies might invest in specific IT projects in order to learn about the technology, or to better gauge possible returns. This is especially true of new technologies. For example, an organization may wish to invest in developing and maintaining a Home Page on the Internet (World Wide Web) as a pre-cursor to investing in an electronic commerce system or even an Intranet. In sum, it is conceivable that IT investments might be partially, or even wholly, motivated by other-than-financial incentives. As such, different forms of governance might be used to oversee these projects (e.g., joint ventures, one-time contracts). Consideration of these motives, and their different forms, leads to our eighth proposition:

P7b: *The degree to which organizational, or governance goals, are met by an investment in IT can also constitute an appropriate indicator of organizational performance.*

Future Research

This chapter has attempted to review and synthesize our knowledge regarding the assessment of the value of information technology to organizations. In doing so, a synthesized model containing six constructs has been proposed, and its possible operationalization discussed in the context of existing research. While this synthesis may contribute to future research by providing a parsimonious review and presentation of the knowledge that exists in this field of information systems, it remains that the foregoing discussion has been largely theoretical, and that empirical support for the model does not yet exist.

While consensus might be near for the IT investment, IT usage, and organizational performance constructs, the remainder of the model suffers from a lack of valid, accepted measures. Organizational Economics has just begun to be used in our field, and the construct of IT governance within the context of this model remains purely theoretical. Similarly, our discussion suggests that IT deployment and IT conversion effectiveness also need considerable development. As such, the challenge facing researchers is to develop, test, and validate appropriate measures for the model's constructs, and apply these to a series of longitudinal cases.

Conclusion

This chapter has investigated the role of IT and examined how IT adds value to information intensive organizations. Research in this area is in the early stages of development but there is a significant level of consensus among researchers regarding models and approaches and promising areas of investigation. We have tried to build on this base, synthesizing the results in order to extend the analysis into a new and promising area of investigation. This type of research is of vital interest particularly to the practice of IT management. We hope that the elaboration of the synthesized model will stimulate further research. We hope that our ideas will be challenged, our measures refined, and our propositions put to the rigors of empirical testing. There is a real need to add to our present understanding of information technology, its application within organizations, and its impact on our notions of organization and society in the future.

Endnotes

[1] Because this model (and subsequent models) are reproduced in their original form, some terminology is not consistent. In particular, "information technology" is used interchangeably with "IT Investment."

[2] We have used the term "usage" in preference to the term "utilization" (as found in Trice and Treacy) to avoid the potential confusing connotation associated with utilization. That is, utilization often refers to the percentage of

total capacity of a particular resource (e.g., an automated drill press may operate at a 90% utilization rate). In their model development, it is apparent that Trice and Treacy are not referring to utilization levels, but to usage.

[3] Revenues can increase in a company for many reasons other than increased sales. Depending on the industry, some forms of interest income, income from the sale of real estate, and other extraordinary items can dramatically alter the revenue growth picture of a company. These revenue items are usually not affected by IT. For this reason, McKeen and Smith (1993b) argue that only revenue generated by the business of the company proper should be included in the measurement of performance for the purposes of IT research.

Chapter 2

A Road Map for IS/IT Evaluation

William E. Wehrs
University of Wisconsin-LaCrosse

This research offers a tentative "road map" to the "bewildering array" of approaches to economic evaluation of information systems (IS) and information technology (IT). To structure the road map, a two-dimensional framework is proposed. The time frame of evaluation distinguishes ex ante and ex post approaches. Level of aggregation partitions the approaches into individual, intermediate, and economy levels. Using this structure, reference theories and associated methodologies are examined. Decision theory provides a point of reference at the individual level. Information Economics (IE) is distinguished from Multiple Attribute Information (MIA) evaluation. MIA provides a foundation for user-oriented methodology such as User Information Satisfaction (UIS). Both IE and MIA are related to Cost Benefit Analysis (CBA) methodology. Ex post approaches above the individual level are predominantly based on production theory. The structure is also employed to examine empirical research. At the individual decision maker level, laboratory experiments have not shown conclusive results. At the aggregate economy level, a decline in labor productivity has coincided with more widespread use of IT — the "productivity paradox." At the intermediate levels, until very recently, field studies had not provided evidence of positive evaluation results.

According to Srinivasan (1985):
Measurement of the effectiveness of a management information system (MIS) is an issue that has generated much debate and consequent research interest over the years... The spectrum of

approaches that have been suggested to deal with this complex issue presents a bewildering array to a researcher whose intention is to include MIS effectiveness as a dependent variable in a study, or to a practicing manager who wants to get a clear indication of the quality of the MIS being used. (p. 243).

The sheer magnitude of investment in IS/IT commands the attention of academics and practitioners. According to Kriebel (1989), in the late 1980's roughly 50% of new capital investments by major corporations were for IS or IT. The *Wall Street Journal* (King, 1994) indicates that by the early 1990's corporate spending on IT amounted to $200 billion measured in dollars of 1987 purchasing power and was growing dramatically. Correspondingly, managers have attached critical importance to measurement of the effectiveness of these massive investments. Over the past decade and a half, the Society for Information Management (SIM) has periodically surveyed its members to determine the most critical issues in IS management. Beginning with the initial survey in 1980, there have been five such surveys. In these surveys, IS/IT effectiveness measurement has been among the top 20 critical issues. Most recently, Brancheau, Janz and Wetherbe (1996) indicate that in 1994 IS effectiveness measurement ranked 11th, up from 16th in the prior 1990 survey.

The purpose of this research is to illustrate the logical structure for evaluation of IS/IT. It offers a road map providing a broad context, selected detail, and the critical relationships necessary for understanding this topic. With regard to "evaluation," a strict interpretation of goal and standard of comparison is adopted — the assignment of a monetary value that represents the value of the system to the organization. Other forms of what often is called IS/IT "evaluation" are examined in comparison with economic evaluation. In a market economy, financial "success" is a necessary condition for viability. Moreover, financial evaluation provides a common denominator to managers, allowing them to compare both IT and non-IT expenditures.

Framework

As a starting point, IS evaluation can be structured via a two-dimensional framework based on the time frame and/or the level of aggregation involved (See Figure 1).

The evaluation process can be undertaken either *ex ante* or *ex post*. *Ex ante* evaluation focuses on the IS investment decision and the goal is to guide resource allocation. The purpose of *ex post* evaluation is to justify the costs that have been incurred and provide a guide for similar future expenditure. Evaluation at either stage has its own peculiar problems. Since it necessarily involves the unknown future, *ex ante* evaluation involves risk or uncertainty and presents forecast-

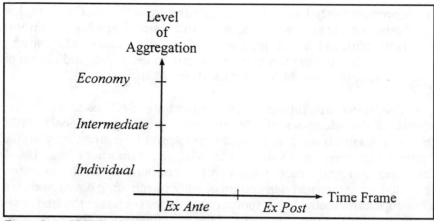

Figure1. An IS/IT Evaluation Framework

ing problems. *Ex post* evaluation presents problems of valid inference. To what may *ex post* performance (or lack thereof) be attributed? Is investment in IS a contributing factor, and if so, to what extent? What are the other endogenous or exogenous variables that also contribute?

Moreover, *ex ante* and *ex post* evaluations differ with respect to the nature of the entity being evaluated (Chismar, Kriebel, & Melone, 1985, p. 5). Is the entity a product, a process, or both? *Ex ante* evaluation focuses on a hypothetical information system of general design only as a product. Assuming this hypothetical product of the development process was properly implemented, given its design parameters, would it be effective in dealing with the decision problem? In *ex ante* evaluation, the product alone is necessary for the determination of hypothetical effectiveness. On the other hand, *ex post* evaluation confounds the actual product and the actual implementation process. For an information system to actually be effective, it must not only be well-designed (i.e., a "good" product), it must also be properly integrated into the organization. In *ex post* evaluation, the product and process are jointly necessary for the determination of actual effectiveness.

The evaluation process can take place at several alternative levels of aggregation. Identification of these levels is somewhat arbitrary. This research partitions IS evaluation into three levels: individual, intermediate, and economy. At the individual level the focus is on an IS as it effects individual decisionmakers. At the economy level, evaluation of information technology (IT) focuses on IT's effect on the growth rate of the entire economy. At this level a distinction is often made between industrial sectors (e.g., manufacturing and service). The intermediate levels of aggregation include work group/department, SBU, organization, and industry.

Reference Theory/Methodology

Reference theories and/or methodologies for IS evaluation may be associated with either decision theory or production theory. In turn, these may be classified in terms of the basic framework (See Figure 2).

Decision Theory

Reference theories for IS evaluation based on decision theory have been identified (See Table 1). Information Economics (IE) is a reference theory for *ex ante* IS evaluation at the individual level. IE was developed, primarily by Marschak (1968, 1971), as a reference theory for *ex ante* IS evaluation at the individual level. The normative model of individual decisionmaking under risk is a good starting point for the examination of IE (Demski, 1972). This model has the following components:

S   set of "states of nature" $(s \in S)$

p(s) probability distribution defined over S

A   set of "actions" available to the Decision Maker (DM), $(a \in A)$

Z   set of "outcomes" resulting from action-state pairs $(z \in Z)$

w   "outcome" function that maps action-state pairs into outcomes [i.e. $z = w(s,a)$]

u   DM's utility function mapping outcomes into utility levels [i.e., $u = u(z)$]

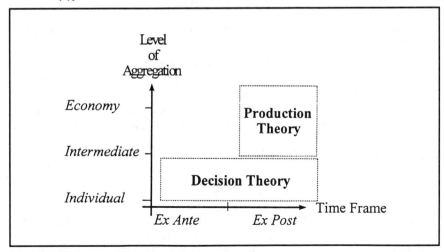

Figure 2. Reference Theories & the Framework

Reference	Roadmap Contribution
Information Economics (IE)	
Demski (1972)	Presentation of the IE model
Emery (1971)	Observations on the origins of information value
Hilton (1981)	Identification of exogenous sources of value and associated theorems
Ahituv (1981, 1982) Barua, Kriebel, & Mukhopadhyay (1989)	Application of IE to evaluation in IS
Multiple Information Attribute Evaluation (MIA)	
Keeney & Raiffa (1976)	Presentation of multiple attribute decision theory
Ahituv (1980)	Application of MIA to evaluation in IS

Table 1: Decision Theory: Key References & Roadmap Contribution

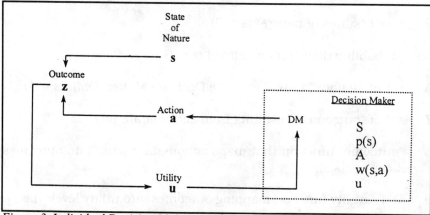

Figure 3. Individual Decision Making Under Risk

The DM is assumed to choose an action (a*) that maximizes the expected value of her utility: E(u | a*). The DM does not observe actual states (s) with certainty, and must choose an action (a) in view of the prior probability distribution p(s). Figure 3 provides a characterization of the relationship between components in this model.

The IE model supplements the model of decision making under risk by introducing an "information system" (h). Specifically, after formulating the model above, but before making an action choice, the DM receives a "signal" from h:

Y   set of signals (y ∈ Y) for system h.

Before the DM receives the signal, her judgment regarding the state of nature likely to prevail is encoded in the probability distribution p(s). After receiving the signal (y), the relevant distribution is given by:

p(s|y) conditional probability distribution given that the DM has received signal y from information system h.

In this context, the distinguishing feature of "information" is that the conditional probability distribution is not identical to the original distribution for some s. Information effects the decision problem by providing the DM with revised (improved) estimates of the likelihood of state occurrence.

The conditional distribution p(s|y) is a posterior distribution which is the end result of a probability revision process based on Bayes law. This posterior distribution is derived from the original distribution [p(s)] over S and a prior conditional distribution over Y:

p(y|s) conditional probability distribution that the information system h will emit the signal y given that state s has occurred.

The DM's perception of the information system is most directly expressed in terms of this prior conditional distribution over Y. The collection of such prior distributions for all s forms a Markov matrix.

After the DM has received the signal (y) from h, the expected utility of the optimal action is given as: E(u|a*,y,h). This notation serves to emphasize that determination of the optimal action is based on a given signal emanated by a given information system. If the DM "adopts" information system h, then the maximum expected utility to the DM over all signals emanating from h is given by: E(u|a*,h). Figure 4 provides a characterization of the relationship between components in the model that now incorporates the effect of information system h on the decision problem.

These expected values provide the components for a theoretical representation of the value of an information system. The gross expected value of information system h [GV(h)], also called the demand value, is the maximum value that a DM would be willing to "pay" in

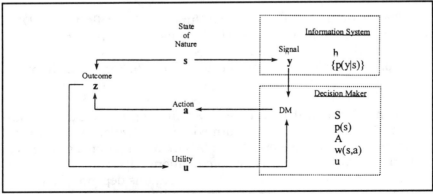

Figure 4. The Information Economics Model

utility units for the use of information system h: GV(h) = E(u|a*,h) - E(u|a*). This value representation is the expected utility difference between adopting system h and making decisions without an information system at all (i.e. the "null" system).

The IE model provides several insights into the theoretical structure of information system evaluation. Information does not have intrinsic value, but rather the value of information is based on the benefits it provides for its users and/or the organization. In particular, in the IE model the source of value for an information system is the improvement of probability estimates for the occurrence of states which affect the payoff from a decision. The value of an information system is relative (comparative) in nature. Since GV(h) is the difference between E(u|a*,h) and E(u|a*), the value of an information system is the expected payoff difference between use of the system in question and the "null" system. Furthermore, in terms of GV(h), Hilton (1979, 1981) points out that there are two sets of factors at work to determine the value of an information system: (1) exogenous factors that are external to the information system, and (2) the information system itself.

Four exogenous factors are evident:

1. the DM's technology and environment as reflected in the outcome function (w);

2. the DM's relative preference for outcomes and attitudes towards risk as reflected in her utility function (u);

3. the DM's initial uncertainty about some aspect(s) of her technology and environment characterized as the degree of uncertainty in the prior distribution over states of nature (p(s));

4. and the DM's flexibility as reflected in the structure of her action set (A).

The structure of the outcome function (w) reflects the DM's *perception* of a complex system which transforms act-state pairs into outcomes (Hilton, 1979, p. 416). This function represents the DM's model of the decision problem (See Ackoff, 1967). For a given information system, the DM chooses an optimal action on the basis of that perceived model.

In the IE model, an information system is represented as a Markov matrix. The Markov matrix is formed as a collection of conditional probability distributions over "signals" emanating from a given information system. There are as many conditional distributions as there are states of nature upon which the distributions depend. If a Markov matrix is an adequate representation of what is commonly understood to be an "information system," then the attributes of information and/ or an information system should also be representable within that framework. The information attribute most readily characterized through the IE model is accuracy. A perfectly accurate information system is one for which there is a one-to-one relationship between states of nature and signals. Under these circumstances, the main diagonal of the Markov matrix contains unit probabilities and all off-diagonal elements are zero.

The IE model is criticized (Kleijnen 1980a, 1980b; Treacy, 1981) for its assumptions regarding (1) the extent of knowledge required by the DM, (2) the rationality of the DM, and (3) the simplicity of the model. Not only must the DM know S, A, and w; but also she must be able to specify prior probabilities over states p(s), and the "accuracy" of the information system in terms of the Markov matrix p(y | s). The IE model is static in nature and assumes an individual DM. The choice of an action as well as the choice of an information system must often take time into account — it is a dynamic situation. Moreover, in an organizational setting, very often choice of action and choice of information system are group rather than individual decisions.

From the viewpoint of the MIS community, perhaps the most telling criticism of the assumptions of the IE model focuses on the primitive manner in which the "system" is characterized in the IE model. The Markov matrix most directly represents a feature of the information forthcoming from a system, and only very obliquely the system itself (Keen, 1982). The IE model does not incorporate components which represent the fundamental design parameters that define a system (e.g., data, hardware, etc.). The system as a process is only identifiable in terms of its output and the extent to which that output can represent value-related attributes (e.g., accuracy, timeliness, etc.) is also limited (Kleijnen, 1980a, 1980b).

This latter shortcoming of the basic IE model has been addressed by Barua, et al. (1989). These authors recognized that the choice of system design variables determines the output attributes of the information system. Accordingly, they developed an expanded version of the IE model that incorporates system design parameters and their relationship to output attributes. As an illustration of how such an expanded model might be employed to evaluate alternative information systems, they employ a dominance approach in an attempt to identify optimal design parameters with respect to the DM payoffs for a specific set of exogenous factors.

In summary, while subject to criticism, the IE model does provide a valuable conceptual framework (Kleijnen, 1980a), and it does demonstrate a rigorous approach to defining the value of an information system and an analytic strategy for the development of theory (Keen, 1980). The model's ability to separate the exogenous factors (i.e., the decision problem and decision maker) from the system itself as sources of value is especially important.

There is another approach to evaluation of IS that proceeds from a decision theory perspective. While there is no well-received label for this approach, it can be described as Multiple Information Attribute (MIA) evaluation. The approach is based on an effort to formulate the DM's utility function for information, and then evaluate alternative information systems in terms of that function. The arguments of the utility function are information attribute measures produced by a specific information system

Keeney and Raiffa (1976, pp.66-68) provide a formal statement of the general multiattribute value problem. The components of the problem include:

A   a set of actions or alternatives available to the DM ($a \in A$).

$X_1(a),....,X_n(a)$ n indices of value associated with n outcome attributes given choice of alternative (a), where X_i is the ith attribute and x_i is a specific magnitude of the ith attribute.

Assuming that the DM "knows" the relevant set of alternatives (A), the specification of attributes suitable for a given decision problem is logically the first task faced by the DM. There is no risk or uncertainty in this decision problem. Given a choice of (a), the outcome in terms of n attribute measures is known with certainty by the DM. However, logically the second task faced by the DM in this setting is to resolve the value tradeoffs implicit in the multiple decision criteria (i.e. attributes of an outcome). Formally, such a resolution requires:

v   a scalar valued function (i.e. value function) where $v(x_1,....,x_n) \geq v(x_1',....,x_n')$ if and only if $(x_1,....,x_n)$ is preferred or indifferent to $(x_1',....,x_n')$.

Given such a value function v, a rational DM chooses an alternative (a) so as to maximize v. This approach serves to indirectly compare various magnitudes of the different attributes through their effect on v.

There have been numerous attempts to identify the attributes generally associated with information (Zmud, 1978). Kleijnen (1980a, Ch. 6) provides a listing of eleven information attributes found in the literature and a framework intended to distinguish between independent (i.e., nonredundant) attributes. His list includes: timeliness, accuracy, aggregation, report mode, retention time, privacy & security, reliability & recovery, scope, user-machine modes, flexibility, and multiple users.

Ahituv (1980) maps the problem of *ex ante* information system evaluation into multiple criteria decision theory. In this formulation, the set of alternative actions (A) is a set of candidate information systems pertinent to a given information problem {h}. In determining which system to select, an information evaluator (the decision maker in this context) elicits the information preference structure of the system user. In doing so, the evaluator must (in principle):

1. identify the relevant attributes of information;

2. measure each attribute, i.e., x_i, $i = 1...n$;

3. specify the "marginal" utility function of each attribute;

4. and specify the joint utility function over all attributes i.e. v.

If these steps have been accomplished, it remains to employ a suitable algorithm to maximize the joint utility function and thereby identify the optimal information system. Figure 5 provides a characterization of the relationship between components in the MIA model.

Due to their common roots in decision theory, portions of the MIA approach correspond with the IE model. Both include a utility function. Furthermore, accuracy, an "information attribute," is characterized in terms of a feature of the Markov matrix in the basic IE model. However, in the MIA approach, these components are combined differently. As opposed to the IE model where two choices had to be made, an action and an information system, in the MIA approach there is only one — the information system. MIA evaluation and IE differ in the arguments of the utility function. In MIA, preferences are stated over information attributes rather than decision problem outcomes as in IE. In MIA, there is a focus on the information system itself in terms

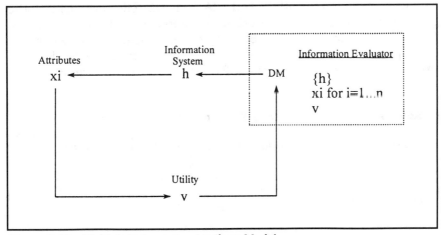

Figure 5. The Multiple Information Attribute Model

of its user-interpreted attributes, and not on the benefits generated by the system serving the users in their decision making capacity.

The MIA approach provides no links to the decision problem towards whose solution the information system is intended to contribute. There is no model of the relation between the system and decision outcomes. Such a model is implicit in the user's preferences. The assumption is that the user knows best — the user knows the decision problem. Furthermore, without a model of the decision problem, there is no means to incorporate non-IS (exogenous) factors that contribute to value.

In summary, a major difference between IE and MIA evaluation is the source of value for an information system. In IE, value is seen as being derived from the outcomes of decisions facilitated by the IS. In MIA, value is seen as derived from the user directly with no explicit recognition of the decision problem that the user faces. The unique contribution of the MIA approach is that it promotes the user as the primary locus of "value" for the information system. In doing so, it provides a theoretical base for a variety of user oriented evaluation methodologies that appear in the literature.

Cost Benefit Analysis

In comparison with IE and MIA, Cost-Benefit Analysis (CBA) is much more of a methodology than a theory (See Table 2). As the terminology suggests, it involves a comparative examination of the costs and benefits of a project. There are a host of analysis and design textbooks that illustrate the use of CBA for the evaluation of investment in information systems. Emery (1971), and King and Schrems (1978) provide more detailed expositions. Sassone (1988) offers an up to date review of a variety of methodologies that broadly fall under the guise of CBA.

CBA is related to both IE and MIA. Since IE relies primarily on the gross value calculation, the primary emphasis of IE is on benefits. Emery emphasizes (1971, p. 6) IE specifies what should be known in principle to properly measure benefits, namely a model of the decision problem that incorporates the effect of alternative information sys-

Reference	Road Map Contribution
Sassone (1988)	Application of CBA to IS/IT Evaluation
Kaplan (1986)	Adjustments to CBA techniques
Dos Santos (1991)	The Options approach

Table 2: Cost Benefit Analysis: Key References and Road Map Contribution

tems. Keeney and Raiffa (1976, p. 20-25) discuss CBA as a multiattribute value problem. That is, CBA can be characterized as a decision problem in which the outcome attributes take the form of a cost measure C, and r benefit measures $B_1, B_2, ..., B_r$. They emphasize that these benefit measures may be in different units of measurement. In this regard they point out that some means of condensing the benefits into a single (monetary) measure is needed. They suggest that it is necessary to construct a set of conversion factors (i.e., shadow prices) to accomplish this. They also point out issues of time discounting in situations where there are t future time periods over which a stream of costs and r streams of benefits occur. The decision criterion is a scalar valued function whose arguments include the costs and benefits for a given project. Sassone and Schaffer (1978) identify nine alternative criteria and advocate the use of Net Present Value (NPV) in those circumstances where the problem structure allows it.

CBA applied to the evaluation of information systems became established practice when transactions processing dominated information services activities. In that type of environment, the benefits of automating existing data handling processes largely took the form of enhanced efficiency. These cost savings were relatively straightforward to quantify. However, in a modern context, computer-based information systems are more directly concerned with effectiveness. Decision Support Systems (DSS), Expert Systems (ES), and Executive Information Systems (EIS) all have "improved decisionmaking" as a primary objective. More recently, Strategic Information Systems (SIS) focus on "competitive advantage" as the major benefit.

Keen (1975) was one of the first to point out the problems of using CBA in more modern information systems environments. A major problem has been how to measure benefits associated with such systems. Hogue and Watson (1983) present the results of a field study of eighteen DSS's in which they inquired into the methods employed to evaluate the proposed (*ex ante*) DSS. They found that only 23% of the companies specifically considered both the costs and benefits of the DSS, only 17% quantified the benefits, and all the quantified benefits were in the form of cost saving. Moreover, in an *ex post* sense, 94% of the companies made no formal attempt to measure the financial impact of the DSS after it became operational. Matlin (1982, p. 191) states the reason that managers exert little effort to find or document the benefits of information systems is that they "intuitively know that most of the benefits of information systems investments are intangible, difficult to measure, and difficult to relate to profit results." Assuming the continued use of capital budgeting techniques such as CBA, Chismar (1986, p. 4) has suggested that the consequence of this problem is that information technology will tend to be under funded. In particular, underfunding would occur in comparison with non-IT projects for which the benefits are more concrete.

Sassone and Schaffer (1978, p. 166) "... consider the costs and benefits of a project as lying along a spectrum of 'quantifiability,' ranging from intangibles through incommensurables to market goods." They define intangibles as effects (i.e., costs or benefits of a project) involving non-economic "values" that are not susceptible to measurement. Incommensurables, however, may be readily measured, but not in money terms. Finally, market goods are any good or service exchanged through a market and hence possessing a market price — a direct measure of economic value. A significant problem facing the analyst is how far to go in "converting" apparent incommensurables into monetary terms. The conversion process itself is based on the use of "shadow prices" for the incommensurables. Shadow prices are non-market monetary values imputed to a good or service. These, in turn, are used to monetize associated incommensurable effects. The construction of shadow ·prices requires a methodology, and is not a costless activity.

It is noteworthy that in their discussion of CBA as a type of multiattribute value problem, Keeney & Raiffa (1976) identify the lack of a mechanism to cope with uncertainty as a problem. The benefits for certain types of systems may be subject to uncertainty. For example, strategic systems, especially those that have interorganizational features, can be subject to network externalities. A network externality exists when a user's demand for a network services depends on the demand of other users (McAndrews, 1993). When evaluating investment in an interorganizational system providing network services (unless the investing organization can compel users to participate) the likelihood of participation by target users may be unknown, and this in turn can make the determination of likely system benefits uncertain.

The ex post application of CBA poses another problem distinct from the issue of measurement alone. For the sake of exposition, assume that appropriate ex post financial measurement is feasible and that it has been done. Recall that according to the IE model, the value of an information system is established in a comparative or relative manner. Relative value determination poses problems for *ex post* analysis. An alternative has been chosen and implemented. Actual value should be measured. But in comparison to what? Gremillion and Pyburn (1985) have pointed this difficulty out with regard to the determination of benefits for a DSS. They argue that one of the reasons that benefit determination for a DSS is so difficult is that it requires a counterfactual comparison. That is, the comparison of actual payoffs associated with employing the DSS, versus the hypothetical payoff for an alternative that was not chosen. Lincoln (1986) refers to this as the problem of the "contentious comparator."

Kaplan (1986) argues that managers should not abandon CBA to evaluate investments in information technology, but that appropriate adjustments to the traditional use of CBA must be made when it is employed to evaluate a modern IT investment such as computer integrated manufacturing. In particular, Kaplan points out that in choosing comparator(s) for the analysis, the status quo alternative of current market share, selling price, and costs may be a poor choice. The appropriate comparator may well be a situation of declining cash flows, market share, and profit margins based on a foregone strategic opportunity that may be undertaken by competitors. Kaplan (1986, p. 92) also suggests that the conservative valuation of intangible benefits at zero is essentially a preference for "being precisely wrong rather than vaguely right." In this regard, he suggests CBA based sensitivity analysis in which managers first estimate how large intangible benefits must be to justify the proposed investment. In a manner similar to Kaplan, using CBA as a point of reference, Clemons (1991) offers some guidelines and principles to structure ex ante investment decisions for strategic information systems.

Several authors have suggested that modern IT investment might better be treated as expenditure on Research and Development (See Keen, 1981; Gremillion & Pyburn, 1985; Curley & Pyburn, 1982; Curley & Henderson, 1989). Keen (1981) argues that it is more appropriate to view a DSS as a form of innovation involving research and development than as a capital investment. Such an approach is also appropriate for investment in IT infrastructure. IT infrastructure are IT resources that are shared by functional areas or business units in a organization. Examples include networks and operating systems. Specific business application systems are built on top of such infrastructure. Investment in infrastructure provides an organization with the flexibility to subsequently develop and implement new application systems. This flexibility has business value. Dos Santos (1991) has demonstrated how financial options theory can be employed to estimate this value in a CBA context.

In summary, while CBA has a long history as an evaluation methodology in MIS, its *ex ante* use with modern information systems often poses benefit quantification problems, and its *ex post* use poses an arbitrary choice of comparator. In the literature, a good deal of attention has been focused on the former problem. The IE model provides a structure for analysis of benefits in the case of decision support systems. The failure to fully measure system benefits in dollar terms implies that information technology may be underfunded in comparison with alternative investment projects possessing more concrete benefit measurements. In view of this, if CBA is employed to evaluate investment in IT, an analyst must make appropriate adjustments to consciously account for problems encountered in this application of the methodology.

Reference	Road Map Contribution
Bailey & Pearson (1983) Ives, Olson, & Baroudi (1983)	Widely employed instruments used to measure UIS
Goodhue (1986) Chismar, Kriebel, & Melone (1985)	Criticisms of UIS as a surrogate of effectiveness

Table 3: User Information Satisfaction: Key References and Roadmap Contribution

User Information Satisfaction

Partly as a response to the benefit quantification problems of CBA, methodologies based on more readily available surrogate measures of effectiveness have been developed. According to Melone (1990) the two most frequently used are user satisfaction and system use, and of the two user satisfaction is the most popular (See Table 3). Ives, Olson, and Baroudi (1983) introduce the concept of User Information Satisfaction (UIS) as a tool for the evaluation of information systems.

> The decision to install an information system necessitates a choice of mechanisms to determine whether an information system is needed, and once implemented, whether it is functioning properly. User information satisfaction (UIS) is one such evaluation mechanism. UIS is defined as the extent to which users believe the information system available to them meets their information requirements. UIS provides a meaningful "surrogate" for the critical but unmeasurable result of an information system, namely, changes in organizational effectiveness.... UIS is a perceptual or subjective measure of system success. It serves as a substitute for objective determinants of information system effectiveness which are frequently not available. Theoretically, the determination of information system value is a matter of economics; the costs of system operations and development are subtracted from the actual benefits (in improved organizational effectiveness) to obtain net value of the system to the organization. In practice, however, this may not be a simple determination... (p. 785)

A large number of studies have developed measures of UIS. The work of Bailey and Pearson (1983) is an example of how these techniques can be used to develop a measure of UIS.

> The literature generally agreed that satisfaction in a given situation is the sum of one's feelings or attitudes toward a variety of factors affecting that situation. ..The applicable definition of

satisfaction is the sum of the user's weighted reactions to a set of factors,

$$S_i = \sum_{j=1}^{n} R_{ij} W_{ij}$$

where
R_{ij} = The reaction to factor j by individual i
W_{ij} = The importance of factor j to individual i
(p. 531).

Operationalization requires two steps; identifying a set of "factors" that are related to satisfaction, and developing a survey instrument (i.e., questionnaire) that incorporates a technique for scaling an individual's reactions to each of the factors. Part of the survey instrument development should include tests for reliability and validity.

UIS can be viewed as a methodology based on MIA evaluation. The "factors" of UIS correspond to the attributes of MIA. The factors used by Bailey and Pearson (1983) were identified through a literature review, and interviews with data processing professionals and managers. The resulting list of factors was tested for "completeness" using critical incident analysis. The first step ultimately resulted in the identification of 39 factors. These included such information attributes as accuracy and timeliness.

As with attributes, each factor must be measured for a given individual. Bailey and Pearson (1983) employed six semantic differential adjective pairs with a seven step scale for each factor. Four of the pairs were averaged to get a value of R_{ij}. One of the pairs was used to get a value for W_{ij}. The resulting instrument was then administered to the managers who participated in identifying the factors. The survey data was then employed in testing for validity and reliability. Ives, Olson, and Baroudi (1983) have altered and further tested the Bailey and Pearson instrument. They advocate the adoption of the modified instrument as a standard measure of UIS.

UIS has been subject to criticism by academicians. Iivari (1987) summarizes the criticism and categorizes the "problems" of UIS. A fundamental criticism has been leveled by Goodhue (1986), Chismar, Kriebel & Melone (1985); Melone (1990); and Chismar & Kriebel (1985). These authors argue that the UIS literature exhibits a lack of attention to a theoretical base for the construct of UIS, and rushes to measure what has not been adequately defined and/or linked to objects of ultimate interest.

Goodhue (1986) focuses on the lack of theoretical development evident in a number of empirical studies that attempt to link user attitudes to features of information systems either as an antecedent or consequent. An example of this is the Delphi approach employed by Bailey and Pearson (1983) for the identification of "factors." Goodhue uses the research literature on job satisfaction for the development of a theoretical model of information system satisfaction.

Chismar, Kriebel, and Melone (1985), and Melone (1990) logically attack the assertion that UIS is a meaningful surrogate for economic effectiveness at the organization level. They argue that to assert that user satisfaction is a surrogate for effectiveness requires a strong relationship between user satisfaction and effectiveness. The strongest relationship would be a causal relationship. A causal relationship requires the joint presence of necessity and sufficiency as conditions of the relationship. Melone (1990, p. 79) contends that necessity is a "more prevalent" justification for employing UIS, and that "few" such authors claim user satisfaction is a sufficient condition for effectiveness. Melone then concludes that "in the strictest sense, the construct (UIS) cannot be a surrogate for effectiveness."

Chismar et al. (1985) pursue this approach by arguing that a case against UIS as a necessary condition for effectiveness can be made on the grounds of either economics or behavioral science. The economic argument largely follows from differences in scope between UIS and organizational effectiveness. UIS is a construct at the level of the individual while organizational effectiveness is a construct at a higher level of aggregation. Economists have recognized that goal incompatibility, sub-optimality, and conflict based on individually rational behavior can lead to situations where "the relative satisfaction experienced by an individual through use of an information system may have...no relation to the value realized by the firm for services received" (1985, p. 8). The behavioral science argument anticipates the work of Goodhue (1986). That is, Chismar and Kriebel (1985, p. 46) point out that the job satisfaction literature shows little empirical evidence that satisfied workers are more productive.

The UIS approach has been extended to apply to the entire information services function. Dickson, Wells and Wilkes (1988) present a comprehensive framework intended to identify the entire choice set of factors/criteria that could be employed in an assessment of the IS function. Miller and Doyle (1987) propose a 38-item instrument of which 36 items were drawn from two other studies. Each item describes a factor presumed pertinent to user satisfaction with the IS function. The instrument was administered to 276 managers in 21 firms. The respondents were instructed to answer on a seven step scale in terms of actual performance within their organization. In the absence of a referent system, responses to each item in the instrument are interpreted as the respondent's perception of the overall performance of the IS function within the respondent's organization. Data gathered from the respondents were analyzed to determine the reliability and validity of the instrument.

Criticism of UIS is related to a lack of theoretical basis and a lack of empirical work validating a relationship between subjective assessment outcomes and economic performance. However, examination of the UIS literature reveals that differences between the critics and proponents of UIS extend beyond views on the adequacy of theoretical background and empirical validation. In particular, these differences appear to be rooted in different attitudes regarding the value of information — in particular the distinction between the IE and MIA approaches. The two approaches have fundamentally different arguments in their respective utility functions. On the one hand, IE suggests that information has no intrinsic value, but rather it derives value based on the associated decision problem and the economic consequences of outcomes for the DM. On the other hand, advocates of UIS see the user directly as the source of value.

> Information systems are thus conceived as utilitarian in nature. Their performance measures seek the value of the system in terms of purposeful serving of the clients interest... User attitudes are thus measured because individual assessments of information systems are held to matter." (Swanson, 1988, p. 251-2)

Production Theory

For *ex post* analysis of effectiveness at aggregation levels above the individual, economic production theory is the most frequent theoretical foundation. According to IE, the value of information is derived from the economic outcomes of decisions in which it is employed. However, the concept of the value of information and information systems that produce it, lose these theoretical underpinnings at aggregation levels above that of the individual decision maker and individual information system. At these levels a production paradigm is most often employed as a basis for analysis (See Table 4). Production models link inputs and outputs. IT is one of the inputs that may create output value. It is noteworthy that CBA may be viewed as a production approach. CBA involves an implicit relation between cost (as input) and benefit (as output).

The basic theoretical construct employed either explicitly or

Reference	Roadmap Contribution
Jonscher (1983)	Aggregate economy production model with information sector
Kauffman & Kriebel (1988)	"Intermediate" production related to business value
Mukhopadhyay & Cooper (1993)	Firm level parametric approach to production theory

Table 4: Production Theory: Key References and Road Map Contribution

implicitly is the production function. A production function relates (maximum) output to a given set of inputs with a given technology. A simple production function relating output (Q) of some good or service to inputs of labor (N) and capital (K) could be stated in general form as:

$$Q = f(N, K)$$

When employing this construct to examine relationships between information technology and output, capital and (sometimes) labor is disaggregated into IT and non-IT components. Different combinations of N and K may be employed for a given level of output Q. Selection of the least cost input combination for a given output level depends on input and output prices. In general, the investment decision to purchase more of one of the inputs (e.g., IT capital) should be based on a comparison of increments to output and increments to cost resulting from the incremental input. The productivity of capital is defined in terms of the increase in output from a unit increase in K with other inputs held constant (i.e., $MP_K = \partial Q / \partial K$). Of particular interest is the productivity of IT capital.

In empirical studies, in order to actually measure the productivity of an input such as IT capital, the form of the production function must be specified, in most circumstances. A widely used specification is the Cobb-Douglas production function. A simple version of this production function in parametric form is:

$$Q = N^\alpha K^\beta$$

In this production function, the parameters α and β are referred to as output elasticities for the respective inputs. Output elasticities are another measure of productivity and may be interpreted as the percentage change in output resulting from a one percent increase in the respective input with the other inputs held constant.

Data Envelopment Analysis (DEA) is an empirical technique that has been used to determine the impact of IT on the efficiency of an organization or a sub-unit of an organization. DEA can be employed when performance is measured in terms of output transformed from input(s), and where the nature of that transformation may be represented by a production function. In this use at least one input must be a measure of IT. Such a model is well suited for analysis of the efficiency with which inputs are transformed into outputs. In order to employ a production model it is necessary to estimate production function characteristics from data representing inputs and outputs for organizations or sub-units in the environment to be analyzed. There are two broad approaches to such estimation; parametric and non-parametric. With a parametric approach, the analyst must specify the assumed functional form of the production function in order to employ conventional econometric techniques. As a non-parametric approach, DEA requires less stringent assumptions about the form of the production function. In the evaluation of IT this is an advantage since there is often little *a priori* knowledge of the production function.

As an introduction to intermediate level studies of IT evaluation, Bakos (1987) and Crowston and Treacy (1986) provide literature reviews and calls for work. Both Bakos and Crowston and Treacy offer "linkage" models that have characteristics of a microeconomic production function linking resource inputs to output. The significance of these models is the suggestion that the impact of IT on performance is mediated by Structure and Processes. Bakos points out (p. 16) that empirical inquiry into the direct link between IT and organizational performance is very difficult. Crowston and Treacy deal with Bako's concern regarding the mediating effect of structure and processes in greater detail. They argue that the articles they cite investigate the *direct* link. They go on to suggest that the likelihood for successfully measuring IT input effects on economic outputs would be much greater if such studies carefully modeled the hypothesized process that linked such inputs with economic outputs.

Business Value Linkage (BVL) correlation, is a statistical methodology for the *ex post* evaluation of IT. It can be viewed as a direct effort to model and estimate the parameters of the process, characterized by Crowston and Treacy (1986), that links IT input with economic output at the organization level. By its nature, the analysis is problem dependent. The modeling and estimation is carried out on a case by case basis.

BVL correlation is loosely based on microeconomic production theory. The hypothesized stochastic relationships between input and output are not production functions in a strict sense. They are offered as a structural representation of the web of relations linking IT, and other resource inputs, to higher order economic outputs (e.g., profit). Kauffman and Kriebel (1988) provide a statement of this approach.

A distinction between different types of output is a critical feature of BVL correlation. The analysis distinguishes between intermediate and higher level output impacts of IT. Ultimately the goal is to measure the impact of IT on economic variables observable at the organization level. However, the connection between IT input and the output in question may not be transparent. BVL correlation partitions the set of organization level economic variables into two subsets; those on whom the hypothesized impact of IT is direct, and those on whom it is indirect.

While there may be an estimable direct connection between some higher level economic variables and IT, given the diffuse impacts of modern information systems, it is likely that the impact of IT on many higher level variables will be the indirect result of a more complex process. In such a process, intermediate output(s) resulting from IT may be lower level economic or incommensurable variables. Assuming for the sake of exposition that this component of the model is recursive, and composed of only two stages, BVL correlation requires that the analyst validate the impact of IT on an intermediate output by means of statistical hypothesis testing. If a statistically significant association is found to exist, then a second stage may be required to estimate the relationship between the direct intermediate output and the indirect, higher level, economic output(s). For example, in general algebraic terms:

$$O_I = g(IT, X_I)$$
$$O_{HL} = h(O_I, X_{HL})$$

where:

O_I	= Intermediate Output
IT	= Information Technology Input
X_I	= Intermediate Exogenous Factors
O_{HL}	= Higher Level Output
X_{HL}	= Higher Level Exogenous Factors

BVL correlation has been suggested as a methodology that can be directly useful to managers. The *ex post* effectiveness information it provides may assist managers in *ex ante* evaluation of similar systems or in the incremental enhancement of the system under examination. Kauffman and Kriebel (1988) identify the "steps" that managers must take to implement the methodology. The outputs on which IT is presumed to have an impact are defined by management. Although evidence of economic impact is sought at the firm level, the focus is on evaluation of a specific system. The IT input variable often takes the form of a categorical variable that accounts for the physical presence or absence of the system for a given observation.

Empirical Research

Individual Level

From an outcome perspective, at the individual level (See Table 5) MIS evaluation falls prey to problems of measurement. Individual decision maker(s) employ a specific (individual) IS to assist them in making decisions that produce economic outcomes. Nevertheless,

Reference	Road Map Contribution
Dickson, Senn, & Chervany (1977)	Overview of laboratory experimentation in IS
Sharda, Barr, & McDonnell (1988) Benbasat, DeSanctis, & Nault (1991)	Reviews of empirical evaluation in IS employing laboratory experiment
Jarvenpaa, Dickson, & DeSanctis (1985)	Issues in laboratory experimentation in IS

Table 5: Individual Level: Key References and Road Map Contribution

using actual field data it is extremely difficult to isolate ex post outcomes at the individual level. Observed data typically represent the joint impact of multiple decision makers employing multiple systems. This is a problem unique to the individual level. Field data is seldom, if ever, available at that unit level.

The difficulty of isolating individual outcomes has led academics to explore an alternative approach. With respect to Van Horn's (1973) taxonomy of empirical research methodologies in MIS, laboratory studies are a methodology which allow one to isolate the relationship between IS parameters and outcome measures. A particular type of laboratory study may be employed for evaluation purposes at the individual level. Dickson, Senn, & Chervany (1977) describe such experiments:

> Man-machine experiments or, as they are frequently called, experimental gaming, imply the creation and use of an artificial decision making environment. A simulator is used to define a specific type of decision, at a specific level of complexity and a specific decision making environment. The application of experimental gaming methodology enables the researcher to control the nature of the information system utilized by the experimental subjects. Consequently, information system characteristics may be varied in order to determine how changes impact the decision outcome. This experimental control is one of the major advantages of this research approach (p. 915).

As the Dickson et al. description suggests, the primary use of this methodology has been to explore the relationship between system design parameters and outcomes. However, this methodology provides a framework for MIS evaluation. That is, it becomes MIS evaluation if the experimental design distinguishes between experimental and control groups on the basis of access or no access, respectively, to an MIS.

Under these circumstances, this methodology resembles the IE model in several respects. Since the value of decision outcomes may be derived from the decision simulator, the value of the information system is based on decision outcomes. Moreover, value is established in the same comparative sense as embodied in the gross value equation of IE. That is, the outcome difference between experimental and control groups reflects the difference between use of the information system in question and the null system. In most instances, the IS is provided to the subjects. Therefore, since cost is not taken into account in those cases where the IS is provided, value is established in a gross rather than net sense. Finally, when appropriate incentives are provided to the subjects, the experimental design can serve to encourage rational behavior on the part of the decision maker.

There are a number of laboratory studies that focus on MIS evaluation. Sharda, Barr, and McDonnell (1988) review laboratory studies of MIS/DSS effectiveness, and Benbasat, DeSanctis, and Nault (1991) review and assess empirical research on management support systems. Both reviews contain at least one component that specifically focuses on laboratory experiments whose experimental design dictated availability or non-availability of a computer-based decision aid for the experimental and control groups.

In their examination of the literature, Sharda et al. (1988) identify twelve laboratory studies (including their own paper) with an experimental design focused on the evaluation of effectiveness. Of these, ten of the twelve studies employed individual decision makers. Five of the twelve employed profit as the performance criterion in a simulated decision environment. On the basis of their review, Sharda et al. (1988, p. 144) conclude that "field and laboratory tests investigating superiority of DSS over non-DSS decisions show inconclusive results." In their own laboratory experiment, Sharda et al. attempt to rectify what they believe are methodological shortcomings that may have led to inconclusive results.

Benbasat et al. (1991) examine ten laboratory experiments and one field experiment involving individual decision makers. Of these eleven experiments, nine were DSS and two were expert systems. In a manner similar to Sharda et al., Benbasat et al. (1991, p. 21) conclude that, "Empirical investigations into the performance effects of DSS availability have been inconclusive. While in some studies use of DSS improved performance, in several studies unaided users performed as well as aided users."

The most oft-cited criticism of laboratory experiments is that of external validity. Can conclusions based on laboratory experiments be generalized to the world of experience? In particular, are the results of experiments with business students generalizable to how business-men behave? Alpert (1967, p. 207) concludes that the best approach is to use businessmen rather than business students as subjects. Hughes and Gibson (1991) also found that students and actual managers behaved in significantly different ways in an experimental setting involving a DSS generator.

The decision simulator in the experiment provides the mapping from the action set to states of the world. As such it must be linked to the decision task faced by the subjects. Courtney, DeSanctis, and Kasper (1983) focus on issues associated with the computer-based simulator. The authors express concern over the high software development costs incurred in building a decision simulator, and the lack of research continuity and replicability associated with the proliferation of simulators.

Jarvenpaa, Dickson, and DeSanctis (1985) examine issues concerning the decision task facing the subject. Since the impact of an experimental treatment on decision making effectiveness depends on the task, a wide array of decision tasks (i.e. excessive task diversity between experiments) contributes to incomparable research. Moreover, if the experimental task is too complex for the subject, the results of the experiment are not a valid reflection of the experimental treatment. In the IE model, the extent of knowledge assumptions require that the DM knows "enough" that she can precisely predict outcomes given action-state pairs. From this point of view, the author's concerns regarding task complexity are analogous to being sure that the DM has the necessary knowledge.

The empirical literature on MIS evaluation at the individual level shows the laboratory experiment to be the dominant research methodology. However, the results of laboratory experiments focusing on MIS evaluation do not clearly demonstrate superior performance by individuals for whom a MIS was available. Since laboratory experiments in MIS are subject to a variety of problems, these research outcomes may reflect issues with the research methodology. Among the problems cited are: (1) external validity, (2) proliferation of decision simulators, and (3) excessive diversity and complexity of experimental tasks.

Aggregate Economy

Futurists such as Bell (1973) and Naisbitt (1982) were the first to identify the growth in information production. They noted that the apparent shift in industrial emphasis from manufacturing to services was actually a shift from direct production of goods to a more indirect production of goods and services based on the intermediate product, information. This shift was most evident in the changing composition of the labor force, from blue- to white-collar. However, in the midst of the growth in information production, beginning around 1973, the U.S. economy experienced a substantial reduction in its rate of economic growth resulting from a decline in the rate of growth of labor productivity (See Denison, 1979). The fact that a growth in information production coincided with a decline in the growth rate of average labor

Reference	Roadmap Contribution
Denison (1979)	The aggregate productivity slowdown
Roach (1984)	Relations between information production and productivity
Baily & Gordon (1988) Brynjolfsson (1993)	Analysis of and reasons for the productivity slowdown
Panko (1991)	A case for measurement error

Table 6: Economic Level: References and Road Map Contribution

productivity (ALP), has not gone unnoticed. As a public issue, it has been termed the "productivity paradox" (See Table 6).

In order to investigate whether these two trends are related, it would be useful to break down the aggregate ALP data to compare the productivity of information and non-information workers over the relevant time span. While ALP may be separately calculated for the manufacturing and service sectors from published data, such measures do not directly focus on the relative productivity of information and non-information workers. That is, manufacturing industries employ information workers, and service industries employ non-information workers. Roach (1984a) has employed aggregate data reorganization techniques, originally advanced by Porat (1977) to measure "partial" productivity for information workers and production workers across industrial sectors. Such workers are identified in terms of their job classifications. Roach's data (1984a, p. 7) indicate that following 1974, the decline in total ALP has coincided with an increasing proportion of information workers with lower measured productivity than their goods-producing counterparts.

However, it is possible that the observed difference in productivity between information and non-information workers over the time span was due to a difference in the amount of capital equipment that each type of worker had available to them at that time. In two other papers, Roach (1984b, 1987) examines reorganized aggregate data on capital accumulation as it pertains to information production. Roach (1984b) subdivides business fixed investment and capital stock data into several categories. Two of these, high-technology and basic industrial, are intended to represent "functional" categories of capital that support information production and goods production, respectively. These investment and capital stock data are combined with labor force data that has been reorganized in a manner similar to that employed to derive "partial" productivity measures. That is, the aggregate labor force is subdivided into information workers and production workers. This all results in time series data showing investment/labor and capital/labor ratios for high-tech capital per information worker and basic industrial capital per production worker. These data indicate that by the late 70's, the investment in high tech/information worker ratio exceeds the investment in basic industrial/production worker ratio. Consequently, with a lag, by the mid 80's the high tech capital/information worker ratio exceeded the basic industrial capital/production worker ratio.

If one assumes that a low early productivity performance of information workers was due to a low level of IT capital per worker, these data indicate that the rapid accumulation of IT capital should subsequently mitigate the problem. Moreover, production theory indicates that the increasing relative size of the information labor force provides additional "leverage" for the impact of the IT capital/information worker ratio on the productivity of information workers.

Baily and Gordon (1988) report on their study of the productivity slowdown and its status as of the mid-1980's. Their examination of the average labor productivity data takes place within the context of traditional industry groupings. They conclude that, while capital investment trends and leverage would tend to favor information worker productivity as compared with production worker productivity, the data indicate the opposite outcome.

Brynjolfsson (1993) and Baily and Gordon (1988) offer four explanations for the paradox: lags, redistribution, mismanagement, and mismeasurement.

First, fundamental structural changes in methods of production take time to be absorbed by the economy. The labor force has to be (re)trained and organizations must learn to productively employ new technology. During this period of adjustment productivity may actually decline at first. However, after the adjustment, gains should be rapid.

Second, extensive strategic use of IT by organizations may simply lead to the redistribution of wealth and not a net gain to society. A competitive advantage to one firm implies a disadvantage to other players in that organization's competitive environment. Therefore, successful use of IT at the organizational level, may be associated with a minimal effect on aggregate productivity data. This reason suggests that strategic success stories at lower levels of aggregation are compatible with poor productivity performance in the aggregate.

Third, IT may encourage waste and inefficiency if IT managers focus on inappropriate measures of the flow of services that IT provides. Information overload results when the performance of IT is based on the amount of information available or generated rather than its value to the organization.

Fourth, the stagnation of real wages in some occupations may be the result of nonmonetary compensation in the form of improved working conditions based on the use of IT. To the extent that this is true, since measurement of the real value of output is based on the real value resources consumed in its production (Note that this is especially the case for the service industries.), this means that the real value of output in industries employing those occupations is understated. Alternatively, IT may be providing valuable services to the customers of the service sector industries that are not being picked up in the official output data. This is the quality issue. In the aggregate, price deflators are employed to adjust money-denominated time series data from nominal to real terms. Therefore, from an aggregate measurement perspective, if price deflators for consumer service expenditures do not adequately capture quality improvements created by IT, then expenditures and output are understated in real terms.

This last explanation suggests that the apparent lack of an economy level labor productivity boost based on substantial investment in IT capital may result from measurement error. Productivity studies require valid output data. The national income and product account procedures for the valuation of service sector output are largely based on labor input. This measurement approach would seem to make productivity conclusions for the service sector based on the ratio of output to labor input highly suspect.

Panko (1991) presents a spirited case for measurement error. His analysis is based on a detailed examination of the manner in which the aggregate data is gathered by the Bureau of Labor Statistics and subsequently processed to produce productivity estimates. He argues that the data are sufficiently suspect that there is no compelling reason to believe that information worker productivity is stagnant or that, if it were, a compelling case could be made for investment in ineffective IT as a cause.

Baily and Chakrabarti (1988, p. 92-101) develop and employ a simulation model based on the redistribution and mismeasurement explanations in order to investigate whether these factors could account for the observed behavior of the aggregate data. The authors model the behavior of a single "firm" in an "industry" composed of similar firms. All the firms provide a regular product as well as customer service and marketing activities. The customer service output is included with respect to reason four, and marketing output corresponds to the (distributional) issue of reason two. However, as opposed to the actual economy, in the model both customer service and marketing are measured outputs. In addition to the price of the regular product, the output amounts of customer service and marketing enter the demand function for the regular output of the firm. While information capital is employed to produce all three outputs, the production of customer service and marketing is assumed to be more information capital intensive.

Baily and Chakrabarti use the model to simulate the impact of a 20% per year decline in the price of information capital for ten years. The simulation results suggest the following:

(1) Information capital is used more intensively in all activities as the price falls.
(2) Since the production of customer service and marketing is more information capital intensive, these two types of output rise more than regular output.
(3) When information capital and "information" labor are poor substitutes in producing customer service and marketing (and consequently information capital intensive production techniques require more rather than less labor) the ratio of regular output to "information labor" declines.

In an innovative paper, in an attempt to circumvent problems in to be an "information system," then the attributes of information and/ or an information system should also be representable within that framework. The information attribute most readily characterized through the IE model is accuracy. A perfectly accurate information system is one for which there is a one-to-one relationship between states of nature and signals. Under these circumstances, the main diagonal of the Markov matrix contains unit probabilities and all off-diagonal elements are zero.

The IE model is criticized (Kleijnen 1980a, 1980b; Treacy, 1981) for its assumptions regarding (1) the extent of knowledge required by the DM, (2) the rationality of the DM, and (3) the simplicity of the model. Not only must the DM know S, A, and w; but also she must be able to specify prior probabilities over states p(s), and the "accuracy" of the information system in terms of the Markov matrix $p(y \mid s)$. The IE model is static in nature and assumes an individual DM. The choice of an action as well as the choice of an information system must often take time into account — it is a dynamic situation. Moreover, in an organizational setting, very often choice of action and choice of information system are group rather than individual decisions.

From the viewpoint of the MIS community, perhaps the most telling criticism of the assumptions of the IE model focuses on the primitive manner in which the "system" is characterized in the IE model. The Markov matrix most directly represents a feature of the information forthcoming from a system, and only very obliquely the system itself (Keen, 1982). The IE model does not incorporate components which represent the fundamental design parameters that define a system (e.g., data, hardware, etc.). The system as a process is only identifiable in terms of its output and the extent to which that output can represent value-related attributes (e.g., accuracy, timeliness, etc.) is also limited (Kleijnen, 1980a, 1980b).

This latter shortcoming of the basic IE model has been addressed by Barua, et al. (1989). These authors recognized that the choice of system design variables determines the output attributes of the information system. Accordingly, they developed an expanded version of the IE model that incorporates system design parameters and their relationship to output attributes. As an illustration of how such an expanded model might be employed to evaluate alternative information systems, they employ a dominance approach in an attempt to identify optimal design parameters with respect to the DM payoffs for a specific set of exogenous factors.

In summary, while subject to criticism, the IE model does provide a valuable conceptual framework (Kleijnen, 1980a), and it does demonstrate a rigorous approach to defining the value of an information system and an analytic strategy for the development of theory (Keen, 1980). The model's ability to separate the exogenous factors (i.e., the decision problem and decision maker) from the system itself as sources of value is especially important.

There is another approach to evaluation of IS that proceeds from a decision theory perspective. While there is no well-received label for this approach, it can be described as Multiple Information Attribute (MIA) evaluation. The approach is based on an effort to formulate the DM's utility function for information, and then evaluate alternative information systems in terms of that function. The arguments of the utility function are information attribute measures produced by a specific information system

Keeney and Raiffa (1976, pp.66-68) provide a formal statement of the general multiattribute value problem. The components of the problem include:

A   a set of actions or alternatives available to the DM ($a \in A$).

$X_1(a),....,X_n(a)$ n indices of value associated with n outcome attributes given choice of alternative (a), where X_i is the ith attribute and x_i is a specific magnitude of the ith attribute.

Assuming that the DM "knows" the relevant set of alternatives (A), the specification of attributes suitable for a given decision problem is logically the first task faced by the DM. There is no risk or uncertainty in this decision problem. Given a choice of (a), the outcome in terms of n attribute measures is known with certainty by the DM. However, logically the second task faced by the DM in this setting is to resolve the value tradeoffs implicit in the multiple decision criteria (i.e. attributes of an outcome). Formally, such a resolution requires:

v   a scalar valued function (i.e. value function) where $v(x_1,....,x_n) \geq v(x_1',....,x_n')$ if and only if $(x_1,....,x_n)$ is preferred or indifferent to $(x_1',....,x_n')$.

Given such a value function v, a rational DM chooses an alternative (a) so as to maximize v. This approach serves to indirectly compare various magnitudes of the different attributes through their effect on v.

There have been numerous attempts to identify the attributes generally associated with information (Zmud, 1978). Kleijnen (1980a, Ch. 6) provides a listing of eleven information attributes found in the literature and a framework intended to distinguish between independent (i.e., nonredundant) attributes. His list includes: timeliness, accuracy, aggregation, report mode, retention time, privacy & security, reliability & recovery, scope, user-machine modes, flexibility, and multiple users.

Ahituv (1980) maps the problem of *ex ante* information system output measurement, Bresnahan (1986) approaches the impact of IT on the financial services sector in terms of implied social welfare gain resulting from technical advances in mainframe computers. Bresnahan treats purchases of IT capital by the services sector as if they were made for its customers. He then infers the social gain to those customers on the basis of the financial services sector derived demand for computers. He concludes (p. 753) that "compared to expenditures on computers, the spillover to adopters of computers (i.e., financial services firms) and their customers has been large." Large is interpreted here to mean 1.5 to 2 orders of magnitude larger than expenditures. Using this approach, Bresnahan cannot distinguish how that gain is allocated between the industry and its customers. However, the results do indicate that the welfare gain is much larger than traditionally measured expenditures.

At the aggregate economy level, evaluation of the effectiveness of information technology is based on its impact on economic growth. The aggregate data show a post-1973 decline in the rate of economic growth caused by a decline in labor productivity. This decline in labor productivity has coincided with the emergence of an information intensive economy. A reorganization of the aggregate data appears to show that the decline in labor productivity was due to an increasing proportion of information workers with lower productivity than non-information workers. Reorganized data also appear to show that increasing capitalization of information workers does not appear to have improved their productivity. A variety of potential reasons for these results have been offered. The most frequently cited reason is measurement error. While there may be several sources of measurement error, the difficulty of measuring output in the information intensive service industries is a significant factor.

Reference	Roadmap Contribution
Kauffman & Weill (1989)	A review of intermediate statistical studies from a methodology perspective
Input & Output Ratios	
Cron & Sobol (1983)	Firm-level analysis & bimodal performance
Alpar & Kim (1990)	Comparison of ratio & parametric production analyses
Business Value Linkage	
Banker, Kauffman & Morey (1990)	Successful use of value linkage at firm level
Business Level Aggregate	
Loveman (1988)	Parametric application with non-positive evaluation results
Barua, Kriebel & Mukhopadhyay (1995)	BVL at the SBU level with positive results
Brynjolfsson & Hitt (1993)	Recent parametric application with positive results

Table 7: Intermediate Levels: Key References and Roadmap Contribution

Intermediate Levels

The intermediate levels cover a broad spectrum of aggregation. Substantial research activity at this level has been spurred by the lack of evidence of positive IT impacts in the aggregate, and by intense interest in the employment of IS at the organization level (See Table 7). At this level of aggregation the research activity falls into three broad groups: Ratio studies, Applications of BVL analysis, and Business Level Aggregate evaluation studies.

Ratio studies examine the association between a ratio representing IT "input" and a ratio for organization "output." These exploratory statistical analyses are largely bivariate and tend to employ cross-section data. In particular, there is little attempt to model or statistically account for input variables other than IT that could affect firm performance.

Included in the first group are Cron and Sobol (1983), Harris and Katz (1988), and Bender (1986). In an early and oft-cited study, Cron and Sobol employed data on medical supply wholesalers made available from a trade association survey. The authors separately employed three different categorical IT input variables; computer ownership, number of software capabilities, and type of software capability. Four measures of firm-level financial performance were used: pretax return on assets, return on net worth, pretax profits as a percent of sales, and average five year growth. The performance variables were also employed as categories by grouping the firms into quartiles. Chi-square tests of independence were performed between each of the performance variables and each of the IT input variables. Five out of the twelve chi-square tests were statistically significant at the .05 level or lower. Via inspection of the categorical distribution of the data, in two of the five cases the authors observe what they interpret as bimodality in the performance variable. That is, high IT input is associated with both high and low performance quartiles.

Harris and Katz (1988) employed data on life insurance companies from a trade association survey. Their output measure is the ratio of non-interest operating expense to premium income — the expense income ratio. Their IT input measure is the ratio of IT expense to non-interest operating expense — the IT expense ratio. These authors also grouped their data into quartiles. These data are displayed as relative frequencies in a cross-tabulation of the quartile groups for the two variables. Their analysis is based on an inspection of this cross-tabulation. On the basis of this inspection the authors conclude (1988, p. 129) that their "findings do suggest very clear and strong empirical relationships."

Bender (1986) uses life insurance company data from the same trade association survey as Harris and Katz. However, Bender uses the ratio of general expense to premium income as the output measure, and a variety of input variables. The author finds a significant (at the

.05 level) simple correlation between the expense to premium ratio and total information processing expense as an input measure. He also groups the ratio of information processing expense to general expense (i.e., the IPE/EXP ratio) into seven categories, and calculates the mean expense to premium ratio for firms in each category. Inspection indicates that these group means appear to achieve a minimum. From this Bender concludes (1986, p. 29) that "a range in the IPE/EXP ratio of 15% to 25% seems to produce optimum results in the life insurance industry.

In an interesting study, Alpar & Kim (1990) develop a dataset of banks at the firm level. They analyze this dataset using two different methodologies. On the one hand, they transform their bank data to formulate ratio variables corresponding with those Cron & Sobol (1983) used with medical supply wholesalers and with those that Bender (1986) employed with life insurance companies. Alpar & Kim employed the resulting ratios in statistical analyses utilized by Cron & Sobol and by Bender, respectively. On the other hand, they employed the same dataset to estimate the parameters of a multi-input production model. Their statistical results from the ratio data sets showed no significant association between IT input ratios and firm performance ratios. However, the econometric results from the production model indicated a significant cost reduction effect from IT. They conclude that a ratio approach is not appropriate for the measurement of IT impact because the approach does not allow for the effects of other exogenous factors (other than IT) on firm performance.

Business Value Linkage analysis is loosely based on production theory. The hypothesized stochastic relationships between input and output are offered as a structural representation of the relations linking IT, and other resource inputs, to intermediate and higher order outputs. A first stage examines intermediate production relations linking IT and intermediate output. In a second stage, intermediate outputs are linked to firm level financial outcomes. The analysis is largely problem dependent. The modeling and estimation is carried out on a case-by-case basis.

Because BVL correlation has only recently emerged as a methodology, there are few studies that have employed it to evaluate IT systems. The largest number of DVL correlation studies to date focus on employment of Automated Teller Machines (ATM's) in the banking industry. Banker and Kauffman (1988) evaluate the impact that ATM's have on one output; bank branch deposit market share. They employ a model from the marketing literature as the basis for regression analysis to estimate an intermediate relationship. Their results indicate that the deployment of ATM's is not a statistically significant determinant of this output variable. However, they did find that ATM network membership choice was significant. While Banker and Kauffman focused on a general cross section of banks when ATM technology was relatively mature, Dos Santos and Peffers (1991) examined banks that were early adopters of ATM technology. They found that early adoption of the technology increased efficiency for the average bank and did allow banks in certain locations to acquire a short-lived gain in market share. Kauffman and Kriebel (1988) present an illustrative example in which both BVL correlation and DEA are employed. The authors propose a technique in which BVL correlation is first employed to provide estimates of deposit contribution and teller hour reduction by ATM. As a second step, these estimates of ATM "output", along with various inputs, are submitted to DEA for the determination of relative ATM efficiency.

In a study exhibiting the use of sophisticated statistical analysis, Banker, Kauffman & Morey (1990) analyze the intermediate output impact of a cash register point-of-sale and order-coordination system at Hardee's fast food restaurants. The intermediate output that is hypothesized to be affected by this technology is material waste. In a sense, the author's reverse the procedure suggested by Kauffman and Kriebel (1988). They first employ DEA to obtain deterministic estimates of inefficiency for input resource use for each restaurant. In a second stage they form test statistics based on groupings of the restaurants in terms of system deployment and other mediating factors. Results indicated that a certain type of restaurant was likely to experience a significant reduction in materials waste via use of the system. While the authors did not engage in a formal analysis of higher level impacts, they were able to employ the intermediate results to pinpoint the financial benefits to Hardees of system deployment in selected restaurants.

Venkatraman and Zaheer (1990) employ a technique equivalent to BVL correlation to evaluate a system that electronically links independent insurance agents with a carrier. Specifically, the study focuses on the property and casualty subdivision of the insurance market. The authors investigate the impact of a proprietary commercial policy processing system that has been installed by one carrier with some of its independent agents. From the perspective of the carrier, four outputs are identified; (1) (increases in) total written premiums, (2) number of policies in force, (3) commissions, and (4) new business policies. A quasi-experimental design is employed in which a random sample of agents that are electronically-linked with the carrier are matched (using several criteria) with similar agents that are not linked. t tests for mean difference in an appropriate transformation of the output variables between the treatment groups are performed. It is noteworthy that this statistical approach is equivalent to regression analysis in which an experimental treatment is associated with a dummy (0-1) independent variable. Further, in lieu of directly incorporating them in the estimated relation, the matching process between groups is intended to control for the direct exogenous factors at the intermediate level. The authors found that the presence of this system was generally not a statistically significant determinant of the transformed output variables (i.e., availability of the system did not lead to a statistically significant mean difference for three out of four performance measures).

Business Level Aggregate IS evaluation studies tend to be parametric applications of production theory. Along the lines of Alpar & Kim (1990), the authors rigorously model a parametric relation between multiple inputs (including IT) and economic performance at the firm level.

Loveman (1988) employs formal econometric techniques to investigate IT productivity impacts at the strategic business unit (SBU) level. In his analysis, Loveman utilizes the Management Productivity and Information Technology (MPIT) database. These data result from a survey covering approximately 60 manufacturing business units from about 20 firms. The data are annual data for five years, either 1978 to 1982 or 1979 to 1983. This yields a pooled total of approximately 300 observations. The data set has several noteworthy features. The value of capital equipment is divided into IT capital and non-IT capital, and all balance sheet and income statement data are available. Consequently, input and output data are available for estimation of a production function that measures the contribution of IT and other conventional non-IT input variables to firm economic output. The database also includes information on such strategic variables as business unit market share. Finally, input variables are divided into two parts by use; the value of the input used directly in production, and the value used in management.

Loveman specifies three sets of models, all of which are based on a Cobb-Douglas production function. Output is taken to be the real value of sales less inventory change (Q). Inputs include the real values of materials expenditure (M), non-IT purchased services expenditures (PS), total labor compensation (L), non-IT capital (K), and IT capital (C). All output and input variables are expressed as growth rates.

The first set of models is static in nature. The time pattern of the effect of investment in IT on output is not taken into account. A representative stochastic equation for the static models is:

$$q = \alpha + \beta_1 \, m + \beta_2 \, ps + \beta_3 \, l + \beta_4 \, k + \beta_5 \, c + e_1$$

where: lower case letters refer to growth rates of the respective upper case variables, and

e = stochastic disturbance.

The parameter β_5 represents the output elasticity of IT capital. It is a measure of the percentage change in the real value of output for a one percent increase in IT. In general β_5 should be strictly positive. If it is zero or negative, based on economic theory, this would imply that the marginal product of IT capital is zero or negative and therefore less than a strictly positive marginal cost. Under these circumstances, further investment in IT capital would decrease economic output and hence be irrational.

The second set of models is dynamic. That is, the term involving c in the static equation is replaced with a sum of terms to capture the lagged effect of the growth in IT capital in prior periods on current output.

$$\text{i.e. } \beta_5 \text{ c is replaced by } \sum_{i=1}^{n} \beta_{5i} \, c_{t-i}$$

In a third set of models, Loveman exploits the capabilities of the data set to specify a "production of management" model. Since the MPIT data distinguish between production and management values of inputs, the author specifies a two-stage model in which management labor, management non-IT capital, and management IT capital are inputs to a "management" output. In turn, "management" output is an input (along with M, PS, and the production counterparts for labor, non-IT capital, and IT capital) in the production of economic output (Q). Substitution for "management" allows the specification of a single equation to estimate relevant parameters.

Estimates of β_5 from the static models tend to be significantly different from zero, but negative! Estimates of the β_{5i}'s for some of the dynamic models produce a concave pattern that might be expected as the impact of IT investment on output rises and then falls over time. However, the majority of these parameters are also significantly different from zero and negative. Loveman reports that estimation of parameters in the "production of management" model did not produce sensible results for management input or for inputs into the production of management. Loveman summarizes the results of parameter estimation as follows (p. 20); "Despite the broad range of models proposed ..., the data speak unequivocally: in this sample, there is no evidence of strong productivity gains from IT investments."

Barua, Kriebel & Mukhopadhyay (1995) utilize a BVL-type approach with the dataset employed by Loveman (1988). Barua et al. identify five intermediate level variables of interest to these manufacturing SBU's: capacity utilization, inventory turnover, a relative quality measure, relative price, and new products. For each of these intermediate variables, the authors specify a linear model where the independent variables include economic input variables and industry specific exogenous variables. IT capital is included in the former set. In contrast to Loveman's results, IT capital was statistically significant and of the expected sign for all the intermediate level variables. According to the authors (p. 20), "Unlike the production function approach (used by Loveman), our two-stage model enables us to open up the "black box" of IT usage, and detect and measure IT impacts where they occur."

Brynjolfsson & Hitt (1993) produce results which also contrast with Loveman's, however they (like Loveman) employ a production function approach, but with a different dataset. Brynjolfsson & Hitt specify a Cobb-Douglas production function very similar to that of Loveman. In particular, it includes separate independent variables for IT and non-IT capital. Their dataset is at the firm, rather than SBU level, covers the period 1987 to 1991, and includes data on 380 large manufacturing and service firms. This gave them a total of over 1,000 observations. Employing this dataset to estimate the parameters of the Cobb-Douglas function produced estimates of the output elasticity of IT capital that were positive, large and statistically significant. In fact, after converting the elasticity estimates (in percentage points) to dollar equivalents, these estimates imply a return on investment (ROI - the increase in output value per dollar increase in input) that averaged 54% in manufacturing and 68% in the combined sample for both manufacturing and service firms. According to the authors (p. 50), "While our paper applies essentially the same models as those used in earlier studies, we use new firm-level data which is more recent, more detailed and includes more companies. We believe this accounts for our sharply different results."

Summary

This research is intended to provide some coherence to the "bewildering array" of approaches that have been hypothesized or employed for the economic evaluation of IS. Examination of this area in terms of time frame and level of aggregation reveals similarities and differences with respect to both theory and empirical research.

IE and MIA have common roots in decision theory — a normative approach to the choice of an information system. They differ in terms of the source of value for the IS. In IE, value is derived from decision outcomes facilitated by the IS. In MIA, value is derived from the user directly with no explicit recognition of the decision problem the user faces. In promoting the user as locus of value, MIA provides a theoretical base for user-oriented methodology such as UIS. CBA, as a methodology, can be viewed either as a special case of MIA or as a bridge to a production approach to evaluation. Production theory approaches also are distinguished in terms of the extent to which factors other than IS/IT are explicitly recognized as contributing to economic value.

Empirical research at the individual level is predominantly in the form of laboratory experiments. At higher levels of aggregation field studies are prevalent. A common thread in this *ex post* evaluation, is a lack of significant evidence for a positive relationship between IS or IT and economic performance. However, recent work at the intermediate levels has provided evidence of positive relationships.

Management Strategies for Information Technology Investment

What guideposts does the roadmap provide to the practitioner? The suggestions that come out of the literature can be related to the two-dimensional framework that was employed to structure examination of that literature. Figure 6 divides the framework area into four quadrants, each of which corresponds to a pertinent time frame/ aggregation pair. The economy level of aggregation is not included within these quadrants on the assumption that managers seeking IS/ IT investment guidance are not public policy makers.

In quadrant one, the manager seeks to examine IS/IT investment ex ante (before the fact) with respect to an individual system, or with output effects for an individual decision maker. Under these circumstances the manager faces serious measurement problems with respect to benefits. In analyzing the investment opportunity the manager should consider some type of experimentation, if feasible, in an effort to investigate whether hypothesized benefits would be forthcoming. Such experimentation might be in a controlled, laboratory setting. Alternatively, a prototype could be implemented in a pilot setting with due regard for data collection on likely mediating factors. If CBA is employed, the manager should undertake sensitivity analysis in an attempt to identify the value of intangible benefits necessary to

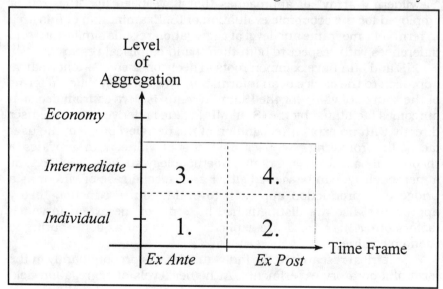

Figure 6. Quadrants in the Evaluation Framework

justify the investment.

In quadrant two, the manager seeks to examine an individual IS/IT investment opportunity in an *ex post time* frame. In this context benefit measurement is less difficult than in the *ex ante* case, and surrogate measures such as UIS are available. Careful consideration should be given as to whether surrogates are appropriate for the system in question. In particular, how objective or knowledgeable are those from whom perceptions would be solicited? If CBA is employed, what is the comparator to be employed? Finally, aside from the system as a product, how well was the implementation process handled?

In quadrant three, the manager is considering investment in technology or systems *ex ante*, but the technology or systems have impacts on multiple individuals and perhaps the entire organization. The manager should be brave and prepare. This is the most difficult, and possibly the most consequential quadrant. Not only is benefit measurement difficult, but it is confounded with issues of valid inference. However, recent *ex post* evidence at this level has shown promise that productivity benefits are available. *A priori* modeling of likely linkages and exogenous factors is helpful. Production models have been the most useful here. Such modeling may serve to structure the decision problem for the manager. Moreover, it serves to pave the way for subsequent measurement and ex post evaluation.

Finally, in quadrant four, the manager is considering higher aggregates *ex post*. In evaluating the outcomes, serious attention needs to be paid to linkages, and exogenous factors should be measured and statistically controlled. It may not be possible to trace significant linkages all the way to financial effects, but incommensurable impacts may prove decisive. While productivity benefits have been evident from recent evidence, the manager should carefully examine to whom those benefits accrue. Is it enough that they accrue to other players in the organization's operating environment, such as customers?

Chapter 3

The Relationship Between Firms' Information Systems Policy and Business Performance: A Multivariate Analysis

Niv Ahituv
Stan Lipovetsky
Asher Tishler
Tel Aviv University

Since business success is usually measured by financial figures, it is reasonable to conjecture that investments in Information Technology (IT) should have an effect on common financial measures of business success. Hence, it would be reasonable to expect that there are significant correlations between the variables that represent the information systems of a firm, and the variables that account for its economic performance. However, such relationships were not always found, entailing, consequently, the term "The Productivity Paradox."

This study presents and analyzes the relations between the economic characteristics and the information systems (IS) attributes of very large U.S. firms (listed in Fortune 500). These relations are estimated by a multivariate model applied to the 1991 data of 80 firms. When the firms are classified into four groups according to their financial performance, then systematic and positive relations between IS attributes and economic variables of the firms become apparent. In particular, very profitable firms exhibit the highest investment and

The authors wish to thank P. Ein-Dor, R. Giladi and S. Neumann for helpful comments and suggestions.

expenditures of IS per employee. These results shed some new light on the phenomenon entitled "The Productivity Paradox," particularly that the results partially contradict the paradox..

Apparently, "successful" firms allocate relatively more budget (per employee) to IS; this budget is directed to salaries to professional personnel, to distribution of end-user workstations, to processors, and to training. The applicability of the findings to management policy towards IT is presented at the end of the article.

Introduction

Since business success is usually measured by financial figures, it is reasonable to conjecture that investments in Information Technology (IT) should have an effect on common financial measures of business success. Otherwise, why would management decide to invest in IT? Hence, it would be reasonable to expect that there are significant correlations between the variables - denoted *attributes* - that represent the information systems of a firm, and the variables - denoted *economic variables* - that account for its economic performance. Moreover, it would be reasonable to expect that financial data about IT investments and expenditures reflect a certain policy or strategy exercised by management towards the scope of employing IT in the organization.

Studies on the effectiveness of IT investments can be classified into some levels. Studies at the upper level attempt to investigate the impact of IT on the national economy as a whole (macroeconomics) by inquiring into variables such as GNP, productivity and the like (Roach, 1989, 1991). Not much success has been found here, entailing the term "The Productivity Paradox" referring to the lack of revealed impact of IT investments on the economy.[1] The second level refers to an industry as a whole. Some results have indicated that IT may have an impact on firms in an industry. e.g., the life insurance industry (Harris and Katz, 1989), the valve industry (Weill, 1992). However, Ahituv and Giladi (1993) could not typify industries by relationship between IT and performance variables. The third level deals with individual firms and tries to see whether those investing more in IT gain something out of it. This level is the focus of the current study. (The fourth and fifth levels deal with the impact of a specific IT application on the firm and the individual user, respectively. They are beyond the scope of this study).

Most of the empirical support for the claim that IS expenditures and investment in information technology improve the performance of firms comes from individual case studies and anecdotal material (see, among others, Cron and Sobol (1983), Porter and Millar (1985), Clemons and Row (1988), Wiseman (1988), Venkatraman and Zaheer (1990), Banker, Kauffman and Morey (1990), and Dos Santos and

Peffers (1992)). In addition, studies that employ recent firm-level data find that ISs have made a substantial contribution to the output of firms (see Brynjolfsson and Hitt (1993), Lichtenberg (1993)). However, most empirical studies (Ahituv and Giladi (1993), Kauffman and Weill (1989), Kauffman and Kriebel (1988), Dos Santos, Peffers and Mauer (1993), and Weill (1992)) find very low systematic relations between firm performance and IS. For an extensive review of previous studies, see Kauffman and Weill (1989), Dos Santos and Peffers (1993), Dos Santos, Peffers and Mauer (1993), Weill (1992), and Brynjolfsson (1993), Brynjolfsson and Hitt (1993).

Two major obstacles to the direct estimation of the relations between a firm's economic variables and its IS attributes are (1) the lack of a comprehensive microeconomics theory of the IS of a firm, and (2) the unavailability of reliable price indices for IS attributes and, in particular, for an aggregate measure of IS expenditure.

In principle, the relations between the IS attributes and the performance of a firm can be deduced from microeconomics theory by a profit maximization (or cost minimization) process. However, unlike other inputs (labor, energy, etc.), but like management, ISs are difficult to quantify or even to define precisely. Therefore, it is impossible, or at least difficult, to employ the standard theoretical model of profit maximization (cost minimization), which uses the prices of all inputs relevant to the production process.

Brynjolfsson (1993) and Brynjolfsson and Hitt (1993) list these reasons for the "Productivity Paradox" phenomenon:

- Measurement problems. It is hard to isolate and measure the impact of IT;
- Organizational surviva. In many cases organizations invest in IT in order to survive rather than to profit;
- Consumer surplus. In many cases the consumers benefit from a better or cheaper product or service; this would not be reflected in the bottom line of the financial statements;
- Delayed effects. There is a time gap between the investment in IT and the fruits engendered from the investment;
- Mismanagement. The investments in IT are poorly managed, hence they are not effective.

In this study, we find a high and positive overall correlation between the IS attributes and the economic variables that represent firms' performance. However, we show that the effect of the IS attributes on firms' performance cannot be well approximated by a simple or even a multiple regression model. We suggest that the "productivity paradox" (see Brynjolfsson (1993)) may arise from the failure to account properly for the heterogeneity of firms' use of their inputs (labor, IS, etc.). Our results suggest that firms that are less efficient in their use of inputs (*IS* included) exhibit poor performance, a natural result that should not be attributed solely to the *IS*. The multivariate model that we employ (see Tishler and Lipovetsky (1993) Tishler, Lipovetsky and Giladi (1994) and Lipovetsky and Tishler (1994)) controls for the heterogeneity of firms and classifies our sample into four relatively homogeneous groups. The simultaneous analysis of all *IS* attributes together makes sense, since it is most likely that management make the investment and expenditure decisions on all attributes simultaneously rather than on one attribute at a time. These decisions reflect the overall policy of management toward the exploitation of IT in the organization. Hence, such an analysis, if performed using a sound statistical method, emulates the managerial decision process.

The major contribution of this study is to classify the firms in our sample into several relatively homogeneous groups. This classification implies that the effective use of *IS* should be tied to other efficiency measures of the firm. Hence, the contribution of a firm's *IS* to its performance cannot be assessed in isolation, but must be analyzed together with other factors.

The results show that highly profitable firms use the greatest amounts of *IS* attributes per employee. These firms seem to be efficient in their use of labor; they exhibit the highest average per employee measures of increase in profits and sales, sales, equity and assets.

The next section of this chapter describes the data. Firms are classified into four homogeneous groups in the following section and then these groups are described. Then you will find the initial analyses of the relations among *IS* attributes and economic variables with the data being analyzed by canonical correlation and by canonical covariance. Finally the results are summarized and some concluding remarks provided.

Data

Data on several economic variables and various *IS* attributes for the year 1991 were collected from *Fortune* and *Computerworld* magazines, respectively. This was performed by comparing the lists published in the two magazines and retrieving the data for matching companies. The economic variables that describe the overall activity of the firm are: Sales[2] (*S*); change in sales from the previous year (ΔS); profits[3] (*P*); change in profits from the previous year (ΔP); assets[4] (*A*); stockholder equity[5] in the firm (*E*); and number of employees (*L*). The attributes that describe the *IS* policy of the firm are: total *IS* budget (*B*); value of the main processor(s) that the firm owns (*C*); the amounts, from the *IS* budget, that were spent on wages (*W*), and on employee training (*T*); and the number of *PCs* within the firm (*Q*).

The selected IS attributes represent various IS policy aspects in organizations. For instance, the first two attributes (B and C) reflect the size of investments and expenditures of IS. The third and fourth attributes (W and T) show the effort directed to human resources (this was before the era of massive outsourcing). The last attribute (Q) represents the proliferation of end user computing in the organization.

The data for all these variables (see Table 1) were available for 80 firms whose names are listed in Table 2. The data exhibit large variability in firm size, technology and use of IS. The main source of heterogeneity among the firms is *firm size* as reflected by some of the economic variables. Thus, to allow a meaningful interpretation of the relations among IS and economic variables across firms, and to control for firm size, we normalize the data, dividing each economic and IS variable by the number of employees of the firm. The six normalized economic variables are organized in the vector f

$$f = (S / L, \Delta S / L, P / L, \Delta P / L, E / L, A / L), \qquad (1)$$

and the five normalized IS attributes are organized in the vector m

$$m = (B / L, C / L, W / L, T / L, Q / L), \qquad (2)$$

The six normalized economic variables and the five normalized IS attributes for all 80 firms are organized in an (80(6) matrix F, and an (80(5) matrix M, respectively. Table 1 presents summary statistics for the 80 firms using the original and the normalized economic variables and IS attributes.

The firms in the sample are very heterogeneous. The standard deviations are larger than the average values for all the original economic variables and for most of the economic variables normalized by the number of employees. The variability of the IS attributes, in absolute value as well as when normalized (divided) by the number of employees, is phenomenal. Thus, we decided to classify the firms into more homogeneous groups in order to intelligently analyze the relations between the IS attributes and the economic variables across all firms. The hypothesis we wanted to check claimed that there are differences among the groups with respect to the correlation between economic variables and IS attributes within each group.

Classification of Firms

There are many ways to classify (namely, to partition) the 80 firms into groups with similar characteristics. One can use multivariate methods such as eigenvector analysis, canonical correlation, factor analysis, discriminant analysis etc. (see Press (1972), Rao (1973), Takeuchi, Yanai and Mukherjee (1985), Tishler and Lipovetsky (1993)), or employ simpler ad hoc procedures derived from economic theory or from simple observation of the data (see Greene (1990)). Here we present several such analyses, all of which lead, surprisingly, to similar classifications.

No.	Variable	Minimum	Average	Maximum	Standard Deviation
	Economic Variables:				
1	S: Sales ($ million)	331	10702	88963	14258
2	ΔS: Change in sales ($ million)	-1362	146	1303	444
3	P: Profits ($ million)	-2258	415	2122	626
4	ΔP: Change in profits ($ million)	-3118	-69	377	490
5	A: Assets ($ million)	134	16879	174429	28472
6	E: Equity ($ million)	-207	3606	22690	3808
7	L: Employees (thousands)	1	68	450	91
	IS Attributes:				
8	B: IS budget ($ million)	5	292	2900	430
9	C: Value of main processor ($ million)	1	99	900	157
10	W: Expenditures on wages in B ($ million)	2	124	1305	196
11	T: Expenditures on training in B ($ million)	0	10	174	22
12	Q: Number of PCs (thousands)	1	33	350	56
	Normalized Economic Variables (per 1000 Employees):				
13	S/L: Sales	58.5	207.4	1299.1	176.6
14	(S/L: Change in Sales	-55.4	5.3	106.2	17.5
15	P/L: Profits	36.5	11.0	86.0	16.7
16	(P/L: Change in profits	-20.2	0.1	10.6	5.1
17	A/L: Assets	17.0	502.0	7766.0	1120.0
18	E/L: Equity	-76.6	3.5	455.5	82.4
	Normalized IS Attributes (per 1000 Employees):				
19	B/L: IS budget	0.5	5.7	38.3	6.1
20	C/L: Value of main processor	0.0	2.0	12.2	2.3
21	W/L: Expenditures on wages in B	0.2	2.3	3.8	2.2
22	T/L: Expenditures on training in B	0.0	0.2	1.0	0.2
23	Q/L: Number of PCs	0.0	0.5	1.5	0.3

Table 1: Summary of the 1991 Data (80 firms): Absolute Values and Values per 1000 Employees

a. Direct Eigenvector Analysis

Consider the following data-generation process (simple model) of the normalized data:

$$F_{ki} = \mu \, a_i \, c_k + e_{ki}, \tag{3}$$
$$M_{kj} = \phi \, b_j \, c_k + u_{kj}, \tag{4}$$

where μ and ϕ are normalizing constants; the parameter a_i denotes the effect of the ith economic variable; the parameter b_j is the effect of the jth IS attribute; and the parameter c_k stands for the effect of the kth firm. Note that the firm effect, c_k, is identical in both (3) and (4).

The firm effect, c_k, classifies the firms according to all the IS attributes and economic variables (see Lipovetsky and Tishler (1994), and Giladi, Lipovetsky and Tishler (1993) for details and examples).

b. Canonical Correlation Analysis

The values of the components of the "scores" (the linear aggregates) derived from canonical correlation analysis (CCA) between the data sets M (the IS attributes) and F (the economic variables) provide another natural classification of the firms in our sample. In CCA, we maximize the pairwise correlation of these two linear aggregates, each being a weighted average of the variables in the respective data set (M or F). These weights are chosen in the maximization process and can be interpreted as the contribution (importance) of the variables in each data set to the formation of the set's aggregate.

c. Eigenvector Analysis with Three-Way Matrices

The data (displayed in Table 1) are very heterogeneous, in particular with respect to the IS attributes. It is imperative to control for this heterogeneity in order to develop a relatively simple model to approximate reality. We account for this heterogeneity as follows. Let

$$Z_{ijk} = (f_i / m_j)_k, \tag{5}$$

where Z_{ijk} denotes the ratio of the ith economic variable (in the vector f) to the jth IS variable (in the vector m) of firm k. Thus, Z_{ijk} denotes the *intensity* of the economic variable i in the firm's IS attribute j. This formulation controls both for firm size and for the heterogeneity of the use of IS across firms. We can visualize the data Z_{ijk} as follows. First, consider a two-dimensional (6x5) matrix Z^k for a given firm k. The ith row presents the ith (in its location in the vector f) economic variable, divided by each of the five IS attributes in the vector m. To allow a meaningful comparison among the six elements of the ith row of Z^k, we divide each element in Z^k, by the square root of the second moment of this ith variable across all 80 firms. This normalization ensures that all elements in Z^k exhibit the same unit of measurement and a uniform variance, i.e. the values of the parameters of our model (see expression 6) can easily be compared. Augmenting the 80 matrices Z^k (one for each k, where $k=1,....,80$) yields the cubic (6x5x80) matrix, Z. The matrix Z contains information on all the ratios (f_i/m_j) for all six economic variables and five IS attributes across all 80 firms. Now we can specify the model using a data-generation process that determines Z_{ijk} as follows,

$$Z_{ijk} = \lambda \, a_i b_j c_k + \varepsilon_{ijk}, \tag{6}$$

where $i=1,....,6$; $j=1,....,5$; $k = 1,....,80$. The term λ is a normalizing constant and ε_{jk} is an error term with mean zero. The interpretation of (6) for our data is as follows. The parameter a_i denotes the effect of the ith economic variable; the term b_j is the effect of the reciprocal of the *j*th *IS* attribute; and c_k is the effect of the *k*th firm.

Several methods to estimate the a_is, b_js and c_ks are analyzed in Lipovetsky and Tishler (1994) and in Tishler, Lipovetsky and Giladi (1994).

d. Univariate Discriminant Analysis

The classification methods described above, and even simple observation, all indicate that *P/L* (profits per employee) is the parameter that best differentiates the firms in our sample. This is true whether we consider the original (unnormalized) variables or the variables normalized by the number of employees. Simple observation suggests that the 80 firms in our sample can be classified into the following four groups:

1. P / L < 0	9 firms	
2. 0≤P / L < 10	40 firms	
3. 10 ≤ P / L < 20	18 firms	
4. 20 ≤ P / L	13 firms	(7)

Applying univariate linear discriminant analysis (see Rao (1973)) to the 80 firms according to *P/L* yields the following four groups:

1. P / L <1	12 firms	
2. 1≤P / L < 11	39 firms	
3. 11 ≤ P / L < 21	17 firms	
4. 21 ≤ P / L	12 firms	(8)

Clearly, commonsense and simple observation yield in this case results that are almost identical to those obtained by the univariate discriminant analysis.

e. Multivariate Discriminant Analysis

We applied multivariate linear discriminant analysis (Rao (1973), Press (1972)) to classify the 80 firms in our sample into four groups (denoted α, β, λ and δ) based on the ranges specified in (7) or (8). This classification is according to all the 23 variables and attributes (in their original units and normalized by the number of employees) listed in Table 1. This method gives a classification, presented in Table 2, that is almost identical to the classifications given in (8). That is, only six firms that were placed by univariate discriminant analysis very close to the boundaries of the groups, moved into neighboring groups. 74 Firms were classified in the same groups that were obtained from univariate discriminant analysis.

Table 3 presents the squared distance between the centers of the four groups. Clearly, the distance between groups α and β and group λ and δ is large relative to that between β and λ. That is, the two neighboring groups in the center (groups β and λ) are more similar to each other than to their immediate neighbors on the other side. Thus, we expect groups α and δ to be more distinct than the other groups in

No.	FIRM	P/L	GROUP	No.	FIRM	P/L	GROUP
1	Abbott Laboratories	23.8	γ	41	International Shipholding	19.6	γ
2	Air Products & Chemical	17.0	γ	42	J.B. Hunt Trans. Service	2.9	β
3	Airborne Freight Corp.	2.2	β	43	J.P. Morgan & Co.	86.0	δ
4	Ameritech Corp.	15.8	γ	44	Johnson Controls, Inc.	2.2	β
5	AMR Corp.	-2.1	α	45	Johnson & Johnson	17.7	γ
6	American Brands, Inc.	16.8	γ	46	KeyCorp	14.3	γ
7	Ashland Oil, Inc.	4.4	β	47	Kimberly-Clark Corp.	12.3	γ
8	AT&T	1.6	β	48	Kmart Corp.	2.5	β
9	Baltimore Gas & Electric	26.3	δ	49	Levi Strauss Associates	11.1	β
10	Banc One Corp.	19.3	γ	50	Lockheed Corp.	4.3	β
11	BankAmerica Corp.	20.7	γ	51	Martin Marietta Corp.	5.2	β
12	Bankers Trust NY Corp.	55.2	δ	52	Massachusetts Mutual Ltd.	17.8	γ
13	Bell Atlantic Corp.	-2.9	α	53	McDonnell Douglas Corp.	3.9	β
14	Bergen Bruswig Corp.	17.2	γ	54	MCI Communications Co.	19.8	γ
15	Bethlehem Steel	-27.9	α	55	Merck & Co.	56.3	δ
16	Black & Decker Corp.	1.4	β	56	Monsanto Co.	7.5	β
17	Branett Banks, Inc.	7.0	β	57	Nordstorm, Inc.	4.4	β
18	Bristol-Myers Squibb Co.	38.4	δ	58	Northeast Utilities	29.8	δ
19	Carolina Freight Corp.	0.1	β	59	Northrop Corp.	5.5	β
20	Carolina Power & Light Co.	46.2	δ	60	Northwest Airlines	-0.1	β
21	Caterpillar, Inc.	-7.5	α	61	PepsiCo, Inc.	3.2	β
22	CoreStates Financial Corp.	16.9	γ	62	Procter & Gamble Co.	18.9	γ
23	Corning, Inc.	10.3	β	63	Raytheon Co.	8.3	β
24	Deere & Co.	-0.6	α	64	Roadway Services Inc.	5.1	β
25	Dillard Dep. Stores, Inc.	6.4	β	65	Rockwell International Co.	6.9	β
26	Dow Chemical Co.	15.1	γ	66	Rohm and Hass Co.	12.6	β
27	Dresser Industries Inc.	4.6	β	67	Sara Lee Corp.	4.9	β
28	Duke Power	30.1	δ	68	Schering-Plough Corp.	32.0	δ
29	Eastman Kodak Co.	0.1	α	69	Sears, Roebuck & Co.	2.8	β
30	Federal Express Corp.	0.1	β	70	Southwest Airlines	2.7	β
31	FMC Corp.	7.1	β	71	Southern Co.	28.8	δ
32	Ford Motor Co.	-6.8	α	72	Textron, Inc.	5.8	β
33	General Dynamics	6.3	β	73	The Boeing Co.	9.8	β
34	Gillette Co.	13.7	β	74	The Duns & Bradstreet Co.	8.7	β
35	Grumman Corp.	4.2	β	75	The Home Depot, Inc.	8.9	β
36	GTE Corp.	9.8	β	76	Toys R Us Inc.	8.5	β
37	Hawaiian Airlines (HAL)	-36.5	α	77	Unocal Corp.	4.2	β
38	Humana, Inc.	5.0	β	78	Upjohn Co.	28.1	δ
39	Ingersoll-Rand Co.	4.8	β	79	Wal-Mart Stores Inc.	4.4	β
40	Inland Steel Industries Inc.	-14.8	α	80	Winn-Dixie Stores, Inc.	1.6	β

Table 2: Classification of the 80 Firms by Multivariate Discriminant Analysis

terms of the economic variables and *IS* attributes that we are considering.

Description of the Four Groups

Table 4, which can be declared as the **central table** of this study, presents, for the four groups of firms, the mean values of the variables and attributes that we analyze here, and the corresponding mean

Group	α	β	γ	δ	Number of Firms
α	0	29.3	55.8	125.4	9
β		0	12.5	51.9	44
λ			0	24.4	16
δ				0	11

Table 3: Squared Distance and Number of Firms

values when all the variables and attributes are normalized by the number of employees (to control for firm size). Several interesting results emerge from Table 4, many of which can be detected by simple observation even before employing any statistical analysis. Group α includes the largest firms (in terms of sales, assets, equity, number of employees and *all* the *IS* attributes) in our sample. At the same time, group α includes the "big losers;" it exhibits the worst performance in terms of profits, change in profits, and change in sales. Group β includes the smallest firms in terms of assets and equity. The firms in group β are, on average, the second largest in terms of sales and number of employees, as well as all the *IS* attributes. We call the firms in group β "small winners," since they show small positive, though declining, profits. Judging by average profits (and possibly change in profits), the ultimate measure of a successful firm, Group λ includes "winners," and the firms in group δ are the "big winners." Groups λ and δ exhibit similar values for assets and equity, but group δ seems to be much more efficient in the use of inputs - labor as well as all *IS* attributes. Group δ exhibits higher profits and greater increase in profits than group λ.

Labor seems to be the key economic variable in the analysis. Group δ, which includes the "big winners," exhibits the highest value, per employee, for the entire set of economic variables and *IS* attributes. On the other hand, groups α and β feature the smallest values for the set of the economic variables per employee, together with the worst performance in terms of profits and change in profits. Similarly, group δ features the highest values of the *IS* attributes per employee, group λ is second, group α is third with values similar to those of group λ, and group β is a distant last. The firms in group δ are obviously the most efficient in their use of *IS* and labor, and exhibit the highest overall and per employee profits. Group λ is second in efficiency and profits.

Before proceeding to the statistical analysis, we would like to make two notes. First, one may question the logic of analyzing *IS* attributes and economic variables of the same year. It may be argued that *IS* investments and expenditures in a certain year should bear fruit in subsequent years (Brynjolfsson, 1993). However, since we analyze cross-sectional data, in which each firm may be at a different stage of its *IS* and economic investment program, our results are of a long-run nature. Furthermore, we estimated our models using one or two lags of the *IS* attributes. The results are fairly similar to those found in 1991 above, but sample size was reduced to only 20 observations. Hence, we present the results based only on data for 1991.

The second note refers to "visual observation" of Table 4. Even before performing any statistical analysis, it is seen that the general

No.	Variable		GROUP			
			α (losers)	β (small winners)	γ (winners)	δ (big winners)
	Economic Variables:					
1	S:	Sales ($ million)	17690	11278	8535	5833
2	ΔS:	Change in sales ($ million)	-238	156	236	292
3	P:	Profits ($ million)	-474	388	679	864
4	ΔP:	Change in profits ($ million)	-710	-33	62	121
5	A:	Assets ($ million)	30371	10795	22236	22384
6	E:	Equity ($ million)	5422	3025	3940	3956
7	L:	Employees (thousands)	89	86	38	21
	IS Attributes:					
8	B:	IS budget ($ million)	488	306	222	175
9	C:	Value of main processor ($ million)	158	111	64	56
10	W:	Expenditures on wages in B ($ million)	204	134	94	68
11	T:	Expenditures on training in B ($ million)	14	11	8	4
12	Q:	Number of PCs (thousands)	44	39	24	11
	Normalized Economic Variables (per 1000 Employees):					
13	S/L:	Sales	172.0	147.0	314.6	322.2
14	Δ(S/L:	Change in Sales	-8.5	3.9	11.2	13.4
15	P/L:	Profits	-11.0	5.4	17.7	41.6
16	ΔP/L:	Change in profits	-6.5	-0.6	2.5	4.7
17	A/L:	Assets	233.6	162.0	835.0	1600.0
18	E/L:	Equity	45.3	43.6	115.9	227.4
	Normalized IS Attributes (per 1000 Employees):					
19	B/L:	IS budget	5.5	3.9	6.9	11.3
20	C/L:	Value of main processor	2.2	1.4	2.3	3.8
21	W/L:	Expenditures on wages in B	2.3	1.6	2.9	4.2
22	T/L:	Expenditures on training in B	0.1	0.1	0.2	0.3
23	Q/L:	Number of PCs	0.5	0.4	0.7	0.7

Table 4: Mean Values of Economic Variables and IS Attributes (Absolute Values and Value per 1000 Employees)

trend indicates an increase in the normalized IS attributes from group α to group β. This trend is particularly clear between the two extreme groups, α and δ. Note also that the average firm in δ is smaller in terms of sales and number of employees than the average firm in the other three groups.

Hence, if one tends intuitively to associate S/L and P/L with efficiency, B/L and C/L with IS resource exploitation, and Q/L with computing power distribution and End User Computing (EUC) in the organization, it can be argued that "thin" organizations tend to be more efficient and more IS-intensive. Causality, however, cannot be proven.

Firms' Performance and IS Structure—Simple Models

As shown in Tishler, Lipovetsky and Giladi (1994), if the sample firms are organized into homogeneous groups, there exist positive and sometimes strong relations between the economic variables (representing the firms' performance) and the IS attributes (representing the firms' IS policy). However, the use of simple or multiple regression models to estimate these relations yields inappropriate approximations to reality. At best, these methods can indicate the direction and, possibly, the order of magnitude of the relations between the sets of economic variables and IS attributes. Table 5 presents the pairwise correlations between each economic variable per employee paired with each IS attribute per employee for all firms together and for each group separately. Generally, these correlations are low, except in group δ. It is interesting to observe that profits are positively correlated with each of the IS attributes and, in particular, with IS budget (B/L) and wages in IS budget (W/L), in all groups. Nevertheless, the results in Table 5 are insufficient for policy analysis regarding the optimal IS structure for a particular firm.

Table 6 presents, for all firms combined and for each group of firms separately, the regressions of each economic variable (representing firms' performance) on the entire set of relevant IS attributes. Regressors that were both insignificant and did not contribute to the R_q of the regression were eliminated. Clearly, the squared correlations in the regressions are higher than those of the respective pairwise correlations (each economic variable with each IS attribute separately). Nevertheless, the correlations in Table 6 are relatively low, with the exception of those for group δ (the "big winners"). Furthermore, due to the multicollinearity of the data, these models feature many unreliable estimates, as well as many negative coefficients. This renders them unsuitable for determining the optimal IS structure of the firms in our sample.

All Firms	B/L	.51	-.10	.58	.09	.83	.67
	C/L	.35	.14	.31	-.03	.27	.46
	W/L	.53	-.07	.53	.11	.76	.67
	T/L	.38	.06	.38	-.06	.41	.45
	Q/L	.32	-.06	.31	.02	.46	.45
α	B/L	-.34	.39	.48	-.51	.16	.34
	C/L	.06	.02	.25	-.87	.39	.41
	W/L	-.00	-.02	.34	-.74	.33	.49
	T/L	.17	.30	.26	-.79	.57	.43
	Q/L	-.57	.41	.53	-.33	-.07	.28
β	B/L	.46	-.45	.26	-.40	.33	.43
	C/L	.28	-.40	.16	-.30	.13	.25
	W/L	.35	-.37	.29	-.28	.22	.32
	T/L	.32	-.29	.20	-.32	.37	.33
	Q/L	.20	-.34	.02	-.22	.28	.18
γ	B/L	.07	-.04	.39	.13	.29	.52
	C/L	.24	.36	.22	.28	.11	.12
	W/L	.19	.06	.34	.20	.19	.49
	T/L	.13	.17	.14	.01	-.10	.27
	Q/L	.07	-.02	.18	.12	.58	.50
δ	B/L	.97	-.64	.79	.07	.98	.72
	C/L	.37	.23	.07	-.17	.25	.41
	W/L	.99	-.56	.81	.16	.99	.78
	T/L	.68	-.44	.50	-.39	.65	.48
	Q/L	.81	-.65	.53	-.25	.75	.86

Table 5: Pairwise Correlations of Firms' Economic Variables and IS Attributes

Canonical Correlation Analysis by Groups of Firms

The effect of the *IS* attributes on the performance of firms, as expressed by the economic variables, cannot be well approximated by a simple or a multiple regression model. Therefore, we shall now use canonical correlation analysis (CCA) to estimate the relations between these data sets.

CCA is a straightforward extension of the simple (pairwise) correlation of two variables applied to the multivariate case. The major difference between CCA and simple correlation lies in the way the variables are expressed. Unlike simple correlation, in CCA the correlation is between two (weighted) aggregates, each based on several variables. These weights are determined by obtaining the

Group	IS Attributes	S/L	ΔS/L	P/L	ΔP/L	A/L	E/L
			Economic Variables				
	constant	108.05	5.09	2.04	-0.31	-241.62	27.91
		(4.38)	(1.84)	(0.97)	(0.37)	(2.65)	(2.84)
	B/L	-	-0.69	1.58	-	194.71	7.98
			(1.87)	(6.27)		(13.53)	(6.03)
All	C/L	-	2.09	-	-	-69.09	5.26
Firms			(2.08)			(1.80)	(1.47)
	W/L	42.86	-	-	0.69	-	-
		(5.51)			(1.93)		
	T/L	-	-	-	-7.24	-1390.90	-
					(1.73)	(2.54)	
	Q/L	-	-	-	-	-	-
	R^2_{adj}	0.27	0.04	0.33	0.03	0.75	0.45
	constant	196.61	3.24	-24.17	-0.59	165.32	-31.32
		(7.07)	(0.21)	(2.74)	(0.33)	(2.90)	(0.58)
	B/L	23.49	6.33	-	-	-	-
		(1.92)	(2.20)				
	C/L	-	-	-	-2.72	-	-
					(4.65)		
α	W/L	-	-22.19	-	-	-	32.70
			(2.18)				(1.48)
	T/L	-	40.89	-	-	-	-
			(1.12)				
	Q/L	-0.292	-	0.025	-	543.60	-
		(2.59)		(1.67)		(1.82)	
	R^2_{adj}	0.44	0.32	0.18	0.72	0.22	0.13
	constant	97.30	13.37	5.11	1.35	27.44	27.25
		(5.94)	(4.42)	(5.89)	(1.88)	(0.44)	(4.73)
	B/L	45.21	-5.79	-	-2.02	141.22	15.89
		(3.58)	(2.61)		(3.64)	(3.02)	(3.58)
	C/L	-	-2.88	-	-	-	-
			(1.42)				
β	W/L	-77.08	10.38	1.41	3.63	-311.6	-27.78
		(2.72)	(2.07)	(2.76)	(2.93)	(3.03)	(2.79)
	T/L	-	-	-	-	797.5	-
						(1.66)	
	Q/L	-	-	-0.005	-	-	-
				(1.91)			
	R^2_{adj}	0.30	0.25	0.12	0.27	0.25	0.28

Table 6: Regressions of Economic Variables on IS Attributes

Group	IS Attributes	S/L	ΔS/L	P/L	ΔP/L	A/L	E/L
				Economic Variables			
λ	constant	255.2 (1.84)	18.42 (1.69)	16.13 (13.76)	2.29 (1.84)	-211.50 (0.60)	61.41 (3.83)
	B/L	-43.42 (1.01)	-3.58 (1.91)	0.23 (1.6)	-	-	-
	C/L	-	7.74 (2.47)	-	1.49 (2.26)	-168.46 (2.48)	-17.25 (2.97)
	W/L	122.9 (1.21)	-	-	-	-	14.82 (2.39)
	T/L	-	-	-	-13.69 (1.93)	-	102.97 (1.96)
	Q/L	-	-	-	-	2.01 (3.93)	0.037 (1.54)
	R^2_{adj}	0.00	0.22	0.09	0.17	0.48	0.47
δ	constant	165.02 (8.07)	29.89 (6.50)	29.70 (5.49)	5.27 (3.96)	-709.30 (6.15)	-45.20 (1.09)
	B/L	13.93 (11.40)	-	-	-	-	-
	C/L	-	1.90	-1.44	-	-108.93	-
	W/L	-	-	4.10 (4.52)	0.71 (2.30	643.37 (33.26)	9.51 (1.82)
	T/L	-	-	-	-13.46 (2.73)	-	-314.58 (3.59)
	Q/L	-	-0.038 (4.96)	-	-	-	0.51 (4.98)
	R^2_{adj}	0.93	0.71	0.65	0.37	0.99	0.88

Note: t-statistics are in parentheses.

Table 6: continued

maximum correlation between the two aggregates. The following presentation briefly formulates the basic mathematical expressions of CCA.

Let

$$\zeta = F\alpha \qquad (9)$$

and

$$\eta = Mb \qquad (10)$$

where ζ is an (80x1) vector of an aggregate measure (a weighted average) of firms' performance (one aggregate measure per firm), and η is an (80x1) vector of an aggregate measure (a weighted average) of IS. The terms a and b represent (6x1) and (5x1) vectors of constant parameters. The term a_i denotes the weight of the ith economic variable in the aggregate measure of the economic performance of the firm. The term b_j is the weight of firm's jth IS attribute in the aggregate measure of the firm's IS.

The relation (closeness) of the firms' performance to their *IS* structure is measured by the correlation, ρ, between ζ and η:

$$\rho = \frac{\text{cov}(\zeta,\eta)}{[\text{Var}(\zeta)\,\text{Var}(\eta)]^{1/2}} = \frac{\zeta'\eta}{[(\zeta'\eta)(\eta'\eta)]^{1/2}} = \frac{\alpha'R_{FM}b}{[(\alpha'R_{FF}\alpha)(b'R_{MM}b)]^{1/2}} \quad (11)$$

where $R_{FM} = F'M$; $R_{MM} = M'M$; and $R_{FF} = F'F$. Since M and F include standardized variables, then R_{FM}, R_{MM}, and R_{FF} are correlation matrices.

Specifically, we seek to estimate a and b to maximize σ, the correlation between ζ and η. That is,

$$\max_{a,b} \rho \quad (12)$$

Forming the Lagrangean function for ρ in (11) subject to $\eta'\eta = 1$ and $\zeta'\zeta = 1$ we have

$$L = \zeta'\eta - \lambda/2\,(\zeta'\zeta - 1) - \mu/2\,(\eta'\eta - 1), \quad (13)$$

which yields the conventional CCA solution (see Tishler and Lipovetsky (1993), Lipovetsky and Tishler (1994))

$$(R_{FF}^{-1}\,R_{FM}\,R_{MM}^{-1}\,R_{MF})\,\alpha - \lambda^2\alpha$$
$$(R_{MM}^{-1}\,R_{MF}\,R_{FF}^{-1}\,R_{FM})\,b = \mu^2 b, \quad (14)$$

and at the optimum, $\lambda = \mu$, and $\rho_{max} = \lambda_{max}$.

Table 7 presents, for the set of all firms and for each group of firms separately, the maximal canonical correlations between M (all the *IS* attributes) and various subsets of the economic variables. The first six rows of Table 7 give the maximal canonical correlation of each economic variable separately with the set of all the *IS* attributes. Since no aggregation is performed on the economic variables, the results are similar to those obtained by the multiple regression of each economic variable on the set of all five *IS* attributes. Most correlations are much higher for groups α (big losers) and δ (big winners) than for the other two, less homogenous groups, or for the set of all firms combined. The canonical correlations of group δ are particularly high, suggesting a very strong correlation (connection) between the *IS* attributes of a group δ firm and its economic performance.

The real power of CCA is demonstrated in rows 7-13 of Table 7. The economic variables that represent the size of the firm (sales and assets) are given in rows 7 and 8. Clearly, the overall correlation of firm size with M (the *IS* attribute matrix) is much higher than that for a single measure of a firm's performance. Again, the connections between the *IS* attributes and firm size are particularly high for groups α and δ. In group δ, the correlation reaches .99, an extraordinarily high value.

The correlation between firms' *IS* attributes and their economic performance, as measured by profits and equity, are given in rows 9 and 10. Very high correlation exists between the ultimate measures of a firm's success - profits and equity - and the *IS* attributes.

Rows 11 and 12 present the correlations of firm's *IS* attributes to the economic variables that measure firm's long-run performance (assets and equity), and short-run performance (profits and sales). The final row presents the correlations of the set of all the economic variables with the set of all the *IS* attributes. Generally, these correlations are very high, suggesting that detailed, and possibly simultaneous, models are likely to show a strong and positive effect of the *IS* attribute on the economic variables of these firms.

An interim conclusion from Table 7 is that there may indeed be high correlations between *IS* attributes and business performance. These correlations are particularly visible in the two extreme groups, i.e., the "losers" and the "big winners." Apparently, the aggregate variable composed of the five normalized *IS* variables is sufficient to distinguish among the four groups of firms. Again, more profitable,

No.	Economic Variable	All Firms	GROUPS α	β	γ	δ
	Each Economic Variable Separately:					
1	Sales (S/L)	.53	.79	.59	.38	.99
2	Changes in sales (ΔS/L)	.27	.81	.55	.60	.93
3	Profits (P/L)	.59	.56	.40	.51	.96
4	Change in profits (ΔP/L)	.24	.90	.57	.54	.79
5	Assets (A/L)	.87	.73	.56	.76	.99
6	Equity (E/L)	.69	.58	.58	.79	.97
	Measures of Firm Size:					
7	S/L, A/L	.87	.92	.70	.78	.99
8	S/L, ΔS/L, A/L	.88	.93	.70	.78	.99
	Firm Performance Indicators:					
9	P/L, E/L	.69	.76	.58	.80	.98
10	P/L, ΔP/L, E/L	.70	.99	.65	.81	.98
	Long-Run Economic Indicators:					
11	A/L, E/L	.87	.88	.61	.79	.99
	Short-Run Economic Indicators:					
12	S/L, (S/L, P/L, ΔP/L	.74	.99	.67	.87	.99
	Full Set of Economic Variables:					
13	S/L, (S/L, P/L, (P/L, A/L, E/L	.89	.99	.74	.97	.99

Table 7: Maximal Canonical Correlations Between Subsets of the Economic Variables and all Five IS Attributes (normalized per 1000 employees)

"thin" and efficient firms, tend to use *IS* more intensively.

Intercorrelations (Canonical Covariance) Analysis

CCA shows that strong and positive correlations exist between the sets of economic variables and *IS* attributes. However, like regression analysis, CCA is useful for making predictions but, due to multicollinearity between the economic variables and the *IS* attributes, CCA may fail to accurately estimate the marginal effects of each *IS* attribute on the performance of the firm. The effect of multicollinearity in CCA, or in regression analysis, on the accuracy of the estimated parameters occurs, at least partially, due to the inversion of the moment matrices R_{MM} and R_{FF} (see (14)). Therefore, we suggest using an estimation method that does not require the inversion of matrices, and is therefore less prone to multicollinearity. In this method, titled Intercorrelations Analysis (denoted IA, or canonical covariance), we maximize the covariance, rather than the correlation, between the aggregates η and ζ in expressions (9) and (10) (see Tishler and Lipovetsky, 1993).

Specifically, IA is formulated as follows:
$$\max_{a,b} c = \text{cov}(\zeta, \eta) = \zeta'\eta = \alpha'R_{FM}b, \tag{15}$$

subject to the normalization $a'a = 1$ and $b'b = 1$.

The Lagrangean function is
$$L = \zeta'\eta - \lambda/2 \, (\alpha'\alpha-1)-\eta/2(b'b-1). \tag{16}$$
which yields, after some manipulations, the following solution

$$(R_{FM}R_{MF}) \, \alpha = \lambda^2 \, \alpha$$
$$(R_{MF}R_{FM}) \, b = \lambda^2 \, b, \tag{17}$$

and at the optimum, $\lambda = \mu$, and $\lambda_{max} = c_{max}$.

Clearly, (17), like (14), is an eigenvector problem. However, (17), unlike (14), does not require the inversion of moment matrices and, hence, may be less affected by multicollinearity in M and/or F. Formally, IA can be obtained as the approximation of the covariance matrix R_{FM} by an outer product of two vectors (see Lipovetsky and Tishler (1994) and Tishler, Lipovetsky and Giladi (1994)),

$$R_{FM} = \lambda \, \alpha \, b' + \varepsilon \tag{18}$$

where ε is a matrix of random errors with mean zero and constant variance. Estimation of a and b in (18) by least squares,

$$S = \min_{a,b} ||\varepsilon||^2 = ||R_{MF} - \lambda \, \alpha \, b'||^3, \tag{19}$$

yields the solution in (17). Finally, it is shown in Tishler, Lipovetsky and Giladi (1994) that, at the optimum,

$$S = ||R_{FM}||^2 - \lambda^2_{max} = ||R_{FM}||^2 (1-\lambda^2_{max}/||R_{FM}||^2). \qquad (20)$$

Thus, the goodness of fit, q, of the estimation problem (15) (or (19)) is defined to be

$$q = \lambda^2_{max}/``R_{FM}||^2, \qquad (21)$$

where $0\leq q \leq 1$.

Table 8 presents the estimates of the vectors of weights a and b for the set of all firms and for each group of firms separately. Note that the interpretation of a and b in (15) (or (18)) is identical to that of a and b in (9)-(10). That is, a_i is the weight of the ith economic variable in the aggregate measure of the firms' performance. The term b_j is the weight of the jth IS attribute in the aggregate measure of IS.

The results in Table 8 show that all the IS attributes correlate positively to the performance of the firm (the weights of all the IS attributes are positive for all groups of firms in our sample). Generally, the effects of all the economic variables, except changes in profits (ΔP) and sales (ΔS), are fairly robust across the groups of firms considered here. The effects of ΔP (represented by a_4) and ΔS (by a_2) on all the firms combined is almost zero due to the high volatility of ΔP and ΔS across the four groups. The intensity of the five IS attributes are usually determined by the medium- to long-run management strategy of the firm. Hence, theoretically, they should have little or no impact on the short-run performance of the firm (which is manifested by the changes in sales and profits). In all the cases, however, except for group α, the IS budget (B/L) and the wages for IS personnel (W/L) have the most

Weights	Variables	All Firms	GROUP α	β	λ	δ
	Economic Variables					
a1	S/L	.42	-.10	.45	.20	.53
a2	ΔS/L	-.02	.22	-.50	.09	-.33
a3	P/L	.43	.38	.27	.45	.40
a4	ΔP/L	.04	-.72	-.42	.24	-.05
a5	A/L	.58	.33	.36	.43	.51
a6	E/L	.54	.42	.42	.71	.44
	IS Attributes					
b1	B/L	.59	.41	.58	.56	.55
b2	C/L	.30	.49	.39	.22	.14
b3	W/L	.56	.47	.45	.53	.55
b4	T/L	.36	.52	.45	.20	.37
b5	Q/L	.35	.32	.32	.57	.48
Goodness of fit		.98	.81	.97	.77	.95

Table 8: Intercorrelation Analysis by Groups of Firms: Weights of Economic Variables (α) and IS Attributes (b)

significant effect on the performance of the firm. The importance of the value of the main processor (C/L) is highest in group a (the "big losers") and declines as we move in the direction of the "big winners;" that is, the effect of the value of the main processor on the firm's performance remains positive but diminishes as we move from losers to winners. This observation may be attributed to the greater decentralization of computing power (EUC) among members of group δ. In other words, in a decentralized managerial setup, the effect of mainframe computers diminishes. Note also the trend in the attribute expenditures on training in IS per employee (T/L), whose correlation is highest in group α - the group that includes firms that spend, on average, the most on training in IS. It may be attributed to the need to do more training in a mainframe environment.

Conclusions

At the beginning of the article we mentioned that an analytic microeconomic model of IS in the firm is not yet available. Nevertheless, the findings of this study shed some light on the relationship between IS and business performance. It is shown that if a modeling is constructed in such a way that it accounts for the heterogeneity of firms, one can derive some interesting results.

The analysis presented here centered first on the classification of the sampled firms into relatively homogeneous groups. The multivariate model that was employed controls for heterogeneity among firms and partitions the sample into four relatively homogeneous groups. Once this was accomplished, the overall correlation between the IS attributed and the economic variables became high within each group.

In particular we see that more "successful" firms spend more budget (per employee) on IS, spend more money on IS related wages and training, and invest more in equipment (main processors and PCs). This was supported by high values of canonical correlation (Table 7).

Although the sample was very heterogeneous, a relatively homogeneous structure is observed within each of the four groups of firms. Within each of the groups (except α - the "losers"), all the IS attributes exhibit positive and high correlation with profits, sales, equity and assets. The analysis suggests that firms can be classified according to efficiency in their use of inputs, high profits correspond to better use of inputs.   Hence, this results cast doubt on the existence of the "productivity paradox."

Another goal of the study was to identify the marginal effects of the IS attributes on various economic variables of the firms. The model provides meaningful and reasonable estimates of these marginal effects (given by the weight vectors a and b in Table 8). It is shown that the leading IS attribute in all the firms together and in the majority of the groups (except group α - the "losers") is the budget per employee. This indicates that investments and expenditures related to information technology are considered an important policy vehicle among firms' management. Other policy-related factors that may have an effect are the distribution of PCs, wages and training.

We do not claim that the correlations identified here prove causality nor do they formulate a rigorous microeconomic model. Further research is needed to establish those. Still, the applicability of the study to IS policy and management decision is quite clear. Companies belonging to the "successful" groups should maintain their relatively high investment and expenditures related to IT. The money should be mostly directed to wages to professional personnel and to the distribution of end user workstations. Those are the preferred budgetary items. Companies belonging to the "less successful" groups should assign more budget to IT, and shift current budget from mainframes to salaries and end user workstations.

Endnote
[1] The term "Productivity Paradox" was later expanded to the other levels of IT effectiveness as well.

Chapter 4

Client/Server Technology: Management Issues, Adoption, and Investment

Amarnath C. Prakash
Texas Tech University

Global competition is forcing many of today's organizations to find new ways to manage their operations in order to survive. Client/Server (C/S) technology provides the vehicle to reengineer and reevaluate organizational processes in order to improve organizational productivity and performance. Organizations find C/S technology compelling for a number of reasons such as improved customer satisfaction, reduced computing cost, increased organizational productivity, and rapid application development.

In this chapter, important and practical issues surrounding the successful management and adoption of, and investment in client/ server technology are presented and discussed in detail. A C/S adoption framework based on the considerable experience and knowledge gained in managing C/S technology projects successfully by leading Fortune 500 companies is presented. A management payoff matrix that is designed to assist information technology managers to identify critical areas of C/S technology application and develop payoff estimates is proposed. Finally, a C/S investment evaluation portfolio to assess the feasibility of migration efforts in organizations is provided.

In a competitive business world, it is necessary for organizations to take advantage of every opportunity to reduce cost, improve quality, and provide service. Most organizations today recognize the need to be market driven, to be competitive, and to demonstrate added value

(Martin, 1994). Toward this end, many organizations have turned to flattening their management hierarchies. With the elimination of layers of middle management, the remaining individuals must be empowered to make the strategy successful. A critical success factor for this is the availability of quality information at the right time. Information technology (IT) is an effective vehicle for providing this information to support the implementation of this strategy. Specifically, the client/server (C/S) model for business computing facilitates this by providing power to the desktop, with information available to support the decisionmaking process and enabling decisionmaking authority (Jander 1994).

The Gartner Group, a team of computer industry analysts, noted a widening chasm between user expectations and the ability of information system (IS) organizations to fulfill them. Client/server technology has proved its capability to bridge this chasm (Smith and Guengerich, 1994). According to a recent IDC estimate, there will be 100 million C/S networks by 1998. Reflecting this trend, corporations worldwide are charging ahead with their plans for C/S computing by migrating their business applications from a mainframe-centric environment to a client/server platform (Jander, 1994). However, migrating to C/S from traditional mainframe systems has often been riddled with a variety of technological and management problems (Schultheis and Bock, 1994).

Case studies on C/S migration in organizations have consistently demonstrated that the success of C/S migration efforts often hinge on management's approach to and understanding of the critical issues surrounding the adoption of C/S technology (Smith and Guengerich, 1994; Nickerson, 1993). Firms that have successfully managed their C/S migration moves also indicate a better understanding of the various issues in the adoption of C/S technology within their organizational contexts pointing to the importance of having a C/S adoption framework to guide migration efforts (Schultheis and Bock, 1994; Yourdon, 1994). In addition to the right approach and basic understanding of C/S technology, the relationship between investments in C/S technology and its perceived payoffs is a critical one (Steger, 1995). This link has often frustrated senior managers' attempt to evaluate the contribution of C/S technology to the bottom line as the relationship between IT and productivity has been widely discussed but little understood (Brynjolfsson, 1993). Hence, if IS/IT managers have to have a good chance of succeeding in their C/S migration efforts, then they should be able to demonstrate the investment payoffs of using C/S technology to their top management (Borkovsky, 1994).

In this chapter, important and practical issues surrounding the successful management and adoption of, and investment in client/server migration that have been presented above are further articulated and discussed in detail. In order to better understand the complexities involved in C/S migration and to provide various perspectives on the subject, well-documented case studies will be used to explain some of the important concepts and realities of managing the C/S migration project successfully in organizations. This chapter also taps into the considerable experience and knowledge gained in managing C/S migration projects successfully by leading Fortune 500 companies and provides a C/S adoption framework which could serve as a blueprint for companies wishing to embrace the technology successfully. A management payoff matrix that is designed to assist IS/IT managers to identify critical areas of C/S technology application and develop payoff estimates is proposed. Finally, a C/S investment evaluation portfolio to assess the feasibility of migration efforts in organizations is provided.

Before we begin to understand the issues surrounding C/S migration, it is important that some of the terms involved in this discussion are clearly understood. The most common misconception is concerning client/server computing and the underlying technology (Nickerson, 1993). In order to put things in the right perspective and frame, we discuss below some of the concepts and principles associated with C/S computing.

What is Client/Server Computing?

Client/server computing is an environment that satisfies the business need by appropriately allocating the application processing between the client and the server processors (Smith and Guengerich, 1994). In a typical C/S setup, the client requests services from the server; the server processes the request and returns the result to the client. The communications mechanism is a message passing

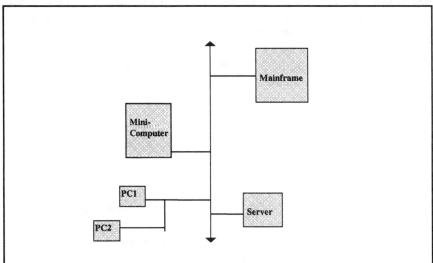

Figure 1. A Modern Client/Server Architecture

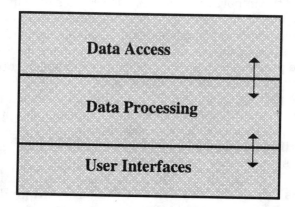

Figure 2. Client/Server Application Model

interprocess communication (IPC) that enables distributed placement of the client and server processes. Thus, it is important to remember that the client/server computing model is a software model, not a hardware definition. Figure 1 illustrates a popular version of modern day client/server architecture found in many organizations.

Because the C/S environment is typically heterogeneous, the hardware platform and operating system of the client and server are not usually the same. Effective C/S computing will be fundamentally platform-independent (Jander, 1994). Changes in platform and underlying technology should be transparent to the user. It has been demonstrated that information systems built with transparency to the technology, for all users, offers the highest probability of solid ongoing return for the technology investment (Yourdon, 1994). Consequently, tools which isolate developers from the specifics of any single platform, assist developers in writing transparent, portable applications. Thus, application processing in a business context can be construed as a three-component structure (see Figure 2) in which there is continual interaction among the data access, data processing, and user interface components. Data access includes the graphical user interface (GUI) and stored data access, while the data process component incorporates the business logic aspects of the applications, and the user interface component links services with other applications (Smith and Guengerich, 1994).

The use of technology layers provides this application development isolation. These layers isolate the characteristics of the technology at each level from the layer above and below (Panepinto, 1993). This layered layout is fundamental to developing client/server applications. The rapid rate of change in these technologies and the lack of experience with the "best" solutions implies that we must isolate specific technologies from each other (Smith and Guengerich, 1994).

Advantages of Client/Server Computing

Organizations want to take advantage of the low-cost and user-friendly environment that existing desktop workstations provide. Client/server computing and the underlying technology provides the capability to use the most cost-effective user interface, data storage, connectivity, and application services (Schultheis and Bock, 1994). The client/server model provides the technological means to use previous investments in concert with current technology options (Jander, 1994).

Client/server computing moves the data capture and information-processing functions directly to the knowledge worker or end-user. Client/server applications integrate the front and back office processes because data capture and usage become an integral part of the business rather than an after-the-fact administrative process (Steger, 1995). Some of the unique advantages that C/S computing provides include quicker system development, better production system performance, user-friendly graphical interface, and increased flexibility (Martin, 1994).

Migrating to C/S technology solutions also have proved to be beneficial to small and medium businesses alike. Although small and medium businesses typically have much modest IT budgets to spend, migration to C/S technology systems is on the rise (Steger, 1995). Smaller organizations have an equally greater need for sharing information on a cross-functional basis, desktop computing, and faster customer responsiveness. Client/server technology and its features allow small and medium firms to share information on local area networks (LAN) and process data locally at various terminals or nodes. Small businesses with their custom-specific requirements and data handling often turn to C/S technology to implement their information solutions.

Having gained a perspective on client/server computing and its advantages, it is important for organizations to identify the various issues surrounding the management of C/S migration efforts.

Management Issues in C/S Migration

Management issues surrounding the migration to C/S include costs of retraining IS personnel, perceived immaturity in technology, lack of adequate management tools, security issues, and threats to functional stability of applications (Schultheis and Bock, 1994). The organization climate and culture issues have often been ignored risking the failure of C/S projects in organizations (Prakash, Janz, and Wetherbe, 1996). Users and systems integrators agree that making conscious decisions about changes to the organization structure is integral to taking advantage of C/S technologies (Gow, 1991). These changes not only include technological improvements, but also involve reorganization of personnel, workflows, and procedures (Borkovsky, 1994). The key to successful management of C/S migration in organizations has been the development of a detailed blueprint listing the anticipated problem areas, payoff projections, and personnel-work matches made in the realm of new technology implementation (Yourdon, 1994). While technical issues surrounding adoption of C/S technology can be challenging, prior research has proved that improvements in technology have yielded only marginal improvements in productivity performance whereas accompanying improvements in management aspects of technology have resulted in more than 200% improvement in organizational performance (Janz, Prakash, and Frolick, 1996). Thus a common theme that runs across success stories in C/S migration projects is the awareness of and sensitivity to the management aspects of C/S migration.

In addition to the consideration of the above management issues involved in migrating information systems to a C/S environment, it is important for organizations to understand and assess the client/server adoption process before they can plan for its successful management (Prakash, Janz, and Wetherbe, 1996). With the help of successful case studies in organizations and findings from earlier research (Prakash, Janz, and Wetherbe, 1996; Steger, 1995; Yourdon, 1994), we propose a C/S adoption framework.

Adoption of Client/Server Technology

Client/Server technology is more than just a technology; it provides a foundation to build better relationships with end-users and make organizational changes (Van Kirk, 1993). The major characteristics of C/S technology include the logical separation of the client processes and the server processes, the operation of each on separate machines, the ability of the server to support multiple clients simultaneously, the ability to change the server without affecting the clients, and the ability to change a client without affecting other clients or server (Lile, 1993). Organizations find C/S technology compelling for a number of reasons such as improved customer satisfaction, reduced computing cost, increased organizational productivity, and rapid application development (Nickerson, 1993). However, as C/S technology is being increasingly adopted by organizations (Caldwell, 1996), C/S migration has often floundered on the inability of organizations to view the technology in the right perspective (Steger, 1995). When an organization adopts C/S technology or decides to migrate existing systems to a C/S platform, it necessitates a fundamental change in the way business processes are perceived (Yourdon, 1994). A significant part of this change is the willingness to change (Jander, 1994). One way to look at this change is to perceive the adoption of C/S technology as an innovation. An innovation is an idea, product, or process that is new to an adopter (Hage and Aiken, 1967; Rogers, 1983).

Based on the premise that innovations diffuse because of perceptions of using innovations (Moore and Benbasat, 1991), this study focuses on new and potential adopters. Although intention does not always lead to actual adoption, it is significantly related to adoption and is the best available measure for products that are in the early stages of their life cycles (Morrison, 1979). Thus, in order to predict and better understand the adoption intention of C/S technology in organizations, which is still in its early stages of its lifecycle (Yourdon, 1994), we adopt an innovation diffusion theory approach.

Research Study

Innovation diffusion theory (Rogers, 1983) posits that perceived innovation attributes that influence adoption include: relative advantage, compatibility, complexity, observability, and trialability. In addition, these factors have been observed to predict future rates of innovation adoption in many instances (Ostlund, 1974; Teo et al., 1995). It has also been suggested that the perception of innovation attributes may have an impact on the outcome of implementation success (Brancheau and Wetherbe, 1990). Thus successful adoption of C/S technology can be predicted and assessed if we can isolate those factors that significantly influence the adoption intention of C/S technology.

Given the growing importance of C/S technology, it is important for both researchers and practitioners to identify those factors that influence the successful adoption of the technology into organizations. Two important research questions that merit investigation include:

1. What are the factors that significantly influence the adoption intention of C/S technology in organizations?
2. Given the importance of some of these factors, which factors are critical for the successful deployment of C/S technology in organizations?

Figure 3 below proposes a research model to help us investigate C/S technology adoption in organizations. The model integrates the attributes of innovation intention based on innovation diffusion theory with successful adoption of C/S technology in organizations.

Operationalization of the Research Constructs

Relative advantage is the degree to which using an innovation (C/S technology) is perceived as being more advantageous than using its precursor (some other technology). It leads to increased efficiency, effectiveness, and increased economic gains (Davis et al., 1989; Rogers, 1983). Relative advantage was also found to be an important factor influencing adoption in a meta-analysis of innovation studies (Tornatzky and Klein, 1982). The importance of relative advantage as a predictor of adoption intention was confirmed in a study of C/S technology adoption in financial markets (Holland et al., 1994; Martin, 1994) and in marketing channels (O'Callaghan et al., 1992). Hence, relative advantage is hypothesized to vary positively with adoption intention and adoption success.

H1a: The greater the perceived relative advantage of using C/S technology, the more likely the present intention of an organization to adopt it.

H2a: The greater the perceived relative advantage of using C/S technology, the more likely the successful adoption of C/S technology in organizations.

Complexity is the degree to which using and understanding an innovation (C/S technology) is perceived as a difficult task. Martin (1994) proposes that complexity in a C/S technology context can be assessed from both a technical and business perspective. Researchers have suggested that a complex innovation reduces likelihood of adoption because it requires more skills and effort in order to adopt

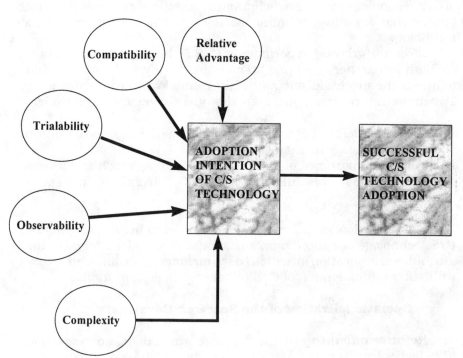

Figure 3. C/S Technology Adoption Model

(Cooper and Zmud, 1990; Dickerson and Gentry, 1983). Complexity has been widely recognized as an inhibitor of adoption (Grover, 1993; LaBay and Kinnear, 1981; Rogers, 1983). Hence, complexity is hypothesized to vary negatively with adoption intention and adoption success.

H2a: The greater the perceived complexity of using C/S technology, the less likely the intention of an organization to adopt it.

H2b: The greater the perceived complexity of using C/S technology, the less likely the successful adoption of C/S technology in organizations.

Compatibility is the degree to which using an innovation (C/S technology) is considered as consistent with existing organizational values, experiences, and needs. In the context of C/S technology, it can be assessed in terms of technical compatibility (with existing hardware and software) and organizational compatibility (with current objectives, culture, and functioning) (Yourdon, 1994; Nickerson, 1993). Grover (1993) found that compatibility was a predictor of information technology innovations. Also positive empirical association between compatibility and adoption behavior has been found (Holak and Lehmann, 1990; Ettlie et al., 1984). Hence, compatibility is hypothesized to vary positively with adoption intention and adoption success.

H3a: The greater the perceived compatibility of using C/S technology, the more likely the intention of an organization to adopt it.

H3b: The greater the perceived compatibility of using C/S technology, the more likely the successful adoption of C/S technology in organizations.

Trialability is the degree to which using an innovation can be carried out on a limited basis prior to adoption. Rogers (1983) argues that potential adopters are likely to feel more comfortable with innovations that can be experimented, thus increasing the likelihood of adoption. In the C/S technology context, there have been calls made to adopt the technology at the individual unit level (Borkovsky, 1993), while some others have suggested that C/S technology must be implemented at an enterprise level in order to be successful (Martin, 1994; Yourdon, 1994). However, given the overwhelming anecdotal evidence of the criticality of enterprise-wide adoption for successful C/S adoption, we hypothesize a negative association of trialability with adoption intention and adoption success.

H4a: The greater the perceived trialability of using C/S technology, the less likely the intention of an organization to adopt it.

H4b: The greater the perceived trialability of using C/S technology, the less likely the successful adoption of C/S technology in organizations.

Observability is the degree to which using an innovation (C/S technology) generates results that are observable and can be communicated to others. Demonstrability of an innovation in the form of results has a strong impact on adoption decision (Zaltman et al., 1973). Similarly, Rogers and Shoemaker (1971) suggest that ease and effectiveness with which results of using an innovation can be communicated to others have a significant influence on adoption decision. In the context of C/S technology, the need for tangible results is more critical because of the high risk and level of investment involved in the effort (Jander, 1994; Martin, 1994). Though several studies have reported no significant relationship between observability and adoption behavior (Bouchard, 1993; Holak and Lehmann, 1990), given the nature of the C/S environment and the technology we hypothesize that observability will vary positively with adoption intention and adoption success.

H5a: The greater the perceived observability of using C/S technology, the more likely the intention of an organization to adopt it.
H5b: The greater the perceived observability of using C/S technology, the more likely the successful adoption of C/S technology in organizations.

There has been substantive and diverse research on innovation diffusion (Brancheau and Wetherbe, 1990; Rogers, 1983; Tornatzky and Klein, 1982). All questions were phrased from the perspective of both actual and potential adopters (Moore and Benbasat, 1991) and anchored on a 7-point scale from extremely disagree (1) to extremely agree (7). Items on relative advantage were based on C/S literature (Yourdon, 1994; Jander, 1994). Questions on compatibility were adapted from Grover (1993) and O'Callaghan et al. (1992). Questions on complexity were adapted from Bouchard (1993), Grover (1993), and Dickerson and Gentry (1983). Questions on observability and trialability were modified from Moore and Benbasat (1991).

Research Methodology

Intention to adopt C/S technology is defined as the degree of willingness of the respondents to make full use of C/S technology as the best course of action. Hence, adoption intention for C/S technology is assessed by asking respondents to indicate, on a scale of 1 to 7, the relative importance of adoption intention attributes in their adoption decision. The respondents also identify those attributes that either facilitate or hinder successful adoption of C/S technology in their organizations.

The survey methodology was adopted to conduct this research. The target respondents are key IS employees from *Fortune 500* organizations. Pilot-testing of the survey instrument was carried out to strengthen construct validity and to ensure unambiguity in the questions.

In order to overcome several acknowledged conceptual and methodological problems (Moore and Benbasat, 1991; Meyer and Goes, 1988; Tornatzky and Klein, 1982) in prior innovation diffusion literature, several measures are taken. First, innovation characteristics are examined simultaneously. Second, reliable and replicable measures are developed with the help of prior empirical work. Third, successful C/S technology adoption will be measured using multiple responses. Finally, the survey instrument was strengthened by incorporating items from similar, prior research settings. For more details regarding the research plan and methodology, please refer to the paper by Prakash, Janz, and Wetherbe (1996).

Results and Implications

The model relating the five factors to successful adoption of C/S technology in organizations was significant at 1% and accounted for 32% of its variance. Complexity, relative advantage, and trialability were predictors of successful adoption of C/S technology in organizations. This shows that organizations may be unwilling to adopt (or migrate to) C/S technology if they consider it beyond their ability to comprehend and use (Steger, 1995). Also, organizations need to be convinced about the relative advantage of using C/S technology over other proprietary and/or mainframe-based systems (Yourdon, 1994). Trialability or the ability to experiment on a small scale (for example, at the departmental level) is perceived to be an important factor that influences the decision to migrate to C/S platforms (Schultheis and Bock, 1994).

Thus the research study identified the critical factors that impact the consideration of C/S technology in organizations. While the isolation of these generic factors will help IS managers to deal with change effectively in their organizations, it is important to note that there may be additional environment- and organization-specific factors that also may impact the decision to migrate to a C/S environment (Prakash, Janz, and Wetherbe, 1996).

The question "Should we invest in C/S technology" has been a major one that has been plaguing IS management for a long time (Yourdon, 1994). The plethora of arguments both for and against the issue has only served to obfuscate real issues behind the decision (Steger, 1995). Given this scenario, it is necessary for IS management to come up with a framework or matrix that will identify areas of impact and address the issue of "payoff" so that a rational decision can be made either way.

Client/Server Management Payoff Matrix (MPM)

Client/server computing grew out of a desire to push computing power and decisionmaking down to the users. However, because of a variety of organizational and technical factors involved in the adoption and use of C/S technology, IS managers are often unable to prioritize their application development portfolio and develop a blueprint for implementing the technology in their organizations (Gow, 1991). Further, implementation of information technology has always been inextricably linked with the returns on investment (ROI) principle (Brynjolfsson, 1993). With increased budget spending on IT, the expectations regarding the returns on IT investment have spiraled in recent years (Caldwell, 1996). To meet these ever-increasing expectations, IS managers are having to look into specific areas where C/S technology can have the maximum impact and result in increased performance. These performance indicators tend to be different for manufacturing and service sectors (Alpar and Kim, 1990).

In the case of manufacturing sector, firms consider capacity utilization, inventory turnover, new product introduction, and product quality as prime indicators (i.e., potential areas of C/S application) of C/S investment (Barua, Kriebel, and Muhopadhyay, 1991). In service-related industries, quality of service, variety of service, speed, and responsiveness are rated high in the area of IT investment (Brynjolfsson, 1993).

The critical components that constitute the core of a C/S computing application consists of hardware, software, networking, user training, and procedures (Panepinto, 1993). The hardware component includes platform (such as UNIX, mainframe, PC, and workstation) issues, processing capacity, speed, and interoperability. The software component refers to both the operating software and the application software, while the networking component includes protocol, conversion, and connectivity-related issues. User training and procedure components of a C/S application are responsible for establishing detailed training plans for end users, procedures for data conversion, and people-related management tasks.

Based on the above two dimensions (viz., C/S components and payoff areas), a comprehensive C/S management payoff matrix (MPM) that will assist IS managers on identifying key areas (i.e., those that can yield maximum ROI) for implementing C/S technology is proposed below. Consistent with our discussions above, a MPM is proposed for

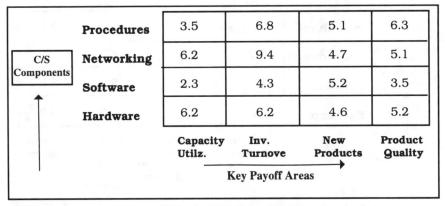

		Capacity Utilz.	Inv. Turnove	New Products	Product Quality
	Procedures	3.5	6.8	5.1	6.3
C/S Components	Networking	6.2	9.4	4.7	5.1
	Software	2.3	4.3	5.2	3.5
	Hardware	6.2	6.2	4.6	5.2

Key Payoff Areas

Figure 4. Management Payoff Matrix (MPM) for C/S Migration in the Manufacturing Sector

organizations in both the manufacturing and service sectors.

Management Payoff Matrix for the Manufacturing Sector

In the domain of IT investment, the payoff areas in manufacturing companies include capacity utilization, inventory turnover, new product introduction, and product quality (Barua, Kriebel, and Mukhopadhyay, 1991). Capacity utilization refers to the ability of C/S technology (or applications) to utilize the available production capacity, whereas in the area of inventory management, C/S technology could facilitate lower process cycle times and inventory overheads. C/S technology also reengineers business processes and promotes organizational learning leading to new product development and introduction (Schultheis and Bock, 1994).

The proposed management payoff matrix assists IS managers in estimating payoffs in certain key areas by rating the contribution of the various C/S components in terms of weighted averages. A typical MPM planned by IS managers in a manufacturing organization would resemble Figure 4 below. A comparison of the total weighted values in the same column across the key payoff areas gives the relative payoffs that would result from investment in C/S applications in those areas. Similarly, a comparison of the total weighted values in the same row across the various C/S components gives the individual contribution or relative importance of each of those components in a given key payoff area.

The proposed MPM provides IS management with a comprehensive yet simple tool to project realistic payoff estimates and prioritize their IS development portfolio. It also provides insight into the criticality of the various C/S components in turn assisting them in the planning and deployment of an enterprise-wide information system based on the C/S environment.

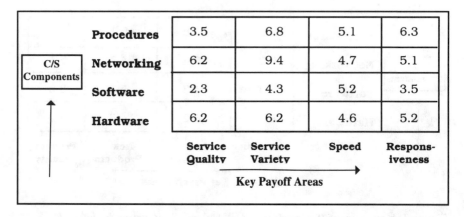

C/S Components		Service Quality	Service Variety	Speed	Responsiveness
	Procedures	3.5	6.8	5.1	6.3
	Networking	6.2	9.4	4.7	5.1
	Software	2.3	4.3	5.2	3.5
	Hardware	6.2	6.2	4.6	5.2

Key Payoff Areas

Figure 5. Management Payoff Matrix (MPM) for C/S Migration in the Service Sector

Management Payoff Matrix for the Service Sector

In the service sector, areas of IT investment include quality of service, variety of service, speed, and responsiveness (Brynjolfsson, 1993). Quality of service refers to the improvement of service either in the form of increased efficiency and effectiveness. Variety of service is the ability to provide a wide range of services to customers, while speed refers to the cycle time to service customers' requests. Responsiveness is the ability of the firm to respond to customer needs and requirements in a timely and orderly manner.

The proposed management payoff matrix assists IS managers in estimating payoffs in certain key areas by rating the contribution of the various C/S components in terms of weighted averages. A typical MPM planned by IS managers in a service organization would resemble Figure 5 above. A comparison of the total weighted values in the same column across the key payoff areas gives the relative payoffs that would result from investment in C/S applications in those areas. Similarly, a comparison of the total weighted values in the same row across the various C/S components gives the individual contribution or relative importance of each of those components in a given key payoff area.

The proposed MPM provides IS management with a comprehensive yet simple tool to project realistic payoff estimates and prioritize their IS development portfolio. It also provides insight into the criticality of the various C/S components in turn assisting them in the planning and deployment of an enterprise-wide information system based on the C/S environment.

While knowledge of the adoption process and the areas of potential impact assists IS management in planning for the migration to C/S environment, measuring the investment payoff in the continuing use of C/S technology is becoming more difficult (Caldwell, 1996). Though the difficulties of measuring payoffs in technological investments have continually plagued IS executives (Bryjolfsson, 1993), there is a growing consensus that investments in information technology like other capital investments need to be justified (Clemons, 1991). In the area of C/S investments, this problem is further compounded because of the magnitude of investments that have taken place in the last decade (Caldwell, 1996).

Based on a variety of both successful and unsuccessful case studies (Smith and Guengerich, 1994) and sponsored research (Prakash, Janz, and Wetherbe, 1996), a C/S Investment Evaluation Portfolio (CSIEP) is proposed. This portfolio seeks to maximize returns on investments made in the area of C/S computing by providing a broad, pragmatic but integrated perspective on the subject.

Client/Server Investment Evaluation Portfolio (CSIEP)

As business environments become ever more competitive, there is an increased emphasis on operational efficiency, improved product and service quality, and responsiveness (Mooney, Gurbaxani, and Kraemer, 1995). Many business organizations have sought to use C/S technology as a means to achieve these objectives (Caldwell, 1996). Indeed, organizations are making significant investments in IT such as C/S technology, currently accounting for about 50% of annual capital investments (Kriebel, 1989).

Productivity is the fundamental economic measure of a technology's contribution (Brynjolfsson, 1993). With this in mind, CEO's and line managers have increasingly begun to question their huge investments in computers and related technologies. This is especially true in the case of investment decisions made in the area of C/S technology and computing systems (Caldwell, 1996). The lack of good quantitative measures for the output and value created by IT has made the MIS manager's job of justifying investments particularly difficult (Brynjolfsson, 1993).

IT Investments and Business Value

The business transformation literature highlights how difficult and perhaps inappropriate it would be to try to translate the benefits of IT usage into quantifiable productivity measures of output. Intangibles such as better responsiveness to customers and increased coordination with suppliers do not always increase the amount or even intrinsic quality of output, but they do help make sure it arrives at the right time, at the right place, with the right attributes for each customer (Brynjolfsson, 1993). In spite of the difficulties associated with IT measurement, a framework for evaluating the investment value in C/S technologies is a much needed one (Caldwell, 1996).

A number of studies of IT productivity and business value, defined as the contribution of IT to firm performance, have appeared (Cron and Sobol, 1983; Bender, 1986; Loveman, 1994; Strassman, 1990; Harris and Katz, 1991; Weill, 1992; Brynjolfsson and Hitt, 1993; Lictenberg, 1993; Markus and Soh, 1993; Hitt and Brynjolfsson, 1994). Many of these studies were conducted using only firm level output or end-product based measures of value. In a C/S context, where payoffs are usually long-term and difficult to measure (i.e., intangible), this kind of approach may provide little value for IS managers. What is required is analysis of the impact of C/S technology on intermediate business processes, which would generate considerable insight into the creation of value through C/S technology, and provide IS management with a tool to evaluate current and future investments in C/S application systems. Process-oriented studies in the area of IT that have appeared are interesting and illustrative of the value of process studies (Banker and Kauffman, 1988, 1991; Banker, Kauffman, and Morey, 1990). Also, the importance and benefits of adopting process oriented perspectives of business value are well recognized within the academic literature (Crowston and Treacy, 1986; Bakos, 1987; Gordon, 1989; Kauffman and Weill, 1989; Wilson, 1993) and its perceived significance by practitioners is indicated by the recent interest in process innovation and reengineering (Davenport, 1993; Hammer and Champy, 1993).

A Business Process Framework for Evaluating C/S Technology Investments

The business value of IT such as C/S technology is a joint technology-organization phenomenon (Mooney, Gurbaxani, and Kraemer, 1995). Hence in order to conduct a realistic investigation of this phenomenon and to develop a meaningful C/S investment evaluation portfolio (CSIEP), theoretical perspectives of both technology and organizations, and their interaction is necessary.

Since one of the central objects of analysis in this research is business processes, it is important to develop a typology of such processes. A business process has been defined as a "specific ordering of work activities across time and place, with a beginning, and end, and clearly identified inputs and outputs: a structure of action" (Davenport, 1993, p.5). Adopting Davenport's classification all business processes can be categorized into operational processes, management processes, and strategic processes. These categories also correspond to the three possible areas of C/S technology investment (Steger, 1995). We distinguish between operational, management, and strategic C/S investments as follows: C/S Investments could be in the domain of operational management with processes that embody the execution of tasks comprising the activities of an organization's value chain; investments in the area of management may include processes and activities associated with the administration, allocation, and control of resources within organization; and C/S investments in the strategic area could include processes such as IS planning, forecasting, and new market development.

Prior research has considered IT (in general terms) impacts along operational and managerial dimensions. For example, Malone (1987) suggests that, in general, organizational technologies consist of production and coordination technologies. Ciborra (1985) and Gurbaxani and Whang (1991) discuss the impact of information technology on both operational costs and costs of coordination and control. In order to evaluate IT business value, the key business processes within each core business area must be identified and the linkages and contributions of IT to those processes defined (Mooney, Gurbaxani, and Kraemer, 1995).

Value chain analysis (Porter, 1985), in which organizational activities are depicted as technologically and economically distinct processes that must be performed in order to do business, provides a useful backdrop for considering the impact of IT (such as C/S technology) on operational, management, and strategic business processes or investment areas. Operational business processes are affected by C/S technology enabled applications such as flexible manufacturing, CAD, data capture devices, imaging, and workflow

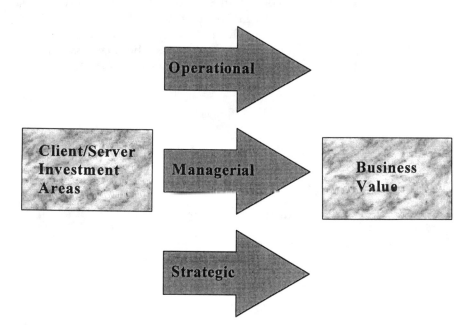

Figure 6. A Process-Oriented Model of C/S Technology Investment

systems. C/S technology can improve the efficiency of operational processes through automation, or enhance their effectiveness and reliability by linking them. Management business processes are enhanced by improved availability and communication of information facilitated by C/S technologies. Electronic mail, C/S databases, and videoconferencing can improve the efficiency and effectiveness of communication, thus contributing to management processes (Yourdon, 1994). Equally, perhaps more importantly, C/S technology can be applied to support interorganizational business processes, particularly the end-to-end linking of value chains of one organization with those of another, in order to achieve competitive or strategic advantage (Benjamin and Wignand, 1995; Prakash, 1996). Figure 6 depicts the proposed model of C/S Technology investment.

Davenport (1993) identified nine opportunities for process innovation through IT: automational, informational, sequential, tracking, analytical, geographical, integrative, intellectual, and disintermediating.

In the area of C/S technology implementation, past research has shown that business benefits are generated through a set of overlapping factors which are transactional, decision-oriented, and reengineering-driven in nature (Caldwell, 1996). In order to arrive at a C/S technology specific and parsimonious model (or portfolio), we can consolidate these opportunities under three broad categories: automative, informative, and transformative.

Further, we propose that C/S technology can have three separate but complimentary effects on business processes. It is through these effects on business processes that C/S technology creates value. First, automative effects refer to the efficiency perspective of value deriving from the role of C/S technology as a capital asset being substituted for labor. Within this dimension, C/S technology value is derived prima-

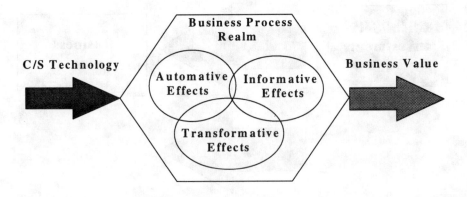

Figure 7. Dimensions of C/S Technology Value

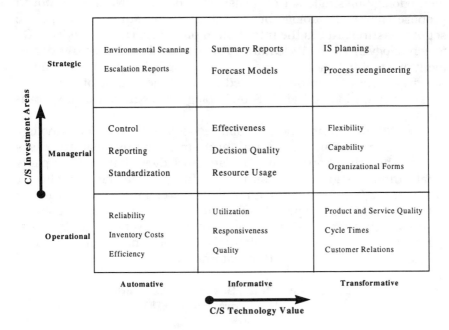

	Automative	Informative	Transformative
Strategic	Environmental Scanning Escalation Reports	Summary Reports Forecast Models	IS planning Process reengineering
Managerial	Control Reporting Standardization	Effectiveness Decision Quality Resource Usage	Flexibility Capability Organizational Forms
Operational	Reliability Inventory Costs Efficiency	Utilization Responsiveness Quality	Product and Service Quality Cycle Times Customer Relations

C/S Investment Areas

C/S Technology Value

Figure 8. Client/Server Investment Evaluation Portfolio (CSIEP)

rily from impacts such as productivity improvements, labor savings and cost reductions. Second, informative effects emerge primarily from C/S technology's capacity to collect, store, process, and disseminate information. Following these effects, business value (i.e., ROI) accrues from improved decision quality, employee empowerment, decreased use of resources, enhanced organizational effectiveness, and better quality. Third, transformative effects refer to the value of deriving from C/S technology's ability to facilitate and support process innovation and transformation (e.g., business process reengineering). The business value associated with these effects will be manifested as reduced cycle times, improved responsiveness, downsizing, and service and product enhancement as a result of reengineered processes and redesigned organizational structures. Figure 7 provides an illustration of these effects.

Client/Server Investment Evaluation Portfolio

The C/S investment areas (i.e., business processes) can be combined with the dimensions of business value to derive a portfolio that can be used to evaluate the investments in C/S technology. This portfolio is shown in Figure 8 below. The evaluation portfolio provides a structure within which to consider the business value impacts of an existing or planned C/S technology investment. Indeed, consistent with Banker, Kauffman, and Mahmood (1993) and Brynjolfsson (1993), we have argued against the appropriateness of a single methodology or single set of measures. The objective here is not to propose a new methodology for assessing C/S investments or a specific set of measures. Nor is the intention to propose a causal model of C/S technology investments leading to business value. Thus, no endorsement of a technological imperative is intended. The proposed evaluation framework is simply intended as a new lens that offers a new perspective on looking at C/S technology investments in organizations.

On the one hand, the portfolio recognizes that C/S technology impacts operational, managerial, and strategic business processes and on the other hand, it further acknowledges that such impacts create three distinct business values. In applying the portfolio for evaluating C/S investments, an organization should identify the key investment areas (i.e., operational, managerial, and strategic business processes) that contribute to the achievement of overall organizational goals, and then consider the potential impacts of the technology along automative, informative, and transformative lines.

Using the Client/Server Investment Evaluation Portfolio (CSIEP)

Figure 8 above describes a set of generic measures that have been successfully applied in a multi-firm study of IT business value (Kraemer, et al., 1994). This scheme, while not universally applicable, forms the basis of a general C/S technology investments evaluation scheme. It may appear that these measures are simply variations of traditional measures of efficiency and effectiveness that continue to reflect the traditional output measures of "MIS impact" studies. However, migration to C/S technology in an organizational context, is implemented through the business application portfolio, reflecting and justifying the use and suitability of this approach.

An unique contribution of this portfolio is the move away from form-level output measures, particularly financial measures, of business value in favor of process oriented measures. Thus, the sample metrics shown in Figure 8 are defined at the process level, rather than at the firm level. The measures may seem dominantly reflective, but the proposed portfolio is not meant to be a comprehensive evaluation scheme, but to illustrate one application of the portfolio. We acknowledge that a plethora of other metric and value systems exist (Bakos, 1987; Attewell, 1991; Symons, 1991), but they do not address C/S technology investments.

Within this proposed portfolio we are still faced with the difficulty of assessing the business value of *specific* C/S technology effects on *specific* processes. For example, informative effects on say, the procurement process, may be difficult to measure. It might be argued that we are still left with the task of explicitly measuring the actual business value of these individual effects, which is further complicated by the lack of appropriate metrics that are available to measure the true business value of an IT investment (Brynjolfsson, 1993). It could further be argued that operational and managerial business processes are empirically inseparable, as are automative, informative, and transformative effects of C/S technology on these processes.

Management Strategies for Information Technology Investment

The management of IT is becoming increasingly complex due to the diversity of available technologies and the strategic importance of this resource to the achievement of business goals (Morgado, Reinhard, and Watson, 1995). In the last decade, business organizations have invested huge sums in information technology, yet the profitability of these investments has not been fully demonstrated (Bergeron and Raymond, 1995). While Roach (1987) was one of the first seriously to question the bottom line implications of IT, it was not until 1993 and following intensive research that a first study by Brynolfsson and Hitt (1993) found computer ROI to average 54%. Another study by the same researchers indicated that computers have not resulted in measurable improvements in business performance (Hitt and Brynolfsson, 1994).

In spite of the bleak picture these results provide, effective management strategies that steer IT to positively impact the bottom line have been adopted by organizations (Chan and Huff, 1993; Raymond, Pare, and Bergeron, 1993). However, for strategic choices to make an impact on performance, they ought to be supported and facilitated by the appropriate information infrastructure. A firm that is more analytical, more proactive and more future-oriented in its outlook requires access to external networks, on-line databases and executive support systems (Bergeron and Raymond, 1995). Conversely, information technology choices shown to have the greatest bottom line impacts (well known case studies exist in the airline, insurance, and distribution sectors) resulted in radical changes in the firm's strategic orientation.

Thus the management of IT investment with the help of well orchestrated strategies and tools (such as the adoption framework, management payoff matrix, and the evaluation portfolio) proposed in this chapter cannot be overemphasized. IT investment by itself, be it transactional, managerial, or strategic in nature, provides no assurance of bottom line improvements (Bergeron and Raymond, 1995). In an increasingly complex, uncertain and global business environment, firms needing to maintain or increase performance levels must adopt a stronger strategic posture (i.e., must be more aggressive, proactive, analytical and future-oriented), and must insure that IT management follows suit (Vitale, Ives, and Beath, 1986). This means aligning the strategic positions and use of IS with organizational objectives and providing the required support in terms of data, applications and technology.

Recommendations for Practitioners

From the above discussion, it is clear that IS managers and executives charged with the implementation of client/server technology in organizations need a checklist to follow before they sit down to chalk out investment strategies in the area of IT. Based on this research study, we offer below a checklist in the form of "lessons learned from the trenches" to IS practitioners who wish to increase their chances of successfully deploying and using C/S technology in their organizations.

• *Never Underestimate the Importance of Training.* One of the most important lessons learned by companies that failed to implement C/S solutions concerns the criticality of training both the developers and the end-users. In order to effectively implement C/S technology, IS managers have to understand a variety of issues including architectures, methodologies, programming tools, diagnostic software, hardware configurations, and security. Awareness of capabilities and pitfalls of emerging technologies such as C/S technology can be brought about only by methodological and focused training that addresses all the above diverse and interrelated issues.

• *Have a committed Project Champion.* Senior and responsible people who are convinced about the viability and indispensability of C/S technology must be entrusted with the planning, deployment, and use of C/S solutions. Many organizations' C/S migration efforts have floundered on the rock of uncertainty engendered by the lack of a suitable project champion. Given the complexity of technological, organizational, and management issues surrounding the implementation of C/S technology solutions, a project champion to head, plan, and steer the C/S migration project is not only important but imperative.

• *Involve Users in the C/S Migration Project.* Client/server computing (and the accompanying technology) grew out of a desire to push computing power and decisionmaking down to the users. Users need to be involved at all stages of the project so as to increase the chances of project success. This research finding is not surprising considering the evolution and history of C/S technology in the first place. With the advent of desktop computing and the proliferation of end-user computing, users' demands for greater responsiveness and computing independence began to grow. Managers and executives in charge of C/S migration projects need to remember the pivotal position that users occupy in the C/S debate in most organizations and accordingly, involve users at the planning, design, and implementation phases of systems development.

• *Create Cross-Functional Teams.* Client/server technology solutions usually tend to impact more than one functional area because of its "distributed" nature. Hence, it is important to promote positive interdependence and create cross-functional teams from user departments where possible and set team-level performance objectives such that individuals can only succeed if the team succeeds. Thus focusing all goals and performance toward those goals known by the group in a supportive team environment helps to encourage individual accountability and promotive interaction.

• *Encourage Skills Transfer.* C/S technology requires well-rounded skills in the form of mainframe and desktop skills, interpersonal skills, team work capabilities, domain knowledge, and project management. In order to do this, identify resident "experts" on teams and provide incentives for them to teach others through informal workshops, mentoring, or on-the-job guidance. Stressing the importance of having back-up capabilities not only helps to encourage a teaching/learning environment, it also provides assurance that critical skills will be available.

Conclusion

With the advent of the internet and proliferation of distributed networks, client/server applications and accompanying migration strategies have assumed a greater criticality (Prakash, 1995). While true success stories have not been too many, organizations have not altogether discarded the possibilities that C/S provides (Prakash, Janz, and Wetherbe, 1996). Research into the conceptual underpinnings and practice of C/S technology has yielded and continues to provide interesting, useful information that organizations can apply (Yourdon, 1994). Future research should address both theoretical as well as practical perspectives on C/S migration. Some of the areas that would benefit from research include: C/S implementation strategies, Systems development practices and methods for developing C/S business applications, and Impact of emergent technologies (such as the internet) on successful C/S deployment.

In order to carry out these and other kinds of research, a concerted and orchestrated research stream should be launched with the help of both academics and professionals in the IS area. Addressing the ever-changing and varied issues surrounding C/S technology is no longer a technology imperative, but a business one. Organizations, in order to survive in a highly competitive global business environment have to be proactive with the learning and applying of newer, emergent technologies such as client/server technology. This can be achieved only if we develop a broad perspective and understand all the issues surrounding the technology.

As discussed above, a clear understanding of the C/S phenomenon from a multi-faceted perspective is a critical success factor in the successful adoption of and migration to a C/S technological environment. This chapter's unique contribution has been in the following areas:

1. Adoption of Client/Server Technology
2. Investments in C/S Technology Applications
3. Evaluation of C/S Technology's contribution to Business Value
4. Management Payoff Matrix to assist IS management

Chapter 5

Toward An Understanding of EIS Implementation Success

Sanjay K. Singh
University of Alabama at Birmingham

An EIS is a class of information system designed to facilitate the decisionmaking processes of executives. These systems are not only high profile, but also expensive in nature. Therefore, the successful implementation of an EIS is politically and economically very important. The success of an EIS depends upon many factors. One is that an EIS should support the strategic management process (SMP). Past research to explain this factor has been anecdotal in nature. This study empirically investigated the relationship between the measures of EIS success (acceptance, usage, satisfaction, and improvement in performance) and the level of support provided by the EIS to the different phases of the SMP (environmental analysis, strategy formulation, strategy implementation, and strategic control). Data were collected through a survey questionnaire administered to EIS professionals and executive users from 51 organizations. Multiple regression analysis was used to test the hypothesized relationships. It was found that the measure of EIS success were related to providing support for the SMP.

Times are tough for IS executives. Corporations are still searching for productivity payoff from the significant IT investments made in the past decade. As a result, IS managers are under relentless pressure to justify further investments and to adopt newer measures of system effectiveness (Sullivan-Trainor, 1993). Increasingly, CEOs are demanding that the effectiveness of IS be measured by its degree of support for the strategic management process (SMP) of the organization (Drucker, 1995; Moad, 1994; 1993; Bacon, 1992).

Executive Information Systems (EIS) are designed to support and facilitate the SMP (Singh, Watson, and Watson, 1995). Recently, EISs have diffused throughout the organization and people have started calling them Everybody's Information System or Enterprise Information System (Messina and Singh, 1995). These systems besides being high profile in nature, are also quite expensive to develop and implement. The failure of an EIS not only results in wasted resources but also the lost confidence of top management in IS. Thus, it is important for organizations, to assure the successful implementation of an EIS.

Given the importance of systems like EIS, one would expect many studies examining their factors for success. While, there are some case studies documenting the reasons for success or failure (e.g., Belcher and Watson, 1993; Watson and Glover, 1990), the IS literature is generally lacking in empirical investigation of EIS implementation success. This paper attempts to develop measurements of EIS success and, based on data collected from 51 North American organizations, empirically test them in relation to its support for the SMP.

The chapter begins by identifying how an EIS can support the SMP. Then, the measures of EIS success are developed and the hypotheses to be tested by the study are presented. Next, the research method is described, followed by the study results and a discussion of the findings. The chapter concludes by examining managerial implications of the research findings.

Literature Review

This section reviews the literature pertaining to the relationship of an EIS and the SMP, and identifies measures of EIS implementation success.

EIS and Support for the Strategic Management Process

An EIS is a class of information system designed for use by senior level executives. These systems provide on-line information about the internal and external operations of an organization, and contain features like electronic mail, querying, and modeling (Watson, Rainer, Koh, 1991; Rockart and Delong, 1988). The primary objective of an EIS is to provide readily accessible information, in an user friendly format, to support strategic decision making (Elam & Leidner, 1995).

In today's dynamic and turbulent environment, IT is a necessity for strategic decision making (Drucker, 1995). Many researchers have

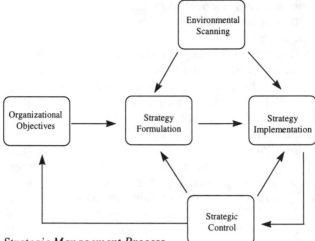

Figure 1: The Strategic Management Process

conjectured that the main purpose of an EIS should be to support the SMP (Singh, Watson, and Watson, 1995; Crockett, 1992). While numerous studies have been conducted showing benefits to users and organizations, few attempts have been made to link the EIS with the overall management process of an organization. Developing such a focus would greatly aid the successful implementation of an EIS (Crockett, 1992; Paller and Laska, 1990).

In order to understand how an EIS can support the SMP, we first need to define the process itself. The SMP begins with the determination of an organization's objectives. These objectives can be strategic, administrative, or operational in nature (Hofer and Schendel, 1978). Strategic objectives are long term in nature, dealing with the organization's future course of action. Administrative objectives are the structural policies and procedures required to implement the strategic objectives. Operational objectives are the decisions that acquire, allocate, and monitor resources to achieve the strategic objectives.

The objectives are then transformed into the established results through the formulation and implementation of strategies (Hofer, et al., 1984). While there is no general consensus of the exact phases of the SMP, Andrews (1987) has identified the following as the most accepted components — environmental scanning, strategy formulation, strategy implementation, and strategic control (see Figure 1). In order to comprehensively support strategic decision making, an EIS should support all these phases (Crockett, 1992).

Organizations begin the SMP with an analysis of their internal and external environment (Daft and Lengel, 1986). An EIS can facilitate environmental scanning by providing information about the task environment (e.g., customers, suppliers, competitors, and labor supply) and the general environment (e.g., technical, political, legal, economic, and socio-cultural).

In the strategy formulation phase, SWOT analysis is used to develop alternative strategies that the organization will adopt (Andrews, 1987). The different strategies are then evaluated on various financial and non-financial criteria and the best strategies are selected for implementation (Galbraith and Kazanjian, 1986). An EIS can facilitate these processes by collecting and disseminating plans and programs from different parts of the organization, and by aiding in the development of budgets through its decision support capabilities (McAullife and Shamlin, 1992; Thierauf, 1991).

The best strategies are then executed in the implementation phase. This process requires the allocation of resources and responsibilities. At the same time, performance measures are constantly monitored against established benchmarks to detect unfavorable variance. Based on the variance results, strategies are either refined or discarded. While many macro-organizational variables have to be designed for the successful execution of strategies, the establishment of an information system is a key factor in the strategy implementation and control processes (Lorange, Scott Morton, and Ghosal, 1986).

EISs are suited to support the business processes required to implement and monitor the strategies because most of these systems are built on existing corporate databases of an organization (van den Hoven, 1996; Singh, Watson, and Watson, 1995). Further, EISs can also support the implementation and control processes by providing features that allow: the flow of information across functional areas and organizational hierarchies; exception reporting; and, capabilities to drill down to lower levels of detail (Crockett, 1992).

Implementation Research

There are numerous definitions of the term implementation in the MIS literature. According to Lucas (1981a), " ... the implementation of a computer-based information system is an ongoing process which includes the entire development of the system from the original suggestion through the feasibility study, system analysis and design, programming, training, conversion, and installation of the system" (p. 14).

Implementation is sometimes used to refer to the last stage of the system analysis and design process (Lucas, 1981b). In the present context, however, the meaning of the term is much broader in scope, from development to integration into its organizational setting. Research in the implementation of information systems can be reviewed from three perspectives: theories, factors, and processes.

Theories provide insights and factors for future research dealing with ideas and propositions regarding implementation (Lucas, 1981b; Galbraith, 1979). Process research, on the other hand, explains system development phenomena, and suggests how to proceed with system implementation. This type of research provides an understanding of what, why, and how something happened and is concerned with understanding relationships among users and designers, and their perspective of the design process (Kraut, Dumais, and Koch, 1989; Srinivasan and Davis, 1987; Lucas, 1981a; Ginzberg, 1979).

Finally, factor research is aimed at identifying and studying factors associated with implementation success (Baronas and Louis, 1988; Tait and Vessey, 1988; Ives and Olson, 1984). A large number of factors important in the implementation process has been identified through this type of research. The current study primarily falls under the category of factor research.

There are many important factors in the successful implementation of an EIS (Watson and Frolick, 1993; Rockart and Delong, 1988). One of the most important factors is that the EIS should support the SMP. During the course of case studies conducted by Volonino and Watson (1991) and Rockart and Delong (1988), the authors observed that all successful EISs were explicitly linked to one or more phases of the SMP. This paper examines empirically how supporting the SMP can lead to EIS implementation success.

Measures of EIS Implementation Success

Measuring the success of an information system is a complex and difficult process (Rainer and Watson, 1995; Zmud, 1979). The problem is compounded in the case of an EIS due to the evolutionary nature of the system, without neatly defined completion dates. Even though most firms are able to evaluate costs, the benefits of the system are often intangible and difficult to quantify, and savings cannot be demonstrated with certainty (Belcher and Watson, 1993; Houdeshel and Watson, 1987). In a previous study, it was found that most firms assess the costs of an EIS, but did not do traditional cost/benefit analysis (Watson, Rainer, Koh, 1991). Therefore, due to the problems involved in direct measurement, researchers often rely on surrogate measures to study implementation success.

In the current study, two different approaches of measuring EIS implementation success were adopted. First, the traditional measures of systems success as developed by Lucas (1981a, 1981b), Lucas, Ginzberg, and Schultz (1990), and Venkatraman and Ramanujam (1987) were used. In their view successful implementation is reflected by the acceptance of the system by users, the usage of the system, user's satisfaction with the system and, the impact of the system on user performance. These four constructs measure change and improvement in the decision-making process, and are used for hypotheses testing. The second approach, termed the GAP measure, is based on the service quality measurement derived from the marketing literature (Zeithaml, Parasuraman, and Berry, 1993, 1990; Parasuraman, Berry, and Zeithaml, 1988, 1985). This measure is computed by analyzing the difference between the objectives for developing an information system and the actual support provided to those objectives by the system. The GAP measure is intended to complement our understanding of the traditional measures of EIS implementation success.

Traditional Measures

Voluntary acceptance of a system is a measure of the proclivity to use that system. Without acceptance, there is no inclination to accommodate and include the system within the management process (Applegate and Osborne, 1988). On the other hand, use is the actual experience of incorporating the system, implying that a change in the behavior of the end user has taken place (Barki and Huff, 1985; Fuerst and Cheney, 1982; Cheney and Dickson, 1982).

However, measures of acceptance and usage should be considered concurrently because one may accept a system conceptually but find it difficult or impossible to use. Ginzberg (1978) noted that usage by itself was an inadequate measure, because given the choice between an unsatisfactory system and no system, users will use the unsatisfactory system. But systems that are adopted voluntarily should have a high level of usage because users must have perceived some benefit from the system (Lucas, 1982).

Another widely used measure of system success is user satisfaction (Raymond, 1987; Zmud, 1979). Even when actual usage can be measured, success ultimately depends on how well the information system supports the end user. If the user perceives the system as providing valuable information not available elsewhere, the system designer can be relatively confident of user satisfaction with the system (Mahmood and Medewitz, 1985; Ives and Olson, 1981).

The post-adoption evaluation of a system is best operationalized by measuring the impact on user performance. When evaluating an EIS, a desirable measure would be the difference in performance or effectiveness based on the results obtained from decisions made using the system as compared to decisions that would have been made without the system. Venkatraman and Ramanujam (1987) identified 12 key factors to measure the success of strategic systems as reflected by the improvements in the SMP. Their instrument can be adopted to measure the impact of an information system on the performance of executive users (Tyran, et al., 1992).

GAP Measure

In addition to using the traditional methods, the GAP method was used to assess the successful implementation of an EIS. GAP measure can be assessed by comparing the importance of different objectives for developing the system and the support provided to those objectives by the system (Gronroos, 1982; Sasser, Olsen, Wychoff, 1978). For an

EIS, objectives are the motivations for its development, while accomplishments are the actual support of the motivating factors through the EIS. The difference between original expectation and actual support provided for a range of objectives will indicate the success of the EIS (Pitt and Watson, 1995).

While this concept of EIS success is derived from the marketing literature (e.g., Zeithaml, Parasuraman, and Berry, 1993, 1990; Parasuraman, Berry, and Zeithaml, 1993; 1991; 1988; 1985), support for adopting this measure can be found in the IS literature (e.g., Watson, Pitt, and Kavan, 1995; Conrath and Mignen, 1990; Rushinek and Rushinek, 1986). Although the GAP measure is used in the context of EIS, it could be readily adopted to measure the implementation success of any information system.

Development of Hypotheses

There has been a noticeable shift in the focus of many EISs, away from particular end users and toward an organizational perspective. Providing support to the SMP is a key factor in the implementation success of an EIS (Singh, Watson, and Watson, 1995; Rockart and Delong, 1988). This study attempts to examine empirically the relationship between the various measures of EIS implementation success and its support of the SMP. To accomplish this, a set of research hypotheses were formulated based upon the literature review of

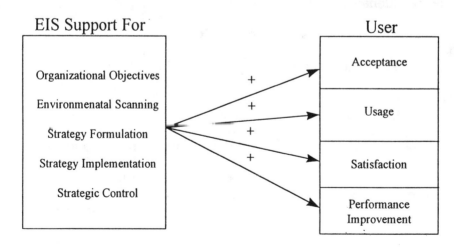

Figure 2: Research Hypotheses

strategic management, EIS, and MIS implementation literature. More specifically, the hypotheses are:

H_1: The acceptance of an EIS is related to its support of the SMP

H_2: The use of an EIS is related to its support of the SMP

H_3: The satisfaction with an EIS is related to its support of the SMP

H_4: The improvement in user performance due to an EIS is related to its support of the SMP

The independent variables are the support provided to the organizational objectives, environmental scanning, strategy formulation, strategy implementation, and strategic control phases of SMP. The dependent variables are the traditional measures of EIS success - acceptance, usage, satisfaction, and the impact on user performance. A positive relationship was anticipated for all the hypotheses, i.e., the higher the level the support for the SMP phases, the more successful the EIS will be in the organization (see Figure 2). The research methodology employed to test these hypotheses is described in the next section.

The Study

A survey questionnaire was used to collect data for testing the hypotheses. This section describes the development of the instrument, data collection, demographic information, descriptive statistics, and the operationalization of the variables.

Instrument Development

Two sets of questionnaire items were developed based on previous research (e.g., Watson, Watson, and Singh 1995; Daft, 1991; Lucas, Ginzberg, and Schultz, 1990; Andrews, 1987; Venkatraman and Ramanujam, 1987; Scott Morton and Ghosal, 1986; Hofer and Schendel, 1978). Questionnaire A (see Appendix C) contained items to measure the objectives for developing an EIS, the support provided for those objectives, and the support for the different phases of the SMP provided by the EIS. This questionnaire was completed by EIS professionals, who should be knowledgeable about the content and features of the EIS. Questionnaire B (see Appendix C) assessed the measures of EIS implementation success and was completed by executive users.

Suggestions from EIS professionals, executive users, and consultants were used to guide the construction of the questionnaire, which in turn ensured the content validity of the instrument (Carmines and

Zellers, 1978). The development process went through six rounds of modification to determine the questions and the format that was used prior to pre-testing the instrument.

A pilot study was conducted to further validate the instrument. The initial versions of the questionnaires were mailed to ten organizations from several geographic regions in the United States, representing manufacturing, government, services, retailing, and mining industries. These organizations used a mixture of vendor supplied software and custom built EIS systems. The respondents (i.e., EIS professionals and executive users) indicated that the content of the questionnaires were appropriate for measuring the support provided to the SMP and assessing the success of an EIS. Based on the promising results from the pilot test, a mass mailing was made.

Data Collection

A mailing containing a cover letter, questionnaire A (one copy) and questionnaire B (two copies) was mailed to EIS professionals at 315 firms listed in The University of Georgia's EIS database. The database consists of firms known or likely to have an EIS. Created from a variety of sources, the database is believed to provide a representative sample of firms with an EIS and has been used in previous studies (e.g., Watson, Watson, and Singh, 1995; Watson and Frolick, 1993).

The cover letter requested that the recipient complete questionnaire A and forward the two copies of questionnaire B to two executive EIS users within their organization. Collecting data from executives is a difficult proposition. Keeping this in mind, two copies of questionnaire B were sent, with the hope of getting back at least one completed questionnaire. In cases where both copies of questionnaire B were returned, the completed instrument from the user in the highest position was used.

Seventeen surveys were returned as being undeliverable. Of the remaining 298 firms, EIS professionals from 60 firms responded by completing questionnaire A. Executive users from 40 firms responded by completing questionnaire B.

Five weeks after the initial mailing, a follow-up mailing with a cover letter, copy of questionnaire A, and two copies of questionnaire B was sent to the non-respondents. EIS professionals from 14 firms reported having an EIS. Users from 11 firms completed questionnaire B. Altogether 74 usable responses were received from EIS professionals and 51 responses were received from EIS users. All data analyses were performed on the sample of 51 firms from where both EIS professionals and executive users had responded.

Demographics

All the organizations that participated in the study are located in

North America, with average gross revenues of $ 2.2 billion (see Table 1). The average age of the EISs in the study was 43 months. The majority of the EIS professionals hold middle-management positions and most of the EIS users are senior-level executives in their organizations (see Tables 2 and 3, respectively).

Operationalization of Variables

The independent and dependent variables were measured using multiple items to improve measurement properties (Nunnally, 1978).

Particulars	
Types of Industry	*Percent*
Manufacturing	31
Government	14
Banking/Finance	12
Computer Software/Services	08
Retail	06
Insurance	06
Others	23
	100%
Gross Revenue (in dollars)	*Percent*
Under 100 million	13
100-200 million	08
200-1000 million	10
1000-5000 million	12
	100%

Table 1. Organization Characteristics (n = 51)

Particulars	
Job Titles	*Percent*
IS Manaager	52
Systems Analyst	19
Director of EIS	16
Vice-President	05
CIO	02
Consultants	06
	100%
Actively involved in the development of EIS	70%
Actively involved in the current operation of EIS	84%
Years of job experience (mean)	11
Years spent with an EIS (mean)	03

Table 2. EIS Professional Characteristics (n = 51)

Particular

Job Titles	Percent	
Director		33
Vice President		25
Manager		15
CIO		11
CFO		08
President		<u>08</u>
		100%

Primary Area of Work Experience

Planning		31
Finance/Accounting		28
Marketing		16
Research		10
Product Development		08
Production		04
Other		<u>03</u>
		100%

Average time spent/week with the EIS (in hours)	5
Years of job experience (mean)	17

Table 3. Executive EIS User Characteristics (n = 51)

EIS professionals were asked to indicate on a scale of 1-7, the level of support provided to the different activities within each phase of the SMP, thereby operationalizing the independent variables (see Appendix A). Dependent variables were operationalized by asking executive users to indicate on a scale of 1-7, their acceptance of the system, usage of the system, satisfaction with the system, and the impact of the system on the management process (see Appendix B).

For the GAP measure, EIS professionals were given a list of factors important in the development of the EIS (Watson, Rainer, and Koh, 1991; Paller and Laska, 1990; Rockart and Delong, 1988). The respondents were asked to rate the importance of each of the factors in motivating the development of the EIS, and, second, to rate the level of support provided by the EIS to each of the factors (see Table 6). The difference between the two ratings, weighted by the importance of each factor, averaged over all the factors, gave a measure of EIS success for each participating organization. In general, the index of EIS success is given by the formula:

$$GAP = \frac{\sum_{i=1}^{N} IF_i(SF_i - IF_i)}{N}$$

Variables	# of Items	Mean	S.D.	α	1	2	3	4	5	6	7	8	9
1. Organizational Objectives	3	4.60	1.11	.78	1.00								
2. Environmental Scanning	9	3.32	1.33	.86	.55	1.00							
3. Strategy Formulation	9	3.83	1.23	.85	.44	.72	1.00						
4. Strategy Implementation	9	4.30	0.95	.76	.43	.55	.64	1.00					
5. Strategy Control	9	4.50	1.04	.76	.18	.29	.51	.78	1.00				
6. System Acceptance	5	5.19	1.38	.90	.47	.31	.24	.52	.36	1.00			
7. System Usage	1	4.64	1.61	--	.25	.23	.19	.48	.50	.72	1.00		
8. User Satisfaction	8	4.90	1.05	.86	.30	.16	.13	.45	.32	.70	.49	1.00	
9. Performance Impact	10	4.43	1.02	.85	.39	.34	.40	.46	.32	.68	.50	.65	1.00

Note: *All the correlation >.25 are significant at or below .05 level.*

Table 4. Matrix of Intercorrelation Among Test Variables (n = 51)

GAP = Measure of EIS success
IF = Importance of the factor in motivating the development of the EIS
SF = Support of the factor through the EIS
N = Number of factors being considered

Questionnaire A contained 39 items to measure the level of support provided to the SMP and 13 items for the GAP measure of EIS success. Questionnaire B contained 23 items for the traditional measures of EIS success. The mean value of the responses to the multiple items addressing each dimension was taken as the measure for that variable.

The instruments were tested for reliability using the Cronbach's (1951) alpha test applied to inter-item scores. The means, standard deviations, and the intercorrelation among the study variables are provided in Tables 4. All alpha coefficients indicate a satisfactory level of internal consistency among the multi-item scales. The values of the alpha ranged from .76 to .92, which are generally within the .80 criterion value for inter-item reliability. Further, the intercorrelation among the study variables showed no evidence of extreme multicollienarity (e.g., r's in excess of .80).

Presentation of Findings

Data Analyses

Multiple regression analysis was used to test the hypothesized relationships. The independent variables for the four hypotheses — support for organizational objectives, environmental scanning, strategy formulation, strategy implementation, and strategic control —

were regressed on each of the measures of EIS success — acceptance, usage, satisfaction, and impact on performance, respectively. The multiple regression model used to test each of the hypotheses was as follows:

$$Y_i = \beta_0 + \beta_1 X_{i1} + \beta_2 X_{i2} + \beta_3 X_{i3} + \beta_4 X_{i4} + \beta_5 X_{i5} + \varepsilon_i$$

where,

Y_i = EIS success measure
X_{i1} = Support for organizational objectives
X_{i2} = Support for environmental scanning
X_{i3} = Support for strategy formulation
X_{i4} = Support for strategy implementation
X_{i5} = Support for strategic control

The F-test was used and all significance were tested for $p < .05$. In each analysis, the significance of the beta weights were also examined. In addition, the regression equations were investigated for aptness of model by analyzing the residuals. No problems were found with the normality of residuals. The results from hypotheses testing appears in Table 5.

The means and standard deviations of the factors used for the GAP measure are presented in Table 6. The factors are rank ordered by the level of support provided by the EIS. While a casual perusal of Table 6 would indicate that all the motivational factors for the development of the EISs were being supported, the GAP measure of EIS success indicates otherwise. A simple difference of the means does not take into account the importance of a factor to the organization. For example, on a scale of 1 to 7, let's assume the importance of factor A in the development of the EIS is a 2 and the level of support provided to the factor is 3. On the other hand, let's say, the importance of factor B in the development of the EIS is a 5 and the level of support provided to

	Variables t statistics (p value)					Test Statistics	
	Organizational Objectives	Environmental Scanning	Strategy Formulation	Strategy Implementation	Strategic Control	F statistics (p value)	R^2
Acceptance (H₁)	2.491 (.0165) *	0.154 (.8781)	-1.452 (.1534)	2.192 (.0336)*	0.187 (.8523)	5.824 (.0003)*	.3929
Usage (H₂)	1.023 (.3316)	0.830 (.4108)	-1.791 (.0801)	0.838 (.4065)	2.133 (.0384)*	4.523 (.0020) *	.3345
Satisfaction (H₃)	1.432 (.1592)	-0.352 (.7268)	-1.361 (.1803)	2.288 (.0269)*	0.019 (.9848)	3.501 (.0093) *	.2800
Performance (H₄)	1.462 (.1506)	-0.343 (.7328)	0.773 (.4437)	1.300 (.2003)	2.412 (.0200)*	3.424 (.0105)*	.2756

*Note: * denotes significant below .05 level*

Table 5. Result from Regression Analyses

Motivating Factors	Importance of the Factors in Development		Level of Support for the Motivating Factors	
	Mean	SD	Mean	SD
Provide timely and faster access to information	5.58	1.24	5.75	1.14
Extract and integrate data from different source	5.10	1.35	5.40	1.45
Monitor organizational performance	5.04	1.19	5.33	1.30
Provide information about the organization's CSF	5.02	1.49	5.32	1.58
Improve inter-organizational communication	4.98	1.30	5.28	1.34
Improve effectiveness of senior executives	4.77	1.66	4.97	1.78
Increase responsiveness to customer satisfaction	4.61	1.61	4.72	1.76
Improve organizational planning and control process	4.35	1.32	4.53	1.63
Need for competitive information	4.30	1.73	4.48	1.74
Improve quality of goods and services	4.28	1.65	4.43	1.91
Increase span of managerial control	4.24	1.57	4.42	1.75
Assist in cost-cutting measures	4.12	1.58	4.22	1.65
Assist in team building	3.77	1.55	3.93	1.74

Table 6. GAP Measure of EIS Success

the factor is 6. While the difference between the support of the factor and its importance is 1 in both cases, what this scenario does not take into account is that factor B is more important to the organization. Thus, if we weighted the difference by the importance of the factor, the difference now becomes 2 for factor A and 5 for factor B.

Using this analysis, 12 companies reported a negative number for their GAP measure. This means that their EIS was not supporting the factors important for the development of the system. When the weighted differences of the individual factors were averaged, the following three factors revealed a negative value: improve the effectiveness of senior executives (-1.15); need for competitive information (-.91); and assist in team building (-.55).

Results

Univariate statistics on the independent and dependent variables are presented in Table 4. The results show that the support provided through the EIS was highest for the organizational objectives, followed by strategic control, strategy implementation, strategy formulation, environmental scanning. Among the organizational objectives, the highest support was for operational objectives, followed by administrative and strategic objectives.

The results from multiple regression analysis are presented in Table 5. As hypothesized, the acceptance, usage, satisfaction, and impact on user performance were significantly related to the support provided by an EIS to the different phases of the SMP. However, the support for strategy implementation and control were most significant in explaining the variance of the relationships. Support for environmental scanning and strategy formulation did not have much impact on the success of an EIS.

Variables	1	2	3	4	5
1. GAP Measure	1.00				
2. Acceptance of the system	.34	1.00			
3. Use of the system	.60	.48	1.00		
4. User satisfaction	.45	.65	.60	1.00	
5. Impact on user performance	.68	.52	.68	.64	1.00

Note: All correlations are significant at .05 level or below

Table 7. Correlation of GAP and Traditional Measures of EIS Success

An investigation of the beta values reveal two interesting points. First, the betas for environmental scanning and strategy formulation were negative. Secondly, the significant betas for strategy implementation and strategic control alternated between the four hypotheses. These values may be due to the relatively high correlation between environmental scanning and strategy formulation (.72), and strategy implementation and strategic control (.78). Theoretically, the high correlation makes sense. According to Andrews (1987), the SMP is actually demarcated into two important parts; strategy formulation and strategy implementation. One begins strategy formulation with environmental scanning, and ends strategy implementation with strategic control.

The univariate analysis of the importance of the factors in motivating the development of the EIS and the support provided to those factors by the EIS, indicates that the system is being primarily used for accessing organizational information (see Table 6). At the same time, the GAP measure indicates that the factors for improving the effectiveness of senior executives, need for competitive information, and team building are not being supported. Further, the GAP measure of success was correlated with the traditional measures of EIS success (see Table 7). The results indicate that all the correlation are significant.

Discussion

The findings of this study suggest that the implementation success of an EIS is related to its support of the SMP. All four measures of EIS success — acceptance of the system, the use of the system, user satisfaction with the system, and the impact of the system on user performance were related to the level of support provided by the EIS to the different phases of the SMP. This result is consistent with and expands on the findings of Volonino and Watson (1991) and Rockart and Delong (1988). Through case studies, these researchers had concluded that supporting the different phases of the SMP was a key to successful EIS implementation.

Drucker (1995) states that due to the complex and diverse nature of information required for decision making, companies need to use information technology for the SMP. The results of this study suggest that EIS are being used to support SMP, with more emphasis on the implementation and control than formulation of strategies, as predicted by Crockett (1992). Almost all EISs are built on corporate databases from which financial and accounting data are obtained. The strategy implementation and control processes are based on these information, which is readily accessed and delivered through an EIS.

The fact that support for organizational objectives (except H_1), environmental scanning, and strategy formulation were not significant in the hypothesized relationships, is hardly surprising. A lot of data used in these processes are soft (e.g., rumors, predictions) in nature. Often, these types of information are difficult to capture in an EIS (Watson, et al., 1996). Besides, these processes require a lot of personal interaction with other organizational members, for which computer based systems are not completely adequate (Jones and McLeod, 1986; Daft and Lengel, 1986). Overall, EIS are being used more to facilitate the exchange and presentation of accounting/financial data and not much to enhance activities that require interpersonal communication.

The results of the GAP analysis support the above findings. The motivating factors that are part of the implementation and control of strategies were the most supported factors by the EIS. For example, the top three factors supported by the EISs (i.e., timely access to information, integration of data from different sources, and monitor organizational performance) are all integral part of strategy implementation and control. On the other hand, factors involving presentation and exchange of soft information and interpersonal communications were the least supported factors (e.g., assist in team-building, increase span of managerial control).

The GAP analysis indicates that out of 13 factors, three were not being supported as anticipated. They are: improve effectiveness of senior executives; need for competitive information; and assist in teambuilding. An analysis based on this approach allows organizations to focus on supporting the factors that are important for the development of an information system. The organization can work on improving the support provided to the critical factors, whose GAP measures are negative, in the next iteration of system development. This is possible because almost all EISs are developed and implemented using the prototyping method (Watson, Watson, and Singh, 1995).

To summarize, the results from both hypotheses testing and GAP analysis point to improvement in supporting the organizational objectives, environmental scanning and strategy formulation for further success of the implementation of an EIS. Finally, the GAP measure of

EIS success was correlated with the traditional measures of EIS success. The results in Table 7 indicate that there is a significant relationship between these two measures of success. Thus, traditional measures of success might be complemented with an approach similar to the GAP measure for a richer insight to the factors contributing to the successful implementation of an EIS.

Management Strategies for Information Technology Investment

The importance of information technology in the strategic management of an organization is becoming critical (Drucker, 1995). At the same time, executives are demanding that IT investment be measured by its impact on the strategic management of an organization (Sullivan-Trainor, 1993).While many top executives still shy away from the use of computers, for the majority of decision makers, computer-based systems have become an indispensable tool. However, prior to the popularity of EISs (or similar systems by different names), there were hardly any alternatives for executives worth pursuing. But with the advent of systems like an EIS, the integration of computer technology in the SMP of an organization is on the rise (Elam & Leidner, 1995).

The findings of the study suggest that EISs are used primarily for the implementation and control of strategies. Information for these activities comes from the financial and accounting information already existing in the corporate databases. However, executives surveyed in this study have indicated there is a need for more environmental information, both internal and external, to the organization, that will help them in formulating strategies. While some organizations are capturing soft information and environmental data (critical for the less deterministic process of strategy formulation), there needs to be more integration of such tools for greater diffusion and use of EIS within an organization. With the advent of the World Wide Web (WWW), Intranets, and Lotus Notes, organizations can enhance the value derived from their EIS by incorporating features to access and communicate internal and external environmental information (Haley and Watson, 1996; van den Hoven, 1996).

Recently, the practice of data warehousing has become very popular. Tools and techniques are emerging that allow managers to be more proactive in the decision making process. MIS managers should be able to recognize that data warehouses are a variation of the EIS. Analytical processing of data warehouses should be integrated in the design process of any EIS, for it has great potential in supporting the strategy formulation phase of SMP.

Finally, the scope and focus of an EIS is no longer limited to an executive. Almost everybody in a corporation is demanding systems that are capable of delivering the right information in the right format at right time. Information that was only available to executives in the past decade are now readily accessible by a wider audience. There are many reasons for the diffusion of this technology. First, the price/performance ratio of hardware and software is improving dramatically, thereby, pushing computer based systems further down the corporate hierarchy. Second, the growth of Intranets has put a wide variety of corporate information at the fingertips of the average employee. But most importantly, companies are realizing the value of timely information in the turbulent and dynamic business environment in which they are operating. Information is time, money, and knowledge. To survive in the global marketplace, any attempts to restrict information access is suicidal. Thus, large number of organizations are doing whatever is necessary to provide all their employees with access to appropriate information.

Naturally, such an undertaking is complex and constitutes a large investment. As a result, companies are adopting prototyping approach in the development and implementation of an EIS (Watson, Watson, and Singh, 1995). Using this approach, the EIS within a company can evolve with the growing demands from and the changing information needs of the employees. Further, realistic cost/benefit analysis for systems like an EIS is extremely difficult. While it is easy to evaluate the costs associated with the tangible resources (e.g., software, hardware, personnel), the intangibles (both the cost and the benefit) are almost impossible to measure. In the absence of precise and reliable evaluation techniques, the GAP index can be used by organizations to measure the success of information systems, EIS or otherwise. The GAP measure will help assess what the expectations were at the time of developing a system and the success of the system in fulfilling those expectations. While the GAP measure cannot be substituted for cost/benefit analysis, the technique can certainly be used to evaluate technology productivity payoff.

Finally, there are many other important factors in the successful implementation of an EIS (e.g., information requirements, personnel, database design). The current research addressed the importance of only one such factor, i.e., the support provided by the EIS to the SMP. In order to build a comprehensive theory of successful EIS implementation, the collective importance of other factors needs to be examined.

Appendix A: Final Measurement Scale of the Organizational Use of Executive Information Systems (Sample Questions)

Environmental Scanning Phase

In this phase of the management process, information is gathered from the **external** and the **internal** environments of the organization. Based on such information, **strengths** and **weaknesses** of the organization are matched with the **opportunities** and **threats** for the organization.

1. Please indicate the extent to which your EIS covers the following categories of information (**circle** a number on the scale).

Categories	No coverage					Significant coverage	
a. Political information (e.g., legislation pertinent to the organization)	1	2	3	4	5	6	7
b. Economic information (e.g., interest rates, employment rates)	1	2	3	4	5	6	7
c. Technical information (e.g., new product manufacturing process)	1	2	3	4	5	6	7
d. Demographic information (e.g., changing population patterns)	1	2	3	4	5	6	7
e. Customer information (e.g., number of orders placed)	1	2	3	4	5	6	7
f. Competitor information (e.g., latest product promotion strategies)	1	2	3	4	5	6	7
g. Supplier information (e.g., time schedule of delivery, defect rates)	1	2	3	4	5	6	7
h. Labor information (e.g., availability of skilled labor in workforce)	1	2	3	4	5	6	7
i. International information (e.g., potential export market)	1	2	3	4	5	6	7

Appendix B: Final Measurement Scale of User Evaluation of Executive Information Systems (Sample Questions)

For the following questions please **circle** a number on the scale.

1. Please indicate the extent to which the EIS **contributes** to your job performance.

No contribution					Significant contribution	
1	2	3	4	5	6	7

2. Please indicate the **extent** to which the EIS helps you achieve your organization's objectives.

Small Extent					Significant extent	
1	2	3	4	5	6	7

3. Please indicate the **impact** of the EIS on the following activities.

Activities	No improvement					Much improvement	
a. Adapting to unanticipated changes	1	2	3	4	5	6	7
b. Identifying new business opportunities	1	2	3	4	5	6	7
c. Identifying key problem areas	1	2	3	4	5	6	7
d. Helping motivate employees	1	2	3	4	5	6	7
e. Communicating top management's expectations down the line	1	2	3	4	5	6	7
f. Fostering management control	1	2	3	4	5	6	7
g. Fostering organizational learning	1	2	3	4	5	6	7
h. Enhancing innovation and solution to problems	1	2	3	4	5	6	7

Appendix C: Item and Scale Characteristics

Items (Questionnaire A)	Mean	SD	α
Organizational Objectives	**4.60**	**1.11**	**.78**
Operational objectives	5.27	1.34	
Administrative objectives	4.43	1.74	
Strategic objectives	4.09	1.45	
Environmental Scanning	**3.32**	**1.33**	**.86**
Customer information	4.23	2.07	
Competitor information	4.03	1.94	
Technical information	3.52	2.24	
Supplier information	3.43	1.97	
Economic information	3.41	2.05	
Demographic information	2.94	2.00	
Labor information	2.90	1.88	
International information	2.74	1.69	
Political information	2.64	1.73	
Strategy Formulation	**3.83**	**1.23**	**.85**
Extract/integrate data from varied sources	5.47	1.34	
Provide information about firms' CSF	5.15	1.59	
Decision making capabilities	4.11	1.95	
Gather strategic plans from within the firm	3.54	2.16	
Consolidate strategic plans	3.43	1.92	
Analyze growth/diversification options	3.37	1.81	
Compare strategic plans	3.27	1.76	
Match products with target markets	3.05	1.72	
Identify life cycle strategies for p oducts	3.05	2.03	
Strategy Implementation	**4.30**	**.95**	**.76**
Exchange information among fuctional areas	5.29	1.54	
Access consolidated financial/operational data	5.23	1.51	
Exchange information among organizational levels	5.07	1.56	
Access detailed financial/operational data	4.76	1.75	
Access timely information about projects	4.13	1.87	
Help communicate organizational values	3.76	1.94	
Budgeting process	3.49	1.79	
Allocate resources to business activities	3.29	1.80	
Match job requirements/persona qualifications	2.33	1.58	
Strategy Control	**4.50**	**1.04**	**.76**
Monitor financial/operational information	5.29	1.71	

Items	Mean	SD	α
Highlight financial/operational information	5.23	1.55	
Drill down to detailed levels of information	5.19	1.72	
Facilitate comparison of actual/intended results	4.98	1.56	
Facilitate responsiveness/accountability of managers	4.45	1.78	
Monitor market share of products and services	4.05	2.06	
Provide explanation for variance in results	4.05	1.58	
Monitor customer satisfaction	3.64	2.09	
Monitor worker performance	3.60	1.97	

Items (Questionnaire B)	Mean	SD	α
System Acceptance	**5.19**	**1.38**	**.90**
Encourage others to use EIS	5.70	1.47	
Voluntarily Chose EIS	5.50	1.60	
Importance of EIS in accomplishing job	5.19	1.48	
Reliance on EIS	4.92	1.42	
Impact on job if EIS is not available	4.62	1.56	
User Satisfaction	**4.90**	**1.05**	**.86**
Accuracy	5.37	1.18	
Currency	5.23	1.45	
Relevance	5.19	1.46	
Timeliness	5.19	1.35	
Time Period	4.90	1.46	
Completeness	4.54	1.48	
Scope	4.15	1.54	
System Usage	**4.64**	**1.61**	**.85**
Performance Impact	**4.43**	**1.02**	
Identify key problem areas	5.07	1.61	
Help achieve organizational objectives	4.90	1.43	
Foster management control	4.82	1.58	
Adapt to unanticipated changes	4.54	1.39	
Foster organizational learning	4.50	1.59	
Contribution to job performance	4.47	1.55	
Communicate management's expectations	4.39	1.72	
Enhance innovations and solutions	4.27	1.53	
Identify new business opportunities	3.78	1.59	
Help motivate employees	3.60	1.58	

Chapter 6

Investments in Reusable Software: A Study of Software Reuse Investment Success Factors

David C. Rine
George Mason University

Robert M. Sonnemann
U.S. Air Force

This research supports the thesis that there is a set of success factors which are common across organizations and have some predictability relationships to software reuse. For completeness, this research also investigated to see if software reuse had a predictive relationship to productivity and quality. A literature search was conducted to identify a set of software reuse success factors. The individual success factors were grouped into the following categories: management commitment, investment strategy, business strategy, technology transfer, organizational structure, process maturity, product-line approach, software architecture, availability of components, and quality of components. A questionnaire was developed to measure software reuse capability, productivity, quality, and the set of software reuse success factors. A survey was conducted to determine the state-of-the-practice. The data from the survey was statistically analyzed to evaluate the relationships among reuse capability, productivity, quality, and the individual software reuse success factors. The results of the analysis showed some of the success factors to have a predictive relationship to software reuse capability. Software reuse capability also had a predictive relationship to productivity and quality. Based on the research results, the leading indicators of software reuse capability are: product-line approach, architecture which standardizes interfaces and data formats, common software architecture across the product-line, design for manufacturing approach, domain engineering, management which understands reuse issues, software reuse advocate(s) in senior management, state-of-the-art tools and methods, precedence of reusing high levevl software artifacts such as requirements and design versus just code reuse, and trace end-user requirements to the components (systems, subsystems, and/or software modules) which support them.

Investments in Reusable Software

In this chapter, we examine a part of the problem of building an information technology (IT) infrastructure. We examine the IT infrastructure of businesses involved in the development of software products. The software products of these businesses are those built by a software engineering process. Hence, these products are generally 'large scale,' and these businesses are generally devoted to building product lines and families of software products within given application domains. Therefore, it is reasonable to consider the possibility of leveraging software reuse in attempting to increase reliability and decrease costs and effort of producing software products. Hence, the part of the IT we wish to examine is that part of software development businesses dealing with reusable software components and architectures as part of the infrastructure of product development. In this chapter we therefore examine software reuse investment successs factors, and it is our premise that software businesses applying software engineering will find these software reuse investment success factors useful within their software business management.

Many organizations in both the private and public sectors are proposing to invest, and have already invested, large sums of money, time and resources into software reuse with the hope of improving their competitive edge through greater productivity in the software development process and higher quality in the software products developed. Various technology organizations such as the Virginia-based Software Productivity Consortium (SPC), the U. S. Government-based Software Technology for Adaptable, Reliable Systems (STARS) program and U. S. Department of Defense-funded Software Engineering Institute (SEI) have proposed certain conceptual frameworks for reuse. While some organizations naively equate software reuse with a particular technology, such as object-oriented technology, in fact it is becoming quite clear that successful software reuse practice has much more to do with organizational management, infrastructure, and technical factors unrelated to object-oriented technology. In this paper we will report on our comprehensive *Study of Software Reuse Investment Success Factors*, and, from this study, proposed an effective 'model' for investment in software reuse (Sonnemann, 1995).

The Problem

Many software development organizations believe that investing in software reuse will improve their product and process productivity and quality, and are in the process of planning for or developing a software reuse capability. Unfortunately, there is still little data available on the state-of-the-art-practice of investing in software reuse. A 1991 study of Japanese Software Factories stated that in 1991 the Japanese software factories were the only organizations successfully applying software reuse (McCain, 1991). This 1991 study and a second 1992 study of U.S. software developers covering 29 organizations (Frakes, 1995) are, until now, the only major studies involving a large number of organizations. The majority of current information available on software reuse investment comes from the literature, which contains unproved theories or theory applied in a limited way to a few pilot projects or case studies.

Our research (to be reported in this paper) investigated the relationships between software reuse investment, productivity, and quality, as well as many of the theories proposed by the literature to provide greater software reuse capability (i.e., what are the success factors for software reuse).

Conclusions

Investment in software reuse is predictive of productivity and quality. However, a product-line management approach and a software architecture technology approach are higher predictors of productivity and quality than software reuse alone.

This study, like the previous 1992 study, found no relationship between software reuse capability and the library approach (i.e., the strategy of collecting a large set of components from previous projects and making them available to other projects; a.k.a., the junkyard approach).

The organizations sampled in this study with the highest software reuse capability (and investment) have the following features:

- product-line approach,
- architecture which standarizes interfaces and data formats,
- common software architecture across the product-line,
- design for manufacturing approach,
- domain engineering,

- software reuse process,
- management which understands reuse issues,
- software reuse advocate(s) in senior management,
- state-of-the-art reuse tools and methods,
- precedence of reusing high level software artifacts such as
- requirements and design versus just code reuse, and
- trace end-user requirements to the components (systems, subsystems,
- and/or software modules) which support them (Sonnemann, 1995).

Rationale

This research may help many organizations to change their approach to software reuse. This change will be at some cost, investment, and risk. Would it be reasonable for an organization to make a major investment in software reuse based on these research results? After all, the statistical analysis only shows that a relationship exists between the independent variables and software reuse capability. Also, what other observations support the conclusions that these practices are high predictors of software reuse capability and are worth the cost, investment, and risk required to implement them?

Research Method

Background

Software reuse is widely believed to be the most promising technology for significantly improving software quality and productivity (Frakes, 1992). It is believed that constructing systems from existing software components should shorten development time, lessen duplication across projects, and lower development costs. One can easily see the productivity gains from not writing code. (Tirso, 1993). In plain language, reuse is based on the principle of not reinventing the wheel. (Troy, 1994). Constructing systems from existing operationally proven software components can lead to increases in quality (Sommerville, 1996; Tirso, 1993).

Unfortunately, software reuse has proven difficult to achieve. Organizations attempting to implement a software reuse program face both technical and non-technical problems. Technical problems include interchangeability and classification. Non-technical problems include changing the organizational structure, processes, and culture, as well as the up-front investment to build a software reuse infrastructure.

The manufacturing and construction worlds have successfully implemented a product-line approach to reuse for many years. It is commonplace for these industries to assemble parts into products and use the same part in more than one product within a product-line family. So, what is the problem with doing this in software? The problem, for example, is that what are routine procedures in other engineering disciplines are research areas in software engineering, e.g. domain analysis, interchangeability of parts, and common architecture across product lines.

Domain Analysis. Looking for commonality and variability across products, i.e., domain analysis, is standard operating procedure in manufacturing. However, domain analysis is a research area in software engineering. The United States (U.S.) Advanced Research Projects Agency (ARPA) Domain Specific System Architecture (DSSA) project is working with universities, government laboratories, and industry to perfect this technology (Tracz, 1994; Armitage, 1993). Other than a few ongoing pilot projects, it will be a while before this technology becomes commonplace in software engineering.

Interchangeable Parts. Software engineering remains a term of aspiration. The vast majority of computer code is still handcrafted from raw programming languages by artisans using techniques they neither measure nor are able to repeat consistently. Before the industrial revolution, there was a nonspecialized approach to manufacturing goods that involved very little interchangeability and a maximum of craftsmanship. If we are ever going to defeat this software crisis, we are going to have to stop this hand-to-mouth, every-programmer-builds-everything-from-the-ground-up, pr-eindustrial approach (Gibbs, 1994).

In April 1994, the National Institute of Standards and Technology (NIST) announced that it was creating an Advanced Technology Program to help engender a market for component-based software. Financial incentives and marketing pressures will force companies to find cheaper ways to produce software. Even when the technology is ready, components will find few takers unless they can be made cost-effective. And the cost of software parts will depend less on the technology involved than on the kind of market that arises to produce and consume them (Gibbs, 1994).

Common Architecture Across Product-Lines. Defining a common architecture across product lines is a fundamental problem that is complementary to developing interchangeable parts. Structured modeling focuses on defining an interchangeable architecture with predictability. This interchangeable architecture defines the ground rules, i.e., interface requirements, which all the programmers must follow. This method forces the software to behave like hardware components and provides an engineering framework for system integration. Information architecture focuses on defining the "building codes" for system integration. This method is modeled after the processes used by the construction industry to assemble buildings from existing components. Building codes are proven design models based on years of experience. If the builder, i.e., software engineer, follows these rules, the structure will go together with minimal problems. The 1993 Air Force Scientific Advisory Board advocates the use of this building code, permit, and inspection process for system acquisitions. Domain modeling looks at the commonality and variability across systems. Knowing the amount of variability of the systems in the problem domain would help define the extent of the problem of their interoperability. Determining commonality, i.e., duplication, among systems is the first step towards identifying potential reuse components and architectures.

Reuse Failure Modes Model. Technical problems associated with reuse include, but are not limited to, finding, understanding, testing and integrating components and sub-architectures [Sommerville 96] Insight into the software reuse implementation problem can be had by considering the probabilistic aspects of the reuse failure modes model. The seven software reuse failure modes are: (1) No attempt to reuse; (2) Part not integratable; (3) Part not understood; (4) Part not valid; (5) Part does not exist; (6) Part not found; (7) Part not available. Each failure mode in the model can be assigned a probability. When this is done, an overall probability of reuse failure, or success, can be calculated. Although this is a simplifying assumption, the easiest way of calculating an overall probability is by assuming independence of the failure modes. The overall probability of reuse success then is given by: Prob(reuse success) = Sum of $(1 - f_i)$, where f_i is the probability of failure mode i. The probability of reuse failure is: Prob(reuse failure) = 1 - Prob(reuse success). This model emphasizes that even if a reuse program is quite good, and the probability of reuse failure at any step is low, the overall probability of successful reuse can still be relatively low. Assume, e.g., that each failure mode has a 0.10 probability and there are seven failure modes. The probability of successful reuse will then be only 0.48 (Frakes, 1994c).

These same failure modes could apply to doing a literature search in the library. For example: part not found; could be the article is available in the library, but the title does not match the keywords used by the library user. The following section will expand on the library metaphor.

Library Metaphor. One attractive metaphor for reuse is the library of software documents, with authors, publications, and librarians. The library metaphor focuses on the management of these documents. This introduces librarians, catalogs, classification schemes, and browsing to the reuse field and has inspired several researchers to investigate various retrieval schemes based on faceted classification, keywords, or free-text document retrieval. Other researchers are investigating the interoperability and interconnection of local and branch libraries, and the problems of interlibrary loan, copyright, etc. (Griss, 1993).

The library metaphor can be broadened into a trading infrastructure concept. The elements of a marketplace are derived from suppliers offering parts and customers requiring parts. Therefore, information about offerings and requirements is necessary. Let us continue the metaphor where 'parts' are software components. To store and advertise the parts to be traded, a repository for holding the parts as well as their descriptions is needed. The probability of a parts exchange also depends heavily on the trust in or quality of the parts. Because quality is a rather unclear word, we introduce the term certification level here, which means a well defined guaranteed completeness and defect rate level of the offered parts. Closely related to this is the issue of maintenance, for two reasons. First, the potential parts user wants to have a clear view of the dependencies that the overall products have on others. A product-lifetime guarantee for the included part is normally expected. Secondly, if a part is repetitively used in different contexts, the economical benefits are best when there is only one centrally maintained version of the part. As in any trading environment, some kind of accounting is required in order to record exchanges and associated costs and savings, and to measure the effectiveness of the trading infrastructure (Wasmund, 1993).

A library must be focused on the needs of the consumers or users. When someone thinks of reuse, the picture that comes to mind is their garage that has many shelves holding many "parts" that they have saved because they think they might be valuable some day. What is wrong with this metaphor? The junkyard approach to reuse comes from the traditional way of thinking about the problem. It reflects the ad hoc approach that might be used by an individual programmer. The whole point is to develop a repository of components that are actually usable. This is where many companies fail; they put parts in the initial library that are not relevant to the population of people using them. Organizations acquire components and make them available before they understand their domain and the needs of their software engineers. Or the organization incorrectly thinks that by simply getting a library they have a program. Fonash (1993) presents a concise description of why the Department of Defense (DoD) Reuse Initiative failed using the "library" approach, i.e., lack of a consumer focus.

Our discussion of the library and manufacturing metaphors is a good background for the next topic, how to evaluate the reuse capabilities of an organization using the Reuse Capability Model (RCM). Having a library will get an organization a "level 2" in the RCM rating, which is just above having an ad hoc approach to software reuse, a "level 1" in the RCM rating. An organization moves up the RCM rating scale through incorporating reuse into their software development processes, including maintenance, and continual process and product improvement to ensure that reusable software components meet user needs, i.e., strong customer focus (SPC, 1993b).

Reuse Capability Model. Advanced Research Projects Agency (ARPA) has funded a number of software reuse projects to further the practice, such as the *Reuse Adoption Guidebook* (Davis, 1994; SPC,

1993). This guide was developed by the SPC under contract to the Virginia Center of Excellence for Software Reuse and Technology Transfer. This document also conatins a Domain Assessment Model and a Reuse Capability Model (RCM), as well as questionnaires to support each. The RCM is most important to our research because it provides a method for determining the software reuse capability of an organization (SPC, 1993).

The RCM has five levels each building upon the previous level. This hierarchical structures is very similar to the SEI Capability Maturity Model (CMM). The RCM levels are from lowest (level 1) to highest (level 5):

Level 1- Ad hoc - no reuse process.
Level 2- Opportunistic - libraries supporting projects.
Level 3 - Integrated - reuse and development process integrated.
Level 4 - Leveraged - distinct product-line life cycle with specialized
         processes
Level 5 - Anticipating - applications optimize reuse.

Hence, the RCM provides a way of categorizing and determining an organization's software reuse level. Given this knowledge, one has a "yardstick" with which to evaluate other relationships, such asthe 12 questions in the next section.

Research Questions - A Proposed Model of Software Reuse Success Factors. Our literature search uncovered a number of possible software reuse success factors, as well as a reuse relationship with productivity and quality. This section addresses productivity and quality together, and each of the possible software reuse success factors individually. The questions derived from our literature search and related theoretical work presents us with a model comprising a theory of software reuse success factors.

After reviewing literature (including Bell, 1993; Boehm, 1987, 1992; Frakes, 1992; 1993; 1994a; 1994b; 1995; Griss, 1993; Joos, 1994; Lim, 1994; O'Connor, 1994; Parnas, 1976; Tirso, 1993; Troy,1994) the following questions were introduced:

Productivity and Quality
Question 1. Is software reuse level predictive of productivity?
Question 2, Is software reuse level predictive of quality?

After reviewing literature (including Fafchamps, 1994, 1993, 1994a, 1994c, 1995, Griss,1993, Joos, 1994, McCain, 1991; O'Connor, 1994; Tirso, 1993; Tracz, 1986, 1989), the following questions were introduced:

Management Commitment
Question 3. Is management commitment predictive of software reuse level?

After reviewing literature, (including Card, 1994; Frakes, 1993, 1994a; Griss, 1993; Joos, 1994; McCain, 19 91; O'Connor, 1994; Staringer, 1994; Tirso, 1993; Tracz, 1986, 1989; Troy, 1994] the following questions were introduced:

Investment Strategy
Question 4. Is investment strategy predictive of software reuse level?

After reviewing literature, (including Card, 1994; Fafchamps, 1994; Frakes, 1993, 1993b, 1995; Griss, 1993; Joos, 1994, O'Connor, 1994; Tirso, 1993; Troy, 1994) the following questions were introduced:

Business Strategy
Question 5. Is business strategy predictive of software reuse level?

After reviewing literature, (including Card, 1994; Fafchamps, 1994; Frakes, 1993; 1993c; 1995; Griss, 1993; Joos, 1994; McCain 1991; O'Connor, 1994; Tracz, 1986, 1989; Tirso, 1993; Troy, 1994; Wasmund, 1993) the following questions were introduced:

Technology Transfer
Question 6. Is technology transfer predictive of software reuse level?

After reviewing literature, (including Boeing 1994; Fafchamps, 1994; Frakes, 1993; Griss, 1993; Loral, 1994; O'Connor, 1994; SPC 1993; Troy, 1994; Unisys 1994; Wasmund, 1993; Withey, 1993) the following questions were introduced:

Organizational Structure
Question 7. Is organizational structure predictive of software reuse level?

After reviewing literature, (including Bell, 1993; Card, 1994; Frakes, 1994b, 1995; Griss, 1993; Tirso, 1993; Troy, 1994; Wasmund 1993) the following questions were introduced:

Process Maturity
Question 8. Is process maturity predictive of software reuse level?

After reviewing literature (including Fafchamps, 1994; Frakes,

1993a, 1994a; Griss, 1993; Joos, 1994; McCain, 1991; O'Connor, 1994; Parnas, 1976; Staringer, 1994; Tracz, 1986, 1989; Wasmund, 1993) the following questions were introduced:

Product-Line Approach
Question 9. Is product-line approach predictive of software reuse level?

After reviewing literature (including Abowd, 1993; Armitage, 1993; Boettcher, 1994; Cohen, 1994; Frakes, 1994a; Ferrentino, 1994; Gacek, 1994; Griss, 1993; Kogut, 1994; Leary, 1994a, 1994b; O'Connor, 1994; Staringer, 1994; Troy, 1994) the following questions were introduced:

System Architecture
Question 10. Is system architecture predictive of software reuse level?

After reviewing literature, (including Bell, 1993; Frakes, 1992, 1994b; Griss, 1993; O'Connor, 1994; Staringer, 1994; Tirso, 1993; Troy, 1994; Wasmund, 1993) the following questions were introduced:

Availability of Components
Question 11. Is availability of components predictive of software reuse level?

After reviewing literature, (including Basili, 1991; Bell, 1993; Bollinger, 1991; Cards, 1994; Frakes, 1992, 1994b; Griss, 1993; McCain, 1991; O'Connor, 1994; Sommerville, 1996; Tirso, 1993; Tracz, 1986, 1989, Troy, 1994; Wasmund, 1993) the following questions were introduced:

Quality of Components
Question 12. Is quality of components predictive of software reuse level?

Problem and Research Hypothesis

This research hypothesizes (Sonnemann, 1995) that there is a set of success factors which are common across organizations and have some predictability relationships to software reuse. Hence, our research hypotheses are that (1) software reuse level is predictive of productivity and quality; and (2) management commitment, investment strategy, business strategy, technology transfer, organizational structure, process maturity, product-line approach, system architecture, availability of components, and quality of components are predictive of software reuse level. The questions associated with each of the hypotheses were previously presented.

Research Approach

In this section, we summarize the research approach taken by means of six steps.

Step 1. Define a set of software reuse success factors. This was done by conducting a literature search to utilize the best theory recorded in the literature. This step includes our first version of a model comprising success factors for software reuse. This is derived from the previous section.

Step 2. Down-size the number of success factors to those with the highest probability of impacting software reuse. This was done by comparing and contrasting software reuse lessons learned from the literature search, as well as utilizing the results of the previous software reuse empirical studies (Frakes, 1994c; Griss, 1993). The downsizing was required to limit the number of questions in the questionnaire (questionnaire-survey instrument), which in turn increases the chances that someone will fill out the questionnaire. This step includes the refining of the model comprising success factors for software reuse.

Step 3. Developing a questionnaire to survey industry and government and to gather empirical data to answer the research questions and to validate our hypotheses. The questionnaire evaluated the organization's environment (stratification of the population), qualifications to answer a given question (reliability of the data - is the data based on a domain analysis or best guess?), reuse capability (level on the SPC's Reuse Capability Model), and the presence or absence of success factors. The questionnaire-survey instrument was further improved by means of pre-survey validation procedure.

Step 4. Print and distribute the questionnaire. Because of the immaturity of the practice of software reuse and lack of a completely defined statistical population to sample, highly randomized sampling was determined not to be feasible. Hence, nearly four thousand surveys were distributed. The cost of preparing, printing and distributing the instrument was supported by U.S. Department of Defense government funding.

Step 5. Collect and analyze the data. The statistical tool JMP from SAS (SAS Institute, Inc.) was used to analyze the data. After determining the normality of the data, the correct method for determining if a given independent variable is predictive of the dependent variable was used. The dependent variables were software reuse level, productivity, and quality. The independent variables were management commitment, investment strategy, business strategy, technology transfer, organizational structure, process maturity, product-line approach, system architecture, availability of components, and quality of components.

Step 6. Report the results. A summary of results relevant to the paper is presented in the next section. This step includes the empirical validation of the model comprising success factors for software reuse.

Results

This section describes the results of the 1995 software reuse survey and answers the research questions listed in the previous section. Of the 3,750 questionnaires sent out, results from 109 responses are presented.

Results by Question

This section summarizes the state-of-the-practice for software reuse.

Demographics. Ninety-nine projects were reported, covering 83 organizations from five countries. The projects covered different domains from embedded to management information systems. The primary end users of the products developed by the projects were well distributed among government, commercial, internal, research and development, and other with government being slightly larger. Respondent's roles in their organization (senior management, application engineering, domain engineering or reuse repository, consultant to include academia and other) varied greatly with consultants being the smallest group with 11 and application engineering being the largest with 41. Fifty-six percent of the projects were supported by domain engineering, and of these 54 percent believed the domain engineering support was effective and efficient. Sixty-eight percent of the projects were supported by software reuse repository, and of these projects, 52 percent believed the repository support was effective and efficient, i.e., Reuse Capability Model (RCM) level 2. Twenty percent of the projects used application engineering to develop 100 percent of their reusable software components. Another 20 percent of the projects used domain engineering to develop greater then 70 percent of their reusable components. Fifty percent of the organizations had a precedence of developing similar products in the past. Forty percent of the projects had a stable environment.

Technology Transfer. Forty-four percent of the projects believed their organizations had effective to extremely effective software reuse programs. The responses to the barriers to software reuse averaged out to be: 70 percent non-technical and 30 percent technical. Seventy-one percent of the respondents believe developing an effective and efficient software reuse infrastructure requires significant investment and substantial time to mature. Twenty percent of the projects have seen senior management demonstrate their support for software reuse by allocating funds and manpower over a number of years. Forty-two percent of the respondents reported that there is a corporate sponsor(s) in senior management who advocates and supports developong a software reuse capability. Sixty-seven percent of the respondents reported that there are respected technical leaders in the organization advocating software reuse. Twenty-three percent of the respondents reported that pilot projects were used effectively to refine software reuse "best practices" prior to adopting them for routine use. Fifteen percent of the respondents reported that the organization has an effective software reuse working group to advocate software reuse, as well as provide guidance and assistance throughout the organization. Seventeen percent of the respondents reported that the organization has an effective software reuse education and training program. Twenty-six percent of the respondents reported that education for senior management is the most important aspect of their software reuse education and training program. Twenty-one percent of the respondents reported that manager(s) understand software reuse issues. Nine percent of the respondents reported that projects document their software reuse lessons learned, which in turn are used to improve the organization's software reuse process.

Software Reuse Strategy. Forty-five percent of the respondents reported that their organization tends to specialize, building variations of products for different customers. Thirty-seven percent of the respondents reported that applications the organization develops are well understood by project team members. Twenty percent of the respondents reported that their organization is taking a library approach to software reuse. Thirty-seven percent of the respondents reported that their organization is taking a preferred parts approach to software reuse. Twenty-one percent of the respondents reported that their organization is taking a design for manufacturability approach to software reuse. Of those with a software reuse repository, 24 percent do customer surveys to determine what reusable components should be placed in the repository. Of those with a software reuse repository, 18 percent do market analysis of their products and their competitor's products to determine what reusable software components should be placed in their repository. Of those with a software reuse repository, 20 percent have established a candidates' library to eliminate duplication among their projects. Nine percent of the respondents reported that they have an effective requirements analysis tool which links their most common end-user requirements with the reusable software component(s) which satisfy them. 42 percent of the respondents reported that their software development process supports a product line. The respondents reported that their organization's software reuse strategy plans to reuse the following artifacts: 62 percent requirements, 61 percent specifications, 78 percent design, 90 percent code, 69 percent documentation, 69 percent test cases, 58 percent data. 18 percent of the respondents reported that the software reuse technology used by the organization is leading edge. Eighty-five percent of the respondents reported that the majority of their software reuse technology (techniques, practices, methods, tools, etc.) is being (was) developed internal to the organization. Twenty-nine percent of the respondents reported that their organization assigns its best software engineers to producing reusable software components. The responses to the organization's strategy for developing reusable software components averaged out to be: 50 percent reverse engineering and 50 percent forward engineering. Thirty percent of the respondents reported that they have a good set of highly effective and available horizontal (across domains) reuse components. Thirty-five percent of the respondents reported that they have a good set of highly effective and available vertical (domain specific) reuse components. Twenty-one percent of the respondents reported that they have done a thorough domain analysis of their products. Forty-one percent of the respondents reported that they have a good understanding of the commonality and variablity of their products. The responses to the commonality and variability across the organization's products (software reuse potential) averaged out to be: 50 percent commonality and 50 percent variability. Sixty percent of the respondents reported that they have a common architecture across their product line. Forty-two percent of the respondents reported that their architecture has proved useful in standardizing interfaces and data formats. Thirty-two percent of the respondents reported that their architecture has greatly simplified re-hosting their applications to different platforms. Eighteen percent of the respondents reported that their architecture has lessened the need to make reusable software components highly generic or flexible because the environment in which they will be used is well-defined and fixed.

Software Reuse Capability. The percentage of reusable software components used in the identified project averaged out to be: 23 percent reused developed components from other projects, 13 percent reused commercial off-the-shelf components, 20 percent developed components for reuse by other projects, 44 percent developed components unique to the identified projects. The software artifacts reused from other projects by the identified project were: 41 percent requirements, 42 percent specifications, 55 percent design, 81 percent code, 51 percent documents, 37 percent test cases, 30 percent data. The respondents reported their highest priority motives for implementing software reuse were: 46 percent reduce development and maintenance costs, 23 percent faster time to market, 12 percent write less new code, 6 percent improved reliability, 5 percent reduce redundancy across projects. The respondents reported that their top three motives for implementing software reuse were: 27 percent reduce development and maintenance costs, 17 percent faster time to market, 14 percent improved reliability, 12 percent write less new code, 10 percent reduce redundancy across projects, 7 percent do less maintenance, 4 percent better understanding of customer requirements, 3 percent better bid estimates, 2 percent successfully enter new markets, 2 percent increase market share, 2 percent better workload estimates. 29 percent of the respondents reported that they observed significant improvement in the previously mentioned areas. 19 percent of the respondents reported that they have a critical mass of reusable software components which enables them to develop effective proto-types with real functionality in a relatively short time. Fourteen percent of the respondents reported that they have a critical mass of reusable components to draw upon which gives them leverage in negotiations with customers (driving them to more generic require-ments in trade for shorter development time). Forty-one percent of the respondents reported that they are able to assemble new products much faster than they could two years ago. Forty-three percent of the respondents reported that their reusable software components are considered highly valuable by project team members. Twenty percent of the respondents reported that management has created new business opportunities that take advantage of the organization's software reuse capability and reusable assets, i.e., RCM level 5. Twenty-one percent of the respondents reported that their decisions to bid on new projects or enter new markets are based heavily on their software reuse capabilities. Twenty-six percent of the respondents reported that they have fewer software components to maintain due to the effectiveness of their software reuse program. Twenty-five percent of the respondents reported that their reusable software components have proven through operational use to be highly reliable. Seventeen percent of the respondents reported that time spent on maintenance (correcting defects) has decreased.

Software Reuse Capability

Given the importance of measuring software reuse capability for this research, it was measured six different ways in the questionnaire using:

1. The Reuse Capability Model (RCM)
    Level 1, Ad Hoc - no process (default level),
    Level 2, Opportunistic - libraries supporting projects,
    Level 3, Integrated - reuse and development integrated,
    Level 4, Leveraged - reuse process measured,
    Level 5, Anticipating - creates new business.
2. The respondents rated their organization's software reuse program
    Level 1, N/A, we do not have a formal software reuse program,
    Level 2, Minimally effective - benefits are not clear,

Level 3, Effective - has observable benefits,

Level 4, Highly effective - benefits are predictable,

Level 5, Extremely effective - provides a competitive edge to gain
   market share.

3. The software artifacts reused from other projects by the identified
   project

   Level 1, Reuses code only or no code reuse,

   Level 2, Reuses code and something else,

   Level 3, Reuses design, code, and something else,

   Level 4, Reuses requirements, design, and code,

   Level 5, Reuses all seven artifact types.

4. Their horizontal and vertical reuse capability

   Level 1, Default level,

   Level 2, Mildly Agree on both questions or a single Strongly Agree
      or a single Agree,

   Level 3, Mildly Agree on one question and a Strongly Agree or Agree
      on the other question,

   Level 4, Agree on both questions or one Agree and one Strongly
      Agree,

   Level 5, Strongly Agree on both questions.

5. The percentage of reusable software components (reused developed
components from other projects and reused commercial off-the-shelf
components) used in the identified project

   Level 1, 0-20,

   Level 2, 21-40,

   Level 3, 41-60,

   Level 4, 61-80,

   Level 5, Greater than 80.

6. Measurement 5 plus developed components for reuse by other
projects

   Level 1, 0-40,

   Level 2, 11-69,

   Level 3, 70-84,

   Level 4, 85-94,

   Level 5, Greater than 95.

The RCM, measurement 1, proved to be unstable and continually
scored the lowest correlations with the other measurements. The RCM
is a hierarchical model with each level building on the previous level.
The RCM produced substantially different results depending on
whether the level questions were answered bottom up or top down. The
six measurements for software reuse capability did not correlate very
well. Measurements 5 and 6 were the exception. They correlated well
with each other because measurement 5 is a subset of measurement
6.

A hybrid measurement was developed from measurement 5

(which favored reverse engineering) and measurement 6 (which favored forward engineering) to solve the poor correlation problem. Given the small sample size, the new reuse capability measurement used three levels (high(H), medium(M), and low(L)). A second hybrid measurement was also developed which further identified the extremes (very high(VH), high(H), medium(M), low(L), and very low(VL)). Very low was assigned to projects scoring level 1 on both the percentage measurements 5 and 6 and is a subset of the low in the H-M-L measurement. Very high was assigned to projects scoring level 5 on both percentage measurements 5 and 6 and is a subset of high in the H-M-L measurement. Bothe the H-M-L and the VH-H-M-L-VL measurements correlations with the other reuse capability measurements were significant.

The VH-H-M-L-VL and the H-M-L measurements (software reuse capability or level) were used to evaluate the predictability of the various independent variables. The strength of the relationships between software reuse capability and the independent variables were assigned based on the highest F Ratio resulting from the H-M-L and the VH-H-M-L-VL analysis using the following scale:

Verbal Relation   **Highest F Value at 95 Percent Confidence**
No Relationship   - less than 5 or the Prob > F is high,
Weak Relationship - 5 to less than 7.5,
Relationship   - 7.5 to less than 10.0,
Strong Relationship - 10.0 or greater.

In the reports on the research questions reported below in section 3.3, with each verbal relation there is also reported the numerical valued relation in the triple form (Questions, Highest F Value, Prob > F Value). We use the verbal relation reporting because it is easier to understand in that form. The Questions are those on the survey questionnaire experimental instrument. For the most part, we have only reported data in those cases where there is a relationship. The key things we looked for in our Oneway Anova are the means for each group, a strong F ratio (strength of the relationship) and low Std Error for each of the means with no Std Error twice the size as another. For example, under *Productivity_*below we have *Research Question 1.* Is software reuse level predictive of productivity?

Based on the reuse capability data there is 'a *strong relationship* between reuse capability and having the ability to create new business opportunities. (67, 13.3066, 0.0000)' because in the Analysis of Variance of RCM Level 5 Q67 By RC H-M-L F Ratio is 13.3066 (Analysis of Variance of RCM Level 5 Q67 By RC VH-H-M-L-VL F Ratio is 7.5371), Prob > F is 0.0000; and in the Means for Oneway Anova, Means for Levels (1, 2, 3) are (2.97222, 4.19231, 4.87500), and Std Errors are

(0.25708, 0.30250, 0.27267).

Research Questions

In this section research questions stated in the section "*Research Questions: A Proposed Model of Software Reuse Success Factors*," will be answered.

Productivity
Research Question 1. Is software reuse level predictive of productivity?
Based on the reuse capability data there is:
- a *relationship* between reuse capability and the organization achieving its productivity goals. (62, 9.0941, 0.0000)
- a *relationship* between reuse capability and having the ability to assemble new products much faster than two years ago. (65, 9.7023, 0.0000)
- a *strong relationship* between reuse capability and having the ability to create new business opportunities. (67, 13.3066, 0.0000)
- a *weak relationship* between reuse capability and an organization's decision to bid on new projects or enter new markets. (68, 6.5313, 0.0022)
- a *relationship* between reuse capability and having fewer software components to maintain due to the effectiveness of their software reuse program. (69, 7.8528, 0.0000)

Quality
Research Question 2. Is software reuse level predictive or quality?
Based on the reuse capability data there is:
- a *relationship* between reuse capability and reusable software components have proven through operational use to be highly reliable. (70, 7.76179, 0.0000)
- *no relationship* between reuse capability and time spent on maintenance (correcting defects) has decreased. (71, 3.9801, 0.0051)

Management Commitment
Research Question 3. Is management commitment predictive of software reuse level?
Based on the reuse capability data there is:
- a *relationship* between reuse capability and senior management has demonstrated their support for software reuse by allocating funds and manpower over a number of years. (13, 9.3650, 0.0002)

Investment Strategy
Research Question 4. Is investment strategy predictive of software reuse level?

Based on the reuse capability data there is:
- *no relationship* between reuse capability and developing an effective and efficient software reuse infrastructure requires significant investment and substantial time to mature. (12, 0.7398, 0.5673)

Business Strategy

Research Question 5. Is business strategy predictive of software reuse level?

Based on the reuse capability data there is:
- *no relationship* between reuse capability and an organization taking a library approach to software reuse. (24, 2.7021, 0.0355)
- a *weak relationship* between reuse capability and an organization taking a preferred parts approach to software reuse. (25, 5.5387, 0.0054)
- a *strong relationship* between reuse capability and an organization taking a design for manufacturability approach to software reuse. (26, 11.1518, 0.0000)
- a *relationship* between reuse capability and doing customer surveys to determine what reusable software components should be placed in the software reuse repository. (27, 8.3863, 0.0005)
- *no relationship* between reuse capability and doing market analysis to determine what reusable software components should be placed in the software reuse repository.
- *no relationship* between reuse capability and establishing a candidates library to eliminate duplication among projects.
- *no relationship* between reuse capability and an organizational strategy to develop reusable software components using reverse engineering (or forward engineering).
- *no relationship* between reuse capability and who in the organization develops the reusable software components (application engineering or domain engineering).
- a *weak relationship* between reuse capability and an organization assigning its best software engineers to develop reusable software components. (35, 6.0105, 0.0035)

Technology Transfer

Research Question 6. Is technology transfer predictive of software reuse level?

Based on the reuse capability data there is:
- a *strong relationship* between reuse capability and having a corporate sponsor(s) in senior management who advocates and supports developing a software reuse capability. (14, 15.7704, 0.0000)
- a *weak relationship* between reuse capability and having respected champions in the organization advocating software reuse. (15, 7.0549, 0.0014)
- a *weak relationship* between reuse capability and using pilot projects

to refine software reuse "best practices" prior to adopting them for routine use. (16, 5.7776, 0.0044)

- a *relationship* between reuse capability and having an effective software reuse working group to advocate software reuse. (9.4718, 0.0002)
- *no relationship* between reuse capability and having an effective software reuse education and training program.
- *no relationship* between reuse capability and education for senior management being the most important aspect of our software reuse education and training program.
- a *strong relationship* between reuse capability and having managers who understand software reuse issues. (20, 10.2890, 0.0001)
- a *weak relationship* between reuse capability and projects documenting their software reuse lessons learned.

Organizational Structure

Research Question 7. Is organizational structure predictive of software reuse level?

Based on the reuse capability data there is:

- a *strong relationship* between reuse capability and having a domain engineering section. Crosstabs analysis used since answers were Boolean.
- *no relationship* between reuse capability and the effectiveness of the domain engineering section.

Product-Line Approach

Research Question 9. Is product-line approach predictive of software reuse level?

Based on the reuse capability data there is:

- a *strong relationship* between reuse capability and having a software development process built around a core set of reusable software components as the foundation for their products. (31, 15.5181, 0.0000)

System Architecture

Research Question 10. Is system architecture predictive of software reuse level?

Based on the reuse capability data there is:

- a *strong relationship* between reuse capability and having a common software architecture across the product-line. Crosstabs analysis were used.
- a *strong relationship* between reuse capability and having a software architecture which has proved useful in standardizing interfaces and data formats. (43, 12.2454, 0.0000)
- a *relationship* between reuse capability and having a software architecture which has greatly simplified re-hosting applications to

different platforms. (44,8.6967, 0.0003)

- *no relationship* between reuse capability and having a software architecture which has lessened the need to make reusable software components highly generic.

Availability of Components

Research Question 11. Is availability of components predictive of software reuse level?

Based on the reuse capability data there is:

- a *relationship* between reuse capability and having a critical mass of reusable software components which enables an organization to develop effective prototypes with real functionality in a relatively short time. (63, 8.3804, 0.0005)
- a *strong relationship* between reuse capability and having a critical mass of reusable components to draws upon which gives an organization leverage in negotiations with customers (driving them to more generic requirements in trade for shorter development time). (64, 13.7882, 0.0000)
- a *strong relationship* between reuse capability and having a horizontal reuse capability. (37, 10.0625, 0.0001)
- a *strong relationship* between reuse capability and having a vertical reuse capability. (38, 12.3504, 0.0000)

Quality of Components

Research Question 12. Is quality of components predictive of software reuse level?

Based on the reuse capability data there is:

- a *relationship* between reuse capability and reusable software components being considered highly valuable by project team members. (66, 9.5374, 0.0000)
- *no relationship* between reuse capability and reusable software components being certified to some quality levels.

Results of our research also included relationships between reuse capability and the software engineering process and the maturity of the software engineering process. However, we have chosen to report on this work separately. Interested readers may refer to Sonnemann (1995).

Further Multivariate Statistical Analysis

Because of the low response rate in our sampling, it was decided to use statistical techniques (methods) that do not require the assumption of large samples. Hence, we used F test values to justify the assumption of the equality of variances, which isneeded in the t test where the t test is applied to test the differences between the means (Hoel, 1954) of the variables in our study.

Our analysis demonstrated that many success factors behave significantly differently. In some cases, software reuse capability steadily increases with increased levels of a success factor, while other success factors only make a difference going from low to medium to high software reuse capability groups. This is why the statistical analysis of Questions versus Reuse Capability were run. Many of the relationships are dynamic and will change as an organization's software reuse capabilities increase.

If someone were to develop a software reuse model and migration guidebook as follow-on to this study, they would have to have a good understanding of the relationships among the independent variables. Using the data from this study one could do multivariate analysis to better understand the interactions (multiplier effects, reverse correlations, etc.). For a proof of concept, using an analysis from our study, let us consider the following independent variables:

1. Product-line approach,
2. Architecture standardizes interfaces and data formats,
3. Design for manufacturability approach,
4. Preferred parts approach,
5. The organization assigns its best software engineers to developing reusable components,
6. The organization has a precedence of developing similar products in the past,
7. There are respected technical leaders in the organization advocating software reuse,
8. The organization has an effective requirements analysis tool which links their most common end-user requirements with the software components which satisfy them.

The statistical analysis of Questions versus Reuse Capability were was used to select variables including both strong predictors and non-predictors of software reuse capabilty.

The following table summarizes the results of the multivariate analysis of the variables selected. F Ratios have been rounded up to the next whole number. In all cases, Prob > F is not significant and equal to or close to 0.0000.

Table summarizing the results of the multivariate analysis F Ratios

	PL	A	M	PP	BD	P	T	R
Product-Line (PL)	**16**	**21**	22	18	13	10	16	14
Architecture (A)	**21**	**13**	18	13	13	8	15	12
Manufacturing (M)	22	18	12	13	14	7	17	13
Preferred Parts (PP)	18	13	13	6	10	5	9	8
Best Develop (BD)	13	13	14	10	7	6	9	8
Precedence (P)	10	8	7	5	6	1	6	5
Technologist (T)	16	15	17	9	9	6	8	11
Requirements (R)	14	12	13	8	8	5	11	6

The F Ratio for PL versus software reuse capability is 16. The F Ratio for A versus software reuse capability is 13. The F Ratio of PL and A combined versus software reuse capability is 21, and so forth.

Management Strategies for Information Technology Investment - Conclusions and Contributions

This section contains our interpretations of the research results presented in the previous section.

State-of-the-Practice

The low response rate to the survey and the answers to the questionnaire indicate that software reuse practices are not institutionalized in our software development and maintenance organizations. However, some companies within narrow, well-defined domains have had great success (increased market share) due to their software reuse capabilities.

It was surprising that the literature search, authors provided almost no responses. The authors were contacted to find out why. In general they said that they did not respond because the questionnaire was to measure software reuse in practice (requiring knowledge of an individual software development or maintenance project). They pointed out that they were theorists and not practitioners. We were surprised to learn that the majority of the articles referenced in the study were based on theory without any practical application.

Top Predictors of Software Reuse Capability

Based on the results of this research, the top individual predictors of software reuse capability are:

1. commonality across products,
2. software reuse process,
3. domain engineering,
4. design for manufacturability approach,
5. product-line approach,
6. software architecture - standardizes interfaces and data formats.
7. common software architecture across the product-line,
8. leading edge reuse technology,
9. management understands software reuse issues,
10. strong influential individual(s) in senior management who advocate(s) and support(s) developing a software reuse capability,
11. kind of software artifacts (requirements, design, code, documentation, test cases, data) reused.

Research Results Matched Predicted Results

The listed software reuse predictors are believed because they are consistent with predicted results in other areas. Prior to beginning the experiment (questionnaire and survey), relationships were identified that could be expected to be true based on the literature theory and on common sense. From this, a model based on a set of possible reuse success factors was proposed. These relationships occurred as predicted and so the model was validated. The following examples show some of the strong relationships to software reuse capability that were expected, and show that the research results were validated to be true.

As expected, a strong relationship was found between software reuse capability and:

1. percentage of reused components in their project,
2. respondent's intuition about their software reuse capability,
3. availability of reusable components to build or assemble systems,
4. reuse potential (amount of commonality across their products),
5. simplest way to achieve reuse (assign project team members to similar projects, so they reuse their own code).

Because of the low response rate in our sampling, it was decided to use statistical techniques (methods) that do not require the assumption of large samples. Hence, we used F test values to justify the assumption of the equality of variances, which is needed in the t test where the t test is applied to test the differences between the means ([Hoel, 1954) of the variables in our study.

Measurement of software reuse capability produced strong F Ratios (> 10) when compared to:

1. percent of components reused from previous projects and percent of commercial off-the-shelf components reused in the project,
2. percent of components reused from previous projects, percent of commercial off-the-shelf components reused in the project, plus percent of developed components for reuse by other projects,
3. respondents self-assessment of their reuse program,
4. respondents self-assessment of the amount of reusable components they have,
5. respondents self-assessment of their horizontal reuse capability,
6. respondents self-assessment of their vertical reuse capability,
7. respondents self-assessment of their understanding of the amount of commonality and variability across their products,
8. respondents self-assessment of the amount of commonality across their products,
9. respondents self-assessment of whether project team members are assigned to similar projects.

Observations of real-world practices, personal experience, interviews with industry experts, and textbook concepts on operations research, systems engineering, and manufacturing, all indicate that the practices associated with top predictors of software reuse capability match the successful practices used in hardware manufacturing. It is a well substantiated belief, based upon years of data, in this industry, that product lines, architecture, design for manufacturability, and domain engineering increase productivity and quality. Moreover, similar observations indicate that the practices associated with top predictors of software reuse capability match sound business practices. Most organizations do studies and analyses to determine if a given practice is cost effective to implement. The greater the potential to reuse components (the greater the savings or profits), the more likely an organization will implement and invest in reuse practices.

In this chapter we have reported on our comprehensive Study of Software Reuse Investment Success Factors [Sonnemann 95], and, from this study, proposed an effective 'model' for investment in software reuse.This research established metrics for measuring software reuse capability, and in doing so developed a model which normalized the influence of an organization's reuse strategy (reverse or forward engineering), validating this model using real world data. Hence, the research has given managers of software engineering projects a strategy for investing in reusable software.

A major goal of software engineering product development is to increase productivity and quality. Our research has shown that there is a strong relationship between software reuse success and productivity. So how does one achieve software reuse success? Our research has shown that there is a strong relationship between the independent variables business strategy (e.g., design for manufacturability approach), technology transfer (e.g., corporate sonsorship advocating and supporting development of a software reuse capability), organization structure (e.g. having a domain engineering section), product-line approach (e.g., a software development process built around a core set of reusable software components as the foundation for product development), system architecture (e.g., a common software architecture across the product-line, to standardize interfaces and data formats) and availability of components (e.g., reusable components to leverage with customers, driving them to more generic requirements in trade for shorter development time), and the dependent variable software reuse success. Therefore, large scale software business investment in these six or more factors, which we have measured, will payoff in improved productivity.

Chapter 7

Information Technology Investment Payoff: The Relationship Between Performance, Information Strategy, and the Competitive Environment

Susan A.R. Garrod
Purdue University

A fundamental premise of strategic management is that a firm's performance is a function of its strategy and its environment. The environment is an important moderator of the value of the firm's strategic resources, and it is the source of information demands placed on the firm. In order to assess the moderating effect that the competitive environment has on the information resources of the firm, a contingency framework is developed based on the resource-based view of the firm. The information strategy specified by the framework is based on the organization's capabilities to process and exploit information within varying contexts of environmental uncertainty and complexity. An appropriate fit between the firm's information strategy and the environment is desired in order to enhance its performance and potentially create a competitive advantage based on the deployment of those information resources. This framework represents a first step in integrating the works of strategy, organizational theory, and information systems to study the value of information technology. It is intended to be used to guide investments to support specific organizational capabilities in order to realize an information strategy that is appropriate within a given competitive environment.

The competitive environment creates information demands which affect a firm's ability to carry out its business strategy (Bourgeois, 1985; Daft, 1986; Daft, and Lengel, 1986; Galbraith, 1977; Miller, 1986, 1987, 1988; Mintzberg, 1979; Thompson, 1967; Wernerfelt and Karnani, 1987). At the same time, information technology is potentially available worldwide for firms to use to meet the information demands of the environment (Bell, 1979; Bradley, 1993; Egelhoff, 1991; Hepworth, 1990; Huber, 1990; Jonscher, 1994; Malone and Rockart, 1993; McFarlan, 1984; Porter and Millar, 1985; Rockart and Short, 1991; Scott Morton, 1991).[1] Although this technology surrounds us, researchers and managers alike have had difficulty defining its specific value in supporting a firm's competitive advantage (i.e., see research summaries in Wilson, 1993; Markus and Soh, 1993; Mahmood and Mann, 1993).

Past research neglects consideration of the competitive environment that drives the need for information, and it is fragmented between the fields of information systems, organizational theory, and strategy. Several early and high-profile case studies described how particular firms achieved benefits from information technology (Cash and Konsynski, 1985; Clemons and McFarlan, 1986; Clemons and Row, 1988; McFarlan, 1984; Neo, 1988; Porter and Millar, 1985), but the claims have been difficult to support empirically and the individual case studies are not generalizable to a wide range of firms (Bailey and Chakrabarti, 1988; DeLone and McLean, 1992; Markus and Soh, 1993; Wilson, 1993; National Research Council, 1994). The short-lived nature of the benefits to some firms has led to questions concerning the sustainability of the advantages derived from the technology (Earl, 1988; Sheppard, 1991; Sethi and King, 1994). Sheppard (1991) observed that the inability to foresee which information technology applications will create a competitive advantage, and which will not, is a major organizational problem.

Prior organizational theory research examines the firm's information processing mechanisms for dealing with uncertainty and complexity (Daft and Lengel, 1986; Galbraith, 1973, 1977, 1994; Lawrence and Lorsch, 1967; Nadler and Tushman, 1978), but it ignores the rich capabilities of modern information technology. Information systems research focuses on the capabilities of the technology and suggests that firms should align their business strategy and organizational structure with their investments in information technology (i.e., Earl, 1988; Egelhoff, 1991; Henderson and Venkatraman, 1994; Lee and Leifer, 1992; MacDonald, 1991; Mahmood and Mann, 1993; Orlikowski and Robey, 1991; Venkatraman, 1991). Unfortunately, the theories developed within this body of research have not taken into consideration those aspects of the competitive environment that drive the firm's need for information.

The framework presented in this chapter depicts a contingency relationship between a firm's information strategy and its *competitive environment* by combining prior theories from strategy, organizational theory, and information systems. The resource-based view of the firm is used to organize these diverse bodies of research, and hence brings to center stage the value of the firm's information resources and capabilities within specific environmental contexts. The framework suggests that the firm's performance and competitive advantage can be influenced by its ability to align its organizational capabilities with those factors in its competitive environment that create the need for information.

The remainder of this chapter is organized into three parts. It begins with a development of the major theoretical constructs. The framework is then used to assess the value of organizational capabilities to process and exploit information in the context of the competitive environment. Finally, the managerial issues are addressed by examining how this information strategy framework can be operationalized and used to analyze the extent to which organizational capabilities supported by information technology are likely to contribute to a firm's competitive advantage.

Theoretical Developments

Two widely held beliefs within strategic management are that a firm's performance is a function of its strategy and its environment (Hatten, Schendel and Cooper, 1978), and that a firm's success is a function of its information or luck (Dierickx and Cool, 1989). Information is considered by many to be a rich resource for the firm and a potential source of wealth (Doz and Prahalad, 1991; Hennart and Park, 1994; Hepworth, 1990; Jonscher, 1994; King et al., 1989; Lucas and Baroudi, 1994; Mangaliso, 1995; Orlikowski and Robey, 1991). While luck - those outcomes and good fortune which could not be predicted ex ante - will not be eliminated, more effort can be devoted to understanding the contribution of *information* to the firm's performance if it is used as a strategic resource.

The resource-based view of the firm proposes that a firm can derive a sustainable competitive advantage if management develops and exploits unique and valuable resources and capabilities (Selznick, 1957). A fundamental assumption of this theory is that firms are heterogeneous in their resource endowments (Wernerfelt, 1984) and in their ability to create and deploy strategic resources (Dierickx and Cool, 1989). Strategic resources have a particular value to the organization, and they cannot be easily traded, purchased, imitated, nor do they have readily-available substitutes.[2] Moreover, they are woven into the organizational capabilities of the firm in complex and ambiguous ways. Strategic resources can be categorized as knowledge-based or property-based resources (Miller and Shamsie, 1995). Property-based resources convey a strategic advantage largely through their ownership, whereas knowledge-based resources contribute to a firm's strategic advantage by the way they are deployed within organizational information-based capabilities. This implies that while many firms may own similar physical resources, the use of the resources within the firm will differ greatly according to its competencies and know-how.

The firm's organizational capabilities are developed over time largely through its information-based processes.[3] These processes are carried out within its value chain of activities as it transfers information between tasks required to create its products and services (Porter, 1985, 1986). Hambrick (1982) observed that firms are heterogeneous both in the level of information they can acquire and in their organizational capabilities to exploit that information.[4] Hence, the firm's ability to acquire, create, and use information resources is an important source of resource heterogeneity that can lead to a competitive advantage.

Information is a knowledge-based resource with unique properties that warrant discussion at this point because they contribute to the strategic nature of the information resources and capabilities of the firm. Information can by duplicated and used simultaneously by a firm without increasing costs or depleting the information (Jonscher, 1994), and it can be substituted for traditional resources such as labor, inventory levels, transportation, capital, location, distribution center (Hepworth, 1990). Information has a very generalized applicability as it is the basis for all managerial activities (Bartlett, 1986), which allows it to be used in multiple firm processes, products and services (Hepworth, 1990; Jonscher, 1994). Information can be used to control other technology-based processes, including manufacturing or distribution technology (Yates and Benjamin, 1991). Finally, information is generated as a by-product of automation processes and thus can be exploited as a resource of the firm's own processes (Zuboff, 1988; Monnoyer and Philippe, 1991).

While the firm's strategic resource heterogeneity is a potential source of competitive advantage, the specific contribution of the resources to the firm's performance must be evaluated within the context of its competitive environment. The firm's product market strategy defines its competitive environment, which in turn determines the level of uncertainty and complexity it faces (Galbraith and Nathanson, 1978; Govindarajan, 1988; Miles and Snow, 1978; Rumelt, Schendel and Teece, 1991, 1994; Thompson, 1967). The environment creates a double-edged sword, by creating opportunities for the firm as well as moderating the value of its resources (i.e. Ansoff, 1965; Chandler, 1962; Hatten, Schendel and Cooper, 1978; Kotha and Nair, 1995; Learned, Christensen, Andrews and Guth, 1965; Miller and Shamsie, 1995; Prescott, 1986; Rumelt, Schendel, and Teece, 1994; Tan and Litschert, 1994). While the environment includes all factors external to the firm, the dimensions of *uncertainty* and *complexity* are closely linked to the information resources and capabilities required by the firm (Daft, 1986; Galbraith, 1977; Lawrence and Lorsch, 1967; Miller, 1986, 1987, 1988; Miller and Friesen, 1982, 1983; Miller and Shamsie, 1995; Mintzberg, 1979, 1983; Rumelt, Schendel, and Teece, 1991; Tan and Litschert, 1994; Thompson, 1967).[5] Within this research, environmental uncertainty is defined as *the dynamic nature of crucial factors external to the firm, such that their fluctuation is difficult to predict.* Environmental complexity is defined as *the number of factors and interdependencies that are crucial to the firm's performance, including societal demands for minimal levels of performance or information services.*

Information can serve as a resource that the firm can use to combat environmental uncertainty and complexity in a variety of ways. In such competitive environments, the performance of the firm is related to its knowledge-based and information capabilities (Bartlett and Ghoshal, 1993; Burgers, Hill and Kim, 1993; Kotha, 1995; Rockart and Short, 1991), especially its ability to acquire and process information (Garud and Nayyar, 1994). Miller and Shamsie (1995) demonstrated that knowledge-based resources and capabilities are most valuable in uncertain environments, whereas property-based resources are most valuable in stable and predictable environments. Information can be used to enhance competitive flexibility by creating a wider range of strategic options that the firm can exercise (Wernerfelt and Karnani, 1987; Lucas, 1996; Sanchez, 1993; Scott Morton, 1991). The information acquisition and processing capabilities of the firm can reduce the level of uncertainty it faces as compared to other firms (Daft, 1986; Daft and Lengel, 1986; Galbraith, 1977, 1994; Jauch and Kraft, 1986; Nadler and Tushman, 1978), and coordinating capabilities enable the firm to handle complexity and improve operating efficiency (Chandler, 1962, 1977, 1990). Initial considerations of the firm's information processing capabilities were described by researchers from the standpoint of organizational structure, managerial hierarchy, and interpersonal communication techniques (Daft, 1986; Daft and Lengel, 1986; Galbraith, 1977; Mintzberg, 1979, 1983; Nadler and Tushman, 1978; Thompson, 1967). With the advancements and widespread availability of modern telecommunications and computing technologies, it is now appropriate to consider the role of information technology to enhance the firm's strategic position.

We have seen that the environmental dimensions of uncertainty and complexity create the information drivers required by the firm, and these consequently determine the strategic value of the firm's information-based resources. However, it is the organizational processes that employ the information resources which create the strategic advantage. The firm's information processing abilities determine the extent to which it acquires information from the environment, transfers it throughout the organization, and integrates it within its processes (Cohen and Levinthal, 1990; Henderson and Cockburn,

1994). Thus, information technology does not serve as a strategic resource merely by ownership alone; its strategic value is revealed when it supports organizational capabilities.

Innovation and coordination are the organizational capabilities for which a firm can use information technology to meet the demands of its competitive environment. *Innovation* occurs when a new idea or procedure is adopted by a firm or within an industry (Daft, 1978; Swanson, 1994). Innovation can take place in the firm's administrative processes, business process, or the products and services produced by the firm (Clark, 1987; Swanson, 1994).[6] Innovation prolongs the strategic value of the firm's resources by exploiting them in novel ways (Daft, 1978), creating causal ambiguity of the outcomes of innovative processes (Lippman and Rumelt, 1982), and creating additional uncertainty for its rivals (D'Aveni, 1994, 1995; Jauch and Kraft, 1986). The result is that competitors have difficulty in imitating or duplicating the use of similar resources (Miller, 1987; Miller and Shamsie, 1995).

Miller and Friesen (1982) found that the degree of innovation of the firm's strategy was significantly related to its use of information processing mechanisms. Miller (1987) later found that successful firms in uncertain environments were those that pursued innovative strategies, thus identifying an important link between innovation, the environment, and performance. When a firm operates in an unpredictable context, it must develop products and processes repeatedly in innovative ways (D'Aveni, 1994, 1995). Therefore, it can be concluded that the only resources which can have any strategic value are those which can be used in innovative ways.

Information technology is an important resource for innovation, which can be used to realize product innovation as well as industry transformation. It creates new avenues by which firms may enter existing industries, create new industries, or reposition themselves within their original industry and change their competitive scope (Henderson and Venkatraman, 1994; Kambil and Short, 1994; Keen, 1988; Venkatraman, 1991). At the same time, it can change the way a firm competes through re-organization of the value chain and coordination of tasks within the firm. (Das, Zahra and Warkentin, 1991; Dos Santos and Peffers, 1993; Hammer and Champy, 1993; Porter and Millar, 1985; Rockart and Short, 1991; Wang and Seidmann, 1995; Yates and Benjamin, 1991).

Along with innovation, *coordination* is an important aspect of the firm's information-based capabilities. Coordination refers to the organization's means of controlling complex tasks between interdependent entities, and widespread use of coordination methods enhances the information-processing capacity of the firm (Ebers and Ganter, 1991; Galbraith, 1994; Galbraith and Nathanson, 1978; Malone and Rockart, 1993).[7] The necessity for coordination is driven by the level of complexity confronting the firm, arising out of known

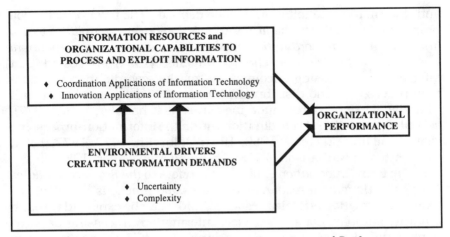

Figure 1: Environmental Drivers, Information Resources, and Performance

factors which impact interdependent processes and which must be controlled in order to conduct the work efficiently.[8] Whereas innovation is seen as an entrepreneurial task of management, coordination is seen as an administrative task (Schendel, 1985). The coordination ability of the firm is revealed through its integrating mechanisms and inter-organizational linkages, and it has been shown that information-intensive organizations rely extensively on such mechanisms (Bakos, 1991; Cash and Konsynski, 1985; Haeckel, 1995; Hagström, 1991; Hepworth, 1990; Malone et al., 1994; Porter and Millar, 1985).

Information technology can be a valuable resource to organizations when it coordinates tasks by processing large amounts of information rapidly, and when it exploits information through innovations in the firm's processes, products and services. For example, it can benefit the firm by creating new processes and adapting old ones (Bradley et al., 1993; Hagström, 1991; Malone and Rockart, 1993; Scott Morton, 1991), coordinating activities through multifunctional and multilevel networks (Chandler, 1986; Glover and Goslar, 1993; Rockart and Short, 1991; Yates and Benjamin, 1991), increasing information flow and information processing over traditional means (Clemons and Row, 1993, Hammond, 1993; Lee and Leifer, 1992), increasing the speed of organizational responses to environmental changes (Lucas and Baroudi, 1994), and implementing innovative business strategies (Haeckel, 1995; Haeckel and Nolan, 1993; Pine, 1993; Wang and Seidmann, 1995). Therefore, the strategic value of information technology should not be evaluated solely by the level of financial investment, but rather through the level of investment in organizational processes that rely on the technology.

To distinguish between the coordination and innovation functions of the organizational capabilities that are proposed within the information strategy framework, the references to "information processing" and "information exploitation" will be defined. The term *"information processing"* will refer to *the firm's knowledge-based capabilities to use information as a coordination mechanism between interdependent tasks in the firm's value chain.* Joncher (1994) suggested that information processing encompasses market coordination, production, processing, and distribution functions. This is consistent with Chandler's use of coordination mechanisms (Chandler, 1962, 1977), as well as the notion of coordination within the information-processing view of the firm (Egelhoff, 1982, 1991; Galbraith, 1973, 1977, 1994; Galbraith and Nathanson, 1978; Tushman and Nadler, 1978).

The term *"information exploitation"* refers to *the firm's capabilities to apply information resources or processing functions in innovative ways.* Information is itself a resource, and it can be exploited through innovative applications. Likewise, information processing applications could also be categorized as innovative if they consist of new means of coordinating the firm's tasks. However, not all information processing activities will be considered innovative. The innovative activities using information technology will be those that use the technology in ways that are new to the firm or to the industry in which it operates (Swanson, 1994), and thus have not been institutionalized as societal demands for minimum performance levels or information services. For example, automatic teller machines (ATMs) in consumer banking are no longer innovative since they have been institutionalized as a requirement for doing business (Attewell, 1994; Lacity, Wilcocks, and Feeny, 1996). The innovation in the information processing activities may be realized through new transfers of knowledge within the firm or between firms, or it may be realized through new uses of information that is a by-product of other processes that may even be routine or ordinary for the firm. In general, information exploitation will require some adaptation of organizational processes and technology to create the new processes (Scott Morton, 1991; Hagström, 1991; Malone and Rockart, 1993; Bradley et al., 1993).

In summary, the resource-based view of the firm was used to established that a firm's information strategy is based on two dimensions of organizational capabilities - information processing and information exploitation - and two dimensions of the competitive environment - uncertainty and complexity. Environmental uncertainty is created when firms have difficulty predicting the dynamic fluctuation of customer demand and competitive forces in its environment that are crucial to its performance, such as varying consumer preferences, industry rivalry, technological developments, regulatory influences, or other factors that the firm cannot control. In contrast, environmental complexity is created when the firm is faced with interdependent processes and tasks or societal demands for expediency and service. These interdependent tasks create intense information demands for the firm, which in turn necessitate the coordination of the tasks in order to meet the expected level of performance. The dimension of "information processing" refers to the firm's use of information to coordinate interdependent tasks crucial to the performance of the firm, and it largely determines the efficiency of the operations conducted by the firm.   The dimension of "information exploitation" refers to the firm's ability to capitalize on the information through innovative applications within the firm or within its products or services. Figure 1 depicts the relationship between the environmental drivers for information, the firm's information resources and capabilities, and its performance.   A firm that is able to exploit information, not only to coordinate traditional activities, but also as an integral component of its products or services - is raising the "information stakes" for the industry in which it competes by making it more difficult for rival firms to survive because it is increasing the uncertainty they face. Thus, information technology resources can contribute to a firm's competitive advantage if the firm adopts an *information strategy" to decrease its level of uncertainty through exploitative uses of information technology and to control its level of complexity through information processing techniques.*

Information Strategy Framework

The Information Strategy Framework depicts the relationship between the firm's information-related organizational capabilities and its environmental drivers for information.   These dimensions - the firm's capacity for *information processing* and *information exploitation*, and environmental *uncertainty* and *complexity* - suggest two key propositions that define the framework, specifying a contingency relationship between the firm's information capabilities and the information demands of its competitive environment.

Proposition 1 - "Information processing": Knowledge-based capabilities supported by information technology will have the greatest strategic value in complex environments when they are used to *coordinate interdependent processes.*

Corollary 1.a: Information processing capabilities supported by information technology will have minimal value in simple environments because sophisticated coordination mechanisms are not needed in such cases.

Proposition 2 - "Information exploitation": Knowledge-based capabilities supported by information technology will have the greatest strategic value in uncertain environments when they support *innovative applications* of information resources.

Corollary 2.a.: Information exploitation capabilities supported by information technology will have minimal value in stable and predicable environments because of the higher value of property-based resources over knowledge-based resources in such environments.

Corollary 2.b.: Information processing capabilities supported by information technology will have less value in uncertain environments than information exploitation capabilities supported by similar technology, due to the ambiguity inherent in the uncertain environment which reduces the ability to coordinate processes.

Corollary 2.c: Information exploitation capabilities supported by information technology will be better able to sustain a competitive advantage than information processing capabilities supported by similar technology, due to the difficulty rival firms will have in duplicating the innovative processes.

The firm's performance is not an explicit dimension of this framework, but rather it is based on the degree of "fit" achieved between the information-based capabilities of the firm and its environmental context. Not all competitive environments have the same levels of uncertainty and complexity, and therefore not all firms require the same degree of innovation and coordination capabilities. In addition, the dynamics of the environment should be taken into consideration when evaluating the "fit" between the capabilities and the environment. If the environment is one where complexity increases while uncertainty remains fixed at a relatively low level, then communication networks and services that are optimized for the specific coordination tasks are most valuable. However, as the level of environmental uncertainty increases, the most valuable information resources will be those that can support general applications and which can be flexibly adapted to changing situations. This suggests the use of general-purpose communication networks that can support a variety of applications simultaneously over the same network (Hagström, 1991; Scott Morton, 1991). For instance, integrated services digital networks (ISDNs, including France's Minitel) and other networks that support a wide range of voice, data, image, and video services would fulfill this need. Increasing environmental complexity requires a greater emphasis on coordination, whereas increasing environmental uncertainty requires a greater focus on innovation. As a firm faces both uncertainty and complexity, then capabilities are needed that encompass both innovation and coordination.

One factor that contributes to a firm's information processing and exploitation capabilities is the variable information content of its processes and products. Once information is encoded, it can be stored, processed, and transmitted with information technology (Monnoyer and Philippe, 1991; Turban, McLean, and Wetherbe, 1996). In industries such as banking, insurance, and financial securities,

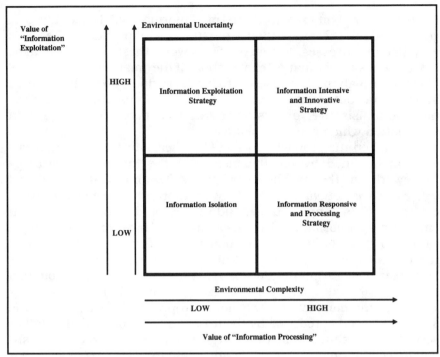

Figure 2: Information Strategy Framework

where the product or service is based on information, it is straightforward to envision how information technology can be used to process or exploit the information. However, even non-information processes can be manipulated such that they create information that can be encoded, processed, transmitted, and used to make decisions. The information can be encoded through the use of sensors, monitors, and other measuring devices. For instance, at a hydraulic equipment firm, monitors can be used to assess the performance of machinery and the data collected by the sensors can be transmitted to an expert system where it is interpreted to determine when pre-emptive maintenance is needed. Some maintenance operations can be performed by remotely controlling the equipment. This saves the use of maintenance personnel for only those situations that cannot be handled remotely, thus enabling the staff to serve a larger geographic region or carry out additional tasks required by the firm (Monnoyer and Philippe, 1991). In another instance, a ski resort can measure and analyze weather and snow conditions and then combine this data with the resort scheduling database to determine when artificial snow should be produced and how long the ski season should be extended (Turban, McLean and Wetherbe, 1996).

Zuboff (1988) describes these types of information processes as "automating" and "informating" (sic). Automated process are those that are used to encode information and coordinate tasks through the use of information technology, and these fall into the category of "information processing" within the information strategy framework.

In contrast, Zuboff created the term "informating," to identify processes that use the information generated as a by-product of the firm's automation processes. Within our framework, these processes can be categorized as "information exploitation" if they make innovative uses of that information. Hence, even if a firm's products do not have a high information content, it is possible that the manufacturing, distribution, administrative, or customer interface processes are rich in information which can be exploited.

Based on the propositions stated earlier, four information strategies are defined by the dimensions of the information strategy framework, and they are shown in Figure 2. The first strategy is labeled *information isolation*. This strategy is appropriate when the firm's environment is simple, stable, and readily predictable. In such an environment, information-based resources will have minimal strategic value, so there is little justification for the firm to invest in such resources. The competitive advantage of these firms rests on other resources besides information-based resources. Examples of such industries includes highly regulated or labor intensive industries where information technology is not appropriately substituted for the services or goods produced by the firm. For instance, small retail or service establishments fit this category, as well as those establishments requiring manual labor, personal talents, or creative efforts that cannot otherwise be replaced or which cannot take advantage of the unique aspects of information resources. This category also includes low market share niche firms whose business strategy creates a relatively protected competitive environment (Woo and Cooper, 1982). (While some might find it hard to imagine that any such industry exists, consider one example to be award-winning culinary chefs who operate exclusive small restaurants with very limited menus and who accept only cash payments for their services.)

The second strategy is labeled the *information exploitation strategy*, and it is appropriate for firms that operate in an environment which has a high degree of uncertainty but not an excessive amount of complexity. In this environment, there are a limited number of well-known constraints and interdependencies which the firm must coordinate, so automation and efficiency gains of coordination technologies, beyond the basic level required to operate in the industry, would have minimal value. Rather, the uncertainty inherent in the environment requires innovative uses of information. Capabilities and investments that enhance the information content of the product or service sold by the firm will contribute more toward the goal of achieving a competitive advantage as compared to those that are intended to improve the firm's task efficiency. In environments with a relatively low degree of complexity, competitors would be able to easily imitate capabilities that are based on automation. Any advantage conveyed by such investments would be very short-lived once rival firms are able to duplicated it. However, the uncertainty of the environment enhances the value of the innovative applications of the information contained in the products and services, and affords the firm a more sustainable competitive advantage.

The innovative influence is heightened if it is applied at the level of the product or service such that it impacts the underlying business and administrative processes as well. For example, firms that specialize in assembling information for specific customer needs base their competitive advantage on their ability to obtain information that their competitors do not have or assemble it in ways that are customized for their client's needs. One such firm specializes in selling information about people and businesses to other firms. Another firm integrates an expert system with its customer service functions in order to diagnose equipment problems real-time during customer "trouble" calls. The expert system combines the individual customer's product history of prior service calls with the information on the operation of that specific piece of equipment in order to diagnose the cause of the event. In a third example, a financial securities firm combines information from customer comments during calls with account information and financial product information, and it analyzes the data in order to recommend specific financial instruments to the customer that would fit most appropriately with his or her investment style and interests. For instance, if a customer expressed interest in the past in a specific product which the firm didn't carry at that time, this customer's desire would be noted so that he or she could be informed when such a product became available. In another case, if the account information reveals that a certificate of deposit or bond is soon reaching a maturity date, the customer would be given specific suggestions of alternative investments to consider at that time.

As the aforementioned examples suggest, the industries generally suited to this type of information strategy experience rapid shifts in product supply and customer demand, or have customers who value specialized services and products over mass efficiency. The firm's competitive advantage rests to a large extent on the firm's ability to evaluate its customers, anticipate their needs or desires, and satisfy them with a customized service or product. The customer's satisfaction will be based to a large extent on the 'information content' of the product, which includes pricing information that enables them to purchase the lowest-priced product that best fits their individual needs or preferences. Examples of such industries includes personal financial services, insurance, travel and leisure services, entertainment services, mortgage banking, educational services, personalized shopping and other retail services, information searching and personalized publication services, personalized retail and shopping services, and customized manufacturing.

The third strategy is labeled the *information responsive and processing strategy*. It is the appropriate strategy for firms faced with complex yet fairly certain and predictable environments. These firms face a large number of known constraints or interdependent relation-ships, and the value of coordination capabilities to gain efficiencies is highest in such environments. Many of these constraints are likely to be driven by societal demands for information and efficiency. This information strategy is based on a firm's ability to process information to coordinate the interdependent activities, and therefore information technology investments and organizational capabilities are required that enhance operating efficiency.

A word of caution is in order regarding this strategy. Although the recommended use for information resources is to enhance efficiency, the low level of uncertainty of the environment coupled with the predictable level of complexity will allow competitors to duplicate the capability relatively easily, unless it is tightly coupled with other resources of the firm. In such an environment, the firm's non-information resources will also have significant strategic value. Examples of industries facing this environment include consumer banking, large retailers, mail-order retailers, and mass manufacturers of non-technical or low-technology products.

The "*information responsive and processing strategy*" is possibly the most common example of firms using information technology. For instance, a travel service firm involved in automobile roadside assis-tance, insurance, and travel planning found that it could work more efficiently if had a network that facilitated communications between its headquarters and independent member offices, and if it consolidated its many customer databases and shared the information between its business units. In another instance, a soft-drink bottling company found that the productivity of its sales representatives increased if it provided wireless order processing and better systems coordination with the distribution center. It found that orders processed in this way had fewer errors and were filled more rapidly to be shipped to the retail customers.

Another fairly common illustration of this type of strategy is in the area of Electronic Data Interchange (EDI). For instance, a manufac-turer of electronic and computer-related products responded to re-quests from its large customers to process purchase orders and price quotes electronically. This firm then linked these order processing systems to its own manufacturing and customer service systems in order to be able to respond more quickly to customers' orders as well as service requests. In a closely related example, but one targeted at the mass market as well as corporate customers, businesses are creating electronic product catalogs so that individual customers can access and search on-line, for instance, through the World Wide Web. The electronic catalog is most useful when it is integrated with the firm's inventory, purchasing, and distribution systems so that it enhances efficiency through coordination of these interdependent functions. In yet another example, firms are providing non-personalized customer support through on-line electronic databases that customers can access and search for answers to their own questions. This service is generally offered at no cost to the customer, and it expends few corporate resources while providing some level of service. If a customer demands a greater level of service, then more personalized services are available for a substantially greater cost. These examples demonstrate that although efficiency gains are important to the firm's operations, they alone are not likely to produce long-term strategic advantages. Information processing capabilities coupled with the firm's other strategic resources would be able to convey more strategic value than the use of information resources alone.

Finally, the fourth strategy is labeled the *information intensive and innovative strategy*. This strategy requires the most intensive use of the information-based resources because the firm must control high levels of complexity while also facing high levels of uncertainty. Hence, both innovative and coordination applications of information will have high strategic value to such firms. For instance, industries facing this type of environment include high-technology industries, investment banking, and industries undergoing transformation as a result of changes in governmental regulations, global, or political factors. The firm's competitive advantage will rest on small differences between its ability to coordinate interdependent tasks and innovatively use information as compared to the capabilities of its rivals, and hence such applications are generally highly guarded corporate secrets. Innovation will be especially useful in altering the effective uncertainty faced by the individual firms in the industry. A firm which can create uncertainty for other rivals through successfully innovating its own process and products will have effectively expanded the value of its information resources. The ability for a firm to use its information-based resources to drive industry transformation, and the efficiency that can be attained in coordinating interdependent operation during the transformation, will be two important determinants of the sustainability of its competitive advantage.

One interesting case of a firm implementing this type of strategy concerns the marketing of products and extending credit to individuals who have been denied credit cards with other companies due to their risky credit history. Uncertainty is created by customer credit worthiness. Complexity is driven by the financial aspects of credit card issuance, coupled with issuing private credit cards, merchandising, costs of printing and mailing catalogs, and establishing cable-TV shopping ventures. This firm coordinates credit histories and credit-issuance information with catalog merchandising to a niche group of people — low to mid-income households. They make innovative and personalized use of very specific customer data on name, address, marital status, age, birthdays, number of children, hobbies, etc. For instance, rather than mass mailing to all customers, they mail catalogs and offer promotions individually to customers when they are most likely to buy merchandise - around the time of family birthdays and other holidays. By storing and accessing approximately 500 pieces of information on each customer, this firm identifies the most credit-worthy customers and markets merchandise to them when they are most likely to make a purchase.

Another example reveals that innovative analysis of customer data can result in non-electronic ways of customizing the customer's experience in dealing with the firm. In this case, a convenience store with a very limited amount of display space is able to maximize sales by changing the inventory mix throughout the day, based on its knowledge of the types of products customers purchase at different times of day (Turban, McLean, and Wetherbe, 1996). This store analyzes data of purchases made as a function of the time of day, and configures its merchandise accordingly. This same store also coordinates inventory purchases through a central distribution center that serves other branches of convenience shops, in order to reduce costs and enhance the efficiency of its ordering, inventory, and distribution while still obtaining the inventory specifically suited to the needs of its customers.

In a very different scenario, a petroleum company is using advanced information technology in a very innovative way in order to exploit information as well as coordinate relationships in order to streamline interdependent tasks. This firm is using high-speed telecommunications networks to transmit oil exploration data gathered at sea to geologists so that they can analyze the data real-time, the goal being to locate oil more quickly and reliably than the traditional method of boring holes in the ocean bottom and analyzing soil sample data at a later time. With this same information technology, this firm is also supporting collaborative work activities to reduce or eliminate the need for travel, through videoconferencing, file sharing, and remote information search activities. Thus, the firm has developed its capabilities to use a common information technology platform to support both innovative and coordination applications that it believes are crucial for its competitive success.

These four information strategies describe organizational capabilities that are posited to fit best in four different competitive environments, depending on the level of environmental complexity or uncertainty facing the firm. The payoff of the information technology investment for firms operating in each of these environments is dependent not on the level of investment in the technology, but rather on the access to the technology and in its deployment for the purpose of achieving the widest reach for those organizational capabilities that have the greatest value in the specific competitive environment.

The framework can be used not only to analyze information technology investments and applications for the current competitive environments, but also to assess overall environmental changes and hence the requisite changes in the strategic value of the information-based resources. For instance, some firms which originally faced an environment of low complexity and uncertainty may find that the level of complexity increases, or conversely the level of uncertainty may increase. These changes suggest different action for the firm to take in order to derive the most value from its strategic resources. While there are suggestions that both complexity and uncertainty are increasing for all firms at a rapid rate (D'Aveni, 1994, 1995), past researchers frequently confounded the two environmental dimensions of uncertainty and complexity, and earlier information technology frameworks ignored the effect of such environmental conditions. This framework allows for a more careful analysis of such dynamic events which will in turn provide more specific answers regarding how a firm can achieve a competitive advantage through its use of information technology.

The value of the framework to researchers rests largely on its operationalization which accounts for the firm's innovation and coordination processes, the extent to which those activities persist throughout the firm, and the richness of the technology supporting the activities. This requires distinguishing between activities that are isolated to a limited number of the firm's functions versus those that are widespread throughout the firm, identifying activities which extend beyond the firm's boundaries by means of an interorganizational or a public telecommunications network, and taking note of the networking technologies that are supporting the activities. Classifying the firm's capabilities in this way provides a rich view of its information processing capacity, beyond that provided by schemes that merely focus on the information technology or applications such as e-mail or videoconferencing, and it is also more powerful than those that only assess the social or procedural aspect of the firm's "networking" activities while ignoring the technologies. The classification scheme specified for this framework combines both the applications and the technology to evaluate the firm's knowledge-based capabilities.

Although the firm's environment encompasses many factors, the environmental conditions of uncertainty and complexity can be operationalized by examining the volatility, number, and interdependencies among factors that have a significant influence on the firm's performance. Environmental uncertainty has been operationalized in past research by considering the volatility of demand and competitive factors faced by the firm, such as customer demand, competitive market conditions, rivals' product design and pricing dynamics, relations with suppliers, technological factors, labor markets, governmental regulations, financial and socioeconomic conditions (Amit and Schoemaker, 1993; Daft et al., 1988; Garud and Nayyar, 1994; Miles and Snow, 1978). Environmental conditions have been operationalized from both a subjective and objective point of view. Managers' ability to perceive environmental conditions is a function of their ability to acquire and interpret information (Hambrick, 1982), and as a consequence, the perceived environmental conditions will often times vary from the objective conditions that exist (Downey, Hellriegel, Slocum, 1975). The overwhelming majority of environmental measures are based on data collected via surveys of the manager's perception of the competitive environment (Lawrence and Lorsch, 1967; Miller, 1986, 1987, 1988; Miller and Friesen, 1982, 1983; Pine, 1993). However, there has been an increased use of objective measures of the environment, such as: market and technological volatility, and the rate of product and process innovation (Bourgeois, 1985; Ghoshal and Nohria, 1989; Nohria and Ghoshal, 1994); competitive intensity (Ghoshal and Nohria, 1989; Downey, Hellriegel, Slocum, 1975; Nohria and Ghoshal, 1994); price volatility (Downey, Hellriegel, Slocum, 1975); technological intensity, as measured by a high R&D to sales ratio (Osborn and Baughn, 1990); volatility in customer demand (Jauch and Kraft, 1986); technological dynamism and entropy, as measured by content analysis (Kabanoff, Waldersee, and Cohen, 1995); variability in industry growth rates (Dess and Beard, 1984; Lawless and Finch, 1989). In addition, the number of firms entering and exiting an industry is yet another measure of uncertainty, as well as the numbers of mergers and acquisitions in an industry, as these events directly change the competitive landscape between industry rivals.

Measures for complexity assess the intensity of interrelationships that are created by the firm's operations, and they provide a view of the firm as a "system" of operations to be controlled (Nohria and Garcia-Pont, 1991). These measures include: the number and variety of organizations with which a firm must interact (Lawless and Finch, 1989); and increases in the size and scope of the firm's product market, and diversification into other markets (Chandler, 1962, 1977, 1990; Ghoshal and Nohria, 1989; Hagström, 1991). Finally, process-level measures have also been used to assess complexity, such as increasing numbers of transactions (Attewell, 1994; Bakos, 1991; Wang and Seidmann, 1995). Another option that some researchers have selected is to rely on proxies for the firm's environment, rather than measure it directly. Such proxies include organizational structures that are most likely to exist in complex environments (Egelhoff, 1991) or periods of time in the history of an industry where there is increased volatility (Miller and Shamsie, 1995). A combined use of different types of measures will provide more detailed information about the environment.

The final phase of operationalizing the framework pertains to the firm's performance. Although performance is not a separate dimension described by the framework, the contingency relationship set up by the framework is intended to maximize the firm's performance within its competitive environment. The performance effects of the use of the knowledge-based capabilities for information processing and exploitation will be revealed at three levels: a) the product, service, or process level; b) the firm level; and c) the industry level. Ideally, the product, service, or process-level effects should not be isolated, but should appear throughout the firm (Hepworth, 1990; Jonscher, 1994; Chandler, 1962; Clark, 1987). For instance, these effects will be most readily observed when a firm sells information and coordinates its delivery through telecommunications networks (Jonscher, 1994), automates or informates (sic) its products and processes (Zuboff, 1988), increases the number of transactions it processes (Landauer, 1995); expands the types of customers served (Monnoyer and Philippe, 1991), or adapts its products or processes so that they may be more easily coordinated, resulting in increased speed and throughput flow (Hepworth, 1990; Jonscher, 1994; Chandler, 1962). Likewise, the performance effects are revealed when the firm reduces the model cycle time to design new products or deliver services (Davidow and Malone, 1992; Dyer, 1996); substitutes information for a traditional resource (i.e. labor, inventory levels, transportation, capital, location, distribution center) by creating electronic linkages, electronic communication, electronic matrixing; electronic workflows, production automation, electronic customer/supplier links (Hepworth, 1990; Lucas and Baroudi, 1994); changes its organizational structure to as it coordinates its tasks in new ways (Bartlett and Ghoshal, 1993; Hagström, 1991; Hedlund and Rolander, 1990; Lucas, 1996), or alters its method of decisionmaking to take better advantage of the uncertainty-reduction capabilities that are available with the information technology (Galbraith, 1994; Glover and Goslar, 1993; Hammer and Champy, 1993; Molloy and Schwenk, 1995; Malone and Rockart, 1993).

There are many firm-level performance measures that can indicate the extent to which the firm's information processing and exploitation capabilities are supporting its competitive advantage. Growth-related measures include: average annual growth in sales (Attewell, 1994; Davidow and Malone, 1992; Jauch and Kraft, 1986; Kotha and Nair, 1995; National Research Council, 1994; Nohria and Ghoshal, 1994; Tan and Litschert, 1994); increases in market share (Attewell, 1994; Burgers, Hill and Kim, 1993; Jauch and Kraft, 1986); expansion into distinct product market areas (Chandler, 1990). Efficiency measures include: sales growth vs. human resource growth (McKeen and Smith, 1993); increases in economies of scale (Chandler, 1962, 1986, 1990); cost reduction through reduced inventories and inventory holding costs (Bradley et al., 1993; Scott Morton, 1991; Dyer, 1996). Quality improvement is measured by a reduction in the defect rate (Dyer, 1996). Flexibility of response is measured as the range of responses possible from the firm (Bartlett and Ghoshal, 1993; Ebers and Kanter, 1991; Galbraith, 1994; Galbraith and Nathanson, 1978; Lucas, 1996). Measures of geographic scope related to competitiveness include: geographic range of coordination and integration (Porter, 1986; Kambil and Short, 1994); geographic range of information dissemination (Bradley et al., 1993; Scott Morton, 1991); geographic flexibility in terms of the geographic speed of response; integration of activities to create global scale in niche markets (Bradley et al., 1993; Scott Morton, 1991). Measures of competitiveness assess the longevity or durability in terms of a firm's survival and effectiveness over the long-term (Bartlett and Ghoshal, 1993). Financial indicators of profitability such as return on assets and return on investments are not recommended since they have not been useful in demonstrating the strategic value of information technology investments (Landauer, 1995; National Research Council, 1994).

Some performance effects may also be revealed in industry measures (Bradley, 1993), such as industry transformation with respect to product or service development, industry boundaries blurring, and the creation of new industries, however these will be more difficult to detect due to the aggregation of many additional factors at the industry level. Researchers have had difficulty using industry measures to evaluate increases in productivity that can be attributed to information technology (Baily and Chakrabarti, 1988; Landauer, 1995; Loveman, 1986, 1990; National Research Council, 1994; Strassman, 1990), but indicators related to industry transformation and growth may be useful (Kotha and Nair, 1995; National Research Council, 1994). The performance measures must be aligned with appropriate measures of the firm's information exploitation and processing in order to accurately indicate the results of the organizational capabilities.

The information strategy framework presented in this section is a vehicle to analyze an organization's ability to process and exploit information according to the demands created by the environmental uncertainty and complexity. The theoretical justification for the framework is based on the role the environment plays in moderating the value of a firm's information-based capabilities. In its basic form, the model identifies four information strategies: a) in an environment of low uncertainty and complexity, the firm's information-based resources will be of little strategic value, and thus its strategic advantage would not be enhanced by investing in information technology; b) in an environment with high uncertainty and low complexity, the firm's ability to exploit information can be a valuable strategic resource in order to offset the uncertainty of the environment and to create potentially greater uncertainty for its rivals; c) in an environment with low uncertainty and high complexity, the organization's information processing ability can be a valuable resource to control complexity by using information technology to coordinate interdependent processes, but this technology alone is unlikely to create a sustainable competitive advantage; and finally, d) in an environment with high uncertainty and complexity, a firm's ability to process and exploit information are both very valuable as strategic resources in order to compete in this information-intensive environment. Firms in this fourth competitive scenario must carefully balance both innovative and coordination roles of the information technology so as to gain strategic value from both types of processes. The remainder of this chapter is devoted to examining the application of this framework by managers and the limitations that affect its use.

Management Strategies for Information Technology Investment

The information strategy framework is a useful tool to assist managers in determining how a firm should invest in information technology and develop strategic capabilities for using this technology within the firm's competitive environment. The framework has illustrated that firms do not all require the same information technology investments. However, it has been difficult to know what investments and capabilities are needed in specific competitive circumstances (Sheppard, 1991).

This framework can be used to guide the information technology investment decisionmaking process by identifying the organizational capabilities to be supported by the technology that are most crucial to the firm's performance in a particular competitive environment. By addressing the issue of these organizational capabilities along with the technology, a more complete picture is created concerning the role of the information technologies within the firm which operates in a particular environment. Better knowledge of this organizational impact can aid, for instance, in deciding the extent to which the systems should be optimized for specific applications or generalized for flexibility; in determining the extent of education and training required in order for the employees to develop the necessary competencies required by the organization; in determining the processes that can be outsourced and those that should be developed in-house; or in determining the extent of the firm's use of the public telecommunications infrastructure versus private or industry-based inter-organizational networks. It can also be used to assess how existing systems are meeting the necessary innovation and coordination tasks and the extent to which they are deployed throughout the organization.

In addition to identifying the value of information-based resources to the firm, the framework implies the role that other resources play in potentially contributing to a firm's competitive advantage. For instance, it indicates that an organization in a simple and stable environment must derive its competitive advantage from resources other than information-technology. In an organization that is faced with high complexity and which uses information technology for coordination, the technology may be able to enhance the firm's efficiency, but it should not be expected to create a sustainable advantage through coordination alone. While it can apply information technology for efficiency gains, but it must also rely on other resources for its competitive advantage. A firm that operates in an uncertain environment with a low level of complexity should not expect to achieve strategic value from systems designed to enhance efficiency. It would derive more strategic value by exploiting the information content of its products and services to better target customers, to move quickly to adapt to their changing demands, and, to the extent possible, to personalize the products and services it sells. Finally, the firm in an information intensive environment will derive considerable strategic value from its information technology, so long as it deploys the technology for both innovative and coordination applications.

The discussion up to this point has used this framework to make comparisons between firms in different industries. However, it is also a useful tool to the individual manager who would like to conduct the analysis within one industry. For instance, it could be used to assess differences in information strategies between firms within the same industry, in order to make comparisons of one firm's competitive position over another. In addition, the environment within a given industry may not present a uniform context for all firms. Consider, for example, the real estate industry where some firms will be faced with very different environmental contexts depending on the housing supply, demand, prevailing prices, and economic conditions in the region where they conduct most of their business. Real estate firms operating in such differing environmental contexts would benefit from different information strategies. Finally, an individual manager can use the framework to evaluate new information requirements facing his or her firm as environmental conditions change, whether these changes occur due solely to external forces or whether they occur as the firm alters its business strategy. If management makes the decision, for instance, to add additional sites in a region with similar customer demographics, it is effectively increasing its environmental complexity but not significantly altering its uncertainty. The information technology needs should be planned at the same time the firm decides to expand in order to be able to coordinate the activities of the entire firm in an appropriate and organized manner. In contrast, if the firm decides to enter global markets where it has no experience, it will require a different approach when planning and designing its information technology applications in order to meet the demands of the increased uncertainty as well as complexity that it will face.

The information strategy framework is designed to be useful for analyzing firms regardless of their size. By having as its central focus the environmental conditions facing the firm, it presents issues that are as much a concern to entrepreneurs of start-up businesses as it is to managers of multinational corporations. In fact, it might be argued that the use of information technology can potentially have a greater impact on the success of small firms as compared to larger ones because the information resources may form a larger proportion of the firm's overall strategic resources, and they may enable it to leverage a

greater proportion of organizational capabilities beyond its boundaries. Evidence of this effect can be seen with the start-up firms that
use the Internet to become global competitors and that operate with a
very small number of employees. Earlier frameworks that focus on the
firm's structural transformation (i.e. Venkatraman, 1991) or strategic
alignment (i.e., MacDonald, 1991) do not as readily address the
concerns of entrepreneurs nor managers of small niche business who
are faced with changing competitive environments.

While the information strategy framework may be useful in a wide
variety of situations, it also has some obvious limitations. First, while
there are four strategies defined by the framework based on the
designations of the environmental conditions, there will clearly be
varying degrees of both environmental complexity and uncertainty
that a firm will face beyond the "low" and "high" levels discussed
earlier. In addition, hybrid strategies such as an Innovative-Responsive
strategy may be employed by a firm attempting to transform its own
business strategy or alter the way in which business is conducted in
a particular industry. Parsimony of the framework has to be balanced
with reality, and the strategic types as well as the environmental
conditions are intended to be illustrative guides to assist in evaluating
the contribution that particular organizational capabilities supported
by information technology may have on a firm's performance.   No
single model contains the necessary number of factors to describe the
real competitive position faced by the firm. The contribution of this
particular framework is to emphasize the role of the environment when
determining the information technology investments that should be
made and the organizational capabilities that should be supported by the
technology in order to obtain any strategic value from the investments.

A second limitation of the framework pertains to its inability to
specify in great detail the particular types of innovation or coordination
that are most useful for meeting the demands of specific types of
environmental uncertainty and complexity. However, the first step to
elaborate on the role of the environment has been made in order assess
the variation in the value of information resources in different competitive contexts. Many empirical studies will be needed to test the various
dimensions of the model, and through these studies more details will
be revealed regarding the value of specific capabilities supported by
information technology.

In conclusion, this chapter describes a contingency framework
that defines the fit between a firm's information strategy and its
environmental context. The framework is strongly grounded in strategic management and organizational theory research, with its primary
focus being the resource-based view of the firm as an organizing
mechanism to integrate relevant concepts from the information processing view of the firm and information systems research.   It
describes four "information strategies" that rely on the use of informa-

tion technologies to support organizational capabilities to process and exploit information within particular environmental contexts of uncertainty and complexity. The framework serves as a tool that researchers and managers can use to analyze the firm's information resources and the unique role that information technology can play in enhancing the firm's organizational capabilities.

Endnotes

[1]"Information technology" is commonly defined as the computer and communications systems used to acquire, encode, transmit, store, and process information (Banker et al., 1993; Hepworth, 1990; Jonscher, 1994; Madnick, 1991; McFarlan, 1984; Porter and Millar, 1985).

[2]The term 'resources' refers to physical, financial, and human resources as well as organizational knowledge and capabilities. For a detailed discussion of strategic resources, see: Barney, 1991; Conner, 1991; Dierickx and Cool, 1989; Peteraf, 1993; Wernerfelt, 1984.

[3]For strategic perspective of the firm's organizational capabilities see: Amit and Schoemaker, 1993; Bartlett and Ghoshal, 1993; Black and Boal, 1994; Burgers, Hill and Kim, 1993; Das, Zahra and Warkentin, 1991; Davidow and Malone, 1992; Doz and Prahalad, 1991; Egelhoff, 1991; Galbraith, 1994; Garud and Nayyar, 1994; Hamel and Prahalad, 1996; Henderson and Clark, 1990; Keen, 1988; Lee and Leifer, 1992; Prahalad and Hamel, 1990; Rockart and Short, 1991; Teece, Pisano and Shuen, 1992; Wilson, 1993.

[4]Hambrick (1982), observed that competitors differ not only in the amount of information that they have from their competitive environment, but even if they have the same information, they differ in their ability to perceive its implications or form a response.

[5]Uncertainty is defined in organizational theory as the lack of information and the inability to predict outcomes or determine the impact of outcomes on the firm's operations (Tushman and Nadler, 1978; Daft, 1986; Daft and Lengel, 1986; Daft et al., 1988). Environmental uncertainty is caused largely by dynamic forces (Mintzberg, 1979; Miller and Friesen, 1982). Environmental complexity refers to a large number of constraints that require the firm to act with sophisticated information (Mintzberg, 1979, 1983). Complexity is also associated with interdependencies between processes or organizations (Lawless and Finch, 1989; Tan and Litschert, 1994), and with the size and systemic nature of the firm (Chandler, 1962, 1977, 1990; Ghoshal and Nohria, 1989; Hagström, 1991). Interdependencies can arise between the firm and other organizations, or between the firm and other environmental factors such as governmental regulations or socioeconomic factors.

[6]Swanson (1994) established a typology of information system innovations. Innovations realized within the technical system alone have negligible strategic impact. Those enacted in administrative process are of greater importance because they also influence system design. Innovations that are part of business processes such as manufacturing or distribution have a more significant impact because they create a feedback effect on administrative processes. Innovations associated with the end products and services of the firm have the widest range of influence in the organization because they affect the business, administrative, and information systems of the firm, as well as the firm's direct interface with the customer.

Clark (1987) assesses the impact of innovation according to its "transilience" which he defines as "the capacity of an innovation to influence the firm's existing resources, skills, and knowledge." (Clark, 1987: 61). Clark's transilience framework describes how various types of innovation affect two distinct domains of the firm: the technological or production capabilities of the firm, and the customer or market domain of the firm.

[7] Coordination results in increased throughput and utilization of the firm's resources by controlling the interdependencies created internally in the firm between its tasks, as well as external interdependencies between the firm and its distributors, suppliers, and buyers. (Chandler, 1962, 1977). Traditional coordination mechanisms are defined as rules, regulations, programs, goal setting and planning, vertical (formal) information systems, lateral relations, special reports, direct contact between individuals, integrators, liaison roles, task forces, teams, group meetings, and matrix designs (Egelhoff, 1982, 1991; Galbraith, 1977; Galbraith and Nathanson, 1978; Tushman and Nadler, 1978). Advanced coordination techniques have been shown to be useful in controlling complex interdependent processes (Chandler, 1962, 1977, 1990; Bakos, 1991; Malone, Yates, and Benjamin, 1994). Firms have traditionally dealt with complexity by decentralizing the organization to reduce the amount of information required of each task, and then coordinating the interdependent tasks conducted by the separate entities using formal and informal communication techniques and organizing structures (Lawrence and Lorsch, 1967; Galbraith and Nathanson, 1978; Mintzberg, 1979; Gupta and Govindarajan, 1991). Middle managers have traditionally played a major coordinating role for the firm, serving as the integrating mechanism between decentralized yet interdependent firm operations. The outcome of a firm's coordination ability is exhibited by its efficiency, growth in scale of operations, and growth in its geographic and market scope (Chandler, 1962, 1977, 1990; Kambil and Short, 1994).

[8]Some authors refer to task-related interdependencies as contributing to internal organizational uncertainty. Rather than to confuse internal versus external uncertainty, these internal interdependencies are considered to contribute to the complexity which the firm must coordinate, since their sources and dynamics are readily predictable within the firm.

Part II
Conceptual Approaches to Measuring Information Technology Investment Payoff

Introduction to Part II

Mo Adam Mahmood, University of Texas at El Paso
Edward J. Szewczak, Canisius College

This section contains papers which are concerned with offering various conceptual approaches to measuring IT investment payoff. These approaches may be classified as mathematical/formal, metamodel, rational–economic, activity versus function-based, strategic, value-based, and hybrid.

The paper by H. Joseph Wen and Cheickna Sylla picks up where the Wehrs paper leaves off by proposing a new evaluation and selection approach for IT investment that combines an integer goal linear programming approach and the analytical hierarchy process in a single multi-objective multi-criteria decision model. Though highly mathematical and formal in nature, the new procedure has three considerations in mind: a) both tangible and intangible benefits should be evaluated for all types of IT investment; b) the assessment of risk is important and required in the IT evaluation process; and c) intangible benefits and risks should be evaluated prior to tangible benefits and risks. By incorporating the analytic hierarchy process that quantifies subjective intangible benefits and risk factors into the procedure, the authors hope to mimic human decision making in a realistic fashion by accounting for human priorities and preferences.

The chapter by Marvin Trout, Arun Rai, Suresh Tadisina and Aimao Zhang can also be characterized as highly mathematical and formal. It discusses the formulation and use of efficiency ratio models (similar to data envelopment analysis models) which represent true ratio productivity measures. These models estimate the weights of inputs (such as operating budgets, capital expenditures, and staff size) and outputs (such as new system completions, number of lines of code implemented, and client evaluations). The efficiency measures can in turn be related to organizational performance measures using regression analysis. This approach, it is argued, is an important addition to previous efficiency analyses for IT because it has the capability for advising how IT operational and capital expenditures appear to be amortized over future time periods. This is important since these expenditures is expected to have carry forward effects on output measures. The approach can, therefore, be used by an information systems department to demonstrate high efficiency in its use of past investments and to increase confidence in higher management in both the existing level of investments and any proposed increases. Information Systems managers can also use results of the mathematical analysis to press for strategic directions of change.

The use of a contingency model to justify telecommunications investment is the subject of the chapter by Kathleen Molnar and Ramesh Sharda. Their proposed model provides a framework that is similar to a model which is already familiar to telecommunications professionals, i.e., the Open Systems Interconnection (OSI) model developed by the International Standards Organization. Molnar and Sharda put forth a 7-level Outcome-based Systems Investment model which may serve as a "metamodel" to identify the value added as well as the costs as justification criteria for the tangible and intangible benefits of a proposed telecommunications investment. It incorporates overlapping economic theory from three areas: information economics, organizational performance, and industrial organization. The authors point out that the model is not a new methodology so much as it is a new way of looking at existing methodologies and applying them to different aspects (levels) of the telecommunications investment decision. In spite of the fact that the Molnar and Sharda model is not empirically validated, the flexibility and completeness of the model can help a firm achieve a better understanding of the benefits and costs of technology and of how a proposed telecommunications investment fits into an overall corporate strategy.

Rick Gibson uses a rational, economic approach to measuring software process improvement payoff. The model he uses is the capability maturity model (CMM) developed by the Software Engineering Institute at Carnegie Mellon University. The CMM is intended as a common sense application of process management and quality improvement concepts to software development and maintenance. Its guiding principle is that the quality of a software product is directly related to the quality of the process used to produce it. To consistently improve software products the process used for developing them should, therefore, be understood, defined, measured, and improved. As a software process grows from ad hoc to one under statistical control, productivity increases and rate of failure decreases. Using the CMM as a model, a variety of improvement performance constructs have been operationalized and quantifiably measured by companies such as Hewlett-Packard, Motorola, Schlumberger, and Texas Instruments, and by the U.S. Department of Defense and the National Aeronautics and Space Administration. The author presents this data to establish an argument for adopting the CMM model to guide IT investment decisions.

The issue of evaluating an IT investment's costs and benefits is approached by Erik Rolland and Roy Maghroori by considering the role of four general leadership strategies for implementation. These strategies are status quo strategies, total quality management strategies, reengineering strategies, and vision institutionalization strategies. Since the IT leadership role is very often multifaceted, the authors argue that different business strategies are needed for different business processes. Each of the four strategies are associated with various categories of costs and benefits, which may vary according to the circumstances associated with the implementation of the strategy. IT implementation costs generally fall into human resource, equipment, capital investment, and productivity categories. IT implementation benefits relate to productivity, costs, quality, production cycle, and information availability. As a simple example, status quo strategies rate low on all cost categories, while vision institutionalization strategies rate high on all cost categories. The same may be generally said about the benefits of the two strategies. The authors believe that their approach can detect ill aligned goals and processes and help to determine which strategies and investments are needed to bring IS processes into alignment with corporate goals.

Murugan Anandarajan and Asokan Anandarajan propose an activity based approach to determining the cost of an IT investment, focusing specifically on cost determination of client server systems. Activity based approaches have been applied to determining costs in hospitals and banks but have yet to be used to cost computerized applications. The authors argue that traditional costing methods have proven ineffective in analyzing and reporting information system costs because of an overemphasis on function and not on detailed activities. Conventional costing categorizes costs as direct material, direct labor, and overhead based on the assumption that there is a direct causal relationship between output and costs incurred. However, by failing to account for various hidden costs (such as costs incurred during planning, design, and prototyping), the accurate determination of information system project total cost is inhibited. By focusing on activities rather than broad functions, the authors argue that managers will get a micro-level view of what is happening at each phase of the system development life cycle, and hence be able to conduct more effective cost-benefit analysis of potential IT investment projects.

Emphasis on intangible factors in the evaluation of IT investments should be a part of any complete cost-benefit analysis. Ram Kumar cites the need to look beyond cost savings in evaluating IT benefits. Such benefits as improved customer service, improved product quality, and better flexibility are often the result of IT investments but are hard to quantify in a convincing fashion. Kumar focuses on the idea of organizational flexibility as one way of understanding the business value of IT. He operationalizes the concept of flexibility using the ideas of stimulus, response, and ease of response (time, cost, scope). When combined with Michael Porter's value chain model, where each part of the value chain is thought of as consisting of multiple processes, it is argued that areas may be identified where flexibility may add value to organizations. Examples of IT-driven organizational flexibility are presented in distinct areas of the value chain (logistics, operations, marketing, and sales) as well as across different areas of the value chain. Among the advantages of this approach is that organizational flexibility may be viewed as a source of competitive advantage and that IS investments can add significant business value by enhancing organizational flexibility.

Kurt Engemann and Holmes Miller provide a methodology for managing the risks of IT investment which involves a number of possible approaches. They focus on two categories of IT risk: disaster recovery and information security. The methodology involves three phases. The first phase (Assesment) of the methodology identifies targets, threats, control alternatives, and relevant costs and losses for these alternatives. The second phase (Estimation) determines specific estimates of costs, losses, and probabilities relevant for analysis. The third phase (Evaluation) conducts detailed analyses and evaluations to select the best alternatives. The third phase may involve different primarily quantitative approaches depending on the problem at hand. Cost-benefit analysis and decision analysis are appropriate for situations involving decision making under risk, assuming the probabilities of events can be accurately estimated. Where these probabilities can not be associated with events, use of ordered weighted averaging operators can be used in the selection of an optimal alternative in the face of uncertainty. In any event, the attitude of the decision maker must be taken into account when using these approaches. Besides being risk averse or risk seeking, the decision maker may also be optimistic or pessimistic. Decision makers do not always behave "rationally," i.e., on the criteria of optimizing expected value. Engemann and Miller discuss a hybrid approach which provides the flexibility of modifying event probabilities to reflect a decision maker's degree of optimism. Finally, an approach using "the weighted medium" may be useful in situations where the payoffs for IT risks are nonnumeric, i.e., situations where ordered objects (not numbers) are combined.

Being conceptual in nature, the various models present prescriptive (as opposed to descriptive) approaches. In Part III, various approaches are discussed in the context of case studies which provide empirical support for approaches used in actual business practice.

Chapter 8

A Road Map for the Evaluation of Information Technology Investment

H. Joseph Wen
Cheickna Sylla
New Jersey Institute of Technology

The decision to acquire a new information technology poses a number of serious evaluation and selection problems to managers, because the new system must not only meet current information needs of the organization, but also the need for future expansion. This chapter describes many strategic implications involved in the selection decision, and the inherent difficulties in: (1) choosing or developing a model, (2) obtaining realistic inputs for the model, and (3) making tradeoffs among the conflicting factors. Tangible and intangible benefits factors as well as risks factors must be identified and evaluated. The chapter provides a review of ten major evaluation categories, and available models which fall under each category, showing their advantages and disadvantages in handling the above difficulties. This chapter offers the following two main contributions. It proposes a road map to guide the decision maker in choosing the most appropriate methodology in his/her evaluation process. The chapter also offers a new evaluation and selection procedure combining Integer Goal Linear Programming and AHP in a single hybrid MOMC model. A Goal Programming methodology with zero–one integer variables and mixed integer constraints is used to set goal target values against which IT alternatives under consideration are evaluated and selected. AHP is used to structure the evaluation process clearly providing pairwise comparison mechanisms to quantify subjec-

tive (non-monetary) intangible benefits and risks factors, and a proce-
dure to verify the decisionmaker's consistency in providing data to the
model.

Information technology is becoming the primary factor to the survival of most organizations. As a result, the fields of manufacturing, business services, and their supporting information systems are experiencing significant contemporary trends. These trends include, but are not limited to, the tremendous advances in computer hardware and software, and the prodigious advances the globalization of information networks. With these advances, information technology (IT) has grown from being a means of automating data processing to being the critical infrastructure for doing business today. According to Ian (1989), firms spend between 1.5% and 3% of their revenue on information technology. By 1986, more than half a trillion dollars had already been spent on information systems (*Business Week,* 1986); and roughly one third of the annual capital investment by US corporations is in IT (Bryan, 1990). The growth rate of information technology expenditures has been and continues to be extremely rapid. Clearly, IT more than any other technology is judged to be the most critical success factor of a business organization in today's global competitive market. Yet, many CEOs are doubtful if they are getting reasonable values on their investment in IT. (Maximizing values from this large and growing investment in IT is a major concern of CEOs.) Much like the CEOs, researchers as well as educators wish to be able to measure the economic viability or contribution of IT related investment projects as one would do for other business projects.

However, measuring the value-add due to IT investment, such as market opportunity, better decisionmaking, management of the organization's boundaries, management and development of people, and competitive advantage, is difficult. This is because most of IT benefits are qualitative, indirect, and diffuse. For instance, a decision support system (DSS) may improve managers' decisionmaking capability, but it is difficult to predict the extent to which the DSS will actually lead to better decisions, and even if it does have the desired effect. Putting any kind of value on the better decision in itself may present a new range of problems. In addition, many of the impacts that IT creates are "ripple effects" inside and outside an organization, which makes the IT investment evaluation process even more complex.

IT has been used in many ways to achieve a wide range of different objectives. The different types of systems and the wide range of objectives suggest that we may need a wide range of evaluation methods, some suitable for evaluating one type of system and some suitable for other types. However, in the real world there are very few pure cases. For instance, most of decision support systems have database components that are part of other transaction processing systems. On the other hand, a well-designed transaction processing system, e.g., American Airlines' reservation system, can improve productivity, provide competitive advantage and many other intangible benefits.

This chapter (1) examines existing analysis methodologies, (2) proposes an evaluation process, and (3) offers a new applicable method based on management science, information science, economics, and psychology to evaluate returns of IT investments. The remaining sections of this chapter are organized as follows. Section 2 discusses the IT investment benefits and risks involved in IT evaluation. Section 3 reviews IT investment evaluation methods and discusses the strength and weakness of each of the available methods. Section 4 describes the proposed evaluation process and maps the process to the methods discussed in the previous sections. This is followed by a description of the proposed new evaluation method in Section 5. The last section of the chapter concludes with a summary and possible avenues for future research.

Information Technology Benefits and Risks

According to Kauffman and Weill (1989), the best IT investments are those which help to maximize the value of the firm. They also contend that to maximize the value of the firm, IT investment decisions need to be able to maximize IT benefits while minimize IT risks. There are three reasons why knowing IT benefits and risks is important. First, some IT benefits are lost through inappropriate management, while some are lost because they are not recognized by the management in the early IT planning stage. Second, it is important to identify the benefits to be measured prior to selecting applicable evaluation methods. This is because some methods are suitable for evaluating tangible benefits while others are more suitable for intangible benefits. Finally, the recognition of risk as an important component in IT investment decision making has long been recognized (McFarlan, 1981). IT investment must recognize that the future is uncertain, thus any evaluation method must recognize this fact in order to lead to correct decisions and recommendations.

Information Technology Benefits

In general, the benefits of IT investments can be classified into four broad classes, the purpose of which is to (1) decrease effort and operating process performance; (2) facilitate management support; (3) gain competitive advantage; and (4) provide a good framework for business restructure or transformation. The following sections briefly define these four broad classes.

Effort and Operating Process Performance. If IT is used to substitute for human effort and automate tasks and business processes, the major benefits are likely to be an increase in system effectiveness and efficiency. Possible benefits include cycle time reductions, headcount reductions, reduction in communication time and related printing costs, increased income from product/service quality improvements, timeliness and accessibility of data, activity-based cost improvements, operating process improvements relative to industrial benchmarks, transformation of data into information, distribution of information, transforming information into desired outcomes, and growth without corresponding increase in overheads (Applegate, 1996; Farbey, Land, and Targett, 1993).

Management Support. If IT investment is to facilitate new ways of managing, the benefits can be summed up as management support. The benefits include, for example, decreased time to decision, improvement in decision time and quality, improved communications, standardization, respond quickly to changes in the law, better control, increased flexibility, compatibility with customer's systems, more effective use of the sales force, and improvement of the quality of working life. Published books by Applegate (1996), Farbey, Land, and Targett (1993) discussed IT investment issues based on management support.

Competitive Advantage. If IT is being exploited for competitive advantage, the ultimate goal is to cause competitive inequality. Here, the benefits of IT investment include improved operating margins relative to competitors, increased market share, differentiation in new products and services, creation of unique product features, buyer and supplier power, switching costs and search-related costs, customer and supplier switching costs, preemptive strikes, first mover effects, positional advantages and timing, integration with company strategy, and leverage of a firm's intrinsic strength. See Seth and King (1994).

Business Transformation. If IT is being used to restructure or transform the tasks, operations and procedures involved in the business processes, the investment characteristics can be summed up under the label 'business process reengineering (BPR).' The benefits of this type of IT investment include, for example, allowing business process redesign, assisting business network redesign, facilitating flatter organizational structure, changing the symbols and the image of the organization, and altering the organization's boundaries to allow new forms of cooperation such as teams and work groups without geographic restrictions. Thus, emphasis on increasing the firm internal as well as external efficiency. The reader is asked to refer to Farbey, Land, and Targett (1993) for more coverage on this topics.

Information Technology Risks

IT has provided many benefits to corporations over the years. Presently, we are living in a global information society with a global economy which is increasingly dependent on the creation, management and distribution of information resources. However, investments in information technology are subject to higher risks than any other capital investments for several reasons. First, their components are comparatively fragile in terms of machine breakdown, hard disk crash, and ability to survive in a disaster. Second, information systems are likely to be the target of disgruntled workers, protester, and even criminals. They can also fall in the hands of the competitors. Finally, the decentralization of information systems and the use of distributed processing have increased the difficulty of design, development, management, and protecting information systems.

We classify IT risks into two general classes: (1) physical risks; and (2) managerial risks. Each of these classes is described briefly below.

Physical Risks. Physical risks include the vulnerability of computer hardware, software, and data. Hardware is the most visible part of information systems. Because of its accessibility, hardware can be subject to theft, sabotage and other crimes against the owners. Software related crimes occur in three ways: piracy, deletion, and alteration of software. Both hardware and software are also subject to the threats of natural disasters, malfunctions, and obsolescence. The possible loss of valuable data is another major physical risk faced by information systems. Reconstructing lost data can be very costly and time-consuming. An actual exposure of lost data can leak important inside information to competitors.

Managerial Risk. Some IT investments failed because the managerial risks in systems design, development, and implementation that involve both general management and information systems management. The managerial risks include (McFarlan, 1981): (1) failure to obtain the anticipated benefits; (2) costs of implementation that vastly exceed planned levels; (3) time for implementation that is much greater than expected; (4) unexpected end-user resistance or lack of interest in the system; (5) performance of resulting systems that is unable to support mission-critical tasks; and (6) incompatibility of the system with the later development of the mainstream IT.

Review of IT Investment Evaluation Methods

A review of the current literature offers several representative IT investment evaluation methods which should be of interest both to practitioners and researchers. Most IT evaluation methods for tangible benefits are designed to compare costs of investment alternatives or attempt to provide procedures for the quantification of benefits and risks. Such methods tend to rely on the help of technical personnel to provide management with accounting data for evaluation. While methods for intangible benefits put emphasis on the process of obtaining agreement on objectives through a process of exploration and mutual learning. Such methods tend to rely on a thorough understanding of the opportunities and the threats of failure of the IT investment.

IT Evaluation Methods for Tangible Benefits

The major categories for tangible benefits include: (1) return on investment, (2) cost-benefit analysis, (3) return on management, and (4) information economics.

Return On Investment (ROI). ROI methods have been widely discussed as possible evaluation procedures for IT investment. Recent coverage in the literature include works by Farbey, Land, and Targett (1993), Au and Au (1992), Horngren and Sundem (1987), and Radcliffe (1982). The rate of ROI is defined as the profit or return divided by the investment required to help obtain the profit or return of a firm. ROI methods are supported by a number of formal capital investment appraisal techniques (see Farbey, Land and Targett, 1993). The best known are those based on evaluating the current value of estimated future cash flows on the assumption that future benefits are subject to a chosen discount factor. The basic assumption of ROI methods is that an investment today should yield a positive return in the future. Thus, time value functions are used extensively to provide an analytical framework.

There are three commonly used ROI methods, net present value (NPV), discounted cash flow (DCF), and payback period. NPV and DCF calculations base their discount rate on an interest rate regarded as appropriate by the financial managers of the organization, while payback period method does not require an assumption of fixed interest rates. Methods based on payback simply requires an IT project to repay its investment over a prescribed period. Using the above methods, various investment alternatives can be evaluated using several possible interest rates. In general, all ROI methods require the estimation of cash flow rates. Trial and error evaluations can be used for different interest rates based on data which satisfy accounting criteria and which are legitimized by appearing in financial statements. Clearly, ROI methods do not include intangible benefits in the evaluation process. These methods favor using benefits which are directly attributable, often, but not necessarily, in the form of direct cost savings.

Methods based on ROI are generally regarded as more theoretically correct and practically feasible approaches to capital investment appraisal. Such methods are also commonly accepted in many organizations as the standard ways for capital investment projects selection. Generally such methods compare the returns from a range of IT investment alternatives, and select the ones which provide the best returns. The key assumption is that the expected outcomes of the investment can be calculated. Thus, ROI should be the natural choice for a company committed to rigorous financial disciplines and expecting directly measurable savings from their IT investments.

ROI methods, however, are unable to capture many of intangible benefits that IT brings to the organization. Often, surrogate measures are used under various assumptions in order to have input which fit the models. Clearly, ROI methods are designed to measure the "hard," quantitative, monetary impacts of capital investment, but in reality IT, in many instances, deliver benefits that are predominately "soft." For example, how can one puts a dollar figure on "better control," "more effective use of the sales force," and or "improvement in the quality of working life in the work environment or to customer?" Indeed, most of IT investments today would not be qualified as satisfactory if they are evaluated based on most ROI methods.

Cost-benefit Analysis (CBA). Cost-benefit analysis tries to overcome the problem of ROI by finding some surrogate measure for intangible costs or benefits which can be expressed in monetary terms (King and Schrems, 1978; Emery, 1973). For example, if one of the objectives of introducing an IT is to increase the customer satisfaction, the benefit may be expressed in terms of the saving in the cost of returned products and reducing the number of customer complains. The approach attempts to deal with two problems namely: (1) the difficulty of quantifying the value of benefits that do not directly accrue to the investor in the project, (2) the difficulty of identifying the benefits or costs which do not have an obvious market value or price (i.e., intangible factors). Therefore, CBA method is useful where the costs and benefits are intangible, but the method requires the existence of abroad agreement on the measures used to attach a value to the intangibles. On the other hand, if there is broad disagreement on the appropriate form of surrogate input values, other methods should be considered (see for example Farbey, Land, and Targett, 1993).

Return on Management (ROM). Strassmann (1985) argues that IT serves primarily to help the management do its job. Therefore, he introduced a concept of value-added productivity measurement system as an approach to identify the impact of information technology on business unit performance. In his approach, all measures of productivity use the simple ratio of "output/input." Thus, the main problem is how to define the output of management. Strassmann defines the output of management as management's "value-added," which is simply everything left after subtracting all the direct operating costs from the value-added due to direct labor. Strassmann proposes an index of the total performance of management due to the introduction of IT. This index is obtained by dividing the management value-added by the costs of management. Strassmann argues that this index has none of the undesirable attributes of ROI methods, since it does not get weighed by the imprecision of asset accounting. Instead, it focuses on the most important impact of information technology, i.e., on the value-added by management generated by the IT in excess of management's total costs.

The advantage of the ROM methods is that they concentrate on the contributions of IT to the management process. The disadvantage is that the residual assigned as the value added by management cannot be directly attributed to the management process. The methods may well be best used as a complement some of the most classical methods, in particular for *ex post* evaluations.

Information Economics (IE). Information Economics is a variant of cost-benefit analysis, tailored to cope with the particular intangibles and uncertainties found in information systems projects (Parker and Benson, 1987). It retains ROI calculations for those benefits and costs which can be directly ascertained through a conventional cost-benefit process. However, the decision making process used in IE methodologies is based on a ranking and scoring technique of intangibles and risks factors associated with the IT investment. It identifies IT performance measures and use them to rank the economic impact of all the changes on the organization's performance caused by the introduction of the IT. Here also, surrogate measures are often used for most intangible and risks factors which are hard to estimate.

The strength of the IE methods is that it links the quantification and comparison approaches with qualification approaches. The limitation of IE, however, is that it does not deal with the mechanism but only with its outcomes (Ahituv, 1989). Another limitation is the focus on simple, idealized settings that can be modeled with applicable mathematical models, often requiring many simplifying assumptions. Clearly, real-world information systems involve complex relationships, variables and parameters; even when rigorous models can be formulated they cannot be solved analytically (Bakos and Kemerer, 1992).

IT Evaluation Methods for Intangible Benefits

Multi-objective, Multi-criteria (MOMC). This method attempts to develop a general measure of utility where utility is defined as the satisfaction of an individual's preferences. The method is based on the belief that people's behavior is determined to some extent by their feeling that their preferences are recognized. People appraise the relative usefulness of different desired outcomes in terms of their preferences and they rank goals by applying a preference weight to each goal. Where there are many stakeholders, the best IT investment is that which will deliver the highest aggregate utility or which provides the highest overall measure of satisfied preferences Models based on MOMC methods have been developed by Kenny and Raiffa, 1976; Land, 1976; Vaid-Raizda, 1983; Chandler, 1982 and other researchers.

The MOMC method is probably best applied to complex projects which attempt to meet the needs of many different users and where the benefits are intangible. The method is able to explore the value of a set of system proposals in terms of relative preferences for different system features. Also, consensus on the most desired system attributes is achieved by means of a thorough exploration of alternatives and preferences. However, the MOMC method does not provide any data for an ROI calculation which can be used to compare an investment justified by the use of a standard cost-benefit analysis. Development of MOMC-based methods are still in their infancy, but they have already generated a great deal of interests and discussions among researchers.

Value Analysis (VA). This method emphasizes value rather than cost. The method is based on the following three assumptions. (1) innovation is value driven and not cost driven; (2) intangibles can be identified and subjectively assessed but rarely measured accurately, as surrogate measures are often used to satisfy the requirement for most inputs; (3) an inevitable clash exists between the persons driven by cost and those driven by effectiveness. This method was developed and used by several researchers such as Keen, 1981; Melone and Wharton, 1984; Money, Tromp, and Wegner, 1988; Rivard and Kaiser, 1989.

The analysis begins with the observation that most successful innovations are based on enhancing value added rather than on cost savings. A multi-stage iterative process begins with a prototype system. Rather than developing extensive specifications, the analysis provides simple models that can be expanded and modified until all complex aspects of the problem are included. Users are asked to provide the analyst with feedback on the values and limitations of the solution obtained from the prototype. The main difference between other IT evaluation methods and VA is that the former methods directly aim at a final solution, while the latter uses an evolutionary process to get to a "satisficing solution" which may be further improved.

Advantages of VA include: (1) quick identification of user requirements to establish agreed values for outputs, which would normally be classed as intangible; (2) improved communication between analysts and users, which gives decision makers some assurance that the benefits can be realized by means of prototype demonstrations; (3) incremental evaluation of benefits and costs, which enables management to continue the evaluation process or stop at any time; (4) an evolutionary approach, which results in user-tailored systems; and (5) providing greater user satisfaction than traditionally developed systems. However, the method has several disadvantages: (1) establishing the required surrogate values and developing a prototype can be a long and costly process; (2) the method's lack of an initial estimate of final costs and benefits, which may commit management to unexpected future expenditures; (3) without target estimates for "final solution values", existing program revisions can be significant.

Critical Success Factors (CSF). This method is used to explore the potential value of information systems. The approach is based on early works by (Rockart, 1979) who proposes the concept of the "success factors." It invites the analyst to explore with executives the factors, which are in their opinion, critical to the success of the business in particular, the factors that are important for the functions or activities for which the executives are responsible. Issues can be ranked by the executives into levels of importance.

The implementation of methods based on CSF involves comprehensive interviews of key managers to obtain their views about business mission, objectives, and current problems. After the interviews, the managers' opinions are cross-tabulated, compared, and ranked. From a group discussion about the divergence of opinions an agreement about systems investment priorities is expected to emerge.

The advantage of the method is that it provides a focus on the issues which are regarded as important by the respondents. It also heavily relies on prototyping and pilot installations before proceeding. In this regard, the technique takes advantage of lessons from the disciplines of organizational learning, adaptive planning, and personal development. The CSF method may be considered to provide the right antidote against some of the worst excesses for conceiving accurate, but meaningless, payback numbers obtained from accounting-oriented cost-benefit analysis.

IT Evaluation Methods for Risks

Real Option (RO). Although the DCF and NPV methods appear to cope with IT risks by the choice of discount rate (Brookfield, 1995; Dixit and Pindyck, 1994; Myers, 1977). However, in practice the methods can lead to erroneous conclusions in the face of uncertainty even when the apparent range of interest or the existence of certain types of risks are possible. Also, the method can lead to the possibility of unexpected outcomes (Brookfield, 1995). This is because NPV analysis ignores the time series interactions among contingent investments, and the possible consequences of delayed effects from the expected benefits and costs. In this sense, real option analysis recognizes the incremental value arising from flexibility. The fact that flexibility gives rise to additional value is a recognition of the altered probability distribution of potential outcomes and its impact on risk exposure. In other word, when a significant degree of uncertainty in outcomes for IT investments, the waiting game might produce substantial benefits.

The value of waiting is a reflection of the costs associated with an irreversible investment. That is, if there is an element of a sunk cost in an investment, then once the investment has been made the sunk cost is incurred. If an investor is making investment decisions on the basis of NPV, then it is almost certain that miscalculations will be made if embedded options are not recognized. In this context, the identification of real options helps to explain the value of flexibility by demonstrating that managers are not miscalculating investment outcomes and are acting rationally.

The method uses three basic types of data: (1) current and possible future business strategies; (2) the desired system capabilities sought by the company, and (3) the relative risks and costs of other information technologies choice that could be used. The method can help assess the risks associated with IT investment decisions, taking into account that business strategies and system requirements may change.

Portfolio Approach (PA). Portfolio approach focuses on three important dimensions that influence the risk inherent in an IT investment (McFarlan, 1981). These include:

- Sizes of the projects and workload to be handled by the system. Note that the larger the dollar expense in the projects, the larger the workload, levels of staffing, the amount of time, and the larger the number of departments affected by the IT, the greater the risk.
- Experience of management with the technology. Because of the greater likelihood of unexpected technical problems, IT risk increases as familiarity of the system team with the hardware, operating systems, database handler, and project application language decrease.
- Capability in handling complex highly structured project. The highly structured projects usually carry less risk than projects which are less structured, their outputs are more subject to the manager's judgment and hence are vulnerable to change.

The portfolio approach suggests that a company not only assesses relative risk for a single IT project, but also develop an aggregate risk profile of the IT investment. For instance, in an industry where computers are an important part of product structure, managers should be concerned when there are no high-risk projects. In such a case, the company may be leaving a product or service gap which may present an opportunity for the competition to step in. On the other hand, a portfolio loaded with high-risk projects suggests that the company may be vulnerable to operational disruptions when projects are not completed as planned.

Delphi Approach (DA). The Delphi approach is a technique in which several experts provide individual estimates of the likelihood of future events associated with the decision situation. The estimates are collected and distributed to all experts. All experts are then asked if they wish to modify their initial ratings based on inputs from other experts. After all inputs are collected, final individual values are evaluated and summarized. If the results are reasonably consistent, final overall values are assessed for all. If any inconsistency is detected, the experts will be asked to discuss the instances of inconsistencies and attempt to reach a compromise on the final value. This and other final values will be adopted and used to compute the risks associated with the investment. This approach is particularly useful for the risk analysis of a new IT investment where the risks

Evaluation category	Model/procedure examples	Measures of IT benefits factors	Measures of IT risks	Major advantages	Major limitations
ROI	NPV, DCF, Pay-back period formulas	tangible	discount rates, surrogate measures	mainly quantitative focus on efficiency	no intangible, reliance on accounting data
CBA	cost/benefits formulas	tangible factors	same as ROI	mainly quantitative focus on effectiveness	surrogate measures for intangible factors
ROM	productivity based formulas	tangible, labor value-added as intangible	not addressed	mostly qualitative measures of efficiency	limited quantitative measures, assumptions hard to meet
IE	same as ROI supplemented with ranking and scoring	tangible and some intangible	surrogate measures, risks with ranking and scoring	qualitative and quantitative measures	major simplifying assumptions and models
MOMC	math models and multistage iterative processes	tangible and intangible	several measures of utility and risks	mainly quantitative, multiple and conflicting objectives	relatively new in MIS, still in development
VA	multistage, evolutionary process	tangible factors	not addressed	tangible factors	prototyping, need several revisions to final results
CSF	multistage, evolutionary process	user's surrogate measures	user's surrogate measures	intangible factors, centered on effectiveness	highly qualitative process
RO	multistage process	tangible and intangible factors	surrogate measures for risks and costs	many intangible, centered on effectiveness	highly subjective and qualitative
PA	Financial models	measures for cost savings	direct measures of risks	higher efficiency	mainly quantitative
Delphi Approach	multistage, evolutionary process	user's surrogate measures	user's surrogate measures	tangible and intangible factors	highly qualitative
Goal AHP	math models, iterative process	tangible and intangible	direct risks, user's surrogate measures	higher effectiveness	relatively new procedure

Table 1: Major Methodologies Used for Evaluating IT

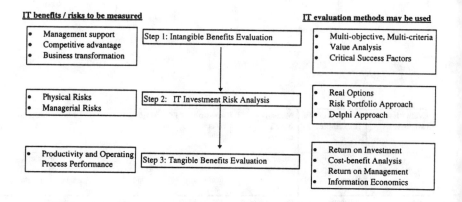

Figure 1: A Road Map for the Evaluation of IT Investment

involved in the investment may be primarily unknown or unfamiliar to managers.

A Road Map for the Evaluation of IT Investment

Previous discussions have provided the information which make it possible to decide which evaluation method is suitable for a particular IT investment (summarized in Table 1).

A road map for the evaluation of IT investment, as shown in Figure 1, is based on the following three major considerations. (1) The process suggests that the evaluation of both tangible and intangible benefits should be carried out for all types of IT investments. Although each type of IT investment may require a different evaluation emphasis (e.g., quantitative versus qualitative, and tangible versus intangible) most IT investments involve both quantitative and qualitative benefits to a certain degree. (2) The process also urges that assessing the risk of IT investments is important and required in the IT evaluation process to ensure that the benefits are greater enough to offset the risks. Most evaluation methods assume wrongly that appropriate human skills and controls that will ensure success, but this is not true involved with the investment. (3) The process recommends that the intangible benefits and risks should be evaluated prior to tangible benefits. This is because research in cognitive psychology suggests that an individual confronted with a simultaneous consideration of both qualitative and quantitative factors tends to assign greater salience to concrete factors at the detriment of more abstract criteria (Simon, 1965; Slovic, 1972; Hogarth, 1980). The proposed process, therefore, suggests that decision makers perform an assessment of intangible benefits prior to tangible benefits. To use the map, one first recognizes the benefits and risks to be measured on the left and then selects an appropriate evaluation method on the right.

The Proposed Hybrid MOMC Model

Developing Subjective Inputs with AHP

The evaluation procedures examined in the preceding sections are mainly geared toward establishing the economic merit of an IT investment. Thus, they are intended to evaluate if the benefits of an IT investment outweigh its costs and risks. Although all of the methods discussed above are not designed to compare two or more IT investment alternatives, they can be used for such an objective. However, such comparisons cannot be done directly. Furthermore, most of the above methods do not explicitly incorporate intangible and risks factors in the evaluation process. As seen in the summary table, most methods require that the users provide surrogate measures to estimate the intangible and risk factors. In this section, a hybrid model is used to include both objective and subjective measures of the benefits and risk factors involved in an IT investment. This model combines an integer goal programming approach and the Analytic Hierarchy Process (AHP) approach and is hereby referred to as Goal with AHP (GAHP). The GAHP is a structural decision model which allows decision makers to identify all the tangible, intangible and risk factors involved in the IT investment situation. All these factors are organized in a hierarchical structure and quantified through the AHP.

GAHP allows the decision maker to establish priority levels for the objective criteria, and to assign weights to the subjective criteria using AHP according to his estimates of their relative importance in investment decision. The criteria can be ranked into priority levels according to the decision maker preference. The purpose of establishing priority levels and weights is to thoroughly incorporate the decision maker's preference in terms of goal targets and relative values for the benefits and risks associated with the IT investment. An aspiration level is a specific value associated with the desirable or acceptable level of achievement of an objective. The evaluation and selection process done in GAHP uses: (1) an integer linear goal programming model which uses all the decision variables and associated constraints to select the most appropriate IT from a set of candidates under consideration, and (2) AHP to determine values for the subjective criteria, and to mimic the human decisionmaking process incorporating a realistic and easy to understand mechanism to check for inconsistencies in dealing with difficult to estimate intangible and risk factors.

The integer linear goal programming model uses zero-one decision variables and does not require translating multiple and conflicting goals into a one dimensional objective criterion. The model is solved through a hierarchical optimization in which weights are implicitly assigned by creating preemptive priorities.

Formulating the Goal Programming Model

Decision Variables. Assume the purpose of the decision model is to identify an appropriate IT alternative of a particular business operations. Relevant decision variables are the candidates IT investments X_j and their associated slack variables are described below.

$X_j = 1$ if candidate IT j is accepted,
$X_j = 0$ otherwise, and
Y^+_i is the positive slack deviation from goal i (the amount of over achievement).
Y^-_i is the positive slack deviation from goal i (the amount of under-achievement).
m: is the number of alternative IT candidates under consideration.
n_1: the number of components in the general intangible benefits included in the evaluation,
A_{ij}: the evaluation value of general intangible benefit i in IT choice j (j = 1, 2, ..., n; i = 1, 2, ..., n_1)
GI_i: the target level (aspiration level) for the general intangible benefit i (i = 1, 2, ..., n_1)
n_2: the number of technological intangible benefits included in the evaluation,
B_{ij}: the amount of the technological intangible benefit i in IT choice j (j = 1, 2, ..., n; i = 1, 2, ..., n_2)
TI_i: the target level (aspiration level) for the technological intangible benefit i (i = 1, 2, ..., n_2)
n_3: the number of components in the tangible benefits included in the evaluation,
C_{ij}: the amount of the tangible benefit i in IT choice j (j = 1, 2, ..., n; i = 1, 2, ..., n_3)
TF_i: the target level (aspiration level) for the tangible benefit i (i = 1, 2, ..., n_3)
n_4: the number of the risk factors included in the evaluation,
D_{ij}: the amount of the risk factor i in IT choice j (j = 1, 2, ..., n; i = 1, 2, ..., n_4)
R_i: the target level (aspiration level) for the risk factor i (i = 1, 2, ..., n_4)

Note that the tangible factors are by definition measurable in quantitative units, however, in order to maintain parity among all tangible factors included in the evaluation, these quantitative values should be normalized to allow the tangible factors with greater desirable qualities to have a larger effect in the selection process. We can use the notation c_{ij} where

$$c_{ij} = \frac{C_{ij}}{\sum\limits_{j=1}^{n_3} C_{ij}}$$

is used to ensure that any tangible factor measured will be compatible with other tangible factors used in the evaluation. For instance, factors such as cost reductions, data storage capability and operating speed, number of added business procedures made possible with the new IT, etc. Note that the above c_{ij} formula may need to be altered to fit other IT evaluation goals under consideration.

The general goal of this selection problem is to choose the most appropriate *IT* candidate who closely meets the decisionmaker's aspiration level reflected in the right hand of equations (2) - (6). The objective function will minimize the deviation from the target levels (to be indicated by specific values for the terms seen in the right hand side). If for instance R_t reflect s a maximum amount of risk not to exceed, the objective function should minimize for the given risk factor *I.* If the goal is to maximize a certain tangible benefit such as throughput level indicated by TF_i, then objective function will focus on minimizing . The objective function should be formulated according to the decision maker's preference and a preemptive priority approach can be used to solve the model. The overall objective function can be written as:

$$\text{Min } [\sum_{i=1}^{n1}(PT_i{}^+YT_i{}^+PT_i{}^-YT_i{}^-), \ \sum_{i=1}^{n2}(PIT^+YIT^+ + PIT^-YIT^-), \ \sum_{i=1}^{n3}(PTI^+YTI^+ + YTI^-YTI_-),$$

$$\sum_{i-1}^{n4}(PR_i{}^+YR_i{}^+ + PR_i{}^-YR_i{}^-)] \tag{1}$$

Subject to:

Constraint reflecting that at most one IT alternative should be selected, which can be written as:

$$X_1 + X_2 + X_3 + \ \dots\dots \ + X_n - Y^+{}_i + Y^-{}_i = 1 \tag{2}$$

The general intangible benefits goal constraints are formulated as:

$$\sum_{j=1}^{n} A_{ij} X_j - YIT_i{}^+ + YIT_i{}^- = GT_i, \ \text{for i=1, 2, ..., } n_1 \tag{3}$$

The technological intangible goal constraints are formulated as:

$$\sum_{j=1}^{n} B_{ij} X_j - YIT_i{}^+ + YIT_i{}^- = TI_i, \ \text{for i=1, 2, ..., } n_2 \tag{4}$$

The tangible benefit goal constraints are formulated as:

$$\sum_{j=1}^{n} C_{ij}X_j - YT_i^+ + YT_i^- = TF_i, \quad \text{for } i=1, 2, ..., n_3 \tag{5}$$

The goal constraints for the risk factors are formulated as:

$$\sum_{j=1}^{n} D_{ij}X_j - YR_i^+ - YR_i^- = R_i, \quad \text{for } i=1, 2, ..., n_4 \tag{6}$$

$$X_j = \{0 \text{ or } 1\} \tag{7}$$

Where are the penalty weights PIT_i^+, PIT_i^-, PTI_i^+, PTI_i^-, PT_i^+, PT_i^-, PR_i^+, PR_i^- are associated with the priority of the given goals as desired by the decision maker. Note that the + (i.e., plus) terms indicate the positive components (i.e., amount of deviation above the target), while the - (i.e., minus) apply to the negative components. The decision variables X_i, and deviation variables Y_i^+, Y_i^-, YIT_i^+, YIT_i^-, YTI_i^+, YTI_i^-, YT_i^+, YT_i^-, YR_i^+, YR_i^-, are restricted to be non-negative. Their values are derived from the model solution.

The terms A_{ij}, B_{ij}, C_{ij}, and D_{ij} are derived from the analysis of the pairwise decision matrices associated with the tangible, general intangible, technological intangible, and risk factors using Analytical Hierarchical Process described below.

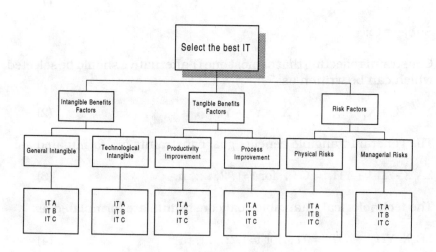

Figure 2: Hierarchy for the IT-Selection Process

Constructing the Analytical Hierarchy Process

The Analytical Hierarchical Process (Saaty, 1980) is a multicriteria evaluation methodology which incorporates a procedure to mimic human decision making and to verify consistency in the process. AHP consists of four major steps:

1. Modeling the decision problem by breaking it down into hierarchy of interrelated decision elements and alternatives. Here the main objective of the problem, i.e., the selection and evaluation problem, is broken down into hierarchy of interrelated criteria and subcriteria. As seen in Figure 2, the a hierarchy of IT evaluation and selection problem includes our three main criteria, namely, tangible, intangible and risk factors. Note that in our case, the tangible factors may be decomposed into productivity improvement and process improvement related benefits, which may be further decomposed. Similarly, the intangible factors may be decomposed into general intangibles and technological intangibles and related benefits. Finally, the risk factors may be decomposed into physical and managerial risks and related factors. All of these factors may be further decomposed as required by the decision maker.
2. Developing judgmental preferences (called preference matrices) of decision alternatives for each criterion and judgmental importance of the decision criteria by pairwise comparisons.
3. Computing relative priorities for each of the decision elements through a set of numerical calculations, called matrix normalization procedure.
4. Aggregating the relative priorities to arrive at a priority ranking of the decision alternatives, achieve by computing eigein vectors of the matrices. Note that this normalized principle vector of the pairwise matrix is the resulting evaluation (weight) of the corresponding IT alternative (factor).

Once the hierarchy has been constructed, the decision maker begins the prioritization procedure to determine the relative importance of the elements at each level. The elements at each level are compared pairwise with respect to their importance to other elements at the same level. Thus, a number of pairwise comparison matrices are created starting at the top of the hierarchy and working down to the lowest level. Note that in the process of creating these matrices, AHP allows the decision maker to express his preference between every two elements verbally as equally important (or preferred, or likely), moderately more important, strongly more important, very strongly important, or extremely more important. These descriptive preferences would then be translated into numerical ratings: 1, 3, 5, 7, and 9, respectively, with 2, 4, 6, and 8 as intermediate values for compromises between two successive qualitative judgments. That is, AHP uses a nine-point subjective "judgmental" rating scale seen described in Saaty (1980).

Since its initial development, AHP has been applied to a wide variety of decision problems involving evaluation and selection decisions, including those related to economic planning, energy policy, health, conflict resolution, project selection and budget allocation. For a comprehensive review, refer to Zahedi (1980).

The judgmental scale used in AHP enables the decision maker to incorporate experience and knowledge in an intuitive and natural way. This scale is insensitive to small changes in decision maker's references, thereby minimizing the effect of uncertainty in his evaluations. Furthermore, AHP allows the decision maker to verify and correctly adjust any inconsistency in his pairwise comparisons. Inconsistency can be calculated through a series of additional matrix manipulations (seen described in Saaty, 1980). The decision maker is able to change "preferences" and to test the outcome if the inconsistency level is high. There is a commercial software package, "Expert Choice," which performs the AHP analysis·in an interactive fashion. Results can be exported into an Excel Spreadsheet package for further calculations to solve the integer goal programming formulation of the selection problem.

Conclusions

The decision to acquire a new Information Technology poses a number of serious evaluation and selection problems to managers, because the new system must not only meet current information needs of the organization, but also the need for future expansion. This chapter describes many strategic implications involved in the selection decision, and the inherent difficulties in: (1) choosing or developing a model, (2) obtaining realistic inputs for the model, and (3) making tradeoffs among the conflicting factors. Tangible and intangible benefits factors as well as risks factors must be identified and evaluated. The chapter provides a review of ten major evaluation categories and the available models which fall under each showing their advantages and disadvantages in handling the above difficulties.

The chapter discusses the fact that intangible benefits cannot be directly measured in quantitative units, and shows a variety of qualitative measures applicable to intangible factors in the evaluation processes. There are two general approaches are proposed in the literature in dealing with intangible and risk factors. One approach uses various surrogate measures, while the other applies measures based on weighted sum. There is no unique methodology in deriving or using surrogate measures. The weighted sum techniques assign weights to the intangible benefit and risk factors on a ratio scale (Siha, 1993). For instance, in using the weighted sum approach, each candidate IT being evaluated is given a score with respect to each intangible benefit and risk factor using the 0-100 scale, and the assigned weights are then normalized by dividing each weight by the sum of total weights for the intangible and risks respectively. Each evaluation score is then weighted by multiplying the evaluation by the sum of the weights. The overall score for each IT alternative is determined by summing its weighted evaluation scores with respect to all the benefits and risk factors included in the evaluation process.

Sullivan (1986) offered a similar method in his "Linear Additive Model," to come with a ranking of alternative candidates being evaluated. Note that only a few models seen in Table 1 use similar evaluation procedures, in which the measures of intangible factors is obtained by multiplying the weights of the intangible factors by the user's subjective ratings. The main weakness with such procedures is that they omit a measure of inconsistency on the part of the decision maker in providing the inputs on the ratio scales. Clearly, inconsistencies can occur when the relative merits of the input values does not correctly reflect the decision maker's preference structure.

This chapter provides several enrichments to the evaluation of Information Technology. It offers: (1) a comprehensive review of the various methodologies available in the literature, (2) a structured summary table comparing the methodologies showing their advantages and disadvantages, and (3) the procedures used in handing tangible, intangible and risk factors. This chapter offers the following two main contributions. It proposes a road map to guide the decision maker in choosing the most appropriate methodology in his evaluation process. The chapter also offers a new evaluation and selection procedure combining Integer Goal Linear Programming and AHP in a single hybrid MOMC model. A Goal Programming methodology with zero-one integer variables and mixed integer constraints is used to set goal target values against which IT alternatives under consideration are evaluated and selected. AHP is used to structure the evaluation process clearly, providing pairwise comparison mechanisms to quantify subjective (non-monetary) intangible benefits and risks factors, and a procedure to verify decision maker's consistency in providing data to the model. The results derived from the AHP are used as inputs to the goal programming model and selection process. Clearly, IT evaluation is a complex problem and one should expect the decision maker to face a considerable opportunity to provide inconsistent inputs and make other mistakes. AHP process allows the decision maker to measure and incorporate checking for his inputs and rankings in the evaluation process. Thus, unlike the major ten categories discussed earlier and summarized in Table 1, the hybrid model proposed in this chapter allows the evaluation and selection process to mimic correctly the human decision making process. The hybrid method is based on two well-grounded multi-criteria modeling approaches which complement each other well in dealing with both objective data (i.e., tangible benefits) and subjective data (i.e., intangible benefits and risk factors). The authors are working on a computer code and numerical examples to illustrate the proposed model. Several experimental investigations will be performed using real evaluation and selection scenarios with practicing IS managers. The results will be published in an appropriate IS journal.

Chapter 9

A New Efficiency Methodology for IT Investment Analysis Studies

M.D. Troutt
Kent State University

Arun Rai
Georgia State University

S.K. Tadisina
Southern Illinois University at Carbondale

Aimao Zhang
Southern Illinois University at Carbondale

This chapter discusses the application potential of some techniques centered on efficiency ratio modeling to assess the organizational value of Information Technology. These models use a productivity/efficiency imputation technique. They apply to situations in which measures of inputs and outputs are available either longitudinally for one organization or cross-sectionally for multiple organizations. Variants of regression and correlation models have been dominantly used to empirically examine the IT value question. In addition, Data Envelopment Analysis has been used by some researchers. The present approach was stimulated by that work which can be applied to the same type of data, but essentially determines only technical and scale efficient units. However the present models are true ratio productivity measures which we call simply Efficiency Ratio models. These models estimate input and output weights which permit comparison of differences in the importance or impacts. The theoretical basis is the Maximum Decisional

Efficiency estimation principle. The ER analysis seeks to relate output efficiency to dollar inputs. The resulting efficiency measures can in turn be related to other organizational performance measures via routine regression analysis. A particular efficiency ratio model called the historical composite is developed and illustrated on hypothetical data.

This chapter will discuss the application potential of some techniques centered on Efficiency Ratio (ER) modeling to assess the organizational value of Information Technology (IT). These models use a productivity/efficiency imputation technique. They apply to situations in which measures of inputs and outputs are available either longitudinally for one organization or cross-sectionally for multiple organizations.

The organizational value of IT continues to be a hotly debated issue among practitioners and academics. There is skepticism regarding the wisdom of increased IT spending in view of some empirical evidence that seems to suggest that IT investments produce negligible benefits (Loveman, 1994). Brynjolfsson (1993) notes that these early studies may not have demonstrated that IT investments yield value for organizations because of mismeasurements of outputs and inputs, lags in learning and adjustment, redistribution and dissipation of profits, and mismanagement of IT.

Variants of regression and correlation models have been dominantly used to empirically examine the IT value question. Weill (1992) used regression models to examine the relationship between IT investments and various aspects of firm performance using data collected from the valve manufacturing industry. Mahmood and Mann (1993) used canonical correlation to assess the impact of IT investments on organization performance using data reported in Computerworld on the top 100 IT spender organizations. Hitt and Brynjolfssom (1994) used seemingly unrelated regression to examine the relationship between IT investment and various measures of performance. In addition, Data Envelopment Analysis (DEA) has been used by some researchers such as Mahmood (1994).

We note some aspects which, if handled effectively by the proposed analytical methodology, should prove useful in the study of IT value.

1. Mukhopadhyay et al. (1995) note that treating IT as one factor is a major limitation of past research. IT investments consist of multiple dimensions. For example, investments may be classified as dollars spent on hardware, software, staff development, maintenance, etc. Alternatively, they could be classified based on type of organizational information system, such as strategic or transactional. Multiple measures of investments should be handled by the methodology.

2. Performance variables can be conceptualized at either the firm or process level. Barua et al. (1995) propose a two-stage analysis of intermediate and final output variables for measuring IT contributions. In either stage, multiple measures are typically needed to assess performance. These measures can be either financial or non-financial. Multiple measures of performance should be handled by the methodology.

3. Mukhopadhyay et al. (1995) observe that previous studies have used cross-section or short time series data. However, IT investments often show value after some time lag. These lagged effects can be due to learning curves that organizations need to overcome in their use of new technologies. As IT investments are "consumed" over time, it is important to amortize inputs. The methodology should have a mechanism to amortize IT investments over time.

The present approach was stimulated by work with Data Envelopment Analysis (DEA), (Charnes et al. 1995, Troutt et al. 1996, Mahmood, 1994). DEA can be applied to the same type of data but essentially determines only technical and scale efficient units. However, the present models are true ratio productivity measures which we call simply Efficiency Ratio (ER) models. These models estimate input and output weights which permit comparison of differences in the importances or impacts. The theoretical basis is the Maximum Decisional Efficieny (MDE) estimation principle (Troutt, 1995 and Troutt et al. 1995).

The rationale for use of the ER methods may be introduced as follows. In the IT investment setting it is generally straightforward to measure expenditures in various categories and time periods as inputs. However, benefits of outputs are not generally available in dollar terms. Instead various other measures must be relied upon. These measures may include for example, lines of code measures, projects and project size measures, and managerial and customer satisfaction measures. Despite lack of dollar benefit equivalents of such measures, these ER models can nevertheless impute weights to those measures which relate them to the inputs. Time periods and/or organizations under comparison are sought for which the efficiency ratio is highest. Thus the weights indicate the importance of various output measures in relation to the relevant input expenditures. When at least one input is in dollar terms, all weights may be given dollar interpretations.

ER analysis therefore seeks to relate output efficiency to dollar inputs. However inputs can also include non-dollar measures such as staff size, team size, memory capacities, etc. by considering inputs as negative outputs. The resulting efficiency measures can in turn be related to other organizational performance measures via routine regression analysis.

Estimating the organizational payoff of investments in IT is the central problem of this volume. This chapter seeks to inform the problem area in three ways. First we propose a methodology for estimating the efficiency of an IT department or function over time. We argue that this methodology will serve IT investment decisions as a surrogate for actual dollar benefit estimates. Specifically, an IT department which can demonstrate high efficiency in its use of past investments can give management more confidence in both the existing level of investments and in any proposed increases. This methodology also will suggest how such efficiencies may be improved.

Secondly, this methodology is proposed as a building block in a more comprehensive attack on the central problem. Overall organizational performance can be regarded as dependent on the efficiencies of its major subcomponents. Thus period-by-period efficiency measures for not only the IT area, but also the other major functions of the organization could serve as predictor variables in regression models of financial performance. Put simply, large capital and operational expenditures in the various functional areas of the organization may not necessarily lead to high performance in a period, if their efficiencies are sufficiently low. Figure 1 gives a framework for this viewpoint. After more fully developing the concepts and techniques discussed

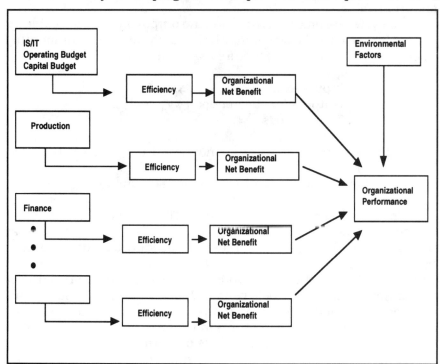

Figure 1. Comprehensive model of the relationship between organizational function efficiencies and performance.

here, we elaborate further on this framework.

A third related use of these methods is in connection with cross-sectional and combined studies. By concentrating on comparative efficiency across different IT departments, IT scholars can study determinants, preconditions, and correlations of high versus low efficiency departments.

Assumptions

The ER method we propose is somewhat similar to the set of techniques called DEA, (Charnes, et al. 1995). Readers familiar with that topic will recognize that the data requirements for the present efficiency approach are similar to those of DEA. However, there are a number of important differences between DEA and this proposed approach which are detailed further below.

Thus we suppose that a set of data consisting of input and output measures are available for the IT department or function of an organization. Let x_{ij} be the level of input i in time period j. We assume there are i=1, ..., I inputs. Initially, there are two inputs consisting of operational budgets and capital expenditures. We also assume there are outputs of various types r = 1, ..., R, and denoted for time period j by y_{rj}. Some common types of input and output measures for IT are shown in Table 1.

Lastly, we assume that the input and output data are available for j=1, ..., N time periods, which may be at yearly, quarterly, or monthly intervals. Thus the data structure assumed is of the form

Inputs for time period j : x_{ij}, i=1, ..., I
Outputs for time period j : y_{rj} , r=1, ..., R
Time Periods : j=1, ..., N

As in DEA, such measures are nonnegative; that is $x_{ij} \geq 0$, and $y_{rj} \geq 0$ for all i, r, and j.

Operational budgets and even more so, capital expenditures, have the property that their effects may tend to be felt over several time periods beyond their actual occurrence. Thus the impacts at successive time points can be regarded as actual expenditures used in that time period as well as portions of earlier expenditures which appear to be used in that time period also. In this way, our model has the capability of suggesting how budgets appear to be amortized over future time periods. We believe that this capability is an important addition to previous efficiency analyses for IT. For example, large operational or capital expenditures in the current time period can be expected to have carry forward effects on output measures in future time periods. As an instance, extra staff on hand now can build systems and procedures which benefit future output or quality levels.

Inputs	How Measured	Comments
Operations Budgets	Current Dollars[1]	Possible subdivisions if data permits
Salaries	—	—
Software Licenses	—	—
Outsourcing Expenditures	—	—
Staff Development	—	—
Capital Expenditures	—	—
Hardware Acquisitions	—	—
Hardware Upgrades	—	—
Other System Upgrades	—	—
Staff Size	Actual Costs	Possible alternatives to salaries
Systems Analysts	—	—
Programmers	—	—
Clerical	—	—
Managerial Staff	—	—
Outputs		
New System Completions	Actual Costs	May be subdivided into system type (e.g., transactional or strategic)
Systems Maintained	—	
Number of Lines of Code Implemented	—	
Lines of Code Maintained	—	
Customer Satisfaction Measures	Actual Counts	These are assumed to persist in observed values until a change is encountered, that is, they are not expected to be updated at each period.
On-time Systems Delivered	Likert Scale	
Client Evaluations		
Management Evaluations	—	
"Whereputs"[2]		
System Interuptions other than routine scheduled downtime	Number of occurences, hours total hour down time. Frequency within period.	These may be considered either as inputs or negative outputs. While this category is a legitimate and necessary output of the IT period function, smaller is better. Thus we suggest they be considered as inputs or negative outputs.
Late System Deliveries	Number of Projects behind schedule at start of Period.	If these deliveries were expedited, they would increase outputs. Since smaller is better, they may be considered as inputs or negative outputs.
	Total months behind - all delayed projects - at start of period.	

[1]   It is assumed that the CPI index is used to adjust past dollars to current dollar equivalents.

[2]   In some cases, it may not be immediately clear whether a measure should be considered as an input or output. We call these "whereputs."

Table 1: Typical Inputs, Outputs, and "Whereputs" for IT

Organization of the Chapter

In Section 2, the general modeling approach is explained and its theoretical background is developed. Section 3 discusses distribution assumptions and validation issues. Section 4 compares these approaches to canonical correlation and DEA. Section 5 gives a computational illustration with our recommended model. Section 6 discusses further applications and limitations of the approach. Section 7 provides a technical conclusion and Section 8 suggests some strategies for managerial use.

Model Development

Productivity/Efficiency Ratio Models

Define nonnegative output multipliers, π_r, by π_r = dollar benefit, in current dollars, per unit of output type r, when the system is *fully efficient*. We may also call π_r the relative output priority of type r.

Let x_j^0 be the operational budget expediture in period j. Then define λ_k^0 by λ_k^0 = the portion of a budget expenditure in any period which has its effect in the same (k=1), or later, k >1, period. We assume that k=1, ..., M^0, so that

$$\sum_{k=1}^{MO} \lambda_k^0 = 1, \ \lambda_k^0 \geq 0.$$

Similarly define λ_s^c for capital expenditures. We assume s=1, ..., M^c, with

$$\sum_{s=1}^{Mc} \lambda_s^c = 1, \lambda_s^c \geq 0$$

for all s. As with the π_r multipliers, the λ_k^0 and λ_s^c are defined with respect to efficient time periods.

Therefore, the total dollar benefit in the current period, j, of all outputs is given for any efficient period by

$$\sum_{r=1}^{R} \pi_y^0 \, y_{rj} \tag{2.1}$$

The total dollar inputs relevant for period j is somewhat more complicated, consisting of portions of current and past operational and capital expenditures. For any efficient period j it is given by

$$\sum_{k=1}^{MO} \lambda_k^0 \, x_{j-k+1}^0 + \sum_{s=1}^{Mc} \lambda_s^c \, x_{j-k+1}^c \tag{2.2}$$

Thus for example, the first term in the leftmost sum is $\lambda_1^0 x_j^0$ giving the amount of the operational budget of period j which benefits the same time period. The second term is $\lambda_2^0 x_{j-1}^0$. This term gives the portion of the previous operational budget which benefits the current (j) time period, and so on.

In periods of *perfect efficiency*, the full current dollar effect of expenditures is realized in terms of current dollar output value. Therefore, if j is an efficient time period we expect (2.1) and (2.2) to be equal. However, for inefficient time periods we expect (2.1) to be less than (2.2). Let e_j be defined as the productivity or efficienty ratio for period j, where e_j is the ratio of (2.1) to (2.2). Namely,

$$e_j = \sum_{r=1}^{R} \pi_r \, y_{rj} \Big/ \sum_{k=1}^{MO} \lambda_k^0 \, x_{j-k+1}^0 + \sum_{s=1}^{Mc} \lambda_s^c \, x_{j-k+1}^c \qquad (2.3)$$

We next consider ways in which the parameters π_r, λ_k^0, and λ_s^c might be estimated subject to their known properties. These properties may be described by the requirement that any such estimates should belong to the following constraint set, CS.

$$\text{CS:} \qquad \sum_{k=1}^{MO} \lambda_k^0 = 1, \; \sum_{s=1}^{Mc} \lambda_s^c \qquad (2.4)$$

$$\pi_r \geq 0, \; \lambda_k^0 \geq 0, \; \lambda_s^c \geq 0 \text{ for all } r, \, k, \text{ and } s. \qquad (2.5)$$

The parameters M^0 and M^c may be specified by managerial or analyst judgement. However, the model itself may suggest good values for them. Namely, if sufficient data are available, one would expect efficiencies to be greatest when the correct values of those parameters are used.

The Maximum Decisional Efficiency (MDE) principle (Troutt, 1995) is a recently introduced approach to parameter estimation problems of the present kind. This principle first selects an average or aggregate of the e_j such as Σe_j and then estimates the parameters as those values which maximize Σe_j subject to constraints CS.

The MDE principle therefore requires different criteria for optimization depending on which aggregate measure of efficiency is used. Here we consider the Historical Composite (HC) criterion. If the outputs or inputs for all historical periods are added together, respectively, then the ratio of their sum is a measure of average efficiency over that time span.

This model and its solution algorithm are discussed in the next subsection, along with some relevant strengths and weaknesses.

However it is useful to simplify the above notations somewhat. Notice that the denominators of the e_j involve current and past inputs. It is more convenient to assume one input vector, x_{ij} -for each period j.
Thus define

$$x'_{ij} = \begin{cases} x^0_{j+i-1} & \text{for } i=1, ..., M^0 \\ x^c_{j+i-1} & \text{for } i = M^0+1, ..., M^0 + M^c \end{cases} \qquad (2.6)$$

Similarly define ξ_i by

$$\xi_i = \begin{cases} \lambda^0_i & \text{for } i=1, ..., M^0 \\ \lambda^c_s & \text{for } i = 1, ...,M^c \text{ and } s=i-M^0 \end{cases} \qquad (2.7)$$

Then by dropping the prime on x_{ij}' we may write the efficieny ratios as

$$\Sigma_r \pi_r y_{rj} / \Sigma_i \xi_i x_{ij} \qquad (2.8)$$

and the constraint set CS becomes

CS: $$\pi_r \geq 0, \xi_i \geq 0 \qquad (2.9)$$

$$\sum_{i=1}^{M0} \xi_i = 1 \sum_{i=M0+1}^{M0+Mc} \xi_i = 1 \qquad (2.10)$$

The HC Model

In this model, what may be called a *Historical Composite* (HC) efficiency score is constructed by separately adding all outputs and inputs to make an overall efficiency score for all past time periods. This leads to model HC given as follows.
HC:

maximize $\Sigma_j \Sigma_r \pi_r y_{rj} / \Sigma_j \Sigma_i \xi_i x_{ij}$ $\qquad (2.11)$

s.t. $\Sigma_r \pi_r y_{rj} \leq \Sigma_i \xi_i x_{ij}$ for all j. $\qquad (2.12)$
$\pi,\xi \in$ CS

(Note that the constraints $e_j \leq 1$ have been expressed in the form (2.12) as more convenient for linear programming solution.) Also if we define

$$Y_r = \Sigma_j y_{rj} \text{ and } xi = \Sigma_j x_{ij} \qquad (2.13)$$

then the objective function of (2.11) may be simplified to

$$\Sigma_r \pi_r y_{rj} / \Sigma_i \xi_i x_{ij} \qquad (2.14)$$

Thus, problem HC estimates the π and ξ weights as those values which give the best overall historical efficiency subject to all individual periods having efficiencies not exceeding unity.

Problem HC is known as a linear fractional programming problem. It may be converted to a linear programming problem by use of the Charnes and Cooper (1962) transformation. (The derivation is available from the first author.)   The result is linear programming problem HCLP.

HCLP: maximize $\Sigma_r u_r y_r$ (2.15)

s.t. $\Sigma_r u_r y_{rj} \leq \Sigma_i v_i x_{ij}$ for all j   (2.16)

$$-w + \sum_{i=1}^{MO} v_i = 0 \qquad (2.17)$$

$$-w + \sum_{i=MO+1}^{MO+Mc} v_i = 0 \qquad (2.18)$$

$\Sigma_i v_i x_i = 1$ (2.19)
$u_r, v_i \geq$ for *all r and i*
$w \geq 0$ *(see remark following)*

Remark on w: Strictly speaking, w is required to be positive. However, since this condition is expected to hold except for specially constructed pathological situations, it does no harm to treat w as a regular nonnegative linear programming variable in problem HCLP.

Following solution of problem HCLP, the corresponding π^* and ξ^* solutions may be obtained from the u^*, v^*, and w^* solutions by the reverse transformation. Namely,

$\pi_r^* = w^{-1} u_r^*$ for all r   (2.20)
$\xi_i^* = w^{-1} v^*_i$ *for all i.*   (2.21)

Thus, problem HC is easily solved by a simple linear programming problem, which may be regarded as a strength of this approach.

A further strength of the HC model is its performance in producing weights which tend to be nonzero. When applied cross-sectionally to different units the model was called the Industry Aggregate (IA) model in Pettypool (1989). In that study the MER and HC (IA) approaches were compared with DEA ratio models on several data sets. The HC (IA) model tended to produce solutions with strictly positive elements ($\pi_r > 0$, $\xi_i > 0$) more frequently than did the other two efficiency models. Analysts and clients of such analyses tend to be skeptical when a model yields a zero optimal weight for an input or output which they believe to be important. It appears that in that study, this problem arose much less frequently for the HC (IA) model than for the MER and DEA ratio models. Presumably similar results should be expected in the present HC setting.

Distributional Assumptions

The HC Model

For this model the most natural density assumption appears to be given by

$$g_\alpha(e) = c_\alpha \exp (\alpha e) \qquad (3.1)$$
$$\text{where} \qquad c_\alpha = \alpha (\exp (e)-1)^{-1} \qquad (3.2)$$

and $0 \le e \le 1$, Troutt (1995). Thus validation of the model can be approached by analysis of the e_j^* scores associated with an optimal solution (π^*, ξ^*). If for some such solution (they need not be unique), and any $\alpha > 0$, the sample e_j^* fit the density g_α, then the model gains a degree of validation. Such general tests-of-fit as the Durbin test can be conveniently done in a spreadsheet model setting, say, since the cumulative distribution function (cdf), $G_\alpha(e)$ is available in the following closed form.

$$G_\alpha(e) = \{\exp (\alpha e)-1\}/\{ \exp (\alpha)-1\}. \qquad (3.3)$$

What-if trials may be performed using various values. If none of these tests-of-fit appear acceptable, we may consider outliers and a flexibility property of the decisional efficiency measure, e_j, described below.

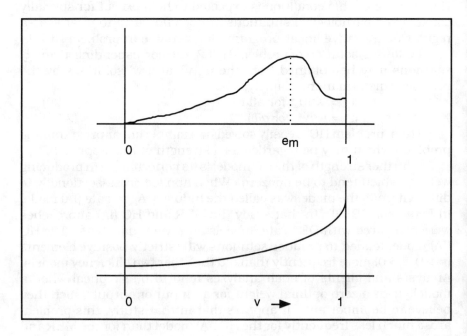

Figure 2. In the top figure, sample values above e_m are suspect as outliers. The bottom figure is the general form of the g_a density, regarded as a more ideal pattern for the decisional efficiencies.

The bounds, $e_j \leq 1$, can be shown to be active for at least one j. However, if active for more than one j, then concern for possible highliers (large outliers) is present. For a density model such as g, the probability of any particular point in the interval [0, 1] is zero. Because of the active constraint property just mentioned, we know that one e_j will have to be 1.0 in value. But the probability of any other e_j having this value is zero. Thus if we have y > 1 with unit efficiency ratio, then y-1 of these become suspect as highliers.

However, a further possibility is that insufficient output and input measures are being used in the current model to permit discrimination among the top performers. To guard against this possibility the length of time over which amortization is assumed to be effected should be expanded before considering deletion of some of these suspected highliers. If after expanding the model variables there are still multiple unity solutions, we suggest trial outlier deletions and re-solving of the model. The model with the fewest unity ratings and maximum average (of retained observations) would seem to be most preferred.

Additional aspects of model quality are discussed in Troutt et al. (1996). Power transformations such $e_j' = e_j^p$, p > 0 are also suitable decisional efficiency (DE) measures. In fact, any monotone increasing positive function of e_j is also a plausible DE measure.

Another view of highliers is possible if sample histogram for the full model appears as in Figure 2. By deletion of sample points above e_m, a more ideally shaped histogram results for the g_α family of densities.

Some supporting arguments for this approach are as follows:
• When data are sufficiently ample.
• Units with uniformly high inputs and/or uniformly low inputs will tend to appear highly efficient regardless of how the weights are set.

Thus, the high end performers are expected to give poorer information about the ideal weights. Als, combinations of high outputs and/or low inputs might be due to windfall situations or other accidental data patterns.

Data Requirements, Constraints and Resampling

As a rule of thumb in regression analysis, analysts are often advised to follow the 10k rule. This suggests that at least ten data points should be available for each parameter (k in number) to be estimated. Given the data-fitting similarities between regression and the present model, we may propose an analogous rule.

Let us focus on nonnegative parameters. The 10k rule applies to ordinary parameters which can be positive or negative. Such variables can be represented as the difference of nonnegative variables. That is

$$\beta_i = \beta_i^+ - \beta_i^- \text{ with } \beta_i^+ \geq 0, \ \beta_i^- \geq 0 \qquad (3.4)$$

Moreover, if $\beta_i > 0$ we set $\beta_i^+ = \beta_i$ and $\beta_i^- = 0$, with similar handling for $_i < 0$. If 10k data points are sufficient for k β's, then this should also be sufficient for 2k variables of the β_i^+, and β_i^- (i.e. nonnegative) type. Thus by proportionality, 5k observations should be sufficient for k variables of this type. That is, since the $\pi_r = \pi_r^+$ and $\xi_r = \xi_r^+$, 5k observations should suffice for k variables of the π_r and ξ_r type.

Note that each data point contributes one inequality to the present models. It might also be reasonable to include constraints of the form

$$\lambda 1 \geq \lambda 2 \geq \lambda 3 ...\text{etc.} \tag{3.5}$$

for the amortization weights. Each such inequality appears to be equivalent, in the sense of added information, to half an additional data point. This is because an equality is logically equivalent to two inequalities.

Putting these observations together for the HC model, let N^d be the required number of data points (in addition to the given constraints). Let $n(\lambda)$ be the number of additional constraints of the form (3.5). Let k be the number of π and ξ variables. Because there are 3 equalities, we obtain the following number of required observations.

$$N^d + n(\lambda) + 6 \geq 5k \tag{3.6}$$

or $\qquad N^d \geq 5k - n(\lambda) - 6 \tag{3.7}$

As an example, suppose we have three outputs. Let there be four amortization fractions for operating expenses and six fractions for capital expenditures; all required to be in decreasing order. Then

$$\lambda_1^0 \geq \lambda_2^0 \geq \lambda_3^0 \geq \lambda_4^0 \tag{3.8}$$

$$\lambda_1^c \geq \lambda_2^c \geq \lambda_3^c \geq \lambda_4^c \tag{3.9}$$

These therefore yield $n(\lambda) = 3 + 5 = 8$; and $k = 13$. Therefore we require

$$N^d \geq 5k(131) - 8 - 6 = 51. \tag{3.10}$$

Hence these assumptions appear suitable for 51 monthly observations. However, some data losses occur due to the lagged input variables which in this case extend back six periods. Therefore, we finally require at least 57 months of historical data for this example. It is assumed here that all dollar data are inflated to current dollar terms by use of the CPI or other index.

If sufficient data are not available for the intended model, we recommend a resampling technique. For example, a multivariate normal distribution may be fitted to the data in hand. Then additional data may be obtained by simulating from that distribution. For additional techniques in bootstrapping and resampling, see Simon and Bruce (1994).

Data Zeroes

It is expected that zeroes will occur in some applications, especially in periods for which no new capital expenditures come on-line.

However, zeroes may also occur in the output data depending on how, for example, customer satisfaction and quality items are measured. Zeroes in either of these cases present no problem for the models here, so long as an output vector does not contain *all zeroes*. We assume that input vectors of all zeroes are not possible. This leaves the case of how to handle all-zero output vectors, if present.

While this case deserves futher study, the following accommodation appears plausible. We suggest to add a dummy output variable y_0, all values of which are unity. The optimal multiplier assigned to that output variable therefore serves as a nonnegative intercept term for the efficiency numerators.

Combined Models

Various combined models can be constructed but are subject to several subtleties. For those models we may use index $j=1, ..., N$, to denote units being compared, and $t=1, ..., T$ as time periods of historical data available on these units. The simplest case results when the input and output parameters are homogeneous across units; and decisional efficiencies, e_{jt}, are also homogeneous, in the sense that they may be assumed to follow the same distribution. In this case the indexes j and t may be pooled. Some other combined model cases have been considered in Troutt and Gribbin (1996).

Modeling Comparisons

Canonical Correlation

The present models appear similar to the following kind of constrained, error-weighted canonical correlation model,

$$\Sigma_r \pi_r y_{rj} \leq \Sigma_i \xi_i x_{ij} + \varepsilon_j \Sigma_i \xi_i x_{ij} , \; \pi_r, \; \xi_i \geq 0, \; \varepsilon_j \leq 0, \qquad (4.1)$$

which could, in principle, be fitted by a criterion such as

$$\min_j \Sigma \, \varepsilon_j^2 \qquad (4.2)$$

It can be checked that this implies $e_j = 1 + \Sigma_j$, so that in terms of the efficiencies, the criterion (4.2) becomes

$$\min_j \Sigma \, (1 - e_j^2) \qquad (4.3)$$

We believe this criterion may be objectionable for several reasons. First if we look at the terms one at a time, then the term involving e_j is $(1-e_j)(1-e_j)$. If e_j is large (i.e. close to 1.0) then $1-e_j$ should receive a large weight in the minimization process, in order to force it close to zero.

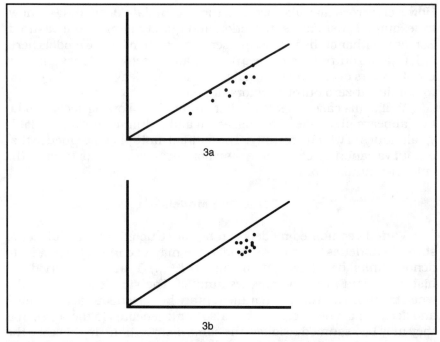

Figure 3. Ideal clustering of data in relation to the efficient frontier is depicted in Figure 3a. Normal clustering is depicted in Figure 3b.

However the weight such terms receive will be $1-e_j$ itself, a small weight in that case. We conjecture that this criterion will seek e_j distributions which are centered on some intermediate average value, perhaps 0.5.

Also it is not known for which density assumption (4.3) becomes an MLE procedure. We conjecture further that this density may be of normal form and again concentrated on some intermediate value in the interval [0, 1]. If this conjecture is correct, then the resulting e_j estimates might appear to be rather more random than purposeful. On the other hand, the proposed models explicitly acknowledge purposeful behavior in that the g densities are monotone increasing with modes of unity. For these models, high efficiencies should be more frequent than lower ones, as would be consistent with purposeful behavior of high performance.

These ideas can be visualized to some extent by Figures 3a and 3b. If these figures represent projections of candidate efficient hyperplanes, then Figure 3a is preferred in the sense that the imputed efficiencies tend to cluster around 1.0 to a greater extent than those in Figure 3b. In some sense, clearly deserving of further study, there appears to be a greater consensus on the efficient frontier in Figure 3a than in Figure 3b. In Figure 3a, we may say that efficiencies tend to focus on 1.0 and appear to be deliberate in origin. While in Figure 3b, they appear to be more random. Clearly one would prefer to believe that IT management, as well as all management for that matter, will tend to exhibit the first form of behavior.   Put differently, good management and high efficiency should be purposeful rather than accidental.

DEA

The models proposed here are also similar to common weights DEA models. See, for example, Dyson and Thanassoulis (1988), Cook et al. (1992) and Roll, et al. (1991). See also Anderson and Peterson (1993). In fact, they may themselves be considered as common weights DEA models.   DEA models can indicate which outputs or inputs need improvement for *inefficient units* and also provide a number of possible directions for such improvements.   The present models suggest optimal directions in terms of the weights.   More importantly the present models address what may be called the *Miller Time Curse* that winners (fully efficient units) incur in a DEA application. By this we mean that DEA weights are not given model-specific meanings, and therefore those declared fully efficient have nowhere to go except "to celebrate." The estimates in the present models, however, show directions of improvement even for those found fully efficient. These models, therefore, appear potentially more suitable for continuous improvement than do the standard DEA models.

HC Model Data Illustration

Sample Data Set

Here we construct a dataset of three output measures and two inputs analogous to operating expenses x^0, and capital expenditures x^c, respectively. The x^0 values are assumed to amortize over two periods, and the x^c values over three periods.   We assume the amortization fractions are all nonincreasing. This leads to the following specific form of the HC model.

Example HC Model:

$$\text{maximize} \qquad u_1 Y_1 + u_2 Y_2 + u_3 Y_3 \tag{5.1}$$

$$\text{s.t.} \quad u_1 Y_{1j} + u_2 Y_{2j} + u_3 Y_{3j} -v_1 x_{1j} \; -v_2 x_{2j} -v_3 x_{3j} -v_4 x_{4j} -v_5 x_{5j} \leq 0 \text{ for all } j \tag{5.2}$$

$$v_1 + v_2 - w = 0 \tag{5.3}$$

$$v_3 + v_4 + v_5 - w = 0 \tag{5.4}$$

$$v_1 x_1 + v_2 x_2 + v_3 x_3 + v_4 x_4 + v_5 x_5 = 1 \tag{5.5}$$

$$v_2 - v_1 \leq 0 \tag{5.6}$$

$$v_4 - v_3 \leq 0 \tag{5.7}$$

$$v_5 - v_4 \leq 0 \tag{5.8}$$

$$u_r \geq 0, \, v_i \geq 0, w \geq 0 \tag{5.9}$$

$$y_r = \Sigma_j y_{rj}, x_i = \Sigma_j x_{ij} \tag{5.10}$$

Note that (5.3) and (5.4) may be simplified first to

Variable	Weight
y_1	-0-
y_2	2.558
y_3	0.740
$\lambda_1^{\,0}$	0.656
$\lambda_2^{\,0}$	0.344
$\lambda_1^{\,c}$	0.344
$\lambda_2^{\,c}$	0.344
$\lambda_3^{\,c}$	0.312

Table 2: Optimal Weight Solutions for the HC Model Example Problem

$$v_1 + v_2 - v_3 - v_4 - v_5 = 0 \qquad (5.11)$$

where w is given by either $v_1 + v_2$ or $v_3 + v_4 + v_5$. That not all of these variables can be zero is obvious, showing, along with nonnegativity, that w must be positive. Furthermore, artificial variables can be avoided if (5.11) is replaced by both

$$v_1 + v_2 - v_3 - v_4 - v_5 \leq 0 \qquad (5.12)$$
and
$$-v_1 - v_2 + v_3 + v_4 + v_5 \leq 0 \qquad (5.13)$$

Also (5.5) can be relaxed to the inequality form

$$v_1 x_1 + v_2 x_2 + v_3 x_3 + v_4 x_4 + v_5 x_5 \leq 1 \qquad (5.14)$$

since the shadow price of that constraint will clearly be positive.

For illustration, an artificial data set for this model was developed as follows. Observations of the form $y_1\ y_2\ y_3\ x_1\ x_2$ were generated as multivariate normal with centroid, (10, 25, 15, 50, 30), and covariance matrix, SIG, given by

$$SIG = \begin{vmatrix} 1 & 0.4 & 1.4 & 0.3 & 0 \\ 0.4 & 4 & -0.4 & 4.8 & 0 \\ 1.4 & -0.4 & 4 & 0 & 0 \\ 0.3 & 4.8 & 0 & 9 & 0 \\ 0 & 0 & 0 & 0 & 9 \end{vmatrix} \qquad (5.15)$$

The Cholesky factorization matrix method described in Law and Kelton (1982, page 269) was implemented in SAS/IML (1990). The rule of thumb proposed earlier suggests that 34 observations should be used. However two lags were necessary to account for the three-period amortization of the second input.

Interpretation

The results on variable weights are shown in Table 2.

The zero weight assigned to variable y_1 can be rationalized by noticing that the correlation between y_1 and y_3 is 0.7 from (5.15). Thus

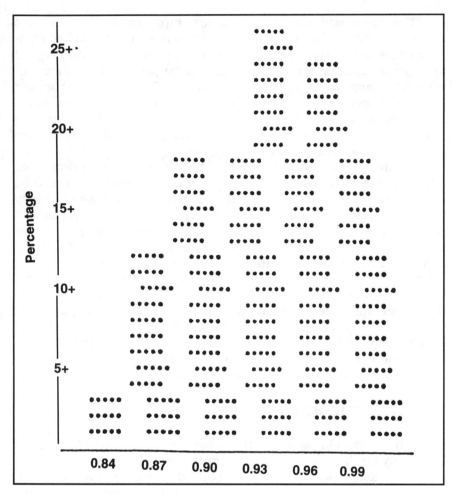

Figure 4. SAS/IML Histogram of Decisional Efficiencies for the HC Model Problem.

the output weights can be regarded as having reasonably good face validity. In terms of the dollar units used to measure the inputs, output y_1 is not valued; while output y_2 is valued at 2.558 per unit, and output y_3 is valued at 0.740 per unit. Thus it appears that output y_2, which might represent a customer satisfaction measure, is being more highly valued. It follows, in that case, that improvement of output y_2 should be prioritized for further improvement of efficiency.

The average efficiency for this model is 0.935. If the data were from a real case, it would appear that IT expenditures have had very good returns to the organization over the data period. As more periods evolve, the trend of the average efficiencies can be monitored. Reasons for upward or downward trends should be sought. Reasons for improvement might include various system innovations that should be enhanced still further.

The amortization factors for the first input variable, x^0, indicate that about 66% of these expenditures influence same period efficiencies; while 34% carry over to the next period. For the second type of input expenditures, x^c, 39% influence same period efficiencies; another 34% carry over to the next period, and 31% carry over to the next subsequent period. If the data were from a real case, the analyst might wish to compare these results to the models with larger amortization periods. Ideally, the amortization percentages should stabilize after some number of such periods.

Figure 4 is the SAS/IML histogram of the computed decisional efficiencies (e_j values) for this example. While the average value of 0.94 can be regarded as quite high, it will be noted that the apparent density is not a good match to the monotone increasing density model (3.1) but resembles the top density in Figure 2. However, it should be noted that this data was generated from a normal (i.e., random) density. Thus it is not surprising that the data do not evidence the expertise pattern which would be expected from actual managerial data. This is further evidenced by observing from Figure 4 that the modal value of the decisional efficiencies does not appear to be unity. Their pattern is therefore more analogous to Figure 3b, indictative of random rather than purposeful behavior, as is known to be the case in this example. If this data were in fact from a managerial setting, then highlier deletion experiments would be appropriate.

Limitations and Extensions

A theoretical limitation of the ER approach proposed here is the possibility of different weights on outputs arising from expenditures in different categories. The present models do not distinguish between dollar inputs from operational expenses and capital expenditures (apart from their amortization effects). If it is considered essential to differentiate between various input types, then the following approach can be taken at the expense of some more complicated models. In place of the π_r parameters, we may consider a technological coefficient matrix of the form $\{a_{ir}\} = A$. This amounts to finding a π_{ir} for each input type i. Assuming efficiencies of any type i are of equal status, then the above models may be adjusted by replacing the e_j components by the corresponding e_{ij} components.

Returning to Figure 1, we note that the IT function does not operate in isolation. Thus, to address the penultimate question of IT investment impacts on organizational financial performance without regard for efficiencies of the other parts of the organization would appear to be highly problematical. A possibly effective strategy may be outlined as follows. By performing similar efficiency studies on the major subfunctions of the organization, a set of efficiency measures may be obtained for each period and each subfunction. As a first approximation, we may combine efficiencies of serially linked subfunctions as the product of their individual efficiencies. In this way an overall efficiency for the organization could be constructed for each period. These efficiencies might then be considered as explanatory variables, along with competition and other organizational environment descriptors. A regression model to predict financial performance of the organization with such internal efficiency measures appears promising for explaining the various impacts on overall performance.

Technical Conclusion

This chapter has outlined a new approach to inter-temporal efficiency analysis of an IT department, or cross-sectional analysis of several such departments. The methodology may be regarded as an alternative to regression, canonical correlation and DEA methods. The essential features of the methodology are: (1) emphasis on purposeful rather than random behavior, (2) meaningful weights on inputs and outputs, (3) direction of improvement for both efficient and inefficient units, (4) dollar value imputation for outputs of efficient units or periods, and (v) ease of handling the estimation of input amortizations or carry-over effects.

The HC model can be solved by a simple linear programming formulation. Fitting of these models follows steps similar to constructing regression models. See Neter et al. (1985) and Madansky (1988). These steps include outlier experiments, agreement testing of distributional assumptions, and face validity of estimated weights.

Managerial Strategies for IT Investment

We suggest here a few strategies based on use of the new methodology. First, the HC model may be routinely monitored and updated. This model will generate the following information:

1. An indication of past periods which were most efficient. By identification of these periods and their associated investments, either operational or capital, both IS and corporate management will have a basis for deciding which types and amounts of IT investments have been most useful.

2. IS managers can use the results, especially on output dollar values (π_r), for strategic directions of change. Those outputs with highest imputed values can be prioritized for further improvement.

3. Large and/or increasing values of these efficiencies will give higher management confidence that past IT investments are being well

spent in the sense of good imputed returns per dollar spent.

4. Comparative uses of the methodology, both between IS departments, and between other functions of the organization, can be
expected to indicate opportunities for improvement in overall
efficiency.

5. By regression studies using efficiency adjusted impacts to explain
financial performance, the impact of efficiency increases on overall
performance can be assessed, not only for IT investments, but for
other organization functions as well.

6. Periods of increasing or decreasing efficiencies can be examined for
their probable causes, and appropriate managerial actions can
then be taken.

Chapter 10

OSI-Based Model for the Justification of Telecommunications Investment: A Conceptual Framework

Kathleen K. Molnar
St. Norbert College

Ramesh Sharda
Oklahoma State University

The problems of selecting and justifying telecommunications investments have increased as investment costs have continued to rise due to the evolution and changes in technology and standards due to organizational requirements of integration and globalization. Traditional financial analyses or competitive advantage analyses alone are no longer convincing models. We propose a generalizable, contingency model for telecommunications investment decision making unifying the justification methods used for telecommunications investment based on the Open Systems Interconnection (OSI) model developed by the International Standards Organization. Just as the OSI model provides a framework to guide the development of computer networks, the proposed 'Outcome–based Systems Investment' model will provide a 'metamodel' to guide the justification for telecommunications investment. The proposed conceptual OS–Investment model uses a seven–layer structure outlining the appropriate factors which should be considered at each level of the investment decision, suggests the value–added and costs that need to be considered and proposes decision technique(s) which may be used to justify the investment decision. We suggest how the OS–Investment model could be employed in practice and speculate on the use of this model for IT investment management strategies.

Information Technology (IT) has changed dramatically from stand-alone equipment and applications to computer-based networking using telecommunications to connect formerly distinct IT equipment in the office (OECD, 1992). However, the justification for investing in this technology has not undergone a comparable transformation. In fact, the justification problem has become even more magnified. The problems of selecting and justifying telecommunications investments have increased as investment costs have continued to rise due to the evolution and changes in technology and standards due to organizational requirements of integration and globalization. Business executives are looking for ways to justify this ever-increasing investment in technology through the use of economic business models.

Traditional financial analyses or competitive advantage analyses alone are no longer convincing models. Justification of technology applications must be linked to either improving the performance of the existing organization or improving the chances of success for new business opportunities and strategies (Parker and Benson, 1989). Cash flow analysis does not adequately deal with 'real' value (Lay, 1985) and studies are inconclusive on whether or not investments in IT have actually increased productivity (Ives and Learmonth, 1984; McFarlan, 1984; Venkatraman and Zaheer, 1990; Brynjolfsson, 1993). Hitt and Brynjolfsson (1996) suggest that it is also possible for firms to realize productivity benefits from IT, without seeing a higher bottom-line profitability which further complicates IT justification. In addition, a variety of different models exists (Grover and Goslar, 1993; Sabherwal and King, 1992; King and Premkumar, 1989; Parker and Benson, 1989), none of which has produced a widely agreed upon approach.

We propose a generalizable, contingency model for telecommunications investment decision making unifying the justification methods used for telecommunications investment. This model provides a framework that is familiar to telecommunications professionals, the Open Systems Interconnection (OSI) model developed by the International Standards Organization. Just as the OSI model provides a framework to guide the development of computer networks, the proposed 'Outcome-based Systems Investment' model will provide a 'metamodel' to guide the justification for telecommunications investment. The key to both models (OSI and OS-Investment) is to make the subject more manageable by reducing the study of the whole to the study of its individual parts. The proposed OS-Investment model can be used to identify both value-added and costs as justification criteria for the tangible and intangible benefits of telecommunications investment.

The model is a conceptual proposal at this stage. That is, the detailed applicability of specific decision criteria and modeling techniques for a specific type of investment is not empirically validated. However, the problem of justification of investments in information technology is still begging for a solution managers can understand. Since the OSI model is already quite familiar to IT professionals in general and telecommunications professionals in particular, we hope that our proposed framework will become a subject of serious applicability testing in the 'real world.'

This chapter is organized as follows. In the next section, we provide a review of the literature to offer a unified view of selected streams of research in IT justification. Then, an OSI-based investment model is developed. We propose how the OSI model could be employed in practice. Finally, the chapter concludes by speculating on the management strategies for IT investment.

Background and Literature Review

The strategic resource for an organization is information. The strategic infrastructure to use that information is telecommunications. A communications technology provides business value in three areas: efficiency (increased productivity), effectiveness (better management), and innovation (improved products and services) and impacts three primary areas: compression of time, overcoming the restrictions of geography, and the restructuring of relationships (Hammer and Mangurian, 1987). In order to maximize the usefulness of information to a business, it must be managed correctly; costs must be tied to the production, distribution, security, storage and retrieval of all information (Kendall and Kendall, 1992). Management must be

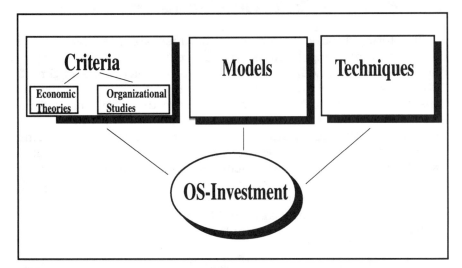

Figure 1: Dimensions of Telecommunications Investment Research

able to determine the potential value of the technologies used in the management of information.

The literature on telecommunications investments ranges from theoretical articles on justifying the technology itself (Dos Santos, 1991; Hammer and Mangurian, 1987; Lay, 1985) to justifying the economic value of the use of the technology (Semich, 1994; Brynjolfsson, 1993; Bakos and Kemerer, 1992; Barua, Kriebel, and Mukhopadhyay, 1991; Parker and Benson, 1989; Schell, 1986; McFarlan, 1984). Empirical articles have studied the impacts on effectiveness and efficiency in terms of productivity on using telecommunications (Venkatraman and Zaheer 1990) and the 'business value' of the technology (Mukhopadhyay, Kekre and Kalathur, 1995).

Our metamodel for Outcome-based System Investment is concerned with three main areas of telecommunications investment research: justification criteria, investment models, and measurement and evaluation techniques (Figure 1).

The next section describes studies on justification criteria for ascertaining the value of telecommunications through economic theories and organizational analysis. Then various theoretical IT investment models are described, followed by a section on that reviews various measurement and evaluation techniques which can be employed by the decision maker in justifying telecommunications investments. The development of this literature clearly shows a trend away from traditional cost-benefit methodologies and quantitative measures towards more subjective or qualitative measures (Powell, 1992). In order to provide a logical and meaningful picture of telecommunications investments research, it is necessary to integrate these diverse theoretical and empirical results into a comprehensive framework.

Justification Criteria

The term investment refers to "commitments of resources made in the hope of realizing benefits that are expected to occur over a reasonably long period of time in the future" (Bierman and Smidt, 1988, p. 4). Since the fundamental goal of the firm is generally considered to be the maximization of value, the justification of telecommunications investments is the measurement of the value of the investment to the organization. But given the difficulty in measuring telecommunications investments, how does the decision maker justify the telecommunications investment decision? Some researchers in this area base their work on economics, while others take an organizational perspectives approach.

Economic Theories. Bakos and Kemerer (1992) state that there are typically five characteristics of IT that drive economic studies:

1. Scale: Information systems typically require large capital investments and they offer substantial economies of scale.

2. Externalities: The benefits realized by individual users of IT increase as more users adopt compatible systems.

3. Uncertainty: Potential adopters of IT face substantial uncertainty regarding the actual benefits of the technology. Occasionally, this uncertainty remains even after an organization has deployed the technology.

4. Switching Costs: Information systems can impose significant switching costs on their participants.

5. Information Costs: IT can reduce customers' costs of obtaining information about prices and product offerings of alternative suppliers as well as suppliers' costs of communicating information about their prices and product characteristics to additional customers.

Additionally, Bakos and Kemerer categorize the research of IT justification into six areas of economic theory: Information economics (IE), production economics, economic models of organizational performance, industrial organization (IO), institutional economics (agency theory and transaction cost theory) and macroeconomic studies. Our proposed OS-Investment model incorporates overlapping economic theory from three of these areas: information economics, organizational performance and industrial organization.

Information Economics is driven by the notion that information has economic value. Information Economics is "a system of weights and measures that quantifies intangible benefits and ranks proposed projects by their expected contribution to business objectives" (Pastore, 1992, p. 66). Information Economics breaks IT investment into three decision factors: tangible cost/benefit analysis, intangible benefit analysis and intangible risk analysis (Semich, 1994). In practice, tangible and intangible corporate objectives are laid out and assigned a relative weight. Proposed systems then receive scores in each business objective and risk category, based on their potential impact on that objective.

Economic models of organizational performance discuss organizational efficiency and competitive advantage. The use of organizational performance economics in IT investment is the attempt to model organizational efficiency and document the organizational benefits resulting from investments in information technology (Bakos and Kemerer, 1992).

Industrial organization economics studies business behavior and its implications for the firm's conduct and market structure and in this case, the use of IT to sustain market power. Industrial organization economics applied to IT studies is the strategic impact of the investment in IT in order for firms to acquire and sustain market power

(Bakos and Kemerer, 1992).

Organizational Studies. Another way of looking at the telecommunications investment decision is by examining the factors which influence an individual organization's investment decision. Various researchers have identified, through empirical studies, a myriad of factors influencing the technological decision processes (e.g., Grover, Goslar and Segars, 1995; Ellis, Jones and Arnett, 1994; King and Teo, 1994; Grover and Goslar, 1993; King and Sabherwal, 1992; Sabherwal and King, 1992; Neo, 1988). Ettlie (1986) proposes that the factors which influence these processes can be divided into three categories. First, the attributes of the proposed new technology itself can influence the decision processes. Examples of factors in this category involve; perceived benefits, technological sophistication and implementation costs. The second category of factors consists of the characteristics of the organization attempting to incorporate the new technology. Examples of factors in this category are: organizational strategy and policy, degree of fit and skills. The third category of factors consists of the external environment of the organization attempting to incorporate the new technology. Examples of factors in this category are; suppliers, competitors and economic resources of the organization.

Investment Models

In order to understand the telecommunications investment decision, many models (from financial to economic) have been proposed for justifying technology. Venkatraman (1994) proposes a framework of telecommunications-enabled business transformation which is based on two-dimensions, the range of telecommunication's potential benefits and the degree of organizational transformation. He states that the range of potential benefits increases from the first level (localized exploitation) to the final level (redesign of the business scope). The higher levels of transformation indicate potentially greater benefits; they also require a correspondingly higher degree of changes in organizations. Therefore, he states that each organization should first identify the transformational level where the benefits are in line with the potential costs of the needed organizational change and then proceed to higher levels as the demands of competition increases.

Keen and Cummins (1994) use the quality profit engineering framework which identifies where and how the proposed services will contribute to the organization's economic health. This quality profit framework identifies six targets of economic opportunity: (1) profit management and alerting systems, (2) traditional costs, (3) quality premium costs, (4) service premium costs, (5) long-term business infrastructure costs, and (6) revenues.

King and Premkumar (1989) propose a conceptual model of strategic telecommunications planning which uses inputs, processes and outputs. Inputs are the organizational mission, objectives and strategies. Processes are the business, technology, organizational and environmental elements. Long-term, medium-term and short-term planning are the outputs.

Parker and Benson (1989) develop a model for enterprise-wide information management which consists of four levels. Level 1, the primary function identifies the specific business functions based on the product and the way it is delivered. Level 2, the enterprise organization, represents the planning, organizing, implementing and controlling resources required for the primary function of the organization. Level 3, business strategy, provides the strategic alternatives of cost leadership, differentiation and focus. Level 4, the environment, represents the external forces at the macroeconomic level (that is, the economic, social and political forces). In terms of financial justification, Parker and Benson state there are three types of IT applications: substitutive (substitute machine power for people power), complementary (increase productivity and employee effectiveness for existing activities), and innovative (maintain or give competitive edge). The five techniques of enterprise-wide information economics which they use in their model are: 1) traditional cost/benefit analysis, 2) architecture-based cost/benefit analysis, 3) benefit acceleration model analysis, 4) hedonic wage model analysis and 5) innovation risk analysis. The type of information technology application determines which analytical tool is to be applied. Techniques 1 and 2 are used for substitutive applications, 3 or 4 for complementary applications and, 5 for innovative applications.

Weill and Olson (1989) classify a telecommunications investment into three different types of investment decisions: strategic, informational and transactional. Strategic investment is guided by long-term goals to gain a competitive advantage usually by using the technology in a new way for the industry at that time. Informational investment is generally guided by medium-term goals and provides the infrastructure to support management control, planning, communication and other management functions. Transactional investment is usually made to reduce the costs of doing business. Weill (1990) states that a firm should develop a balanced portfolio of the three types of IT investment to suit both its strategy and level of IT experience. Each of the three types of IT investment contain different objectives and risks and the portfolio should balance the risk versus gain. Determining the appropriate level of telecommunications investment allows the decision maker a clearer picture of the investment decision.

Keen's model (1988) divides telecommunications investments into radical, innovative, incremental and operational moves and states that businesses should focus on the benefit side of the cost-benefit equation and know where to put the emphasis. That is, the various levels of telecommunications investments should be evaluated differently. "For radical moves, a strong focus on value is called for with costs defined in terms of a floor. For innovative moves, emphasize value but also be more detailed in indicating costs components and ranges. For incremental moves give equal weight to benefit and cost, but treat them separately and in that order. And for operational moves, be very precise about costs, since that is the issue here; the firm does not need to make the change and the real benefit is the cost impact (p. 195)."

Many of these telecommunications investment models appear to be an expansion of the traditional three-layer systems classification (transactional, operational, strategic). We suggest that expanding an investment model to seven layers provides additional insights into the types of costs and value-added issues that need to be considered. This expansion allows for a better analysis of the costs and values-added that need to be considered in telecommunications investment decisions as well as what decision techniques would best help measure these values. The process of actually justifying telecommunications investments involves how the decision is made; therefore, the next step is to determine how the decision maker operationalizes (what methods or measurement techniques) the investment decision.

Measurement and Evaluation Techniques

There are a variety of measurement and evaluation techniques which can be employed by a decision maker in justifying telecommunications investments. Klammer (1994) outlines model groupings of various strategic investment management decision tools. Single criterion or traditional financial models are used to analyze individual or mutually exclusive projects. These economic justification techniques typically calculate a specific numerical result that is compared to a single quantitative criterion. Examples include net present value, internal rate of return, discounted cash flow and return on investment (King and Schrems, 1978; Kanter, 1970). These models have significant limitations since these techniques do not consider nonfinancial strategies, synergies and long periods of investment.

Multiple criteria decision models such as deterministic models, multiple attribute decision models (MADMs) and strategy-based MADMs, use many quantitative and qualitative criteria and evaluate several mutually exclusive projects taken one at a time (Carter, 1992). Other models such as the portfolio models use both quantitative and qualitative criteria and can evaluate groups of related projects. Segev (1995) outlines seven portfolio techniques in order to evaluate corporate strategy including the Boston Consulting Group matrix, the GE/McKinsey model, the Shell/DPM model, the Hofer-Schendel product-market evaluation portfolio model, the ADL Life-Cycle model, the Hussey Risk Matrix and the Cardozo-Wind risk-return model. These portfolio investment models are, however, time-consuming and expensive to prepare and require extensive data to be effective.

Powell (1992) states that current evaluation techniques of telecommunications are an outgrowth of the traditional cost-benefit methodologies or applications of standard accounting techniques which can be classified into objective and subjective techniques. Objective techniques seek to quantify system inputs and outputs in order to attach value to them. These include such techniques as cost/ benefit analysis (King and Schrems, 1978; Kanter, 1970), graphical cost/benefits analysis (Shoval and Lugasi, 1988), MIS utilization techniques (Martin and Trumbly, 1986), value analysis (Keen, 1981), option valuation (Dos Santos, 1991), multiple criteria approach (Chandler, 1982), simulation technique (Kanter, 1970), and decision theory (Clemons, 1991; Schell, 1986). Subjective techniques rely on the attitudes and opinions of users and system builders. These techniques include user attitude surveys (Hamilton and Chervany, 1981), user utility function (Ahituv, 1980), AHP (Roper-Lowe and Sharp, 1990), and Delphi evidence (Senn, 1978; North and Pyke, 1969). Other techniques combine the objective and subjective approaches such as value chain analysis (Rainer, et al., 1991), MADM (Carter, 1992), speculative risk grid analysis (McGaughey, et. al, 1994), portfolio models (Segev, 1995) and cost modeling (Busch, 1994). Powell (1992) suggests that these standard techniques could be applicable to IT investment with some caveats. When measuring IT investments one

Evaluation Method	Main References
Objective:	
Cost Benefit Analysis (ROI/DCF)	King & Schrems (1978); Kanter (1970)
MIS Utilization	Martin & Trumbly (1986)
Simulation	Kanter (1970)
Decision Theory	Clemons (1991); Schell (1986)
Graphical Cost/Benefit	Shoval & Lugasi (1988)
Multiple Criteria	Chandler (1982)
Option Value	Dos Santos (1991)
Value Analysis	Keen (1981)
Subjective:	
User Attitude Survey	Hamilton & Chervany (1981)
User Utility Function	Ahituv (1980)
AHP	Roper-Lowe & Sharp (1990)
Delphia	Senn (1978); North & Pyke (1960)
Both:	
MADM	Carter (1992)
Value Chain	Rainer et al. (1991)
Speculative Risk Grid	McGaughey et al. (1994)
Portfolio Models	Segev (1995)
Cost Modeling	Busch (1994)

Table 1: Strategic/IT Investment Evaluation Methods

must also consider the subjective factor of strategic justification in terms of competitive edge, entry barriers and critical success factors. An overview of strategic/IT evaluation techniques and main references are presented in Table 1. Independently, each of these techniques have significant drawbacks in estimating telecommunications investments. More research is required in this area to determine the most appropriate calculation(s) necessary for evaluating telecommunications investment decisions.

In summary, as Powell (1992, p. 29) points out, "Information technology investment is more difficult than many other investment decisions because the cost and benefits are hard to identify and quantify and the intangible factors present are likely to be significant." Powell also states that there are currently seventeen identified IT evaluation methodologies and suggests that since a 'new' method would not likely solve this problem "...a last attempt might be to investigate how currently available techniques might be employed and possibly amended to overcome some of the difficulties raised..." Following this reasoning, the proposed OS-Investment model does not propose a new methodology, but attempts to communicate a view of examining telecommunications investment decisions that is likely to be familiar to IT managers as well as other key decision makers in an organization.

The objective is not just to capitalize on an acronym that is familiar to telecommunications managers, but also to use the underpinnings of the familiar OSI model to develop guidelines for measurement and evaluation techniques and modeling tools. The next section proposes the Outcome-based Systems Investment model.

Development of the OS-Investment Model

Technological justification has been studied from many different perspectives (e.g., Schell, 1986; Keen, 1988; Keen and Cummins, 1994; King and Premkumar, 1989; Parker and Benson, 1989). Our proposed metamodel is organized into different units of analysis in an attempt to coordinate these perspectives. We use the terms model and metamodel interchangeably to describe this model because it can serve as a standalone entity or can be used to define the specific models, decision techniques, and measurement criteria to be used in a specific investment. The value of technology can be viewed, in terms of the organization, as a network of value-added/costs interacting with its environment or value-added/costs between organizational units or in terms of individual value-added/costs. By considering justification separately from technical viability, a more accurate estimate of the economic impact of a project or investment can be determined.

Our proposed metamodel is based on the hierarchy (levels) of IT applications and the foundation for each of these levels depends on the

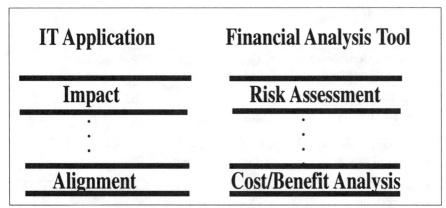

*Figure 2: Spectrum of IT Applications and Financial Analysis Tools
Adapted from Parker and Benson (1989)*

character of the business itself. Parker and Benson (1989) introduce the 'business value linkage' framework which links the value-added chain to financial justification.   They propose a spectrum of IT applications ranging from improving the performance of the existing enterprise (alignment) to improving the chances of success for new business opportunities and strategies (impact). Alignment-oriented applications of IT focus on maintaining competitive position and proven practices.   Impact applications focus on gaining competitive advantage and technology domain. The type of IT application then determines which financial analysis tool is applied ranging from measurement (i.e., cost/benefit analysis) to evaluation (i.e., risk assessment) techniques (Figure 2). Our proposed model expands the type of IT application (based on economic and organizational justification criteria and previous theoretical investment models) and financial analysis tools (based on previously outlined measurement and evaluation techniques) to seven layers using the OSI model as a framework.

The OSI data communications model was developed to establish standards for data communications networks. "The purpose of the standards developed for the OSI architecture model is to provide a common basis for interconnecting dissimilar open systems" (Keen and Cummins, 1994, p. 281). Similarly, the purpose of our value added/ cost model based on OSI is to provide a common basis for evaluating the dissimilar approaches of value-added and cost analysis.

"The OSI model is a seven-layered generic structure that defines communications tasks and functions to be carried out by specific protocols, but it does not specify the particular protocols to be used...Each layer in the model provides interface services to the adjacent higher layer in the structure...the actual physical transfer of information is between adjacent layers of one system until it reaches the bottom physical layer; then it is transferred across the network to the corresponding physical layer of the receiving system..." (Keen and

Value-Added		Costs
Changes in Market Structure (External Environment)	7. Application Layer (Risk Management)	Research and Development
Competitive Advantage (Business Strategy)	6. Presentation Layer (Value Analysis)	Reorganize/Restructure Education and Training
Production Economics (Strategic Business Unit)	5. Session Layer (Value Restructuring)	Administration
Core Competency (Primary Business)	4. Transport Layer (Option Pricing)	Operations
Increased Revenues (Value Acceleration)	3. Network Layer (Value Acceleration)	Maintenance and Support
Efficiency/Quality (Value Linking)	2. Data Link Layer (Value Linking)	Software and Development
Direct Benefits/ Cost Reductions	1. Physical Layer (ROI Analysis)	Hardware

Figure 3: Outcome-Based Systems Investment Model

Cummins, 1994, p. 281). Accordingly, the proposed Outcome-based Systems Investment model uses a seven-layer structure that defines the value-added and costs at each level depending upon the technological investment opportunity of the business. As in the OSI model, each layer provides information to the adjacent higher layer and only the necessary layers become involved. The following sections describe each of the seven OSI layers: 1) in terms of data communications, 2) in terms of the value-added and cost analysis model and 3) in terms of suggested procedures that could be used in employing the OS-Investment model for telecommunications investment justification. In the proposed OS-Investment model, the information from the pertinent 'value-added' layers and the corresponding 'cost' layers (Figure 3) are determined. Keen (1988) recommends first establishing the benefit of the technology while keeping costs separate, giving the net business value. While the cost and value-added models are not directly comparable, the OSI model serves as a valid framework to identify what 'value-added' and cost considerations might be appropriate for each investment. We next describe each layer of the OSI model as well as our proposed OS-Investment model.

Physical Layer

The OSI physical layer specifies the physical interface and is concerned with transmitting data bits over a communications circuit.

This layer deals with the mechanical, electrical, functional and procedural characteristics to establish, maintain, and deactivate the physical link. This is the only layer in which data actually moves between separate systems.

This layer in the OS-Investment model is concerned with the physical benefits/costs and hardware or the perceived benefits factor of the technology. The value-added physical layer in the OS-Investment model is the direct and indirect benefits and cost reductions due to: elimination of personnel, reduction of inventory and management costs, reductions due to less waste and the elimination of obsolete materials and better distribution of resources. The costs physical layer is the fixed costs of the technology such as the hardware costs. These costs include the computer and communications equipment, facilities costs and common carrier line charges.

Traditional cost/benefit analysis approach for items that can be directly calculated applies to this layer. Level 1 calculations are traditional capital budgeting decisions using return on investment (ROI) techniques using discounted cash flow (DCF) analysis (e.g., King and Schrems, 1978; Kanter, 1970). Level 1 should be calculated if the technology will affect only localized internal operations of the business. The fixed costs related to the technology such as the hardware and facilities costs along with the benefits due to reduction of inventory, elimination of personnel, etc. are estimated and cash inflows and outlays based on the appropriate discount rate should be computed.

Data Link Layer

The OSI data link layer manages the basic transmission circuit established in the physical layer and provides for the reliable transfer of data. The data link layer packages the data for transmission, unpackages data upon receipt, and handles error detection during transmission. Its chief function is error correction.

This corresponding layer in the OS-Investment model is concerned with error correction through efficiency and quality and defining data transmission through software and development. This layer deals with the increases in efficiency and quality related to the technology. The value-added characteristics include the smoothing of operational flows, reduced volume of paper handled, and rise in level of service quality and performance. These calculations use Information Economics value linking justification. Value-linking is a technique to assess costs that enable benefits to be achieved in other departments through a ripple effect (Parker and Benson, 1987). The cost data link layer is concerned with the software and development costs associated with the technology. These include such things as software costs, file conversion costs, development and performance of acceptance tests and documentation and vendor installation charges.

Level 2 calculations should be performed if the investment will contribute to improvements in efficiency and quality within the organization. Level 2 calculations include estimated benefits due to increases in efficiency and quality or additional values 'linked' to the new technology. The software and development costs associated with the technology are included in the calculations at this level. Decision theory techniques (Clemons, 1991; Schell, 1986) could be used here.

Network Layer

The OSI network layer is primarily concerned with network addressing, establishing and terminating connections across the network and the routing of information through the network. When a message is received, the network layer is responsible for partitioning it into blocks or packets and at the receiving end, reassembling it into the original message.

This layer in the OS-Investment model is concerned with routing the information through value acceleration (Parker and Benson, 1987) as well as addressing (maintaining and supporting) the business operations. The value-added network layer is based on increase in revenues due to increased sales because of better responsiveness, improved services and faster processing of operations (internal efficiency). Increases in revenues are due to improvements in services throughout the organization including additional values 'linked' to the new technology (such as increased performance and capability) and resource sharing. These calculations involve using Information Economics value acceleration methods which causes benefits to be received more quickly. The cost network layer focuses on the costs associated with the maintenance and support of the technology. These include costs of transforming operational procedures, and hardware and software maintenance costs.

Level 3 should be calculated if the investment is expected to increase revenues due to improvements in services throughout the organization. The increase in revenues associated with the addition of the technology are included in the calculations as well as the costs associated with the maintenance and support of the technology. For level 3, decision support tools such as multiattribute decision model (MADM), analytical hierarchy process (AHP) and Hurwicz's principle (Carter, 1992) or the graphical cost-benefit approach (Shoval and Lugasi, 1988) may prove useful.

Transport Layer

The OSI transport layer provides reliable, transparent transfer of data between separate systems or data administration. The transport layer controls the quality of the entire transmission, ensures network facilities are used efficiently, and ensures the integrity of the entire message from its origins to its destinations.

The OS-Investment model's transport layer is similarly concerned with the operations of the business or the core competency (organizational strategy factor). The value-added transport layer is concerned with how the technology affects the primary function of the business (its core competency). The value-added is faster decision making by faster access to information and determining the 'true' value of a project. A major portion of the value of new IT projects accrues from future projects that use the technology. Few benefits are obtained from the initial project. One of the values-added obtained by an organization is experience in the use of the technology. The 'true' value of a first-stage project is the traditional user-oriented benefits, plus the benefits of second-stage projects. These results are transportable to other parts of the organization. New technology projects that provide the firm the opportunity to invest in future projects that are risky, are more valuable than projects that will only offer an opportunity to invest in less risky projects. In addition, if that investment opportunity is available for a long time, the value of the new technology increases. The lower the correlation between the development costs and revenues of future investment opportunities, the greater the value of the new technology (Dos Santos, 1991). The cost transport layer deals with the costs associated with operating the network. These costs include additional operating personnel and security, backup and control costs.

Level 4 calculations should be estimated if the technology will have an effect on the core competency of the organization. Level 4 is concerned with the additional benefits obtained by future projects which will require the technology, or a project's contribution to management's need for information on core activities. Costs such as those associated with operating the new technology including personnel and security costs are included in these calculations. Option pricing techniques such as the model suggested by Dos Santos (1991) could be used here to capture the potential of IT to support strategic alternatives in the future. These techniques are mainly used for evaluating multiple proposals with varying prices and capabilities. Scores are assigned based on a proposed project's value to corporate business objectives and risks.

Session Layer

The OSI session layer provides the control structure for communication between applications or network administration activities. The session layer establishes and controls the dialogue between the two communicating applications and acts as a moderator.

The OS-Investment session layer is concerned with administration and providing the control structure (key resources) for the organization. The value-added session layer is concerned with how the technology affects the strategic business unit (organizational policy factor). IT can change the value of key resources by reducing the cost of integrating and coordinating economic activities. This increases the potential production economies, such as scale, scope and specialization that can be exploited (Clemons and Row, 1991). The costs session layer deals with the costs associated with the administration of the network. These costs also include additional personnel for network administration and costs associated with additional vendors.

Level 5 is concerned with how the technology affects the strategic business unit by reducing the costs of key resources and exploiting economies of scale, scope and specialization through the use of the technology. Level 5 should be calculated if the investment is expected to affect the value of key resources or the support functions of the organization. Costs which are included at this level include administration of the technology. Lucas, Weill and Cox (1993), suggest using four perspectives in measuring performance: financial perspective, customer perspective, business-process perspective and organizational learning perspective. The financial perspective measures relative market share, increased margins and cashflow. The customer perspective can be measured by on-time shipments, profit margins, and customer satisfaction. The business-process perspective is measured by manufacturing cycle time, order entry time, process yield, and inventory turnover. The organizational learning perspective is the ability to sustain innovation and make improvements and might be measured by percentage of sales derived from products using the technology or number of successful products innovations due to the technology during the year. The Delphi approach (Senn, 1978; North and Pyke, 1969) may prove useful in evaluating these estimates. If the technology would supply resources to the core activities, i.e. a support function, value restructuring techniques are required. This technique estimates the effects the technology contributes to each employee/department level. Value restructuring analysis techniques could also be used here. Value restructuring analysis assumes that because a function exists within an organization, it has some recognized value, based on economic theory (Parker and Benson, 1987).

Presentation Layer

The OSI presentation layer is primarily responsible for formatting data. It transforms the data to provide common communication services. This layer negotiates, selects and maintains the syntax of the information being transferred between the application processes. It transforms data from the format of the sending application to a compatible format and performs code conversion, data compression and data encryption when needed.

The OS-Investment layer at this level is concerned with reorganizing and restructuring when needed and negotiating and selecting the best business strategy (business strategy factor). The value-added presentation layer deals with how the proposed technology will affect the business strategy (that is, the affect the technology has on the firm's competitive advantage). Keen (1988, p. 194) states that "the formal proposal for any major investment must look at both cost and value" and that business criteria should drive technical planning. He states that telecommunications is a strategic capital investment for reasons such as:

1. operational necessity-to keep up with the base level of service in one's industry
2. defensive necessity-to protect one's market
3. competitive opportunity-to steal an edge
4. breakaways and preemptive strikes-to changes the rules of the game for competitors

However, in order to effectively evaluate strategic capital investment, management must first understand how technology affects competition. Porter and Millar (1985) identify three ways that technology affects competition: (1) it alters industry structures, (2) it supports costs and differentiation strategies and (3) it spawns entirely new businesses. They state (p. 50) that "a business is profitable if the value it creates exceeds the cost of performing value activities. To gain competitive advantage over its rivals, a company must either perform these activities at a lower cost or perform them in a way that leads to differentiation and a premium price (more value)." Barua, Kriebel and Mukhopadhyay (1991, p. 330) discuss the strategic impacts of IT investment and demonstrate that the "outcome of competitive advantage versus strategic necessity depends on several factors, including the relative IT efficiency of the competing firms, the similarity of their products or services, and the opportunity to price the IT-related services." The costs presentation layer is concerned with education, training/retraining, reorganization and restructuring expenditures.

Level 6 deals with how the technology will affect the firm's competitive advantage. One technique suggested by Keen (1981) when knowledge, accuracy and confidence about issues for innovation are unknown, is value analysis. Value analysis asks simple questions most managers would naturally ask. The first step establishes the value by defining an operational list of benefits (i.e., what exactly will I get from the technology?) and determining a cost threshold. Financial, technical, project, functionality and systemic risks are then balanced against strategic necessity. Information Economics innovation and investment valuation or value analysis techniques can be used here since they are useful for new, unprecedented applications of technology. Innovation and investment valuation is applied when the financial issues change from measuring to evaluating and choosing among new, untried and unproven alternatives. These techniques consider the value and benefit of gaining and sustaining competitive advantage, the risk and cost of being first, and the risk and cost of failure (Parker and Benson, 1987).

Application Layer

The OSI application layer is responsible for coordinating communications between applications that reside in different systems linked across a network. The application layer is used to standardize generic elements common to different classes of applications. This layer is the source or ultimate receiver of data transmitted. The application layer contains the management functions necessary to provide services to the users of the OSI environment.

The application layer in the OS-Investment model is the source of the information through research and development and the receiver through changes in market structure due to the technology (environmental uncertainty factor). The value-added application layer is concerned with how the technology affects the business in relation to the external environment and in changing market structure. "The competitive significance of a technological change depends neither on its scientific merit nor its effect on the ability of the firm to serve market needs per se, but on its impact on industry structure" (Porter, 1983, p. 2). Dos Santos, Peffers and Mauer (1993) provide empirical support for the case study evidence linking innovative IT investments with competitive advantages for firms. The cost application layer is concerned with continuing research and development and associated costs and risk assessment. Strategic telecommunications investments are based mainly on innovation, investment valuation and risk assessment. These type of investments deal with how the technology will affect the firm's competitive advantage in terms of first-mover and strategic business advantages. This level of investment is concerned with management vision and organizational objectives which would change market and industry structure. Furthermore, this level is usually very complex and has high research and development costs. Weill (1990) suggests that IT investment made to create competitive advantage is risky and has high potential payoff for only a few successful adopters.

Level 7 is concerned with changing market structure and research and development costs. Level 7 calculations are considered if the investment will have an effect on industry structure. First-mover advantages as well as research and development costs should be estimated. IO risk assessment methods are used here. Techniques such as cost modeling as suggested by Busch (1994), Speculative Risk Grid and Pure Risk Grid as suggested by McGaughey, Snyder and Carr (1994) and Value Chain Risk analysis as suggested by Rainer, Snyder and Carr (1991) may be used at this level. Overall, resources should be concentrated on those investments perceived to have the greatest commercial potential.

OS-Investment Model Overview

Now that the OS-Investment model for justifying technology investment has been outlined, it can be compared to the previously mentioned IT models. By using this model, businesses can focus on the 'level' of the model that is appropriate to the investment. By partitioning the value-added and costs into hierarchical segments, managers are better able to view and evaluate the justification process for telecommunications.

Quality profit engineering (Keen and Cummins, 1994) can be integrated into this model. Traditional cost analysis and revenues are the basis for levels 1 and 2, quality and service premium costs can be found at level 3, profit management and alerting systems are levels 4 and 5, and long-term business infrastructure costs are levels 6 and 7. In the King and Premkumar (1989) model, the process elements contain the justification for telecommunications. The technology process element corresponds to level 4; the business process element corresponds to level 5; the organizational process element is level 6; and the environmental process element corresponds to level 7. In the Parker and Benson (1989) enterprise-wide information management model, their primary function layer equates to the transport layer (4); the enterprise organization is the session layer (5); the business strategy layer is the presentation layer (6); and the environment is the application layer (7).

Keen's model (1988) states that businesses should focus on the benefit side of the cost-benefit equation and know where to put the emphasis.

> "For radical moves, a strong focus on value is called for with costs defined in terms of a floor. For innovative moves, emphasize value but also be more detailed in indicating costs components and ranges. For incremental moves give equal weight to benefit and cost, but treat them separately and in that order. And for operational moves, be very precise about costs, since that is the issue here; the firm does not need to make the change and the real benefit is the cost impact (p. 195)."

Radical moves require consideration of all seven levels. Innovative moves involve the first six layers. Incremental moves involve the first five layers. Operational moves may involve the first four layers.

The flexibility and completeness of the OS-Investment model can give managers a better understanding of the relationship between value-added and costs analysis of technology and how a proposed technological investment fits into the overall corporate strategy (business plan).

Questions		Costs/Value-Added/Technique
Will the new technology have an effect on industry structure?	7. Risk Management	1) Estimate first-move adv. 2) Add in R&D costs 3) Cost model/risk grid/value chain
Will the new technology affect the firm's competitive advantage?	6. Value Analysis	1) Determine cost threshold 2) Add in educ., retrain, restruct 3) Balance the risks vs. strategy
Will the new technology affect the value of key resources/support facts?	5. Value Restructuring	1) Estimate key resource reduct. 2) Include techn. admin. costs 3) Delphi/value restructuring
Will the new technology have an effect on the Core Competency?	4, Option Pricing	1) Estimate add. benefits of future 2) Include personnel and security 3) Option pricing/option valuation
Will the new technology increase revenues due to service improvement?	3. Value Acceleration	1) Estimate income in revenues 2) Add in maintenance & support costs 3) Use decision support tools (AHP)
Will the new technology contribute to Efficiency/Quality?	2. Value Linking	1) Estimate add. values "linked" 2) Add in software and dev. costs 3) Use decision theory techniques
Will the new technology affect only localized internal operations?	1. ROI Analysis	1) Estimate expected cash flows 2) Compare to expected outlays 3) Use DCF techniques

Figure 4: OS-Investment Model Questions and Techniques

Procedures for Using the OS-Investment Model

Each of the model constructs must be operationalized at each of the seven levels. Each 'level' of this model has a corresponding question. An affirmative response at the highest 'level' question indicates the 'level' of the investment decision and becomes the superset of analysis techniques. Decision makers need to ensure that the 'level' of investment decision being considered fits into the organization's overall technology investment portfolio. Weill (1990) states that a firm should develop a balanced portfolio of IT investment to suit both its strategy and level of IT experience. Each type of IT investment contains different objectives and risks and the portfolio should balance the risk versus gain. Weill also suggests that an IT investment made to create competitive advantage is risky and has high potential payoff for only a few successful adopters. If it does, the model

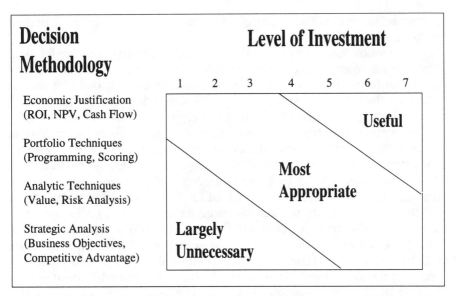

Decision Methodology	Level of Investment

Figure 5: Investment Decision Method and Level of Investment
Adapted from Meredith and Hill (1987)

construct(s) for that 'level' of investment decision are then operationalized by performing the appropriate calculations (Figure 4) for each level of affirmative response.

The investment calculation techniques suggested (in Figure 4) for each level are merely guidelines. Many methodologies, both objective and subjective, have been proposed for evaluating IT investments (Powell, 1992). Although each level involved in the investment decision should technically be calculated, in higher level decisions it is generally recognized that ROI-type calculations are not relevant since they cannot usually be associated with measurable financial gains or losses and should be considered as a sunk cost (Weill and Olson, 1989; Robinson, 1985). Meredith and Hill (1987) have examined the appropriateness of different approaches to investment justification and state that the relevance of economic, portfolio, analytic and strategic considerations is dependent on the level of system integration (Figure 5). The critical factor, according to these authors, is not the technology itself, but the intended use of the investment. More research in this area is required to determine the most appropriate calculation(s) necessary for the telecommunications investment.

In addition, it is not suggested that every calculation for every level involved be performed in this OS-Investment model. A fisheye view as proposed by Jones (1996) is suggested in employing telecommunications decisions using this model. That is, the level of the particular telecommunications investment decision should be emphasized while suppressing, but retaining global detail. The factors and calculations for the level of the telecommunications investment is the most detailed.

However, the rest of the 'picture' is still included, but to a lesser degree of detail.

The following example illustrates an application of the model. The first step is to make sure that the telecommunication project investment conforms to the open system standards and procedures put in place by the entire telecommunications strategic plan, i.e. the overall technology investment portfolio of the organization. The next step is to determine the type of investment decision the organization is considering. For telecommunication investments, that will only affect the primary business function; only the value-added and costs for the first four layers need to be considered. For example, if a small organization is considering an initial LAN in which improvements in efficiency and quality **within** the organization would be expected to occur, only the first four layers of the model would be calculated. The first consideration is to add all the potential benefits that would occur due to the addition of the LAN. This includes all direct benefits and cost reductions due to the LAN, along with the estimated additional values gained by the organization 'linked' to the new technology, plus the increases in revenues due to the LAN, plus the additional benefits obtained by future project requirements (knowledge and experience). Then, one needs to estimate all the potential costs due to the addition of the LAN such as additional hardware, software, development, maintenance, support, personnel and security costs. Finally, we may use an appropriate decision support technique to validate the final decision such as the AHP (Roper-Lowe and Sharp, 1990) or option valuation model techniques (Dos Santos, 1991). It must be remembered that each telecommunications investment will be seen differently by every company. That is, a LAN for a small organization who has not previously been networked will place the investment higher on the model (level 3 or 4) than a LAN for a large organization who already has several in place (level 1 or 2). This is part of the flexibility of our proposed model: the decisionmaker decides what level of the model they should consider based on their individual organization and circumstances.

Although the telecommunication investment should be viewed from the 'big picture,' only the value-added and costs for the appropriate level need to be computed. In keeping with the fisheye view, the most important considerations should be at the highest level, or in the previous hypothetical case, level 4 (core competency). In this case, if the investment will effect the core competency of the organization, the major estimations should be based on the additional benefits which will be gained by future project requirements and the additional costs of increased personnel and security to manage the investment. Although the lower level benefits and costs are important considerations, these will most likely be overshadowed. In most organizations installing an initial LAN, the major concerns are not the cost of the hardware and software, but the costs of operating, maintaining, supporting and protecting the integrity of the LAN in the future. On the value-added side, the LAN is seen as a first step in networking the organization and although the technology is expected to increase revenues, the main goal is usually to view this as a stepping stone to future telecommunications investments.

Management Strategies for Information Technology Investment

"Investing in telecommunications is inherently a business gamble. The technology is expensive, rapidly changing and complex" (Keen, 1988, p. 5). How then does management determine the potential value of these technologies to its business strategy? The OS-Investment metamodel suggests one approach through the use of an open systems framework. Open systems interconnection is based on the concept of cooperating distributed applications. OSI is concerned with the exchange of information between open systems and not the internal functioning of each individual system. The capability of systems to cooperate in the exchange of information and in the accomplishment of tasks is paramount.

The proposed OS-Investment model is also concerned with the concept of open systems. "A firm should be conceived of as an economic value-adding transformation through representing the firm as an open system..." (Betz, p. 253). When a firm is viewed as an open system it can be seen that the whole, as defined by OS-Investment, is more that the sum of its parts. The OS-Investment model provides a common framework of reference when referring to value-added and/ or costs and the relationship between them. It provides for the exchange of information between the value-added/cost levels and is concerned with the exchange of information between these two 'systems' in the accomplishment of a task (investment justification). The interrelationships between the value-added and cost levels highlights the complexity and may provide insight into the nature of the investment decision. In addition, by compartmentalizing functions into layers, managers are better able to identify and evaluate the justification process for telecommunications.

Justification for an investment is based on two key questions: What is the project worth to the business? and Does the business have the necessary resources to invest in the technology? (Parker and Benson, 1987) By separating benefits from costs, these two questions can be answered and more importantly justified. Dean and Sharfman (1996, p. 388-389) found that "...managers who collected information and used analytical techniques made decisions that were more effective than those who did not." Informed managers are therefore more likely to make more successful decisions. In addition, power and politics have been recognized as influencing management objectives (Markus, 1981). By providing a comprehensive look at the estimated costs and benefits, it is hoped a more rational management decision can be made.

It is suggested that the proposed OS-Investment model is merely a communication vehicle which presents decision criteria in a way that is familiar to telecommunications decision makers and therefore might allow for more successful telecommunications investment decisions. The model outlines the appropriate factors which should be considered at each level of the investment decision, suggests the value-added and costs that need to be considered and proposes decision technique(s) which may be used to justify the investment decision. In addition, the proposed OS-Investment model helps in evaluating the 'fit' of the technology to the organization's IT plan by determining the level of the investment.

However, the model is only speculative at this point and many questions remain to be resolved. For example, choices of analytical techniques suggested at each layer are only our proposal based on our interpretation of the literature and still need to be validated and/or refuted. The techniques may really not be exclusive to a specific layer. While there is an implied hierarchy in the layers, it may be conceivable to have a system that only relates to some non-adjacent layers. The concept of a band for selecting the appropriate layers (as in Figure 5) is another issue to be validated.

Our purpose in presenting a conceptual model that requires considerable further development is to invite practitioners and academic communities to explore the concept of a familiar framework to address the problem of IT justification, a problem that has been the subject of much study but of relatively few practical results. For practitioners, we propose that technical managers could use this model as a guide to justify telecommunications investments to middle and upper-level managers, by outlining the factors which need to be considered in the telecommunications investment decision. We believe that a guiding metamodel such as this proposed OS-Investment model would help in determining the appropriate cost and value-added questions to be asked and calculations to be performed. For academicians, this prescriptive model can provide a foundation as well as a direction for future cohesive and focused research by determining which subset(s) of techniques are most appropriate for justifying specific telecommunications investments. We recognize the need to test the efficiency and effectiveness of the OSI approach in actual telecommunications investment decision problems.

We suggest a case study approach to validate this model and we invite other researchers to collaborate with us on testing the use of this model. Further research is required in order to support this proposed framework in determining:

1. the appropriate level(s) of the model,
2. the most important value-added and costs, and
3. the most appropriate decision technique(s),

which should be applied in order to justify telecommunications investment decisions. "As with any major business strategy, technology's contribution is only as real as its impact to the bottom line" (Research-Technology Management, 1996, p. 6). This proposed OS-Investment model is one approach to help justify telecommunications investments' bottom-line.

Chapter 11

Measuring Software Process Improvement Payoff

Rick Gibson
American University

    The purpose of this chapter is to distill concepts from software engineering practice and the process improvement literature that may be used to justify Information Technology (IT) process improvement investments. Such investments have reached threshold levels that have triggered senior management reactions centered on determining the associated contributions and payoffs. More than ever, such assessments of IT value are needed in order to evaluate decisions regarding new technology investment, outsourcing, cost reduction or reorganization. Created by breaking the rules that govern the way IT systems are perceived, strategic information systems create a direct link between a company's business objectives and the information processing resources needed to support them. Since such radical changes in fundamental relationships defy traditional measurement approaches, such as productivity increases, they should be judged by their impact on customers.

    Confronted with a lack of consensus among researchers and practitioners regarding IT investment payoff, it seems appropriate to return to first principles. The reference discipline of economics has long established the importance of residual factors of productivity, which include process improvement factors. Accepting the basic quality tenet that process improvements lead to product improvements has taken the software industry on a journey guided by process improvement models such as the CMM. The real–life examples of CMM–based process improvements described in this chapter are obvious and significant. This chapter's search for evidence of IT investment payoff adopts a microeconomic canonical approach. Information supplied by IT investment is a scarce resource, which is in high demand and as such, lends itself to study by methods from the discipline of economics. Economic theory provides the instruments to model the value added by a service industry, such as IT, with the sub–discipline called cost–benefit analysis. The conclusions reached suggest that using process improvement models to operationalize the IT investment and performance constructs have provided indisputable measures of IT payoff. Senior managers must be apprised of these benefits so they continue to provide the information processing resources needed to support a company's business objectives.

The increasing use of information technology (IT) by business enterprises for strategic purposes has resulted in a conceptual revolution in the information systems field that shows no sign of abating. Investments in IT have reached threshold levels that have triggered senior management reactions centered on determining the associated contributions and payoffs. More than ever, such assessments of IT value are needed in order to evaluate decisions regarding new technology investment, outsourcing, cost reduction or reorganization. Created by breaking the rules that govern the way IT systems are perceived, strategic information systems create a direct link between a company's business objectives and the information processing resources needed to support them. Since such radical changes in fundamental relationships defy traditional measurement approaches, such as productivity increases, they should be judged by their impact on customers. The purpose of this chapter is to distill concepts from software engineering practice and the process improvement literature that may be used to justify IT process improvement investments.

This chapter's search for evidence of IT investment payoff adopts a microeconomic canonical approach. Information supplied by IT investment is a scarce resource, which is in high demand and as such, lends itself to study by methods from the discipline of economics. Economic theory provides the instruments to model the value added by a service industry, such as IT, with the sub-discipline called cost-benefit analysis. Scott Morton (1991) introduces a perspective on IT that focuses on the new power available to fundamentally alter work by qualitative manipulation of information and heuristics. He uses the analogy of the Industrial Revolution steam engine's impact on business to suggest the step-function change expected from widespread use of the "information engine." Since IT systems create associations between logic and raw data, the principal constraint on these systems is the limitation of software in representing these associations. It is therefore appropriate to consider software to be the product supplied by IT investment. Software is a highly complex, ill-defined product with a unique development process. Bandinelli et al. (1995) note that software process improvement has become one of the most important research areas for government and private industry.

IT Investment Measurement Problems

Accurate measurement of IT costs and benefits are especially problematic for at least four major reasons. First, there is no such thing as starting anew in the IT environment—no firm can abandon the very substantial computer and communications investments made over many years. Efforts to reliably estimate development time and costs are usually classified as either Prototyping (essentially an outcome-based control strategy) or Systems Development Life Cycle (an input or behavior-based approach preferred by risk averse practitioners). Second, due to the nature of the technology, system capacity cannot be increased continuously, but must follow a cycle starting with substantial excess capacity in a new system that has no marginal value. Hardware supply problems are compounded by the fact that information systems utilize a highly volatile technology. For example, the cost effectiveness of computer processing and storage technology has improved by a factor of 10^6 in just thirty years. Investment and staffing uncertainties combined with the high ratio of fixed to variable costs results in extreme difficulties in developing capacity estimates. Third, a non-trivial question remains as to exactly what is meant by the term information—a uniquely expandable, substitutable, transportable, diffusive, and shareable entity. Care must be taken to avoid inappropriate application of concepts developed for the management of more tangible things, such as the concepts of property or depreciation. Fourth, the IT department's inability to quantify an objective such as "improves service" is a disadvantage in competition for the organization's financial resources. Attempts to do so have caused queuing models to dominate the computer performance evaluation literature. Mendelson (1988) notes that attempts to embed a general queuing model into the standard microeconomic framework to study price and capacity decisions have resulted in guidelines that contradict common maxims. Queuing effects are not self-regulating, so congestion results in a delay cost inflicted on the rest of the system. With delays, the IT budget cannot be balanced due to the delay cost that is paid by the users but not collected by the IT department. So, when taking user delay into account, low system utilization is acceptable.

One method of introducing IT measurement issues is to briefly present some of the key ideas of the preeminent researchers of this problem without any attempt to assign priorities to their contributions. Nearly a decade ago, Strassmann (1988) warned that measurements of information and technology were required for budgeting computer investments, but that conventional ratio-analysis methods were misleading. He showed that there is no point in comparing one firm's IT budget with other companies as a percentage of sales or any other internal variables. The external marketplace is the competitive equalizer, and must be included in all evaluations.

Brynjolfsson (1993) is among the small but growing number of researchers attempting to understand the relationship between IT investments and productivity. He attributes dismal reports on IT productivity to four mistakes. One is mismeasurement, as shown by the unmeasured quality improvement that has resulted from automated teller machines used by the banking industry. A second mistake is the failure to account for the time required for IT investment payoff due to adjustment lags, which may be as long as five years. Third, redistribution of profits has not yet spread from benefiting individual firms to entire industries. A fourth mistake is mismanagement such as use of heuristics for IT decisions rather than rigorous cost/benefit analysis.

Later, Brynjolfsson (1994) reminds us that not too long ago the business press described the productivity paradox of computers—billions spent without increasing worker output. More recently, more positive correlations were revealed between computer investment and output. He warns that much work is still needed and that focus on aggregate productivity statistics is distracting and meaningless.

Mahmood et al. (1996) provide several guidelines that emerged from a study of productivity of software projects. They contend that either function points or source lines of code are appropriate as single productivity measures—if used consistently, but multidimensional inputs (e.g., hours spent by process stage) and outputs (e.g., SLOC and number of modifications) are needed. Their study was motivated by the large amounts of money spent on software and the obvious fact that even modest productivity improvements would save billions of dollars.

Parker and Benson (1988) explain that in order for enterprises to gain a competitive edge, the way IT is financially justified must also change. Cost-benefit analysis is not adequate for evaluation of IT applications, except when dealing only with cost-avoidance issues. Information economics, which measures and justifies IT on the basis of business performance, is a better method. One technique used in information economics is value linking, which involves assessment of benefits achieved in other departments in calculating the contribution of IT. Another technique is value restructuring, which assumes that if a function exists in an organization it has some value. This suggests consideration of IT investments as analogous to those of research and development or the legal department.

Mendelson (1988) blames the mutual partial ignorance of providers and users of IT for failed efforts to determine its value. Within an organization there exist reasons for both IT managers and functional managers to seek to improve IT systems regardless of cost, resulting in a proliferation of costs and ineffective systems. Information is perceived as a powerful, sensitive resource; resulting in a tendency to expand, to maximize the systems that provide it. Also, for IT personnel, their labor market value and self-concept are based on attainment of state-of-the-art skills, thus creating desires for technological capabilities and costs in excess than what is optimal for their required contributed to the organization.

An elegantly simple investment management strategy comes from Davis (1996). He reminds us that software began in a rational era when software was developed and good work was obvious and utilized. The 1980s ushered in the empirical era and the philosophy of software engineering technology—baseline your process, introduce the new method, compare results—but this overlooked development team skill, which is a key variable we cannot control or measure. Davis argues for a synthesis era guided by simple tenets. If a new method has an obvious positive effect on productivity or quality, then adopt it. If the effect is questionable, then the benefit is likely minor, so do not bother.

Information Technology: What's the Value?

Classical economic theory suggests that demand is directly related to the perceived value for any product. For an unusual product such as information, the magnitude of this perceived value to business managers is based solely on the information's utility in supporting decision making. This utility is affected by the information's timeliness, accuracy, presentation mode, completeness, and degree of

Past	Present
Financial	Holistic and political
Cost savings, Tactical	Opportunity, Strategic
Less than two years for ROI	Greater than three years for ROI
Single business area	Multi/cross-functional
Small, then monolithic systems	Modular, then incremental systmes
In IT departments	In business departments
Technically risky	Organizationally risky
Standalone systems	Interdependent and infrastructure
Pre-project	Ongoing
Project maangement	Change and benefits management
Technology driven	Business driven
Involved experts only	All stakeholders involved
Quantitative and intangible benefits	Qualitative and social issues

Table 1: IT Investment Appraisal Factors (Source: Serafeimidis, 1996)

aggregation. Under such conditions, and where the evaluation of IT personnel is based on quality of service, not efficiency, IT personnel are likely to overinsure against failure or error by developing elaborate, inefficient, though highly effective systems. This economic theory was verified by Katz (1993), who surveyed U.S. organizations to determine how they measured the business value of IT. He discovered two major categories of value: information systems department performance and impact of IT on the business. Effectiveness of IT was not an issue or concern.

More recently, Serafeimidis (1996) summarized past and present information systems evaluation factors to improve understanding, as shown in Table 1.

Wilson (1988) grouped 160 measures of IT into seven assessment methods: productivity (efficiency of expenditure), user utility, value chain (impact of IT on goals), competitive performance, business alignment, investment targeting, management vision. Comparably, DeLone and McLean (1992) develop a thorough taxonomy to argue convincingly for a consideration of six categories of measures of IS success: system quality, information quality, use, user satisfaction, individual impact and organizational impact. They warn that arbitrary selection of items from these categories is unlikely to provide a valid measure of success.

Clark (1992) notes that the IT literature provides little specific guidance on IT contribution to the bottom line, but does provide some areas that need assessment and some representative performance measures such as: reliability of service, technical performance, business plan support. In contrast to other functional areas, assessment of IT at the enterprise level was not judged as useful; instead arguing that if each project was acceptable on a cost/benefit basis, then the sum was beneficial. This flawed reasoning ignores subsystem interface, synergy and suboptimization issues.

Jones (1995) suggests that best-in-class companies may provide the best idea of what to measure to determine IT value. Such firms, which include AT&T, Hewlett-Packard, and Microsoft measure: quality, productivity, soft factors (processes, tools, infrastructure, skills, training) and business measures (portfolio size, growth rate, replacement cost, usage, market share).

Information Technology: What's the Cost?

Accampo (1989) contends that traditional methods of cost-benefit analysis can be hard to apply to activities in which the key commodity is information that must be delivered when and where it is needed. New methods of cost justification are needed, which treat IT as an asset whose function is to manage key information flows that improve productivity and decision support.

Software has an extremely low variable cost after development and is difficult to price because it has value only as ascribed by its application. Unlike hardware, competitive software development does not require low cost inputs and components to be successful. Instead, software uses relatively high-cost inputs in the form of highly educated individuals.

Consider the contention by Parker and Benson (1988) that changes from standalone, functional application-oriented systems to database oriented enterprise-wide systems have been caused primarily by a reversal of the traditional constraint as applied to the resource mix—hardware costs are becoming less expensive and personnel costs for development and maintenance costs are soaring.

Mendelson (1988) attributes hardware cost declines to both supply factors and demand factors. Supply factors include: learning curve effects, integration efficiencies, regenerative feedback, and modularization. High demand has been sustained by the multipurpose nature of general purpose hardware, which can be subsequently customized by software. Unlike hardware with its well-defined costs and acquisition alternatives, software cost structures are vague. How do you compare software programs, or prove equivalence between specification and design? Do you develop software or buy it?

One indisputable conclusion that can be drawn from the preceding discussion is that there is more conflict than consensus regarding the software component of IT investment. The next section prescribes state-of-practice software process improvement models as a rational, economic solution to this dilemma. Although several process improvement models exist, the rationale for a chapter focus on the approach taken by the Software Engineering Institute will be presented.

Process Improvement Efforts as Investment Frameworks

Software development, like every production process, employs some specific balance of technique, tools, and materials calculated to produce the desired output. Fagerberg (1994) explains that, in economics, this principle is concisely referred to as the production function:

$$Y = [K + L + TFP]$$

Where Y is the gross domestic product, K is capital stock, L is labor input and TFP is a residual total factor of productivity to account for productivity not captured by the main variables and due to process improvement factors such as technology or education. Clearly, the production function suggests a focus on both product and process innovation due to new technology.

Software development as a process is an old idea, but began reemerging in the 1980s because of shortcomings in software productivity and quality. Competitive pressures on the software development industry at home and from abroad led many organizations to examine their software development processes. Heineman et al. (1994) observed that organizations began to realize that the key to improving the results of their software development operations was to focus on the software process by which the operations were performed.

Smith and Cusumano (1993) compared classic and PC software developers. Their findings as related to process improvement are as follows:

- IBM Federal Systems Company (Houston)—process improvement is critical in the drive to zero defects. The formal process is Causal Analysis and Defect Prevention.
- IBM Application Business Systems—after early efforts directed at schedules, ABS shifted process improvement efforts to quality using Causal Analysis and Defect prevention along with a Process and Quality Improvement department to introduce and spread new process ideas.

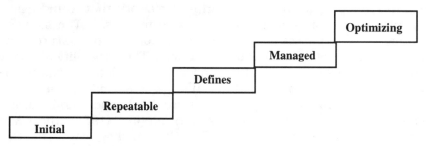

Figure 1: Capability Maturity Model

Immature Process	Mature Process
Ad hoc; process improvised by practitioners and management.	Work is done in a consistent, defined, documented and continuously improving way.
Procedures not rigorously followed or enforced.	Development efforts are supported visibly by management and others.
Highly dependent on current practitioners, key individuals.	Individual performance is still important, but institutionalized processes endure after the people who originally defined them are gone.
Product functionality and quality may be compromised in order to meet schedules.	Product and process measurement is used.
Use of new technology is risky	Disciplined use of technology.
Quality if difficult to predict	Process fidelity is controlled, audited and enforced.

Table 2: Maturity Concept (Source: Curtis and Paulk, 1993)

- Fujitsu—A Total Quality Control Program, which extends to subsidiaries and subcontractors forms the process improvement program.
- Hewlett-Packard—process improvement is driven by individual developers. Changes agreed to by developers include improved quality, shortened cycle time, or improved engineer productivity. Sources of ideas include the Corporate Quality and Technology Groups. Assessments are used to determine change areas.
- Microsoft—new process ideas come directly from teams, adopted by trying best practices, not through dictated usage.
- Lotus—each project chooses its own process, thus improvement does not occur.

The Software Engineering Institute (SEI) was established in 1984 and awarded to Carnegie Mellon University. The SEI's mission is to provide leadership in advancing the state of the practice of software engineering to improve the quality of systems that depend on software. In November 1986, the SEI with assistance from the Mitre Corporation began developing a process maturity framework that would assist organizations in improving their software process. The software process capability assessment methods developed by the SEI are being used by a growing number of organizations. The Capability Maturity Model (CMM) was developed under a federally funded program by the SEI as a common-sense application of process management and quality improvement concepts to software development and maintenance. Though now associated with Humphrey (1989), the CMM foundation is with Shewhart's plan/do/check/act cycle from the Bell telephone Labs in the 1930s, and further expounded by Deming (1986). The principle behind the CMM is that the quality of a software product stems, in large part, from the quality of the process used to create it. To consistently improve software products, the process used for developing them should be understood, defined, measured, and

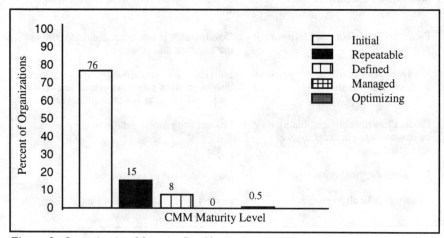

Figure 2: Organization Maturity Profile

improved. Five basic levels of process maturity, shown in Figure 1, have been defined to describe this progression from an ad hoc software process to one that is under statistical control. Increases in maturity are associated with increasing productivity and decreased risk of failure.

The typical Level 1 (initial), crisis-driven, organization has serious cost and schedule problems and uses ad hoc development. At Level 2 (repeatable), the organization, although still intuitive and too dependent on key individuals, has installed project management controls and learned to manage costs and schedules. As such, it is able to repeat previously attempted tasks. In level 3 (defined), the process is well understood because the organization has introduced a structured framework for software development and dedicated resources to process improvement. At level 4 (managed), the process is measured and controlled by established relationships that are understood quantitatively. Data are available to establish improvement priorities and to support technology and tool investment. Variations in early life cycle activities can be analyzed rigorously to determine their effect on later activities.   Finally, at level 5 (optimizing), process data are collected automatically and used for continuous measured improvement in response to new and evolving issues.

Curtis and Paulk (1993) comment on the maturity concept by contrasting mature and immature process impacts on organizations, as summarized in Table 2.

Of course, there are other maturity models besides the CMM, such as the Software Productivity Research model developed by Jones (1994), the ISO 9000 standard, the International Standards group for Software Engineering Software Process Improvement and Capability Determination (SPICE) model, and the Quality Improvement Paradigm. Saiedian and Kuzara (1995) suggest that the existence of other maturity models is prompting companies to extend the CMM and make it more applicable. Grady (1992) notes that the CMM was not the first evaluative model, but it is the one that is gently forcing companies to look at software practices from an engineering perspective. As seen in Figure 2 (from Zubrow, 1995), most firms remain at lower maturity levels.

Hersch (1993) observed that process improvement efforts have encountered many of the same productivity and payoff measurement problems as IT in general.   Investment payoff data are presented in the next section to establish an argument for adopting the CMM as a model to guide IT investment decisions.

Process Improvement Results

Specific suggestions on how to measure process improvement costs and benefits are described by numerous researchers.   For

Company	Improvment Focus	Results
Bull HN Information Systems	Customer Report Defects	10% reduction per year
Hughes Aircraft	Coding Defects per Stage	80% of defects found in coding stage prior to unit or integration testing.
Hughes Aircraft	Cost reduction	50% reduction in cost overruns—an estimated annual savings of $2 million.
Schlumberger	Average difference between estimate and actual completion times	Reduction from 35 weeks to 1 week
Schlumberger	Productivity	30% increase in productivity. Business value recognized on the $170,000 spent over 3 1/2 years was calculated at 1.5 times the annual budget.
Texas Instruments	Comparison of two projects: A at Level 1 B at Level 2	Cost per line of source code: A = $10.20 B = $3.60 Number of defects per thousand lines of source code. A=6.9 B=2.0

Table 3: Benefits of CMM-Based Improvements (Source: Herbsleb et al., 1994)

Process Improvement Category	Range	Median
Total yearly costs of SPI activities	$49,000-1,202,000	$245,000
Years engaged in SPI	1-9	3.5
Cost of SPI per software engineer	$490-2004	$1375
Productivity gain per year	9%-67%	35%
Yearly reduction in time to market	15-23%	19%
Yearly reduction in post release defect reports	10-94%	39%
Business value of SPI investment (dollar return for each dollar invested)	4.0-8.8	5.0
Early detection gain per year	6-25%	22%

Table 4: Summary Findings (Source: Herbsleb et al., 1994)

example, Rozum (1993) categorizes software process improvement costs as recurring costs and nonrecurring costs, and savings result from finding errors earlier or making fewer errors or increased process efficiency or decreased maintenance or increased productivity. Other researcher's categories span a wide spectrum that includes: productivity, calendar time, quality and business value. Although such parameters are measured in a variety of ways by different organizations, changes within organizations over time can be reported with a reasonably assumed consistency. The remainder of this section reports an array of results divided into the three sources of the reported data: Software Engineering Institute (SEI), National Aeronautics and Space Administration (NASA), and the U.S. Department of Defense (DoD).

Software Engineering Institute Process Improvement Results

The Software Engineering Institute (SEI) maintains a database of assessment results. Information provided to the SEI is kept confidential and can only be released with permission from the assessed firms.

	Very Important	Important	Less Important
Highest Cost	Functional Specification	Requirements Definition	Prototyping
High Cost	Develop User Interface Code	Unit Test Research	
Low Cost	System Test	Project Planning	Process Quality Improvment
Lowest Cost	Project Management	Training	

Table 5: Strategic Alignment Matrix (Source: Nejmeh, 1995)

Payoff Area	CMM Level 1	CMM Level 2	CMM Level 3
Ability to meet schedules	39%	55%	80%
Ability to meet budget	40%	55%	70%
Product quality judged as good or excellent	75%	90%	100%
Productivity judged as good or excellent	55%	65%	85%
Customer satisfaction judged as good or excellent	75%	70%	100%

Table 6: Payoff by Maturity Level (Source: Goldenson and Herbsleb, 1995)

In Table 3, results from several firms were obtained by Herbsleb et al., (1994) to demonstrate the variety of ways that improvement performance constructs have been operationalized and measured.

A summary of their findings for thirteen organizations (Bull HN, GTE Government Systems, Hewlett-Packard, Hughes Aircraft Co., Loral Federal Systems, Lockheed Sanders, Motorola, Schlumberger, Siemens Stromberg-Carlson, Texas Instruments, USAF Oklahoma Logistics Center, USN Fleet Combat Direction Systems support Activity) is shown in Table 4.

Herbsleb et al. (1994) measure percentage gain per year like a nominal compound interest rate to avoid exaggerated performance figures arrived at by simply dividing total gains by total years. They measure productivity in terms of lines of code (LOC) per unit of time and early detection of defects; quality as number of post-release defect reports; business value as ratio of measured benefits to measured costs.

Nejmeh (1995) provides a useful strategic alignment matrix for comparing costs and values of process activities, adapted here, in Table 5, to include only relevant CMM activities. Note that some high-value activities have correspondingly low costs. For example, project management is acknowledged as very important, and can be implemented at very low cost. In contrast, high cost status reporting is judged as least important.

Goldenson and Herbsleb (1995) studied a cross-section of software organizations and found that process improvement does have a measurable (and statistically significant) payoff in a variety of areas detailed in Table 6. Note the increasing percentages corresponding to higher maturity levels.

Measurement	CMM Level 1	CMM Level 2	CMM Level 3
Process Compliance	0%	43%	50%
Resource Stability	0%	14%	25%
Requirements	0%	25%	75%
Defect Statistics	40%	71%	100%
Defect Profile	20%	71%	75%
Cost Data	25%	100%	100%
Productivity (Delivered LOC)	20%	86%	75%
New LOC	40%	86%	100%
Percent Reuse	0%	71%	75%
Effort Estimate to Complete	80%	71%	50%
Rework Effort	0%	29%	50%
Schedule Variance	20%	100%	100%
Earned Value	0%	57%	75%
Average number of metrics	11	19	22

Table 7: Metric Compliance by CMM Level (Source: Brodman and Johnson, 1996)

Metric Category	Measurement	Benefits
Productivity	Increase	2.5 to 130%
Quality	Defect reduction	10-80%
	Error rate reduction	45%
	Product error rate	2 down to 0.11 per KLOC
Cost	$ saved/$ invested	1.5/1 to 7.7/1
	Project dollars saved	2 to 3.4 million
Schedule	Within estimate	5% of estimate
	On-time deliverables	from 51 to 94%
	Completion	50% down to 1% late
Effort	Rework reduction	10%
	Test time	10 test hours per one analysis hour

Table 8: Maturity Payoff (Brodman and Johnson, 1996)

Department of Defense Process Improvement Results

The U.S. Department of Defense (DoD) is one of the world's largest consumers of computer software as an integral part of military defense systems. Yeh (1993) reports on the lack of quality in many software products purchased by the DoD, and the resulting guidelines issued to insure software quality. Boehm's (1993) analysis of DoD software investment technology portfolio using a Return-on-Investment (ROI) analysis suggests that the 1994 investment in software technology is paying back $5 for every $1 invested. Moreover, by considering cost savings from three sources: software reuse (work avoidance), process improvements (working smarter), and improved tools (working faster), he contends that a ROI of 27:1 is possible by the year 2008.

Schedle Performance Index (SPI)	CMM Level 1	CMM Level 2	CMM Level 3
2			+
			+
			+
			+
	+	+	+
1	+	+	+
	+	+	+
	+		
	+		
	+		
0			

Table 9: Scatter Plot of SPI Versus CM Rating (Source: Lawlis et al. 1995)

CPI	CMM Level 1	CMM Level 2	CMM Level 3
2			
		+	
		+	
		+	
		+	
		+	
		+	
		+	+
		+	+
		+	+
1	+	+	+
	+	+	+
	+	+	
	+	+	
	+	+	
	+		
	+		
	+		
	+		
0			

Table 10: Scatter Plot of CPI Versus CMM Rating (Source: Lawlis et al., 1995)

Brodman and Johnson (1996) also examined ROI for DoD software. They note the lack of a consensus on the term ROI. They started with the textbook definition, which notes that investing to improve productivity involves foregoing the use of those funds for other purposes. Payback from the future stream of gains returns the capital invested. Then they found a contrast in the U.S. industry definition of ROI, which measures investment in terms of effort (labor hours not dollars) exclusive of capital expenditures, which are considered minimal. Returns are also described in terms of value (not dollars).

They found that software organizations involved in process improvement report the following increases in measured effort and cost: new data collection efforts were 7% of total effort, the cost to fix design defects increased from 0.75 to 2% of project cost, and the cost to fix code defects increased from 2.5 to 4% of project cost. Their detailed study of metric compliance by Capability Maturity Model (CMM) level resulted in the trends shown in Table 7.

The data in Table 7 suggest that mature organizations are tracking high payback areas such as stability of requirements, causes of defects, cost, productivity and percentage reuse. Clearly, increased effort and costs are associated with process improvement, but the payoffs of these activities are also measurable, as detailed in Table 8.

Finally, and perhaps most usefully, Lawlis et al. (1995) suggest a

Improvement Area	Baseline (1980s)	Current (1993)
Product Reliability (average errors per developed KLOC)	4.5	1
Average Reuse rate	20%	61% FORTRAN
	90%	Ada
Cost (in staff months)	490	210
Development cycle time (months)	28	16

Table 11: NASA Process Improvement Benefits (Source: NASA-GB-001-95)

Cost Performance Index (CPI) and a Schedule Performance Index (SPI) be used to demonstrate the correlation between higher maturity levels and successful performance. The SPI is calculated by dividing the budgeted cost of work performed by the budgeted cost of work scheduled. Index values equal to 1 indicate on-schedule or budgeted cost performance, with values below 1 showing schedule or cost slippage. Such an index can be applied across a variety of firms. Tables 9 and 10 show scatter plots of SPI and CPI values for DoD projects (individual projects are represented by +) examined at a point in time when they were less than 80% complete. The 80% cut-off controls for crisis-mode anomalies that occur near scheduled completion dates.

Note the significant improvement in schedule performance at higher CMM levels. The CPI is calculated in an analogous manner using budgeted and actual costs of work performed, with results shown in Table 10. The increase in costs, as evidenced by the higher CPI values is attributed to additional project management tasks required at Level 2.

National Aeronautics and Space Administration Process Improvement Results

The National Aeronautics and Space Administration (NASA) experience suggests minimal costs associated with establishing and operating process improvement programs. NASA used the CMM as a model for their own process improvement program. Overhead to the developers (participation, interviews, completing forms, training) will not exceed 2% of the total project development cost. Full-time support staff for collecting, validating and archiving data ranges from 3 to 7%. The real cost is that of several full-time analysts, which may require 6-15% of the total development budget. The analysts are needed for designing studies, developing new concepts, writing standards and improvement guidelines. Corresponding NASA benefits are portrayed in Table 11.

NASA's successful experience with process improvement programs is captured in a list of key management guidelines. NASA suggests: limit scope (start small); produce specific products the first year (concepts, baselines, handbook); assure developers of their role in driving the change (analysts are helpers), proceed slowly. Their recommendations, as well as other strategies, are included in the last section of this chapter.

Management Strategies for IT Process Improvement Investment

This concluding section returns full-circle to the senior management concerns that served as the introduction and impetus for this chapter. The approach taken herein has been to address concerns regarding the efficient allocation of scarce resources to IT systems by application of ideas from the reference discipline of economics. Since the principal constraint on these systems is the limitation of software in representing data-logic associations, software served as the focal point for these discussions.

Confronted with the lack of a consensus among researchers and practitioners regarding IT investment payoff, it seems appropriate to return to first principles. The reference discipline of economics has long established the importance of residual factors of productivity, which include process improvement factors. Accepting the basic quality tenet that process improvements lead to product improvements has taken the software industry on a journey guided by process improvement models such as the CMM. The real-life examples of CMM-based process improvements described in the previous section are obvious and significant. We can distill from these examples the following guidelines for improving overall IT investment success:

- Internal, firm-specific measures are necessary but not sufficient for IT evaluation. The external marketplace is the competitive equalizer, and must be included in all evaluations. The CMM guidelines include the best practices from world-class firms and provide a focus on customer satisfaction.
- Improvement efforts must start small. IT professionals seem oblivious to concerns about scope; they routinely deal with changes of great magnitude. However, process improvement efforts require organization-wide commitment and target projects should be carefully chosen. This suggestion comes primarily from NASA's process improvement experience. It is further supported by Hewlett-Packard's Grady (1992), who contends that the most promising area for demonstrable process improvement is defect analysis (such as defect density before and after changes), which may yield a series of small (5-10%) gains.
- Measuring process improvement results remains a challenge. There remains the need to identify and measure outcomes of interest (in this case, payoff). Demonstration of improvements necessitates the ability to plot changes over time and control for variable units of

measurement. Establishing a causal link between the changes and the measures is vital.

- Leave experimental efforts to researchers. Established process improvement models and measurement methods abound. In fact, measurement is a decade-old sub-industry consisting of over 50 companies and nonprofit groups such as the North American Software Metrics Association and The Society of Cost Estimating and Analysis.
- Useful return-on-investment values are calculated in terms of labor effort and value—not dollars. The language of upper management remains dollars, and so translation will be needed.
- More mature organizations are tracking high payback areas such as stability of requirements, causes of defects, cost, productivity and percentage reuse.
- It is generally agreed that efforts to improve one measure of performance, e.g., productivity, are offset by decreases in another, e.g., quality. Customer expectations, personnel experience, and technologies all exhibit volatility and may influence the measures.
- Novel metrics, such as the SPI and CPI have been introduced. Additional techniques should be identified and empirically tested.
- Process improvement efforts have been shown to repair schedule problems. This is especially significant in an industry where late delivery is a chronic illness.

In conclusion, using process improvement models to operationalize the IT investment and performance constructs have provided indisputable measures of IT payoff. Senior managers must be apprised of these benefits so that they continue to provide the information processing resources needed to support a company's business objectives.

Chapter 12

Enhancing Corporate Investment Decisions for IS/IT: The Role of Leadership Strategies

Erik Rolland
Ohio State University

Ray Maghroori
University of California

Through this chapter, we propose a conceptual framework for evaluating costs and benefits associated with investments in IS/T, based upon four general leadership strategies for implementation. We present the four strategies for information systems and technology investments, and delineate the various categories of costs and benefits associated with each of the strategies. Our goal is to provide guidelines for managers to recognize the strategy and technology investments necessary to succeed.

Over the past three decades, information systems have developed from being pure transaction processing systems to real decision making tools. Whereas the information systems 30 years ago automated and simplified tedious processing tasks, they today serve an active role in decisionmaking at all organizational levels. Indeed, in this information age, it is hard to imagine that organizations that do not actively pursue the use of technology in decision making can survive in the long run. However, it is not always clear from past practice and research to what extent, and in which dimensions, the investment in technology has benefited organizations. The reasons for this may come from the difficulties experienced in finding and measuring appropriate quantitative and qualitative performance indicators. A major underlying factor for the lack of success that many companies have experienced with technology investments, may be due to the absence of guidelines on how to integrate IS/T (information systems/information technology) successfully with corporate strategy. Furthermore, it is our contention that the costs and benefits of technology are functions of the implementation. In other words, costs and benefits will vary depending on how IS/T is employed in an organizational context, and depending on their relation to organizational goals and processes. This chapter identifies four general IS/T leadership strategies determining implementation, and outlines the broad categories of costs and benefits associated with these strategies.

Strategy and IS/T Investment

Past research in strategic management often stresses the importance of aligning business processes with corporate goals (Dess & Miller, 1993). Further, in order to enhance the business processes, it has been argued that IS/T should be leveraged in these processes (Hammer & Champy, 1993). As indicated by Hammer & Champy, effective organization often make use of IS/T in pursuing corporate objectives, to gain a competitive advantage. In addition, the strategic focus on technology, and alignment of IS/T to corporate goals, are often reflected by investment in technology in a particular industry group. Although there is not always a positive correlation between investment in technology and improved quality or productivity (i.e., Brynjolfson & Hitt, 1993; West & Courtney, 1994; Mahmood & Mann, 1993), managers from certain industries (such as manufacturing) will typically accredit technology as the reason for increased productivity (Kelley, 1994; Barua, Kriebel and Mukhopadyay, 1995). The health care industry is typically associated with poor productivity, and is a prime example of misalignments of IS/T investments and corporate goals. Whereas the health care industry embodies 13-14% of the GDP in the US, the spending on IS/T is typically only 1-2% of the operating budget. Compare the IS/T spending with 10% for banking, 6-7% for insurance companies (BusinessWeek, Feb. 21, 1994). In the health care industry, paper records are still dominant, and about 30% of patient information needed during a typical clinical visit is missing (BusinessWeek, Feb. 21, 1994). Only about 10% of the 6,600 hospitals nationwide have discovered the benefits of IS/T. The reason for this pattern lies clearly in the health care systems definition of their business: patient care is their business, and not technology. Our own anecdotal evidence confirms this myopic view. During a recent health care conference in Southern California, only two out of 10 health care providers mentioned technology or information systems as a part of their strategy. Successful companies can no longer afford to exclude themselves from being in the information (systems) business. Their information systems strategy must be an integral part of corporate goals and strategies (Abernethy & Guthrie, 1994; Mahmood, 1995; Mahmood, 1993; Mahmood & Soon, 1991). This is exactly where many health care providers, and other companies, so far have failed. The main reason for these failures may be the lack of guidelines for the IS manager on how to align IS strategies with corporate goals. In this chapter we present a framework for IS/T investment strategies that includes aligning information systems and technology with other corporate goals and strategies. First, we discuss four different management strategies, and then we outline a process-focused technique that identifies the appropriate strategy to be applied to each process. Further, we discuss the cost/benefits of the investments associated with these strategies.

Management Strategies for Information Systems Executives

IS/T management strategies determine the choices for the IS leader in employing information technology and systems to achieve corporate goals. This choice affects the entire posturing of the firm, and may be a significant factor in determining the future of the organization (Kettinger et al., 1994). Moreover, the leadership choice prescribes the investment in IS/T. IS leadership choices are broad, but can usually be classified into the following four categories:

- Status Quo Strategies
- TQM Strategies
- Reengineering Strategies
- Vision Institutionalization Strategies

These strategies are exhaustive: you are either in a favorable situation (status quo), where all you need to do is make sure you continue to stay in this position; or you are in a position where you realize that you must take some action to improve your business operations (TQM, Reengineering, or Vision Institutionalization). If you currently have business processes in place, some or all of these either need minor (TQM) or major (Reengineering) changes to become efficient. If you have no or few realized business processes, you need to implement such processes (Vision Institutionalization). We discuss all these strategies further in the following paragraphs.

Status Quo Strategies. There are organizations in which the IS/T function is in full compliance with corporate goals. In such organizations, the IS/T processes are well defined, well designed, and well managed. Often these organizations are on the cutting edge of their industries. Superior organizations are not created by accident. Rather they are the result of right mix of vision, policy, procedures, technology and people. Thus, it is important to recognize that at times the best type of IS leadership is to simply provide support for the existing system of vision, policy, technology and procedures. Under these circumstances, the best IS/T management strategy is to maintain a status quo.

The Status Quo Strategies must be sensitive to two considerations: 1) The business environment and the nature of the competition change continuously, and 2) Even the best run organizations must remain receptive to the notion of continuous improvement. This is particularly true with respect to IS/T, given the rapid changes in technology. Thus, Status Quo Strategies for IS/T can be divided into two categories:

1. Strategies to sustain strategic business advantages due to IS/T: This type of leadership is aimed at making sure that the IS/T supports the organizational policies and procedures, and leverages any sustainable strategic advantages to ensure that the firm maintains its position (assuming that one or more sustainable advantage exists). The information systems aspects of such a strategy would normally include continual investigation of new IS/T advancements to improve efficiency of current business processes. For example, a banking institution may want to investigate the possibility of distributing account statements via e-mail or the Internet, as opposed to current practices (printing and mailing).

2. Strategies to support current business operations: Even a management strategy based upon maintaining status quo does strive to do things better. However, the main emphasis here is not on change, rather it is making sure that the existing system of policies, procedures and technologies has adequate support and resources so that it can survive. The information systems aspects of such a strategy could often include continual support for user training/education; support for — and maintenance of — data structures that are flexible (non-proprietary, if possible), and independent of specific vendor solutions.

TQM Strategies. Total quality management as a business philosophy is aimed at improving quality. To improve quality, one may have to deal with major and radical transformation of business processes; however quite often, and when interpreted rather narrowly, TQM deals with gradual and continuous improvement.

There may be circumstances where, from an IS perspective, the fundamental structure of the IS/T role in the business is sound, but where various elements of the IS processes and procedures may need improvement. The assumption is that through gradual and continuous reform we will be able to improve all products and services associated with IS/T processes.

TQM implementation within IS/T requires training, employee participation, and managerial commitment. There is no end when it comes to TQM implementation — TQM is a continuous process.

True implementation of TQM goes beyond mechanics associated with statistical control process and quality assurance. As one commentator pointed out correctly, TQM is largely an "attitude and mental process." The task of the IS leadership is thus to create and share this attitude with the rest of the organization. In this context, quality needs to be implemented from the top down (Deming, 1986).

A successful TQM program, in relation to IS/T processes, requires total organizational reform. In this context, as Armand Feigenbaum suggests, it is the task of leadership to mobilize the knowledge, the skills, and the attitudes of every person in the organization (Feigenbaum, 1983). Successful implementation of TQM in IS processes requires that involved employees believe in it and are fully convinced about its merit. Also, all IS personnel should be satisfied with their own conditions within the firm. Indeed, as Fred Smith, president of Federal Express, commented: customer satisfaction starts with employee satisfaction. Furthermore, no TQM program will succeed unless all those who are involved with IS/T processes are fully involved and are willing to make it work.

It should be understood that TQM is not just a set of tools or techniques. Instead it is a paradigm for doing business — a management philosophy. As such, TQM should not only be used for the technical aspects of MIS, but also for systems development and systems selection (Mathieson & Wharton, 1993). An example of innovative TQM applied to the administrative (purchasing) side of MIS is currently seen at the California DMV (Saxon, 1995). Here, numerous vendors and consulting firms are invited to serve on an advisory panel for the $260 million project aimed at updating the DMV technology from 1960's mainframes to a 1995 client/server structure. In return for serving on the advisory panel, the companies are allowed to bid for more than one part of the overall project (purchasing/contracting regulations of the State of California do not normally allow more than one successful bid from one organization on any project).

The information systems aspects of TQM would typically include measures to ensure customer satisfaction, as well as compliance with corporate goals. Such measures entail (among others) focused and goal oriented investigation of new tools to improve efficiency of current systems that are deemed insufficient, as well as active use of systems analysis and design techniques to improve on data structures, information flow, processing times, and user friendliness. The total hardware and software configuration is designed to create a "quality information system," that assures total customer satisfaction (Keith, 1994).

Reengineering Strategies. General management strategies employing a reengineering approach are based upon the assumption that the fundamental processes of the organization need radical transformation, and that continuous improvements are not adequate to correct the structural weaknesses of the system. In the context of IS/T, reengineering would require radical transformation of one or more processes involving IS/T.

This radical transformation or restructuring is reengineering (or business process reengineering - BPR). BPR is a one-time activity that can be applied to various aspects of the business operations, to different IS processes, and to different projects at different times.

Total quality management is a philosophy, and a paradigm for doing business. Reengineering on the other hand is a tool: it is a set of techniques for rethinking business processes, and then in particular, rethinking the general role of information technology in relation to corporate strategy.

Thus, reengineering in the IS context requires change — lots of change. Thus, there will be all types of employee resistance (both inside and outside the core IS department) that must be overcome. Cognizant of this, a good reengineering program should create positive incentives for change. These incentives must be aimed at both IS employees and IS customers. In particular, it is important that IS personnel are convinced that they will not be affected adversely by the reengineering outcomes. IS personnel should be convinced that reengineering would not necessarily result in downsizing, and that the change will create new opportunities. Reengineering IS processes requires creativity, hard work, and commitment. It requires a clear vision regarding alternative structures for IS integration in performing the various business functions.

The information systems aspects of a reengineering strategy may include a thorough analysis of information flows, both within the organization and between the organization and other involved parties. It may also include creation of new work flows and/or information flows, and the implementation of appropriate technologies that allow for proper communications and rapid processing. The benefits of such reengineering projects have been proven and documented in the business press, as well as in past research. AT&T recently reengineered its Consumer Communication Services organizations, a unit responsible for the software changes required for new products and services. Through reengineering, they were able to reduce the amount of steps in the process from 250 to 100, and at the same time reducing the cycle time by 75%. These reductions in cycle time enabled the company to increase its production capacity by 50% at no extra cost (Cross et al., 1994). Several reengineering initiatives at CIGNA Corporation reported a total saving of more than $100 million over a five-year period

(Caron, Jarvenpaa and Stoddard, 1994). In this period, operating expenses were reduced by 42%, cycle times improved by 100%, customer satisfaction was up by 50%, and quality improved by 75%.

Vision Institutionalization Strategies. Quite frequently, organizations are created by individuals with a vision. The vision is usually about creating a new product or service — about fulfilling a need. This is the common heritage of many entrepreneurial organizations. However, vision alone is not enough to create a successful organization. Vision has to be translated into, among others, a business plan, financing, marketing, resource allocation, information systems planning, and recruitment. Vision is the root of all organizations. Yet, roots are not adequate to create fruits and flowers unless there are intermediaries. Trunks, branches, and leaves are the intermediaries needed to transform ideas into products and services, and further into profits and market shares. Information systems and technology make up an increasingly larger amount of these trunks, branches and leaves.

It is noteworthy that during the past 20 years many organizations have invested heavily in IS/T. However, it is not unusual to find that in many such organizations, IS processes have not been successfully integrated with corporate strategy. In many industries, this is exemplified with the failure to increase output while heavily investing in technology (e.g., Brynjolfson & Hitt, 1993).

For many industries, the IS forms the backbone of the business. Many new organizations require an IS management strategy aimed at institutionalizing the vision, and implementing this backbone. Often entrepreneurial firms fail to succeed because they are lead by visionaries who fail to recognize the importance translating vision into programs, and aligning technology with corporate goals. German social scientists Max Weber (translated reference: Weber, 1947) recognized this phenomenon nearly 100 years ago when he correlated the development and maturation of organizations with the development of processes associated with institutionalization.

Institutionalizing IS in an organization requires strong leadership. The IS leader must secure expertise, both in business operations and technology, to ensure that the right technology is matched up to proper business processes (Scrupski, 1994). This task is one that starts with blank sheets, and gradually maps business processes and information flow (e.g., Goodhue et al., 1992).

The management strategies discussed above are often not that distinctly different from each other. There are overlaps. We only aim at identifying some fundamental choices that IS leaders have to make. Also, we like to stress that there are costs associated with each strategy. These costs must be weighed against their respective benefits. In particular, we have lately seen numerous firms overspending on TQM and BPR, only to end up in bankruptcy proceedings (BusinessWeek, Aug. 8, 1994). A proper discussion of costs and benefits (of TQM and BPR) is too situation specific to be considered herein, and we refer our readers to the popular business literature for a general discussion of this topic (BusinessWeek, Aug. 8, 1994). In the next section we will provide some guidelines to choosing an appropriate strategy based on the alignment of goals and processes.

Management Strategies for Information Technology Investment

In the above sections, we have identified four different management strategies for IS leaders.   From a managerial perspective, the crucial question remains which strategy to choose. Before we proceed, and only to provide a preliminary answer, we admit that the leadership role in IS/T is often multi-faceted: we need to use different strategies for different processes. There is not one single management strategy that fits all processes. Thus, in order to determine which management strategy is appropriate, we need to analyze each process independently. We will assume in the further discussion that the corporate goals are known to the IS manager, and that all processes that involve the business operations are known as well (the business processes can for example be mapped efficiently using information flow and context diagrams — see e.g. Yourdon & Constantine, 1986). We also assume that large and complex processes are broken down into appropriate sub-processes.   Thus, we use the term process to describe all processes, even those that are sub-processes of larger processes.

A general model for mapping IS/T processes to corporate goals

Assuming that all business goals (corporate strategy) and all processes are known, we now seek to determine which of the four possible strategic management actions are appropriate for a certain process. Recall the definition of these strategies:

1. **Status Quo Strategies.** IS/T is currently doing fine. We wish to provide support so that existing systems continue, or to sustain a competitive advantage. Scan environment for trends and new tools.
2. **TQM Strategies.** IS design is basically OK — some fine-tuning may be necessary.
3. **Reengineering Strategies.** IS processes require radical change. There is no, or little, support for business goals.
4. **Vision Institutionalization Strategies.** Immature or non-existent IS processes — inadequate to support goals (lots of vision, very little process).

These four situations are depicted in Figure 1. The vertical axis is a measure of increasing focus (from the IS/T side) on the vision and corporate goals, whereas the horizontal axis is a measure of extent of

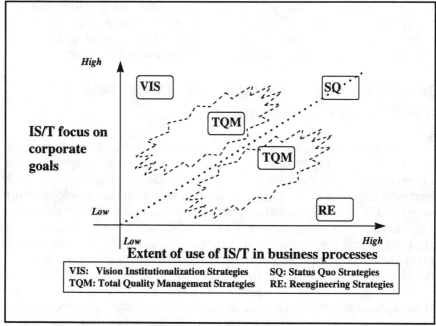

Figure 1. Alternative IS strategies

use of IS/T in the business processes. An efficient organization must simultaneously focus on both IS/T use in business processes and goals to be effective. The top-right situation (in Figure 1) depicts the need for status quo strategies, where the IS process is properly aligned with corporate goals. This is the alignment businesses should strive to achieve. The situations in the middle of the figure (marked "TQM") depict the need for TQM strategies, where some fine-tuning of the IS process is needed for better alignment with corporate strategy. Further, we here also seek to make the IS process more efficient. This situation may occur anywhere along — and on either side of — the dotted diagonal line. Reengineering strategies (bottom-right) will typically be needed when the IS process exists, but the process is not properly aligned with goals (it requires radical change). This situation could occur anywhere along the horizontal axis. Institutionalization, or creation, of an IS process is needed when corporate vision requires technology/IS, but no (or little) IS structure is there to support them: we are in need of better IS/T support for institutional goals (top-left). This situation could occur anywhere along the vertical axis.

In choosing an appropriate strategy, one must assess the efficiency of IS/T in the various processes. We caution that the evaluation of IS effectiveness often is considered a subjective one. An accountant may have a completely different view of the information systems' efficiency than does an IS person. Neither may be right: the ultimate acid test is if the information systems support the overall organizational goals and strategy. Thus, we seek in the following section to objectively compare the goals with the processes.

A procedure for determining appropriate strategy for an IS/T process

Whereas we outlined a general model for the mapping of corporate goals and processes above, we now seek to determine which strategy is appropriate for each process.   The mapping of appropriate IS management strategies are depicted in the flowchart given in Figure 2. We evaluate each process individually by answering a set of questions as follows:

Each process is first investigated by answering the question "Could IS/T be applied to the process?"   If IS/T cannot be applied to the process in question, then we may stop analyzing this particular process. We may wish to rethink such processes in the long run, to check if IS/T can be applied in the future (maybe due to newly available technology).

If IS/T can be applied to the process, we check to see if it indeed has been applied. If IS/T has not been applied, then the most appropriate strategy for managing the IS process is institutionalization of the corporate goals.

If IS/T has been applied in the process, then we should seek to answer if it is indeed efficiently supporting the corporate strategy. If so, then we have reason to be content with the situation. Under these circumstances, the most appropriate strategy is Status Quo.

If IS/T is not supporting corporate goals for the process in question, we need to know if the process can be fixed with minor improvements. If this is the case, then the most appropriate strategy is TQM. Otherwise, we need to completely overhaul the process by employing a Reengineering Strategy.

In the above section, we have provided an analytical method for selecting appropriate strategies for corporate management information systems. Considering the method outlined above, we recommend one strategy per process. However, complex processes may require the use of more than one strategy.

The issues pertaining to the cost/benefits in investment in IS/T have been debated widely in the literature (Brynjolfson & Hitt, 1993; West & Courtney, 1994; Mahmood & Mann, 1993), and as most experts would readily admit, there are no authoritative conclusions with regards to the costs and benefits. While it might be difficult to come up with a general statement regarding cost/benefits of IS/T, the costs and benefits would vary according to the circumstances associated with the implementation of the strategy.   However, cost and benefits of IS/T are a function of the various strategies outlined above, and can be broadly characterized in relation to resources and relative benefits. In the next section, we will provide a conceptual framework

Process Evaluation

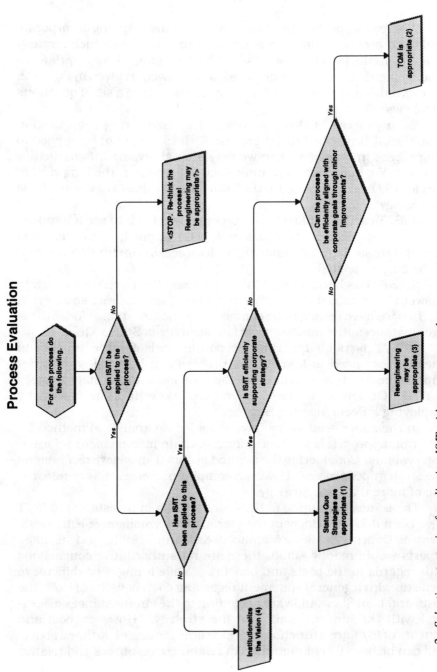

Figure 2. Selecting strategies for aligning IS/T with corporate goals

for classifying costs and benefits associated with the strategies discussed above.

The cost and benefits of IS/T strategies

The notion of costs and benefits are rather complex, since they could be subject to various interpretations of corporate goals and strategies. Further, the costs and benefits may be a combination of tangible and intangible factors. Regardless of these considerations, the costs and benefits are likely to be a function of the implementation strategy. Thus, we suggest that costs and benefits can be categorized broadly. More specifically, we suggest that cost associated with IS/T implementations typically belong to the following categories: human resource, equipment, capital investment, and productivity (see, e.g., Davidson, 1993). Similarly, we evaluate the benefits of IS/T along the following dimensions: productivity, cost, quality, production cycle, and information availability. These are all further discussed below.

Equipment costs may constitute a major expense category for IS/T implementation. Even though hardware costs are generally decreasing, the rapid pace of change in technology causes this component to be quite substantial. Furthermore, the increasing functionality in software causes increased hardware requirements and the need for frequent software updates. In addition, maintenance and support costs for both the hardware and software are generally consuming an increasing share of any IS/T budget.

While IS/T costs are often focused on equipment, an ever more important component of cost is related to the human resources. Human resource costs are typically related to hiring, firing, and training of employees. Implementation of IS/T requires people with new skills, who can leverage the technology in the firm. Further, due to process automation and redesign, may result in outplacement of some employees. Finally, implementation of new technology will require training or retraining of existing employees. All of these would result in cost to the organization.

Process changes due to the use of the above strategies may require changes or additions to the physical structures These capital investment costs are comprised of such items as network design and implementation, new buildings or structures, and financing costs.

Productivity costs are based on temporary decrease in productivity due to the change itself, and due to the employees involvement in the analysis, design or implementation of the new business processes.

In Table 1, we outline the relative costs of the previous proposed strategies. Since the actual costs of implementing the four strategies would depend on the particular situation, we categories the costs only on a relative scale: low, medium, and high.

We see that Status Quo strategies require very moderate resources in all categories. This is due to the fact that the business

| Strategy | Human Resources | | Equipment | | Capital | Productivity Decrease | |
	Hire/Fire	Training	Hardware	Software		Involvement	Change
SQ	Low	Low	Low	Low	Low	Low	Low
TQM	Low	Med	Low	Med	Low	Med	Low
RE	High	High	Med-High	Med-High	Med-High	High	High
VIS	High	High	High	High	High	High	High

Table 1. Cost of IS/T-Strategies

processes are sound. We only maintain our positions through scanning the environment, and making very minor adjustments to the processes.

TQM would typically require low hiring/firing cost, but medium training costs. Software costs are likely to be medium, but hardware costs are often low due to the fact that a TQM strategy would require only incremental changes in the processes. Furthermore, the productivity costs are medium due to employee involvement in the TQM process itself.

Reengineering typically implies medium to high costs in all categories. This is due to the major changes required in a reengineering process. These changes may affect the employees, the equipment, capital needs as well as temporary productivity losses.

Vision institutionalization may require higher costs than reengineering, since this strategy involves creating new processes from scratch. Thus, most resources needed in the processes must be acquired.

Benefits associated with our leadership strategies discussed above can be categorized into five major groups: productivity increase, cost decrease, quality improvement, production cycle compression, and added information availability. Several of these benefits may, to some extent, be interrelated. However, for analytical purposes, we discuss them separately.

The sound implementation of an IS/T strategy often leads to increased productivity, resulting in cost savings. Therefore, many IS/T investments are motivated by these two benefits.

Implementation of IS/T based processes may often result in better consistency of processes and products, and therefore improve quality. Thus, while improved quality may not be the primary goal of our strategy, it is often a byproduct.

In a global and competitive marketplace there is a growing need for reducing production cycles. Production cycle compression refers to decreased product-to-market time, and it may be a necessity for competitiveness. Proper implementation and use of IS/T in the business processes, such product design, will typically contribute to cycle compression.

To enable high quality decision-making in a firm, the

decision-makers need to have timely access to information about the company operations. Information availability, related to company operations, consists of two elements: information about the process itself (such as costs and processing time per units completed; failure rates, etc.), as well as information about the products involved in the process (quantity produced, inventory availability, etc.). The major strength of utilizing IS/T in business processes is its ability to create, store, and manipulate such information.

In table 2 we outline the relative benefits of the previous proposed strategies. Again, since the actual benefits from implementing the four strategies would depend on the particular situation, we categories the benefits only on a relative scale of low, medium, and high.

As seen from Table 2, benefits associated with Status Quo strategies are relatively low. This is due to the fact that current business processes only marginally can benefit from additional investments. Indeed, the information availability may increase due to the scanning of the environment, which may lead to higher quality products. Having said this, we are cognizant of the fact that an investment in a Status Quo strategy may be beneficial in the long-run, since it would reduce the necessity of major business process adjustments.

A TQM strategy has a relatively low impact on all benefit categories, since it promotes incremental changes. Accordingly, any investment in a TQM strategy would be relatively low, as compared to reengineering. Reengineering may lead to medium to high impacts on the benefits, since it typically results in streamlined and more efficient processes. In comparison, a vision institutionalization strategy normally leads to high impact on all the benefits.

Quantifying the above benefits is often a difficult task. However, when possible, they can typically be quantified as follows: Productivity changes are measured in units/time-period, while cost is measured in cost per unit. Quality is measured in the standard failures per a certain quantify (often 1,000), and production cycles are measured in time from planning to market. Information availability is measured relatively in timeliness, accuracy, and detail of the information — in other words how well it supports high-quality decision-making.

It is worth noting that a large proportion of reengineering and TQM

Strategy	Productivity increase	Cost decrease	Quality increase	Production cycle decrease	Increase in information availability
SQ	n/a	n/a	Low	n/a	Low
TQM	Low	Low	Low	Low	Low
RE	Med-High	Med-High	Med-High	Med-High	Med-High
VIS	High	High	High	High	High

Table 2. Benefits of IS/T-Strategies

efforts have indeed ended in failure (e.g., *BusinessWeek*, August 8, 1994). The result of such a failure is obviously that the benefits would not be realized, or that they would not be realized to the extent that they exceed the costs. In our opinion, such failures can often be characterized by misaligned processes and goals. The benefits discussed above do assume that the goals and the resulting processes are indeed fully aligned. Thus, if we fail to achieve these goal/process alignments, the benefits cannot be fully realized.

Summary and Conclusions

The importance of investigating the strategic impact of IS, and the IS implications of strategic business planning have been empirically verified in recent research (Premkumar & King, 1994; Earl, 1993). It is not surprising that companies where technology has a leading position in strategic management, and thus where IS/T based processes are strongly focused on corporate goals, are the most successful ones. A prime example of this is found in the package shipping industry: at Federal Express, perhaps the most successful company in its niche, technology and technology-based problem solving personnel (mathematical programming, and information systems) serve as main players in strategic management (Hinson, 1995). At American Airlines, another company that has a strong strategic focus on the interrelationship between goals and technology-based processes, the resulting high-tech yield management system is responsible for increasing annual revenues by $500 million (Gray, 1994). Companies, such as American Airlines and Federal Express, are market leaders because they have had a vision of fitting technology into their most senior strategic think-tank, and focused on using technology as an integral part of their strategy (Hinson, 1995; Palvia et al., 1992). These companies have implicitly complied with the framework of process alignment/investment presented herein, and the results can also be seen by bottom-line performance. Obviously, the cost of this technology focus is substantial (Hinson, 1995). On the other hand, the health care industry, as described in the introductory sections, is an example of the opposite. In this industry, the investment costs in IS/T are generally lower than those of any other industry group (only 1-2% of the operating budget), demonstrating that they often have not focused on integrating IS/T into their business processes.

In a successful company, the corporate vision or strategy must include an IS/T dimension, otherwise the benefits from IS/T investments will not be maximized. Further, in such companies there are adequate, appropriate and institutionalized IS processes in support of these corporate goals and visions. In this chapter, we have described four strategies that can help identify the areas where IS investments are necessary to fully align IS processes with corporate goals. We have further outlined the potential categories of costs and benefits associated with each particular strategy. Our research can be used as a framework for detecting ill-aligned goals and processes, and determines which strategies and investments are necessary to bring the organizational processes into alignment with the goals.

While we have asserted that successful companies indeed make IS/T investments that cater to the full alignment of corporate goals and processes, we did not present any empirical results supporting this hypothesis. We have in this research presented a theoretical framework for IS/T alignments/investment, with associated potential investments and benefits. We will attempt to empirically analyze the usefulness of this framework on past data in our future research.

We wish to thank two anonymous reviewers for their help in vastly improving this research.

Chapter 13

Using an Activity-Based Approach to Determine the Cost of Client/Server Systems

Murugan Anandarajan
Saint Joseph's University, Philadelphia

Asokan Anandarajan
New Jersey Institute of Technology

Client/Server (C/S) computing is one of the most discussed topics in the field of information systems in the 1990's. C/S systems represent a fundamental shift in information systems architecture; a shift that has not been witnessed since the evolution of batch to on-line systems. However, the benefits of these system have not been fully realized. Recent surveys indicate that information systems managers perceive the development, implementation, and monitoring of a C/S system to be costly. The managers also noted that the manner in which costs are accumulated, analyzed and allocated under conventional accounting systems provide them with information that distorts the true costs of implementing a C/S system. Under conventional techniques, many costs of implementing a C/S system are hidden and difficult to identify.

The purpose of this chapter is to show how an activity-based approach can be used to help managers identify the true costs of implementing a C/S system. This study proposes a theoretical framework for setting up an activity-based system for a C/S life cycle. In addition it provides insights into how the costs of a client/server system can be analyzed and monitored. This framework will also help information systems managers control disproportionate costs because such costs can be traced back to their roots. More effective cost monitoring and control will help to ensure that the full potential of C/S systems are realized and the benefits outweigh the costs of implementation.

Organizations in the 1990's are facing a turbulent business environment characterized by an increase in globalization, fierce competition, and corporate volatility. These factors have accelerated the mean time to obsolescence of most business applications. In such an environment it is imperative that an organization be able to act quickly—to take advantage of its business opportunities, react to competitor action, and to be first in the market with a new product or service. The flexibility to maneuver can be expressed in terms of the *'reach and range'* of an Information Systems (IS) architecture (Keen, 1991). 'Reach' refers to whom you could reach through the information systems; 'range' defines what information could be shared. By expanding the reach and range of its IS, an organization can obtain greater maneuverability and enhance the information processing power of their employees, thereby attaining competitive advantage. An IS architecture that expands an organization's reach and range is the Client/Server system (Boar, 1994).

Client/Server (C/S) systems can be defined as *'a process architecture which allows applications to be developed as efficiently as possible, exploiting the capabilities of personal workstation client and intelligent server computers'* (Elbert and Martyna, 1993). The concept of C/S systems began to emerge in the early 1980's with the advent of intelligent desktop machines and computer network architectures (Wecker, 1979). In its simplest form, a C/S system is a configuration of clients (microcomputers or workstations) and servers (microcomputers, workstations, and/or large-scale computers such as mainframes) communicating with one another over a network. The clients request the task to be done; the server(s) performs the application and returns the information to the client over the network. Each component in the system (clients, servers, software, and networks) concentrates on the tasks that it does best. This leads to optimization of the information system.

C/S computing has been propounded as the most promising application architecture of the future (Benjamin and Blunt, 1992). This is evident by the number of organizations that are developing and implementing C/S systems with a view to empower their work force. In 1992 only 5% of all organizations in the U.S had applications based on the C/S architecture (Simpson, 1994). This figure rose to 60% by 1995. This rapid growth in C/S computing can be attributed to a combination of several factors. This includes factors such as faster and cheaper hardware components, open standards, as well as the advent of graphical user interfaces and fourth-generation languages.

However, while C/S systems in most part have been beneficial to organizations, it has proved to be more costly than initially estimated. According to a recent survey, over 50% of all C/S systems eventually cost more than anticipated (Baum, 1996). This has made it difficult for managers to justify future Information Technology (IT) investment in C/S systems. This shortfall can be attributed to the fact that many of the costs in a C/S computing environment are hidden and therefore are not properly identified by the traditional costing methods that are typically used managers (Hufnagel, 1994). This is because the traditional costing methods tend to merely 'expense' costs of development, design, and other related expenditure that are incurred in the various phases of a C/S's life cycle. In addition, these costing methods fail to account for many types of expenditure that are popularly referred to as *hidden costs*. A recent survey conducted by Price Waterhouse indicated that fewer than 40% of IS managers could accurately identify and relate costs to individual activities in the development, implementation, and maintenance of their C/S systems (Geishecker, 1996). This lack of reliable and accurate cost information has undermined the decision-making ability of the managers in making IT investment decisions.

This paper proposes the use of an activity-based approach for costing C/S systems. The activity-based approach is more suitable for a C/S environments which tend to be more labor intensive. Traditional costing approaches, on the other hand, are more suitable for mainframe-based environments, which are more capital intensive. The next section discusses the traditional and activity-based costing methods. This is followed by the development of a theoretical framework for applying the activity-based approach to C/S systems. The paper concludes by discussing the managerial implications of this framework.

Costing C/S Systems

Traditional Costing Approach

Many organizations use traditional costing methods to identify the costs of developing, implementing, and maintaining information systems. These costs are typically categorized as direct material, direct labor, and overhead. This methodology attempts to trace overhead costs to the final output and is therefore based on the assumption that there is a direct causal relationship between output and the costs incurred (Turney, 1989). While this costing method was suitable for the capital intensive mainframe environment (labor:capital ratio of 20:80), it is inappropriate for a labor intensive C/S development environment that has a labor:capital ratio of 80:20. In the case of labor intensive environments, such as those represented by C/S systems, the traditional costing methods do not facilitate accurate costing for the following reasons:

1. Traditional costing methods tend to allocate costs by *function* than by the *activity* that generates them. This results in misallocation of costs.
2. Since traditional costing is capital intensive, costs incurred during planning, design, and prototyping are merely expensed and set-off against revenue in the income statement (Raffish, 1991). Therefore, these hidden costs are treated as "sunk" for the purposes of decision making and not considered in the initial investment calculations. A list of common hidden costs are given in Table 1.

These hidden costs can be categorized broadly into technology costs and non technology costs and are discussed below.

Hidden Technology Costs: Since most IT personnel have main-frame based skills, a complete skills assessment has to be conducted to determine whether the skill of existing personnel are compatible with the requirements of a C/S environment. This could result in extensive training or restaffing of IT personnel. According to a study conducted by the Forester Research Group, the costs of shifting an employee from a host computing environment to a C/S environment could approximate between $10,000 to $15,000 per head. Such costs tend to be hidden under conventional costing methods. 'Hidden' implies that the costs are accumulated by function and may be included as a component of (for example) information systems or administrative department overhead. The costs are now hidden because it is more difficult to identify and attribute them to specific projects.

Source	Hidden Costs
People	• Cost of training/retraining staff
	• Cost of replacement staff
	• Cost of relocating staff
	• Productivity losses
	• Cost of end-user support
Multiple locations	• Costs associated with:
	— Multiple points of failure
	— Multiple points of entry
	— Multiple backup requirements
Multiple Vendor Support	• Costs associated with:
	— Ensuring compatibility
	— Multiple site licensing
	— Document preparation
	— Version maintenance

Table 1: Examples of Hidden Costs in a Client/Server Development Environment

The nature of C/S computing implies multiple, heterogeneous, and disparate systems, with multiple points of entry. These systems typically have multiple backup requirements, multiple possible points of failure, and therefore require multiple copies of software. The management of the C/S systems and the associated costs of administrating software distribution and site licensing spiral upwards as multiple servers are added. However, these costs are not accounted for separately (and therefore not brought to management's attention) since traditional costing is functional rather than activity oriented. Other hidden technology-based costs include the cost of C/S system downtime and connection failures which usually increase proportionately with the number of servers and networks.

Hidden Non-Technology Costs: As mentioned earlier C/S systems are more labor intensive relative to the mainframe environment. Labor costs such as those given below are typically ignored or vastly underestimated in determining the cost of implementing and operating a C/S system:

i) *Costs of system planning*, includes costs relating to the management of a more complex IS as well as keeping abreast of rapidly changing business needs.

ii) *Costs of lost productivity*, includes the time spent when personnel attend training sessions. In addition to lost training time, it is estimated that the cost of lost productivity approximates $20,000-$30,000 per employee during training (Baum, 1996).

iii) *Costs of increased development demands*, in terms of time spent by programmers creating more complex applications and interfaces.

iv) *Costs of system and application maintenance*, which includes keeping track of the C/S system updating, and the effects of such updating throughout the applications life cycle. Additional costs include the incremental costs of integrating the new systems and applications into the new C/S architecture.

The above mentioned hidden costs are typically considered as overhead and is accumulated by functions. This manner of accumulation prevents effective identification and attribution of costs to a C/S project, since these costs are now merged with a variety of other functional costs.

Activity Based Costing Approach

Activity-Based Costing (ABC) is an alternate costing method that gained popularity in organizations. Computer Aided Manufacturing - International (CAM-I) defines Activity Based Costing (ABC) "as the collection of financial and operating performance information tracing the significant activities of the organization to product costs." ABC is not an alternative to the traditional costing approaches, but a costing method that enables management to compute the *exact cost* of producing an output (hereafter referred to as deliverables).

ABC is based on the premise that; (i) an organization's objective is to create certain outputs, (ii) these outputs have characteristics that cause certain activities to take place, and (iii) those activities cost money. While traditional costing systems tend to allocate costs to products or services on a predetermined basis, the goal of ABC is to trace costs to products or services instead of arbitrarily allocating them. ABC has become popular for two major reasons. First, the cost of products and services is more accurately measured by the activity based system and hence expenditure can be allocated to projects more effectively. Second, the activity-based approach helps to identify and control costs. However, in-depth analysis must be conducted to uncover hidden costs so that a proper cost allocation can be obtained. By identifying activities and the costs that relate to each activity, it is possible to obtain greater understanding of *cost drivers* [1] and also identify potential areas for cost savings.

In essence, the activity-based approach is geared towards understanding what activities are involved in the production of the deliverables. The costs of activities are then built up to compute the costs of the deliverable, thus providing managers with better information to make investment decisions.

Steps in Developing an ABC System

In general, the development of an activity-based system involves the following steps:

Conduct Activity Analysis: An activity analysis describes the tasks, time allotted for each respective task, and the deliverables of the process. This step in essence, identifies the way by which an organization uses its resources to produce deliverables. For instance, in a C/S system development environment, it could involve activities such as project planning, data collection, data synthesis, data analysis and recommendations.

Linking the Activities to Costs: The cost of an activity includes all the factors of production used to perform an activity (Brimson, 1991). This includes the cost of items such as people, hardware, software, data, and other such resources which are needed to perform the activity.

Identifying Cost Drivers: A cost driver represents the demand each activity makes on project expenditure. Cooper and Kaplan (1992) emphasize that activity cost drivers are not devices to allocate costs, but instead represent the demand that deliverables make on each activity. For instance, the cost driver for the activity of information gathering would be the number of hours spent on interviews and observations.

The identification, measurement, and control of cost drivers is an essential element for the success of the activity-based system. An inefficient cost driver can cause erroneous decisions to be made. Cooper and Kaplan (1992) have differentiated cost drivers into different categories, namely Unit-related (U), Batch-related (B), and Facility-related (F). These are discussed briefly below:

i) *Unit-related* implies that there is a direct cause-and-effect relationship between cost and activity. Since a direct causal relationship exists, the cost can be directly attributed to the activity. An example of a cost that can be directly attributed is software licensing cost (assuming that the software is needed exclusively for the C/S application).

ii) *Batch-related* implies that a cause-and-effect relationship may be more difficult to identify, since the cost is common to many activities or projects. For example, end-user training hours could be considered an example of a batch-related driver, since end-user training is shared by many projects.

iii) *Facility-related* implies that a cause and effect relationship may be non-existent so that the cost can only be allocated to the activity on an arbitrary basis. Examples of facility-related costs include administration costs and the costs of utilities. While it is known that a certain amount of administration time may be used and some utilities may be consumed by C/S systems, a causal effect is difficult to establish (or may not be cost effective to do so). In such cases, the cost is allocated using an arbitrary basis.

Cost Attribution: In this step, a rate per unit of activity is developed, (for example, cost per employee hour). These rates are determined by managers and information system developers and could vary between organizations. The rate also depends on the nature of the cost driver.

Applying Activity Based Costing to C/S Systems

The activity-based costing framework for the C/S environment is shown in Figure 1. Step 1 identifies the major activities of the C/S life cycle. The second to sixth step creates the activity-based system for the C/S environment. The final step deals with monitoring the performance of the C/S system.

Step 1: Identifying the Activities in the C/S Systems Life Cycle

Prior to applying the activity-based approach to a C/S system, it is important to identify the major activities that take place during the life cycle of the C/S system. These activities can be viewed within a

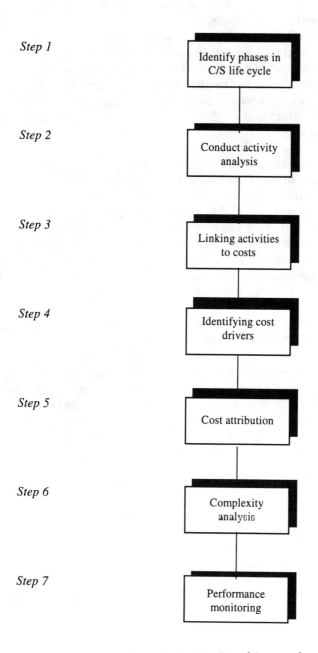

Figure 1: Framework of Applying the Activity-Based Approach to the Client/ Server Development Environment

systems development environment. There are four major deliverables in the C/S development life cycle. Namely, *solution definition, solution development, solution implementation*, and *continuous improvement.* Figure 2, summarizes the activities that must be undertaken to produce these deliverables. The last deliverable from each stage is part of the input for the next phase.

Solution Definition. The solutions definition phase deals with problem identification, and solutions determination.   This phase involves activities such as interviews with end-users and managers to identify the root causes of the problems. Problems are examined in terms of the current environment and all possible causes of the problem are identified and verified. To do this effectively, the following steps are required:

a. The systems analyst must document the existing system design (system design implies both workflows and processes).
b. The system analyst must clearly determine users' needs.
c. Based on the results of the information gathering, the systems analyst defines the end-users' functional requirements.
d. Based on the findings in steps a to c, the systems analyst must review existing information technology to determine whether it meets the organization's needs. In doing so, the current hardware and software should be cataloged and evaluated.

The above steps are followed by the identification of a range of alternative solutions which address the root problems. Each of the alternatives are prototyped for their suitability and ability to solve the problem. Once a suitable alternative is identified, the appropriate technology is selected. This step analyzes currently used technologies and evaluates the potential of both current and potential replacement technologies to meet the requirements of the optimal solution identified above. When this is attained, potential development tools and technologies are evaluated against the projected needs of the optimal solution.

Solutions Development. The Solutions Development stage deals with developing detailed prototypes of the new workflows and processes required by the solutions in the previous phase. It also involves verifying the adequacy and completeness of the solutions determined at the solution definition phase. This is accomplished by a brainstorming session of the work team. This is followed by the documentation of; (i) the problem (ii) the root causes of the problem (iii) the solution, including the hardware and software required and (iv) details of specific personnel requiring educational and training support for effective transition and (v) a list of the improvements that are to be expected as a result of implementing the new system.

The documentation is followed by the design, construction, test-

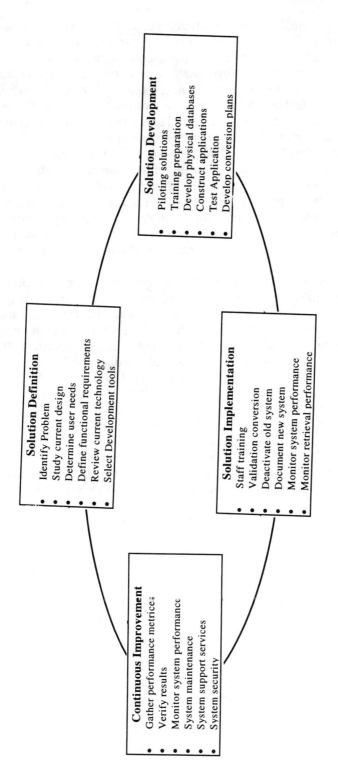

Figure 2: Major Phases in the Client/Server Life Cycle

ing of the physical database structure, and the creation of the conversion plan. In the conversion plan, information systems analysts map existing data sources to their equivalents in the new database and specify all conversion, synchronization, and timing considerations. The systems analysts document a backup plan in the event of a failure when data is being transferred from one system to another. Once this is attained, they design, construct, and test all functions necessary for intefacing with external data when the system is run.

Solutions Implementation. The solutions implementation phase deals with training users, validating data conversion efforts, and implementing process and workflow changes. This is followed by the execution of the migration plan as specified and the incorporation of adequate controls to ensure immediate response to any nonconformance associated with the C/S system. Once the C/S system is implemented, its performance is monitored under actual operating conditions.

Continuous Improvement. This is the most important phase in the C/S system's life cycle. In this phase, enhancements begin to successively refine and extend the application's functionality as the users become more comfortable with its capabilities and the process reengineering changes begin to take hold in the daily operations. It has been observed that as much as 75% of a successfully introduced application's value to an organization is added in the 12 to 18 months following its implementation (Vaughn, 1994).

The key activities involve gathering performance metrics data and verifying that the results expected are achieved. If variances do exist, the work team has to determine the cause and initiate corrective action as required. This stage also entails routine monitoring, optimizing application performance by quickly addressing nonconformances when they appear, and the provision of hardware support services.

Step 2: Conduct Activity Analysis

The foundation for this step lies in identifying the key activities. Identifying key activities will provide a clearer understanding on how costs of producing the final deliverable (i.e., the C/S system) are generated. Responses to the following questions will lead to the hierarchy of C/S activities as illustrated in Figure 3.

• What is the final major deliverable?
• What are the intermediate deliverables?
• What are the sub-activities required to generate the deliverables?
• What precisely has to be done to achieve the sub-activities?.

By responding these questions, analysts can determine the major tasks to be performed, the participants in each activity, and the

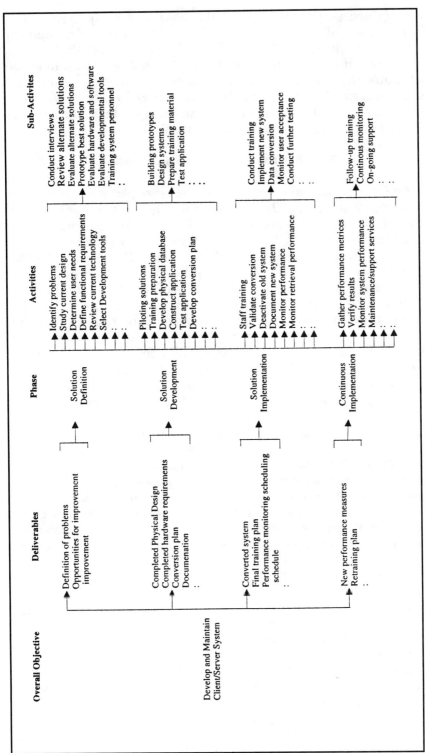

Figure 3: Hierarchy of Activities for a Client/Server System

resources necessary to accomplish the task. This analysis should be conducted for all the major phases in the systems development environment. The hierarchy of activities thus establishes the basis for assembling information that can be used to link activities to costs. Each sub-activity's cost is determined by the amount of time and resources devoted to each. (A distinct advantage of this type of analysis is that if a particular cost is perceived as being too high, the cost can be traced back through the bill of activities).

Step 3: Linking Activities to Costs

An understanding of the nature of the tasks performed will result in a greater awareness of the costs each task generates. For instance, in the solution definition phase (refer to Figure 3), the systems analyst will gather information by means of interviews and observation techniques involving managers and end-users. The relevant cost for this activity can be broken down into the cost per man hour of the systems analyst, as well as the cost per hour of managers and end-users. In a traditional costing environment the latter cost (namely, the non-productive time of managers and end-users) would be ignored (and therefore is a hidden cost). However with activity costing, the costs of both the managers and end-users will be determined by assigning a fraction of the departmental expense to each activity. Similarly, by examining the resources spent on each sub-activity, costs can be attributed to the other phases.

Step 4: Identifying Cost Drivers

Once a link is established between activities and the costs they generate, the cost drivers for each activity should be identified (refer Figure 4). Traditional costing would consider the number of hours spent on information gathering as irrelevant since employees are paid a fixed salary. However, this argument does not take into consideration the concept of opportunity cost. The more time managers devote to this activity (interviewing), then the less time available for other activities that could be financially rewarding to the company. Hence, the number of hours spent represents a lost opportunity to gain revenue for the company and should be attributed to this activity. Similarly, the cost to be attributed for software would be dependent on the number of function points designed.

The final column in Figure 4 categorizes the type of cost driver. This categorization is important because it affects the manner in which the cost is attributed to the project. By definition, while a unit cost can be directly attributed to the activity, a batch cost has to be attributed based on the demand the activity imposes on project costs. If a cost is defined as "facility," there is no real basis for charging the cost and it has to be allocated using an arbitrary basis.

Activity	Nature of Cost Driver	Costs	Cost Driver	Class
Solution Definition Conduct interviews Review alternate solutions Evaluate alternate solutions Prototype best solution Evaluate hardware and software Evaluate developmental tools Training system personnel . .	Hours spent on information gathering Hours spent on prototyping Hours spent evaluating best solutions . . .	Manager salary End-user salary System analyst salary Cost of developmental tools . .	Number of manager hours Number of end-user hours Number of system analyst hours . .	B B B
Solution Development Building prototypes Design systems Prepare training material Test application . . .	Hours spent by system developers Hours spent on preparing training material Hours spent by system testers . . .	Developers' salary Cost of software Testers' salary Cost of training material . .	Number of developer hours Number of tester hours Number hours of preparation time . .	B B U
Solutions Implementation Conduct training Implement new system Data conversion Monitor user acceptance Conduct further testing . .	Hours spent by trainers Hours spent by trainees Hours spent on data conversion Hours spent developers . . .	Manager's salary Training cost Lost productivity . .	Number of trainer hours Number of trainee hours Number of productive hours spent . .	B U U
Continuous Improvement Follow-up training Continuous monitoring On-going support . . .	Hours spent in training Usage of maintenance resources . .	Manager's salary Training cost System maintenance salary . .	Number of trainer hours Number of trainee hours Number of maintenance hours . .	B B

Figure 4: Links Associating Activities, Costs, and Cost Drivers

Step 5: Cost Attribution

Figure 4 illustrates how the cost of activities can be attributed using the cost drivers discussed earlier. For instance, the cost of information gathering can be attributed using cost drivers such as, the cost per hour of the systems analyst, cost per hour of the manager, and the cost per hour of the employee.

Step 6: Level of Complexity Adjustment

The above mentioned steps, however, does not take the C/S level of complexity into consideration. Taking this into account, the costs generated by the activity-based approach as described in steps 2 to 5, may not be applied meaningfully.

In order to ensure that the activity-based approach does generate costs that can be meaningfully analyzed it is essential that the cost estimates consider the complexity of the C/S system and the varying

Project Classification and Analysis Form					
PRIMARY CLASSIFICATION _____ CLASSIFIER'S NAME _____ CLASSIFIER'S DESIGNATION _____				DATE REVIEWED BY AUTHORIZED BY	

In each of the following sections, place a check-mark in the most appropriate box regarding project complexity and

insert a budgeted time

SOLUTION DEFINITION	1	2	3	Estimated Time	Comments _____
• Interviewing managers and users	☐	☐	☐	_____	
• Observing, examining hard copies	☐	☐	☐	_____	
• Matching current needs	☐	☐	☐	_____	
• Software selection	☐	☐	☐	_____	
SOLUTIONS DEVELOPMENT					Comments
• Prototyping	☐	☐	☐	_____	
• Benchmark identification	☐	☐	☐	_____	
• Hardware selection	☐	☐	☐	_____	
• Design & development of system	☐	☐	☐	_____	
• System testing	☐	☐	☐	_____	
• Conversion planning	☐	☐	☐	_____	
• User interface development	☐	☐	☐	_____	
• Document preparation	☐	☐	☐	_____	
SOLUTIONS IMPLEMENTATION					Comments
• Interviews for skills assessment	☐	☐	☐	_____	
• Staff training	☐	☐	☐	_____	
• Installing new system	☐	☐	☐	_____	
• Document preparation	☐	☐	☐	_____	
• Recovery planning	☐	☐	☐	_____	
• Monitoring network performance	☐	☐	☐	_____	
CONTINUOUS IMPROVEMENT					Comments
• Follow-up training	☐	☐	☐	_____	
• Continuous monitoring	☐	☐	☐	_____	
• Check administrative services	☐	☐	☐	_____	
• Hardware, software maintenance	☐	☐	☐	_____	
• On-going support	☐	☐	☐	_____	
• Security and control services	☐	☐	☐	_____	

Legend 1 = least complex   2 = medium complexity   3 = most complex

Figure 5: Determining the Complexity of the Client/Server System

degrees of complexity of the different activities.

Figure 5 shows a document that can be used by managers to record the various degrees of complexity of each activity prior to estimating the costs of the C/S system.

All activities identified in the C/S life cycle are categorized based on degree of complexity, ranging on a scale of 1 to 3; where 1 represents an activity where low effort is needed and "3" represents an activity where considerable effort may be needed. The nature of the category is contingent upon the type of project handled. By comparing the estimated cost with the cost attributed to a project, the manager can determine if the project has been implemented in a cost effective manner (for example, if the budgeted time for a systems analyst on the document had been far exceeded during actual implementation, the adverse variance will be easily noted by the project manager who can institute an investigation).

Step 7: Performance Monitoring

It has to be pointed out that the activity-oriented approach is only a diagnostic tool that provides a means to an end. The end product of the activity oriented approach is to ensure that all costs are identified. Performance monitoring is essential because it will help identify areas of disproportionate cost, the reasons for the excessive cost incurrence (if any), and help to pinpoint responsibility. The activity-oriented approach can only be truly beneficial if used in conjunction with other diagnostic tools that aid in this regard. An example of a diagnostic monitoring tool is shown in Figure 6.

An advantage of the activity oriented approach is that all activities that contribute towards the end-product are identified. As illustrated in Figure 6, a comparison of the budgeted numbers with the actual numbers at the end of the C/S life cycle will highlight adverse variances. It may not be beneficial for IS managers to investigate all variances. The costs of attempting to investigate all variances may far exceed the potential benefits. One solution would be to establish tolerance limits and investigate only those variances that exceed the tolerance level. At each level of activity it is essential to identify the person responsible. This aids in pinpointing responsibility. The variances that are deemed to be worthy of investigation can now be made accountable by the person in charge of that activity. Investigation may help to identify the root causes of inefficiency (if any). If the variance was not controllable by the person in charge of that activity, it could be attributed to inappropriate budgeting. This will also be useful information because it will help to refine budgeted time for future C/S projects.

	Budget			Actual		Variance	Responsibility
	Time	Rate	Cost	Time	Cost		
Solutions Development							
Conduct interviews							
Review alternate solutions							
Evaluate alternate solutions							
Prototype best solution							
Evaluate hardware and software							
Evaluate developmental tools							
Training system personnel							
Solution Development							
Building prototypes							
Design systems							
Prepare training material							
Test application							
Solutions Implementation							
Conduct training							
Implement new system							
Data conversion							
Monitor user acceptance							
Conduct further testing							
Continuous Improvement							
Follow-up training							
Continuous monitoring							
Ongoing support							

Figure 6: Performance Monitoring Sheet

Summary and Conclusions

Most organizations are rushing to introduce C/S computing into their businesses. This is evident from the phenomenal growth of C/S systems in U.S organizations (from 5% to 60% in a four-year period). However, this transition from a host-based computing environment to a C/S environment has been costly for many organizations. Surveys show that over 50% of companies far exceeded their initial budgets. This is attributed to deficiencies of traditional costing approaches which accumulate costs by function and then attempt to allocate those costs to activities. Any such allocation has to be arbitrary at best and the costs attributed to a project may not be accurate. Further, many project specific costs tend to be hidden under conventional systems and management may not be aware that such costs have incurred. Surveys conducted by researchers bear out existing dissatisfaction with conventional techniques. While the problems outlined above have been addressed in manufacturing industries by the implementation of activity oriented procedures, these procedures are still in an infancy stage with regard to service industries. The activity-oriented concept is still novel in relation to the costing of computerized applications.

This chapter recommends the use of an activity-based approach for identifying all related costs including uncovering potential hidden costs of a C/S system. Activity-based systems are based on the premise that an organization's objective is to create certain deliverables; these outputs have characteristics that cause activities to take place; and those activities cost money.

The chapter demonstrates, on a theoretical basis, how an ABC system can be generated by:

a. Clearly understanding the activities that take place to generate the final output by establishing a *hierarchy of activities*.
b. Identifying the costs related to and generated by the activities above.
c. Establishing the cost drivers that link activities and costs.
d. Identifying how all relevant project costs can be attributed to a project, and
e. Setting up a form of budgeting that is contingent on the complexity of a potential project to aid in performance monitoring.

As stated earlier, many organizations discover after the event, that (i) developing and maintaining a C/S system can be a long and expensive event, and (ii) that most times C/S projects over run budgets. This problem has been attributed to non-identification, and distortion of information by traditional costing approaches. The activity-based approach proposed in this study provides more reliable cost information since it identifies and allocates costs in accordance with the activities performed. This activity analysis helps in identifying many costs that are typically hidden in a traditional costing environment. By having accurate information about the true cost of the C/S system, managers can make more effective decisions on whether or not to develop a C/S system.

The activity-based approach ensures that managers at the decision-making stage will be aware about the potential costs they will incur during the development, implementation, and maintenance of the C/S system. Thus, they will be able to conduct an effective cost-benefit analysis before making a final investment decision. The activity-based approach also provides managers with information at a micro-level stage of each phase of the C/S life cycle. This will facilitate investigation and ensure that appropriate action can be taken to remedy the causes of excessive costs.

Certain limitations of this study have to be noted, namely:

• ABC may not be easily implementable for all projects. This study provides a framework for a generalized C/S system only.
• The causal relationship between activities and cost may not be clearly

determinable in all cases.
- The lack of understanding of ABC, especially by accountants specialized in working for service industries, may hinder its acceptance and use.

Management Strategies for Information Technology Investment

This study provides a framework which managers can utilize to accurately determine the cost of a C/S system prior to its development and implementation. This improves the quality of information available to an organization to determine whether investment in C/S systems will be financially beneficial. The framework recommends the identification of activities in the various stages of the C/S development life. The framework proposed in this study allows managers to:

a. monitor performance in a C/S environment.
b. trace disproportionately high costs to their root causes.
c. trace and identifying non-value added hidden costs.
d. determine whether the benefits exceed the costs of implementation.

Overall the activity-based approach will ensure that the true benefits of a C/S system can be attained by maintaining an effective system of cost identification, monitoring, and control.

Endnote

[1] Horngren (1994) defines a cost driver as any factor that affects costs. That is, a change in the cost driver will cause a change in the total cost of a related cost object.

Chapter 14

Understanding the Business Value of Information Systems: A Flexibility-Based Perspective

Ram L. Kumar
University of North Carolina at Charlotte

Investments in information technology (IT) can result in improved organizational flexibility. This article explores the relationship between IT investments and organizational flexibility. A framework for analyzing organizational processes and relating them to flexibility is discussed. Multiple examples from different industries are provided.

Investments in information technologies (IT) constitute a significant portion of organizations' capital budgets. The magnitude and growth of these investments underscore the need for measuring the payoff resulting to businesses from information systems investments. The problem of measuring the business value of IT is an important problem that is of interest to practicing managers as well as researchers (Brynjolffson, 1994; Hitt and Brynjolffson, 1994; Straussman et al. 1988). Initial studies claimed that paradoxically investments in information technology had not produced the degree of productivity increases that were anticipated (Roach, 1991). The literature on IT investment payoff contains studies that claim a significant positive relationship between information technology investments and outputs of organizations (Brynjolffson and Hitt, 1993, 1996) as well as those that are critical of the payoff from using computers (Landauer, 1995). These studies have focused on measuring productivity gains resulting from investments in information technology.

It is generally accepted that measuring the business value of information systems goes beyond evaluating productivity measures. Several intangible factors need to be considered in evaluating the benefits resulting from investments in information systems. A survey of 285 companies conducted by *Information Week* underscores the need to look beyond cost savings in evaluating information technology related benefits (Brynjolfsson, 1994). Improved customer service was identified as the most important benefit of investing in information systems. Cost savings was next in importance, followed by timeliness of customer interactions, improved product and service quality, support for reengineering efforts, and better flexibility. Many of these benefits are interrelated (e.g., support for reengineering and better flexibility), and need to be described in qualitative terms since they are difficult to quantify. Very often, quantification is really a means to an end. The real problem is to convince management that information technology investments add value to the business. While quantification is undoubtedly useful in convincing management of the value of information systems, carefully researched qualitative arguments can also be useful.

It is important to realize that measuring the business value of information systems and justifying investments in information technology involve the same kinds of considerations and methods. The major difference is that of time, with justification being done prior to investment and measurement of business value being a post investment exercise. Problems of quantification of business value apply to justification as well as post investment analysis. Ideally, the results anticipated at the time of justification should have been clearly specified and realized at the time of post investment evaluation and measurement. In practice, however, these results may be significantly different (Keil, 1995).

This article focuses on an important and interesting benefit resulting from information technology investments, namely flexibility. The term flexibility means different things to different people. Hence, this article starts by discussing the multifaceted concept of flexibility and provides a framework for operationalizing the concept of flexibility. Flexibility is then explored in the context of organizations and a framework for analyzing organizational flexibility is presented. The ideas presented are also valid in the context of networked organizations (Malone, Yates, and Benjamin, 1987). The relationship between organizational flexibility and investments in information systems is then examined. The framework for analyzing organizational flexibility is then applied in the context of IT investments. Several examples of organizational flexibility resulting from IT investments are provided.

The managerial implications of this article and guidelines for measuring flexibility resulting from investments in information technology in qualitative terms are provided. A brief discussion of possible quantification of the value of flexibility is also provided.

Understanding the Concept of Flexibility

The objective of this section is to illustrate that flexibility is a multifaceted concept. Different perspectives on flexibility, drawn from literature in the areas of economics, strategic management, and operations management are presented. A simple framework for operationalizing the concept of flexibility is discussed.

Flexibility is a commonly used term in everyday life. We talk about flexible lifestyles and flexible attitudes in the case of individuals. In an organizational setting, we encounter the terms such as flexible organizations (Baharami, 1992) and flexible manufacturing systems (Maleki, 1991). As earlier, many organizations consider flexibility to be a benefit resulting from investments in information technology (Brynjolfsson, 1994). However, the term flexibility means different things in different contexts.

Webster's dictionary defines the term flexible as "capable of responding or conforming to a changing or new situation." It also cross-references the term flexible with the term elastic. The term elastic in turn has several meanings such as capable of easy expansion or contraction, and capable of recovering quickly from depression or disappointment.

The concept of flexibility has interested researchers in several different fields such as economics, organization theory, decision theory, and manufacturing management. Evans (1991) provides a historical review of research on the concept of flexibility. He also discusses the meaning of flexibility and terms such as adaptability, agility, elasticity, resilience, robustness, and versatility that have been

Term	Interpretation
Adaptability	Ability to adjust to a transformed environment
Agility	Swiftness in seizing an opportunity or avoiding a negative outcome
Elasticity	Ability to easily change in response to pressure
Liquidity	Ability to be converted to some other form with minimal switching costs
Resilience	Tendency to rebound or recoil
Robustness	Ability to absorb, deflect effects of unanticipated change
Versatility	Being able to adapt or respond to a range of scenarios

Table 1: Different Interpretations of Flexibility

used instead of flexibility and refers to related literature. Table 1 summarizes major interpretations of the term flexibility based on Evans (1991).

Flexibility in the context of manufacturing operations has been extensively studied. Sethi and Sethi (1990) provide an excellent survey of the research on flexibility in manufacturing. Researchers have identified several different types of manufacturing flexibilities, which include expansion flexibility, product-mix flexibility, process flexibility, and volume flexibility. Table 2 summarizes major types of manufacturing flexibility based on Sethi and Sethi (1990).

Tables 1 and 2 illustrate the multifaceted nature of flexibility. Different views of flexibility may be appropriate in different contexts. However, all definitions of flexibility involve some kind of change (stimulus) and some kind of response to this change. The primary differences is the nature of stimuli and responses. Hence it might be useful to think of flexibility in terms of a stimulus-response framework. This framework is illustrated in Figure 1.

First, flexibility deals with an entity (an individual, organization, machine,...). Second, there is a stimulus or change in the operating environment of the entity that requires a response. Third, it is not always easy to respond to the stimulus. Thinking of flexibility in terms of stimulus, response, and ease of response is a useful way of

Type of Flexibility	Description
Volume	Ability to vary production volume
Expansion	Ability to expand or contract maximum production rate
Product-Mix	Ability to vary product-mix
Process	Ability to vary the manufacturing process by which a product is produced

Table 2: Major Types of Manufacturing Flexibility

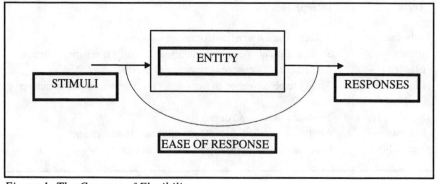

Figure 1: The Concept of Flexibility

operationalizing the concept of flexibility. It is important to realize that it is not always necessary to be reactive and think of a response after a stimulus has occurred. It is possible to be proactive by anticipating stimuli and trying to build appropriate responses. If certain types of stimuli can be anticipated then it is possible to design organizations that can respond easily to these stimuli. The reactive versus proactive nature of flexibility has been recognized and discussed in earlier studies on flexibility (Evans, 1991; Gerwin, 1993). The framework illustrated in Figure 1 will be used in the following sections to examine the relationship between IT investments and organizational flexibility.

Organizational Flexibility

This section examines the concept of flexibility in the context of organizations. The framework for operationalizing flexibility presented in Figure 1 is analyzed and extended in the context of organizations. Porter's value chain concepts (Porter, 1985) are introduced and integrated with the concept of flexibility. A critical analysis of organizational flexibility and its impact on organizational performance is provided.

The strategic management literature recognizes the importance of organizational flexibility and contains interesting ideas on appropriate organizational strategies under different environmental conditions (Wernerfelt and Karnani, 1987). Several studies discuss the need for organizational flexibility. Das and Elango (1995) discuss the fact that organizations in the turbulent business environments of today are recognizing that a static corporate strategy aimed at aligning organizational strengths with the environment does not often result in sustained financial performance. They emphasize the need for strategic flexibility. Aaker and Mascarenhas (1984, p.74) define strategic flexibility as "the ability of an organization to adapt to substantial, uncertain and fast occurring (relative to the reaction time) environmental changes that have a meaningful impact on an organization's performance." The concept of strategic flexibility is also discussed by Evans (1991) and Harrigan (1980, 1985). Boynton and Victor (1991) introduce the concept of "dynamically stable" organizations. They provide examples of organizations that build a stable set of process capabilities that are dynamic enough to deal with a variety of product and customer demands.

Prahalad and Hammel (1990) discuss the benefits of focused organizations with distinctive core competencies. Wernerfelt and Karani (1987) analyze competitive strategy under different types of uncertainty, intensity of competition and the position of a firm relative to competition. They illustrate that flexibility as well as focus may be desirable strategies under different conditions. Several studies point out that the focus that is typically expected in mass production is not necessarily contradictory with the concept of customization (Davis, 1987, Dertouzos, Lester, Solow, and the MIT commission on industrial productivity, 1989). Terms such as "efficient flexibility" and "mass customization" have been used. Das and Elango(1995) present several external and internal factors that organizations should manage in order to achieve strategic flexibility. They identify suppliers, alliances, and multinational operations as being important external factors. Manufacturing flexibility, modular product design, employee flexibility, and organizational structure are identified as being important internal factors that impact strategic flexibility.

Thus the literature reviewed in this section indicates that focus as well as flexibility are important for organizations. Too much flexibility can result in excessive costs and inefficiencies. Too little flexibility can result in rigid organizations that are incapable of responding to changing environments. Managers in organizations need to decide what actions need to be taken achieve the right mix of focus and flexibility.

Figure 2 illustrates the concept of organizational flexibility. Market changes such as changes in customer preferences or competition might result in an organization responding by offering new products or services. Similarly, changes in technology might cause organizations to change organizational processes (for example, the purchasing process might be changed to use Electronic Data Interchange transactions). Examples of organizational change induced by market and technology changes can be found in (Kumar and Crook, 1997). The ease of responding to changes (or degree of flexibility) can be thought of in terms of three interrelated dimensions: (a) cost of response (b) response time, and (c) scope of response (Das and Elango, 1995). One or more of these dimensions may assume a high degree of importance in different contexts. Also, it is important to realize that the term scope of response may mean different things in different contexts. Several examples will be provided in this article to illustrate the context-sensitive nature of scope of response.

Quick response to changing customer needs is an important requirement in the textile industry (Hackel and Nolan, 1993). Clearly time is related to cost, in that quicker response times may mean higher costs. Response time and associated cost are related to the scope of the required response. In some cases, new customer requirements can be easily met (for example, a 5% increase in order quantity or the same product in a slightly different color). In other cases (such as a complete revamping of the product line), the scope of response may be large. In situations such as the above example, organizations may decide to use a strategy of competing on response time and manage the scope of change and associated costs. In other situations organizations could choose to compete on the basis of scope of response (being able to offer a wide range of products in response to changing market conditions)

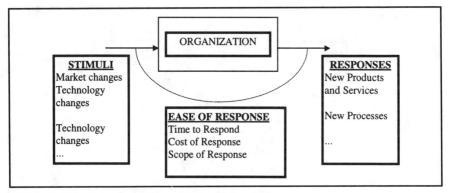

Figure 2: The Concept of Organizational Flexibility

and choose to manage the associated costs and time. Examples of these situations are provided later in this article.

This section has discussed the concept of organizational flexibility from a strategic perspective. The benefits of strategic flexibility may be realized over short or long periods of time. Organizations can also benefit from flexibility in day to day operations (operational flexibility) (Sethi and Sethi, 1990). For example, the availability of multiple machines might facilitate manufacture of a product on one machine if problems are encountered with another machine. Here again, having multiple machines provides flexibility, but the flexibility adds business value only if machines break down and there is a need to use one machine instead of another. Having multiple machines represents unproductive use of capital if each machine is extremely reliable and not expected to break down. Operational flexibility and strategic flexibility could be related to each other. For example, a manufacturing organization that operates in a market where meeting tight delivery schedules is extremely critical could set up an infrastructure consisting of backup machines and personnel and develop meeting tight delivery schedules on time as a competitive niche. Sustainability of this competitive advantage would depend on the nature of the industry and capabilities of competitors.

Thus, strategic flexibility, designed in a proactive manner can provide competitive advantages which in turn would translate into improved financial performance in the long run. Designing strategic flexibility requires managers to identify areas where flexibility can produce business value. However, identification of such areas is not an easy exercise. It is suggested that the value chain model (Porter, 1985), when used in conjunction with the model of flexibility in Figure 2 provides a useful framework for identifying areas where flexibility may add value to organizations. The value chain model suggests that a typical organization can be thought off as consisting of core functions such as (a) inbound logistics, (b) operations (c) outbound logistics (d) outbound logistics (e) sales and (f) service. Value addition occurs to a

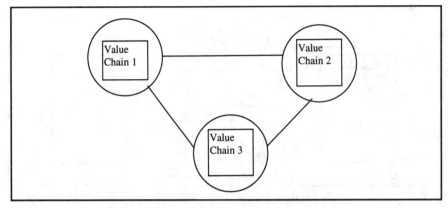

Figure 3: Interconnected Value Chains

product as it moves from (a) to (f). In addition, there are support functions such as purchasing, human resource management, technology management and administration. The nature and relative importance of these functions is likely to vary depending on the type of organization and the industry in which it operates.

So far, this article has focused on single organizations. However, in the information driven economy of today and given the rapid proliferation of computer networks it is realistic to view an organization as part of a network of trading partners (Malone, Yates, and Benjamin, 1987). An organization's trading partners, in turn could be other organizations or individuals. The value chain of each organization is linked to the value chains of trading partners as illustrated in Figure 3.

Each part of the value chain can be thought of as consisting of multiple processes. Figure 4 provides an illustration of the value chain with key supporting processes in the context of a manufacturing organization. It is important to realize that processes can be defined at different levels of granularity. For example, a manufacturing process can be subdivided into different operations. This approach to modeling an organization in terms of the value chain and processes has been termed the value process model (McDonald, 1991). This approach can be applied to a variety of organizations in different industries. The actual terminology used in conceptualizing an organization in terms of the value process model would be terminology that an organization is comfortable with and would depend on the nature of business that the organization is in.

Figure 5 provides an alternative formulation of the value process model in more general terms, and depicts core processes in a service organization such as UPS or Federal Express that provides transportation services for packages. This formulation is based on the work of Rockart and Short (1991).

The value process model can thus be used as a starting point to model an organization. Each process in the value process model can

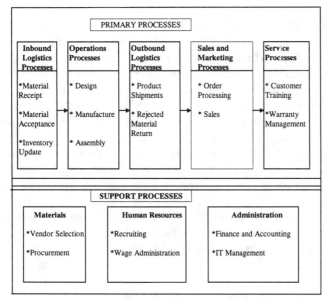

Figure 4: Illustrative Value Process Model for a Manufacturing Organization

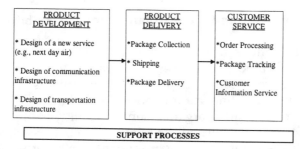

Figure 5: Illustrative Primary Processes for a Transportation Service Provider

then be examined using the concept of flexibility discussed in Figure 2 to identify areas where flexibility is important.

For example, consider a service organization such as UPS or Federal Express. Consider an area in the value process model such as inbound logistics. Collecting packages that need to be shipped is a process in this area. We could try and identify stimuli that impact this process. An example of a stimulus would be a request from a customer to pick up a package from a particular location as soon as possible. Flexibility in inbound logistics would mean that this stimulus should be easy to respond to in terms of time to respond, as well as cost of response. Scope of response may also be relevant in terms of the geographic area where such a service is available. In this case, the ability to collect packages from customers with relative ease is an operational flexibility. However, an organization that is able to do a good job of flexible inbound logistics may use this as a competitive strategy.

In addition to flexibility in different processes in areas of the value chain, organizations could derive flexibility as a result of integration between processes which may belong to different areas of the value chain. For example, integration between marketing and operations might facilitate quick response to customer demand changes. If the integration merely reduces time for processing standard orders then it is an efficiency issue. However, if integration results in quick responses to changes in demand patterns then it is a flexibility issue. Flexibility can also result from integration of processes which belong to different parts of the value chain for different organizations. For example, integration of an organization's marketing, operations and inbound logistics processes with the operation and outbound logistics of a supplier would increase the flexibility of an organization. This flexibility could be the result of being able to respond quickly to changing market conditions by obtaining the necessary raw materials quickly from a supplier.

Information Systems and Organizational Flexibility

Understanding IT and Organizational Flexibility

Previous sections discussed the fact that flexibility in certain areas can add value to businesses. This section focuses on the relationship between information systems investments and organizational flexibility. The important enabling role of information system investments in facilitating organizational flexibility is highlighted. A framework for conceptualizing the relationship between information technology investments and organizational flexibility is presented. This framework emphasizes the fact that investments in information technology often need to be accompanied by other types of investments and process changes in order to achieve organizational flexibility. The value process model described in the previous section along with the concept of flexibility presented in Figure 2 is used to identify several situations where flexibility results from appropriate investments in information systems.

Investments in information systems can play an important role in increasing operational as well as strategic flexibility of organizations. Clemons and Weber (1994) highlight the fact that information technology enables the implementation of flexible, finely tuned "segment tailored" strategies that are much more effective that simple strategies (such as cost leadership, differentiation or niche). Boynton (1993) explores the relationship between "dynamically stable" organizations (organizations that build a stable set of process capabilities that are dynamic enough to deal with a variety of product and customer demands) and information technology. Three classes of information systems that facilitate the achievement of dynamic stability are identified and characterized.

However, it is often the case that these investments in information systems may need to be augmented by additional investments and process changes in order to derive organizational flexibility. Consider the example of flexibility in inbound logistics presented in the earlier section. This flexibility results from investments in information systems (hardware and software), other equipment, people, and changes in operating procedures. Examples of hardware include hand-held scanners to scan in bar codes on shipments, hardware to maintain a database of customers and their pick up requirements and any other required information, and a telecommunications infrastructure that supports customer calls and transfer of information about package routing and delivery status. Examples of software include database management system software to manage databases of customer information and package routing information, and specialized software for routing and scheduling of trucks. Examples of investments in other equipment and people include trucks for pickup of customer packages, and additional personnel for operating these trucks. Examples of changes in operating procedures would include training customer service operators and truck drivers to respond to customer calls for speedy pickup of packages. This may involve a customer service representative identifying a particular truck for pickup of a package, communicating customer information to the driver, and the driver responding to the call.

This view of IT investments resulting in organizational flexibility only if other related factors are effectively managed is similar to the view that IT investments per se do not improve organizational performance unless the investing firms use their resources efficiently (Weil, 1992). In addition to efficient resource usage, the extent to which IT-induced organizational flexibility is impacts firm performance is likely to be influenced by industry structure, nature of competition, and management capabilities of the company (Bharadwaj, Bharadwaj, and Konsysnski, 1996). The effect of IT-induced organizational flexibility on business value is outlined in Figure 6 and is based on the conceptual models proposed by Bharadwaj, Bharadwaj, and Konsynsski (1996), and Weil (1992). Figure 6 focuses on flexibility and its impact on organizational performance. Figure 2 helps to operationalize the concept of flexibility in terms of stimuli, response, and ease of response that may be relevant in a particular context. In the example regarding flexible inbound logistics, figure 6 helps to think about the factors that determine whether flexible inbound logistics could help to provide competitive advantage. Management effectiveness plays an important role in converting IT investments into organizational flexibility in terms of inbound logistics. Also, the impact of organizational flexibility is impacted by management effectiveness in making other decisions (for example pricing of services) relative to competition and the nature of industry. Figure 2 on the other hand,

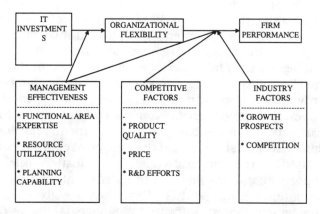

Figure 6: The Relationship Between IT-Induced Organizational Flexibility and Organizational Performance

helps to think about and understand the stimuli, response, and ease of response (time, cost, scope) that would be associated with flexible inbound logistics.

Examples of IT-Driven Organizational Flexibility

This section aims to deepen the reader's understanding of IT-driven organizational flexibility by providing several examples from different industries. Examples illustrating flexibility in different core processes in the value process chain are provided. IT-driven organizational flexibility resulting from integrating different parts of the value process chain is then discussed. Examples of IT-driven organizational flexibility resulting from integrating across value chains of multiple organizations are provided. These examples use the concept of organizational flexibility presented in Figure 2.

IT-driven Flexibility in the Value Process Chain

Flexibility in Logistics. The examples provided in this section emphasize inbound logistics. Similar ideas can be applied to outbound logistics.

Example: transportation services. Inbound logistics refers to the processes of receiving, collecting and distributing inputs required for the final product or service. This portion of the value chain is extremely important in some industries such as transportation services (trucking, parcel and courier services, airlines, railroads, shipping), sanitation services, and some manufacturing settings.

Consider a process such as package pickup for a courier service such as UPS. Stimuli such as changes in traffic patterns at different times of the day and requests from customers for packages are often encountered by such organizations.   Each time such a stimulus occurs, the organization responds by selecting the best route to pickup packages. Speed of response may be important (it needs to be a within reasonable limits). Cost of response is important from the organization's viewpoint. The scope of response would refer to the geographical areas where pickup is available.   An organization that has a high degree of flexibility in inbound logistics would be able to respond to stimuli easily (in terms of time, cost, or scope of response). A telecommunications infrastructure that enables drivers of pickup vehicles to communicate with a control center and pass voice and data messages along with software that decides the optimal routing of vehicles would be an example of an IT investment that results in organizational flexibility. Clearly, investments in IT may need to be accompanied by other investments and process changes (investments in trucks, training, new steps in the receiving process such as scanning in of bar codes on collected packages).   Organizations operating in environments where the frequency and variability of stimuli is high (such as crowded uptown areas or remote areas) would value such IT-driven organizational flexibility highly.   A similar system would be of value for law enforcement agencies who often need to respond to crime reports at short notice.

Example: Financial Services. Customer transactions (such as deposits, withdrawals, requests for purchase or sales of stocks) are key inputs to a financial service industry. Inbound logistics in the context of financial institutions represents managing these inputs. Financial institutions need to cater to a wide range of customer requirements (scope of response) in terms of times at which transactions can occur and locations from which transactions can occur. Time of response as well as cost of response are also important. Traditional branches at fixed locations with a limited number of are not very flexible in terms of catering to a variety of customer needs (expressed in terms of time at which the transaction can occur and locations from which transactions can occur). However, they may offer a wide selection of possible financial transactions. Automated Teller Machines (ATMs) represent an option that has more flexibility than branches in terms of time at which transactions can occur as well as location of transactions, but is still only capable offering a limited scope of response (the customer still has to locate the nearest ATM and these ATMs offer only a limited range of financial services). Internet or electronic banking, on the other hand is extremely flexible in terms of times at which the bank could respond to requests for transactions (in terms of time of response).   In addition, electronic banking can potentially offer a much wider range of financial services (scope of response) than ATMs. These examples illustrate that information technology investments can replace manual systems (tellers working in branches) thus making the organizations more flexible in terms of responding to demand stimuli.

Flexibility in Operations

Example: Flexible Design. Design is an extremely important process in the operations of aircraft manufacturer Boeing. However, given the complexity of Boeing's process there are several sources of uncertainty (stimuli) that require periodic changes in the design. These include suggestions from other designers, problems in manufacturing or assembly, changes in customer requirements, problems that surface during use of aircraft, and the need to produce innovative designs to stay competitive. Each of these stimuli requires responses in terms of design changes. The original design process was often inflexible since it tool long periods of time, involved high cost, and was limited in terms of the scope of changes that could be made.

Boeing realized the importance of flexible design and began using the CATIA (computer-aided three-dimensional interactive application) and ELFINI (finite element analysis system). With this system design teams could work concurrently (with simultaneous access to the design) and suggestions from one designer could easily be incorporated. This was in contrast to the earlier scenarios where versions of designs slowly made their way from one designer to the other in a linear fashion with backtracking where required.

Manufacturing problems could be anticipated and design modifications could be made even before the aircraft was manufactured. This is because the high precision drawings generated by CATIA facilitated the designers to visualize if parts would fit or if adding new subsystems altered the design in undesirable ways. It was also possible to check if the design resulted in a maintainable system because a computer generated mechanic could demonstrate whether a human being could access parts of the aircraft that needed to be maintained. Changes in customer requirements could easily be translated into design changes. The advanced simulation and graphics features facilitated relatively easy creation and on-screen testing of sophisticated, innovative designs.

CATIA thus allowed the designers to respond with a variety of stimuli quickly, at relatively low cost (for making the change), and could accommodate a significant variety (scope) in the kinds of changes that could be made to the design. CATIA involved over seven mainframes and over two thousand terminals and related hardware. In addition, the use of CATIA involved process changes such as concurrent engineering, multi-functional work teams, and on-line design and testing. More information on this application can be found in (Tapscott, 1996, 143-147).

Example: Flexible Financial Products Design. Derivative securities or financial instruments that are based on other assets have become relatively popular in recent years (Marshall, 1989). Several leading financial houses deal in derivative securities. In many financial trading floors, the trader is backed by a computer whiz-kid who is capable of designing derivatives to meet a particular profile of risk and return by sophisticated combination of other securities. This real time design of new derivative products is made possible by a combination of sophisticated mathematical modeling and high performance computing for doing mathematical calculations as well as accessing large amounts of data from networked databases. Such applications of information technology increase flexibility by increasing the scope of response (in terms of customized risk and return properties of derivatives) as well as time of response at a reasonable cost. Additional information on applications of information technology in financial trading are described in (Kaufman, 1995).

Example: Flexible Manufacturing. Several manufacturing organizations worldwide have implemented systems for material requirements planning (MRP). These MRP systems have typically been implemented on mainframes and designed to produce reports from massive amounts of data. However, these systems are often relatively static in terms of supporting changes. Hence, some software vendors have been offering products such as advanced planning system (APS) which add sophisticated decision support capabilities to relatively static MRP software. APS costs between a few hundred thousand dollars and a million dollars and runs on powerful workstations

An example of the use of APS to aid flexible manufacturing is illustrated by the case of Trane Unitaray Products division. This division experienced a sudden surge in demand for cooling units from small businesses affected by Hurricane Andrew in Florida in 1992. APS was used to examine if this surge in demand could be catered to. Material availability, alternative production schedules, and impact on existing customer commitments could be quickly examined. A means of working the additional demand into production plans without disrupting existing orders was found.

Similarly, Compaq computer used APS to cater to an unanticipated demand of 10,000 units of a personal computer model that it was phasing out. It could quickly determine component availability, possible vendors, examine plant capacity and make production decisions in order to meet this demand. Discussions of these flexible manufacturing situations can be found in (Rifkin, 1992).

In general terms, manufacturing settings could encounter a variety of stimuli that require response. Examples of such stimuli include machine breakdowns, problems relating to supply of material, quality problems, changes in volume of production, and changes in product mix. Responses include meeting revised product mix or production targets, or meeting time commitments in spite of machine or supplier problems. The ease with which responses can be made (in terms of time, cost, or scope) often depends on IT investments. These IT investments could be information systems such as APS or sub-systems within manufacturing equipment such as numerically controlled machine tools.

Flexible Marketing and Sales

Example: "Segment-Tailored" Marketing Strategies. Clemons and Weber (1994) discuss the important role of information technology in making fine distinctions in terms of identifying market segments and customizing strategies to meet the requirements of these segments. They argue that organizations could benefit from employing different strategies simultaneously with each strategy being targeted at distinct, carefully selected market segments. For example, it is possible for a travel services firm to offer a different mix of services and service levels to different types of customers based on information about customer preferences cost of services, and value of different services to each type of customer. Sophisticated information systems are used to collect, monitor, and process data regarding profitability of each customer type. The role of information systems is primarily to facilitate flexible (primarily in terms of scope) responses to customer requirements (stimuli), in a reasonably timely and cost effective manner. Multiple examples from industries such as financial services, travel services, and telecommunications services are provided.

Credit card issuers use information systems to collect and monitor data on profitability of individual accounts. These systems enable identification of relatively profitable market segments and customized product or service offerings that would enhance profitability of selected types of accounts. For example, extending credit to teacher couples whose summer income is variable enhances the profitability of the account. Sophisticated computer models based on household and individual data facilitate identification of low-risk customers with high revolving balances (balances that are not paid off each month). These customers are given the opportunity to apply for a specialized low cost card. The bank hopes to profit from the interest on the high revolving balances. A dramatically different marketing strategy is used for other cards which are targeted at high risk customers.

Example: Using Expert Systems to enhance the scope of response. Hammer and Champy (1994, p. 93) discuss an expert systems that a major chemical company has provided each of its customer service representatives with. This system offers advice on the relationship between different products and services offered by the company and helps its employees identify opportunities for cross selling (of other products or services that might interest prospective customers of a related product). Thus, the expert system increases flexibility of response to customer inquiries by altering the scope of response.

Customer Service

Example : Enhancing customer service through flexible customer information. The following excerpt from PR Newswire (January 24,

1985) illustrates an information technology investment that enhances flexibility of customer service by reducing the response time for customer questions as well increasing the scope of response by increasing the types of information that customers can be provided.

> *Inland Steel Company announced today that they will establish the first fully integrated electronic customer communications systems in the industry. Serving the needs of both steel customers and processors, the new system will permit Inland to transmit to them all of the information associated with the purchase and delivery of a steel order, including: price and delivery quotes, order entry, order change, material release, order status, invoicing, shipment notification, and test results. "Establishing this new communications network is part of a larger Inland initiative to improve our service to customers," said Robert J. Darnell, president. "The evolving steel market demands that we meet customers' needs for shorter lead times and fuller information of the status of their orders."*

Integrating Different Areas in the Value Chain

The examples detailed above focused on flexibility in distinct areas of the value chain. IT investments also result in flexibility as a result of integration of processes across different areas of the value chain.

Example: IT-Driven Enterprise Models. Hackel and Nolan (Hackel and Nolan, 1993) discuss the idea that models of how an enterprise functions can be coded in to enterprise wide information systems and describe applications at Mrs. Field's Cookies and Brooklyn Gas Union of New York. These information systems contain core operating procedures that can be applied consistently across the organization, at the same time allowing variation across different location (mass customization). For example, an information system advises each of over 800 stores at Mrs. Field's Cookies on an hourly basis on what cookies to make, in what quantities and how to adjust the baking pattern as the day progresses. The advice is tailored to local conditions (such as demand forecasts and weather conditions) at each store but the same set of guiding principles are applied storewide. These information systems integrate processes across the organization and increase flexibility through speed of response (to changing demand pattern as the day progresses) and scope of response (a different response to each location based on local conditions).

Integrating Processes across Value Chains of Different Organizations

Rockart and Short (1990) and Clemons (1991) provide examples of flexibility resulting from integrating processes belonging to value chains of different organizations. For example, Wal-Mart and its apparel suppliers (such as Wrangler) are connected through a telecommunications network. Sales patterns of Wrangler jeans at different Wal-Mart stores are transmitted to Wrangler. This data facilitates operations planning at Wrangler and shipment of specific quantities of specific sizes and designs of jeans to different Wal-Mart store locations. This system is based on a forecasting model shared by both companies. The model is modified periodically to account for changes in fashion or pricing policies. This system increases flexibility by primarily reducing response time to cater to change as well as enhancing scope (the variety of changes to which can be responded).

Management Strategies for Information Technology Investment

This article has focused on one type of benefit resulting from IT. It has emphasized the fact that flexibility can be an important competitive weapon in the turbulent business environment of the nineties. While organizations are aware of flexibility as being related to IT investments, the nature of the relationship is complicated. Also, the term flexibility can mean different things to different people. The relatively amorphous concept of flexibility can be operationalized using the ideas of stimulus, response, and ease of response (time, cost, scope). This framework for operationalizing flexibility, when combined with the value process model provides a useful means of identifying areas in the organization where organizational flexibility may be of value. IT investments are an important source of organizational flexibility and managers can consciously strive to identify areas where IT investments result in organizational flexibility. It is, however, important to realize that flexibility has associated costs which need to be considered.

The ideas presented in this article are likely to be of use to practicing managers as well as researchers. These ideas can be applied to evaluating the payoff (in terms of flexibility) from existing information systems, as well as for proposing new projects. The following managerial guidelines are likely to be useful in operationalizing the ideas presented in this article.

(1) Organizational flexibility has value in today's uncertain business environments. It might therefore be helpful to consciously think of organizational flexibility as a source of competitive advantage. IT investments can add significant business value by enabling organizational flexibility.

(2) Managers can understand their businesses better by breaking down business operations into processes at different stages of the value chain.

(3) Managers can benefit by examining sources of uncertainty that provide stimuli to different processes and whether the ability to respond easily to these stimuli (in terms of speed, cost, scope) can be a source of competitive advantage.

(4) Managers can study existing and proposed information systems to identify areas where these systems result in organizational flexibility. These areas could be processes at different stages of the value chain or interconnected processes (within an area of the value chain, across areas of the value chain, or across value chains of multiple organizations). The analysis of organizational flexibility and IT investments together with examples and references presented in this article should help in this process. While doing this study, it is important to realize that often it is a combination of IT investments, other resources, and operating procedures that result in organizational flexibility. Hence managers should attempt to identify the mix of IT investments, other resources, and operating procedures that result in organizational flexibility.

(5) Using Figure 6 helps to understand the factors relating organizational flexibility to firm performance.

(6) Steps (4) and (5) above would help to make qualitative statements about the value derived from information systems in addition to other quantitative statements about factors such as cost reductions. It would also help to identify areas where other investments or changes in operating procedures would enhance organizational flexibility.

(7) Managers could proactively use the ideas presented in this article to identify IT investments and other related resources that can provide competitive advantage through organizational flexibility. Qualitative arguments about the business value of IT resulting from organizational flexibility can be made in addition to quantitative arguments.

This article has suggested the use of qualitative statements about IT investments resulting in organizational flexibility. However, it may be possible to quantify the value of flexibility. Flexibility produces value because it generates options (alternative courses of action) for the firm in terms of responding to uncertainty. Kester (1984) provides an easy to understand qualitative discussion about the value of these options. It may seem at first glance that flexibility ultimately results in productivity improvements that can be quantified through financial calculations, but this is really not the case. Brynjolffson and Hitt (1993) discuss the limitations of traditional productivity measures in measuring factors such as responsiveness. Recent advances in capital budgeting have realized the limitations of traditional financial calculations and suggested that the options generated by flexibility can be valued differently (Trigeorgis, 1995). Applications of valuation of flexibility are beginning to emerge and researchers as well as decision makers in organizations are becoming increasingly aware of the fact that flexibility has value and can be valued (Dos Santos, 1991; Kemna, 1993; Kumar, 1995; Sethi and Sethi, 1990; Trigregoris, 1995). The measurement and valuation of flexibility is an interesting, active, and important research area that may help in understanding the business value of information systems.

Acknowledgments:
The research on which this article is based was funded in part by The University of North Carolina at Charlotte, and BarclaysAmerican.

The author is grateful to the anonymous referees for their insightful comments.

Chapter 15

Evaluating Information Technology Investment: A Methodology for Managing Risk

Kurt J. Engemann
Iona College

Holmes E. Miller
Muhlenberg College

Information technology (IT) investment decisions are among the most complex of any investment decisions because of rapid technological change, dynamic cost relationships, and often unclear benefits. IT exists in an environment of uncertainty and applying traditional investment methodologies may ignore key variables and lead to poor decisions. In this chapter, we focus on two categories of IT risk: risks concerned with maintaining business continuity, which we refer to as disaster recovery, and risks associated with information security. We shall present a three phase methodology to incorporate risk into the IT investment analysis: Phase 1 involves assessment of the risks and control alternatives; Phase 2 involves estimation of the requisite probabilities, costs, and losses; and Phase 3 involves evaluation of the alternatives. In addition to providing an overall managerial framework to evaluate alternatives to control IT risk, we shall also discuss various approaches to use when probabilities are not specified according to events; when data is qualitative rather than quantitative; and when a manager's degree of optimism or pessimism affects the assessment of the overall probabilities.

Investment decisions are among the most complicated decisions that managers make, even in well-understood settings such as investments in equipment and facilities. Investment decisions involve uncertainties and must balance the investment's initial and ongoing costs with present and future payoffs. Information technology (IT) investment decisions are among the most complex of any investment decisions. Because of rapid technological change, cost relationships governing IT are more dynamic than other technologies, and benefits often are unclear and difficult to estimate at the time the decision is being made (Alpar and Kim, 1990; Schell, 1986). IT exists in an environment of rapid technological change and uncertainty and applying traditional investment methodologies may ignore key variables and lead to poor decisions (Dos Santos, 1991; Dué, 1992; Keen, 1991).

Since the late 1960s, IT has evolved from automating existing work processes, to serving as a competitive weapon, to facilitating ubiquitous communications and providing platforms for new opportunities (Keen, 1991; Cecil and Hall, 1988). Despite IT's potential benefits, many IT investments have had mixed reviews regarding their impact on the bottomline and on managerial decision making (Kettinger, Grover, Varun and Segars, 1995; Wagner, 1995; Simon, 1990) and measuring their effectiveness by relating IT to organizational performance variables is challenging (Mahmood and Mann, 1993; Mahmood and Soon, 1991).

Selecting an IT investment often involves a detailed analysis. Specific methodologies and even domains differ among organizations, but generally IT payoffs and costs can be analyzed along four dimensions. First is the IT investment's functionality, or how it achieves its announced objectives. This dimension is the one most frequently used, the one most amenable to quantification, and often the only one used when analyzing the IT investment. A second dimension is new capabilities from an operational or competitive perspective (e.g., quicker response leading to decreased product development time). Payoffs here are not as evident as with functionality, and may be more difficult to quantify because of their strategic nature; nonetheless, new capabilities of an IT investment are increasingly well understood. How the investment interacts with the current matrix of IT investments and applications is the third dimension. Here interesting questions include whether the IT investment might create positive synergies which can expand the benefits beyond those particular to the investment itself, or conversely, impose new constraints which result in hidden costs. The final category concerns the risks addressed or created by the IT investment, which is the subject of this paper.

IT risks, though more prominent today than in the past, often are addressed only as an afterthought to the traditional analysis of IT payoffs and costs. Doing so, however, may change the dynamic of costs and payoffs and lead to selecting an inappropriate investment alternative. IT risks come in many varieties. For example, an organization developing an on-line customer information application integrating various databases on different network servers might encounter risks such as: servers and telecommunications not operating as planned, technological obsolescence, software not performing as expected, an interloper accessing and changing data, and incidents of software failure. In this paper we narrow the scope of IT risk and focus on two categories: Risks concerned with maintaining business continuity, which we refer to as disaster recovery, and risks associated with information security. Thus, when we refer to "IT risk" we will mean IT risks only in these two categories. For a discussion of other components of IT risk see Sherer (1992) and National Research Council (1991).

A key tenet of risk management is that risks cannot be eliminated but they can be controlled. The appropriate level of control depends both on the likelihood of the risk occurring and the magnitude of the loss if the risk does occur. Often risks can be quantified and analyzed via decision analysis. When risks cannot be quantified, either because the underlying information does not exist or because it is too expensive to collect, principles of risk analysis can still be applied. These principles include: 1) identifying what can go wrong, by analyzing the underlying threats and possible events; 2) identifying what controls are currently in place to mitigate either the probability of events occurring or the subsequent losses if they do occur; 3) evaluating the current exposure to the organization; 4) identifying new controls that can be implemented to reduce this exposure; 5) evaluating whether these controls should be implemented by investigating the costs and benefits.

These principles can be used to manage disaster recovery and information security related risks in conjunction with IT investments. These mechanisms may include software, hardware, facilities, person- nel, insurance, or external agreements. However, because many options exist to mitigate IT risks, selecting the most appropriate risk control alternative among the many available is itself an IT investment decision. Moreover, which IT investment is "best" may be determined by how it addresses its concomitant risks.

Because disaster recovery and information security deal with events that are infrequent, analyzing these risks as part of the investment decision is challenging. By their nature, controls to mitigate these risks can cause processing inefficiencies and increase capital and ongoing operational costs. For example, backing-up information, implementing hot site processing, purchasing security software and integrating it into system usage, encrypting data and limiting physical access all affect IT investments. As a result ,manag- ers may opt for the least expensive and least system-intrusive solution. Because disaster recovery and information security are aspects of larger IT investments and themselves are technologies which affect systems, operations, and other internal and external organizations, the next two parts of the Introduction will discuss how they affect the larger IT investment decision. In the final part of the Introduction, we will discuss how to incorporate risk into the IT investment decision then we shall present a three phase methodology to incorporate risk into the IT investment analysis: Phase 1 involves assessment of the risks and control alternatives; Phase 2 involves estimation of the requisite probabilities, costs, and losses; and Phase 3 involves evaluation of the alternatives. Finally, we shall discuss some management strategies for IT investment.

In the methodology, in addition to providing an overall managerial framework to evaluate alternatives to control IT risk, we shall also discuss various approaches to use when probabilities are not specified according the events; when data is qualitative rather than quantitative; and when a manager's degree of optimism or pessimism affects the assessment of the overall probabilities.

IT in Disaster Recovery

Disaster recovery is a necessity for any organization that depends on computer processing (Myers, 1993; Tom, 1987). Formulating and defining disaster recovery plans has investment implications. Historically, IT disaster recovery plans were viewed as computer systems issues affecting only data center operations, but now, due to IT's widespread influence, disaster recovery plans must cover the entire service delivery system. For example, a customer service organization using hundreds of terminals connected via a network needs disaster recovery plans for the network servers, the terminals, and external and internal telecommunications. Failure to plan for any one element of the system's availability can affect the entire service delivery system's operation. Given its broad scope, disaster recovery planning has obvious investment implications.

Four generic disaster recovery strategic alternatives can be used (Engemann and Miller, 1992): First, is using a duplicate site which may or may not be used in ongoing operations. Though most costly, this strategy maximizes managerial control over the disaster recovery plan's resources. Second, is contracting with another organization to be the backup site -- for example, two bank's agreeing to provide mutual backup for their check processing facilities. While cost-efficient, this strategy raises business questions of its reliance on an outside party who may be a direct business competitor. A third strategy calls for a processing area to use another area internal to the organization as backup, for example, one data center using another data center in another state or country as backup. The fourth strategy is outsourcing disaster recovery to a third party vendor in the disaster recovery business. Outsourcing vendors often have national networks and expertise, but using an external organization for critical support introduces risks related to outsiders becoming privy to private technological and customer information.

Choosing a disaster recovery strategy usually is an economic decision, based on risks, losses, and costs (Engemann and Miller, 1992). Implementing a duplicate facility is expensive and because of the expense, justifying the decision requires either a business requirement for separateness or the ability to reduce costs by sharing costs via reorganization. Even ostensibly cost-efficient duplicate facilities capable of performing production and systems development may cause externalities which may adversely affect overall system performance and future development efforts.

Finally, often overlooked as a cost of a disaster recovery investment is ongoing maintenance after implementation. Because of interdependencies between organizations and technology, changes by one area of an organization can affect other areas. These changes include implementing new technologies, implementing new procedures or changing capacities.

IT in Information Security

Since organizations began using mainframe computers, information security has been an issue and access control software has evolved to address risks (Baskerville, 1993; Parker, 1981; Sherman, 1992). When computer processing was centralized, implementing information security was relatively easy because few failure points existed and only people with access to the data center could access computing resources.

Client/server architectures and the Internet have placed computing power and access in the hands of "the many," and as a result have changed how organizations do business and have expanded IT risks. Today's networked, open office environments present new information security risks because access to information, even when protected, is ubiquitous (Carley and O'Brien, 1995; Cheswick, 1995; Cohen, 1995; Loch, Carr and Warkentin, 1992). Physical access differences between locked data centers and open offices illustrate this but no less important are the logical access risks that characterize networks and the Internet. Logical access controls depend on security software to protect workstations and networks from threats such as computer viruses, hacker incursions, and disgruntled employees, which can result in disclosure of information, fraud, or modification or destruction of information.

Software security products affect investment decisions and require ongoing maintenance and administration (Hoffer and Straub, 1989; Menkus, 1991; Wood, 1990). Because products often are actively resident in the background when other applications are executing, they can interact with other IT applications and potentially degrade overall system performance.

Both purchased and internally developed software have associated information security risks, apart from risks regarding their functionality (Sherer, 1992; Straub and Collins, 1990; Boehm, 1989; Charette, 1989). Issues for purchased software include the integrity of the code, including the presence of embedded code which could be used to illegally access or disable the system. Internally developed software also can contain embedded code. Moreover, internally developed software increasingly is developed for workstations and networks which now can process applications formerly residing on mainframes. In these environments, the goal is to ensure a similar degree of information security and software integrity as would be appropriate in the mainframe environment, without losing the benefits in quick response and software flexibility that new environments offer.

The Role of Risk in the IT Investment Decision

Risk's role in the IT investment decision must be viewed in the context of the larger IT application. Issues related to disaster recovery and information security manifest themselves in how they affect hardware, telecommunications and software used to meet organizational IT objectives. Though playing a secondary role (see Niederman, Brancheau and Wetherbe, 1991; Brancheau and Wetherbe, 1987), failure to adequately address risk when deciding on IT alternatives can lead to significant losses and avoiding these losses is the benefit of controlling IT risk.

The core of the analysis involves specifying a set of encompassing disaster recovery and information security risk events which represent "what can go wron.g." This involves taking the business apart and looking at it through the eyes of the business manager. Figure 1 presents a schematic of how threats manifest themselves in events and lead to risk exposures in a disaster recovery environment. The relationship of threats, events and controls in information security is analogous.

Risk events arise from generic threats. In our terminology, threats can lead to events which can lead to a loss of assets or a loss of

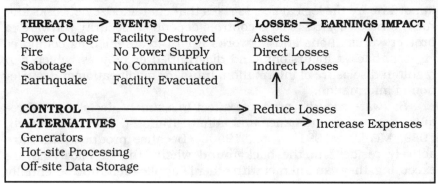

Figure 1: Relationship of Threats, Events and Controls: Disaster Recovery

resources. For example, a fire (a threat) can make a facility unavailable for three days (an event); a hacker (a threat) can access and destroy information in a customer database (an event). Because identifying all possible events is difficult and impractical, the events chosen for the analysis should represent the most relevant exposures faced by the organization. The impact of a control alternative on these events defines the alternative's effectiveness. Control alternatives either reduce the rate of occurrence of a threat (e.g., a halon fire suppressant system reduces the likelihood a fire will occur) or mitigate losses if events occur (e.g., a hot site processing center mitigates losses when a three day fire outage does occur). The methodology next discusses how to operationalize this decision process.

The Methodology

Risk management involves assessing risks, evaluating alternatives and implementing solutions. The methodology presented below focuses on assessment and evaluation. Implementation would be part of the implementation of the overall IT investment. Phase 1 of the methodology (Assessment) identifies targets, threats, control alternatives, and relevant costs and losses for those alternatives. It is an outgrowth of a methodology used successfully by a large bank to identify key information security risks (Miller and Engemann 1996). Phase 2 (Estimation) involves determining specific estimates of costs, losses and probabilities relevant for analysis; and Phase 3 (Evaluation) involves detailed analyses and evaluation to select the best alternatives.

Phase 1: Assessment

The initial step of any risk analysis is understanding what events can occur. The decision maker must decide how to respond to these events, whether by avoiding risks (e.g., eliminating dial-in access to a system to thwart hackers); by changing the likelihood of occurrence of an event (e.g., by installing a sprinkler system to lessen the chance a small fire grows into a large one); by reducing the losses if an event does occur (e.g., implementing a contingency plan); or by assigning the risk to others (e.g., purchasing insurance).

Because IT investment decisions address organizational needs and because the risk components of these investments lead to consequences with business implications, business managers must be involved from the inception to provide direction regarding threats, events, controls, and the appropriate level of risk they are willing to incur. In addition to the direction they provide regarding the quantitative aspects of the analysis, involving business managers provides a forum for them to introduce qualitative issues into the analysis.

Phase 1 involves three steps: Step 1 is to prepare a "talking paper" for senior IT and business managers to elicit their guidance and preferences in IT risks. This paper specifies which targets are relevant in analyzing risk for the IT system, which threats are relevant, and which events should be considered. In this step, control alternatives for these threats are identified and ways to integrate these alternatives within the IT investment are estimated. Finally cost and loss categories are specified.

Step 2 is to present the "talking paper" to senior business and IT managers for their input and modifications. The result of this conversation is a guide for the IT staff to use in the detailed analysis which contains information on IT risk from both a technology and a business perspective. These results can be summarized in a matrix where the relevant targets affected by the IT investment define the rows, and where generic threats define the columns. For example, in a dial-in customer service inquiry system, the targets might include:

- customers
- external telecommunications
- internal telecommunications
- centralized databases
- distributed databases
- software and hardware maintenance
- customer service operations.

The generic threats might include:

- disclosing account numbers, balance information, PIN numbers and transaction details
- inserting "trapdoors" in the code
- changing account balances for fraudulent purposes
- modifying or destroying information
- deliberately destroying hardware
- power outages
- short-term outages (less than one day) that prevent access to computer systems
- short-term outages (less than one day) that prevent access to terminals and support operations
- long-term outages (one day or more) that prevent access to computer systems
- long-term outages (one day or more) that prevent access to terminals and support operations
- outages that destroy terminals and support operations.

Each cell entry in the matrix would summarize comments from the discussion with the senior business and IT managers and provide guidance for detailed analysis regarding specific events, costs, losses, and control alternatives.   For example, a cell entry for the cell: Distributed databases—Disclosing account numbers, balance information, PIN numbers and transaction details might include the following points and directives from the discussion:

- Disclosure of balances would be embarrassing but not result in financial loss;
- Disclosure of an account or pin number could facilitate fraud, and "organized" disclosure is a significant threat;
- Restrict access to databases using need to know criteria;
- Direct attention to controlling access to information which combined could result in theft of funds;
- Investigate an expert systems approach to highlight unusual account activity.

All of these comments would have implications regarding identifying specific control alternatives and analyzing the costs and impact of these alternatives on IT risk.

Step 3 is to take the results of the senior business and IT managers' discussions and develop the details required for the estimation done in phase 2.

Phase 2 - Estimation

Phase 2 involves estimating the costs, losses and probabilities needed for the evaluation methodology of Phase 3.   Estimates of costs and losses are obtained via standard procedures which rely on information contained in the organization's MIS and on expert managerial judgment.

Specific cost and loss categories may vary depending on the specific control alternatives and events, but some general categories include:

- Direct Costs — Costs of hardware, telecommunications, software, ongoing maintenance, ongoing administration.
- Indirect Costs — Constraints on operational efficiency, IT functionality, and future IT and business strategies; and opportunity costs including lost future business due to the presence or absence of specific controls.
- Direct Losses — Loss of physical assets, data, revenue, added personnel costs, penalties.
- Indirect Losses — Future loss of business and other opportunity losses.

In performing the analysis, for each alternative all of the direct and indirect costs would be calculated.   For example, for an organization considering two backup site processing centers, the annualized costs might be as follows (in $1000):

	Backup Site A$_1$	Backup Site A$_2$
Direct Costs		
Hardware	70	50
Telecommunications	25	40
Software	25	25
Maintenance	15	20
Administration	75	100
Indirect Costs		
Constraints	20	25
Opportunity costs	40	50
Total Direct and Indirect	270	310

Direct and indirect losses would be calculated for each relevant event, given that a specific alternative would be implemented. For example, for the above organization suppose the following lists the losses for one such event — a one week outage due to a fire in a transformer which causes the business to use backup site processing:

	Backup Site A$_1$	Backup Site A$_2$
Direct Losses		
Physical assets	50	50
Data	5	5
Revenue	130	55
Added personnel costs	110	45
Penalties	80	25
Indirect Losses		
Future lost business	100	20
Opportunity losses	50	10
Total Losses	525	210

Estimating the probability of events involves reviewing historical data and discussing the events with relevant groups such as the fire department, weather bureau, utility companies, computer virus incident monitoring agencies, police departments, building engineers, reliability engineers, and government agencies. Probabilities also can be estimated by using computer simulations. Computer simulations can blend historical data and subjective opinion to arrive at intuitively acceptable estimates for the occurrence rates for events.

Using probabilities to evaluate the IT investment according to the classical cost-benefit method (see below) can be problematic when data is incomplete or unavailable for specific events, or when the analysis requires incorporating the decision maker's degree of optimism or pessimism. Therefore, alternative methods are required which consider both the nature of the information used to evaluate the IT alternatives, and the behavioral characteristics of the decision makers themselves. The next section discusses several evaluation methodologies which can be used to evaluate disaster recovery and information security control alternatives.

Phase 3: Evaluation

The effectiveness of the IT investment for risk planning may be evaluated after a disruptive event in a postmortem analysis. Postmortems are beneficial in identifying new alternatives and altering existing alternatives, but by definition occur only after the event occurs. Alternatives to a postmortem analysis are computer simulations (Miller and Engemann, 1993) or gaming simulations (Miller and Engemann, 1992). Simulations may be used in conjunction with decision models.

Deciding on the IT risk investment itself involves analyzing costs and benefits. Performing a risk analysis and a cost-benefit analysis should be a formal part of the investment analysis procedure to ensure resources are allocated rationally and all risk exposures are considered when designing the IT application under consideration.

The objective of investing in IT to support disaster recovery and information security is to limit the impact of major disruptions to an acceptable level (Engemann and Miller, 1992). The appropriate type of analysis to use depends on the nature of the available data. We will discuss the role of some approaches in evaluating disaster recovery and information security control alternatives used to support IT investments.

Decision Making Under Risk: Classical Approach

The classical approach is based on cost-benefit and decision analysis and requires estimating costs, benefits, and probabilities, developing net benefits for each decision alternative, and selecting the alternatives with the largest net benefits (Raiffa, 1968; Merkhofer, 1987; Layard and Glaister, 1994). For each risk control alternative, incremental disaster recovery and information security costs presented above are estimated. These can be "stand-alone" such as extra hardware to be used as backup; or they can be "embedded" such as decreased system functionality to deal with information security issues.

Each risk control alternative provides benefits which reduce the risk exposure relative to a base case— for example, no controls at all. The benefits actually are reduction in expected losses due to the control alternative, relative to the base case. For each alternative and each event, disaster recovery or information security losses similar to those presented above would be estimated. The expected losses for the alternative would be the sum of the probabilities of the events multiplied by the losses if those events occurred. The net expected loss of the alternative relative to the base case alternative would be the difference between the expected losses with the alternative and the expected losses under the base case.

The net benefit would be the difference between the net expected losses (i.e., how much the alternative reduces expected losses relative to the base case), and net costs (i.e., how costly the alternative is relative to the base case). When an alternative's net benefit is positive it is preferred to the base case, and the alternative with the largest net benefit is most preferred.

Net benefits may be evaluated using several methods. One is to convert all current and future cash streams are to annual cash streams equivalent to that of an annuity, or to discount all cash streams using present value methods (see Engemann and Miller, 1992; Dos Santos, 1991; Clemens, 1991; Sharpe, 1969).

Analyzing IT investment to manage risk can be aided by a variety of decision models. The model to be used to aid in the selection of the best alternative depends upon the nature of the information describing the situation. Decision analysis is a key tool in the situation in which events can be assigned probabilities and payoffs can be quantified. It integrates the factors influencing the decision, and in many cases it is reasonable to use expected monetary value as the criteria. Risk attitude may need to be incorporated by means of a utility function into the analysis, given the relative monetary size of the events under consideration. Risk attitude measures willingness to assume greater risk for a chance of higher reward, or conversely, to assume less risk at a higher expense.

There are some drawbacks in attempting to apply the classical approach. Many events associated with IT risk either have not occurred of if they have, have occurred with such infrequency that obtaining accurate probability estimates is problematic. Even when probabilities of threats can be obtained —for example, probabilities of fires, power outages, viruses, frauds— translating them into probability estimates for events which specify how these threats manifest themselves is much more difficult. Methodologies from reliability theory such as fault trees can be used (Sherer, 1992; Pate-Cornell, 1984) but as a practical matter, the cost of conducting a comprehensive analyses for all disaster recovery and information security related risks often is impractical. We will illustrate a general model of decision making under uncertainty which is useful in situations where event probabilities are difficult to estimate.

A second drawback to the classical approach concerns assumptions regarding how decision makers reach their conclusions. Beyond being risk averse or not risk averse, decision makers often act differently than utility theory would indicate. For this case, we present a method which modifies the event probabilities to account for a decision maker's degree of optimism or pessimism.

Finally, the classical approach requires accurately measuring the costs and the losses that occur given the occurrence of various risk events (West, 1994; Bender, 1986). Obtaining numerical estimates of costs and benefits ultimately depends on detailed and accurate information and access to the expertise of business and IT managers, particularly when estimating softer figures such as estimates of the security alternatives on IT performance and business impact. We will show a method that is especially useful when the estimation of the alternatives' payoffs is represented on an ordinal scale.

Decision Making Under Uncertainty

In decision making under uncertainty, we do not have probabilities associated with events. The methodology used in the selection of the optimal alternative in this environment depends on the attitude held by the decision maker. The ordered weighted averaging (OWA) operators can be used to help in the selection of an optimal alternative in the face of uncertainty by providing an aggregated value for each alternative (Yager, 1992; Engemann, Miller and Yager, 1996). An OWA aggregation function of dimension n is defined as the function, F, that has associated with it a weighting vector, $W = (w_1, w_2,....,w_n)$, such that: (1) $0 \le w_j \le 1$, and (2) $\Sigma_j w_j = 1$, and for any set of values $a_1,....,a_n$, $F(a_1,....,a_n)$ $= \Sigma_j w_j b_j$, where b_j is the jth largest element in the collection $a_1,....,a_n$.

We can calculate $V_i = F(C_{i1},....,C_{in})$, where F is an OWA aggregation operator. We then select the alternative that has the highest V value. Note that for any W, the OWA aggregation operation satisfies the condition of Pareto optimality. Let $b_{i1},....,b_{in}$ be the ordered set of the payoffs, C_{ij}. The OWA weights, $w_1,....,w_n$, can be interpreted as probabilities of the jth best thing happening. Then $V_i = \Sigma_j w_j b_{ij}$ is the expected payoff in this case. Thus the OWA aggregation provides a kind of expected value similar to that used in decision making under risk except the weights, w_j, are assigned to the preference ordered position of the payoff and not to a particular state of nature. Using this interpretation, the w_j are referred to as dispositional probabilities. The pessimistic strategy is a situation in which a probability of one is assigned to the worst thing happening given any selection of alternative. In the optimistic approach, we are assuming a probability of one is assigned to the probability of the best thing happening. In the normative case, we are assuming equal probability for each of the preference positions. The Hurwicz strategy assigns a probability α that the best thing will happen and probability $1-\alpha$ that the worst thing will happen.

A measure of optimism associated with a set of weights, W, is: Ω $= \Sigma_j (n - j) w_j/(n-1)$. Note that for the optimistic case $\Omega = 1$, for the pessimist case $\Omega = 0$, for the normative case $\Omega = .5$ and for the Hurwicz case $\Omega = \alpha$. Methods to determine a decision makers level of optimism, W, and associated set of weights, W, have been discussed elsewhere (O'Hagan, 1990; Engemann, Filev and Yager, 1996).

The two cases, risk and uncertainty, are special cases of a

formulation using a belief structure (Dempster, 1967; Shafer, 1976). A belief structure, m, on the state of nature Y consists of a collection of non-empty subsets of Y, B_i, and an associated set of weights $m(B_i)$ such that: $m(B_j) \geq 0$ and $\Sigma_j m(B_j) = 1$. The subsets B_i are called the focal elements. $m(B_i)$ can be interpreted as the probability of B_i occurring. OWA operators may be used in selecting an appropriate alternative in situations in which our knowledge about the state of nature is in the form of a belief structure as follows:

1. Determine the w_i, for each different cardinality of focal elements, with the degree of optimism Ω.
2. Determine the payoff collection, M_{ik}, if we select alternative A_i and the focal element B_k occurs, for all i,k.
3. Determine the aggregated payoff, $V_{ik} = F(M_{ik})$, for all i, k.
4. Calculate the generalized expected value, C_i, where $C_i = \Sigma_k V_{ik} m(B_k)$, for each alternative.
5. Select the alternative with the largest C_i as the optimal.

The procedure for determining the best alternative combines the schemes used for both decision making under risk and uncertainty. In a manner similar to decision making under risk, we obtain a generalized expected value, C_i, for each alternative A_i. To obtain this expected value, we use evidential knowledge by means of the weights associated with the focal elements. Note that $m(B_k)$ is the probability that B_k will be the set that determines the state of nature.

Consider the following simplified illustration. The scope of the problem is the threat of power failure to several critical services at a financial institution. There are three alternatives. In the first alternative, no emergency generator is installed - i.e. the present situation is maintained. In the second alternative, a small generator is installed that would permit limited operations to continue in the event of a power outage. In the third alternative, a large generator is installed that would permit operations to continue in the event of a power outage. The costs of these alternatives can be accurately estimated.

Power outages are discretized into events from 0 through 5 days. By estimating the resulting loss of assets, direct losses, indirect losses, and financial impact of insurance and taxes, the financial impact of each event is determined. Costs are annualized and adjusted for insurance and taxes. The payoff matrix, in millions of dollars, is as follows:

	S_0	S_1	S_2	S_3	S_4	S_5
A_1	0	0	-2	-30	-40	-50
A_2	-.2	-.2	-.6	-10	-12	-14
A_3	-.8	-.8	-.8	1	2	3

where event S_j is a power outage lasting j days, and A_1 is no generator, A_2 is a small generator, and A_3 is a large generator.

Limited data are available to determine the probabilities of the events. In the past 20 years, in the immediate area containing the operations center, two power interruptions occurred, each of which lasted less than 48 hours. In a wider area, data showed that approximately one out of twenty outages lasted three or more days. From this data, it was assumed that in any particular year: the probability of no outage is .9 (i.e., 18/20), the probability of an outage lasting one or two days is 0.095 (i.e., 2/20*19/20), and the probability of an outage lasting 3, 4 or 5 days is .005 (i.e., 2/20*1/20).

The costs of each control alternative, and the losses associated with an event of a particular duration are fairly straightforward to determine. This is not the case in determining probabilities of the exact length of the power outage. Therefore, we will use the focal elements as follows:

Focal element		Weights
$B_1 =$	$\{S_0\}$	0.9
$B_2 =$	$\{S_1,S_2\}$	0.095
$B_3 =$	$\{S_3,S_4,S_5\}$	0.005

We recall that M_{ik} is the collection of payoffs that are possible if we select alternative A_i and the focal element B_k occurs. We next determine the payoff collections M_{ik}.

$M_{11} = \{0\}$, $M_{12} = \{0,-2\}$, $M_{13} = \{-30,-40,-50\}$,
$M_{21} = \{-.2\}$, $M_{22} = \{-.2,-.6\}$, $M_{23} = \{-10,-12,-14\}$,
$M_{31} = \{-.8\}$, $M_{32} = \{-.8,-.8\}$, $M_{33} = \{1, 2, 3\}$.

Assume that the decision maker is optimistic with a degree of optimism of 0.75. Using the method proposed by O'Hagan (1990) yields the weights associated with the OWA operators for the required numbers of arguments. We calculate V_{ik}, using these OWA weights. We recall that $V_{ik} = F(M_{ik})$.

$V_{11} = 1.00(0) = 0$
$V_{12} = .75(0) + .25(.-2) = -.5$
$V_{13} = .62(-30) + .27(-40) + .11(-50) = -35$
$V_{21} = 1.00(-.2) = -.2$
$V_{22} = .75(-.2) + .25(.-6) = -.3$
$V_{23} = .62(-10) + .27(-12) + .11(-14) = -10.98$
$V_{31} = 1.00(-.8) = -.8$
$V_{32} = .75(-.8) + .25(.-8) = -.8$
$V_{33} = .62(3) + .27(2) + .11(1) = -2.51$

Finally we use these values to obtain the generalized expected value for each alternative:

$$C_1 = .9(0) + .095(-.5) + .005(-35) = -.223$$
$$C_2 = .9(-.2) + .095(-.3) + .005(-10.98) = -.264$$
$$C_3 = .9(-.8) + .095(-.8) + .005(2.51) = -.784$$

Given the above information, the optimal choice is alternative A_1, no generator. Sensitivity analysis to the coefficient of optimism indicates that A_2, a small generator, is preferred when $a < .57$.

Decision Making Under Risk Using Immediate Probabilities

The process of decision making under risk is characterized by knowledge of the probabilities of the events. The standard procedure in this case is to select the alternative with the highest expected payoff. The attitude of the decision maker has a great influence on the ultimate decision. Risk perception is a function of the payoffs and their likelihood (Mellers and Chang, 1994). The size of the payoff may be the more prominent of the two components (March and Shapira, 1987) . A person may be less likely to engage in risk-taking behavior as the level of perceived risk increases (Dunegan, Duchon and Barton, 1992; Staw, Sandelands and Dutton, 1981). Nevertheless, some decision makers who perceive high levels of risk respond with risk-seeking behavior (Kahneman and Tversky, 1979). Risk propensity is the consistency of a decision maker to either take or avoid actions that he perceives as risky (Sitkin and Pablo, 1992). An individual with high risk-taking propensity is more likely to recognize and weigh positive outcomes, thereby overestimating the probability of a gain relative to the probability of a loss (Brockhaus, 1980; Vlek and Stallen, 1980). An individual with low risk-taking propensity will typically weigh negative outcomes more highly (Schneider and Loppes, 1986).

Decision makers who know the probabilities of the states of nature may not always use the expected value approach exactly. A hybrid model of decision making (Engemann, Filev and Yager, 1996; Yager, Engemann and Filev, 1995) provides the flexibility of modifying the event probabilities (pristine probabilities) to reflect the decision maker's degree of optimism. The optimism modifies the event probabilities in the following way. We represent the decision maker's optimism by an OWA operator with weights (dispositional probabilities) $w_1, w_2, ..., w_n$, where

$$\sum_{j=1}^{n} w_j = 1, w_j \geq 0 \text{ for all } j.$$

The dispositional probabilities satisfy the degree of optimism, Ω, as previously defined. We denote by T a transformation of the second indexes of the set of outcomes a_{ij} associated with the i-th alternative to a new set b_{ij}. $T: (a_{i1}, a_{i2}, ..., a_{in}) \rightarrow (b_{i1}, b_{i2}, ..., b_{in})$, such that $b_{i1} \geq b_{i2} \geq$

b_{in}. For each alternative i, we apply the same transformation T to the set of probabilities p_1, p_2, ..., p_n. We denote the new set of probabilities p^*_{i1}, p^*_{i2}, ..., p^*_{in}. Obviously such a transformation in general doesn't imply p^*_{i1}, p^*_{i2}, ..., p^*_{in}. The original event probabilities are modified for each alternative i, by incorporating the decision maker's level of optimism, into *immediate probabilities*, p'_{i1}, p'_{i2}, ..., p'_{in}, that are defined as follows:

$$p'_{ij} = \frac{w_j\, p^*_{ij}}{\sum_{k=1}^{n} w_k\, p^*_{ik}}$$

We can look at the immediate probabilities as a kind of conditioned probability, that is, conditioned by the degree of optimism. The value of the i-th alternative will be the *immediate expected value* (IEV) that is calculated on the basis of these immediate probabilities, p'_{ij}:

$$IEV_i = \sum_{j=1}^{n} p'_{ij} b_{ij} = \frac{\sum_{j=1}^{n} w_j\, p^*_{ij} b_{ij}}{\sum_{j=1}^{n} w_j\, p^*_{ij}}$$

The decision maker then selects the alternative associated with the optimal IEV. The effect of this modification to the event probabilities is that, for each alternative, the probabilities of preferred outcomes increases and the probabilities of unpreferred outcomes decreases as the level of optimism increases.

To illustrate the application of immediate probabilities consider a situation in which an IT department is considering two backup sites, A_1 and A_2, and no backup, A_3. The following annualized data shows the payoff matrix of cost plus losses (in $1000) and associated probabilities for the three outage durations: S_1, none, S_2, 1 day, S_3, 1 week.

	S_1	S_2	S_3
A_1:	270	390	795
A_2:	310	360	520
A_3:	0	650	3900
P_j:	.8	.15	.05

Given that the decision maker is pessimistic with a level of optimism $\alpha = 0.3$, we find $w_1 = 0.154$; $w_2 = 0.292$; $w_3 = 0.554$, using the method presented by O'Hagan (1990).

The reordered outcomes are:

$b_{11} = 270; b_{12} = 390; b_{13} = 795$
$b_{21} = 310; b_{22} = 360; b_{23} = 520$
$b_{31} = 0; b_{32} = 650; b_{33} = 3900.$

The reordered probabilities under the same transformation of the indexes are:

$p^*_{11} = 0.8; p^*_{12} = 0.15; p^*_{13} = 0.05$
$p^*_{21} = 0.8; p^*_{22} = 0.15; p^*_{23} = 0.05$
$p^*_{31} = 0.8; p^*_{32} = 0.15; p^*_{33} = 0.05$

The immediate probabilities are:

$p'_{11} = .8(.154)/(.8(.154)+.15(.292)+.05(.554)) = .627$
$p'_{12} = .15(.292)/(.8(.154)+.15(.292)+.05(.554)) = .227$
$p'_{13} = .05(.554)/(.8(.154)+.15(.292)+.05(.554)) = .146$
$p'_{21} = .8(.154)/(.8(.154)+.15(.292)+.05(.554)) = .627$
$p'_{22} = .15(.292)/(.8(.154)+.15(.292)+.05(.554)) = .227$
$p'_{23} = .05(.554)/(.8(.154)+.15(.292)+.05(.554)) = .146$
$p'_{31} = .8(.154)/(.8(.154)+.15(.292)+.05(.554)) = .627$
$p'_{32} = .15(.292)/(.8(.154)+.15(.292)+.05(.554)) = .227$
$p'_{33} = .05(.554)/(.8(.154)+.15(.292)+.05(.554)) = .146$

The immediate expected values of the alternatives are:

$IEV_1 = (.627*270 + .227*390 + .146*795)\ \ = 374$
$IEV_2 = (.627*310 + .227*360 + .146*520)\ \ = 352$
$IEV_3 = (.627*0 + .227*650 + .146*3900) = 718$

Therefore alternative A_2 should be selected. Note that the expected values of the alternatives using the original event probabilities and ignoring the decision maker's pessimism would have resulted in selecting alternative 3, as follows:

$EV_1 = (.8*270 + .15*390 + .05*795) = 314$
$EV_2 = (.8*310 + .15*360 + .05*520)\ \ = 328$
$EV_3 = (.8*0 + .15*650 + .05*3900) = 293.$

We can see that the degree of optimism modifies the event probabilities via the OWA weights and therefore the expected values. In this simplified illustration the decision maker with a neutral disposition would not be willing to pay for a backup site, but the pessimistic decision maker would.

We have presented a way to include a decision maker's optimism even when he knows event probabilities. We believe that decision makers do not always act on the criteria of optimizing expected value. After all, probabilities and therefore expected values are long run concepts and the decision maker is faced with an immediate and perhaps non-repeatable decision.

Decision Making with Nonnumeric Payoffs

In some situations it may be difficult to determine numeric payoffs for IT risks. The median provides an aggregation operation which only requires that the aggregated objects are ordered. Thus while the median aggregation, like the average, can work in numeric domains, it also can be used in situations in which we are not combining numbers but ordered objects. A new aggregation operator which is an extension of the median, is called the weighted median (Yager, 1995) (Engemann, Miller and Yager, 1995). With this operator, we can provide an aggregation of weighted objects where the objects to be aggregated need only be drawn from an ordered set while the weights can be numbers.

Assume $D = \{ (w_1, a_1), (w_2, a_2), \ldots , (w_n, a_n) \}$ are a collection of pairs where ai is a score and wi is its associated weight. Assume that the a_i are reordered such that b_j is the jth largest of the a_i. Furthermore, let u_j be the weight that is associated with the a_i that becomes b_j. Thus if $b_j = a_5$ then $u_j = w_5$. Once having the ordered collection $D = \{ (u_1, b_1), (u_2, b_2), \ldots, (u_n, b_n) \}$ to calculate the weighted median, we proceed as follows. We denote

$$T_i = \Sigma i_{j=1} \ u_j,$$

the sum of the first i weights. From this we define the Weighted Median $(D) = b_k$ where k is such that $T_{k-1} < 0.5$ and $T_k \geq 0.5$.

Thus the weighted median is the ordered value of the argument for which the sum of the weights first crosses the value 0.5. The weighted median and the weighted average share the properties of idempotency, commutativity/symmetry, and monotonicity.

Immediate probabilities may be used in conjunction with the weighted median. Consider the following illustration. A company is deciding which of two access control systems to use. Assume the scale of payoffs is: very low (vl); low (l); medium (m); high (h); very high (vh). The payoff matrix is as follows:

	S_1	S_2	S_3	S_4	S_4
A_1	m	vh	vh	vl	h
A_2	vl	vh	m	l	h
p_j	.1	.1	.3	.3	.2

Using the pristine probabilities we find:

A_1	b_i	u_j	T_i	A_2	b_i	u_j	T_i
	vh	.1	.1		vh	.1	.1
	vh	.3	.4		h	.2	.3
	h	.2	.6		m	.3	.6
	m	.1	.7		l	.3	.9
	vl	.3	1.0		vl	.1	1.0

Since the Weighted Median (A_1) = high and the Weighted Medium (A_2) = medium, A1 would be preferred by a decision maker with a neutral disposition.

Now assume that the decision maker is pessimistic with a degree of optimism of 0.3. The OWA weights are $w_1 = .071$, $w_2 = .109$, $w_3 = .167$, $w_4 = .257$, $w_5 = .396$ (using O'Hagans method (1990)). The reordered outcomes are:

b_{11}=vh; b_{12}=vh; b_{13}=h; b_{14}=m; b_{15}=vl
b_{21}=vh; b_{22}=h; b_{23}=m; b_{24}=l; b_{24}=vl

The reordered probabilities under the same transformation of the indexes are:

p^*_{11}=0.1; p^*_{12}=0.3; p^*_{13}=0.2; p^*_{14}=0.1; p^*_{15}=0.3
p^*_{21}=0.1; p^*_{22}-0.2; p^*_{23}=0.3; p^*_{24}=0.2; p^*_{25}=0.1.

The immediate probabilities are:

p'_{11}=.1(.071)/(.1(.071)+.3(.109)+.2(.167)+.1(.257)+.3(.396))=.03
p'_{12}=.3(.109)/(.1(.071)+.3(.109)+.2(.167)+.1(.257)+.3(.396))=.15
p'_{13}=.2(.167)/(.1(.071)+.3(.109)+.2(.167)+.1(.257)+.3(.396))=.15
p'_{14}=.1(.257)/(.1(.071)+.3(.109)+.2(.167)+.1(.257)+.3(.396))=.12
p'_{15}=.3(.396)/(.1(.071)+.3(.109)+.2(.167)+.1(.257)+.3(.396))=.55
p'_{21}=.1(.071)/(.1(.071)+.2(.109)+.3(.167)+.3(.257)+.1(.396))=.04
p'_{22}=.2(.109)/(.1(.071)+.2(.109)+.3(.167)+.3(.257)+.1(.396))=.11
p'_{23}=.3(.167)/(.1(.071)+.2(.109)+.3(.167)+.3(.257)+.1(.396))=.26
p'_{24}=.3(.257)/(.1(.071)+.2(.109)+.3(.167)+.3(.257)+.1(.396))=.39
p'_{25}=.1(.396)/(.1(.071)+.2(.109)+.3(.167)+.3(.257)+.1(.396))=.20

Then using the immediate probabilities we find:

A_1	b_i	u_j	T_i	A_2	b_i	u_j	T_i
	vh	.03	.03		vh	.04	.04
	vh	.15	.18		h	.11	.15
	h	.15	.33		m	.26	.41
	m	.12	.45		l	.39	.80
	vl	.55	1.0		vl	.20	1.0

Therefore by including the decision makers pessimistic disposition, the Weighted Median (A_1)=very low and the Weighted Median (A_2)= low. Now A_2 would be preferred by the decision maker.

Management Strategies for Information Technology Investment

Foresight in disaster recovery and information security planning for IT investments can result in cost effective strategies that avoid losses, reduce the likelihood of occurrence of events, mitigate losses or transfer losses via insurance. State-of-the-art approaches are available and should be appropriately utilized. This chapter has focused on investment decisions which involve choosing among discrete alternatives to support the business continuity planning process (Smith and Sherwood, 1995). This process is systemic and involves many steps from the initial policy statement and defining planning responsibilities, to testing, maintaining and reviewing the plan. A part of the process involves organizing a crisis management team and even, when appropriate, implementing crisis management games (Miller and Engemann, 1992). Thus, the costs of implementing each alterative include systemic elements which can be readily factored into the investment decision using the above methodology. It is key for decision makers to be aware of each option's total cost and not ignore or underestimate all the actions required for business continuity planning.

We have shown how several recent approaches in decision modeling may be used when evaluating the risk control component of IT investments. A decision maker's attitude is an important element of the decision process and may be integrated into a decision model in cases of risk or uncertainty. Immediate probabilities play a key role in blending the decision maker's disposition with event probabilities.

Integrating risk into the IT investment decision requires balancing the quantitative and the qualitative aspects of the decision process. The quantitative aspects involve appropriately using the methodologies described above to estimate costs, losses, and likelihoods of occurrence of threats and events, and to perform rigorous evaluations. Making this happen requires sound information, attention to detail, and in-depth understanding of the IT investment and the internal and external environment that the investment will address.

The quantitative aspects of the decision process necessitate including senior business and IT managers in the process. Two benefits arise form doing this: first, tapping their expertise, particularly on qualitative aspects of the IT investment and the related decisions; and, second, educating the managers on risk issues and obtaining their support. Leaving senior managers in the dark regarding risk issues and the appropriate controls increases the IT investment's risk exposure. If risk events do occur, this results in substantial losses and organizational turmoil; even when events do not occur, exposures which are highlighted—for example, by auditors—can require expensive retrofitting of an implemented IT systems.

The methodology provides a structured way to elicit business manager's guidance and provides a rigorous way to evaluate and choose among alternatives that address the nuances that characterize decision situations. Asking business managers for guidance and presenting them with recommendations is not enough; they must be made aware of risk issues, controls, and methods of rational choice and feel confident that the decisions they make regarding highly improbable events are made with the same rigor as other, more familiar, investment decisions regarding costs and profits.

Using the methodology provides three benefits. First, explicitly considering IT risk in the IT investment decision raises awareness of these risks on the part of business and IT managers, and results in better solutions addressing those risks. Second, the methodology provides an overall approach to identifying risk and developing alternatives. It provides both management structure and analytical rigor to an inherently unstructured problem. Third, it provides the capability of applying newer, state-of-the-art methods to evaluate the risk alternatives which may be used in cases where belief structures, ordinal data, or a manager's degree of optimism or pessimism can affect the decision process.

The evaluation approaches presented in Phase 3 involve varying amounts of analytical effort. The illustrations were computed using spreadsheets as decision support tools. Availability of an integrative decision support system, incorporating the various models proposed here would remove an obstacle for a less technical person to access these methodologies. Another limitation is that the decision maker needs to thoroughly understand the implications of the subjective estimations. Nevertheless, we believe that the decision maker can grasp the concepts presented here and employ them advantageously.

The methodology's strength is it addresses risk issues in a structured fashion and explicitly identifies the limitations inherent in the decision situation. The methodology makes the process stronger and provides a path which ultimately will ensure more complete and robust decisions.

Part III
Case Studies of Measuring Information Technology Investment Payoff

Introduction to Part III

Mo Adam Mahmood, University of Texas at El Paso
Edward J. Szewczak, Canisius College

The papers in this section employ the case study to exemplify various approaches to measuring IT investment payoff. The approaches used include an historical process-oriented case research effort, aligning the IS organization with the business units they serve, identifying the role that the IT will play in the organization, and various forms of triangulation, i.e., using multiple measures to measuring IT investment payoff. While some of these approaches are new, it is interesting to note that, unlike the conceptual approaches proposed in Part II, the paper authors are not necessarily concerned with proposing a novel approach so much as with arriving at effective measures of IT investment payoff which are actually used by business organizations.

Marielle Bergeron and Albert Dexter uses, based on the theory of capital budgeting, a value measurement framework to examine the economic value of financial electronic data interchange (EDI). An historical process-oriented case research strategy is utilized to assess the economic impact of EDI on two Canadian user sites: a corporate originator (buyer) and a corporate receiver (supplier). Only tangible or quantifiable costs and benefits are considered, although the analysis can be supplemented with a subjective evaluation of intangibles. The authors contend that assessing the economic contribution of IT applications on firm performance requires an in-depth understanding of underlying business processes, and that such assessment involves an extensive evaluation of one-time investment costs as well as ongoing net benefits. The authors claim that the evaluation methodology suggested by them can be applied to both ex ante and ex post analysis of financial EDI investments.

Tim Tatum and Peter Aiken report on the experience of the Virginia Department of Transportation which invested in four distinct IT–based reengineering initiatives in different functional areas simultaneously. Management viewed this reengineering as a means for improving current business practices in anticipation of new technology. To compare and evaluate these initiatives, the authors developed a redesign comparison framework to link them to corresponding payoffs in organizational performance and productivity. Tatum and Aiken contend that existing measurement frameworks do not permit the surplus created by reengineering to be redistributed across functional boundaries in an organization. Instead a measurement system that identifies strategic, provider, and customer issues centering on value and that involves useful process/performance measures can itself become a tool for pushing surplus through the organization, thereby turning surplus into productivity. The authors suggest that their redesign comparison framework is an example of such a measurement system.

Jack Callon's paper provides an in-depth analysis of the approach taken by Hewlett-Packard and National Semiconductor Corporation to explain the value of their investment in information system. Callon contends that firms should place a priority on building a management process (involving good dialogue and an ongoing working relationship among the business units involved) that aligns the activities of the IS organization with the business units they support. A firm's financial strategy for IS evolves over time in four phases: 1) the use of budgets as a means of financial control; 2) the development of a business case justifying new IS investment proposals; 3) the creation of a charge out approach, asking users to pay for IS support and services; and 4) the building of a management process to address information systems value questions. The objective of the financial strategy is to control costs, to prioritized the development of new systems or to allocate increasingly larger information systems costs to those that benefit from the use of the computer–based systems. Callon argues that many companies have successfully managed the financial aspects of information systems using the aforementioned strategy.

The task of measuring productivity of end user training services that are dependent on human behavior is extremely difficult especially when the IT is relatively new and untried. Kathryn Marold presents case studies conducted at the University Corporation for Atmospheric Research in Boulder CO; the Oppenheimer Funds of the Oppenheimer Management Corporation; and Coors Brewery, which deal with the companies' efforts to measure the productivity derived from the multimedia computer-based training modules (CBTs). The author states that the various advantages and disadvantages of multimedia CBTs must be considered when investigating the feasibility of utilizing such technology to train employees. Both quantitative measures and qualitative measures used with several methods of evaluation (triangulation) are needed to arrive at a complete evaluation. Marold contends that the more technology training using multimedia CBTs will give a company a better return on their information technology investment. The author emphasizes that a management strategy of evaluation may take years to effectively complete and the management should exercise "blind faith" at first so as to allow new IT to prove its worth.

The importance of considering intangible benefits of IT investment is a theme of the paper by Elizabeth Towell. Innovative Internet applications are often perceived by IT managers and users to provide benefits which are difficult to predict and measure. Towell presents the case of St. George Crystal and of John Wiley & Sons and argues that justification for investment in Internet technology can be made in terms of the role that Internet access will play in the entire organization not as a solution to a single problem or opportunity. Drawing on the work of M. M. Parker, she provides a framework for measuring the business value of Internet investment in an organization. She argues that this investment can be demonstrated, in terms of costs and benefits, along three dimensions: business value, strategic value, and enterprise value. She is, however, quick to point out that it is difficult to compare costs and benefits across dimensions. Successful utilization of the Internet "should be translated into the eventual realization of positive value in each dimension." The author concludes by providing a number of recommendations for management for Internet planning and use.

The case of "CARVE" at Morgan Stanley by Chrys de Almeida and Elizabeth Kennick likewise addresses the intangible: measuring the impact of IT supporting knowledge work. CARVE is a decision support system developed to support the mortgage-backed securities business by helping create securities based on pools of assets. It helps the decision maker determine a structure that maximizes net aggregate proceeds and minimizes costs. It uses a framework to measure payoffs from IT at three levels: knowledge worker level, business process level, and firm level. At the knowledge worker level, the benefits of CARVE include its flexibility as a modeling tool to allow the structurer to focus on business issues, faster and better analyses, and greater confidence in outcomes. At the business process level, benefits include more deals completed and less time to prepare presentations. At the firm level, CARVE has increased profitability and strengthened the firm's competitiveness. The authors maintain that senior management should not try to rationalize investment on IT supporting knowledge work purely on firm level macro measures. They should rather pay close attention to benefits which are subtle and indirect or which may be substantive over the long-term.

Chapter 16

An Empirical Assessment of Financial EDI Value to Corporate Adopters

Marielle Bergeron
Université Laval

Albert S. Dexter
University of British Columbia

Within a cohesive value measurement framework based on the theory of capital budgeting, this study empirically assesses the economic value of financial electronic data interchange (financial EDI) technology to corporate adopters. The evaluation methodology requires an in-depth understanding of the processes by which the technology is implemented and utilized. Both organizational costs and benefits are examined following an historical process-oriented case research strategy. Actual user sites include a corporate originator (buyer) and a corporate receiver (supplier), because these two underlying business processes are managed differently. In contrast to previous research, the evaluation methodology can be applied to both ex ante and ex post analyses of financial EDI investments.

Corporate decision-makers are making significant investments in information technology (IT) often on the basis of blind faith alone in the absence of strong evidence of its positive contribution to organizational performance (Mooney et al., 1995). In the current competitive environment, increasing pressure is put on management to justify these expenditures by quantifying their economic impact to the firm (Dos Santos, 1991; Mukhopadhyay et al., 1995).

Although the IT value stream of research comprises numerous

empirical studies, previous works on specific IT innovations or applications typically follow a baseline or benchmarking approach where functionally related performance improvements are measured for different levels of system utilization. These studies often examined the presence or absence of IT at user and non-user sites (Banker and Kauffma,n 1988; Pentland, 1989; Banker et al., 1990; Venkatraman and Zaheer, 1990; Kekre and Mukhopadhyay, 1992; Srinivasan et al., 1994). While important, this ex post evaluation approach doesn't assess the contribution of an IT investment to organizational performance before the IT investment decision is made by management.

In contrast to previous studies, the value measurement framework developed here is based on the theory of capital budgeting and applies to both ex ante and ex post analyses of investments in financial electronic data interchange (financial EDI) technology. Moreover, previous research appears limited in scope by studying only a subset of benefit variables. The framework taken here is global in scope and comprises an extensive evaluation of financial EDI cost variables as well as benefits over time[1].

A notable exception is the recent work of Mukhopadhyay et al. (1995) on electronic data interchange. Based on a 10-year data set from nine assembly centers of Chrysler Corporation, the authors estimate the total benefits of EDI per vehicle at over $100 which translates to annual savings of $220 million for the company. The study is however, limited to a single dominant buyer firm and the cost of implementing the technology in the organization is not considered.

Consistent with the emerging view that adopting a process perspective holds the key to additional insights into the IT value issue (Davenport, 1993; Mooney et al., 1995), this study follows an historical process-oriented case research strategy to assess the economic impact of financial EDI to a corporate originator (buyer) and a corporate receiver (supplier). This dual perspective of financial EDI value takes into account that the underlying business processes are managed differently. Indeed, corporate originators introduce *outbound financial EDI* into their accounts payable (A/P) and disbursement processes, while corporate receivers introduce *inbound financial EDI* into their accounts receivable (A/R) and collection processes.

Management strategies derived from this in-depth study of financial EDI investments at actual user sites cover both the benefit and cost sides of the value equation from both corporate originator and receiver perspectives. The study also provides a comprehensive and useful set of cost and benefit variables to account for in determining the economic feasibility of future financial EDI investments, or in sustaining and evaluating the organizational value of current financial EDI programs.

Limitations of the study include its limited domain focus using a specific information technology with the underlying business processes which may restrict generalizations to other technologies. Only tangible or quantifiable cost and benefit variables are examined. This approach is thus particularly suitable for valuing investments in operational information systems. On some occasions, we estimated the actual costs and benefits of the technology to participating firms, because some of the firms lacked good data on their IT projects.

This chapter is organized as follows. First, it provides an overview of the financial EDI value measurement framework and research methodology. Then, the actual value of the technology to the participating originator and receiver is assessed. Finally, management guidelines for improving financial EDI investment payoffs are derived from this in-depth study of actual corporate users.

Financial EDI Value Measurement Framework

Financial EDI is a subset of EDI for the computer-to-computer (application-to-application) transmission of payment-related business transactions in a standard format. In the context of this study, financial EDI refers primarily to the exchange of standardized payment orders and remittance advice between organizations. The study was conducted in Canada and this definition is consistent with the original scope of the Canadian banking industry's EDI initiative which excluded the transmission of invoices in EDI format[2]. However, the value measurement framework developed here could readily be applied to the broader analysis which includes the transmission of invoices.

The lack of theoretical analysis has been identified as a major impediment to the quality of empirical studies on IT impact (Crowston and Treacy 1986). The finance literature provides a theoretical foundation for corporate investment decisions referred to as capital budgeting. The financial EDI measurement framework developed here is based on the theory of capital budgeting which states that in order to be profitable or cost beneficial to the firm, the one-time initial investment I_0 in any corporate project must be less than its ongoing net benefits i.e., its ongoing benefits B_t minus its ongoing costs C_t, over N pre-defined periods of time:

$$\sum_{t=1}^{N} (B_t - C_t) - I_0 > 0$$

Several methods or techniques can be used in deciding whether or not to make an investment, such as the payback method, the return on investment, the net present value and the internal rate of return (Fama and Miller, 1972; Myers, 1976; Copeland and Weston, 1983). As illustrated in Table 1, these traditional techniques are all based on the above cost/benefit or net cash flow model for project evaluation.

The model applies to both ex ante and ex post analyses of

Payback Period	Return on Investment
$\sum_{t=1}^{X} (B_t - C_t) = I_0$	$\dfrac{\sum_{t=1}^{N} (B_t - C_t)}{N\,I_0} = \text{ROI}$
where: *X* is the number of time periods to recoup the initial investment.	where: *ROI* equals the average net benefits over the initial investment in percentage.
Net Present Value	**Internal Rate of Return**
$\sum_{t=1}^{N} \left\{ \dfrac{(B_t - C_t)}{(1 + r)^t} \right\} - I_0 = \text{NPV}$ where: *r* is the shareholder cost of capital and *NPV* is the net present value.	$\sum_{t=1}^{N} \left\{ \dfrac{(B_t - C_t)}{(1 + X)^t} \right\} = I_0$ where: *x* is the discount rate for the cumulative net benefits to equal the initial investment.

Table 1: Comparison of Four Investment Evaluation Methods

corporate projects or investments. At the initiation phase, the *expected value* of a project is based on a forecast of future costs and benefits i.e., one-time initial costs (I_0) and ongoing net benefits ($B_t - C_t$). At the post-mortem stage, its *actual value* accounts for realized costs and benefits. In that context, the *investment success* can be expressed either as the extent to which the actual value of the project is positive to the firm (S_1), or the extent to which the expected value of the project is realized assuming only those having positive expected value are accepted (S_2). Both approaches are examined in this study.

S_1 = Actual Value > 0
S_2 = Actual Value > Expected Value > 0

The difficulty of applying the financial model to IS projects arises from various reasons, including the intangibility of many IS costs and benefits (Parker and Benson 1988) and the lack of accurate data on which to base cost and benefit projections (Lay 1985). The former limitation is relevant to financial EDI projects but, possibly, to a lesser extent because of the operational or transactional nature of the technology. This study attempts to alleviate the latter difficulty by providing an extensive set of variables to include in cost/benefit analyses of financial EDI investments.

When the success construct or dependent variable is defined in terms of economic performance, variables such as IS competence and system usage are then considered as explanatory or mediator rather than criteria variables (Kauffman and Weill 1989; DeLone and McLean 1992). As an example, the diffusion strategy of an organization can influence the level of financial EDI adoption among trading partners which, in turn, directly impacts the benefits, and thus the value, of the technology to the initiating firm. In that context, previous factors identified in the literature as potential factors influencing the development and adoption of IOS/EDI systems also impact the success of financial EDI investments (Reich and Benbasat, 1990; Benbasat et al., 1993; Bergeron, 1994).

The definitions of one-time investment costs (I_0), ongoing system benefits (B_t) and ongoing system costs (C_t) were refined to take into account the specific nature of the technology under analysis. Three main sources of information were used to identify potential costs and benefits associated with the implementation of financial EDI in organizational settings: (1) the current EDI literature in both research and practitioner domains[3]; (2) structured interviews with participants from major Canadian financial institutions acting as financial EDI service providers[4]; and, (3) the first author's multidisciplinary experience in the accounting and IS fields.

Initial Investment

The initial investment in financial EDI applications can be divided into two major cost categories: (i) *one-time development costs* incurred by the firm to setup its system or application, e.g., communications hardware/software, mailbox with a network provider and EDI translation software; and, (ii) *one-time adoption costs* to gain acceptance among internal users and external partners e.g., education, training and marketing documentation, and start up software for external partners.

Ongoing Adoption Benefits

Potential tangible or monetary benefits of financial EDI can be grouped into three basic categories: (i) *ongoing payment process savings* derived from a comparison of the cost of processing payments via EDI versus the cost of processing payments under the previous payment method, (ii) *one-time payment cycle gains* resulting from changes in payment frequency and cycle time, and (iii) *other financial EDI benefits* such as the value gained from increased discounts on transacted goods prices, reduced cash discounts lost on late payments and payment process reengineering benefits[5].

This classification is consistent with Parker and Benson (1988) who make the distinction between value linking and value acceleration IT benefits. The authors define value linking benefits as recurring or ongoing benefits related to performance improvements and value acceleration benefits as one-time benefits related to earlier achievements of benefits. The latter benefits encompass the potentially very significant impact of financial EDI on trade credit cycle and firm profitability (Lovejoy, 1990; Keller, 1990).

Ongoing Adoption Costs

The ongoing adoption costs of financial EDI can be divided into three major cost categories: (i) *ongoing roll out costs* incurred by the firm to get more external partners on board, (ii) *one-time system enhancement costs* to improve the functionality of existing payment systems, e.g., automating the application of remittance data and building flexible delivery capabilities for remittance advice, and (iii) *other financial EDI costs* for organizational and business process changes, including the cost of organizational disruption and resistance to change.

Research Methodology

Overall Design

This study follows an historical process-oriented case research strategy. The retrospective history of financial EDI implementation, and its economic impact over time, was reconstituted through the available documentation and structured questioning of key players involved in the process at participating user sites. Access to these firms was gained under the seal of confidentiality as a result of the well-known reluctance of organizations to disclose financial data (Attewell and Rule, 1991; Mukhopadhyay et al., 1995).

Sample User Sites

The study illustrated below was conducted at two Canadian financial EDI user sites, a corporate originator (buyer) and a corporate receiver (supplier), in order to understand both business perspectives, with distinctive organizational and technological environments. As shown in Table 2, the originator is from the public sector, while the receiver operates in the private sector; one firm was already EDI active in non-financial areas, while the other had no prior experience with EDI. Finally, the financial EDI system of one participant is running on a personal computer (PC), while the other system resides on a

	Originator	Receiver
Industry Sector	Public	Private
Number of employees	2,500	4,500
Annual sales (budget)	$150M	$500M
Existing EDI Applications	No	Yes
Financial EDI Platform	PC	Mainframe

Table 2: General Information on Participating Firms

mainframe. We believed that important economic aspects of financial EDI implementation could be uncovered with this complementary case base.

Data Collection

The study followed a triangulation data collection approach combining: (1) extensive structured interviews with key participants involved in the areas of IS/IT, Treasury, A/P and Disbursement, A/R and Collection, Purchasing and Sales; (2) the review of financial EDI project documentation, e.g., business cases and cost/benefit tracking reports; (3) the cross-validation of participant responses with financial records e.g., value-added network (VAN) invoices and bank statements; (4) the gathering of sample data to support the alleged benefits of financial EDI, e.g., cycle time and error/problem reductions; and, (5) reference firms to obtain more information on selected topics related to the study, e.g., postage delays in Canada and the cost of mail distribution within an organization.

A multiple-baseline design across groups (Komaki 1977) was followed for some variables, such as the number of errors/problems and float days. Whenever possible, data were collected randomly for a relatively large number of data points over a period of six months before and after the implementation of financial EDI (e.g., one payment per week). This approach enhances the internal validity of research findings because potential sources of confounding can be more easily ruled out when the quasi-treatment (use of financial EDI) is naturally introduced at different times in independent organizations (Cook and Campbell, 1976).

Financial EDI Value Assessment

Table 3 summarizes the expected and estimated actual value of financial EDI at participating firm sites. Expected value of the originator depicts this firm's analysis, while the estimated actual figures arise from the more complete analysis of our model. The table follows the same structure as the financial EDI value measurement framework described earlier. Results are presented on a cumulative basis for the period of time between the first real-life EDI payment and the on-site research work (i.e., system lifetime in operation).

Outbound Financial EDI Value

At the initiation stage, the participating originator performed an economic feasibility analysis of outbound financial EDI which is reproduced in Table 4. Potential variable unit cost savings were evaluated at $0.39 per payment transaction. At an expected adoption

	Originator		Receiver
	Expected	**Estimated Actual**	**Estimated Actual**
I. SYSTEM LIFETIME			
Time in Operation (in months)		12	21
Development Elapsed Time (in months)		5	7
II. ADOPTION MEASURES			
Level of Adoption:			
Number of Financial EDI Partners	100	19	3
Volume of EDI Payments	8,200	540	650
Volume of EDI Remittance Items	82,000	4,500	52,000
Value of EDI Payments		14M	44M
Rate of Adoption:			
Number of Financial EDI Partners	3%	0.6%	0.2%
Volume of EDI Payments	33%	2%	2%
Volume of EDI Remittance Items	82%	5%	10%
Value of EDI Payments		16%	15%
III. ONGOING NET BENEFITS			
Cumulative Adoption Benefits:			
Ongoing Payment Process Savings	1,800	-2,000	21,000
One-time Payment Cycle Gains		-7,000	-16,000
Other Ongoing Adoption Benefits	3,000		
	1,800	-6,000	5,000
Cumulative Adoption Costs:			
Ongoing Roll Out Costs		4,000	
One-time System Enhancement Costs			
Cumulative Net Benefits	1,800	-10,000	5,000
IV. INITIAL INVESTMENT			
One-time Setup Costs	1,800	4,000	4,000
V. BUSINESS VALUE			
Cumulative Business Value	0	-14,000	1,000

Table 3: Financial EDI Business Value to Participating Firms

level of 8,200 payments, this translates into $3,200 ongoing annual savings. After subtracting $1,400 ongoing fixed costs (bank EDI maintenance fee, VAN mailbox fee and EDI software maintenance), the firm was projecting $1,800 ongoing annual payment process savings. Only *hard* cost/benefit items were considered in the ex ante analysis, although softer potential benefits such as lower product cost, reduced cash discounts lost and labor cost savings were mentioned as potential qualitative benefits.

It took five months to set up the financial EDI environment. The IS function was not involved in the development process because, according to the A/P Manager: "It would have taken too long if they

	Original	Revised
Level of Adoption		
Number of Financial EDI Partners	100	100
Volume of EDI Payments	8,200	8,200
Volume of EDI Remittance Items	82,000	82,000
Variable Unit Cost Savings		
Pre-EDI Unit Costs		
Postage	0.42	0.42
Bank Cheque Fee	0.04	0.04
Cheque Forms	0.12	0.12
Envelope Forms	0.04	0.04
	0.62	0.62
Post-EDI Unit Costs		
Bank EDI Payment Fee	-0.10	-0.10
Bank EDI Invoice Fee	-0.13	-0.13
VAN Payment Fee		-0.16
VAN Kilocharacter Fee		-0.61
	-0.23	-1.00
	0.39	-0.38
Post-EDI Fixed Costs		
Bank EDI Maintenance Fee	600	600
VAN Mailbox Fee	440	440
EDI Translator Maintenance	360	360
	1,400	1,400
Ongoing Net Benefits		
Ongoing Variable Cost Savings	3,200	-3,100
Ongoing Fixed Costs	-1,400	-1,400
	1,800	-4,500
Initial Investment		
Bank EDI Setup Fee	150	150
EDI Translator Software Purchase	1,550	1,550
Modem Purchase	100	100
Bridge Program Development		2,200
	1,800	4,000
Payback Period (in months)	12	n/a

Table 4: Outbound Financial EDI Expected Value

were" and also "When we started our initial program, the IS manager's suggestion was not to go ahead with EDI." At the initiation phase, the firm evaluates the initial investment at $1,800 for bank EDI setup fee, the acquisition of an EDI translation software package on PC and the purchase of a modem.

As shown in Table 4, the payback period method was used to determine the advisability of investing in financial EDI technology. The project was approved by the Vice-President of Finance on the basis that it would take only one year to recoup the forecasted one-time costs of $1,800 with annual net benefits of the same amount. In other words, the cumulative value of financial EDI would break even in one year at the expected level of adoption by the supplier community.

This study revealed that the firm has actually lost $14,000 after one year of system operation. The post-implementation evaluation performed at the time of the research is summarized in Table 3, Column 2. Six key factors explain the negative variance between the expected and estimated actual value of financial EDI: (1) missing payment process evaluation items in the firm's ex ante analysis; (2) a lower level of adoption than expected, and associated costs; (3) the partial IS/IT integration between existing A/P and financial EDI systems; (4) the limited extent of payment process changes introduced by the firm; (5) the economic impact of payment cycle changes as a result of financial EDI implementation; and, (6) other unexpected or non-quantified financial EDI benefits.

Pre-Implementation Evaluation Completeness
In Table 4, Column 1, the firm's expected variable savings of $0.39 per EDI payment transaction were derived by subtracting $0.23 post-EDI variable unit costs (bank EDI fees) from $0.62 pre-EDI variable unit costs (bank cheque fee, cheque/envelope form costs and postage fee). However, EDI payments are actually transmitted to the bank via a value-added network (VAN) which charges $0.77 per transaction at a ratio of two kilocharacters of remittance information per payment.

The firm's overlooking of VAN transaction fees is surprising given that VAN monthly mailbox fees were included in the firm's ex ante analysis as a fixed cost. If VAN transaction fees had been considered at the initiation phase, the analysis would have shown -$0.38 rather than $0.39 variable savings per transaction. At the expected level of adoption, this translates into ongoing net losses of $4,500 in Table 4, Column 2.

A bridge program was developed by the external EDI software/network provider to maintain vendor banking information on the PC and to integrate this information with payment data downloaded from the A/P system on the firm's mainframe. The revised initial investment of $4,000 in Tables 3 and 4 takes into account the $1,500 bridge program not originally forecasted by the firm, as well as user involvement in the development project.

Level and Cost of Financial EDI Adoption
At the initiation phase, the firm's expected benefits were based on the assumption that 100 of its top vendors, representing only 3% of the total number of suppliers but 33% of the annual volume of payments, would receive EDI payment transactions after one year. Hand-signed letters from the Vice-President of Finance were sent to the 100 targeted vendors but the A/P Manager rapidly realized that this kind of mass

diffusion strategy would not work: "When I sent out those letters, I planned them and I made sure I had no other appointments for the following week because I fully expected my phone would be ringing off the hook — people would want to jump into that. I was quite shocked at the vendors' reaction to EDI — the resistance out there." The firm received only three responses.

A one-to-one communication strategy was then adopted and potential vendors were contacted mainly through telephone calls. From the vendor log maintained by the firm, 69 suppliers had been contacted over the year: 19 were receiving EDI payment transactions at the time of the research[6], 46 were at various stages of implementation, and 4 had refused to embark on financial EDI because of costs, reluctance to change existing procedures and lack of requests from other customers. According to the source participant, the 19 early adopters of financial EDI share three major characteristics: (i) they have a client-oriented approach, (ii) they are all proactive firms, and (iii) they are generally larger size companies.

The firm has also organized a one-day seminar to foster a more rapid adoption of EDI by other industry buyers: "When we have three or four more buyers live with EDI, we may all of a sudden have four buyers calling up a vendor at the same week and even a small vendor who relies solely on the industry for its business will have to go EDI. Those buyers will be more aggressive than we are. I have been really nice with the vendors." Indeed, this participating originator has adopted a proactive, non-coercive diffusion strategy of financial EDI among its suppliers, and associated roll out costs are estimated at $4,000 in Table 3.

At the actual level of adoption, annual payment process savings amount to -$1,200 based on the revised cost figures in Table 4, Column 2, (i.e., 540 EDI payment transactions at -$0.38 less $1,400 annual fixed costs). Actual payment process savings are estimated at -$2,000 in Table 3, Column 2, and the negative impact of financial EDI implementation on labor costs explains the difference.

Level of IS/IT Integration

Labor costs for the processing of cheques can be evaluated at $1.53 per transaction based on data gathered at the participating user site[7]. At an actual level of 540 EDI payments, this translates into $800 potential ongoing annual savings. However, the lack of integration between the A/P and financial EDI systems partly explains the negative impact of the technology on labor costs[8].

At the initiation stage, the decision was made by management to implement financial EDI as a standalone system running on an available PC, and this decision results in the creation of new manual payment processing tasks. For instance, the vendor banking information is now maintained on PC by the A/P Manager who also executes the data transmission protocol manually. Transmission security controls imply telephone conversations with the EDI leading bank to acknowledge and authenticate each electronic data transfer. The bank account reconciliator treats EDI payments as cheques and manually flags them as cashed during the month-end bank reconciliation process. These additional recurring financial EDI-specific activities account for roughly 60% of the non-realized labor cost savings.

Extent of Payment Process Changes

The remaining variance is explained by the limited extent of payment process changes introduced by the firm as a result of financial EDI implementation. For example, copies of cheques issued were previously attached to back-up documents (e.g., purchase orders, receipt reports and supplier invoices). The cost of performing this task is included in the estimated $1.53 unit labor cost. However, the activity was not eliminated after the introduction of financial EDI because the transmission report is now cut and used for exactly the same purpose. A similar observation applies to the perforation and filing of paid documents.

According to the A/P Manager, "These procedures will eventually be removed down the road, but sometimes it's better to do changes slowly because we will have better acceptance. When somebody has been doing a task for 20 years, it's this empty feeling that there is something wrong there [by eliminating the task]."

Impact of Payment Cycle Changes

The study reveals that the payment cycle time of the firm has been reduced on average by three days as a result of financial EDI implementation. At an annual interest rate of 6%, this translates into $7,000 payment cycle losses in Table 3, Column 2. It should be noted however, that the A/P policy of the firm is to pay its suppliers 45 days, rather than 30 days, from the invoice date. Consequently, the reduced post-EDI payment cycle time contributes at getting the actual trade settlement date closer to the payment terms negotiated with suppliers at the procurement stage.

The three-day float reduction was introduced by the participating originator which generates EDI payment transactions every three days (as opposed to daily cheques) with a transmission lead time to the bank of two days. Thus, cheque processing delays from 2 to 9 days had been reduced from 1 to 5 days for EDI payments (i.e., -1 to 1 payment initiation days plus 2 to 4 payment clearing days on a calendar basis).

Other Financial EDI Benefits

Nault et al. (1997) demonstrate the positive impact of lump-sum incentives and discounts on transacted goods prices to encourage the adoption of electronic communication innovations. Similarly, Ballance (1992: 27) reported that "Sellers were beginning to enforce terms or, alternatively, negotiate on price with their buyers on the basis of efficient and prompt payment practices."

In this particular case, the bank has waived its cheque fees for the financial EDI corporate adopter on both its Canadian and American dollar bank accounts which represents approximately 80% of other financial EDI benefits estimated at $3,000 in Table 3, Column 2. Lower product cost was also mentioned by the participating firm as a potential benefit of financial EDI but increased discounts on transacted goods prices were not negotiated with suppliers, and according to the Purchasing Manager: "We have to do more work on this area. We have to approach it before the contract is expired."

The remaining balance accounts for realized reduced cash discounts lost on late payments by the participating originator. The evaluation of this benefit variable is based on a detailed analysis of discounts lost comparing six months before and after the first real-life EDI payment with two of the firm's largest suppliers.

Inbound Financial EDI Value

The participating receiver was asked to be the pilot partner in the financial EDI program of its largest Canadian customer. The firm was already EDI active in non-financial areas and the decision to be part of this financial EDI pilot project was promptly made by senior management. According to the Director of Finance, people believed that: "We can't leave this opportunity because it will build a stronger relation with *our client.* It is part of our EDI mission, so let's do it." Therefore, at the time, no cost/benefit analysis was made to support this decision. Since then, the company has developed a formal cost/benefit analysis methodology to assess the profitability of potential EDI trading agreements before entering into them. The first real-life EDI payment was received by the participating organization seven months after the adoption decision date. This period of time mainly reflects the development elapsed time at the payment originator site.

The post-implementation evaluation performed at the time of the research is summarized in Table 3, Column 3. After almost two years of system operation, the cumulative value of financial EDI to the firm is estimated at $1,000, which implies an investment payback period of approximately one year and a half. The positive economic contribution of financial EDI technology to firm performance is explained by five key factors: (1) the low-cost management diffusion strategy of financial EDI; (2) labor cost savings for the automated application of paid invoices in the A/R system; (3) post-EDI incremental transaction receipt charges; (4) the economic impact of payment cycle changes; and, (5) the presence of an integrated EDI environment.

Diffusion Strategy and Cost of Financial EDI Adoption
At the time of the research, this firm was receiving real-life EDI payments from three clients, two Canadian and one American, and two

other customers were at the testing phase. This corporate receiver is not really promoting financial EDI to its clients, and according to the source participant: "It would be a soft sale from an EFT [electronic funds transfer] side. We don't push a lot of advantages of EFT. What we say is if you want to do it, we are able to do it with you as a partner. We kind of soft sell the partnership side of the process. We are not selling them that there is a lot of big savings for them to do this [issuing EDI payments rather than paper cheques]."

On the other hand, the firm pursues a much more proactive diffusion strategy for its outbound EDI invoice capabilities, "because our clients can realize significant tangible benefits almost immediately by cutting down paper work." The firm markets its EDI infrastructure as a value-added service to its customers. The organization has "committed to taking an aggressive approach in such areas as incorporating more trading partners, increasing EDI capacities, updating software, and generally continuing to provide input and support to its customers and the entire EDI community" (extract from a public pamphlet on EDI produced by the firm).

The Director of Finance only considers this project to be a partial success because his original goal was to deal with ten major customers via EDI, but "we have not got anywhere close to the top ten customers." The actual cost of financial EDI adoption by the corporate clientele is negligible because the firm's diffusion strategy focuses on outbound invoices rather than inbound payments. The EDI coordinator estimates the setup of current, non-pilot financial EDI partners at less than $200.

Invoice Reconciliation Labor Cost Savings

From a receiver perspective, the transmission of remittance information in an electronic format eliminates the need to manually reconcile invoices paid by customers in the A/R system. The integration of existing financial and EDI applications is a *sine qua non* condition to the realization of associated potential labor cost savings (Iacovou et al. 1995), and the participating firm has achieved a high level of system integration in this area.

Unit labor cost savings for the application of paid invoices are estimated at $0.24 per remittance item. This evaluation takes into account the fact that the manual invoice reconciliation process of the firm is relatively time-efficient. At the actual level of financial EDI adoption, this translates into $12,500 of the annual savings in Table 3 (i.e., 52,000 remittance items at $0.24). These savings are mainly attributable to the high ratio of 80 invoices on average per payment transaction.

Incremental Transaction Receipt Costs

The firm has established a pickup/courier system with its top Canadian customers to minimize mailing delays. Its two Canadian financial EDI partners were among those, and eliminating express delivery charges results in $4,000 annual savings at an average courier rate of $12 per cheque. However, post-EDI transaction receipt costs exceed these savings by almost 50% in Table 3.

For its Canadian customers, the firm disburses a fixed amount of $4.00 per EDI payment flowing through the Canadian EDI banking network. For its American client, the company is charged a monthly EDI maintenance fee of $300, and a transaction fee of $0.50 per EDI payment flowing through the Automated Clearing House (ACH) system. The firm also incurs EDI network receipt charges estimated at $1.60 per transaction. At the actual level of adoption, this translates into $6,000 annual charges for the receipt of EDI payments and remittance data.

Impact of Payment Cycle Changes

The study reveals that the payment cycle time with the Canadian pilot financial EDI partner has increased by six days after the technology implementation. At an annual interest rate of 6%, this translates into $16,000 payment cycle losses in Table 3. The evaluation is based on a detailed analysis of payments received six months before and after the first real-life EDI payment from the originating firm.

This particular case illustrates the role of EDI technology as a catalyst for correcting problems and streamlining work flows and business processes (Sokol, 1989; Davenport and Short, 1990; Emmelhainz, 1990; Bain, 1992). As explained by the Director of Finance: "If you look at this client, you will find that our payment terms have increased by 6 days. They were paying us 24, and now they are paying 30. So they have already received the financial benefit from better controlling their cash flow. However, that was really only an internal thing to them because we have given them 30 days already, and if they had paid net 30 days, there would be no changes as a result of EDI."

Existing EDI Environment

The development of inbound financial EDI and its integration with the A/R system was relatively straightforward: the firm was already EDI operational in non-financial areas and the A/R system could already process input data from batch files.

The EDI Coordinator evaluates the actual technical effort of implementing financial EDI at 10 hours, 5 hours to update the EDI software and 5 hours for the A/R bridge program, which amounts to less than $500. However, the Director of Finance also mentioned his personal intervention in the business side of the development project. He believes that most of the time spent on the pilot project was for face-to-face meetings and communications with the remote pilot customer. The combination of these aspects explains the estimated actual $4,000 initial investment in Table 3.

Management Strategies for Information Technology Investment

In the context of this study, management suggestions to improve the business value or profitability of financial EDI investments are grouped in two broad categories: (1) strategies aimed at maximizing the benefit side of the value equation, and (2) strategies for controlling associated implementation costs. The suggestions take into account the different business perspectives of corporate originators and receivers. The study also provides a useful set of cost/benefit variables to account for in determining the economic feasibility of future financial EDI investments, or in sustaining and evaluating the organizational value of current programs.

Benefit Management Strategies

Payment Process Savings

From a payment process perspective, financial EDI is potentially more beneficial to corporate receivers than originators. Receivers have relatively higher potential process cost savings per payment transaction. This finding is primarily explained by the fact that paper remittance data on paid invoices are manually applied to the supplier's A/R system, while no data entry is directly associated with the production of paper checks. Demonstrating this result to potential financial EDI partners from the supplier community may facilitate the diffusion effort of originating firms.

Corporate originators as well as receivers should aim at maximizing the realization of potential payment process savings as a result of financial EDI implementation. The following major areas of improvement were identified from case studies: (1) achieving a high level of integration between existing financial and EDI systems; (2) avoiding the use of multiple intermediaries in the transport of electronic payments (i.e., value-added and banking networks); (3) minimizing fixed monthly maintenance charges of third parties involved in the processing of EDI payments; and, (4) ensuring that beneficial payment process changes are effectively implemented in practice.

The magnitude of payment process savings as a result of financial EDI implementation is directly related to the volume of transactions exchanged, rather than the number of partners, even though the latter is the most frequently cited indicator of EDI diffusion (Wrigley, 1991). Considering the cost of setting up new partners, high transaction volume partners should be targeted first. For corporate receivers, the volume of remittance items rather than payments must be considered because payment process savings are mainly derived from automating the application of paid invoices in the A/R system.

Payment Cycle Gains

Financial EDI eliminates some delays in the trade credit cycle (e.g., postage, cheque production and deposit processing delays). A reduction in payment cycle time translates into gains of a positive magnitude to corporate receivers and of a negative magnitude to corporate originators. An increase in payment cycle time would have the reverse impact. Consequently, potential economic gains from reduced payment cycles accrue primarily to the supplier community rather the originators of EDI payments.

Corporate originators may decide to assume this loss and use this positive potential effect of financial EDI on supplier performance as a marketing argument to foster a more rapid adoption of the technology. Alternatively, originators counterbalance the negative impact of shorter trade credit cycles on their own financial performance by different approaches, including: (1) streamlining the cheque production process, (2) increasing post-EDI payment terms, or (3) negotiating increased discounts on transacted goods prices.

Other Financial EDI Benefits

Other than payment process savings and payment cycle gains, potential tangible benefits of financial EDI identified from case studies include: (i) reduced cash discounts lost on late payments, (ii) waived cheque fees by the EDI leading bank, and (iii) increased discounts on product costs. While the reduction of cash discounts lost on late payments is managed internally, the other benefits realization implies negotiations with external agents which must be planned before entering potential financial EDI trading agreements.

Cost Management Strategies

Roll Out Costs

Once an EDI application has been developed, tested and put into production, the term "rollout" is commonly used to refer to the next phase of diffusion among external partners other than the pilot partner. The choice of a diffusion strategy can influence the magnitude of roll out costs incurred by the initiating firm. For example, the participating originator has embarked on a proactive, non-coercive diffusion program of financial EDI, while the participating receiver elected to take a more reactive approach and initiate EDI payment exchanges upon request.

It is predictable that rollout costs on a per-partner basis increase in relation to the extent of interorganizational communications prior to the conclusion of a financial EDI agreement. In that context, a proactive diffusion strategy where the initiator actively promotes financial EDI among its partners in an attempt to convince them of adopting the technology is more costly than a reactive diffusion strategy where the corporate adopter only links up with requesting partners.

The way a given diffusion strategy is carried out or implemented by the firm can also impact its actual level of adoption and associated roll out costs. For instance the following diffusion success factors were mentioned by study participants: (1) the identification of already EDI active, preferably financial EDI active trading partners to link up with first[9]; (2) the need to make contacts with the right individual in corporations, preferably the Vice President of Finance; (3) the conduct of group meetings rather than one-to-one communications with potential candidate partners; and, (4) an initial focus on intra-bank partners because the originator's bank can waive its EDI fees to suppliers.

This is an area where the achievement of a critical mass could potentially bring substantial cost reductions to corporate adopters. As more and more firms become financial EDI operational, it is predictable that the cost of linking up with them would be significantly lower than the cost of an early adopter allocating resources to the education and indoctrination of potential candidate partner firms.

Initial Investment

The magnitude of one-time costs associated with the setup of a financial EDI application depends on a series of factors, including: the existence of an already operational EDI environment in non-financial areas; the financial EDI platform (e.g., PC or mainframe); the level of integration between the financial and EDI systems; the extent of automated controls and security procedures; and, third party pricing and service policies. A forecast of potential ongoing net benefits to the firm should guide the selection of a cost beneficial technological solution.

Summary

This dual case study of financial EDI value to corporate adopters is based on the view that assessing the economic contribution of specific IT applications on firm performance requires an in depth understanding of the underlying implementation and business processes, and implies an extensive evaluation of one-time investment costs as well as ongoing net benefits. This approach applies to both ex ante and ex post analyses of IT investments. Thus, management guidelines for improving future investment success can be derived from a rigorous post-implementation evaluation or post-mortem of existing systems at actual corporate user sites.

While providing a very comprehensive analysis, the study's focus on financial EDI and underlying business processes may restrict generalizations to other technologies. Only tangible or quantifiable cost and benefit variables were examined, and this analysis can be supplemented with a subjective evaluation of intangibles.

Endnotes

[1] The reader will note that the scope of the chapter is purposely narrowly focused on financial EDI costs and benefits. The methodology, however, is general and applicable to the full spectrum of EDI applications within and between organizations. The focus here was to keep the paper manageable in scope.

[2] In the early 1989, the creation of an inter-financial institution EDI committee began a major cooperative EDI initiative in the Canadian banking industry. In contrast to electronic fund transfers, an EDI payment can accommodate the transfer of both funds and remittance data because the Canadian EDI banking network supports virtually unlimited descriptive information about corporate payment.

[3] The financial EDI cost/benefit analysis worksheet developed by NACHA (1993: 25-37) and the empirical study of EDI advantages by Bergeron and Raymond (1992) were particularly useful.

[4] Three of the six major Canadian chartered banks agreed to participate and fund this study: Royal Bank of Canada, Bank of Montreal and Toronto-Dominion Bank. Their corporate client base represents approximately 50% of the total business population in Canada.

[5] The terms "savings" and "gains" also refer to losses, hence to benefits of a positive or negative magnitude to the firm.

[6] Some of the 19 suppliers may in fact receive an electronic print file, a fax or a printout of the remittance information if they are not yet financial EDI capable.

[7] The following tasks for the origination of manual checks are accounted for in the $1.53 unit labor cost: cheque printing, payment association with back-up documents, automatic and manual check signing, payment auditing, special handling, envelope stuffing and mailing, perforation and filing of paid documents, outstanding cheques reconciliation, payment inquiries and error/problem resolution.

[8] Nonetheless, the A/P Manager believes that financial EDI has alleviated the pressure on staff to process an invoice before its due date.

[9] Unfortunately, no directory of financial EDI active firms is available in Canada. The maintenance of such a repertory by the Canadian banking industry would facilitate the adoption of financial EDI by the business community.

Acknowledgment
Financial support for this research project by the Canadian banking industry is gratefully acknowledged. We also thank professors Izak Benbasat and Maurice Levi for their insight and valuable advice.

Chapter 17

A Framework for Assessing IT Investment in Reengineering Initiatives: A Case Study

Tim Tatum
Virginia Commonwealth University

Peter Aiken
*Virginia Commonwealth University and
Defense Information Systems Agency*

Organizations need to be able to evaluate the performance of their information technology investments. Thorough evaluation is difficult without understanding the links between IT investments and corresponding payoffs in organizational performance and/or productivity. Further, understanding these payoffs should be key to subsequent IT investment decisions. The structural similarity of many reengineering initiatives and the fact that many reengineering initiatives are keyed on IT investments, provides an opportunity to begin to address these organizational needs. This chapter describes a framework for assessing IT investment in one organization's reengineering initiatives. During the period 1994-1996, the Virginia Department of Transportation (VDOT) has been concurrently investing in four IT-based reengineering initiatives. For these initiatives, reengineering is seen by management as a means of improving current business practices in anticipation of technology. This chapter details: the VDOT reengineering initiative context; the research motivation and basis of our approach; the framework; two examples of framework application; and some suggestions for future research. Designing a framework for comparing the four initiatives permits VDOT to evaluate its reengineering IT investments by linking them with corresponding payoffs in organizational performance and productivity. In addition, understanding the linkages permits development of better systems and (thus) valid comparisons among the IT investments, and understanding IT investment payoffs in reengineering contexts permits comparisons with investments outside of reengineering contexts.

" ... the most important figures that one needs for management are unknown or unknowable but successful management must nevertheless take account of them" [Deming, 1986, p. 121].

Today, one of the most obvious sets of unknown figures are those relating investment in information technology to quantifiable performance or productivity payoffs. Because it has been difficult to link IT investments to specific organizational performance or productivity payoffs, thorough IT investment payoff analysis has been problematic. This makes it difficult to determine: 1) which, if any of the potential IT investments should be attempted; 2) how much should be invested; and, 3) what resource mixes will yield synergistic investment conditions? IT investment payoff data is crucial to making these decisions.

This chapter presents a case study contributing toward the development of a potential solution. The opportunity to evaluate four reengineering initiatives occurring simultaneously in the same organization has facilitated the development of a comparison framework. The case study also provides an opportunity to evaluate the framework use.

The next section of this chapter describes the organizational context and the four VDOT reengineering initiatives. The literature review (section 3) presents the framework motivation and research basis. We derived the framework presented in section 4 benefiting from: the initiative timing and intensity; preceding research; and the VDOT reengineering initiatives characteristics. In section 5 we illustrate use of the framework with examples from one of the VDOT initiatives. Section 6 concludes the chapter with description of management strategies for assessing IT investments as a part of appropriate reengineering initiatives and some suggestions for future research.

Organizational Reengineering Initiative/IT Investment Context

During the period 1994-1996, the Commonwealth of Virginia's (CoV) Department of Transportation has been investing in four distinct reengineering initiatives in the areas of: finance; maintenance; project planning (contract management); and human resources. (Each initiative is briefly summarized in Figure 1.) While each project is premised on a major IT initiative and aimed at replacing associated legacy systems - the projects are implemented with a reengineering perspective. That is, each project is considered a customer focused, self examination of how the process is performed throughout the organization. Management sees the initiatives as technology-enabled means of improving current business practices. While technology plays a key role in each initiative, VDOT has taken care to ensure the organization does not view any of these as narrowly focused technology-based system replacements.

With just under 10,000 employees and an FY 1995-96 budget totaling about $2 billion, the apparent reengineering project costs are not especially significant or even large investments. (For example, during the course of the reengineering, the organization also began a five year investment of $32 million in an integrated document management project that was considered to be outside the scope of the reengineering efforts.) Senior management understands the organizational dexterity required to implement these initiatives simultaneously and is focusing on formal strategic level coordination among the initiatives.

While indirectly linked, another event has made these four

Construction Management System (CMS)	VDOT is responsible for the construction and maintenance of transportation systems. CMS will foster agency effectiveness and efficiency in contract related activities. The stated CMS goal is 'redesigning contract management practice to provide timely access to relevant contract data' implying this does not currently exist.
Financial Management System II (FMS II)	VDOT requires finance and accounting systems that are compatible with new line operation support systems for construction and maintenance. Implementing new finance and accounting systems will eliminate the likelihood of 'bottlenecks' in the other systems while providing significant cost savings. Multiple project goals include redesigning accounting and purchasing procedures to 1) automate manual tasks; 2) eliminate redundant data entry; 3) decentralize data processing; and 4) provide timely access to relevant financial data.
Integrated Maintenance Management System (IMMS)	Upkeep of the transportation systems requires speedy response to diverse repair needs over a large geographic area. A major project goal is to prioritize maintenance according to need (i.e., allocation distribution could be based on a combination of need and asset condition).
Integrated Human Resource Management System (IHRIS)	The target organization's human capital will undergo significant changes as a result of the other change initiatives. While replacing an aging legacy system, Human Resources (HR) is working to develop a system that will support future organizational needs while exploiting the efficiencies of new technologies. The primary project goal is to support change initiatives in and of the HR function effecting the entire organization.

Figure 1: VDOT Reengineering Initiative Overview

reengineering initiatives undertaken by VDOT more imperative. In addition to the massive change anticipated by the four initiatives, the organization faces a severe resource shortage. In 1994-95, the CoV provided significant incentives (known as the Work Force Transition Act) for employees to retire early or otherwise part service. As a result VDOT lost roughly 13% of its work force. The attrition was organization wide and many departments lost valuable organizational expertise.

Since May 1995, we have been supporting the IHRIS initiative by developing the information and system requirements for the new technology and coordinating the requirements engineering with the reengineering of the associated process(es). We were invited to research and propose a framework comparing the four initiatives. This has provided us a somewhat rare opportunity to observe and compare the four initiatives and the organization as the initiatives are pursued simultaneously. The framework was developed with the intent that it could be applied to a range of project types. Several characteristics make this study of IT investments in reengineering likely to be applicable beyond the scope of the case study.

The first is project feasibility and reasonability. Practitioners realize that only a small percentage of large software-based systems are finished on time and within budget. When selecting IT investments to study, it has been difficult to be certain the project would finish. Reengineering projects in general, and these in specific, have passed several layers of review to screen out infeasible initiatives. Especially initially, reengineering projects can be targeted to 'harvest low hanging fruit' going for 'quick hits' that can be accomplished in nine to twelve months. Short cycle time provides opportunities to evaluate the initiative results rapidly.

Secondly, the structure of the four reengineering initiatives is similar - following the now popular reengineering approach of getting: 'organized, oriented, crazy, and real' shown in Figure 2. In each initiative, the breakthrough design concept and end-state vision provides input to the replacement of existing system functionality. Some initiative requirements call for a commercial-off-the-shelf (COTS) solution, in other instances customized software is required. The structural similarity of reengineering initiatives facilitates analysis. Following the reengineering guidance, each solution is evolved by prototyping and evaluation cycles in 'laboratories' before full scale implementation. This iterative prototyping approach is used with the understanding that it is much more likely that satisfactory solutions will be evolved as opposed to delivered perfectly on the first attempt [Andriole 1990]. (Another benefit is that frequent iterations provide more actual data points for subsequent analysis.)

Third, the success of many reengineering initiatives hinge on successful IT investments. IT investment often plays a major role in reengineering initiative success. Consider a widely reported estimate

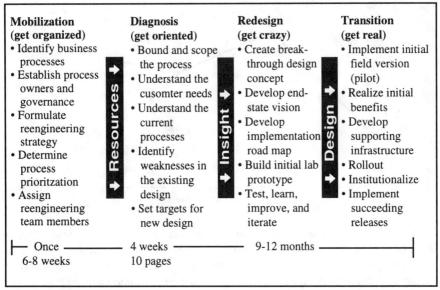

Mobilization (get organized)	Diagnosis (get oriented)	Redesign (get crazy)	Transition (get real)
• Identify business processes • Establish process owners and governance • Formulate reengineering strategy • Determine process prioritzation • Assign reengineering team members	• Bound and scope the process • Understand the cusomter needs • Understand the current processes • Identify weaknesses in the existing design • Set targets for new design	• Create break-through design concept • Develop end-state vision • Develop implementation road map • Build initial lab prototype • Test, learn, improve, and iterate	• Implement initial field version (pilot) • Realize initial benefits • Develop supporting infrastructure • Rollout • Institutionalize • Implement succeeding releases

(arrows labeled: Resources → Insight → Design)

├── Once ──────── 4 weeks ──────── 9-12 months ──────────┤
6-8 weeks   10 pages

Figure 2: Business Process Reengineering Initiative Structure (adapted from Hammer and Company, 1996)

that the reengineering market will grow from $32 billion in 1994 to $57 billion in 1997 [Caldwell 1994]. Of the $57 billion, $40 billion is estimated to be spent on IT investments. Results achieved measuring the payoff of IT investments in reengineering contexts will inform the large IT component of reengineering. It also could be extrapolated to other IT investment contexts.

Research Motivation and Literature Review

Our review of previous research focus primarily on two areas: the emergence of non-traditional measurement systems for use in reengineering contexts; and a study of the published investment comparison frameworks.

Research Motivation

In a widely reported reengineering success story told by Dr. Michael Hammer, Hewlett-Packard used information technology to virtually centralize its purchasing department by connecting and facilitating coordination of dozens of divisional purchasing functions. The savings are reported as $500 million annually! Some (see for example Farrell, 1994) declare these type of results the only true measure of the success whether the reengineered process was imple-mented and then delivered as 'increased revenues, reduced costs, or greater cash flow.'

Reengineering is currently an undeniably popular tool. During

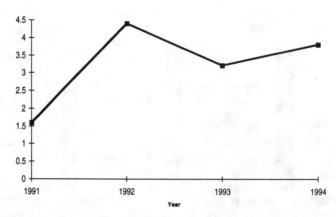

Figure 3: Average number of reengineering initiatives started for the years 1991 - 1994 (Note: In 1991 and 1992, organizations were asked how many reengineering they were sponsoring, in 1993 and 1994 they were asked how many initiative were attempting "radical change of critical business processes and their supporting systems to effect breakthrough gains in performance" (Deloitte & Touche, 1995).

the period 1993-1994 the percentage of organizations reporting as the 'jury still out' on reengineering effectiveness dropped from 27% to 7% and the percentage reporting 'satisfied' increased from 68% to 86% (Deloitte and Touche, 1995). As a result, reengineering is being increasingly implemented as a management tool (see Figure 3).

The top *InformationWEEK* computer firms report investing an average of 23% of their IS Budgets and an average of 3.41% of their annual revenue (representing a combined investment of more than $1.1 billion in reengineering during 1994 (Brynjolfsson & Hitt, 1995). Results similar to HP's are hard to argue with but not all reengineering results are as clear cut. Figure 4 indicates other types of reengineering results can produce organizational surpluses such as satisfaction and time that are not necessarily able to be assessed using financial measures.

Evaluating reengineering results requires a mechanism for tracing surpluses through the organization as they are translated into productivity improvements. IT investments sometimes return quantifiable savings but also can return performance improvement that can be leveraged in support of other strategic goals. The MIT/ *InformationWEEK* study examined two classes of IT investment strategies pursued by organizations. The first strategy (financial savings) focused on cost savings and improved management control type objectives. The second (customer orientation) focused on investments in quality, customer service, flexibility and speed. The latter approach provided organizations with a statistically significant performance improvement (Brynjolfsson & Hitt, 1995).

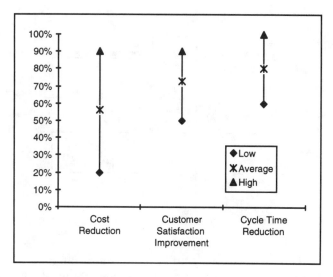

Figure 4: Typical Reengineering Results Ranges (as reported by Hammer and Company 1996).

Customer Focused Value Analysis

Much of the relevant research has its origin in Porter's [1985] value analysis concepts. The basic tenants of value analysis are that organizations should focus on sustaining a competitive advantage by creating and sustaining superior performance and that IT investment should play a role by focusing on core process areas offering strategic opportunities.

The Value Chain Model was developed to highlight specific organizational activities where competitive strategies can be best applied using IT. We have adapted it for use determining the characteristics of IT investment. The model represents the organization as a series of basic activities and classifies them as either 'primary activities' or 'support activities' for each line of business. Primary activities relate directly to the production and distribution of the final product. Support activities enable primary activities (see Figure 5). The concept translates into Hammers & Champy's (1993) concepts of value-added and non-value added work presented in *Reengineering the Corporation.* Increased surplus and organizational processes assessment are consistent with the a customer focus. As a result 'primary functions' take on new definition of customers - as recipients of IT enabled surplus (for those IT-based reengineering initiatives).

The value chain model is used to define customer-provider roles. The value-chain linkages indicate key measurement points at which the four VDOT initiatives should be assessed. Figure 6 illustrates how value chain analysis can be extended to derive linkages between

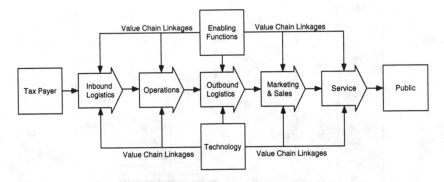

Figure 5: An example value chain analysis outcome based on Porter's model [1985].

organization process outputs and IT investment payoffs. Figure 6 is a close-up of any of the value chain linkages shown in Figure 5. It details our implementation of IT payoff analysis. The organizational direction will determine how far back information will have to be traced to identify the value-chain linkages. At each stage, each of the flows are refined into operational terms in order to make them visible and understood to the organizational operations.

Productivity Paradox

Studies involving IT investment during the 1980s suggested a sharp drop in service sector productivity improvement during a period of significant IT investment. Hypothesis surrounding the paradox include:

• Faulty measurement system - productivity may not generate profit-ability;
• Productivity improvement time lags associated with workplace techno-logical advancements;
• Organizational failure to coordinate productivity initiatives; and
• Combinations of above factors.

A more in depth examination of IT investment at the time demonstrated significant differences between the effects of IT invest-ment in the service and manufacturing sectors of the economy. A 44% ROI was traced to manufacturing sector investment which accounted for only 15% of all IT investment. But the remaining 85% service sector investment demonstrated to have only a 1.9% ROI. The implications of this "Productivity Paradox" triggered doubt concerning potential return of IT investments.

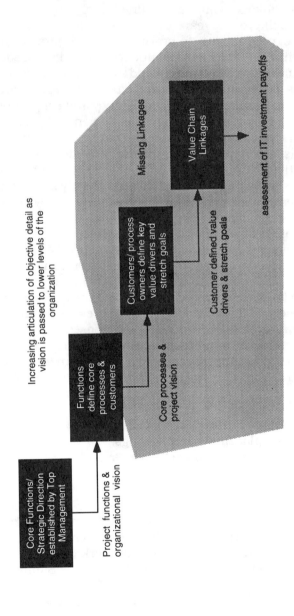

Figure 6: Porter's value chain analysis requires further refinement to facilitate IT investment payoff analysis.

A conclusion offered by Brynjolfsson is that organizations can fail to reap expected IT investment productivity improvements because functional and hierarchical process imbalances may arise. "A successful [technology] intervention to increase performance requires that a number of actions be taken at different organizational levels and that they be congruent in their goals, strategies, actions, and measures" [Brynjolfsson & Hitt 1994]. From an organizational perspective, once the linkage points are defined, real productivity improvements can be achieved by carefully devising measurement systems that facilitate productivity improvements and provide synchronization opportunities. The interdependencies and their associated flows can only be measured and understood through process analysis. Although analysis is required to insure that all linkage point measurement systems maintain strategic consistency and congruence at all organizational levels. This finding is complemented by a National Research Council study that indicates organizational performance is a function of at least seven interrelated criteria: effectiveness, efficiency, quality, productivity, innovation, quality of work life, and profitability. Their attempts to aggregate individual productivity measures or to disaggregate organizational measures were thwarted by the dissimilarity in measures of output (Harris, 1994).

Another Brynjolfsson et al. (1993) study indicates that IT investment changes the fundamental structure of the value chain by facilitating organizational transformation into a value adding network of new, smaller firms that function as component parts. Belcher and Watson [1993] discovered evidence of surplus occurring in soft areas and indicated the need for soft measures. They measured IT investment improvements in quality as opposed to quantity, noting that traditional accounting tools do not trace the ensuing profitability or cost reduction to their respective IT investments. Their concepts of 'hard' and 'soft' IT investment benefits measurement included:

- improved decision making;
- information distribution cost savings;
- services replacement cost savings;
- software replacement cost savings; and
- intangible benefits.

An additional observation was that business value must be measured at least at: individual, departmental, and organizational levels. Simmons concurs noting the existence of a similarly structured IT benefits and measurement framework (Simmons, 1996). The five types of benefits and measures identified by Simmons are:

- Increased Efficiency: Economic, through cost avoidance or reduction;

- Increased Effectiveness: Economic (resulting from the use of the information) and key performance indicators (if value-based management has been implemented);
- Added Value: Usually no direct measure for IT system alone; evaluate return from the entire business strategy;
- Marketable Product: Economic through establishment of market price; and
- IT Infrastructure: Usually no direct measure; corporate policy decision.

Mounting evidence supports the belief that traditional investment measurement systems are not only inadequate for IT investments but are often secondary management considerations in making IT investments. Observers (Simmons, 1996; Drucker, 1995; and Ginther, 1996) conclude that often the executive's primary objectives of IT investment initiatives are non-financial and that understanding the limits of data analysis tools as well as the limits of the data is key to being able to use existing measurement systems.

Measurement Framework Survey

We found two published reports of process cross-comparison and briefly discuss each below.

Process Value Estimation. We found a published use of reengineering as a context for development of a comparison framework reported by Pacific Bell. Pacific Bell developed a process value estimation (PVE) methodology. Noting how "It is hard to stay focused on the mathematics of value when an army of consultants are urging managers to 'Obliterate' or 'Rip Apart' complex business processes" Housel et al. (1995) describe PVE as a means of quantifying and comparing the value added components of pre- and post- reengineered processes. Using PVE, the market process performance is evaluated in terms of the revenue it generates per single change in 'raw material' (or process input). PVE analysis focuses on determining return on investment in processes and measures increased value comparing the amount of value added by a process before and after reengineering. It documents process contribution to surplus for repeatable tasks. This enables Pacific Bell to determine how much value the company is receiving from its investment in any part of the process. The importance of the approach is the emphasis on defining reengineering project phases and the input, output, process-based analysis. We adapted these concepts for use in our framework. PVE appears useful in industries with well-defined repetitive core processes consisting of limited numbers of simple tasks that have well-defined payoffs. Successful application depends on being able to correctly identifying core processes and isolate financial effects of core process changes.

Control Points And Level Of Automation. Lucas et al. (1996) apply two techniques (control points and level of automation) for comparing data flow diagrams as surrogates of the reengineered processes, describing the before and after states. The process comparisons provided feedback on the extent to which two alternative processes overlap. The author proposes them as surrogates of radicalness and difficulty. The techniques also track the following metrics: *obsolescence* - via the percentage of obsolete functions and the extent to which functions have become obsolete; *newness* - via the percentage of changed functions; and *extent of automation* - the nature of the shift of stable functions to more automated categories. Aggregated, these provide indications of *system-wide change* due to the reengineering. The complete comparison framework consisted of both qualitative and quantitative information as shown below. The technique documents operational changes but not strategic issues and may fail to provide guidance facilitating syncretistic Business Process Reengineering (BPR) combinations. From Lucas et al. we have incorporated several metrics (indicated by the check marks "√") in our comparison framework presented in the next section.

VDOT IT Investment Assessment Framework

As shown previously (in Figure 2), the VDOT reengineering initiatives share a common structure. Within this structure, initiative characteristics permitted us to derive a framework for assessing the IT component of the reengineering investment. The framework development process is outlined in Figure 8.

Figure 9 illustrates how identifying the IT investment components, depends on first defining reengineering payoffs and then subtracting those payoff components that are not technology dependent. Figure 10 presents a sample comparison framework. The framework analysis is described below according to its information representation of populated cells (the next section presents two

Qualitative information:	Quantitative data:
√ Changes in organization structure	• Comparison of data flow diagrams
√ Major changes in work flows and functions performed	√ Comparisons of resources required previously
√ Interface changes	√ Investment
√ Major changes in technology	• Return on investment
• Impact on the organization	√ Documents changes attributable to reengineering

Figure 7: Merrill Lynch Process Comparison Framework Metrics [Lucas et al. 1996]

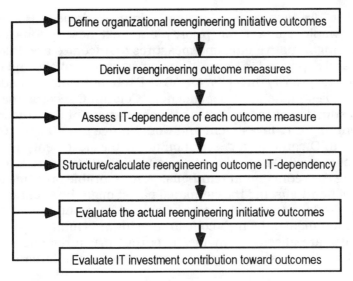

Figure 8: Evaluating IT investments in a reengineering context.

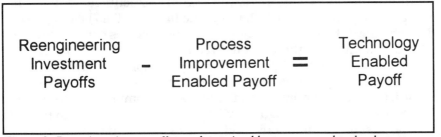

Figure 9: Reengineering payoffs are determined by process and technology enabled payoffs.

	A	B	C	D	E	F	G	H
3	Outcome Measure Priority	Outcome Measure	Expected Outcome IT Dependence	Estimated Outcome Payoff	Estimated Solution Importance	Actual Outcome IT Dependence	Actual Outcome Payoff	Actual Solution Importance
4	1							
5	2							
6	3							
7		Expected Initiative IT Depedency:						
8		Estimated Technology Enabled Payoff:						
9		Estimated Process Improvement Payoff:						
10		Estimated Initiative Payoff:						
11					Actual Initiative IT Depedency:			
12					Actual Technology Enabled Payoff:			
13					Actual Process Improvement Payoff:			
14					Actual Initiative Payoff:			

Figure 10: Sample Comparison Framework.

examples of framework application). Framework cells B4-B6 for example, would contain the priority and text descriptions of the reengineering initiative outcome measures. Outcomes are linked to strategy and expressed in terms of customer-based payoffs and listed according to priority in cells A4-A6. Each outcome measure is evaluated to estimate its IT dependency. Column C records these as subject estimates of the percent that achievement of the outcome is dependent on an IT investment and would range from 0% to 100%.

Column D contains a description of the measurement outcome. For example - cell D4 could describe an outcome measure aimed at measuring the reduction in hand-offs. A measurable outcome is the number of hand-offs and the estimated payoff might be a reduction of three hand-offs in the new process. Column E contains estimates of each measurement outcome's contribution towards initiative success. Percentages are allocated among the output measures and each is assessed for their estimated contribution toward the initiative outcome.

Using this structure, the weighted average can be combined in multi-criteria format to determine what percentage of the total reengineering initiative is IT-based. The figure (cell E7) can be use to describe the outcome IT-dependence. Dependencies can be combined with an estimate of the expected reengineering payoff (cell E10) to determine the expected payoff of the technology component of the investment. Once the reengineering initiative has established a track record, the corresponding 'actual' cells can be computed (cells F4-H6). It is expected that most figures will be revised in response to periodic re-analysis of assumptions and progress. In the same manner described previously, a post implementation weighted average can be recalculated to obtain 'actual' initiative IT dependency and IT investment payoffs. With this information, reengineering payoffs can be allocated among IT-based enablers and process-based enablers and the IT investment can be evaluated and linked to specific organizational performance or productivity payoffs. The next subsection describes the framework analysis leading to its population and use. This is followed by a section illustrating its use with an example.

Initiative reengineering outcome measures must be derived before initiative payoffs can be usefully articulated and evaluated. Outcome measure determination consists of: determining initiative outcomes; mapping measurements to outcomes; process alignment; and evaluation. These represent generalized information flows - gathered and summarized during process development. Framework application is context sensitive and tends to overlap especially between process alignment and evaluation. Figure 11 is a data model describing the information requirements that must result from any attempt to assess IT investment in reengineering initiatives. The model is described

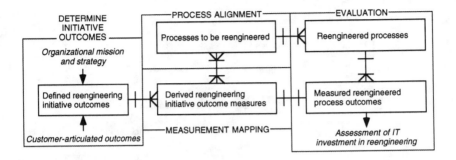

Figure 11: Redesign Comparison Framework

below according to its information flows.

Determine Initiative Outcomes

Determining initiative outcomes provides organizations with a means to assess their reengineering progress. To be most effective, reengineering initiative outcomes are defined best as contributions toward organizational strategy. Typically there are three perspectives of organizational strategy that need to be reconciled. Functional management, initiative sponsors, and customers often have their own perceptions of how they impact are impacted by organizational strategy. In order to be consistent, the expected outcomes must be understood as functionally equivalent by all stakeholders. Strategic outcomes must be linked and documented explicitly. Customers and customer vocabulary must be used to articulate the initiative outcomes. These must document common perception of the outcomes as held by the three stakeholder types. The output is a list of reengineering initiative outcomes requiring prioritization and alignment.

Figure 12 illustrates the complexity of reengineering initiative outcome setting. Initiative outcomes are an important tool for facilitating organizational vertical and horizontal integration. As shown in Figure 11, the end result is that each reengineering initiative is associated with a series of initiative specific outcomes.

Measurement Mapping

Defining and prioritizing outcome measurements is the purpose of measurement mapping. Multiple outcome measures can be linked to each reengineering initiative outcome. Once defined, they can be prioritized as shown on Figure 10. Cells B4-B6 describe specific outcomes that must be sustainable through implementation. There

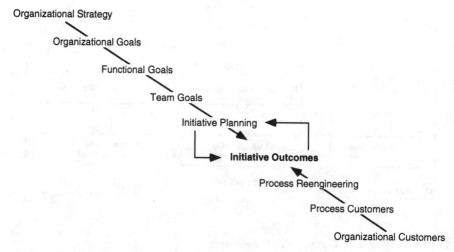

Figure 12: Reengineering Initiative Outcome Setting Complexity.

are a small number of clearly defined outcome measures that provide customer value, support strategic positioning, guide team goals and establish the goals supporting organizational strategies. The output of measurement mapping is the target processes and measurements needed for comparison throughout reengineering. As shown previously in Figure 11, at measurement mapping conclusion, one or more specific outcome measures are derived for each reengineering initiative outcome.

Process Alignment

Process alignment is characterized by the initiation of activities aimed at reinventing the existing process. Outcome measures developed during measurement mapping can be used to guide process and prioritization decisions of the BPR initiative. At the end of this phase, the reengineering initiative outcome measures are associated with processes to be reengineered. As shown previously in Figure 11, a specific outcome can be linked to many processes and each reengineered process can be associated with many outcome measures.

Evaluation

Evaluation involves assessing actual process outcomes against the expected initiative outcomes developed has part of measurement mapping prior to reengineering. The assessment involves refinement of the numbers in cell F4-H6 of Figure 10. At the conclusion of the framework application process each candidate reengineering process is associated with one or more attempts to reengineer it. Each of those reengineered processes are linked with one or more process outcomes. These process outcomes are matched one for one with reengineering initiative outcome measures. From these the success of the initiative can be evaluated and annualized. Once the measured process reengineering outcomes are stabilized, the IT investment can be evaluated by first reevaluating the original IT-based outcome measure percentages to see if the predicted values match the actual percentages. If not, they can be adjusted.

Framework Use Example: the BERT - Hiring Process Outcome Measurement

As part of IHRIS, the VDOT Human Resource - Benefits and Employment Reengineering Team (BERT) is currently reengineering agency's hiring process. BERT defined 'hiring' as providing the human component to work and is working to design and implement a new hiring process that distributes hiring decisions down to lower organizational levels while expanding hiring options. The new process must facilitate hiring practices capable of more closely matching new hires with the work needs and VDOT's work environment.

BERT members received significant input from hiring managers and HR professionals while looking to strategic management for additional guidance. VDOT's strategic plan includes the following points:

- redesign of work processes and procedures that reflect value-added activities;
- distributed authority (empowerment);
- selection on the basis of outcome-based competencies; and
- customer orientation (internal and external).

HR has identified agency managers who have hiring responsibilities as their customers. Hiring manager feedback identified the following drawbacks associated with the existing process:

- short probationary periods fail to reflect seasonal responsibilities;
- inability to respond to short response time requirements that accommodate immediate hiring needs;
- inflexibility to accommodate diverse organizational responsibilities - providing a one-size-fits-all solution; and
- hiring manager's cannot incorporate prospective employee's peers counsel in hiring decisions.

Using process decomposition, this example focuses on two hiring process outcomes: improving the selection responsiveness and improving the fill responsiveness. Both outcomes are measured by customer satisfaction. Figure 13 (selection) and Figure 14 (fill) show application of the framework - assessing the payoff associated with the

IT investments in these two aspects of the hiring process reengineering. The outcome measures for selection (Figure 13) include: increasing the scope of hiring criteria; increasing the degree of localization; increasing the longevity of the applicant pool; and increasing the number of hiring criteria. Figure 14 shows the fill outcome measures as: increasing the number of fill option parameters; increasing the number of fill options; reducing the minimum time to fill a job; and reducing the new employee probationary period. In both figures, Column C contains an assessment of how much each outcome is IT-dependent.

The metrics for each outcome are shown in column D, articulating the expected results in measurable terms. Column E contains the initiative teams collective assessment of each outcome's individual contribution to the total project.

Presently BERT is working to design process that members expect will support expanded and more customer focused processes. Distributing authority requires enabling employees of localities (the customers) with the ability to make their own decisions while being aware of and responsible for the consequences of the decision (legal liabilities, employee perceptions etc.). HR will take on an advisory role supported by IT-based systems, and:

• provide a skills list template on employee applications;
• provide behavioral, competency-based questions to support expanded peer interviewing;
• support the construction and posting of job announcements automatically (point and click environment);
• decentralize/localize the hiring process to the lowest levels of the organization as appropriate; and
• provide employment law training/advice.

The new process involves 1) identifying a work need, 2) identifying and matching the appropriate worker, and 3) filling the position in a manner that matches the work need. For example, a short term need might require a short term hire. Consider an example of the new process at work. Fredericksburg district is short a fiscal technician. The traditional way of getting the work done would be to start the process required to hire a fiscal technician. This initiates the "as is" employment process which has been taking 45-90 days. Using the new process the workgroup supervisor consults a computer-based advisor and asks for advice on getting a task accomplished that is equivalent to hiring a fiscal technician. The next week, a new fiscal technician begins work as a temp.

Once the new processes have been implemented, economic and performance metrics must be broken out in two ways as shown in Figure 15. First, the net improvement must be calculated by subtracting the old process outcomes from the new process outcomes, resulting

	A	B	C	D	E	F	G	H
31	Reengineering Initiative: Benefits and Employment Hiring Process							
32	Reengineering Outcome: improving the selection responsiveness as measured by customer satisfaction							
33	Outcome Measure Priority	Outcome Measure	Expected Outcome IT Dependence	Estimated Outcome Payoff	Estimated Solution Importance	Actual Outcome IT Dependence	Actual Outcome Payoff	Actual Solution Importance
34	1	increasing the scope of hiring criteria	10%	to include knowledge, abilities, and competencies	30%	10%	scope increased to include knowledge, abilities, and competencies	40%
35	2	increasing the degree of localization	60%	2 levels (from central office to residency)	30%	50%	increased localization by 2 levels	30%
36	3	increasing the longevity of the applicant pool	0%	to 90 days will decrease the number of recruiting cycles from 12 to 3 annually	20%	25%	increased the longevity to 60 days decreased recruiting cycles from 12 to 6 annually	20%
36	4	increasing the number of hiring criteria	10%	from an average of 30 to 50/job category	20%	10%	increased by 15 criteria/job criteria	10%
37			Expected Initiative IT Depedency:		23%	(Weighted Average)		
38			Estimated Technology Enabled Payoff:		$115,000			
39			Estimated Process Improvement Payoff:		$385,000			
40			Estimated Initiative Payoff:		$500,000			
41								
42						Actual Initiative IT Depedency:		25%
43						Actual Technology Enabled Payoff:		$112,500
44						Actual Process Improvement Payoff:		$337,500
45						Actual Initiative Payoff:		$450,000

*Figure 13: Sample framework to illustrate the **selection** outcome payoff calculations.*

	A	B	C	D	E	F	G	H
47	Reengineering Initiative: *Benefits and Employment Hiring Process*							
48	Reengineering Outcome: *improving the fill responsiveness (as measured by customer satisfaction)*							
49	Outcome Measure Priority	Outcome Measure	Expected Outcome IT Dependence	Estimated Outcome Payoff	Estimated Solution Importance	Actual Outcome IT Dependence	Actual Outcome Payoff	Actual Solution Importance
50	1	increasing the number of fill option parameters	66%	from 4 to 12 hiring parameters	20%	75%	increased to 8 hiring parameters	50%
51	2	increasing the number of fill options	66%	from 2 currently to six	20%	75%	from 2 currently to seven	30%
52	3	reduce the minimum time to fill a job	75%	from 45 days to 1 day	30%	75%	reduced it to 5 days	10%
53	4	increase new employee probationary periods	0%	from 6 months to 12 months	30%	0%	increased it to 12 months	10%
54			Expected Initiative IT Depedency:		49%	(Weighted Average)		
55			Estimated Technology Enabled Payoff:		$1,467,000			
56			Estimated Process Improvement Payoff:		$1,533,000			
57			Estimated Initiative Payoff:		$3,000,000			
58								
59						Actual Initiative IT Depedency:		68%
60						Actual Technology Enabled Payoff:		$2,700,000
61						Actual Process Improvement Payoff:		$1,300,000
						Actual Initiative Payoff:		$4,000,000

*Figure 14: Sample framework to illustrate the **full** outcome payoff calculations.*

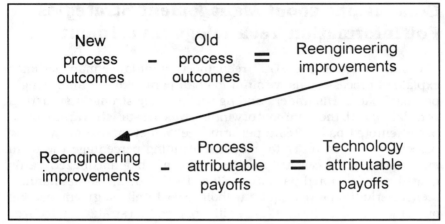

Figure 15: Technology investment payoff calculation.

in the reengineering improvement. Second, subtracting the process attributable improvements would leave the IT investment payoff.

Sample IT investment payoff calculations for the hiring process reengineering outcomes are documented in the two framework applications - Figure 13 and Figure 14. Number and scope of hiring criteria (Figure 13, Rows 37 & 34) improved by 15 and 3 respectively. Additional criteria such as teamwork, customer orientation and innovation are within the expanded areas including ability, knowledge and demonstrated competencies. For the selection outcome, 'increasing the degree of localization' (Figure 13, Row 35) reflects the level of delegation of hiring responsibility. A two level improvement represents authority distribution from the central office to the district office and then to the hiring manager. While 'longevity of the applicant pool' (Figure 13, Row 36) has improved by 30 days (from 30 to 60) the improvement is a result of policy changes rather than enabling technology (Cell C36). Reengineering improvements associated with the fill process are more technology intensive. The fill process (known within the agency as 'the BERT fill options') will employ a desktop application to guide the hiring manager in decision tree format making fill a technology dependent process.

When actual instead of projected outcome measures are available, VDOT will be able to calculate the IT dependency for each reengineering initiative outcome (25% of selection and 68% for the fill outcomes). By applying the real reengineering annual benefits (estimated to be $450K for selection and $4 million for fill) illustrated as examples, the technology investment payoffs can be calculated ($112K for selection and $2.7 million for fill) and used to inform any subsequent IT investment decisions and evaluate the results.

Conclusions about Management Strategies For Information Technology Investment

Dan Saverline, the VDOT reengineering initiative manager once explained process goals within a football paradigm, paraphrasing a popular coach. His understanding was that the strongest statistical correlation with the team goal of winning was the statistic yards gained per attempted pass. Team performance was evaluated on winning percentage but in order to maximize winning percentage the team emphasized a successful practice regiment that maximized yards gained per attempted pass (Saverline, 1996). In the same manner, reengineering initiatives require an indirect goal of aligning reengineering outcome and outcome measures with organization strategic objectives before IT investments in reengineering can be assessed. This chapter has presented an analogous approach to assessing IT investment payoff in reengineering contexts. The framework described here can help management determine its own winning strategy. The framework permits VDOT and other organizations to:

• maintain strategic direction at all levels
• guide development process requirements
• support customer value as it is perceived by the customer
• support continuous improvement
• track business value at the level in which it is added
• provide customer feedback (lagging indicator)
• provide early warning signal (leading indicator)
• foster organizational coordination

In addition, it addresses two payoffs are desired by organization management:

1. Identification of those reengineering initiative outputs that worked well and those that did not and the reasons why. This analysis will provide management with better information for formulating initiative outputs useful to future reengineering efforts.
2. A now possible, cross initiative analysis will give organization management better information on the size and shape of possible investment 'returns.'

Management can use this case study to inform their own IT investment payoff assessment process. IT payoff assessment must accurately reflect organizational complexity in order to guide and support organizational change and aid in determining reengineering initiative success. Reengineering initiatives can be seen as efforts to respond to the transformed set of organizational improvement priorities (Dixon et al., 1994). Often information and management systems do not provide the kind of feedback required to assist personnel working towards reengineering initiative goals. The assessment system must then be aligned with newly defined goals of the altered operating environment. Measurement frameworks such as the one described in this chapter also permit surplus to be redistributed across functional boundaries. By redefining the focus on customers, value, and organizational objectives, accurate IT investment assessment can be accomplished.

One of the best approaches to embracing change is for organizations to adopt measurement and reward systems supporting the changed processes as part of the change strategy. In effect, the measurement system can become a tool for pushing surplus through the organization, turning surplus into productivity. Reengineering's purpose is also to deliver a surplus to the organization, the challenge is how best to apply that surplus to the fulfillment of strategy. A measurement system that identifies strategic, provider, and customer issues centering on value can build measures around the transference of surplus.

Process outcome measures are recently developed however lessons can be learned from software engineering. McCabe (1976) published widely used process measures that effect software performance. Principles that are used to evaluate software engineering practices and alternatives can be applied to business processes (Clark, 1996). In short, process measures aid in documenting process characteristics. They can be used to link to performance indicators and team goals making them useful as continuous improvement tools. In addition, this form of analysis permits the organization to gauge its own organizational capability to take advantage of reengineering opportunities.

In order to facilitate these analysis forms, more specific forms of communication (e.g., process representation) need to be developed. Another promising area is to develop a computer support environment facilitating process development and results maintenance. This would enhance metric collection capabilities and open still further, the observational window. Subsequent analysis could focus on results in five areas:

1. What outputs and/or measurements were able to be successfully compared across the four initiatives?
2. What outputs and/or measurements were not comparable across the four initiatives?
3. What do these results imply for assessing the payoffs of individual reengineering initiatives?
4. What strategies should be refined for additional measuring and assessing of information technology investments?
5. Can the framework be expanded to include a 'knowledge assessment' that would facilitate changing skill requirements?

Acknowledgments
This research has been sponsored in part by the Virginia Departments of Transportation and, of Training & Personnel. Bill Girling is the research initiative architect. John Clark of Comptek assisted in the concept development. Lynda Hodgson collaborated on the project. The authors wish to thank the following organizational reengineering project teams, and in particular, the following individuals for providing us with a opportunity to participate in such an interesting and productive research opportunity:

Project Manager:
Daniel M. Saverline

Team Leaders:
Debbie Mitchell
Sandy Arnett
Alison Anderson
Sandy Fox
Jeff Shrader
Brooke Hawks

Team Members and Participants
Daphne Ashwell, Tim Fortune, Tammy Smith, Tonia Burton, Lezlie Ellis, Joe Staton, Jane Wimbush, Gregg Nolan, Angie Walker, Stan Artis, Cindy Norman, Nancy Berry, Michael Pierce, Theresa Daughtry, Haston Presnell, Ken Lantz, Glenn Macmillan, Jim Barrett

Chapter 18

Achieving Information Systems Value: A Case Study Analysis

Jack D. Callon
San Jose State University

The study that produced the material for this chapter started with a focus on how to deal with the financial implications of client server computing. As often happens, the scope of the study became broader than was originally intended. There is a very simple explanation as to why this happened. Logical, effective approaches to the information systems value issues are not unique to client server computing. They are fundamental to how an enterprise chooses to deal with its information systems financial value issues. Both of the case studies confirm that this starts with the need to establish the best possible working relationship between the information systems organization and the users that they support. The success in accomplishing this is then validated by the level of satisfaction that users have regarding the value of information systems based on what they are charged by the information systems organization.

The two case studies are the Test Measurement Organization (TMO) of Hewlett–Packard and National Semiconductor. They are similar yet different. Both deal with large companies where the information systems organization supports users in multiple locations throughout the world. The Hewlett–Packard TMO example was driven by cost reduction pressures. This triggered a major consolidation of multiple data centers into a single, centralized organization and the posturing of the new information systems organization with eighteen thousand

*worldwide users. The National Semiconductor information systems
redesign took advantage of a new vision for the company. This made
it possible and logical to rethink the posture and relationship of the
information systems organization with those users that it supports.
Both cases were both broad scope and comprehensive in terms of the
evaluation process and the approaches that were implemented.*

Explaining the value of the significant and often increasing cost of
information systems (IS) is a problem for many companies. The
prevailing view is that the solution to this problem is either through
precise measurement or a clever, new cost assessment methodology.
This chapter counters with the contention that a better approach is
building a management process that effectively aligns the activities of
the IS with those that it supports. Good dialogue and an effective
on-going working relationship can do an effective job of explaining the
value of the investment in information systems. This contention is
supported by an in-depth analysis of the approach taken by two
organizations to explain the value of their investment in information
systems: 1) the Hewlett-Packard Test Measurement Division (TMO)
and 2) National Semiconductor Corporation.

Some Basic Premises To Be Substantiated By
This Case Study Analysis

To accomplish this analysis, it is necessary to establish some
basic premises. A first point is that organizations lose sight of the
difference between controlling expenditures and realizing a return on
investment. There is clearly a difference between the value of the
return on IS investments and budgetary control strategies that are
implemented to manage these financial costs. One would expect that
the determination of IS value, the focus on IS use and the controls
gained by financial strategies would be realized through the same
business process. Unfortunately, this is often not the case.

Assessments of the value of the return on IS investments are made
by company executives and operational management. These are based
on support provided by IS in managing the business more effectively
and posturing the organization for the future. The value of IS can be
categorized according to its three potential roles:

1) Efficiency that can be measured by productivity improvements.
2) Effectiveness that involves computer-based support to broaden the
   scope of specific tasks, activities and even complete individual jobs.
3) Competitive advantage through the use of information systems that
   directly or indirectly provide value to customers.

Financial strategies for IS support and services often have a

Evolution of Financial Strategy

Phases	I	II	III	IV
Financial Strategy	Budget	Business Case Post Install Audit	Charge Out System	Management Process

Figure 1

primary objective to control costs, to prioritize the development of new systems or to allocate increasingly larger IS costs to those that benefit from the use of the computer-based systems. Many companies have managed the financial aspects of IS with a four phase approach graphically presented in Figure 1.

Phase I - Budgets as a Means of Financial Control

When an initial computer system is implemented within a company (Phase I) the total cost is often relatively small compared to the total operating cost for the entire company. The primary use of the first computer-based system is often focused on a specific area like accounting, manufacturing or engineering. The managers that use the computer system control its use and are responsible for the related costs. This cost is included in the department budget and the challenge is to accomplish as much as possible with the computer resources without exceeding the budget.

The value of IS in this phase is based on an assessment by those that were responsible for obtaining the initial computer system. This assessment is very subjective unless it is relatively easy to articulate productivity gains or direct personnel cost savings.

Phase II - Business Plan and Post-Installation Audits

Success with computer-based systems within an organization breeds growth in both their use and related costs. An increasing demand for computer-based applications and the related growth in cost often prompts the need for better prioritization of the requests for implementation of new applications. A logical method involves the creation of a proposal in the form of a business case by the responsible user manager. This asks for justification for a new information system by identifying the systems development and operating costs and the business value to be gained. To confirm that the benefits proposed were actually accomplished, a post-installation audit could be made six to twelve months following the actual implementation of the new system. This approach would prioritize all new application requests through a review process. The post-install audit can confirm that the desired value of the new systems was realized through specific benefits. The problem with this approach is that it does not do a good job of tracking cost and benefits. The entire process tends to focus on a particular time frame even if the business case addressed multiple years. This prompts a sentiment that something is needed to accomplish better financial management of information systems.

Phase III - A Charge-Out Approach Asks Users to Pay for IS Support and Services

An axiom based on the growth of IS costs is that users should pay for the information systems support and services that they receive. Implied by this approach is that the cost is justified if the users are willing to pay for it. There are a number of ways that a charge-out process can be implemented directing who pays for what and at what price. The end result is an allocation of all or most of the costs related to information technology within the organization. This approach provides what many feel is better financial control but frequently fails to provide a better way to explain the value of information systems.

Many companies profess satisfaction with a charge-out system since it is logical that those that create and use information systems should pay for them. But a problem arises when a senior executive wants to know the value obtained for the company's very large information systems costs. The answer that one hundred percent is charged out to users often fails to satisfy the executive since a charge-out process simply transfers the cost from the IS organization to the users. A charge-out process spreads the costs among multiple departmental budgets but it does not minimize the cost. More importantly, it does not answer the value question. A general truth becomes evident in this situation. Even the most supportive executive has a pain threshold regarding the cost of information systems. When that threshold is reached, it becomes necessary to provide better answers to the IS value question than "it is all charged out to user departments."

Phase IV - A Management Process to Address Information Systems Value Questions

The focus of a management process must be based on those factors that drive the success of the business. Aligning information systems with these success factors is fundamental to creating an appropriate management process. As stated earlier, the primary role of information systems can be either efficiency, effectiveness or competitive advantage—or combinations of all three. Which of these would be the basis for an appropriate management process is dictated by the key success factors of the business. This is easily said and difficult to accomplish. Two organizations that concluded that it was necessary to create a management process to better address the IS value issues were the two companies that will be evaluated in the rest of this chapter. Their similarities and differences in approach will be highlighted in the final conclusions of the chapter.

Hewlett-Packard Test Measurement Organization: Changing the Way to Think About Information Technology

Introduction

The Test Measurement Organization (TMO) based in Santa Clara, California is the instrumentation product division of Hewlett-Packard (HP). It is the original part of the company founded by David Packard and Bill Hewlett in 1938 in the most famous garage in Palo Alto. Faced with the same increasing competitive pressures as other technology-based companies, a standard part of the HP culture has become "Do more, do it faster and do it with less resources." This seems to be working since HP, unlike a number of its large computer industry competitors, has been able to avoid large financial losses. This record was challenged in 1992 and resulted in a company-wide focus on cost structure that triggered a chain-reaction of business priorities that provided an interesting IS value story. One of the cost reduction efforts prompted the consolidation of fourteen Test Measurement Organization information technology (IT)* organizations into one. Historically, HP had included IT groups as an integral part of the operating units. An evaluation in 1992 concluded that this was not the most cost-effective approach given the dynamics of the business environment and alternatives enabled by distributed systems technologies.

The consolidation of the multiple IT organizations was completed in 1993. Led by Karen Rogge, Worldwide TMO IT Manager, the new organization consisted of three hundred managers and professionals to support a very large, worldwide group of 18,000 users with major operations in the U.S., Germany and Japan. It was obviously important for the new IT organization to evaluate how its users viewed

---

*HP uses IT as the terminology to describe its information systems organizations.

IT systems and support to better understand both their opportunities and challenges. The conclusion was that the users felt that the quality of their systems and support was poor, the charges for IT support were too high, and they didn't particularly like working with the IT personnel.

A number of alternatives were considered to address these complaints. This raised some very important questions. Did the IT organization really understand who it was supporting and what was important to them in terms of IT services? Did it understand how to improve quality and cost-effectiveness? Finally, how would the answers to these questions add up to an approach that benefits both the IT organization and supports the business success of the Test Measurement Organization? The conclusion was to position the IT organization as a business within a business. Users would be treated like customers of the IT organization's business within TMO. While this concept has been around for a long time, it was selected as the best approach for the IT organization to address both short-term and long-term business needs.

The new vision for the IT organization was: "Changing the way people work together by becoming recognized as the experts in integrated information technology services." To accomplish this meant capitalizing on opportunities in process innovation while maintaining and selectively enhancing IT service offerings. By better applying IT capabilities, the TMO customers would be able to improve their business results. The primary goal of the new IT organization can be summarized as follows: to increase customer satisfaction by reducing operational costs and aligning the IT services portfolio to meet the needs of the customer. Guiding principles, summarized in Figure 2, highlighted the importance of the focus of the new model, cost structure competitiveness, organizational implications and the need for business partners.

Customer satisfaction had to be based on what the customer considered important and not what the IT organization felt was needed. Reducing operational costs also meant achieving cost com-

Focus	Invest in major trends in cross-organizational networked solutions and services.
Cost Structure	Achieve competitive cost structure for service offerings.
Organization	Reduce decisionmaking layers and increase responsiveness to business partners.
Partnerships	Forge solid partnerships with internal and external suppliers of information technology services.

Figure 2: Guiding Principles

petitiveness based on outsourcing possibilities and best-of-breed benchmarks. Outsourcing loomed as a possibility if these expectations were not met. Adding to the challenge was the fact that customers were often completely unaware of IT service costs or were at least confused. They also did not trust the cost allocations and couldn't find value in the services that they purchased.

The new IT organization needed to make some fundamental changes if it was to meet the expectations that prompted its creation through consolidation. In addition, it was necessary to focus on the attitude and morale of the IT employees. The consolidation had subjected them to major changes and this needed to be effectively addressed. IT personnel were being asked to wear a business hat and address how they could help run TMO better based on business and not technical results. They were being asked to break away from the traditional mode of providing IT services and allocating costs to one that involved marketing IT services and enumerating services to customers based on customer needs. This represented a culture change for the IT employees and the new model needed their acceptance and commitment to succeed. As indicated in the Figure 3, an agile, skilled and motivated IT team was not just desirable it was necessary to accomplish the objectives of the new IT organization.

Specific Approach

As summarized in Figure 4, this entire endeavor was objective, thorough and required almost two years to complete. The new approach provided a model that realized the primary objective that motivated the entire process. It conveyed a superior value proposition for all information technology products and services at an acceptable cost to the 18,000 employees throughout TMO's worldwide factory and field organizations.

Initial Three Year Objectives

OBJECTIVE	STRATEGY	MEASURE
Increase customer satisfaction	•Increase customer focus •Streamline operational processes •Reduce operational costs	•Customer satisfaction index ratings •Quality/response time •Competitive rates
Increase return on investment	•Evolve scenario planning process •Increase new product offerings	•Market share % •Turnaround time •Market share %
Develop an agile, skilled and motivated team	•Evolve a learning organization	•Motivation •Agility (skill matrix)

Figure 3: Initial Three-Year Objectives

---

1. Understand Customers and Their Needs.
2. Define the Market Segments.
3. Specify Customer Segments.
4. Identify IT Competitors and Partners.
5. Define Products and Services Including Cost Drivers, Pricing Methodologies and Customer Invoicing.
6. Complete Development/Introduction Plan.
7. Develop/Refine Financial Analysis of IT Investments.
8. Identify Potential Problems Regarding the New Model.
9. Document Recommendations/Linkage Issues.
10. Develop First Year Tactical Plan.

Figure 4: Process to Develop and Implement the New TMO IT Strategy

Understand Customers and Their Needs

The process started by developing a better understanding of different types of customers and their specific needs. This was not just what customers say they wanted but what they really needed. Accomplishing this was not easy, but was done by having IT business consultants and in some cases, IT managers ask customers what was important to them. This involved looking at customer business goals and working with the customer to translate these into IT requirements. A technique involving the Hundred Dollar Test was used to accomplish this. A customer was asked, "If you were given a hundred dollars how would you invest the money in IT support and services based on your business goals?" It was not easy to answer the question regarding needs and priorities for IT services, but it was easier for them to make these decisions than for someone in the IT organization to do so. To ensure breadth and depth in the customer point-of-view, a cross section of what was important to the customer was addressed with multiple people and levels within the same organization.

A possible pitfall to this approach is misaligned strategies. The desires of the customer may not correspond to what the IT organization is prepared or even able to do. Conflicts can also arise based on the difference between short-term customer goals and the longer-term implications to the IT organization.

Define Customer and Market Segments

Customer segments were identified by conducting a test of the six value propositions shown in Figure 5. These related to the most important customer needs uncovered in the data collection and customer interviews. The breakdown of the customer segments was specific to the TMO organization. It showed no significant differences

	Customer Need	IT Value Proposition
1	Improve organizational agility and flexibility in a rapidly changing global marketplace.	Increase the ability of the businesses to create and support new geographically dispersed organization structures through worldwide information systems convergence and integration
2	Make TMO organizations more effective by enabling better, more timely decision-making processes.	Improve decision-making capabilities by providing a simple information environment that is accessible to all levels of the organization.
3	Achieve a better return on investments in desktop computing assets.	Increase the efficiency and effectiveness of individual contributors and work groups through better utilization of desktop computing devices.
4	Improve customer satisfaction and return on assets through deployment of signifi-cantly improved (reengineered) processes.	Increase the global competitiveness of the business by delivering services which increase the effectiveness of business process transformation initiatives.
5	Improve sales growth through improved time to market.	Increase the speed and reduce the complexity of transferring design and product information between organizations.
6	Maximize the lifetime return on process and system investments.	Optimize the operations return on investment in mature processes through the selective application of process and technology improvements.

Figure 5: Value Propositions

by businesses but demonstrated segmentation across functions. One segment showed a strong preference for integrated information and access tools across the entire organization. A second group wanted information access, process reengineering and customer-focused ways to facilitate business relations. The third group also had a strong preference for process reengineering with a priority to simplify and increase the speed of ordering TMO products.

This first and very challenging step also grouped IT services into a few logical, standard categories and agreed upon results by the customer shown in Figure 6. The overall TMO IT marketplace was

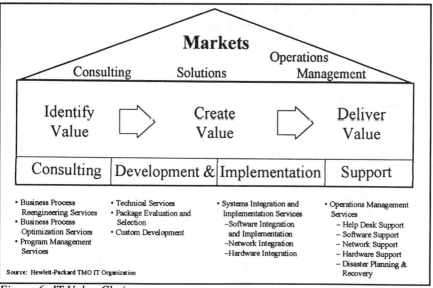

Figure 6: IT Value Chain

divided into three market segments: consulting, solutions and operations management. These market segments were derived from extensive data collection and customer interviews. Customer needs were also placed in three categories: 1) needs that reflect a concern for identifying value, 2) needs that reflect a concern for creating value, and 3) needs that reflect a concern for the delivery of value.

The services offered by TMO IT in these three markets were grouped as follows:

Consulting Services

Customers in the consulting market segment are making IT investments to address needs for function and/or business process planning and to identify breakthrough goals and opportunities that are supported by the following service categories:

1. **Business process reengineering** provides a variety of services including benchmarking, management of change and technology consulting. All of these activities are designed to help the business identify and achieve quantum performance improvements through significant, strategic changes in fundamental business methods. The focus of these services is enterprise-wide business process transformation.

2. **Business process optimization services** are very synergistic with the above consulting services. These include process redesign methodologies, requirements assessment and client consulting. These services focus on helping customers to identify process and technology improvements as part of continuous process improvement programs. They also focus on recreating process and systems linkages after reengineering is completed.

3. **Program management services** ensure that all activities associated with the delivery of customer solutions are integrated and aligned. These services include project management, IT portfolio management and information systems planning.

Solutions Services

Customers in the solutions market segment are making IT investments to create solutions via the integration of technology, software and networks. This includes:

1. **Technology services** to understand new technologies and find new ways of applying them to TMO businesses. The goal is to reduce time-to-market through implementation of technologies to solve business needs.

2. **Package evaluation and selection services** focus on identifying both current and future software packages to support major busi-

ness areas at the enterprise, workgroup and individual level. Key to the evaluation process will be performing an assessment of requirements in business processes and the information infrastructure. Vendor evaluation, selection, negotiation and contract management are also part of this service.

3. **Custom development services** provide the flexibility to develop a software solution where a package does not exist on the market to meet TMO business needs. Software professionals deliver state-of-the-art client/server applications to the TMO business.

4. **Solutions integration and implementation services** take a holistic approach to delivering both package and custom development solutions. Included in this service area are software, network and hardware integration and implementation services.

Operations Support Services

Customers in the operations market segment are making IT investments for the delivery of solutions to keep their operational processes running smoothly and productively. These services deliver value to customers by managing the total computing environment by combining and coordinating all aspects of the operations business. Operations support includes:

1. A reengineered **Help Desk** with multiple access paths to a coordinated response and delivery of all support activities.

2. Access to all aspects of **software, network and hardware support** regardless of platform or network through a single interface with the TMO IT organization. This team can procure and install new hardware and software solutions for the business in one seamless step. This worldwide approach to service delivery ensures consistent quality and effective service in the most economical way possible. It enables business organizations to remain focused on core competencies while the IT organization maintains the production environment and linkages to other HP organizations and business partners.

Identify IT Competitors and Business Partners

A major message to IT organizations from this TMO experience was the importance of determining strategic competencies relative to its part of the HP business and then developing and honing these capabilities. The point is not to get caught up in turf battles but to remember that the IT organization exists to help the business to be as competitive as possible. This dictates the need for a dialogue with both customers and potential vendors. A vendor that offers IT services that are more competitive than the IT organization becomes a potential supplier that can become a business partner. There are also situations where there is a need to develop something that is both new and unique to the TMO organization and this is done internally. On the other hand, a company that can deliver worldwide phone service with world class quality would definitely get the job. Business criteria are always used to dictate the need for both IT competencies and business partners.

Define Cost Drivers, Pricing Methodologies and Customer Invoicing

Once the customers were identified and their needs were determined the cost drivers and prices were then established for each major service category. While it may appear straightforward, establishing prices for every service was not easy.

This resulted in establishing three logical groupings of IT services: 1) operational and infrastructure services that can be managed on the basis of cost per unit of service, 2) strategic investments that change the way business is conducted are based on the total return to the business, and 3) management planning that is based on the percentage of total spending.

Fixed costs were a problem relative to pricing. These costs are often not controllable by a customer in the short run. A customer that wants a new voice service involving a new PBX will face a high fixed cost. Another important consideration regarding pricing was the policy regarding the recovery of all IT costs. While it expected full recovery, the TMO management was willing to accept a deviation of plus or minus five percent of the IT budget if it was supported by business requirements.

After determining the price schedules the IT organization was able to say to customers; "Here is our service and its price. What do you want to buy?" The IT organization was then held accountable for managing competitive rates. The following is a summary of the IT services and the price drivers that were included in the new financial model.

1. **Production Services:** Mainframe-based transaction processing provided in partnership with the Corporate Technology Centers including disaster recovery and print services. Expenses are allocated to customers based on weighted average CPU use plus disk storage space and mailboxes.

2. **Leveraged and Non-leveraged Application Support:** Data access for ad-hoc reporting, implementing software application releases, maintaining scheduling parameters and fixing abnormal job ends. The term "leveraged" suggests that the central organization supplies support to multiple sites, whereas non-leveraged support is provided locally. The leveraged application support price is based on

forecast hours per application suite. Non-leveraged application support is based on cost per person-hour.

3. **PC and UNIX Client Support:** Platform service activities required to provide the personal computing infrastructure to the site customers including hardware, software and problem resolution.   The services also include support and/or administration for personal computers, workstations, networked disk space and computer hardware. Cost is based on the number of clients (users).

4. **LAN Services:** The engineering and maintenance of the site data communication infrastructure equipment performed by network technicians and engineers.   Cost is based on the number of machines and user addresses.

5. **Voice Usage:** The pass-through traffic charge for voice services supplied by Corporate Network Services for Wide Area services and local call service provided by the telephone company.

6. **Voice Services:** The engineering and maintenance of the site telecommunications infrastructure equipment performed by network technicians and engineers. Included in this infrastructure are handsets, PBX phone wiring, voice and voice-mail equipment. Also provided are voice mail administration, telephone operators and directory distribution. The standard cost driver is the number of telephone extensions.

7. **Interactive Video Conferencing:** The use of cross-site video conferencing facilities. Cost is based on the number of hours of video conferencing use.

8. **WAN Usage:** The pass-through traffic charge for user access to remote computers and the Internet.

9. **Application Engineering:** New business functionality through business-specific application modification, development or sourcing. This also includes investigating and analyzing the contribution that technology can make.   The standard driver is cost per person-hour.

10. **Client Solutions:** Custom solutions using universally available tools such as database or worksheet solutions and information access solutions. Cost per person-hour is the standard driver.

11. **Enterprise Consulting and Solutions:** Strategic enterprise-level business process reengineering consulting, development and program management. Software licenses, consulting contracts and

other materials-type items are passed through at cost.

12. **Enterprise Planning and Architecture:** These services, funded
   by TMO Sector/Group, provide enterprise level architecture planning, infrastructure management and strategic planning.

The standard drivers were intentionally kept as simple as possible
to enable the best possible understanding by customers. Volume
usage trends help both the IT organization and its customers align
service demand to best meet business needs on a cost-effective basis.
Process metrics were established to measure results and to serve as
the basis for future planning by both the IT organization and its
customers. Simply stated, process metrics are used to measure what
is important. An example of a metric is Help Desk Call Closure. The
objective could be to close all help desk calls in two hours. When TMO
started to measure IT services, it started to get both results and quality
improvements. Improvements occur when an employee is told the
things that they are going to be measured on in their performance
evaluation that determine their next salary increase.

The next step was to create service level agreements (SLA) that
highlighted service definitions, prices, planned usage volumes, metrics
and service availability. The SLA lists what the IT organization will
provide and what the customer can expect. Treating this as a formal
discussion tool was important. The pricing model and the service level
agreements were new tools that emphasized delivering IT support on
time and on budget based on meaningful, data-driven discussions
between the IT organization and the purchasing customers. Service
level agreements had not previously been used within TMO.

The last step in this phase was to create IT invoices. The billing
approach was changed from allocating expenses that resembled a
general tax to invoicing customers based on actual usage. On a
monthly basis, volume usage information is collected and an invoice
is prepared that includes prices based on the standard service rate.
Customers are billed on a one-month lag. Computer modeling also
helped improve the new financial approach and provided a better
understanding of the cost impact on specific customers.

Senior Management Role

Leadership in establishing the new IT model came from both
business and IT management. HP feels that fundamental change often
does not come from the top but from across the organization. Having
acknowledged that, the new approach received important and strong
support from the senior management within the TMO organization.
The general manager and controller would point out that the IT
organization spent a substantive amount of time looking at volumes
and the related cost factors and what it costs the business. They would

ask managers within the organization whether the cost drivers made sense as a way to measure IT services and to determine IT costs. The answer in most cases was yes. If managers agreed that it was the right approach then any disagreements could be addressed with the responsible IT manager. There were some specific problems, but these were addressed with the responsible general managers to highlight the reasons for the increased costs. This new approach was not perfect, but it was a significant improvement over how IT charges had been managed in the past.

Senior management support definitely facilitated the job of selling the new IT model. The effort also included significant dialogue with users, the budgeting process, seminars for customers and a brochure that identified specific IT services and their cost drivers that was distributed to IT customers.

Results of the New IT Model within TMO

Four major factors were significant in implementing the new IT model. As stated earlier the starting point was looking at what customers valued. This dictated the creation of a customer partnership that necessitated a change in attitude on the part of the IT personnel. The IT pricing structure was then completely overhauled. It went from a general "IT tax" to specific prices for 14 categories of IT services. Service level agreements played an important communicative role between the IT organization and its customers. This clearly helped to reduce emotion and inject reality into the expectations of the customer regarding IT services. The way that IT metrics were measured, collected and communicated to users was used as the basis for future plans. A final important point was the creation of a monthly invoice that clearly and specifically spelled out the IT services that the customer received and the related cost.

In terms of specific results, the financial goals were achieved with the reduction of IT operational costs as a primary factor. The IT organizational consolidation was a major reason for these cost reductions. Additional cost savings were achieved with the new approach and the improved dialogue between the IT organization and its customers. This operational cost reduction provided funds that could be invested in new computer-based support and services which provided an initial momentum for the new IT model.

A shift from tactical to strategic use of IT was accomplished. Operational IT support was reduced from 98 to 82 percent of the IT budget and strategic services grew from one to fourteen percent. A very important gauge of the impact of the new IT approach was a customer opinion survey. The IT customers were asked two questions: 1) How important is it to you that IT do a service well? 2) How well is IT delivering that service? The survey addressed PC support, UNIX support, business application support, business application development, print services, e-mail, networking, telephone and voice services, help desk, communications and business consulting. As bad as the situation had been in the past, the IT organization was prepared for and would probably have been satisfied with ratings of 2.0 on a scale of 4.0. Customer satisfaction was a gratifying 3.1 that confirmed that the new approach was working.

Like many organizations, TMO will continue to evaluate its IT investment portfolio and search for the proper funding level. Both business and IT management has concluded that IT services can be segmented into three main categories with distinct investment strategies and measures. Operational and infrastructure services are managed based on efficiency compared to competitive rates. Instead of focusing on total expenses, the goal is to meet the business demands in the most efficient way possible. The business will drive the volumes and emerging services, while the IT organization will focus on ensuring competitive rates. Strategic investments such as business process initiatives are based on return on investment for the business process. The IT organization has established a partnership with the business process owner to address priority requirements. Finally, management and planning for such things as architecture strategy and vendor management is controlled as a percentage of budget.

Final Conclusions Regarding the Test Measurement Organization

The TMO IT organization clearly recognized the importance of focusing on the customer to address the issue of IT value. In becoming a customer-focused business the definition of the customer changed from "the people that complain about cost allocations" to "the people that the IT organization works with in its marketplace." Steve Hussey, an IT manager within TMO who played a major role in the task force that planned the single, consolidated IT organization as well as the design and implementation of the new IT model, emphasizes the following: Without some rationalization or professionalization of IT services, it is very difficult to have any credibility with business customers. He contends that credibility with customers and their attitude towards IT value is a function of empathy and performance. Too often in an IT environment, one or both of these components is missing. Either good performance is lacking or performance is adequate, but there is not a good connection with the people or the strategies of the business. Empathy is achieved by ensuring IT services are clearly understood and by competitive benchmarking. Performance evaluations by users are relative to their expectations. It is necessary to get emotion out of this evaluation and measurable results into the evaluation process. This was achieved within TMO through service definitions and clear, well-understood pricing so customers would conclude that IT services were truly competitive and not just pushed on them so that someone could save his job.   An important observation according to the people at TMO is that IT cannot be successfully established as a strategic resource until credibility is reached with users regarding the cost-effectiveness of the IT services that they are already receiving.

A critical dimension of this fundamental change was based on the commitment by the IT organization to ensure that its services provide superior value as measured against external benchmarks. To accomplish this, it was necessary to deliver services that provided a competitive advantage and/or addressed compelling business needs. In other cases, value was delivered by acting as managers of outside vendor services. Those capable of delivering comparable IT services were viewed as external competitors and used as reference points to assess the health of internally created products. When these competitors were determined to be a better choice, they were treated as business partners for the delivery of IT services.

A case could be made that a primary reason for treating the IT organization as a business within a business was more for the benefit of the IT organization than the IT users. It played a key role in creating a new attitude, even a new culture within the IT organization.

It is important to remember that this entire effort started because of an emphasis on costs. The significant success of HP in 1995 and 1996 prompts one to forget that the company faced some serious challenges in 1991 and 1992. The founders of the company actually returned from retirement to get the company back on track. The Test Measurement Organization had serious cost problems and a 30,000 item product line that had become cumbersome. The cost emphasis motivated the consolidation of the IT organizations. The managers of the IT organizations then recognized the need to better position themselves with the needs of the current and future business.

This emphasis on cost structure provided strong motivation for both customers and the IT organization to find a better way. The customers had their own pressures and were willing to pay for quality services that would help them address their problems. User management also realized that many employees were dissatisfied, so they were both interested and willing to work to develop a better approach that would improve both the business results and the levels of IT satisfaction.

This entire endeavor was a maturing process—an organizational learning curve. Learning curves are legitimately not the same, so different organizations respond to different business drivers. A major challenge of this entire effort was managing change. HP in general and TMO specifically have done an impressive job in training the IT managers to do the best possible job in managing the IT change implications both within the IT organization and with its customers. The scope of this chapter does not allow the time to discuss this point in specific detail, but it was a key factor in the overall success of this endeavor.

National Semiconductor Redesigns Its Information Systems Organization

Introduction

National Semiconductor Corporation (National), headquartered in Santa Clara, California, focuses on three major markets within the semiconductor industry: analog-intensive, communicative-intensive, and markets for personal systems. Each market is driven by the need for personal productivity and connectivity in the workplace and the home. This forms the basis for the company's overall strategy to concentrate on markets that reward the creation of technologies for moving and shaping information, and lead to such products as Ethernet cards and analog-to-digital interface devices that connect people to electronics and networks.

While the primary intent of this analysis is to focus on an approach used to better articulate the value of information systems through the redesign of the IS organization, it is necessary to understand the company and its business environment to accomplish this. In 1993, National reversed a negative financial trend by achieving both a profitable year and a growth in revenue. This positive performance has continued through 1996 and represents a significant turn-around, especially when compared to losses of $505 million from 1989 to 1992. Its longer term historical performance was not much better. From 1983 to 1992, National had losses in seven of ten years.

The turnaround at National coincided with the arrival of Gil Amelio as President and CEO in January 1991. Although he left in 1996 to become CEO of Apple Computer, Amelio successfully initiated a process of rethinking and repositioning National as a viable player in the dynamic and competitive semiconductor industry. Key to accomplishing this were the following:

- Clearly identifying where the company wanted to go and establishing a roadmap that could be communicated to the people within the organization.
- Clearly defining success.
- Understanding the current status of the organization.
- Establishing metrics to measure progress, determine how good the progress actually was and compare progress against competition.
- Being prepared to change if the business environment of the company changed.
- Gaining acceptance among people within the organization by making them part of the process.
- Being accountable for results by having effective leadership throughout the entire organization.

- Getting individuals to decide whether they are leaders or victims since leaders make things happen while victims complain about what is wrong.

This emphasis on creating a new National provided an excellent opportunity for the Corporate Information Systems organization to better position itself as a valuable resource that could play a major role in support of new business strategies. Phil Lorson of National's IS organization played a key role in the entire redesign and offered the following observation regarding their primary motivation: "The entire effort was all about value. It is fundamental to the purpose, the role and the benefits of any and all information systems endeavors. The overall goal was initially and continues to be to make the most intelligent, best possible IT investment decisions."

Conrad Deletis, Vice President of Information Systems, faced two problems in particular that highlight the challenge to create a new IS organization. The first was an interesting contrast. The IS vice presidents of most of the major U.S. semiconductor companies meet once or twice a year in what is essentially a benchmarking group. Each of these companies hired the same firm to benchmark its data center operations. The National IS managers were pleased to find that they scored significantly better than any of the other companies. National's IS staff then surveyed their major users and they found something quite different. They ran the best data center in their industry but their users did not feel that the IS organization was doing a good job of addressing the demands of the business. There was also a strong sentiment that progress toward leveraging new technologies was slow and the impact on business results was neutral, while the potential was felt to be very high. The users were also critical of the attitude of people in the IS organization which was a deterrent to a good working relationship.

The funding trend for IS was the second part of an important message. The annual budget of the corporate IS organization was in excess of $50 million. The remote sites that run their own IS operations but report to Deletis on a dotted line basis were spending $30 million. User spending for their own IS was estimated to be between $30 and $40 million and was considered to be the fastest growing of the three budgets.

Also influencing the need for a change was a general conclusion by Deletis and his staff that there were significant opportunities for IS to make a major contribution to the success of the company. They felt that the right initiatives were being identified but the proper forces were not in place to deliver the desired computer-based solutions.

National's IS management responded to these challenges by redesigning itself. The goal was not to downsize or to reduce cost per se, but to realign IS with business divisions and business processes, to make IS more responsive to internal customer needs and to make a more valuable contribution to the success of the business. The redesign process looked at the focus, priorities and structure of the IS organization. Most important was the assessment of its working relationship with its customers (users within National as well as external customers and suppliers). This thorough, objective and comprehensive approach fundamentally changed the information systems organization within National. The specifics of the redesign are described below. It involved hundreds of IS and National employees and took ten months to complete. While successful as a separate effort, it is important to emphasize that the IS redesign took advantage of the new environment within National.

The Vision Process To Create a New National Semiconductor

In the summer of 1992, the management team at National built a framework to allow the company to move continuously toward a shared vision. It was an intense effort with high priority and visibility for a basic reason—their future depended on it. The purpose was to describe in compelling terms their vision for the future of the company. They structured their approach around the missions and beliefs of the company, critical business issues and a strategic business plan. Key to this effort was the understanding and acceptance of this new direction by all employees throughout the world, which at that time was 23,000 employees at 11 major locations plus sales offices. Critical business issues identified were:

- Organizational excellence, which includes empowerment, incentives, education and internal communications.
- Operational excellence, which includes cycle time, quality and service issues.
- Strategic positioning, which includes the issues of planning competencies, external relations and benchmarking against industry standards.
- R&D return on investment which includes phase reviews, economic and core competencies issues.
- Financial performance that emphasizes gross profit, break-even and asset management.

The above factors provided guidelines for the internal operations of the IS organization, but also afforded opportunities to make major contributions in addressing these critical business issues. Business strategies described the action plan that guided them to long-term profitability and growth. These business strategies stated that National Semiconductor will meet its objectives by:

- Focusing on markets where success could be realized.
- Developing core competencies.

- Preventing mega-mistakes.
- Exploiting the personal systems market.
- Successfully implementing differentiating product and service strategies.
- Modernizing distribution.
- Developing a management infrastructure.
- Continually improving.

National sought to empower management to become involved in developing the vision and take the new directions to the entire organization. It was necessary, even critical, that employees also became immersed in the process.

Information Systems Organization Role

An effort that complemented the company-wide approach was made by each major function within the business including the IS organization. The following four themes formulated by the IS organization called for change in the way that National did its IS business:

1. Establishing proactive business partnerships with its major customers.
2. Establishing the IS organization as the information control panel of National's spaceship (the new company vision was built around a spaceship theme).
3. Migrating the company from data to information to knowledge for all employees.
4. Moving toward a client/server architecture with standards for applications.

The implication of the first major theme "to be business partners with IT customers so they become successful" was the opportunity to implement newer information technologies more quickly. To do this, senior level IS personnel were assigned as Business Partners to major customers. They were responsible for managing the IS relationship with the customer, acting as a focal point to help guide the use of information technologies for the customer's advantage. This effort started with a training program for IS personnel on how to become an extension of the customer's organization and proactively providing value to them. This meant that the IS people had to have the ability to establish an effective partnership with the user, show commitment to the delivery of high value IS, rally the various IS resources to customer projects and demonstrate a high level of personal initiative. This was not an easy job for many traditional IS people. It dictated a high level of interest in the customer's business and core processes, a broad knowledge of IS resources, a proven track record of accomplishments and effective communication skills.

For the IS organization to function as the control panel of the National spaceship it had to improve its capabilities to provide data, information and knowledge for its customers to operate successfully. The goal was to share knowledge across the company by providing useful information to all employees. This sharing encouraged trust which was necessary to accomplish the transformation of National as a company.

The shift to client/server computing was viewed as necessary as mainframe use started to decline. Major changes in software were also necessary as desktop PC use became more pervasive. To ensure this, network capabilities needed to be established to take advantage of the new technology.

Given these objectives the critical business issues for the IS organization were:

- Achieve results by meeting quality, cost and time commitments for all IS products and services.
- Share knowledge across all sites to maximize synergy.
- Create a proactive value-added partnership with customers.
- Create a modern infrastructure of standards and architecture that permits employees to easily communicate, share information and work together.
- Invest in an information systems staff through incentives, upgraded environment, training, teams and a process orientation.

The Specific IS Redesign Process

The redesign approach shown in Figure 7 involved five phases that included prework, macro redesign, identifying and filling information systems leadership positions, micro design and the implementation of the specific elements of the redesign process. It was driven by customer, stakeholder and best-in-class company evaluations. The entire endeavor took ten months to complete and involved 175 participants on 25 teams from all of National's worldwide locations.

- Prework (1 month)

- Macro Redesign (3 months)

- IS Leadership Positions Identified and Filled (1 month)

- Micro Design (5 months)

* Redesign Implemented (1 month)

Figure 7: The IS Redesign Process

Prework

The prework activities which took a month to complete began by defining the strategic intent of the entire effort, identifying the known factors upon which the intents should be based, completing the plans for the entire project and forming a macro design steering committee.

The strategic intent was to make a quantum improvement in satisfaction for those customers supported by the IS organization, to increase information access by accelerating the adoption of new technology, to leverage worldwide information technology investments and capabilities and to achieve significant productivity gains world-wide through effective use of information technology.

Macro Redesign

The macro redesign was a combination of doing necessary home-work and determining the general approach to be pursued. This part of the process spanned three months. The result of this effort was gaining a very good picture of customer perceptions, expectations and hopes regarding IS products and services. It provided the foundation upon which to base a successful redesign.

Core processes received a great deal of attention in the new business vision process and the IS redesign. The new business model identified four core processes which if made world class would enable the company to become world class. The IS redesign approach was organized around the core business processes shown in Figure 8. Strategy development deals with National's overall business strate-gies.   Value development is product design and engineering, and

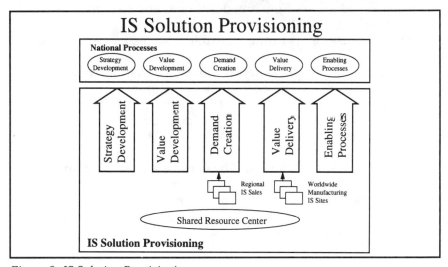

Figure 8: IS Solution Provisioning

demand creation is marketing and sales. Value delivery begins with the customer order entry process and includes manufacturing and any distribution, support and service functions until value is delivered to the customer. Enabling processes are those that make up the corporate infrastructure including finance and accounting, human relations and the information systems organization.

IS solution provisioning groups were created and aligned with the company's core business processes. The first part of the redesign determined that the IS organization is a solution provisioner and not a systems developer. As newly defined solution provisioners they bring solutions to business requirements within National. They are organized to do this consistent with the processes of the company. The IS expertise is not only focused on technology but on the core processes. The challenge was to align the expertise and resources of the IS organization with the core processes of the business with the objective of making them world-class.

In formulating the best approach to accomplish this, over two hundred customers were interviewed in thirteen worldwide locations. The key messages from the customers that make up the marketplace for the IS organization were:

- Be customer oriented by understanding the business and communicating in business and not technical terminology.
- Partner with the business through continuous involvement in business processes to deliver more value.
- Provide a single point of contact to IS services while allowing direct access to IT expertise.
- Have a clear IS vision and establish, communicate and align IS strategies with business partner's goals.
- Provide global access from any desktop to any National system.
- Integrate IS across all functions.
- Provide end-user tools through flexible systems for data access and reporting.
- Build an extended business network by establishing inter-connectivity between National and its customers and suppliers.
- Train and educate end-users on IS supported tools and systems.
- Establish an IS architecture that provides a corporate framework for enterprise-wide standards and tools.

Stakeholders were addressed by surveys and personal interviews. This involved over five hundred personnel in corporate and remote site IS organizations as well as business partners and the corporate steering committee. The consensus messages from these stakeholders was summarized as follows:

- Establish one IS organization.
- Emphasize developing a better understanding of National's business

by IS personnel.
- Establish measurements as defined by internal IS customers.
- Promote skills transformation and training on new information technologies.
- Strengthen worldwide alignment.
- Market IS for internal staff and customers as well as external customers.
- Promote worldwide standards and guidelines for IS planning, development and operations.

Twenty best-in-class company evaluations were made ranging from American Airlines' SABRE organization to ATT Universal Card to the San Jose Sharks hockey team. Major benefits from these evaluations were learnings associated with organizational structures, customer interactions, vendor relationships, skills transformation, human resources issues and internal processes. A Shared Resource Center, which uses a central database to identify technical employees and contractors for departments and projects, was formed as a direct result of these company evaluations.

IS Leadership Positions Identified and Filled

In determining the new structure for the IS organization, the emphasis was on establishing a broad span of control with a flatter organization and self-directed, cross functional teams. A clean slate approach was taken in identifying and filling the leadership positions. All 300 of the IS positions were opened, with 251 filled immediately through an application process. Seventy percent of the applicants

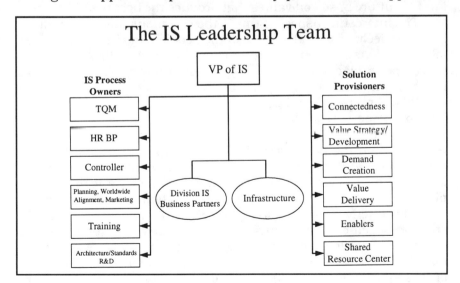

Figure 9: The IS Leadership Team

achieved their first choice for specific positions. Thirty-six percent of these people had new responsibilities and seventy percent reported to new managers. Fourteen people joined the IS organization from non-IS positions within National. It is significant that despite the magnitude of the changes and the possible negative reaction to them, only one person left National.

Twenty-three leadership positions were filled first. While continuing to function in their former capacities, these people became leaders in the micro process to shape the organization in which they would play key roles. The second phase was placing 251 people within the new organization. Once the new processes and positions were defined the remaining personnel were assigned to new jobs. Everyone continued to function in their previous positions until the actual transition to the new organizational structure. The third and final people phase was the transition from old to new jobs. All personnel had to develop a transition plan which dealt with how to terminate their efforts in their previous jobs and move to new responsibilities.

Behaviors, feelings and attributes were important terms used within the redesign process to deal with the "people challenges" of successfully implementing the new structure and processes. A simple picture of this entire redesign process started with capturing all of the business requirements that guide processes and any organizational structure that is put in place. It was mandatory to respond to these requirements. Next was the behavior, feelings, and attributes of the staff. This is the combination of structures and processes together with the feelings, behavior and attributes of the staff that produce the final results. It begins with a requirement and an intent to produce a result with a structure and a set of processes while also creating the kind of culture based on values that produce the best possible result.

The interesting aspect of this is the enormous importance of the behavior, feelings and attributes of the people. An absolutely perfect job can be done in structuring the organization and putting world-class processes in place, but if the personnel do not exhibit a customer focus, team spirit and become highly motivated the best possible results will probably not be realized. If an organization like National had to do one part of the entire redesign process well, it had to be getting people motivated with a spirit of producing the best possible results within the new organizational structure. This will beat the competitor that does not accomplish this part of the process as well. The need to get people charged-up and working as a team was the primary focus of the National IS implementation transition team.

The objective of a flatter IS organization was achieved through the creation of self-directed teams. The data center operation that had earned the excellent benchmark results was previously managed by four director level managers. The new organization eliminated three of these positions and replaced them with self-directed teams. The approximate number of personnel assigned to each of the major support areas in the new Santa Clara IS organization is indicated under the bar reflecting the IS function in Figure 10.

Micro Design

The micro design finalized a new mission for the IS organization. This stated that the mission was to maximize the impact of information technology on business results by aligning IS and business initiatives. Key goals to accomplish this were to discover opportunities where IS could successfully support business objectives, strategies and core processes. This made it critical to link IS and business personnel to do the best possible job and in doing so, leverage systems for successful, productive solutions.

As a result of the micro redesign, IS now has three core processes: Strategy, Provisioning and Delivery. As Figure 11 depicts, strategy drives provisioning which in turn drives delivery. All three processes are closely coupled with the business and the IT market place. Strategy development has become a continuous process within IS. For the most part it is driven by business direction, but in some cases actually influences business direction. Technology trends in the IT market place are also key to IS strategies. Provisioning depends on a strong interaction with the business as solutions are determined and continued until they achieve their business objectives. The provisioning process includes thorough scanning of the IT market place for packaged solution systems components. Acquiring these components is strongly preferred to developing them internally. The IS delivery process provides business partners with ongoing use of computing and communications services. The outsourcing of delivery services is pursued when there is an economic or service advantage to do so.

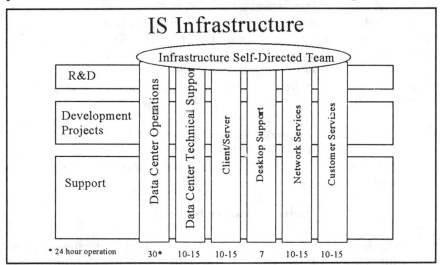

Figure 10: IS Infrastructure

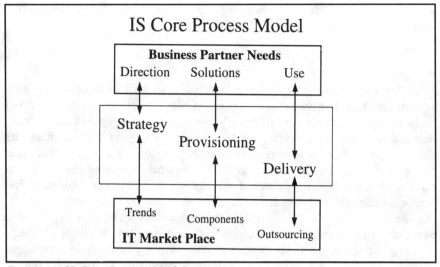

Figure 11: IS Core Process Model

Specific products and services were identified and related processes designed. Budgets were also aligned between user departments and the IS organization. Final IS positions were also filled. As the most detailed part of the entire process, the micro design took the longest to complete and was finished in five months.

Redesign Implementation

The redesign implementation was the responsibility of a transition team made up of six members that was formed after the completion of the micro design. A primary focus of the transition team was on the personnel issues. The actual transition to the new organization was completed in one month. This new IS structure required considerable effort in terms of personnel development. The first challenge was dealing with the new balance between employee responsibilities and those of the now fewer in number managers. It is one thing to say to an employee that she is empowered but what does this actually mean? To answer this question, individual improvement plans were created to reinforce the need for employees to act in an empowered capacity. Career and skill development were addressed by both formal training and individual assignments. Mentoring to provide guidance to people with new assignments and a new mode of operation played an important role.

Positive Results for National

Results after the initial two years since the IS redesign suggest that things are definitely going in the right direction. Customers are working with IS business partners and have been very positive regarding the value that they are receiving from IS products and services. The best endorsement of the level of customer satisfaction is that the demand for IS support has continued to increase.

People have been effectively linked to people so that information and relevant knowledge are providing improvements in productivity through both collaboration and innovation. Improvements in global operations and coordination have been facilitated with both customers and suppliers based on electronic commerce, enterprise architecture and aligned IT strategies. Finally, the IS personnel are excited about the changes made and feel that they are making more of a contribution to the success of the business. The longer term objective continues to be moving all core business processes to world class levels. This has not been accomplished as this is being written, but there is increasing evidence that IT is playing an increasingly important role to enable National to reach this goal.

Lessons learned start with the realization that it is impossible to communicate too much in this type of endeavor. Because of the scope and complexity of the entire redesign, "just check the data" became something very much worth remembering. When things got confusing, making sure that evaluations and decisions were factually based was important. Another major lesson was to involve as many people as possible. This increased the workload and the time horizon to complete some of the steps in the process, but it also built credibility and acceptance by people impacted by the changes. Overhauling an IS organization that was this large in scope and magnitude definitely required both business and IT leadership. A key factor was also the alignment with customer strategies and plans. Finally, it was critical to remember that the people factors and how they were dealt with would determine the success of the entire endeavor.

HP TMO Support of the Basic Premises Regarding IS Value and Financial Strategies

As shown in the chart in Figure 1, TMO tracks the hypothesized financial strategy evolution. It uses budgets to address IT costs within both user departments and the IT organization. It has both formal business proposals and direct negotiations with users to help prioritize the implementation of new IT applications and services. It has used a charge-out process for a long time, which the new financial model restructured. As can be expected, TMO concluded that a charge-out process was not enough to address the IT value questions. A major objective of the new model was to better align the IT support with core business processes and business strategies. One can conclude that in doing so, HP TMO has moved into Phase IV by creating an effective management process. Since the business environment is dynamic, this management process must stay equally dynamic. This entire effort to create a management process was the start of a journey since the objective of the IT organization will continue to be to support the company to achieve business success.

National Support of the Basic Premises Regarding IS Value and Financial Strategies

National also has both IS organization and departmental budgets for IS support. As suggested by the chapter premises this is how and where it started to manage IS expenditures. While it has done so for some time, the new IS structure put more of an emphasis on identifying a justified business case to implement major new IS applications. National has not generally conducted post-install audits. Charge-out systems have existed for a long time and in the past the IS organization worked hard to develop what could be called a metered system. This included a bundled pricing approach that was structured so that it generated sufficient funds to allow the IS organization to do joint studies and prototype systems with users without charging them. Historically, this approach also resulted in a small surplus at the end of the year.

One of the steps taken to enhance the new management process within National was to negotiate IS spending at lower levels within the company. The negotiators were senior IS managers who were given new assignments as individual contributors and an objective of building better working relations with major users. Instead of spending less, the user managers signed up for an increase over what they were previously spending with the central IS organization. The central IS organization budget was no longer something based on a going rate, but one where users "bought the need" for the IS support.

What has really changed with the new approach is the type and nature of the negotiations regarding IS costs. This new approach does involve a significant amount of time for both the user and the IS organization to negotiate costs. Having invested this time the IS customer better understands what they are investing in and the IS organization better understands the customer needs and expectations regarding its services.

The new National process includes 20 possible sources of IS costs for a user but six are probably key investment areas. Previously a customer would request IS support and cost factors were specifically identified and included in the charge as the work progressed. In the new environment a user can ask how much the entire project is going to cost and the IS organization is willing to negotiate an agreement for the total cost. This is a very positive difference for those customers that are under cost pressures and can't risk run-away IS costs. There have been cases where the customer wanted to and was able to negotiate a total cost for the entire year. The National IS organization is also moving to more use of service level agreements to document the understandings reached in the negotiations with its customers.

National now has a new management process in place where it is possible for an IS customer to make discrete investment decisions. This has led these same customers to conclude that they are making better IT investments that are more focused on value-add aspects of running the business, because they are better informed regarding the range of possible IS products and services and their related costs.

Management Strategies for Information Technology Investment

Are the IS value experiences of HP TMO and National Semiconductor unique or are they representative of challenges that are similar to those faced by many IS organizations? As suggested by the chart in Figure 1, the IS value issue evolves over time. Both of the evaluated companies spend sizable amounts of money on information systems. Both of the companies face increasing competitive pressures that dictate the need for computer-based support for core business processes. The combination of these two factors moved the management of the IT resources high enough on the company priority list so that it received the attention, funding and support needed to develop the necessary management process. If other companies parallel the cost trends and information needs, then it is safe to conclude that they already have IS value issues that need to be addressed. On the other hand, they may simply be in an earlier phase. If their IS costs continue to increase, and to do so out of necessity they can expect to face IS value issues at some time in the future.

Is a management process as described in this chapter really necessary to address the IS value question? The experience of these two companies says that the creation of a management process that emphasized a business partnership with their customers was necessary to enable them to better articulate the role and explain the value of information systems to the business. While successful in their efforts, this came at a price that was significant in terms of time and effort on the part of both the user departments and the IS organizations. Both companies provide evidence that the role of IS needs to be an integral part of the way that major resources of the business are managed. In treating IS as an integral part of the business the emphasis must be on how it can better address the needs of the business. Whether it is called "a business within a business" as at HP TMO or an "IS redesign" is not the point. What is important is positioning the IS organization as a business partner to deliver what user departments need and will accept, support, and pay for, based on the fact that it provides value to them.

But isn't a charge-out approach enough to address the IS value question? The answer to this question based on the two case studies and the author's personal focus on this issue since 1984 would have to be no. An IS organization does not gain user or senior management acceptance of the value of information systems based on the accuracy, preciseness, fairness or thoroughness of a bill that is sent to the user based on some charge-out methodology. Much more important is the working relationship of the people within the IS organization and its users. The charging methodologies help but are seldom the determining factor in gaining recognition and acceptance of IS value to the business. The right approach is understanding an overall management process versus a specific technique or methodology.

There are definitely organizations that would argue with this premise since they say that they are satisfied with the use of a charge-out approach. One's view is influenced by the following questions: How large are the IS costs? How satisfied are users with IS support? How important is this resource to the success of the business? Is the IS value issue high enough on the priority list of the business that it will receive the support necessary to create a better management process?

Does the creation of a management process like those of either HP or National Semiconductor change the focus and strategic significance of information systems? In both cases, this was actually the case. The National IS organization had felt for some time that it did a good job of identifying strategic initiatives. When it looked at what it was actually doing on a day-to-day basis, it fell short of its expectations to play a more significant strategic role. It was clearly easier to talk about playing a strategic role then making it a reality. The improved relationships between the IS organization and its customers has played a definite role in changing this strategic role. Statistics cited above provide evidence that the same is true with the HP TMO operation. Both cases support the premise that an effective partnership between the IS organization and its customers is necessary to move IS support and services into a strategic role. When this happens the value issue becomes less of a specific measurement issue. Customers (user management) become more aware of the role of IS, its significance and its VALUE!

Other factors that should influence strategies and plans regarding investments in information technology include the following:

- The role of information technology has shifted from operational support that could be measured by productivity to a much broader range of organizational activities that are more difficult to measure.
- Knowledge-worker technology has the potential to increase performance in more ways than simply enabling work to be done faster and/or more easily. (Qualities that can be measured.)
- IS value answers lie with users (customers) and not financial or cost accounting experts.
- The appropriate factors that drive the success of the business should be the basis of the evaluation of the contribution of information systems, e.g., efficiency improvements through productivity measures, value-add to customers, etc.

• In any of the phases shown in Figure 1 short of Phase IV (management process), a distributed systems approach with a client/server architecture can further complicate attempts to address the information systems value issue. By definition, a distributed system involves the sharing of information systems resources (processors and a network). If it is difficult to assess the value of IS when it is centralized, it can be even more difficult to accomplish this when it is distributed throughout the enterprise.

Final Conclusion

This chapter can logically conclude where it started. It becomes necessary to address the value of IS as it increases in both total cost and importance to the organization. As the costs become significant to the cost of operating the business, it will become necessary to articulate the value of the support and service provided by this organizational resource. How to do this will continue to be controversial since there are those that contend that the real value of IS cannot be measured or that it is not worth the cost of doing so. When an item is sold, isn't the buyer in the best position to determine if they gained value from the purchase? Doesn't this same logic apply to users that are charged for IS support and services? If there is agreement with this premise and the IS costs are growing in both amount and importance, then a management process to address the IS value question probably lies in the near term future.

Recommended Reading

1. Carlson, Walter M. and Barbara C. McNurline, *Uncovering the Information Technology Payoffs*, I/S Analyzer Special Report, United Communications Group, Rockland, Maryland, 1992. This document summarizes fourteen strategies for measuring the value of information systems. Included are methods advocated by Peter Keen, Paul Strassmann, Charles Gold, Paul Berger, Peter Sasssone and commentaries on their findings.

2. Drucker, Peter F., "The Information Executives Truly Need: Redesigning the Corporation Requires a New Set of Tools and Concepts" *Harvard Business Review*, (January-February 1995), p. 55. Once again Peter Drucker challenges you to look at an issue with a very broad and historic perspective. He states that the corporation that is now emerging must be designed around an information skeleton. As such this new approach will define a business as an organization that adds value and creates wealth. The article addresses activity-based accounting as a necessary way to cost an entire economic process. It also discusses price-led costing, value-added analysis, core compe-

tence and benchmarking as important business management (wealth creation) tools.

3. Framel, John E., *Information Value Management*, Journal of Systems Management/December, 1993, pp. 16-41. Mr. Framel provides a methodology entitled "Information Value Management Implementation Steps (IVM/IMP). This approach is based on the premise that everyone within the organization is personally committed to maximizing the value of their operation by managing the value of the information assets that they use. It starts with management understanding of the role of information systems and systematically follows a process that is very similar to the approach advocated in this book.

4. Meyer, N. Dean and Mary E. Boone, *The Information Edge*, McGraw-Hill Book Co., New York, 1987. The major focus of this book is the defense of the premise that the strategic use of information systems can be quantified. Methods to quantify value-added applications are provided and supported by company case studies.

5. Parker, Marilyn M. and Robert Benson, *Information Economics: Linking Business Performance to Information Technology*, Prentice-Hall, Inc., Englewood Cliffs, New Jersey, 1988. The primary emphasis of this book is to thoroughly explore the meaning of value in information systems. The authors content that "the heart of Information Economics is change." They assert that "a business must change to achieve real, enduring value from information technology."

6. Saunders, Carol Stoak and Jack William Jones, *Measuring Performance of the Information Systems Function*, Journal of Management Systems/Spring 1992, Vol. 8, No. 4, pp. 63-82. This article is based on the premise that measurement of the information systems function is a critical issue facing today's executives. It goes on to say that "value is reflected in the ability of information systems to satisfy individual managers' information requirements. It is the assessment issue, not the theoretical model, that dominates current concerns of both managers and evaluators." Unfortunately, the measurements vary over time. This does a competent job of assessing many of the alternatives and factors that can be considered in formulating an approach that will address the information systems value issue.

7. Strassman, Paul A., *Information Payoff: The Transformation of Work in the Electronic Age*, Free Press, New York, 1985. Strassman contends that information value is a product of management. One might want to debate whether this can be consistently measured but the author clearly supports this as the major focal point in addressing the value of information systems.

Chapter 19

Measuring the Success of Implementing Multimedia CBTs in Business

Kathyrn A. Marold
Metropolitan State College of Denver

The addition of multimedia programs in business information systems is becoming widespread. The added modalities accessed by the inclusion of graphics, sound, video, animation, and interactivity results in a more natural, user-friendly product that can be more effective than traditional systems. CBTs—computer based training modules—are one of the most widespread uses of multimedia in the corporate world. Using individualized, "just-in-time" software for training employees promises better, faster training, and makes economic sense to severely strapped company training programs. The acceptance of multimedia CBTs by employees, most of whom are now computer literate and quite familiar with graphic user interfaces (GUIs), is encouraging. Actual frequency of use is not as encouraging. The "electronic tutelage" that CBTs provide could be one of the greatest advantages of new multimedia applications. How to successfully measure the success of these programs is not standardized yet, but companies are beginning to assess the investment payoff of using multimedia CBTs for corporate training. An exploratory study of three large companies suggests that multimedia CBTs can be successfully used for company training, and that there is an acceptable return on the investment.

The Challenge

The portion of a corporation's budget that is allocated to Information Technology is always significant. Twenty to twenty-five per cent of the total operating expenses of a company is often devoted to the Information Technology division. And approximately 33 percent of that sum is expended for end user services (Mahmood and Mann, 1993). Yet accountability for these large sums frequently lags behind measures of the return on the investment of other divisions.

There are many explanations for this situation: the task of measuring productivity of end user training services that are dependent upon human behavior is a true challenge. Human behavior, especially cognitive behavior, is not predictable and does not lend itself to the quantitative measures that other areas of corporate business rely upon. Tying the sums spent on Information Technology—specifically end user training—to company performance is very difficult. Senior management many times does not have a strategic plan for measuring the investment payoff. High performance firms spend more on information technology than low performance firms, but they are frustrated by lack of standard measures for their investments (Mahmood and Mann, 1993). Measuring the productivity of just one area—the multimedia CBTs used for training—seems almost impossible. Yet the significant investment in this newest method of training warrants an investigation.

The Research Question

One of the newest applications of multimedia technology in business systems is the development of CBTs-computer based training modules for employees. These engaging multi-sensory programs, most of which are PC-based, were developed with the promise to train better, more efficiently, more quickly and thoroughly, with a more individual approach, than a human company trainer could accomplish in a longer period of time. They provide a JIT—just in time—approach to company training. Individualized learning is provided precisely when it is needed, regardless of training staff availability. Interactivity and individualized pace are the hallmarks of these modules. The employee is able to spend as much or as little time as necessary to master the material. Recordkeeping is automated. So far, employee acceptance of the CBT style of delivery is encouraging, although as will be further explained, there appears to be an initial "honeymoon" enchantment with the technology that later fades. Will the multimedia CBT and the electronic learning environment replace the human tutor (Marold, 1994; Zuboff, 1988; Vygotsky, 1987)? And more importantly for our purposes here, can a payoff be accurately accessed? The latter is often the question that arises when a company is considering adoption of CBTs for their employee training programs.

CBTs Defined

Today's CBTs are multimedia software products aimed at teaching the user desired skills and concepts through his/her interactions with the computer program, without the intervention of a trainer. Company use of CBT programs preceded the availability of multimedia computing. The first computer-based training programs were mostly text, with occasional graphic enhancements. They were sometimes referred to as CAI (computer-assisted instruction) or CAL (computer-assisted learning), and they occasionally suffered from serious design and execution flaws. As do today's multimedia CBTs, they followed the basic principles of instructional design—with content areas, reenforcement activities areas, and assessment areas that scored the user's mastery of the material and recorded the results. All of the material was closely tied to a set of predefined "learner outcomes" or objectives.

The multimedia CBTs of today are significantly different from the first CBTs, although they follow the same basic principles. First of all, they are more complex and expensive; they demand the latest of hardware, and in great quantities. Combining the traditional text and graphics with audio, animation, full-motion video, and interactivity taxes the most powerful microcomputer hardware. The huge storage requirements (both primary and secondary) that multimedia CBTs require pose a problem—that of investment payoff. For example, one-half minute of uncompressed video can fill a 810 MB (megabytes, or million bytes) hard drive. The uncompressed video requires almost 30 MB per second storage and rapid data delivery, which taxes even a Pentium microprocessor. Microcomputer hard drives now routinely ship with only 2 or 3 GB (gigabytes, or billion bytes) total storage. Video compression standards exist (CODECs), and more sophisticated compression schemes such as MPEG, are advancing rapidly. Hardware to play MPEG video files will soon be available on all PCs that meet the new MPC multimedia standards. Nevertheless, many CBTs require 16 MB and greater of RAM (main memory), and hard disks and CD-ROMs that hold gigabytes rather than megabytes. This is sophisticated hardware for routine PC workstations.

Multimedia CBTs are state-of-the-art, and may as marketing representatives note, reflect an innovative attitude, but at a steep price. They usually contain multisensory presentation of information, animated activities to further explain concepts, review, testing and scoring. They often include full-motion video clips with instructor explanations and typical client interviews. Many include an automated recordkeeping system. All of these elements are presented within an engaging user interface that makes it easy for the user to navigate among the various menus and modules. The prohibitive cost of implementing multimedia CBTs is being challenged by senior management. Are multimedia CBTs really an investment payoff? Given the expensive requirements, how do we justify their use?

Arguments For Multimedia CBTs

Our technology is changing, and the methods with which we train are changing along with it. The multimedia CBT offers training for the new electronic learner who grew up with MTV and video games. The electronic learner is often as comfortable interacting with machines as he/she is with other individuals (*New Media*, 1994). Because of the diffusion of computer technology many companies are now beginning to invest in multimedia for sales and market presentations, and for employee training (Faier, 1993). Multimedia CBTs are a growing trend. And although there is not yet a standard procedure, individual companies are beginning to assess the return on the investment of their CBTs (Hall, 1995). Some first instruments to measure payoff have been developed. From these preliminary assessments, it is possible to develop and recommend a strategic plan for measuring the productivity of these expensive software applications.

Is it prudent for a company to implement CBTs with little prior investigation into the return on the investment? It is enticing to consider using technology for end-user training. However, senior management is beginning to hold information technology accountable for the large sums spent on end user training. They now require more than the distinction of being "the first by whom the new is tried." Companies whose strategic policy is to always be at the forefront of innovation still must have a reasonable payoff for their investments (Andrew, 1995).

The mass diffusion of computer technology, especially of the personal computer (PC), does reduce the risk of implementing this newest method of end user training somewhat (Markus, 1987). An investment in CBTs is not as risky as it would have been several years ago. That is, most employees are now familiar with the ubiquitous microcomputer and the GUI (graphic user interface) software that runs upon it. Computer literacy has increased a full ten per cent in a decade (Hancock, 1995). Studies done in the late 1980s on costs and benefits of CBTs saw a more effective use of employee time, and indicated a generally positive employee attitude (Dean, 1988; Kulik in Baker edition, 1993). Although the jury is still out on the general IT investment (Roach, 1994), the studies specifically on CBTs in academic and business environments indicate reduced instruction time, easier monitoring, and better content retention (Hall, 1995; Carlsson, 1994; Barker, 1989).

In the diffusion of computer technology, behavioral scientists have pointed out that we have even begun to humanize computers, calling them our "second self" (Turkle, 1984). The explosive growth of the Internet and computer communications in general has brought individuals from all over the globe "on-line"(*Denver Post*, 1995, Marold, 1995).   Research shows we personify computers, choosing our "favorite" machines, and using those specific machines when we have a choice (Nass, 1993). Computers have become almost a natural extension of our biological beings, entering into the "everyday" of our lives (Marold, 1994). It is rare today that a new corporate employee does not have at least rudimentary computer skills.   In the Woodstat study of Metsa-Serla, 27 percent of the middle managers considered themselves advanced users of computer based systems, and 41 percent reported extensive prior experience working with computer based systems (Carlsson, 1994). Computers are an accepted part of most of our lives, whether in business, or in a home setting.

In addition, hardware and software costs decrease daily. What cost $10,000 a decade ago now costs little over a thousand (Hancock, 1995). While computer hardware and software are still a significant expense for a large corporation, the annual wages of a large group of company trainers who do not use computer technology for end user training is greater. Perhaps we cannot afford *not* to invest in CBTs. We must ask, " Are custom built multimedia CBTs that require more labs and/or networks but less trainers a cost effective alternative to traditional methods of trainer-led sessions with small groups?"

The topic of the corporate image is also a consideration. Companies that use CBTs are sometimes regarded as forward-looking; they are frequently acknowledged as being keenly aware of individual differences and learning styles (Williamson, 1994). Van Dyke's study of one hundred and twenty individuals included their perception of CAI as a training tool (1972). Males' perception was more positive than females', yet the group as a whole had positive attitudes toward the use of computer aided instruction.   Companies are sometimes highly admired for embracing the "new" technology, and changing with the times. Corporate culture may demand that the company be known as being on "the cutting edge" of technology implementation. The three case studies discussed in this chapter initially chose multimedia CBTs for many of these same reasons. The corporate image conveyed is a significant incentive.

However, managers realize that user efficacy and endorsement cannot be the only criteria a company uses to justify the significant outlay that multimedia CBTs require. A standard metric and a more rigorous means of polling users can help companies develop a strategic management plan for measuring CBT payback. In general, it can be argued that software produced for PC users in the new graphical user environment has much to gain by including multimedia elements. Text, graphics, audio, video, animation and interactivity can be combined to produce highly effective, yet user-friendly programs. All types of software applications are now incorporating multimedia elements. GUIs are the standard. The business use of multimedia elements are common in lecture presentation software, corporate presentation packages, skills training packages such as keyboarding videos, CD-ROM marketing endeavors, and in entertainment software. CBT modules are a natural extension of multimedia (Rawles, 1994). In the realm of learning theory, it can be argued that retention and level of understanding can improve with the addition of modalities (Kliewer, 1993). Although research shows that we have a channel capacity that severely restricts our comprehension when it is exceeded (Miller, 1974), as technology diffuses our culture has been gradually able to successfully absorb more and more. Roger Shank says all learning is the acquisition of new skills WHEN the individual needs it—real learning is "on demand," in other words (Shank, 1995). It can be argued that JIT learning is more effective learning. Multimedia CBTs are individualized learning; because of their interactivity they epitomize "learning on demand." As Bill Gates notes, interactivity means flexibility, and that brings exploration (Gates, 1995). Cognitive psychologists and laymen alike agree that exploration that leads to discovery constitutes true learning. Of the early studies of CBTs in general, the presentation of text alone in the program was always rated as least effective and desirable. Yet, users reported learning more with interactive computer-based modules (Kulik in Barker, 1989; Bannister, 1970).

Still, the argument that "everyone's beginning to do it" isn't strong enough justification from the management perspective. Perhaps the company image is enhanced by implementing CBTs, perhaps employees are accustomed to the technology and even are receptive to computerized instruction, perhaps hardware and software costs have decreased, but what is the return on the investment? The question begs for a strategic plan to assess the payoff.

Arguments Against Multimedia CBTs

An overriding problem with implementing a new technology such as multimedia CBTs is the lack of measures of productivity. Although Negroponte abhors our American preoccupation with productivity whenever a method involves computers, it remains a major concern for the financial directors of companies (Negroponte, 1995). Is there a standardized way to successfully measure the return for the investment in multimedia CBT modules? Not quite yet.

The gnawing problem of how to measure the return for the investment has been approached in very general ways by some corporations. How do you measure quality—quality of learning of those who are trained with CBTs, and the quality of the CBT itself? How do you measure the success of electronic tutelage as opposed to company trainers? End user services cannot control what it cannot measure (DeMarco, 1982). Some of the possible benefits of CBT use are intangible, or at least very difficult to assess. User comfort, personal interaction, and efficacy are hard to measure objectively. Cognitive processes have been traditionally examined in a qualitative way (Marold, 1994.) Human response doesn't neatly equate to dollar amounts. Is a reduction of training staff, but increase in hardware and software, as is often the case when implementing multimedia CBTs, worth it? In a company that decides to adopt CBTs, will trainers be able to successfully transfer their deep knowledge of subject matter to the informational contents of a CBT?   Can they, with the help of a consultant or a developmental team, produce a quality product?   Or should the development of company multimedia CBTs be entirely outsourced, for yet more money and less control?   And how does the company determine if the contractor is competent in the particular field, even though they can produce multimedia training modules? There are many unknowns when embarking on CBT development, and few proven measures once they are implemented. We know instructional design and development of user interface is crucial (Hackos, 1994.) We know recordkeeping will be automated and clearer, but perhaps not satisfactory for the company needs. There are no warranties on developing and/or adopting multimedia CBTs; the risk is significant.

It can be argued that with CBTs, the human element and the subjectivity are lost. Furthermore, CBT development, in-house or contract, is fraught with general production problems: there are design problems, hardware and software compatibility problems, the usual cost overruns, time delays, and so forth. The few studies on ROI from the pioneer corporations are not definitive, and may not apply to the individual company considering multimedia CBTs.

There is the argument of the extensive time lag between planning, designing, implementing the multimedia CBTs and being able to measure their productivity. How long is acceptable for a company to wait before a return is realized? Substantial CBTs can take up to a year or two to develop and yet more time to implement. They can cost many thousand dollars to produce, even in-house; funds and IT employee time are tied up for long periods before summative evaluations can be initiated. Of the three case studies in this research, only one company (COMET) has more than five years of users from which to poll. COMET waited two years to begin an extensive evaluation, in an attempt to compile data for a truer picture. OppenheimerFunds formulated an evaluation strategy within six months, but now must wait a similar period of time to gather final results.   Coors has not developed evaluation plans yet. ROI studies conducted by Storage Tek, Price Waterhouse, and American Airlines (Hall, 1995) can provide only guidelines, not timelines. How soon after implementation it is feasible to measure success, and in what manner do you measure the success of multimedia CBTs? Since multimedia CBTs, rather than the older CAIs, are relatively new, strategic methods of measuring impact are just beginning to be developed. Often, the initial results of comparisons come as long as seven to ten years after the CBTs have been implemented. Ideally, a long range strategy for measuring productivity should begin while the large sums of money are being allocated, yet no standard strategies exist specifically for multimedia CBTs. Nor do companies have a pool of past experience from which to draw; even if they have used CAI and computerized Decision Support Systems in the past, the implementation of multimedia CBTs differs. This means each company is left largely on its own to determine individual methods of measuring productivity. Even as will be seen, there are the beginnings of a strategic plan, there are no quick answers for management. It is a significant risk, without truly standardized measurement methods.

It is also possible to see misleading results from early measures of productivity of multimedia CBTs. As with the COMET results cited in this chapter, there may be an initial approval of multimedia CBTs, followed by a general disenchantment of the method by users. With somewhat of a "honeymoon syndrome" all appears well, and the multimedia CBTs appear to be very successful, then as users become accustomed to the method of training, usage falls (Wilson, 1996). To assume that all is well, and neglect to pursue a strategic plan for measuring productivity can result in false sense of security for companies. Perhaps the novelty of the multimedia CBTs is what carries their use for the first years.

COMET is so convinced of the necessity of continually evaluating their modules with a general strategic plan that they have instituted a budget line item for independent summative evaluation studies with all of their development proposals (Lamos, 1996). For a truer assessment of productivity of multimedia CBTs, companies must pursue measures beyond those initial evaluations.

In addition, one of the most challenging aspects of developing, and even just implementing multimedia CBTs that are outsourced, is the teamwork required of the effort. If the company decides to produce the CBT in-house, where all of the subject matter experts (SMEs) reside, the problem of gathering a qualified production team is a major hurdle. The company is not only making a technology investment, it is making a human resource investment as well. Multimedia programs, out of necessity, are always produced by a cross-functional team of authors, skilled in their own specific areas, working together to take advantage of all media possibilities. As Dean notes, "The production of high quality CBT courses is a challenging process requiring skills in training design." (1988, p. 167). What one team member knows about logic and programming constructs and coding is complemented by his/her teammates' knowledge of composition, layout, writing, use of color, audio and video production, instructional design, and success-ful presentation. Good multimedia software requires knowledge and skills in all of these areas. No one person possesses all of these attributes. Therefore, a team, and a team composed of authors from different disciplines, constitute the standard multimedia development team (Reisman, 1994.)

Thankfully, company trainers and IT employees are often already from many disciplines—information systems, psychology, education and instructional design, sociology, technical writing, journalism and communication. All of these disciplines are frequently represented within the department that handles end user training or company training. The heterogeneous nature of most training staffs is a natural for the successful development of multimedia CBTs. The OppenheimerFunds case study cited here is an example of such an eclectic group of developers. However, meshing such varied individu-als into a team takes cooperation and work. The mix requires strong teamwork skills and a unified commitment by all.

Team multimedia CBT development within a company also re-quires strong management support. The development process as-sumes a cooperative and adventuresome nature. This requires a commitment that recognizes the risk, yet weighs the possible gains for all. This adventuresome environment may not be politically feasible within some companies. As noted, teamwork is vital, and upper management support is a necessity for successful teamwork (Larson, 1989). Companies must be willing to balance the risks and the rewards in order to successfully develop CBTs and train employees using the newest multimedia environments. This is a special challenge in light of the work force reduction that is current within many American corporations (Marino, 1996). Giving employees the freedom to develop CBTs without realizing the return on the investment for five years is desirable, but often not realistic. The production staff needs this liberty in order to succeed, yet top level management often wants quick results. As was noted earlier, there are no known quick measures of results of implementing multimedia CBTs. Executive endorsement and support are just as important as the funding to develop the CBTs.

The implementation of multimedia CBTs requires team effort, strong management support, and flexibility—a study in contrasts. Although the COMET modules were developed for three different weather services, the implementation of the modules cited here were the most successful in NWS (National Weather Service), an organization with strong centralized management. Their use at AWS (Air Force Air Weather Service) and NMOC (Naval Meteorology and Oceanography Command) were not as widespread. The Coors Brewery case cited does not yet have widespread use of their CBTs, either. The OppenheimerFunds case cited has a multimedia CBT that every new employee nationwide is required to complete.

Even with a thorough understanding of all of the arguments for and against multimedia CBTs, if a strong sense of commitment and true teamwork is not present, a company may still not experience a payoff for its significant investment in this new technology.

Finally, there must be the realization that for all of the hype about "new electronic tutelage" and using computers as our ultimate tool—using them as natural extensions of our biological selves—in many areas of computer usage we are not at critical mass yet (Ganger, 1990). What is true in one company or one part of the globe is certainly not true universally. We know that employees still use text as their fundamental means of learning. The COMET data collection indicated that 69% of employees still reach for a book or a user guide instead of an on-line module when they need to learn something. What is more, in the COMET study, data shows that new employees are not introduced to the CBT modules as a matter of course (only 39 % of the time). Therefore, this enormous expenditure on multimedia CBTs is not being used in a most cost effective way. Instilling voluntary usage seems to be a major challenge to the widespread adoption of multimedia CBTs. The final section of this chapter gives some strategic guidelines for managers wishing to begin using and measuring effectiveness of multimedia CBTs.

All of these advantages and disadvantages must be considered when a corporation is investigating the feasibility of adopting multimedia CBTs for their training. Being aware of potential problems is a first step toward successful implementation of multimedia CBTs in business. The second is an awareness of the team commitment such training programs require.

Responding to the Challenge

To develop a strategic management policy for measuring the success of multimedia CBTs, a metric and a method are required. The case study of American corporations evaluating implementation of their multimedia training programs (Hall, 1995) can provide an outline of a strategic plan for measuring the return on the investment of multimedia CBTs. The following case studies add to the possibilities for applying the theory. The entire research project, including the cases cited here, is exploratory and longitudinal: the topic of a strategic plan for measuring the productivity of multimedia CBTs is relatively new, and will evolve with time. As cases are added, and evaluations accumulate, a clearer picture of desirable strategies will emerge.

The Three Case Studies

To those companies that early on committed to using, and even developing CBTs in-house, such as these case studies of COMET, OppenheimerFunds, Inc. and Coors Brewery, the information technology investment has been a difficult but generally rewarding experience (Gnadt, 1996). Although the three companies showcased here are at different stages of implementation of multimedia CBTs, they conclude that the multimedia CBTs that they develop and/or use within their corporations are a worthwhile investment. The COMET program has the most experience, and the most extensive evaluation system. OppenheimerFunds is in the process of implementing a new evaluation plan. Both companies have an ongoing development team for future CBT modules. Coors is in the earliest stages of implementing and evaluating the success of their multimedia CBTs. Implementation of their CBTs is restricted to the Information Technology end user training division.

COMET

COMET is the Cooperative Program for Operational Meteorology, Education, and Training, part of the University Corporation for Atmospheric Research (UCAR) in Boulder, Colorado. They have been authoring multimedia CBTs for meteorologist training for eight years. COMET's multimedia CBTs have been used by the National Weather Service (NWS), the Air Force Air Weather Service (AWS), and the Naval Meteorology and Oceanography Command (NMOC) as part of their distance learning programs. Under the direction of Program Manager Dr. Joseph Lamos, COMET is now producing a module a month for the three weather services. Their earliest modules—the Doppler Radar Interpretation and the Convection Initiation and Boundary Detection were produced in 1992. They have continued building and implementing modules since that time, doing formative evaluations and summative evaluations on each individual module. In 1995, they contracted an extensive summative evaluation of nine modules that spanned six years of the program's history (Wilson, 1996).   The study was a triangulated evaluation, using both quantitative and qualitative measures. COMET's study was one of the most comprehensive attempts at measuring the return for the investment of multimedia CBTs that has been done.   Done by an independent team at the University of Colorado, May Lowry and Dr. Brent Wilson directed a six-month study using personal interviews, quantitative and qualitative questionnaires (394), site visits (17), focus groups (4), and extant data from the records of COMET. As a result of this independent evaluation, COMET was able to measure the payoff of their multimedia learning program for the National Weather Service, the Air Force Air Weather Service, and the Naval Meteorology and Oceanographic Command.

In the case of COMET's data, users indicated that as more modules were introduced, they completed less of each. What is more, the rating on the effectiveness of the material (the content and how it was taught) decreased correspondingly. Tables 1 and 2 show the completion rates and the rating of effectiveness for the first four modules COMET introduced. As each subsequent module was introduced, the completion rate and the effectiveness rating decreased substantially. Whether the introduction of modules were in order of importance—that is, the most important, most needed completed first—had a bearing on the use and effectiveness rating by users, or whether the users tired of, and took for granted technology that first seemed exciting and innovative, or some other variables such as busier schedules, less manpower were responsible for the regular decline, the trend hints at what was described earlier as "the honeymoon syndrome." Tables 1 and 2 show some of the results of the independent evaluation.

Of the three cases sited here, COMET is by far the most experienced at both designing and building multimedia CBT systems and also measuring their productivity. They have the largest base of users, as well. The independent evaluators for COMET sent out 950 surveys to be filled out by participants. They included closed items, and open questions as well (e.g. "How did this CBT compare to other training you have had?" and "In the past year, where did you learn any new meteorological methods or information?") The mailed surveys were followed up with seventeen on-sight visits to locations all over the country. For triangulation, the evaluation team also used focus groups. The evaluation was extensive; however, the actual dollar amount of the return on the investments of NWS, AWS, or NMOC has not been attempted. The perceived value of content of the modules was

Module Number	1	2	3	4
% of Module Completed	90	80	70	68

Titles of Module:
1= Doppler Radar Interpretation, 1992
2= Convection Initiation and Boundary Detection, 1992
3= Heavy Precipitation and Flash Flooding, 1993
4= Forecast Process, 1993

Table 1 : Completion Rates of COMET Modules by National Weather Service

Module Number:	1	2	3	4
Content Effectiveness	4	4.0	3.9	3.6
How material taught	4	3.7	3.7	3.4

Rating from 1-5 (not good -> very good)

Table 2: COMET CBT module Effectiveness Rating

surveyed, but no link between the time and money expended, and the return for them was established. The next case—OppenheimerFunds' plan—is trying to determine dollar value as well.

OppenheimerFunds

OppenheimerFunds is the shareholder services division of Oppenheimer Management Corporation, a national investment corporation. Although there is a small office in New York City near Wall Street, the training for the entire corporation is done in Denver, Colorado. In 1995, the company Training and Development division began in-house production of multimedia CBTs. There is a small team of company trainers (no more than 5) who are charged with the actual development of the CBTs, while the rest of the department continues to train employees in the usual way—small instructor led classes at preset times. By 1996 the first five multimedia CBT modules were developed and deployed on the company network. For the first several months, OppenheimerFunds used the same evaluation forms for their multimedia CBTs that they had used for their small class training sessions. This effectively measured the trainer—in this case, some of the authors of the CBT—but not much of the CBT itself. Table 3 shows some results for the first CBTs OppenheimerFunds implemented. They used a traditional Likert scale 1-5, with 5 as the highest and 1 as the lowest level. They also used some of the more traditional open ended questions, such as:

"What was the most valuable aspect of the CBT?"
or
"Was there anything confusing?"

As can be seen, OppenheimerFunds' experience with multimedia CBTs seems to have improved with each successive administration.
The open-ended questions revealed problems with hardware and software and the amount of content of the modules—too much or too monotonous. Some of the qualitative comments are summarized in Figure 4.

	Dates	3/96	4/96	4/96	5/96	6/96
Level of confidence after using CBT		3.7	3.8	4.3	4.0	4.6
Concepts were clear, understandable		3.5	4.4	4.3	4.3	4.4
Pace of the CBT: too slow -> too fast		3.0	3.0	3.0	3.0	3.0

Table 3: Oppenheimer's CBT Folio VIEWS Evaluations

What was the most valuable aspect of the CBT?

- the interactivity
- the self-paced nature
- ease of use

What could be improved?

- the amount of downtime, system problems
- less keystrokes for each procedure
- needs better organization
- mastery of CD-ROM skills, need more technology training first
- need bigger icons

Figure 4: Qualitative Reponses—OppenheimerFunds Evaluations

The traditional evaluation forms, especially the qualitative open-ended questions quickly became valuable guides as to how to design a new form to better measure the success of the CBT. A new form with something more was needed to measure the productivity of their new multimedia computer based training program. As manager Jane Gnadt noted, they needed to know how many employees were more productive, had better performance evaluations, and better retention rates as a result of CBT training rather than the traditional classes (Gnadt, 1996). This required a new management strategy for measuring productivity of their multimedia CBTs.

The Training and Development division of OppenheimerFunds has recently revamped its CBT evaluation forms, and is using them as well as a Pre- and Post-Baseline Survey. There is still the traditional Training Observation forms, and there is still a five point Likert scale. However, there is now a section of the evaluation form that asks for input on how well the user was able to learn new material using the self-paced nature and the simulations and images of the CBTs. The next phase of the evaluation process hopefully will include things like relating retention and whether the employee used the CBTs or traditional training environment, or items like the number of customer telephone service interactions and whether the employee was trained with the multimedia CBT modules. Oppenheimer has plans for extensive evaluations of their CBTs; they have the advantage of in-house development and quick response to module problems that other companies might not have. OppenheimerFunds' challenge is to produce quality in-house multimedia CBTs to place on the network for all departments to access at any time, without the direction of a company trainer, and to accurately determine the return for the investment in their new endeavor. The management strategy at Oppenheimer is evolutionary, but the company is committed to their CBT development.

Coors

Coors Brewery had to resume CAI training much more cautiously than the other two cases cited—because of a past less than successful experience with text-based CBTs. Coors Brewery is located in Golden, Colorado. It is a third-generation, family-owned brewery, employing some six thousand individuals. The Training Division of Information Technology has recently adopted CBTs to teach employees the ins and out of the *Oracle®* database system (Gardelin, 1996; Nash, 1995). In the past they had used the "Video Professor" series for technology training as well. Their present challenge is not just to realize a return on the investment, but to first affect a change in a deep-seated company attitude. Past experiences with CAI and distributed video stations in each department where employees were released to work on their own at the station were accepted, but not enthusiastically embraced—by management and individual departments alike. Coors still faces the challenge of developing a strategic management plan for measuring the payoff on their current CBT undertaking.

As was noted earlier, the lack of standardized methods is contributing to Coors' "catch-22" situation of not being able to accurately evaluate their CBT training before time and money is spent implementing it. In view of their previous mistakes, they are proceeding cautiously.

Paul Gardelin of Coors Information Technology division notes that past benefits were substantial, despite the margin of acceptance (1996.) Some of the advantages Coors found with using CBTs was that the timing was flexible. This same benefit was noted by almost every study that has been done by companies implementing CBTs (Wilson, 1996; Hall, 1995; Dean, 1988; Kulik, 1993.) Scheduling was easier because it could be at the employee's convenience. However, the employee came to the training facility, or else went to an area of his/her work facilty where a temporary training station had been set up. In other words, he/she could not do the training from his/her desk, as is presently done at OppenheimerFunds. The training was cheaper than instructor-led sessions. However, and was much more flexible. As Price Waterhouse noted in their study on the return on their investment, over five years the cost per learner decreased from $760 to $106 when multimedia training was introduced (Hall, 1995.) The first training at Coors could not be classified as true multimedia CBTs. Yet Coors experienced a similar reduction in employee training costs. Even more cost reduction should be realized with the multimedia training they are beginning. When American Airlines moved from a text-based CBT to a multimedia CBT, they saw an even greater reduction in hours required to train—from 300 to 150 when multimedia CBTs replaced the traditional text-based ones (Hall, 1995.)

In the past at Coors, employees were limited to the availability of one VCR or PC, which were shared by all. Coors had even used hardcopy training books that were dispensed to departments in the past. End-users went to the department conference room to use the setup, one at a time. There are still no plans to network the CBTs at Coors, but they would like to change delivery, providing single user copies on disk or CD to dispense. Employees could then use their own PC's for the CBT session. An eventual method of delivery-provided this current effort is successful-could be to deploy the CBT on a company-wide Intranet network, providing the same Internet Web style browser employees are familiar with, but keeping the network in-house where multimedia delivery would not suffer the same delay in delivery that *Netscape®* based Internet applications currently experience because of limited bandwidth.

The CBTs Coors used in the past have been supplemented with a written test, so no electronic record keeping is employed. Results of end-user training with CBTs are similar to the first Coors experience. If Coors heeds the research on multimedia CBTs, they will note that manual record keeping and pencil tests were a complaint of employees at American Airlines (Hall, 1995.) It seems if a company is to implement multimedia CBTs, the employees also expect electronic testing and evaluation.

Flexibility and individual scheduling makes the CBT program at Coors productive (Gardelin and Barrows, 1996). The employee can stop the session at any time, and pick up later. With the previous experience, there was better mastery of the material; the average mastery was 80%. If one looks at the previous case studies underwritten by MacroMedia:

> There is strong evidence that computer based training results in equal or higher quality of learning over traditional instruction (Hall, 1995, p. 2.)

The greatest benefit that Coors noted with their experiences with CBTs is also one of the hardest to measure in dollar return: consistency of training. The fact that the CBT training was individual was one of the greatest benefits. In the past manual training sessions, one representative from a department was sent to classes. Then the trained one returned to his/her department and trained the others. The element of personal interpretation and mastery was always there. That is, the second generation were trained as the first had interpreted the material; the training was different in every department because everyone interprets classes differently. The CBTs present the "same story" to everyone; there is no "middleman." Then, as with any learning, the individual interprets it his/her own way. This made a big difference in mastery and standardization of training programs. Ray

Barrows of end-user training notes that Coors does not have any firm plans for evaluation of its CBTs' productivity yet, but that is the next step after its widespread implementation (1996.)

All three companies use self-reporting and on-site visits and interviews. OppenheimerFunds future plans for tying required multimedia CBTs to employee performance and retention introduces a more robust quantitative measure. Feedback from series of employees who have used CBTs will be compared with evaluations of those who participated in trainer-led sessions. Likewise, scores on manual assessments will be compared with CBT records. Finally, performance evaluations of groups that trained with the CBTs will possibly be compared with those who trained with company trainer-led sessions. The acceptance of employees to this new type of training (as determined by the self-reports) and their performance on the job, (as determined by performance evaluations, amount of sales, time spent with clients, and so forth) will better quantify the investment these companies have made in their CBT training programs. The three cases cited reflect companies that are concerned that the implementation of multimedia CBTs realize an appropriate return. They plan to continue to expand their CBT programs, and they are anxious for a strategic plan for measuring the productivity of their CBTs.

Management Strategies for Information Technology Investment

From these first-hand case studies of implementation of multimedia CBTs in business and from the past studies on ROI of multimedia, an initial strategic plan can be formulated. As with all new technology implementations, management strategies for investment payoff are necessarily iterative. That is, as more multimedia CBTs are introduced and used within the corporation, the strategies will keep changing and improving. As more and more cases are studied and more and more is learned about what has been done that is right, and what strategies are not effective, a more definitive plan will evolve. Companies can benefit from their own first experiences and from those of others. It is possible to early on devise a strategic plan to guide the measurement of investment payoff of multimedia CBTs, keeping in mind that the plan may change. The importance of having an initial strategic plan— a long range guide for measuring success—is what is important. Just as a company would not embark on introducing a new product or revising its internal structure without a strategic plan, nor should it introduce multimedia CBTs without some strategic plan for measuring the payoff for their investment.

It can be clearly seen from the available data that multimedia CBTs can reduce the total cost of training when compared to instructor-led sessions, that there is less time required for the training, there is employee acceptance, and the retention of material is at least as good as traditional company training programs. The promise of electronic tutelage can be realized, and there can be an acceptable return on the investment if a few basic principles are followed.

Prepare the User

The first recommendation for a strategic management plan for implementing multimedia CBTs is the same end-user perspective for all information technology projects: assuring an educated user. Before the information technology division of a company commits to implementing multimedia CBTs, it should have in place firm plans for ensuring that all employees who will be using the CBTs will have the technical skills necessary to comfortably use the hardware and software necessary to complete the CBT. This means training on the specific system that will be used. It is true that employees of today are more "computer savvy" than those of a decade ago. There are few true cases of cyberphobia in the workplace today; nevertheless, an educated user is paramount to the success of multimedia CBTs. Even a well-designed CBT can be intimidating to the unfamiliar. A very brief orientation to the equipment can make all of the difference. Hackos, DeMarco, Fenrich and many other end-user authorities echo what the data gathered in this study has told us: more technology training will give a company a better return on their information technology investment, including the multimedia CBT investment (Hackos, 1995; Fenrich, 1997).

The cryptic or nonexistent instructions of text-based CAIs of the past gave them a bad reputation. The friendly user interface and on-line help of multimedia CBTs today make them generally intuitive. Yet all of the data from the three case studies cited here indicate that more help with the particular CBT system would have improved its effectiveness. The key to successful multimedia CBT implementation is the same key as with all information technology—a better educated user. Zuboff's view of computers' role of automating and informating our world includes training the end user in all aspects necessary to perform tasks (Zuboff, 1988). Electronic tutelage only works with the educated user. If management recognizes (and provides funds for) training of the user of the multimedia CBTs, there is a greater likelihood of an acceptable return on the investment (King, 1995). This naturally adds to the time and expense of already very expensive multimedia CBTs, but it should dramatically increase chances of success. For this reason, it is the first step in the management strategy for multimedia CBTs—providing for an educated user. Doing needs assessment for types of new technology training required will show a company just how much and what type of specialized training the end-user will need before using a multimedia CBT (Gagne and Briggs,

1992). Assuring technology training for multimedia CBT implementation is the first step in a strategic management plan.

Develop a Measure of Time and Cost of Training

The second management strategy is a quantitative one. It has been noted that multimedia CBTs involve a great deal of time and expense, from planning to implementation. And once implemented, there is a time lag before a return on the investment can be realized. A true evaluation of success may come years after the multimedia CBTs are in place; five years was the standard in this study. Although implementing multimedia CBTs calls for a little "blind faith" on the part of management, measures of cost of training and time invested must be developed. The companies who have developed templates, such as the Storage Tek "Cost Comparison Spreadsheet" and the Pacific Gas and Electric "Decision Aid," have allowed these companies to juxtapose their costs with the time reduction in employee training (Hall, 1995). While waiting until the multimedia CBT has had time to prove itself, a company can track the reduction in time and expense of training. As was noted, OppenheimerFunds is working closely with its corporate statistics division to develop a similar template for time and expense compared to employee productivity.

Since it takes several years to accurately assess the productivity of multimedia CBTs, measures of time and expense should begin immediately, and continue. Both COMET and OppenheimerFunds would have a very different picture of their successes had they stopped with the first formative evaluations. Even if it takes five years to get a credible measure on the return, measures should begin immediately and continue for as long as the CBTs are in place. Management patience and an ongoing, constant collection of evaluative data is good strategy. Giving a multimedia CBT project a five year window for accurate measures is difficult in a world of short term solutions, but it is the recommended strategy. The ongoing formative evaluations give some indication of the direction of success, but measuring the dollar worth of the return on the investment can begin immediately, recognizing that time will give a truer picture. Giving multimedia CBTs time to prove themselves or doom themselves is the second recommended strategy.

Use Multiple Evaluation Methods

Measuring productivity of multimedia CBTs is inprecise at best. At its worst, it is downright misleading. As was noted, any metric so dependent upon human involvement cannot be purely scientific and quantitative. The tangible is intertwined with the intangible. Any measures that involve so many human elements, so many variables to success must be regarded with prudence. By implementing many measures, both qualitative and quantitative, a truer measure of success can be determined. Therefore, as shown with these three cases, several methods of evaluation should be attempted. Gathering ratings on Likert scales, using interviews and focus groups, using written tests, self reports, and open questions—all of these methods should be combined with quantitative measures of cost and time of training to produce a comprehensive measure of productivity. If it is possible to correlate end-user mastery of multimedia CBT material with amount of sales or employee longevity, or other quantitative measures, it should be attempted. Combining several methods of evaluation is termed triangulation; it makes good management strategy to use as many tools as possible to determine the return on the investment of multimedia CBTs. The more quantitative methods such as correlating employee retention with type and depth of training received may occasionaly mislead, but they do make measuring the return on the investment more scientific than the purely qualitative means of measuring productivity of CBTs, such as open questions and observations. Recommended strategic management plans would include using many, diverse means of measuring productivity of the CBTs. By combining methods, it is possible to measure with some degree of confidence the return on the investment in multimedia CBTs.

Can a payoff on an investment in multimedia CBTs be assessed? What is an appropriate strategy for a company to follow to evaluate the return on costs of multimedia training programs? These are the questions this chapter began with. The recommendations for management strategies are the partial answer the study produced. Multimedia CBTs require a huge up-front investment in hardware and software that becomes obsolete practically before it is unpacked. Even if companies lease rather than buy equipment (Inc. Technology, 1995) ,the hardware and software investment for a company that embarks upon a multimedia CBT program is substantial. The time arrives when the investment must be justified.

There is no quick and certain answer to measuring the return on the investment of multimedia CBTs. Despite all of the promises multimedia CBTs make, a sure strategic management plan for measuring their productivity still alludes us. There are only suggestions, and initial attempts. The companies cited here are still searching for the answer to the problem of evaluating the return on the investment when using multmedia CBTs. They are joined by more and more other companies who believe in using technology for training. As the use of multimedia CBTs increases, a clearer management plan will emerge.

In summary, it is often tempting for companies to embrace new technology, and multimedia CBTs are attractive alternatives to traditional employee training. The addition of graphics, sound, animation, video, and interactivity make training programs more enticing, more personalized, and provide "just in time" training. However, determining if the information technology has a payoff is not as easy. Despite the difficulty of measuring a payoff with so many intangible benefits, companies are beginning to assess the return for investment in their multimedia CBTs. From the data gathered, it appears that it can be determined if multimedia CBTs are a worthwhile and rewarding investment. With time and the addition of more case studies, an effective pattern will emerge. With the research begun, however, companies can start looking at investing in multimedia CBTs with the assurance that, indeed, there will be more and more measures of productivity developed to assess this newest method of training. The promise of electronic tutelage can be realized, and it can be measured.

Chapter 20

Business Use of the Internet

Elizabeth R. Towell
Northern Illinois University

For many years, acceptable use policies (AUPs) developed by the Federal Government forbade commercial traffic on the Internet. Relaxation of these restrictions over the past five years, together with a shift in ownership of the Internet, has resulted in the proliferation of commercial hosts. Once a government–controlled, tax–supported endeavor, Internet development is now evolving through private costs based on commercial value. The rapid adoption of the Internet within the organization has been paralleled by a rapidly growing impetus to accelerate realization of value from Internet Investment. This chapter describes a framework for evaluating the costs and benefits of Internet investment. Three recommendations are made: 1) consider Internet planning as an iterative process; 2) plan the overall role of the Internet in the organization; and 3) measure the value of Internet investment in three dimensions: financial, strategic, and enterprise.

A survey conducted in the spring of 1996 investigated business use of the Internet (Feher & Towell, 1996). While over 85% of information technology (IT) managers responding said they were currently using the Internet, only 20% felt strongly that they would realize significant business value from Internet use. The 85% adoption figure is remarkable. For many years, acceptable use policies (AUP's) forbade commercial traffic on the Internet. Beginning in 1991, the Federal Government relaxed restrictions and several large commercial access providers emerged. As of July 1996, there were about 419,000 commercial hosts on the Internet.

The rapid adoption of the Internet within the organization over the last five years can be compared to the adoption of other broad-sweeping technologies such as the personal computer (PC) or the relational database. Phases of IT adoption have been characterized by a stage of identification and initial investment, followed by experimentation and proliferation, followed next by control of the proliferation, and finally widespread technology transfer (Nolan & Gibson, 1974; McFarlan & McKenney, 1983).

It is clear that the use of the Internet in a business setting has entered the proliferation stage (Turner, 1995a). This will be most likely followed by some control of the proliferation, and eventually, maturation. It is equally clear that many IT managers are unable to evaluate the contribution of this new technology within their organization. A top priority for IT managers should be building the business case for Internet investment (Turner, 1995b; Turner, 1995c). This chapter describes a framework for evaluating the costs and benefits of Internet adoption.

What Is The Internet?

The Internet is a set of networks and machines that use the same communications protocol and addressing scheme. The Transmission Control Protocol/Internet Protocol (TCP/IP) reference model utilized for standardizing communication between computers consists of four layers: a network access layer, an Internet layer, a transport layer, and an application layer (Figure 1). This protocol was first developed at University of California, Berkeley, as the Berkeley Software Distribution (BSD) UNIX network protocol. Berkeley's UNIX and this protocol became well established in the academic, research and defense worlds first and later spread to the commercial arena.

Addressing a specific host on the Internet can be done in two ways. The Internet Network Information Center (InterNIC) utilizes a dual

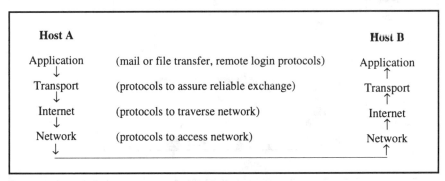

Figure 1: The TCP/IP Model for Communication Between Two Hosts

addressing scheme so that each host has both a dot-separated decimal IP address (e.g., 131.156.1.191) and a hierarchical domain name, in the form *host.domain.* The domain name often expresses type of organization or geographical location. For example, *hayek.cob.niu.edu* is an educational host; *hayek.cob* is a uniquely addressable machine at domain *niu.edu.* There may be many hosts associated with one domain name. The domain name for commercial hosts typically end in *.com.* InterNIC now charges $50 annually for the registration of a domain name.

The Shift In Ownership Of The Internet

Development of the Internet was funded largely by the US Federal Government under the auspices of the National Science Foundation (NSF) for research and defense applications. In the spring of 1995, the NSF shifted the bulk of its funding to a new experimental network called the Very-High-Speed-Backbone Network Service (vBNS).

The main Internet backbone (NSFNET) had been operated and maintained by Advanced Network & Services (ANS), which was set up by a non-profit consortium of state-supported universities in Michigan in conjunction with IBM and MCI. When the NSF eliminated NSFNET funding, this backbone was sold to America Online (AOL). Maintenance of the Internet backbone today is handled by ANS, AOL, and other commercial network service providers like MCI and Sprint. Thus, Internet development, once a government-controlled, tax-supported endeavor, is now evolving through private costs, based on commercial value.

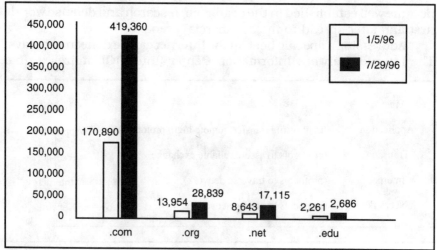

Figure 2: Change in Number of Domain Names Registered by Type, First Quarter 1996

The Growth In Number Of Commercial Domains

An organization known as InterNet Info specializes in the analysis of commercial domains. Their snapshot published for first half of 1996 shows an increase of over 145% in the number of InterNIC registered commercial domains.[1] As of July, 1996, over 89% of Internet domain names were commercial (Figure 2). This rapid growth of commercial domains has been paralleled by a rapidly growing impetus to accelerate realization of value.   Good, meaningful metrics for Internet investment payoffs, however, are not yet available.

Current Limitations of the Internet

The Internet has not yet reached the maturation stage. The most widely discussed limitations today are summarized here:

Unsophisticated Security Protocols-Inadequate security is probably the biggest challenge to widespread Internet adoption. The use of the Internet introduces new security threats for individuals and businesses. Information transferred over the Internet is vulnerable to access, modification, and even destruction by unauthorized parties. Dependence of the medium can lead to additional problems if access is interrupted for significant periods of time. In the survey by Feher and Towell (1996), 60% of the responding IT managers were "very concerned" and another 38% "somewhat concerned" with regard to current Internet security.

Insufficient Search Tools-The associative structure of many Internet documents and their uncontrolled proliferation have contributed to a situation in which it is tedious for businesses and individual consumers to locate useful information.   While there are many products and services which provide searching and indexing tools, they are largely unsophisticated and incomplete. The Internet can be compared to a library where books and even pages within books are organized using a variety of schemes.   Furthermore, no assistance is available from a librarian or comprehensive card catalog.

Common Access-As a commercial medium, the largest obstacle to use of the Internet is public access.   Commerce on the Internet will be hindered until socio-economic barriers fall away. This may come as a result of less expensive computers which can be used primarily as network appliances or by government funding of public terminals in libraries or other institutions.

Limited Bandwidth-Use of the Internet to reach consumers in a meaningful way is also hindered by technological boundaries. The Internet is usually accessed from the home via a 28.8 kilobits per second or slower modem. This inhibits effective use of applications incorporating audio, video, or even larger graphical images. Network transport technologies being developed now promise speeds in the gigabit per second range by the late 1990's but extending significant improvements "the last mile" to homes will take much longer.

Justifying IT Investment

The IT organization is under increasing pressure to make evident its understanding of what constitutes business value and to demonstrate the contribution generated by specific IT investment *before the investment is made.* It is important for IT managers to have a framework for justifying IT investment and to have metrics which define success. Tangible values and costs can be substantiated through financial calculations. Traditional cost-benefit analysis, however, is no longer adequate for most information system applications that are innovative (Parker and Benson, 1987). Many of the early Internet applications are linked to less tangible benefits such as enhanced customer service and quality, improved time to market, or added value to research and development. Innovative IT applications such as these, often provide benefits which can be clearly linked to enterprise goals but are more difficult to predict and measure.

This chapter looks specifically at the business case for Internet adoption. The underlying theme is that the business value of the Internet should be evaluated, not in terms of an isolated situation, but in terms of the *role* that Internet access will play in the organization. Justification for investment and metrics for measuring success should be established on the basis of this overall role. The role of the Internet must be determined by first investigating applications available and

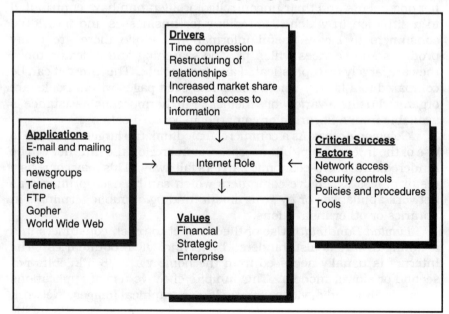

Figure 3: Determining the Role of the Internet in an Organization

drivers for adoption; next by characterizing critical success factors in adoption; and finally by considering the potential values, both tangible and intangible, within a particular organization (Figure 3). The next section discusses key Internet applications and drivers. The third section considers critical success factors and risk unique to this technology. The final section discusses categories of value and proposes a framework for making investment decisions.

Internet Applications and Drivers

There are several applications supported by the TCP/IP protocols that may be used in a variety of ways to address key business concerns. Discussed in the following paragraphs are six applications supported by Internet protocols. Examples of use of these applications illustrate how they relate to business needs. Extended cases are also presented to provide a more comprehensive picture of the role of the Internet in two organizations. Case 1 is application oriented and discusses St. George Crystal and their Virtual Product Exchange. This application allows St. George Crystal to develop products interactively with their customers. Case 2 is process oriented and describes how the well-known traditional print media publisher, John Wiley & Sons, approached the development of electronic print materials on the Internet.

Electronic Mail and Mailing Lists

The Simple Mail Transfer Protocol (SMTP) provides a basic mechanism for transferring messages among separate hosts on the Internet. Features of SMTP include capabilities for messages to be sent to multiple recipients simultaneously, simplified reply addressing, and forwarding of messages. Messages can be created in local editors or local electronic mail facilities. E-mail is quicker than using the postal service and is often cheaper than phone or FAX communication. Electronic mail (e-mail) is the most commonly used Internet application in business (Feher & Towell, 1996).

Software has been developed to maintain lists of the e-mail addresses of users sharing a common interest. The most common of these programs is called LISTSERV, which maintains user lists for about 10,000 different topics. A user subscribing to a LISTSERV list receives all mail sent to the group. The cost of sending many pieces of mail to everyone on a list is the same as sending just one message. The business use of mailing lists is centered on hardware, software and technology concerns. There are 68 lists involving IBM products alone. There are 74 lists with "Internet" in their description with another 24 focusing on the WWW. There are seven lists dedicated to Microsoft products:

• Microsoft Access Database Discussion List
• Microsoft Excel Developers' List
• Microsoft Mail Discussion List
• Microsoft SQL Server Discussion List
• Discussion for Microsoft Visual Basic Data Access
• Microsoft Windows for Workgroups
• WINDOWS: A forum for Q&A, rumors and insights about Microsoft

Mailing lists are used for press releases and product updates as well as the sharing of problems and expertise.

Usenet Newsgroups

Mailing lists facilitate mass distribution of a message to hundreds or thousands of interested recipients. Usenet newsgroups have the same general purpose but are a passive form of the mailing list concept. Usenet is itself a network of machines that store the various groups' postings and move traffic over the Internet. Readers do not receive each communication as electronic mail, but access and read the information stored centrally on a Usenet machine that has been posted for a particular group.

Usenet is divided hierarchically into major categories including biz (business), comp (computers), soc (social topics), clari (Associated Press wire service news), news (Usenet organization news), sci (science), rec (recreation), alt (alternative topics), talk (topics for debate) and misc (miscellaneous topics) and then further divided by specific interest area. There are more than 10,000 Usenet groups such as *misc.invest.fund* and *biz.jobs.offered*. Newsgroups centered on technology, hardware, or software are particularly abundant. Internet users can access information posted to Usenet newsgroups at no cost. They can post questions and read or answer questions on topics of interest as well. Basic questions on a given topic (called Frequently Asked Questions or FAQ's) are often compiled and serve as a very useful reference. Newsgroups can also be used to offer low cost customer support. Digital Equipment Corporation (DEC), for example, posts press releases, product announcements, new services, sales promotions, and information on seminars to the biz.dec group.

Telnet

Telnet protocols provide a user with the capability to log-on to a remote computer via the Internet and perform tasks as if directly connected to that computer. The list of hosts with publicly accessible data is impressive. Libraries, schools, and governmental agencies offer a broad range of services. For example, Cornell Law School offers free access to legal information; Stanford makes campus information available via their Campus-Wide Information System (CWIS); the US Commerce Department's Economic Bulletin Board provides access to current information on economic and employment conditions. There are many commercial applications as well. An Internet user can buy CD's, flowers, or software using telnet. Book Stacks Unlimited in Cleveland, OH allows you to search over 365,000 titles by author, title, ISBN, or keyword and place orders for mail delivery using a credit card.

FTP

The file transfer protocol (FTP) allows users to move files from one system to another. Again, the number of publicly available files on the Internet is remarkable.   One recent estimate of the information available places it in the terabyte range or 1,000,000,000,000 byes of data (Gilster, 1995). Many schools, agencies, and companies allow anonymous users to download programs and informational files to their machines. For example, UPI Newswire releases are available from a host at University of Michigan. The U.S. Government provides images from various NASA shuttles and flights. The National Center for Supercomputing Applications (NCSA) offers many useful Internet programs. A primary business use of FTP is the downloading of software (Feher & Towell, 1996). Patches for known software problems are often available; standard operating system drivers for new hardware devices can usually be obtained by FTP; software upgrades are often distributed this way as well.

Both telnet and FTP can be used in a more restricted way. While many hosts allow any telnet user to login as a "guest" and any FTP user to login as "anonymous," it is possible to provide these services only in a more secure situation, allowing these services only to users entering a valid ID and password.

Gopher

Gopher software was developed initially for organizing campus information at the University of Minnesota. It is widely used today to help users locate and access information on the Internet. The Gopher information client provides users with a hierarchical set of menu choices; Gopher users do not need to remember commands or host names. Several potential actions are possible depending on the menu choice made: the text of a file may be viewed, another Gopher server may be accessed, an indexed search may be performed, a telnet connection may be established, or a file transfer may be initiated. Information is available on Gopher servers from the U.S. Departments of Commerce, Education, Energy, Justice, State, Transportation, and Health and Human Services. There are Gopher-based bookstores on-line including Addison-Wesley, O'Reilly and Associates, and the Electronic Newsstand. Catalog Mart has a Gopher site listing over 10,000 catalogs that can be obtained for free. There are Gopher accessible newspapers, history archives, and genealogy resources. There are even Gopher sites dedicated to listing popular Gopher sites!

World Wide Web

Beginning in 1994, the rapid growth of Gopher traffic gave way to a new phenomenon, a tool also intended for organizing information on the Internet, the World Wide Web (WWW). The WWW was initially developed at the European Particle Physics Laboratory, known as CERN, as a means for sharing information throughout a research organization. The unique features of the WWW are the use of hypertext links and the incorporation of multimedia. Users of the WWW are not constrained to hierarchical menus, but are provided with "hot links" in a document which, if desired, take them to related documents which may reside on the same WWW server or on a different server. This associative structure, while sometimes chaotic, is thought to be a more natural way to store and use information. Documents may incorporate graphics, audio, and video as well as text information.

According to the Internet Domain-Name Database, as of May 14, 1996, 58% of the registered Internet domains had WWW servers.[2] Use of the WWW has grown so rapidly that often its name is used synonymously with the Internet. Addresses in the Uniform Resource Locator (URL) format were developed as part of the specification for the WWW but now are used by WWW clients to point to a wide variety of Internet resources (Figure 4). *http://www.yahoo.com/Computers_and_Internet* is the address for a hypertext document (http stands for hypertext transport protocol) called Computers_and_Internet which is on the server www.yahoo.com.

Electronic Mail
mailto:etowell@niu.edu

USENET Newsgroups
news:comp.ai.genetic

Telnet
telnet://locis.loc.gov/

Gopher
gopher://gopher.gsfc.nasa.gov/

WWW
http://www.yahoo.com/Computers_and_Internet

Figure 4: Examples of URLs for a Variety of Internet Resources

Because of the additional multimedia capability of the WWW, it has become the medium of choice for many business applications on the Internet. Today, one can access the WWW pages of hundreds of passenger airlines. There are WWW pages belonging to jewelers, schools, lawyers, and churches. A company called Blue Chip Cookies with stores in twelve states now describes their line of fresh cookies on the WWW and offers phone, fax, or online ordering of cookies for delivery. They also provide franchise information online. Sheraton Inns offers directory services on the WWW, incorporating pictures, facility information, maps, and directions for their hotels worldwide. Resnick and Taylor (1995) describe six ways the WWW is being used for business: displaying brochures; operating stores; publishing newspapers, magazines, or newsletters; providing customer support; communicating with company investors and shareholders; and setting up a yellow page-style directory service.

Drivers for Adoption

There are a great many pressures and opportunities that might motivate a corporation to consider use of the Internet. Results from the survey by Feher and Towell (1996), provide additional insights into the way businesses are currently using the Internet. The factors for adoption mentioned by IT managers included these top two responses: increasing access to knowledge and entering new markets (Figure 5). The list of drivers for adoption is long and involves many overlapping themes; however most fit in one of these four general categories: streamlining processes or time compression, restructuring relationships with various stakeholders, increasing market share or profits, and increasing access to information or knowledge. St. George Crystal as discussed in Case 1 is a good example of a firm using the Internet

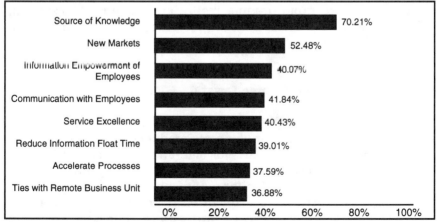

Figure 5: Top Eight Reasons Given by IT Managers for Internet Adoption

to streamline processes. John Wiley & Sons, discussed in Case 2, is more focused on the Internet as a medium for information access.

The survey results also suggested that in the spring of 1996 the top three applications for business use of the Internet were electronic e-mail, research, and downloading software. When asked for planned use of the Internet in the next twelve months, the same three primary applications were indicated, but there was significant growth in two additional areas: Electronic Data Interchange (EDI) and commerce/banking applications. The impact of this trend may be profound. Electronic commerce is expected to reshape the relationship between buyers and sellers in a fundamental way (Mason and Turner, 1995).

The top uses for corporate WWW servers were offering information about the company (92%), offering information about products (62%), and offering service related information (56%). Only 45% of the respondents had a policy in place restricting Internet use in the organization.

Case Analysis 1: The Catalyst Group and St. George Crystal

Introduction

The Catalyst Group is a strategic alliance developed by students and faculty from The Entrepreneurship Program of Northern Illinois University and the Institute for Competitive Manufacturing of the University of Illinois at Urbana-Champaign. Established in 1994, the alliance has been collaborating with a devoted group of American lighting manufacturers to collectively develop strategies for industry members to compete in the face of increasing global competition. Student teams, working on industry defined projects, are capitalizing on the Internet to implement competitive tactics ranging from desktop manufacturing to rapid product realization. One such project involves St. George Crystal, based in Jeannette, PA, and demonstrates the use of a variety of Internet functions to increase their global competitiveness.

St. George Crystal - History

St. George Crystal, the last 24% pure lead crystal manufacturer left in the United States, manufactures products ranging from crystal wine glasses to component parts for high-end crystal chandeliers. As a component supplier to the lighting industry, they have seen an increasing number of U.S. lighting manufacturers shift to a practice of importing less expensive component parts and full assemblies from off-shore producers (primarily countries in the Far-East). While increasing consumer demand has produced an overall growth in the lighting industry of 7% per year, domestic production has been decreasing by nearly 20% per year.

In order to stay in business and increase their competitiveness, St. George Crystal is beginning to implement an Internet-based product realization system developed by The Catalyst Group. Traditionally, each new product design required at least a four month undertaking to develop a customer approved prototype representing a cost of over $6,000. The process starts with the customer idea or requirement for a new product. St. George Crystal's engineers create an artistic sketch of the proposed design and mail or fax this to the customer. If approved, the sketch is drawn using a two-dimensional engineering software package such as AutoCad. This is again delivered to the customer for feedback and corrections prior to the design and creation of a metal mold (the part of the process which involves the most time and consequently cost). If the prototype parts are unsatisfactory, the mold is scraped and the lengthy process is repeated from the artistic sketch stage. The first three-dimensional presentation to the client occurs only after an extensive investment in creating the mold.

Innovation and Solution: Internet-Based System

The task given to The Catalyst Group student team was to reduce the cycle time and cost associated with realizing new products. In the reengineered process, ProEngineer (Pro/E), a powerful three-dimensional engineering software package, is used to replace the traditional 2-D drawing process. This product defines the parameters to create a rapid prototype eliminating the need to create an initial metal mold. In addition, client involvement is enhanced by capitalizing on the rapid communication environment of the Internet. The client is now able to visualize and respond to the new designs, from the initial artistic sketch through to the three-dimensional virtual product representation using VRML (Virtual Reality Modeling Language), within minutes of creation. This process is accomplished through a multi-functional dynamic Website (incorporating text, images, VRML, e-mail, FTP) called the Virtual Product Exchange (VPE). Figure 6 illustrates the VPE and labels each frame in the system. In frame #1 the client chooses from a catalog of option and products. A specific part can be called up into Frame #2 for inspection. Frame #2 serves a variety of functions and as depicted in Figure 6 contains a part in VRML. This VRML is generated by a software program, using the parameters generated by the 3-D drawing done in Pro/E. Other activities which can be performed in Frame #2 include viewing a photo-realistic rendering of the new design (again taken from the Pro/E parameters) or FTP the file for use on an Engineering workstation. Frame #3 is the feedback button (e-mail connection to the design engineer) and can be used by the client to comment on the picture or 3-D model they are viewing in Frame #2.

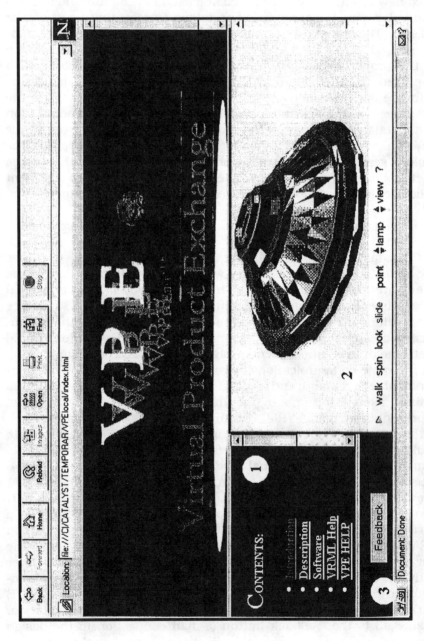

Figure 6: The Virtual Product Exchange Interface

Benefits and By-Products

The Virtual Product Exchange (VPE) tool is intended to do more than just reduce customer response time to design changes. It will reduce the number of iterations the design cycle has to go through by allowing the customer to track and influence the development of the product using the Internet as the platform. The customer will be able to access VPE through the World Wide Web, look at the prototype at the current stage of development and maintain "real time" interaction throughout the design phase. The flow charts shown in Figure 7a and 7b illustrate the differences between the current and proposed system at St. George Crystal.

The solution provided by The Catalyst Group will benefit St. George Crystal by;

• Reducing product time of development from four months to two weeks.
• Eliminating physical prototypes by scraping molds, saving $5K-$10K per development.
• Improving communications between St. George Crystal and its customers

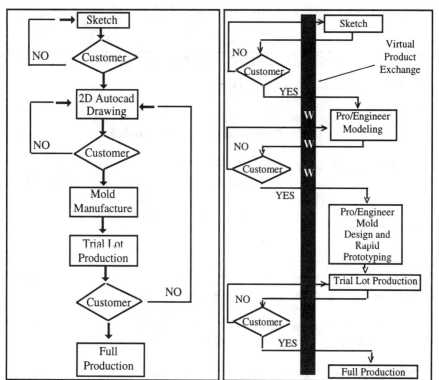

Figure 7a: Current Process Flow Chart   *Figure 7b: Proposed Process Flow Chart*

"Prosumer," a term coined by futurist Alvin Toffler, where the consumer actively engages in the product design process, may well be the shape of things to come via the use of the Internet at St. George Crystal. Problems at St. George Crystal can be quickly resolved, not only because they are more visible to all, but because the feedback loop for information is short. By the end of the project, St. George will have an interactive Web page. The Virtual Product Exchange system harnesses cutting edge technology to enhance the current production process at St. George Crystal. The Web page will be used to communicate with current customers on developing products, to advertise for new customers worldwide and to act as a product catalogue for future products. Members across the value chain share information, collaborate without geographic and time restrictions which previously would have been cost prohibitive if not technologically impossible. The platform independence of the Internet allows for this type of connection and collaboration.

St. George Crystal's vision in forging alliances with suppliers, customers and competitors with shared research to improve conditions for everyone, and the use of the Internet as the solution by acting as the enabler and architecture provider may well be the answer to the problems faced by the lighting industry.

Case Analysis 2: John Wiley & Sons, Inc. Information Technology

Wiley Overview and Background

Founded in 1807, John Wiley & Sons is the oldest independent publishing company in North America. Wiley is a global enterprise that develops and markets print and electronic products and services for the academic, professional, scientific, technical, medical, and consumer markets.

Wiley's goal is to anticipate and serve its customers' professional and personal needs for knowledge and understanding while generating financial results that yield attractive returns for all members of the Wiley partnership: shareholders, authors, and employees.

Five years ago, Wiley embarked on an aggressive strategic program to increase shareholder value by implementing and achieving four fundamental strategies. These strategies are:

- **Invest in core businesses**, through internal development and acquisition, to strengthen market positions in academic, scientific, technical, medical, professional, and consumer publishing.

- **Emphasize continuity products**, including journals, newsletters, annuals, update services, and other products that are sold on a subscription or standing-order basis. Such products, which meet the needs of customers for timely, authoritative information, are a superb business for Wiley, generating predictable revenues and cash flows.
- **Grow globally**, to maximize publishing opportunities in the world's major English language markets, and to break into select regional markets with growth potential. Constantly strive to improve the high quality of sales, marketing, and service contracts with customers around the world.
- **Stay on the leading edge of technology**, to improve support for staff, reduce cost and delivery times in production and manufacturing, and develop new products and services to satisfy customer needs.

One of the notable features of the strategic program is the accelerating investments in, and applications of new technologies. In recent years, Wiley has introduced several hundred technology-based products, including software and CD-ROMs. In addition to investments in electronic products, the use of electronic production technologies is increasing to manufacture print products more rapidly, more flexibly, and at less cost.

Wiley also employs technology to market products. Wiley's first foothold in cyberspace was established in 1993 by opening a "bookstore" in CompuServe. In 1994 Wiley established a presence on the Internet: their "home page" on the World Wide Web (http://www.wiley.com) introduces people around the globe to Wiley and its products.

Still further, technology is a powerful instrument for managing the business. Wiley recently completed the development of CORE, an advanced information technology system that links Wiley locations worldwide on a common systems platform. Because of its many innovative aspects, including the use of Wiley-developed "templates" to write software, CORE was a case study in the MIT Sloan School of Management's prestigious journal, *Sloan Management Review* (Fall, 1994).

Wiley and the Internet

Prior to the advent of the World Wide Web, Wiley initiated a project to establish a connection to the Internet for the purpose of exploring new technologies and methods of product development and delivery. Early in 1993, the Corporate Planning group within Wiley recommended that the Internet be seriously considered as a new media alternative to traditional print publishing. Evidence was mounting that the industry was approaching a period of secular change, and Wiley's scientific, technical, and medical author and customer constituencies were already using the Internet for day-to-day activities including: electronic mail, remote login, file transfer and retrieval, and newsgroups.

Thus, a project team headed by the Information Technology group within Wiley along with representatives from each of the publishing groups, formed a plan that would ultimately provide Wiley with a solid and economical technology capability for Internet publishing.

In June 1993, an aggressive plan was launched which satisfied both the immediate requirement for full Internet connectivity for e-mail, FTP, and telnet services by Wiley staff, and the capability to allow external customers, authors, and others to access information from a Wiley Internet server. Because Wiley staff had little Internet technology experience in UNIX or TCP/IP, a consultant was brought in to provide the necessary technical expertise and more importantly, provide management with the perspective and knowledge to be able to evaluate the business opportunities and risks of publishing on the Internet.

Major elements of the Internet plan included:

• Create a 20-month staged implementation program
• Establish Wiley UNIX host system
• Subscribe and install Internet connectivity via a commercial provider
• Establish full time Internet System Administrators
• Create/purchase front-end user software
• Provide Internet education and training programs
• Create business user-led Internet governance group

Since publishing on the Internet was totally new, no business model or product paradigm existed. It was also essential to limit costs associated with Internet experimentation as Wiley did not have the financial resources to invest in expensive computer and communications equipment.

Organizationally, Wiley is a collaborative, team-oriented company, comfortable and familiar with the traditional publishing venues of printed books and journals. The notion that these traditional businesses might be eroded or replaced by electronic publishing was truly frightening to members of the staff and indeed management. Therefore, the Internet project team included a comprehensive education program for managers, publishers, editors, and others involved with the creation of a new product.

Wiley's Internet Education

The Internet education program began with a series of focus discussion groups with various managers and publishers to gain buy-in for the Internet project.   The goals of the projects were communicated and the need for immediate action was explained. Briefly, the goals were:

• Position Wiley to participate in the emerging movement to electronic publishing
• Expand global internal and external communication capabilities to provide necessary infrastructure to capitalize on emerging opportunities.
• Explore the technical, legal, economic, and business issues surrounding dissemination of information in an electronic environment.

These goals were in the context of a demanding business climate:

• Wiley's evolving business needs require expanded access to electronic communications and publishing.
• Competitors are moving rapidly into the electronic information environment.
• Technologies are new, evolving, and require extensive support.
• Management, technology, and administrative resources are scarce for these technologies and markets.

Following the focus groups, a series of demonstrations was held on the capabilities of the Internet. These were done mostly to small groups using dial-up links to the Internet. Wiley was fortunate that the consultant, Fred Gerkin, was also an instructor at the New York University (NYU) Graduate Business School and had access to full high speed Internet facilities.

The value of this education program cannot be overstated as a fundamental understanding of the underlying Internet technologies was crucial to the formation of sound business and technology plans for electronic publishing.

Wiley on the Web

Closely following the education program was Wiley's development of full Internet access capability. Beginning with a modest 64KB dedicated line and a   SUN1000 server, Wiley experimented with Internet access for a select set of internal users. A full Internet training program was rolled out in parallel with Internet connectivity so that all users would use the Internet appropriately.   A section on proper Internet etiquette was included in the training program to avoid episodes of flaming or access to inappropriate information.

A management committee was established from the start to provide guidance and align business participation in every phase of the project. It was seen as essential that the Internet project not be driven by the technology group.   The management group known as the

Internet Governance Committee formulated policy, process, and product strategies for the corporation worldwide. All business groups including corporate communications were represented on the committee to provide a balanced perspective. As a mid-sized company, Wiley could achieve full participation without creating a bureaucracy.

Before launching into home page development, the Internet Governance Committee researched competitive offerings to determine what designs and formats seemed to work best. It was quickly determined that gaudy displays of large graphical images caused significant response time delays. It was also observed that sequential or linear text-based versions of printed matter, even with hypertext links and images, would not prevail as the model for online offerings. The conclusion was that electronic media products should be interactive with searchable content and be used as research tools or knowledge assistants, rather than as linear documents.

Wiley decided to continue to experiment internally and not to permit external access until a complete and competent offering was available. Although fearful of being perceived by the marketplace as slow to go on the Internet, Wiley decided that it would be far more damaging to present an unprofessional or, worse, boring image.

During the period of Internet experimentation, Wiley technology staff built the infrastructure necessary to support Internet services beginning with e-mail. Part of the justification of the Internet project was a significant cost savings associated with the elimination of several hundred CompuServe e-mail accounts and replacing them with Wiley internal e-mail. At the same time, all e-mail users (about 1000) were given e-mail access to the Internet. This approach of demonstrating a hard dollar cost savings while experimenting with the Internet was attractive to senior management and reduced the risk of the investment significantly. The Internet access infrastructure was upgraded to full T-1, and firewall security, network management, and e-mail capabilities were implemented throughout 1994.

In January 1995, the Internet Governance Committee presented the Wiley home page to the senior management group. The Wiley home page had to pass muster with critical internal and external audiences so could not afford the "this page under development" stage. While not voluminous in content, it projected a professional and complete image that was both thoughtful and thought-provoking.

The process by which the Wiley home page was developed was modeled more as a computer software development project rather than as a book or journal production effort. A software development project goes through phases which include: planning, requirements or specifications, design, construction, testing, and implementation. The book production process was melded with the system development process to integrate marketing, sales, and editorial phases as well. In this manner Internet product development could be standardized so that all Wiley offerings would have a similar look and feel, and operate in a consistent and orderly manner. Additionally, Internet product components could be designed to be reusable allowing subsequent products to be rapidly developed at a significantly lower cost. This aspect of Internet development was contributed by the Information Technology group which pioneered reusable "templates" for Wiley business systems worldwide.

Finally, after marketing preparations were complete, Wiley launched its home page offering to the external world in June, 1995. In the period just prior to the launch of the home page, Wiley provided demonstrations at several industry association conferences attended by engineering and medical professionals. Several of these marketing demonstrations resulted in new business opportunities for Wiley, one of which has become the award winning *Journals of Image Guided Surgery* (IGS). The Wiley team, led by Gregor St. John, Director of New Media, was recognized by an industry association with an award for their high level of excellence in the development of electronic products. According to St. John, IGS is a prime example of what new technology has to offer the public. He cautioned however that "our reservations about using the Internet don't lie with technology; our concerns over copyright protection and security dominate the agenda for Internet publication."

Following the launch of the Wiley home page, a successor team replaced the Internet Governance Committee to continue product development and integrate product responsibilities more closely with the publishing groups. This new entity, called the Internet Product Management Team, provides corporate-side coordination and collaboration for all Internet offerings and functions as a line unit work group rather than as a policy-setting committee. Wiley's approach to electronic publishing has not been to form so-called "New Media" divisions that are isolated from the traditional publishing group. Rather, new media development has been integrated within each publishing group and coordinated by cross-functional work groups.

Since the launch, the number of visitors to Wiley's home page has steadily increased. *Publishing Trends* called the Wiley offering "a refreshingly clear and logically laid-out site." The premiere issue of *Yahoo! Internet Life Web Site Guide* called Wiley's Web page "top notch, well above average and arguably the most interesting site put up by a specific publisher."

Wiley Beyond the Web

The evolution of the Internet compels all participants to constantly evaluate and refresh the content, format, and business models of their electronic products. What does it take to be among the Web's finest? Wiley's recipe includes innovative offerings, easy navigation, and a few surprises such as advisory services, specialty catalogues, and easy local geographical access via a global mirror site capability.

During Wiley's initial period of Internet development, the Internet evolved beyond all expectations. However, few have made profits from this "virtual" industry. The commercial aspects of the Internet, and even the Internet itself are still in a formative stage. In spite of these uncertainties, Wiley remains committed to electronic publishing via the Internet for its publishing activities.

Going forward, Wiley intends to expand its Internet offerings to continually refresh its content on the Internet, as it does with its more traditional products. Above all, a cohesive business strategy coupled with prudent investment in technology should provide the best opportunity for profitable electronic publishing via the Internet.

Critical Success Factors

This section of the chapter considers success factors unique to the Internet and describes the costs and risks associated with adoption. Critical decisions include selecting a provider for Internet access and determining their role, evaluating and implementing security controls, establishing policies and procedures and communicating them throughout the organization, and recognizing and using appropriate Internet management tools.

Choosing a Service Type and Provider. The level of support and cost associated with setting up and maintaining an Internet connection depends on factors such as the size of the company, the applications to be utilized, the number of users to be supported, and the complexity of the existing internal network. The value that the Internet can add to a firm is related to the strengths and weaknesses of the existing infrastructure and the additional requirements brought about by adding the Internet connection. It is critical that a firm's Internet developers and their network experts collaborate on the creation and support of applications (Turner, 1994).

Commercial access providers lease telephone lines and have a full-time network connection. They offer three different types of services. Customers can establish a dialup account with the service provider. These accounts have either a simple command-oriented interface or they are graphical and support point-and-click interaction. Service providers will also help companies, who are able to lease telephone lines themselves, establish and maintain a direct network connection.

Command-oriented dialup accounts, or "shell" accounts, are low-cost and provide unlimited access to most of the information on the Internet. There are major drawbacks to this type of access, however. Users need to recollect and type commands and they are unable to experience the multimedia aspects of the World Wide Web. Shell accounts are slow and lack the ability to support multiple Internet sessions simultaneously.

Shell users aren't actually connected to the Internet; they're connected to the access provider's host which is connected to the Internet. Graphically-oriented dialup accounts require a user to have additional software which supports the TCP/IP protocols, so that a user's machine actually becomes a node on the Internet. This allows the user to run graphical client programs which are mouse-driven and which incorporate pictures, audio, and video data as well as text. The user can also download files directly to his or her machine.

Dialup connections are limited by the capabilities of a modem-accessed, shared telephone line. With a dedicated telephone line companies can connect their local area network (LAN) to the Internet directly. Data transfer rates are dramatically improved and many employees can access the Internet at the same time. The cost of a leased line connection, however, is also dramatically greater. It requires additional routing hardware and software. Connecting an internal network to the Internet also introduces new vulnerabilities and security risks.

Full service providers offer more than the physical connection to the Internet. For example, they can register a domain name and address with InterNIC, create accounts for individual employees, troubleshoot the network end-to-end, facilitate online publishing activities, provide user training, collect statistics regarding traffic to and from a site, list a site in the indexes of popular search engines, provide assistance in response to security breaches, backup electronic mail for a site when it is unavailable, and relay Internet newsgroups to an internal news server.

Service providers also often assist in the creation and monitoring of firewalls. The word firewall originates from the firefighting industry as a physical or logical mechanism for isolating a fire. In networks, a firewall involves software and/or hardware used to isolate one network from another untrusted network. Two techniques are used: one to identify and block certain types of forbidden traffic and the other to identify and permit certain types of non-threatening traffic. Some firewalls focus on one technique and some on the other.

In addition to selecting a type of Internet service and a provider for that service, it is crucial for an organization to determine the relationship that it will have with the provider.

Identifying Security Controls

The new responsibilities resulting from the Internet connection should be determined to rest within the organization or with the service provider; or they can be shared. Internal discussions and those with the provider should serve to identify current strengths and weaknesses, new exposures, and new strategies for security control (Figure 8). The first step is to look at IT assets and their protection in the current environment. This includes assets in many categories. One popular taxonomy divides assets into the following categories: people

---

1. Identify IT assets and their protection in the current environment
• people and procedures
• physical and environmental
• hardware
• software
• communications
• data and information

2. Identify possible problems and new exposures
• more assets
• assets more dispersed
• hard to value certain assets
• cost of risk analysis is greater and results are more difficult to analyze
• more access points increases likelihood of interception of data and the
  potential for denial of service
• more components lead to more misconfigured systems
• added trafic requires more extensive investigation when tacking intrusion or
  tampering

3. Identify strategies for protecting vulnerable assets
• locate critical communication links and important hardware in physically
  secure areas
• encrypt information in transit
• require all access to the Internet via firewall
• use and manage passwords
• monitor system use

Figure 8: Identifying Security Controls

and procedures, physical and environmental assets, hardware, software, communications, and data and information (Pfleeger, 1989). The next step is to identify possible new exposures due to the Internet connection.

What are the chances that sensitive e-mail messages, company files, or credit card numbers will be intercepted? How will the increased complexity affect the audit function? What is the potential for misconfiguring the added software and hardware components? The final step is to identify available security controls for protecting assets identified as vulnerable. These controls might include physically securing critical communication links, using firewalls to protect internal networks from the Internet, using and monitoring passwords, and monitoring system use.

Another key strategy for protecting assets is the use of encryption. Encryption involves the scrambling of plain text documents into unintelligible forms by means of a reversible mathematical formula for transmission over a communications link. Nearly half of the over one thousand cryptographic products on the market as of March 1996 were based on an encryption scheme developed by the National Bureau of Standards known as the data encryption standard (DES).[3] Additional security protocols are being developed specifically for financial transactions on the Internet. Terisa Systems Inc., a company backed by IBM/Prodigy, AOL, Netscape, Compuserve, and several other large firms, has developed products integrating encryption, client/server authentication, and digital signature schemes to secure commerce on the Internet.

Management as well as system administrators need to understand and manage the risks associated with Internet adoption, even though some controls may be implemented by the service provider or through third party products.

Policies and Procedures

After identifying security controls, policies for acceptable use of the Internet must also be selected, documented, and operationalized. Internet security policies vary with the needs and culture of an organization, but the planning process itself is, invariably, critical. The "Site Security Handbook", produced by the Internet Engineering Task Force (IETF) for the Internet community[4], describes seven key issues:

- Who will be allowed to use the resources?
- What will be the proper use of the resources?
- Who will be authorized to grant access and approve usage?
- Who will have system administration privileges?
- What will be the users' rights and responsibilities?
- What will be the rights and responsibilities of the system administrator vs. those of the user?
- Where will sensitive information be stored?

To be useful, corporate policies governing the use of the Internet should also spell out incident handling procedures, covering a vast array of potential policy violations. Policies and procedures should be publicized and discussed at every level of the organization. Two important goals in developing computer security policies are 1) implementing measures which serve to protect assets in a *cost effective* manner and   2) reviewing the process *continuously*, making improvements each time a weakness is found (Fites, Kratz, and Brebner, 1989).

Linking an organization to the Internet radically alters the composition of an organization's network vulnerabilities. Network security policies and procedures should be written to reflect new issues and concerns before the connection is made. There is really no substitute for thorough and creative contingency planning. It takes time to indoctrinate users as to proper use, to operationalize problem reporting, and educate the various host administrators. While robust policies and procedures governing Internet usage are generally considered important, many firms currently using the Internet do not have written policies and procedures specific to Internet usage (Feher and

Towell, 1996).

Internet Management Tools

An integral part of designing Internet policies and procedures is the selection and use of appropriate security management tools. Security management tools assist system administrators in thwarting security breaches. Threats include the interruption of service, the interception of proprietary data or programs, and the alteration of data or programs. Resnick and Taylor (1995) suggest that businesses that connect their computer systems to the Internet are open to three principal risks: interception of e-mail, interception and/or alteration of business and financial records, and interception of credit card numbers.

Commercial products may offer combinations of functions but there are five general categories of security management tools: compliance, intrusion detection, session monitoring, activity logging, and authentication. *Compliance* tools check configurations and settings of security related files such as: account, password, system, and audit files. These parameters can be compared to acceptable levels and deviations can be reported to the system administrator. *Intrusion detection* tools alert the administrator when unauthorized attempts are made to access resources that are protected. *Session monitoring* tools can be used to monitor a suspicious user's activities over a given period of time. Monitoring can be triggered by the system administrator or automatically by certain activities. *Activity logging* tools are used to provide an audit trail of who enters the system, who uses it, and/or how they use it. A record can be created of attempted logins, use of specific commands, or the text of all commands. Software is available to track the percentage of the network consumed by WWW requests and to identify the bandwidth abusers. Tools for securing interchanges, or *authentication* tools, are used to protect client/server interchanges by verifying client credentials and access permissions before an exchange is made.

Management Strategies for Internet Investment

The role of the Internet in an organization should be determined by articulating the drivers for adoption, identifying uses for the various applications within the organization, and determining factors critical to success. The Internet should be seen as a potential resource for the entire organization, not as a solution to a single problem or opportunity.

This chapter is concluded by discussing generic values and risks of IT investment as proposed by Marilyn Parker (1996). A framework for measuring the business value of Internet investment is derived from this work. Finally, recommendations concerning Internet planning are made.

Generic Values and Risks of IT Investment

The productivity of IT investments in recent years has been subject to increasing scrutiny (Brynjolfsson, 1993; Dué, 1993; Dué, 1994). Many recent texts propose the need for a radically new business paradigm in reaction to the increasingly global economy and today's ultra-rapid pace of technological change (Tapscott and Caston, 1993; Estabrooks, 1995; Howard, 1995). Most agree that there is a lack of metrics, particularly for the intangible benefits derived from information technology adoption.

One approach to estimating value and risk criteria that has gained worldwide recognition and application is discussed in Parker (1996). Parker combines tangible and soft measures for a generic set of values and risks: financial values, strategic values, stakeholder values, competitive strategy risks, and organizational strategy risks and uncertainties.

Financial values as defined by Parker (1996), are benefits that are measurable using standard accounting practices such as simple return-on-investment (ROI) or internal rate of return (IRR). Strategic values are externally focused which are generally market oriented and include creation of new markets and product differentiation. Strategic values are often measured by assessment of the contribution to critical success factors (Rockart, 1979; Rockart and Treacy, 1982) or by analysis of competitive advantage (Porter 1980; Porter 1985). Stakeholder values involve benefits to a broad set of business partners: customers, employees, regulators, stockholders, and/or community members. As Parker notes "...while each stakeholder has a different view of value, there are some common themes." Examples of stakeholder values include environmental quality and flexible product lines. Stakeholder value is often measured using multi-factor weighting and scoring. Competitive strategy risks involve external business risks resulting from market dynamics, political realignments, demographic change, and so forth. Organizational strategy risks and uncertainties have an internal focus and include potential losses due to business process redesign, the uncertainty stemming from communication deficiencies, and technical mismatches and dependencies. Both types of risk can be evaluated through various risk modeling techniques.

A Framework for Measuring the Business
Value of Internet Investment

Parker's framework lays a foundation for measuring the business value of Internet investment in a particular organization. The value provided by the Internet in an organization can be seen as three

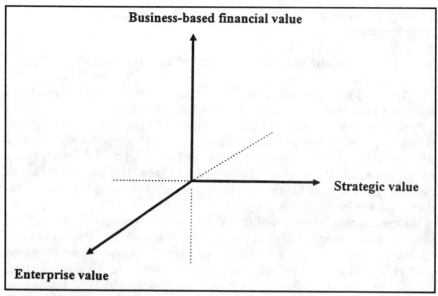

Figure 9: The Three Dimensions of Value in Internet Investment

dimensional (Figure 9). Value, in this context, is defined as the ratio of benefits to costs.

The first dimension involves tangible business value. Costs of hardware, software, network enhancements and services, training and security should be compared to revenues from new markets, improved communication speed, and reduced fax, phone, and mail costs. The second dimension is externally focused. Strategic costs include increased network traffic which decreases efficacy and alienation of potential customers by use of the medium. Strategic benefits include success in new markets, increased market share, and improved customer relationships. The third dimension is internally focused. Enterprise costs involving the Internet include lost productivity due to personal use of the Internet and training needs, as well as employee dissatisfaction. The most important enterprise benefit of Internet adoption is the information empowerment of employees for decisionmaking.

It is sometimes difficult to compare benefits and costs in one dimension to that of another. For example, the trade-off between positive financial value and negative strategic value or positive strategic value and negative enterprise value is generally unclear. This dilemma is expressed in the often used adage "you can't prove competitive advantage through discounted cash flow." The concept of truly successful utilization of the Internet should be translated into the eventual realization of positive value in each dimension.

With the current adoption rate of 85%, it is probably not a matter of whether an organization will use the Internet, but when and how. As depicted in Figure 3, the ideal framework for decision-making involves planning a coherent infrastructure for the Internet which links drivers, applications, and success factors *in light of the goal of realizing maximum positive value in each of the three dimensions of value: financial, strategic, and enterprise.* By demonstrating the merits of the Internet in a particular organization in all three dimensions, an IT organization can build momentum and credibility for future stages of deployment. The next section summarizes the chapter and makes three specific recommendations for Internet planning.

Recommendations for Internet Planning

Recommendation 1: *Consider Internet planning as an iterative process.* The use of the Internet in a business setting is immature. Inadequate security, insufficient search tools, lack of common access, and limited bandwidth are current limitations to its widespread acceptance. Still, there are over 400,000 commercial domains and 85% of IT managers indicate that their organization make some use of the Internet. Consider Internet planning an iterative process that is not likely to end in the next few years. Widespread Internet technology transfer will evolve.

Recommendation 2: *Plan the overall role of the Internet in the organization.* The role of the Internet should be determined by investigating drivers for adoption and applications available and then characterizing critical success factors unique to this technology. There are four prominent themes in Internet adoption: time compression, restructuring of relationships, increasing market share or profits, and increasing access to information. These drivers are evident in the business use of the most common Internet applications: e-mail, newsgroups, Telnet, FTP, Gopher, and the World Wide Web. Critical decisions associated with application development include selecting a provider for Internet access and determining their role, evaluating and implementing security controls, establishing policies and procedures and communicating them throughout the organization, and using appropriate Internet management tools. Use of the Internet should not be evaluated by looking at an individual application, but by looking at the comprehensive infrastructure necessary for Internet development.

Recommendation 3: *Measure the value of Internet investment in three dimensions.* Developing metrics for an information technology investment is difficult but feedback mechanisms are important. It is hard to associate the many benefits and costs of the Internet derived over an extended period of time. It is especially hard to measure intangible, non-financial costs and benefits in such a way that they can be compared to business-based financial value. Avoid comparing the hard and soft measures. Strive for rapid realization of maximum value, i.e., maximizing benefits and minimizing costs in each of the three dimensions: financial value, strategic value, and enterprise value. By demonstrating value in all three dimensions, momentum is built for future stages of deployment.

Endnotes

[1] Obtained via the World Wide Web at URL:http://www.webcom.com/~walsh/stats.html

[2] Obtained via the World Wide Web at http://home.tig.com/cgi-bin/genobject/domaindb

[3] Comprehensive survey results obtained from Trusted Information Systems, Inc. via World Wide Web at URL: http://www.tis.com/crypto/survey.html

[4] Internet document Request for Comments (RFC) 1244, 1991, is available via World Wide Web at URL: http://info.internet.isa.edu/1s/in-notes/rfc/files

Chapter 21

Impact of IT Supporting Knowledge Work: Case of "Carve" at Morgan Stanley

Chrys de Almeida
Saint Francis Xavier University

Elizabeth Kennick
Morgan Stanley

As the investment in information technology supporting knowledge work continues to grow, determining its contribution to a firm's performance becomes an increasingly important concern of business executives. Measures of productivity face serious challenges when dealing with knowledge work. In this chapter, we propose a three–tiered framework for measuring the impact of information technology supporting knowledge work, and based on this framework, we investigate the payoff from the deployment of a new information system supporting mortgage–backed securities structureres at Morgan Stanley. We contend that though payoffs from IT supporting knowledge work may be mostly qualitative, assessing their impact should be no less objective than assessing the impact of other traditional assets. Our framework is a step in the direction of making a disciplined approach to deal with the problem of IT value assessment.

In the emerging post-industrial economy, an increasing proportion of workers engage in knowledge work. The investment in information technology supporting knowledge work continues to rise. At the same time, the environment in which firms compete is becoming more turbulent and volatile. In the highly information-intensive financial services industry, these trends are even more pronounced.

As the investment in information technology continues to grow, determining its contribution to a firm's performance becomes an increasingly important concern of business executives. However, unlike in other more traditional type of investments such as plants and machinery in manufacturing, determining the impact of information technology is difficult because the benefits attributable to IT are more indirect, diffused, qualitative, and contingent than other traditional types of assets, and thus, are hard to quantify (Banker et al., 1993b). In addition, the impact of IT may be distributed among different levels of the enterprise and commingled with other efforts of the organization. Isolating the effects of IT is, if at all possible, a very tedious process. Finally, these effects may also be confounded by hard-to-predict actions over time of the economic, regulatory, and competitive environments in which the firm operates (Mahmood, 1993).

While the problem of assessing the impact of IT supporting knowledge work is not very different from those of IT in general, measuring the impact on knowledge worker productivity is regarded as a central issue. Productivity is as important to the knowledge worker as it has been to the factory worker in the industrial era. Senior managers are as interested in knowing what these productivity gains are and how they can be achieved, as they are in assessing the impact of IT on organizational performance. According to Drucker (1995), the single greatest challenge facing managers is to raise the productivity of knowledge workers, which will ultimately determine the competitive performance of firms. However, whether the use of information technology in knowledge work has led to significant productivity gains both at the firm level and at the individual level is still an issue that needs further study (Davies et al., 1993).

Measures of productivity face serious challenges when dealing with knowledge work. The traditional blue-collar productivity measures used in the manufacturing environment cannot be used to measure white-collar productivity of knowledge workers because the outputs and the inputs in the latter are not as distinct and easily quantifiable (Jurison, 1995) and knowledge work is primarily guided by the cognitive processing of the knowledge worker (Davies et al., 1993). Productivity measures of knowledge work should relate to outcomes rather than outputs (Packer, 1982). Bullen (1995) argues that understanding what and how a knowledge worker does to achieve his or her goals is important to understanding what it means to be productive in that context. Davis et al. (1993) suggest that payoffs from IT supporting knowledge work could be obtained by reducing routine task work, by reducing task complexity, by providing access to accumulated knowledge and expertise, and by supporting knowledge work processes. Drucker (1995) suggests that the greatest productivity gains from knowledge work will come from eliminating what need not be done and concentrating on essential tasks that are needed to accomplish the expected outcome.

The study of the business value of IT is motivated by several factors: High proportion of investment in IT compared to firm's revenue (McKeen et al., 1990), the relative uncertainty about the contribution of IT to the firm's bottom line, the abysmal gains in firm's productivity [Roach, 1989], and the shortcomings of the existing methods and models used to measure the impact (Smith and McKeen, 1991). Measuring the business value created by IT can serve two purposes: 1) ex-ante justification of planned IT and guidance during planning and design stages to maximize its potential payoff; 2) ex-post evaluation and assessment of installed IT during the post-implementation stage to ensure that it delivers the expected payoffs (Konsynski, 1993; Wetherbe, 1993).

In this chapter, we will investigate the payoff from the deployment of a new and innovative information technology supporting mortgage-backed securities structurers at Morgan Stanley. We examine the payoffs using a three-tier framework that includes the firm, the business process, and the knowledge worker.

Mortgage-Backed Securities Business

Background

The creation of structured securities backed either by whole loan mortgages or by Mortgage-Backed Securities (MBS) pools is essentially an arbitrage game. Arbitrage is the trading of related securities which have predictable future value in differing markets, providing an opportunity for profit from price differentials in the markets. MBS trading is based on buying and selling groups of loans (conventional mortgages, home mortgages, home equity lines of credit, leases, etc.). Loans are bought, repackaged, and sold as securities. The payment stream against the mortgage loans serves to collateralize the new securities.

The most fundamental building blocks or the assets of MBS are the loans or mortgages which are purchased from originators. Typically, the bank or mortgage broker which originates a loan later sells it to one of three government mortgage agencies: Fannie Mae, Freddie Mac, or Ginnie Mae. These agencies package the individual mortgages into more generic (easily tradable) security products (pools) and auction them to Wall Street financial firms. The financial firms sell the pools to insurance companies, pension funds, mutual funds, and individual investors. When the original borrowers make their mortgage payments, the cash (principal and interest) is "passed through" to the investor at the other end of the chain.

Agency mortgage pools are also used to create a type of

mortgage-backed product called Collateralized Mortgage Obligations (CMOs). Groups of loans can be organized together to provide aggregated cash flows with varying levels of stability or risk, and then repackaged into securities of different sizes and maturities. The market determines what the packages are worth. MBS traders make money by packaging securities to take advantage of demand from investors who are willing to pay higher prices in order to reduce their cash flow risk.

The introduction of the mortgage agencies in the 1970s made more money available to banks by allowing them to sell the cash flows from the mortgages they wrote, and pass on the risk to investors. The increasing role of Fannie Mae and Freddie Mac in the creation of mortgage-backed US Agency-guaranteed pass-through pools facilitated the transfer of risk, with the Agency taking the credit risk and investors taking the prepayment risk. Changes in tax and securitization laws in the 1980s made it easier and less costly to issue multi-class securities, which helped enlarge the overall market by introducing new investors who took on credit and prepayment risks from sellers (often originators) of mortgages.

Over the past decade, mortgage-backed securitization has evolved from being relatively simple and unsophisticated on the loan collateral side and quite complex on the bond structuring side, to being more complex on the collateral and simpler on the bond-sizing. From 1988 to 1993, the MBS business mostly ran on the supply of single family agency-backed (Fannie Mae, Freddie Mac...) mortgages flooding the market during the refinancing boom. Single-family collateral was inexpensive compared to similar assets, but the timing of cash flows coming back as the loans were paid down was growing in uncertainty. Investors were willing to give up higher returns or pay a higher price to reduce cash flow variance (CFV) for greater security.

In 1994, refinancing dropped off, and single family mortgage yields when compared to other fixed income assets began to tighten, pushing investors to cheaper assets. Home equity loans, among other assets, were originated in greater volume and became available as a cheaper alternative to traditional residential mortgages. These more complex assets required more complex asset cash flow capabilities and scenario capabilities since assets with different characteristics were often sold together and more complex forms of loan loss methodologies (ways of structuring securities to absorb losses from loan defaults or delinquencies) had to be analyzed. In most cases, the asset characteristics and credit enhancement methods were more complex than the allocation of payments among bond classes. Mortgage-backed bonds may be partitioned into several classes or tranches of bonds of serialized priority by which the bonds are redeemed. The focus for structuring MBS today has shifted away from complex bond structures to complex assets as a result.

Players

Three types of players are involved in the MBS business:

1. The mortgage lenders who want to sell off their loans and use the sale proceeds to focus on their core fee business of originating more mortgages;
2. The investors who want to buy these securities to get superior rates of return versus other fixed income assets such as U.S. Treasury Bonds;
3. The financial services companies engaged in MBS trading, which buy the loans, repackage them as securities, and bring them to the market with value added.

Process

The structurer begins the securitization process by looking at the characteristics of the mortgage collateral required to provide cash flows, the characteristics of the collateralized securities, and the method by which collateral cash flow is allocated to the securities. Based on these inputs the structurer determines the appropriate yield that investors require to purchase a given type of security. Then, this yield is used to discount the projected cash flows of the collateralized securities to derive the prices and proceeds of each type of securities. Finally, these proceeds are aggregated and compared to the cost of acquiring the mortgage collateral.

The main goal of the structurer is to determine the MBS structure that would maximize the net aggregate proceeds and minimize the all-in-costs. Several different scenarios have to be tried out before the most profitable structure is picked. The competitiveness of the firm is determined by how well and how quickly these goals are achieved. The ability to produce and distribute results quickly is crucial to the profitability of the operation. But the task is very complex, has several possible combinations to consider, and is very time consuming. Naturally, the performance of the structurer is measured in terms of the efficiency and effectiveness with which these goals are accomplished.

Two types of reports are produced, one for the MBS issuer or trader and the other for the investor. The report to the issuer shows the elements of the transaction that allow it to be judged against alternative structures and non-securitization financing alternatives. The report to the investors show those elements of a security that allow it to be compared to other securities available for sale and provide a basis for determining which securities to invest in. MBS traders use this information to negotiate deals.

What Is "CARVE" ?

The MBS industry had a boom year in 1993. The size of the mortgage market dwarfed almost all other sectors in the fixed income marketplace, ahead of the corporate and municipal bond markets, second only to the U.S. Treasury market. Morgan Stanley was not a market leader in the MBS business at the time, and consequently saw some missed opportunities. By 1994, Morgan Stanley's senior management saw mortgages as one of the most strategic areas in the fixed-income market. Catapulting Morgan Stanley into the top five in this multi-trillion dollar market became their highest priority. Acquisition or development of the necessary resources, including IT resources such as the "CARVE" system, occurred in response to this strategic initiative.

CARVE is a decision support system that was developed to support the mortgage-backed securities structuring process; that is, to create securities based on pools of assets. It has two types of users: the primary users or the structurers who structure MBS securities that are placed in the market; and the secondary users or the reverse engineers who analyze market activity and collect market intelligence.

CARVE has been designed to deal with the current conditions and complexities of the market and has replaced the previous outdated system. The main features of CARVE are:

- a modeling language to model cash flows for different types of assets and to structure the cash flows to create securities out of them.
- a scenario builder to analyze how cash flows are affected by pay downs under different market conditions, and to determine the specific outcome in each situation.

CARVE handles many different types of asset characteristics such as coupon, principal, maturity, and other relevant information about the loans, allowing the structurer to test the impact of altering the terms of an asset or pool of assets. The modeling language allows the structurer to describe a pay down methodology that allocates mortgage cash flows to the collateralized securities in a prescribed order. The user can specify the terms of the assets, determine the allocation of cash flows to the bond classes, and price the resultant securities to determine the structure's profitability. The structure can then be altered and the profitability impact of the alteration can be assessed. CARVE also produces two main reports for the issuers and investors.

Framework for Measuring Impact of Information Technology Supporting Knowledge Work

We contend that the impact of IT supporting knowledge work has to be looked at from three different perspectives: the end-user or knowledge worker level, the business process level, and the firm level. Most previous studies focus on either one or two of these perspectives but not all three, and thus, fails to capture the full impact of IT.

The distinction between knowledge worker gains and process gains is important as knowledge work is an integral part of an entire business process. The gains from knowledge work are not tightly coupled with process outcomes. For example, in the case of MBS trading, the outcome of the business process is the completion of a transaction or a deal. In this process, the structurer's role is to provide the trader with the information required to put together the most favorable deal. Whether the transaction takes place or not is beyond the control of the structurer, though the efficiency and effectiveness of the structurer has a positive influence on the outcome of the process.

A related point is that a process may involve teams or workgroups, and the final process outcome may be determined by the cooperative effort and not just by the aggregate work output of each individual worker. A gain in the productivity of an individual knowledge worker may not necessarily produce gains in the overall process.   The distinction we made above between the knowledge worker level and the process level is helpful in locating not just the payoffs of individual workers, but also payoffs of entire processes with respect to collaboration and coordination of workgroups.

Conceivably, any productivity gain at the end-user level translates into a gain at the process level, and any gain at the end-user or the process level translates into the firm level. However, the macro level measures of performance and productivity may not reflect the productivity gains at knowledge work level. The propagation of productivity gains along this pipeline may be mitigated by other factors, such as the strength of the linkage between knowledge work and the business process, the misfit of IT with the processes and tasks that it supports, or the misalignment of the firm's mission and objectives with the deployment of information technology.

At the end-user or the knowledge worker level, productivity is the source of job enrichment. Productivity gains will result from qualitative and quantitative improvements in their performance. To improve productivity, the workload of the knowledge worker should be focused on professional work, the work that requires the special skills and training of the knowledge worker, the work for which he or she gets paid for. Knowledge workers perform better when they have better control of their work, are able to apply their knowledge and expertise to their tasks more freely, and can extend and adapt their knowledge when necessary. Supporting knowledge workers to do what they do best - creating and disseminating knowledge and information — in the context that they do it, while removing the tedium of routine tasks from their work will also improve personal satisfaction and motivation, which will, over the long term, contribute to improved productivity. Changes in the way people work as individuals and as teams sharing knowledge and expertise in complex environments, or changes in the way work is organized and work flows among the functional units engaged in a business process may have long term implications for organizational performance that transcend financial value of an investment in IT (Lucas, 1993; Parnisto, 1995).

At the individual knowledge worker level, performance is evaluated using measures such as, 1) efficiency based on throughput such as the number of analyses conducted within a specified time, 2) effectiveness based on quality of output such as timeliness, accuracy, completeness, and reliability of results or recommendations, 3) task concentration based on ability to focus on non-routine tasks requiring relevant expertise of knowledge work, 4) task extendibility based on the complexity of tasks such as the scope and scale of models formulated and the nature of the data used, 5) knowledge extendibility based on access to accumulated knowledge and augmentation of organizational learning (Davies et al., 1993; Wilson, 1993; Drucker, 1995; Jurison, 1995).

At the process level, productivity is the source of improved process efficiency and outcome. The most significant productivity gains in process efficiency result from eliminating redundant tasks and concentrating on the essential tasks required to deliver the desired output or outcome. IT should not merely replace an old system or process, but should change, modify, and reengineer the process where necessary and possible. Furthermore, in processes where teams or groups are jointly involved, the productive use of IT should also facilitate the coordination, collaboration, cooperation or any other symbiotic and synergistic relationships among the members of these teams and groups. In terms of process outcome or output, gains in productivity are realized by the increased value added to the products and services, by changes in the nature of products and services, improved quality, increased scale and complexity.

Understanding how IT contributes to process and product improvement and innovation is a way of measuring the impact of IT at the process level (Bullen, 1995). Flexibility and adaptability to changing customer preferences and speed of customizing products or developing new products based on individual customer needs are critical aspects where IT can play a significant role [Parnisto, 1995; Pine, 1993]. Adding value to products and services and increasing their information intensity is an important effect of IT on the firm (Porter and Miller, 1985). IT is an enabler of business change that helps align business process with business strategy (Hammer, 1990; Davenport, 1993; Venkatramen, 1991).

At the firm level, productivity is the main source of competitiveness, profitability, and long-term survival. Productivity measures at firm level have to focus on important goals and missions of the organization. The productive use of a firm's assets should help the firm to assert market leadership, sustain market standing, forge stronger links with stakeholders, and improve profit margins. Firms should also be responsive to changes in the economic, regulatory, and economic environments.

The most widely used measures of IT value are the firm-level financial measures such as profit, revenue, cost, and return on investment (McKeen and Smith, 1993; Panko, 1991; Weill and Olson, 1989; Zimmerman, 1988). These are time tested and proven measures used in business practice to evaluate various types of investments. However, in IT these measures lead to some problems. Traditional accounting and finance approaches used to evaluate competing alternative investments, such as pay back period, internal rate of return, net present value may not reveal a true picture as they impose simplistic linear relationships between value and the cash flow forecasts of IT investments (Westland, 1993). Another drawback of these analytical methods is that they take into account only those costs and benefits that are quantifiable. While some payoffs such as increased revenue or market share are quantifiable others such as increased customer satisfaction, strategic advantage, or changes in way people work and make decisions are not easily quantifiable. These intangible benefits are either quantified through simplistic proxy measures [Herscheim and Smithson, 1988] or sometimes ignored when they cannot be easily quantified (Kaplan, 1986). Value analysis (Keen, 1981) based on the user's perception of IT value is an alternative approach that attempts to overcome this problem.

Impact of CARVE

At the knowledge worker or the structurer level, we looked at what impact CARVE had on the nature of knowledge work, qualitative and quantitative changes in the work including task focus, task simplification, time to complete task, task flexibility and adaptability, and quality of the outcome. We also looked at the behavioral and cognitive aspects including confidence in the outcome, interest, motivation, and learning.

We found that CARVE's most significant payoff is its flexibility as a modeling tool which allows the structurer to focus on the business issues. More time and effort is spent on analyzing potential structures and less on deciding how to analyze. The structurer's knowledge and intuition is used more readily and more often as the structurer is forced to construct a set of rules that tell the model how the structure allocates mortgage cash flows. The task of describing a pay down methodology that allocates mortgage cash flows to the collateralized securities in a prescribed order is much simpler. These methodologies can be very complex and vary greatly for different mortgages and securities structures. The quality of the outcome which is judged on how well a MBS structure maximizes the net aggregate proceeds and minimizes the all-in-costs is improved as more complex structures can be tried and tested.

Significant gains have been realized in terms of efficiency and effectiveness of doing knowledge work. Extremely difficult deal structures are handled very quickly and accurately. The time required to iterate among alternatives and identify the most profitable scenario has been significantly reduced. More complex analysis is handled in less time. More and better analyses are quickly made available to the trader, enabling the traders to negotiate and put through more deals.

As structurers have to interact closely with CARVE in implementing the models, the structurer is forced to understand how the entire structure works from top to bottom. They gain a better insight and understanding of the structures they create. For the novice structurer, this is helpful as a learning tool to gain insightful knowledge.

The abilities to create different structures that fit the market conditions and to gain a better understanding about the structures have raised the level of confidence that the structurers have on the outcomes. As modeling and analysis have become more challenging without being painfully slow and laborious, and cognitive skills are used more extensively, structurers find work more rewarding, and their levels of interest and motivation have increased.

At the process level, we move beyond just strictly the knowledge work. We are interested in assessing the impact of CARVE on the entire business process, on the users of the outputs and outcomes of knowledge work. We will look at effects on the coordination and collaborative aspects among the different stages of the MBS process, the nature of the products and services delivered, including the value added to them and the efficiency with which they are delivered.

As we have seen before, the process of trading mortgage-backed securities involves the buying and selling of securities structured from mortgage loans. The outcome of the MBS process is a transaction or a deal. The outcome can be measured by the size of a deal, number of deals put through, and the complexity of the deal. The first two are responsible for revenue generation, and the last is responsible for improved margins.

MBS traders use information from the outputs produced by the structurers to negotiate deals. We found that CARVE has helped MBS traders complete more deals which are much bigger and more complex than would otherwise be possible. Finance bankers benefit by needing less time to prepare presentations as CARVE delivers reports that are more customized and tailored to the needs of issuers and investors. This facilitates the decision making of the issuers via easier comparison of the securitization and non-securitization options available, and of the investors via better determination of the value of securities being offered.

CARVE has also contributed to better collaboration and cooperation between the structurers and the traders. Traders present new ideas to the structurers, who in turn provide analyses very quickly. This interaction helps traders match the dynamics of the market and the needs of the investors, thus improving the prospect of closing deals.

At the firm level, CARVE's primary impact is as a competitive tool. CARVE has helped Morgan Stanley strengthen its market position by enabling it to respond to issuers and investors much faster and more creatively than its competitors. CARVE has made it possible to complete multi-billion dollar MBS deals that would, otherwise, not have been possible. As a result of CARVE, Morgan Stanley is able to broker partnerships with other firms in putting together mega deals, thus, changing the rules of the marketplace. CARVE has also helped the firm offer better service to its customer by bringing into the market securities that meet the needs of the investors while providing superior rates of return and by offering lenders better opportunities to focus on their core business of providing mortgages by selling off cash flows.

The most predominant way of measuring business value of IT at Morgan Stanley is by the impact on the profitability of the firm, as in money saved in terms of reduced labor, equipment, or storage costs, and money earned in terms of new markets entered, customers serviced, additional revenue generated which would not have been possible without the new technology. CARVE has contributed to increased profitability of the firm by increasing the revenue generating capacity as more, better, and much larger deals can be handled. The ability to produce and distribute results quickly is crucial to the profitability of the operation. But, the task is very complex, has several possible combinations to consider, and is also very time consuming. CARVE handles many different types of assets programmable for different options, enabling securities structurers to quickly try different combinations of assets. They then apply prices based on prevalent market conditions to immediately determine the profit or loss potential.

Finally, we looked at the impact CARVE would have on the firm's competitiveness when regulatory and economic environments change. MBS trading is very susceptible to fluctuations in interest rates, causing huge expansions and contractions in the market. Product demand also fluctuates under regulatory pressure from FFIEC imposed tests on securities, scrutiny on derivatives, etc. Under these circumstances, CARVE can model structures that logically focus on these changes.

Conclusion

In this study, we have looked at the payoffs of CARVE from three distinct perspectives: knowledge worker level, process level, and firm level. As knowledge work is often an embedded process within a business process, and the outcomes of knowledge work may or may not directly affect the process outcome, separating the impact at the knowledge work level and the process level is helpful in obtaining a more accurate measure of the payoffs.

One of the issues which we have not addressed is how to weigh the payoffs at the different levels in relation to each other. As the main objective of a firm is to maximize shareholder wealth, and how the firm sets about it is determined by the management philosophy, different firms will attach different importance or values to each type of payoff.

As we have seen, some payoffs from IT supporting knowledge work may be direct, concrete and immediate. But, there are also several benefits that are either subtle and indirect or may be substantive over the long-term. Senior management, when evaluating different IT investment alternatives, should pay close attention to these aspects. Management should not *a priori* overlook or discard benefits that do not immediately produce bottom line improvements, but rather, determine the payoffs first and then attach importance to those they deem fit.

Management Strategies

Payoffs in IT may be mostly qualitative and hard to quantify, but their assessment should be no less objective than that for other more traditional types of assets. Because the impact of IT is more indirect, diffused, qualitative, and contingent than other types of assets, assessing their impact poses a difficult problem and is often dealt with superficially or ignored. Managers have to adopt a more disciplined approach to IT investment by establishing a very carefully crafted program of measurement and evaluation that will allow firms to collect hard and soft evidence of the business value of any IT investment. Devising a comprehensive set of robust and reliable metrics will help business and IT executives assess IT investments more objectively in a somewhat subjective realm, and thus, gain more confidence over their decisions.

Frameworks, such as what we have proposed, provide a disciplined approach to deal with the IT value assessment problem. It help IT managers recognize the nature of the problem and focus on the critical points at which IT creates business value, namely, the firm, process, and end-user levels. It is important not only to develop a portfolio of metrics at each level but also to discern the relationship among the different metrics at the different levels. This way firms can avoid gross inaccuracies in evaluating the value of IT. On one hand, by relying either only on firm-level macro measures to evaluate the impact of IT, or only on end-user micro measures, the overall payoff may tend to be undervalued. On the other hand, the benefits of IT may tend to be overvalued, if payoffs are measured at each level in isolation and then aggregated, while disregarding how the payoffs at one level is translated to another level. For example, an IT investment on knowledge work, such as CARVE, may increase revenue to the firm as well as enhance the productivity of the knowledge worker. Instead of just adding the two payoffs together, one must factor into the payoff formula their relationship, that is the contribution of one payoff to the other. Finally, a model need to have some built in flexibility to factor in the context in which a firm operates and implements IT, that is, managers should evaluate and rank order the portfolio of metrics based on management expediency.

Measuring the business value created by IT serves two purposes: 1) *ex ante* guidance during IT planning and design stages to maximize the potential payoff of the planned IT; 2) *ex post* evaluation during the post-implementation stage to ensure that the installed IT delivers the expected payoffs. To maximize the payoff from an IT investment, payoff considerations should be emphasized at the systems analysis phase. A top-down approach needs to be adopted in systems analysis, beginning with macro measures of the firm such as revenue generation, down through business process measures, to finally, end-user measures. These will have real implications for the design of the system, and hence the technology-specific measures of the IT investment. This way IT investments can be more cost-effective than tinkering with a system once it is installed.

Managers should not try to rationalize investment on IT supporting knowledge work purely on firm level macro measures because most benefits are generally not measurable by conventional techniques, and also because the real impact of these benefits may be felt in the long-term rather than immediately. Investment on IT supporting knowledge work is an investment on human capital that improves the general well-being of the firm. It makes a firm 'battle-ready' to respond swiftly and effectively to competitive action, customer demands, regulatory changes, or other market disturbances. The true business value of IT may be in hedging downside risk and damage control rather than purely gaining positive returns on the investment.

Acknowledgment
The authors thank John Reynolds, Michael Sternberg, and the Mortgage-Backed Securities and Information Technology teams at Morgan Stanley for their time and the useful information and insights that they offered to make this research a success.

Conclusion
Measuring Information Technology
Investment Payoff: A Summary

Mo Adam Mahmood, University of Texas at El Paso
Edward J. Szewczak, Canisius College

It has been claimed that investment in IT must be made either for strategic necessities or for gaining competitive advantage. During the 1980s, IT investment had increased by about 300 percent to $1 trillion, $800 million of which was invested in the service sector (Gleckman, 1993; Keen 1992). Measuring IT investment payoff has, however, been elusive. Traditional approaches to measuring such payoff have not been very successful. As a matter of fact, they left many senior managers wondering whether the investment has been worthwhile to their companies. Though a reliance on quantitative methods and measures has resulted in some reassuring estimates of the worth of the IT investment, there is a nagging sense that much of the invested resources has resulted in something hard to measure and intangible. Indeed some senior managers wonder if the money and time invested in IT has been squandered. For example, U.S. data demonstrated that information technology investment has not engendered the anticipated improvements in productivity (Roach 1991). Eighty percent of the respondents, in a survey of technology managers in U.K. banks, indicated that technology had fallen short of their expectations (Weil 1988). Parsons et al. (1990) reported that the impact of IT investment on multifactor productivity in the Canadian Banking industry is also low.

The contemporary approaches discussed in this book recognize the limitations of the earlier traditional approaches and attempt to improve on them. The primary outcome of these attempts is a wide variety of approaches with different characteristics. This outcome is consistent with the conclusion drawn by Banker, Kauffman and Mahmood (1993) in their earlier book; namely, that there is no single "holy grail" of IT value research that provides a method for producing useful information for justifying IT investment and measuring payoff from this investment under all circumstances. The diversity of stakeholders in IT investment and of IT investment impacts within an organization precludes any one approach to measuring IT investment payoff. The issue is too multidimensional to allow a simple analysis or a single solution. The approaches presented in this book suggest that a multi-method approach to measuring IT investment payoff holds the greatest promise for assisting senior managers in making this important decision.

The Introduction began by stating the necessity of rethinking traditional approaches to measuring IT investment payoff. In particular, the over-reliance on quantitative measures has led some managers to question the value of their existing IT investments. It was argued that other measures may complement quantitative measures in order to compile a complete picture of the contributions of IT to an organization. Various qualitative measures and process measures may be constructively used in this regard. An analysis of IT investment payoff should include quantitative, qualitative, and process measures whenever possible in order to approach the evaluation of IT investment payoff from all possible angles.

In Part I, the theoretical background for measuring IT investment payoff was presented. A wide range of existing theories relevant to the IT payoff measurement issue were identified. Empirical studies were presented which tested hypotheses that were generated from these theories. The empirical studies involved a range of relevant variables and measures of these variables, which extend from the quantitative to process-oriented. This theoretical background laid the basis for the approaches discussed in Parts II and III and helped to provide a backdrop against which the various approaches may be viewed and compared.

Conceptual approaches to measuring IT investment payoff were presented in Part II. The two mathematical/formal approaches were particularly noteworthy in that they fully recognize the value of considering variables that are other than obviously quantitative or financial. Cost-benefit analysis, though highly quantitative, was given a fresh look in light of a consideration of decision maker's attitude and of risk situations where IT payoffs are nonnumeric. The hidden costs of system development were brought into clear view when the focus of the analysis was switched to the activity and away from the function when costing computerized applications. An emphasis on corporate strategies dominated three of the proposed approaches, suggesting a move away from the quantitative and toward the qualitative and process-oriented.

Part III presented case studies of actual organizations measuring IT investment payoff. These case studies indicated a range of approaches are actually being used to measure IT investment payoff. Two of the case organizations used primarily quantitative approaches, one used process-oriented approaches, two focused on measuring intangibles, and one used a multi-method (triangulation) approach. Taken together these case studies suggest that a multi-method approach which takes into account the different characteristics of the organization being evaluated may be the best way to effectively measure IT investment payoff in a given organization.

In the remainder of this Conclusion, we offer a set of propositions for future research-based on the ideas and results of the authors who have contributed chapters to this book.

Propositions for Future Research

One of the recurring themes in the book chapters is the need to move beyond purely quantitative measures of IT investment payoff. While measures such as NPV, IRR, and ROI provide a financial perspective on the value of an IT investment, clearly other measures are needed to address the multidimensional nature of the IT investment payoff issue. Strassmann's (1990) measure of management quality was a step in the right direction, but his measure was also quantitative in nature. The book chapters suggest either directly or indirectly that qualitative measures and process-oriented measures of IT investment payoff are also needed to effectively round out the analysis of IT investment payoff. This need leads us to the following proposition:

> **Proposition #1**: *The multidimensional nature of the IT investment payoff issue suggests that different categories of measures be created to address the various dimensions. An over-reliance on quantitative/financial measures is not adequate to the task. What is needed is a range of measures which deal with the quantitative, qualitative, and process-oriented aspects of measuring IT investment payoff.*

In their earlier book Banker, Kauffman and Mahmood (1993) remark that the primary goal of the IT researcher seeking to measure the business value of IT "should be to determine the extent to which the variety of newly available methods can be applied in different settings. Limiting ourselves to a single framework or a narrow research perspective at this time will reduce our ability to understand and discover the multiple sources of IT value" (p. 598). The range of alternative approaches to measuring IT investment payoff presented in this book's chapters serve to support this remark. But in addition, the range of approaches also suggests that, given the multidimensional nature of the IT investment payoff measurement problem, a multi-method approach to the problem is to be recommended. The challenge now is to discover which combination of methods works best in a given setting. This leads to the following proposition:

> **Proposition #2**: *The multidimensional nature of the IT investment payoff issue suggests that a variety of methods should be used to*

measure IT investment payoff in a given setting. Finding the best combination of methods to use in a given setting implies that the setting's characteristics be understood and that the multi-method approach chosen be consistent with these characteristics.

Clearly, a "contingency" approach to measuring IT investment payoff is suggested.

Weill (1992) stated that a single measure of IT investment is too broad and should be broken down into IT for different management purposes (e.g., strategic, informational, and transactional).   Barua, Kriebel, and Mukhopadhyay (1995) recommends a process–oriented approach that involves an analysis of intermediate and higher level output measures.   Different approaches to measuring IT investment payoff presented in this book's chapters support these remarks.   This leads to the following proposition.

> **Proposition #3**: *To increase the likelihood of success, measure IT investment payoff at various levels (e.g., low, intermediate, and high) and for different types of IT (e.g., transactional, informational, and strategic).*

Senior Management Guidelines for Measuring IT Investment Payoff

In the next few paragraphs, we offer a number of guidelines to senior managers in order to help them measure IT investment payoff using the contemporary approaches presented in this book:

> **Guideline #1**: *Adopt a multidimensional view of the IT investment payoff measurement issue.*

Traditional approaches to measuring IT investment payoff focused too much on financial measures such as NPV, IRR, and ROI. This focus is too narrow, emphasizing costs and benefits in monetary terms only   While lip service was paid to intangibles, non-monetary considerations were mostly either ignored or discounted.   Of course, while monetary considerations are important and cannot be ignored, a wider view of other dimensions of the IT investment payoff issue may reveal heretofore unseen or unappreciated IT value.

> **Guideline #2**: *Identify and embrace non-quantitative measures of IT investment payoff.*

Quantitative measures of IT investment payoff are comforting and may receive the blessing of the accounting staff.   However, beyond the possibilities of measurement error and inaccurate reporting, quantitative measures only tell part of the story. Events which are not easily quantified may prove to be much more important, and provide insight into IT investment payoff value that is not evident "in the numbers." For example, strategic necessities may compel an organization to invest in IT and benefits derived from these ventures may not be quantifiable.

Guideline #3: *Be open to using a number of approaches to measuring IT investment payoff at the same time.*

The temptation to choose and implement a single method of measuring IT investment payoff should be resisted, even if the method provides a convenient numerical conclusion. Even though using multiple methods to arrive at a conclusion will take more time and in all likelihood cost more money, the overall result may well provide a much clearer and more complete picture of the value of the IT investment. This is particularly true in the case of "emerging" technologies.

Guideline #4: *Measure IT investment payoff at various levels of the organization.*

Most researchers, mainly because of the paucity of data, investigated the impact of IT investment at one organizational level or another. Even though measuring IT investment at various levels will significantly complicate the measuring process and will take more time, the overall results will be more complete and are likely to provide a clearer picture. It is, therefore, worth the time and effort to undertake such measuring efforts.

Guideline #5: *Measure IT investment payoff separately for different types of IT.*

In order to obtain a more precise picture, IT investment payoff should be measured separately for transactional, informational, and strategic IT. This is because measuring these impacts together may confound the overall results and may not provide a clear depiction of the overall effort.

A Comprehensive Bibliography on the Strategic and Economic Value of Information Technology

Mo Adam Mahmood, University of Texas at El Paso
Edward J. Szewczak, Canisius College

The research literature on measuring the strategic and economic impact of IT is still not mature enough and comprehensive enough for us to direct senior managers and researchers to a particular research paper or model that will answer all their questions with regard to investing in IT. The problem is exacerbated by the fact that the research literature in the area is multidisciplinary in nature and no one approach by itself may be suitable for measuring IT investment payoff. The best advice we can give to the senior managers and researchers is this: read widely and find the models that fit your requirements best. This is especially important in view of the fact that the approaches presented in this book suggest that a multi–method strategy to measuring IT investment payoff is more promising than a single approach in assisting senior managers make IT investment decisions.

The contents of this bibliography by no means represent an exhaustive list of references in the IT investment and organizational performance area. These, however, provide a cross–section of some of the most important research studies conducted in the area. This is true in spite of the fact that most of the research studies listed in the bibliography came from the chapters included in this book. We believe these references will be immensely helpful to senior managers interested in investing in IT for gaining competitive advantage and for satisfying strategic and competitive necessities.

Aaker, D.A., & Mascerenhas, B. (1984). The need for strategic flexibility. *Journal of Business Strategy*, 5(2), 74–82.

Abernethy, M.A., & Guthrie, C.H. (1994). An empirical assessment of the "fit" between strategy and management information systems design, *Accounting & Finance*, 34 (2) (Nov).

Abowd, C. et. al. (1993). Structured modeling: an application framework and development process for flight simulators, CMU/SEI–93–TR–14.

Accampo, P. (1989). Justifying network costs. *CIO*, 2(5), 54-57.

Ackoff, R.L. (1967). Management Misinformation Systems. *Management Science*, 14, B147-B156.

Aiken, P. (1996). *Data Reverse Engineering: Slaying the Legacy Dragon.* New York: McGraw–Hill.

Ahituv, N. (1989). *Assessing the value of information: Problems and approaches*, Proceedings of the Tenth International Conference on Information Systems, Boston, MA, 315–326.

Ahituv, N. (1980). A Systematic Approach Toward Assessing the Value of an Information System. *MIS Quarterly*, 4(4), 61–75.

Ahituv, N. (1981). A Comparison of Information Structures for a Rigid Decision Rule Case. *Decision Sciences*, 12, 399-416.

Ahituv, N. (1982). Describing the Information Systems Life Cycle as an Adjustment Process Between Information and Decisions. *International Journal of Policy Analysis and Information Systems*, 6, 133-145.

Ahituv, N., & Giladi, R. (1993). Business Success and Information Technology: Are They Really Related? *Proceedings of the 7th Annual Conference of Management IS*, Tel Aviv University, (in Hebrew).

Allen, T., & Scott Morton, M. (Eds.) (1994). *Information technology and the corporation of the 1990s: research studies.* New York: Oxford University Press.

Alpar, P., & Kim, M. (1990). A Microeconomic Approach to the Measurement of Information Technology Value, *Journal of Management Information Systems*, (7:3), 55–69.

Alpar, P., & Kim, M. (1990). A Comparison of approaches to the measurement of IT value. In *Proceedings of the Twenty–Second Hawaiian International Conference on Systems Science.* Honolulu, Hawaii.

Alpert, B. (1967). Non-businessmen as Surrogates for Businessmen in Behavioral Experiments. *Journal of Business*, 40, 203-207.

Amit, R.. & Schoemaker, P.J. (1993). Strategic assets and organizational rent. *Strategic Management Journal*, 14, 33–46.

Anderson, P., & Peterson, N.C. (1993). A Procedure for Ranking Efficient Units in Data Envelopment Analysis, *Management Science*, 39(10), 1261–1264.

Andrew, D.. & Goldman, J. (1995). The Lunacy of Multimedia: A Parable. Digital. *Educom Review*, 30(6). 36–39.

Andrews, K.R. (1987). *The concept of the corporate strategy.* Homewood, IL: Irwin.

Andriole, S. (1990) *Information System Design Principles for the 90s.* AFCEA International Press.

Ansoff, H.I. (1965). *Corporate strategy.* New York: McGraw-Hill.

Applegate, L.M., McFarlan, F.W., & McKenney, J.L. (1996). Corporate *Information Systems Management,* Irwin.

Applegate, L.M., & Osborne, C.S. (1988). *Phillips 66 company: Executive information system.* (Case study No. 9-189-006). Boston, MA: Publishing Division, Harvard Business School.

Armitage, J. (1993). Process guide for the domain–specific software architectures process life cycle. CMU/SEI–93–SR–21.

Attewell, P. (1994). Information technology and the productivity paradox. In Douglas H. Harris (Ed.), *Organizational linkages: understanding the productivity paradox.* (National Research Council), 13–53. Washington, D.C.: National Academy Press.

Atttewell, P. (1991). Information Technology and the Productivity Paradox. *Markle Foundation/Social Science Research Council Conference on Social Aspects of Computing,* Washington, D.C., September.

Attewell, P. (1991). Information Technology and the Productivity Paradox. Working Paper. Department of Sociology, City University of New York.

Attewell, P. (1993). Why Productivity Remains a Key Measure of IT Impact. International Workshop on The Productivity of Information Technology Investments, Organized by the National Science Foundation, the Organization for Economic Cooperation and Development, and the Massachusetts Institute of Technology, Charleston, S.C., November 11–13.

Attewell, P., & Rule, J.B. (1991). Surveys and Other Methodologies Applied to IT Impact Research: Experience from a Comparative Study of Business Computing, *Harvard Business School Research Colloquium.* Boston, MA: Harvard Business School, 299–315.

Bacon, C.J. (1992). The use of decision criteria in selecting information systems/technology investments. *MIS Quarterly, 16*(3), 335-354.

Bahrami, H. (1992). The emerging flexible organization: Perspectives from Silicon Valley. *California Management Review,* 34 (4), 34–51.

Bailey, J.,& Pearson, S. (1983). Development of a Tool for Measuring and Analyzing Computer User Satisfaction. *Management Science,* 29, 530-545.

Baily, M.N. (1986). What Has Happened to Productivity Growth? *Science,* (234), 443–451.

Baily, M., & Chakrabarti, A.K. (1988). *Innovation and the Productivity Crisis.* Washington, D.C.: Brookings Institution.

Baily, M.N., & Gordon, R.J. (1988). The Productivity Slowdown, Measurement Issues, and the Explosion of Computer Power. *Brookings Papers on Economic Activity,* (2), 347–431.

Bain, A. (1992). Financial EDI at IBM Canada: The Long and Winding Road. *EDI Forum,* 6(1):45–48.

Baker, E.L., & O'Neil, Jr., H.F. Eds. (1994). *Technology Assessment in Education and Training.* Hillsdale, N.J.: L. Earlbaum Associates.

Bakos, J.Y. (1987). Dependent Variables for the Study of Firm and Industry–Level Impacts of Information Technology. In J. I. DeGross & C. H. Kriebel (editors). *Proceedings of the Eighth International Conference on Information Systems.* Pittsburgh, PA. 10–23.

Bakos, J.Y., & Kemerer, C.F. (1992). Recent Applications of Economic Theory in Information Technology Research. *Decision Support Systems,* 8(5), 365–386.

Bakos, J.Y. (1991). Strategic Implications of Inter–organizational Systems, Chapter 11 in Sutherland & Morieux (Eds.), *Business strategy and information technology*, 163–174. London: Routledge.

Ballance, C.S.T. (1992). Financial Electronic Data Interchange in Canada. *EDI Forum*, 6(1): 26–31.

Bandinelli, S., Fuggetta, A., Lavazza, L., Loi, M., & Picco, G. (1995). Modeling and improving an industrial software process. *IEEE Transactions on Software Engineering*, 21, 440–454.

Banker, R.D., & Kauffman, R.J. (1991). *Quantifying the Business Value of Information Technology: An Illustration of the "Business Value Linkage" Framework*. Stern School of Business, New York University. Working Paper.

Banker, R.D., & Kauffman, R.J. (1988). Strategic Contributions of Information Technology: An Empirical Study of ATM Networks. In J. I. DeGross & M. H. Olson (editors). *Proceedings of the Ninth International Conference on Information Systems*. Minneapolis, Minnesota, 141–150.

Banker, R.D., Kauffman, R.J., & Mahmood, M.A. (1993). Information Technology, Strategy and Firm Performance Evaluation: New Perspectives for Senior Management from Information Systems Research. In Banker et al. (ed) *Strategic Information Management: Perspectives on Organizational Growth and Competitive Advantage*. Idea Group Publishing, Harrisburg, PA.

Banker, R.D., Kauffman, R.J., & Mahmood, M.A. (1993). *Strategic Information Technology Management: Perspectives on Organizational Growth and Competitive Advantage*. Harrisburg, PA: Idea Group Publishing.

Banker, R.D., Kauffman, R.J., & Morey, R.C. (1990). Measuring Gains in Operational Efficiency from Information Technology: A Study of Positran Deployment at Hardee's Inc., *Journal of Management Information Systems*, 7, 29–54.

Banker, R.D., Kauffman, R.J., & Morey, R.C. (1990). Measuring Input Productivity Gains from Information Technology: A Case Study of Positran at Hardee's Inc. *Proceedings of the 23rd Annual International Conference on System Sciences*, Honolulu, Hawaii, 120–126.

Bannister, R. (1970). *Case Studies in Multi–Media Instruction*. Mount San Jacinto College. Mt. San Jacinto, CA.

Barker, P. (1989). ed. *Multimedia Computer Assisted Learning*. New York: Kogan Page.

Barki, H., & Huff, S. L. (1985). Change, attitude to change, and decision support system success. *Information and Management, 9*, 261-268.

Baronas, A. M., & Louis, R. (1988). Restoring a sense of control during implementation: How user involvement on system usage leads to system acceptance. *MIS Quarterly, 12*(1), 111-23.

Barney, J. (1991). Firm resources and sustained competitive advantage. *Journal of Management, 17*, 99–120.

Barney, J.B., & Ouchi, W.G. (eds.) (1986). *Organizational Economics*. San Francisco, CA: Jossey–Bass.

Barrington, H. (1971). An Evaluation of the Effectiveness of Instructional Television Presentation Variables. *British Journal of Educational Psychology*, 41(2), 219–220.

Bartlett, C. (1986). Building and managing the transnational: the new organizational challenge. Chapter 12 in Porter (Ed.), *Competition in Global Industries*, 367–401. Boston: Harvard Business School Press.

Bartlett, C., & Ghoshal, S. (1993). Beyond the M–form: toward a managerial theory of the firm. *Strategic Management Journal*, 14, 23–46.

Barua, A., Kriebel, C.H., & Mukhopadyay, T. (1995). Information technologies and business value: An analytic and empirical investigation. *Information Systems Research*, 6 (1) March, 3–23.

Barua, A., Kriebel, C., & Mukhopadhyay, T. (1991). An Economic Analysis of Strategic Information Technology Investments. *MIS Quarterly*, 15(3), 313–331.

Barua, A., Kriebel, C., & Mukhopadhyay, T. (1989). MIS and Information Economics: Augmenting Rich Descriptions with Analytical Rigor in Information Systems Design. In *Proceedings of the Tenth International Conference on Information Systems*, 327-339.

Barua, A., Kriebel, C., & Mukhopadhyay, T. (1991). Information Technology and Business Value: An Analytic and Empirical Investigation. Working Paper, University of Texas, Austin, Texas.

Basili, V., & Musa, J. (1991). The future engineering of software: a management perspective. *COMPUTER*, 90–96, September.

Baskerville, R. (1993). Information systems security design methods: implications for information systems development. *ACM Computing Surveys*. 25(4), 375–414.

Baum, D. (1996). Putting Client/Server in Charge. CFO. *12* (1), 45–53.

Belcher, L.W., & Watson, H. J. (1993). Assessing the value of Conoco's EIS. *MIS Quarterly*, *17*(3), 239–53.

Bell Canada. (1993). Software reuse case study–TRILLIM. *ARPA Report*, September.

Bell, D. (1979). Communications technology — for better or worse. *Harvard Business Review*, May–June, 20–41.

Bell, D. (1973). *The Coming of Post-Industrial Society; A Venture in Social Forecasting*. New York: Basic Books.

Benbasat, I., Bergeron, M., & Dexter, A.S. (1993). Development and Adoption of Electronic Data Interchange Systems: A Case Study of the Liquor Distribution Branch of British Columbia. *Proceedings of the Annual Conference of the Administrative Association of Canada* 14(4): 153–163.

Benbasat, I., DeSanctis, G., & Nault, B. (1991). Empirical Research in Managerial Support Systems: A Review and Assessment. Unpublished Working Paper, June.

Bender, D.H. (1986). Financial Impact of Information Processing. *Journal of Management Information Systems*, 3(2), 22–32.

Benjamin, R.J., & Blunt, J. (1992). Critical IT issues: The Next Ten Years, *Sloan Management Review*, 7-19.

Benjamin, R., & Wigand, R. (1995). Electronic Markets and Virtual Value Chain on the Information Superhighway. *Sloan Management Review.*

Bergeron, F., & Raymond, L. (1992). The Advantages of Electronic Data Interchange. *Database* 23(4): 19-31.

Bergeron, F., & Raymond, L. (1995). The Contribution of IT to the Bottom Line: A Contingency Perspective of Strategic Dimensions. In the *Proceedings of the Sixteenth Conference on Information Systems,* December 10–13, Amsterdam, 167–181.

Bergeron, M. (1994). Measuring the Business Value of Information Technology: The Case of Financial Electronic Data Interchange (EDI) in Canada, unpublished Ph.D. dissertation Vancouver, BC: University of British Columbia.

Berndt, E.R., & Morrison, C.J. (1992). High–tech Capital Formation and Economic Performance in U.S. Manufacturing Industries: An Exploratory Analysis, M.I.T Sloan School of Management, Working Paper #3419, April.

Betz, F. (1993). *Strategic Technology Management,* New York: McGraw–Hill, Inc.

Bhada, Y.K. (1984). A Framework for Productivity Measurement, *BUSINESS,* January–March 27–33.

Bharadwaj, A. S., Bharadwaj S. G., & Konsynski, B. R. (1995). The moderator role of information technology in firm performance: A conceptual model and research propositions. In J. I. DeGross, G. Ariav, C. Beath, R. Hoyer, & C. Kemerer (Eds.). *Proceedings of the Sixteenth International Conference on Information Systems,* 183–188. Amsterdam, The Netherlands: ACM Press.

Bierman, H., & Smidt, S. (1988). *The Capital Budgeting Decision,* New York: Macmillan.

Black J. A., & Boal, K. B. (1994). Strategic resources: traits, configurations and paths to sustainable competitive advantage. *Strategic Management Journal,* 15, 131–148.

Boar, B.H. (1994). *Implementing Client/Server Computing.* McGraw–Hill.

Boehm, B. (1989). *Software Risk Management.* Washington: IEEE Computer Society Press.

Boehm, B.W. (1993). Economic analysis of software technology investments. In T.R. Gulledge & W.P. Hutzler (Eds.) *Analytical Methods in Software Engineering Economics.* Berlin: Springer–Verlag.

Boehm, B., & Papaccio, P. (1987). Understanding and controlling software costs, *IEEE Transactions on Software Engineering,* Vol 14, No 10, October.

Boehm, B., & Scherlis, W. (1992). Megaprogramming (preliminary version), ARPA Paper.

Boeing Defense and Space Group (1994). Experience reports – The Navy/STARS Demonstration Project, *ARPA Report,* 13 July.

Boettcher, K. et al. (1994). A case history: development and use of an information architecture for ballistic missile defense battle management, Command, Control, and Communications (BMC3), *ARPA Report.*

Bollinger, T., & Pfleeger, S. (1991). Economics of reuse: issues and alternatives. *INFO SOFT,* 643–653, December.

Borkovsky, Ed. (1994). Mixed systems development tasks made easier with object technology. *Computing Canada*, 13.

Bouchard, L. (1993). Decision criteria in the adoption of EDI. *Proceedings of the Fourteenth International Conference on Information Systems*, Orlando, 365–376.

Bourgeois, L. (1985). Strategic goals, perceived uncertainty, and economic performance in volatile environments. *Academy of Management Journal*, 28(3), 548–573.

Boynton, A.C. (1993). Achieving dynamic stability through information technology. *California Management Review*, 35(2), 58–67.

Boynton, A.C., & Victor, B. (1991). Beyond flexibility: Building and Managing the Dynamically Stable Organization. *California Management Review*, Fall, 53–66.

Bradley, S. (1993). The role of IT networking in sustaining competitive advantage. Chapter 5 in S. Bradley et al. (Eds.). *Globalization, technology and competition: the fusion of computers and telecommunications in the 1990s*. Boston: Harvard Business School Press.

Bradley, S., Hausman, J., & Nolan, R. (Eds.) (1993). *Globalization, technology and competition: the fusion of computers and telecommunications in the 1990s*. Boston: Harvard Business School Press.

Brancheau, J., Janz, B., & Wetherbe, J. (1996). Key Issues in Information Systems Management: 1994–95 SIM Delphi Results. *MIS Quarterly*, 20, 2, 225-242.

Brancheau, J. C., & Wetherbe, J. C. (1990). Key Issues in Information Systems Management. *MIS Quarterly*, 14(3), 31–39.

Brancheau, J.C. and Wetherbe, J.C. (1987). Key issues in information system management. *MIS Quarterly*, 11(1), 23–46.

Bresnahan, T.F. (1986). Measuring the Spillovers from Technical Advance: Mainframe Computers in Financial Services. *American Economic Review*, 76, 742-55.

Brimson, J.A. (1991). *Activity Accounting: An Activity Based Costing Approach*, Wiley.

Brockhaus, R. (1980). Risk Taking Propensity of Entrepreneurs. *Academy of Management Journal*. 23(3), 509–520.

Brodman, J.G., & Johnson, D.L. (1996). Return on investment from software process improvement as measured by U.S. industry. *Crosstalk*, 9(4), 23–29.

Brookfield, D.(1005). Risk and capital budgeting: avoiding the pitfalls in using NPV when risk arises. *Management Decision*, Vol. 33, No. 8, 56–59.

Browning, J. (1990). A Survey of Information Technology. *Economist*, June 16, 5–20.

Bryan, E.F. (1990). Information systems investment strategies. *Journal of Information Systems Management*, Fall, 27–35.

Brynjolfsson, E. (1993). The Productivity Paradox of Information Technology. *Communications of the ACM*, 36(12), 66–77.

Brynjolfsson, E. (1994). Technology's True Payoffs. *InformationWeek*, 496, 34–36.

Brynjolfsson, E., & Hitt, L. (1993). Is Information Systems Spending Productive? New

Evidence and New Results. In J. I. DeGross & D. Robey (editors). Proceedings of the Fourteenth International Conference on Information Systems. Orlando, Florida, 47–64.

Brynjolfson, E., & Hitt, L. (1993). New Evidence on the Returns to Information Systems, Center for Coordinating Sciences Working Paper #162, MIT, Cambridge, Mass.

Brynjolfsson, E., & Hitt, L. (1996). Paradox lost —Firm–level evidence on the returns to information systems spending. *Management Science*, 42(4), 541–558.

Brynjolfsson, E., & Hitt, L. (1994). Information Assets, Technology, and Organization. *Management Science*, 40, 1645–62.

Brynjolfsson, E., & Hitt, L. (1994). Creating Value and Destroying Profits? Three Measures of Information Technology's Contribution. CCS Working Paper. MIT Sloan School of Management.

Brynjolfsson, E., & Hitt, L. (1995). InformationWeek 500: The Productive Keep Producing. *InformationWeek*, 545, 38–57.

Brynjolfsson, E. Malone, T.J., Gurbaxani, V. & Kambil, A. (1994). Does Information Technology Lead To Smaller Firms? *Management Science*, 40(12), 1628–44.

Bullen, C.V. (1996). Critical Success Factors and Productivity. In Paul Gray and Jaak Jurison, *Productivity in the Office and the Factory*, Boyd & Fraser, Danvers, MA.

Burgers, W.P., Hill, C.W.L., & Kim, W.C. (1993). A theory of global strategic alliances: The case of the global auto industry. *Strategic Management Journal*, 14, 419–432.

Busch, J. (1994). Cost Modeling as a Technical Management Tool. *Research Technology Management*, 37(6), 50–56.

Business Week (1986). The information business, August 25, 82–92.

Business Week (1994). Hospitals attack a crippler: Paper–computers might be America's real health–care reformer, February 21.

BusinessWeek (1994). Quality: How to make it pay. August 8.

Caldwell, B. (1996). Client/Server: Can It be Saved? *Information Week*, April 18, 36–44.

Caldwell, B. (1994). Missteps, Miscues: Business Reengineering Failures Have Cost Corporations Billions, and Spending is Still on the Rise. *InformationWeek*, June 20, 50–60.

Caldwell, B. (1994). Probing the Productivity Paradox. (Editorial). *Management Information System Quarterly*, 18(2). XXV–XXXI

Card, D., & Comer, E. (1994). Why do so many reuse programs fail? *IEEE Software*, 114–115, September.

Carley, W.M., & O'Brien, T.L. (1995). How a Citicorp system was raided and funds moved around the world. *Wall Street Journal*, 226(50), 1, 18.

Carlson, W.M., & McNurline, B.C. (1992). Uncovering the Information Technology Payoffs, I/S Analyzer Special Report, United Communications Group, Rockland, Maryland.

Carlsson, C., Walden, P., & Kokkonen, O. (1994). Strategic Management with a

Hyperknowledge Support System. Proceedings of the Twenty–Seventh Annual Hawaii International Conference on System Sciences, December.

Carmines, E.G., & Zellers, R.A. (1979). *Reliability and validity assessment.* Beverly Hills, CA: Sage University Paper.

Caron, J.R., Jarvenpaa, S.L., & Stoddard, D.B. (1994). Business Reengineering at CIGNA Corporation: Experiences and lessons learned from the first five years, *MIS Quarterly,* 18 (3) (September), 233–250.

Carter, W.K. (1992). To Invest in New Technology or Not? New Tools for Making the Decision. *Journal of Accountancy,* 173(5), 58–64.

Cash, J., & Konsynski, B. (1985). IS redraws competitive boundaries. *Harvard Business Review,* March–April, 134–142.

Caudle, S. L. (1994) Reengineering Strategies and Issues. *Public Productivity & Management Review,* 18, 149–162.

Caudle, S. L. (1994). Reengineering and Information Resources Management. *Public Manager,* 23, 39–42.

Cecil, J. L., & Hall, E. A. (1988). When IT really matters to business strategy. *The McKinsey Quarterly,* 2–26.

Chakravarthy, B.S. (1986). Measuring Strategic Performance. *Strategic Management Journal,* (7), 437–458.

Champy, J., & Hammer, M. (1993). *Reengineering The Corporation: A Manifesto For Business Revolution.* New York: Harper Business.

Chan, Y. E., & Huff, S. (1993). Strategic Information Systems Alignment. *Business Quarterly,* 58(1), 51–54.

Chandler, A.D., Jr. (1962). *Strategy and Structure: Chapters in the History of the American Industrial Enterprise.* Cambridge, MA: Massachusetts Institute of Technology Press.

Chandler, A.D., Jr. (1977). *The visible hand, the managerial revolution in American business.* Cambridge, MA: The Belknap Press of Harvard University Press.

Chandler, J.S. (1982). A Multiple Criteria Approach for Evaluating Information Systems. *MIS Quarterly,* 6(1), 61–75.

Charette, R N (1989). *Software Engineering Risk Analysis and Management.* New York: McGraw-Hill.

Charnes, A., & Cooper, W.W. (1962). Programming with Linear Fractional Functions, *Naval Research Logistics Quarterly,* 9(3 & 4),181–185.

Charnes, A., Cooper, W.W., Lewin, A., & Seiford, L.M., (1995). *Data Envelopment Analysis: Theory, Methodology and Applications.* Boston: Kluwer Academic Publishers.

Charnes, A., Cooper, W.W., & Rhodes, E. (1981). Evaluating Program and Managerial Efficiency: Application of Data Envelopment Analysis to Program Follow Through. *Management Science,* 7(4), 698–697.

Cheney, P.H., & Dickson, G.W. (1982). Organizational characteristics and information systems: An exploratory investigation. *Academy of Management Journal*, 25(1), 170-184.

Cheswick, W. (1995). Is the Internet secure? No. *Computerworld*, 29(22), 95–96.

Chismar, W. (1986). Assessing the Economic Impact of Information Systems Technology on Organizations. Unpublished doctoral dissertation, Carnegie Mellon University.

Chismar, W., & Kriebel, C. (1985). A Method for Assessing the Economic Impact of Information Systems Technology on Organizations. In *Proceedings of the Sixth International Conference on Information Systems*, 45-56.

Chismar, W., Kriebel, C., & Melone, N. (1985). Criticism of Information Systems Research Employing 'User Satisfaction.' Graduate School of Industrial Administration, Carnegie-Mellon University, WP 24-85-86.

Ciborra, C. U. (1985). Reframing the Role of Computers in Organizations: The Transactions Costs Approach. In L. Gallegos, R. Welke & J. Wetherbe (Editors). Proceedings of the Sixth International Conference on Information Systems, Indianapolis, Indiana, 57–69.

Clark, J. Principal Engineer (1996). Comptek Federal Systems, Inc. *Personal communication*. July 18.

Clark, K. (1987). Investment in new technology and competitive advantage. In D. Teece (Ed.), *The Competitive Challenge*, 59–81. Cambridge, MA: Ballinger.

Clark, Jr., T.D. (1992). Corporate systems management: An overview and research perspective. *Communications of the ACM*, 35(2),61–75.

Clemens, C., & Weber H. (1990). Strategic information technology investment: some guidelines for decision making. *Journal of Management Information Systems*, Winter.

Clemons, E.K. (1991). Evaluation of Strategic Investments in Information Technology. *Communications of the ACM*, 34 (1), 22–36.

Clemons, E.K., & McFarlan, F. W. (1986). Telecom: hook up or lose out. *Harvard Business Review*, July–August, 91–97.

Clemons, E.K., & Row, M. (1988). McKesson Drug Company: a case study of Economost — a strategic information system. *Journal of Management Information Systems*, 5(1), 36–50.

Clemons, E.K., & Row, M.C. (1991). Sustaining IT Advantage: The Role of Structural Differences. *MIS Quarterly*, 15(3), 275–292.

Clemons, E. K., & Weber, B.W. (1994). Segmentation, differentiation, and flexible pricing: Experiences with information technology and segment–tailored strategies. *Journal of Management Information Systems*, 11 (2), 9–36.

Cliff, V. (1992). Reengineering becomes the CEO's policy at Mutual Benefit Life. *Journal of Strategic Information Systems*. 1(2):102–105.

Cohen, F.B. (1995). *Protection and Security on the Information Superhighway*. New York: Wiley.

Cohen, S., (1994). A model base for software engineering. *SEI Briefing Charts*, June.

Cohen, W. M., & Levinthal, D. A. (1990). Absorptive Capacity: a new perspective on learning and innovation. *Administrative Science Quarterly*, 35, 128–152.

Computerworld (1992). Framingham, MA: CW Publishing, Inc.

Conner, K. R. (1991). A historical comparison of resource–based theory and five schools of thought within industrial organization economics: do we have a new theory of the firm? *Journal of Management*, 17, 121–154.

Conrath, D. W., & Mignen, O. P. (1990). What is being done to measure user satisfaction with EDP/MIS. *Information and Management*, 19(1), 7-19.

Cook, T.D., & Campbell, D.T. (1976). The Design and Conduct of Quasi–Experiments and True Experiments in Field Settings. M.D. Dunnette, ed., *Handbook of Industrial and Organizational Psychology*. Chicago, IL: Rand McNally College Publishing Company, 224–246.

Cook, W.D., Kress, M., & Seiford, L.M. (1992). Prioritization Models for Frontier Decision Making Units. *European Journal of Operational Research*, 59, 319–323.

Cooper, R., & Kaplan, R.S. (1992). Activity–Based Systems: Measuring the Cost of Resource Usage. *Accounting Horizons*, 1–13.

Cooper, R. B., & Zmud, R. W. (1990). Information Technology Implementation Research: A Technological Diffusion Approach. *Management Science*, 36 (2), 123–139.

Copeland, T.E., & Weston, F. (1983). *Financial Theory and Corporate Policy*, 2nd ed. Reading, MA: Addison–Wesley.

Courtney, J., DeSanctis, G., & Kasper, G. (1983). Continuity in MIS/DSS Laboratory Research: The Case for a Common Gaming Simulator. *Decision Sciences*, 14, 419-439.

Crockett, F. (1992). Revitalizing executive information systems. *Sloan Management Review*, 39-47.

Cron, W. L., & Sobol, M. G. (1983). The Relationship Between Computerization and Performance: A Strategy for Maximizing the Economic Benefits of Computerization. *Information and Management*, 6, 171–181.

Cronbach, L. J. (1951). Coefficient alpha and the internal structure of tests. *Psychometrika*, 16(3), 297–333.

Cross, K.F., Feather, J.J., & Lynch, R.L. (1994). *Corporate Renaissance: The Art of Reengineering*. Cambridge, MA: Blackwell Publishers, 15–16.

Crowston, K., & Treacy, M.E. (1986). Assessing the Impact of Information Technology on Enterprise Level Performance. Proceedings of the Seventh International Conference on Information Systems, San Diego, CA: 299–310.

Curtis, B., & Paulk, M. (1993). Creating a software process improvement program. *Information & Software Technology*, 35, 381–386.

Curley, K., & Pyburn, P. (1982). Intellectual Technologies: The Key to Improving White-Collar Productivity. *Sloan Management Review*, 24, 1, 31-39.

Curley, K., & Henderson, J. (1989). Evaluating Investments in Information Technology: A Review of Key Models. Unpublished Working Paper Prepared for the 1989 ACM SIGOIS Workshop on The Impact and Value of Information Systems.

D'Aveni, R.A. (1995). *Hypercompetitive rivalries.* New York: The Free Press.

D'Aveni, R.A. (1994). *Hypercompetition: managing the dynamics of strategic maneuvering.* New York: The Free Press.

Daft, R.L. (1978). A dual–core model of organizational innovation. *Academy of Management Journal,* 21(2), 193–210.

Daft, R.L. (1986). *Organization theory and design.* St. Paul, MN: West Publishing.

Daft, R. L. (1991). *Management.* Chicago: IL: The Dryden Press.

Daft, R.L., & Lengel, R. (1986). Organizational information requirements, media richness and structural design. *Management Science,* 32(5), 554–571.

Daft, R.L., Sormunsen, J., & Parks, D. (1988). Chief executive scanning, environmental characteristics, and company performance: an empirical study. *Strategic Management Journal,* 9, 123–139.

Das, S.R., Zahra, S.A., & Warkentin, M.E. (1991). Integrating the content and process of strategic MIS planning with competitive strategy. *Decision Sciences,* 22, 953–984.

Das, T. K., & Elango, B. (1995). Managing strategic flexibility: Key to effective performance. Journal of General Management, 20 (3), 60–75.

Davenport, T.H. (1995). Business Process Reengineering: Where It's Been, Where It's Going. In Varun Grover and William Kettinger, *Business Process Change: Reengineering Concepts, Methods, and Technologies.* Harrisburg, PA: Idea Group Publishing.

Davenport, T.H. (1993). *Process Innovation: Reengineering Work through Information Technology,* Boston: Harvard Business School Press.

Davenport, T.H., & Short, J.E. (1990). The New Industrial Engineering: Information Technology and Business Process Redesign. *Sloan Management Review,* 31(3): 11-27.

David, P.A. (1988). Path Dependence: Putting the Past in to the Future of Economics. Stanford University, Dept. of Economics Technical Report, 533.

David, P. (1990). Computer and Dynamo: The Modern Productivity Paradox in a Not Too Distant Mirror. Stanford University Working Paper. Center for Economic Policy Research.

Davidow, W. H., & Malone, M. S. (1992). *The virtual corporation.* New York: HarperBusiness.

Davidson, A., & Herskovitz, M. (1994). *Mortgage–Backed Securities – Investment Analysis & Advanced Valuation Techniques.* Probus Publishing.

Davidson, A., Ho, T., & Lim, Y. (1994). *Collateralized Mortgage Obligations.* Probus Publishing.

Davidson, W.H. (1993). Beyond re–engineering: The three phases of business transformation. *IBM Systems Journal,* 32 (1), 65–79.

Davis, A.M. (1996). Eras of Software technology transfer, *IEEE software,* March:4,7.

Davis, F.D., Bagozzi, R.P., & Warshaw, P.R. (1989). User Acceptance of Computer

Technology: A Comparison of Two Theoretical Models. *Management Science*, 35 (8), 982–1003.

Davis, G., Collins, R.W., Eierman, M., & Nance, W.D. (1993). Productivity from Information Technology Investment in Knowledge Work. In Banker et al. (eds) *Strategic Information Management: Perspectives on Organizational Growth and Competitive Advantage*. Harrisburg, PA: Idea Group Publishing.

Davis, S. M. (1987). *Future perfect*. Reading, MA: Addison Wesley.

Davis, T. (1994). The reuse capability model. *CrossTalk*, The Defense Software Engineering Report, 5–9, March.

Dean, C., & Whitlock, Q. (1988). *A Handbook of Computer Based Training*. New York: Kogan Page Publishing.

Dean, J., Jr., & Sharfman, M. (1996). Does Decision Process Matter? A Study of Strategic Decision–making Effectiveness. *Academy of Management Journal*, 39(2), 368–396.

Deloitte & Touche LLP. (1995). Leading Trends in Information Services. *National Office*, Ten Westport Road, Wilton CT.

DeLone, W.H., & McLean, E. (1992). Information system success: the quest for the dependent variable. *Information Systems Research*, 3(1), 60–95.

DeMarco, T. (1982). *Controlling Software Projects: Management, Measurement, and Estimation*. Englewood Cliffs, N.J.: Yourdon Press.

Deming, W.E. (1986). *Out of the Crisis*. MIT Center for Advanced Engineering Study, Cambridge, MA.

Dempster, A. P. (1967). Upper and Lower Probabilities Induced by a Multi–valued Mapping. *Annals of Mathematical Statistics*, 325–339.

Demski, J. (1972). *Information Analysis*. Reading, MA: Addison-Wesley Publishing Co.

Denison, E. (1979). Explanations of Declining Productivity Growth. *Survey of Current Business*, 59, 8, 1-24.

Dertouzos, M.L., Lester, R. K., Solow, R.M., & the MIT commission on industrial productivity. (1989). *Made in America : Regaining the productive edge*. Cambridge, MA: The MIT Press.

Dess, G.D., & Miller, A. (1993). *Strategic Management*. New York: McGraw–Hill.

Dess, G.G., & Beard, D.W. (1984). Dimensions of organizational task environments. *Administrative Science Quarterly*, 29, 52–73.

Dickerson, & Gentry, J.W. (1983). Characteristics of adopters and non–adopters of home computers. *Journal of Consumer Research*, 10(2), 225–235.

Dickson, G.W., & Wetherbe, J.C. (1985). *The Mangement of Information Systems*. New York: McGraw Hill.

Dickson, G., Senn, J., & Chervany, N. (1977). Research in Management Information Systems: The Minnesota Experiments. *Management Science*, 23, 913-923.

Dickson, G., Wells, C. & Wilkes, R. (1988). Toward a Derived Set of Measures for

Assessing IS Organizations. In N. Bjorn-Andersen, & G. Davis (Eds.). *Information Systems Assessment,* 129–147. Amsterdam: Elsevier Science Publishers.

Dierickx, I., & Cool, K. (1989). Asset stock accumulation and sustainability of competitive advantage. *Management Science,* 35, 1504–11.

Dion, R. (1993). Process improvement and the corporate balance sheet. IEEE software, July, 28–35.

Dixit, A., & Pindyck, R.S. (1994). *Investment under Uncertainty.* Princeton, N.J.: Princeton University Press.

Dixon, J. R., Arnold, P., Heineke, J., Kim, J., & Mulligan, P. (1994). Business Process Reengineering: Improving In New Strategic Directions. *California Management Review,* 36, 96–108.

Dorling, A. (1993). SPICE: Software process improvement and capability determination. *Information & Software Technology,* 35, 404–406.

Dos Santos, B.L. (1991). Justifying Investments in New Information Technologies. *Journal of Management Information Systems,* 7(4), 71–90.

Dos Santos, B.L. & Peffers, K. (1991). The Effects of Early Adoption of Information Technology: An Empirical Study. In Proceedings of the Twelfth International Conference on Information Systems, 127-140.

Dos Santos, B.L., & Peffers, K. (1992). Rewards to Investors in Innovative Information Technology Applications: A Study of First Movers and Early Followers in ATMs. Working Paper, Krannert Graduate School of Management, Purdue University, West Lafayette.

Dos Santos, B.L. & Peffers, K. (1993). Firm level performance effects: a framework for information technology evaluation research. Chapter 23 in R. Banker, R. Kauffman, & M. Mahmood (Eds.), *Strategic Information Technology Management: Perspectives on Organizational Growth and Competitive Advantage,* 515–546. Harrisburg, PA: Idea Group Publishing.

Dos Santos, B.L., Peffers, K. & Mauer, D.C. (1993). The Impact of Information Technology Investment Announcements on the Market Value of the Firm. *Information Systems Research,* 4(1), 1–23.

Downey, W. K., Hellriegel, D., & Slocum, J. W., Jr., (1975). Environmental uncertainty: the construct and its applications. *Administrative Science Quarterly,* December, 20(4), 613–629.

Doz, Y., & Prahalad, C. K. (1991). Managing DMNCs: a search for a new paradigm. *Strategic Management Journal,* 12, 145–164.

Drucker, P. F. (1995). The information executives truly need. *Harvard Business Review,* 73(1), 54–62.

Drucker, P. F. (1995). The New Productivity Challenge. In Paul Gray and Jaak Jurison, *Productivity in the Office and the Factory.* Danvers, MA: Boyd & Fraser.

Drucker, P.F. (1991). The New Productivity Challenge. *Harvard Business Review,* 69, 69–79.

Drucker, P.F. (1993). Drucker on Management: We Need to Measure, Not Count. *WallStreet Journal,* April 13, Section A, 18.

Drucker, P.F. (1994). From Lean Production to the Lean Enterprise. *Harvard Business Review*, March–April.

Dué, R.T. (1992). The real cost of outsourcing. *Journal of Information Systems Management*. 9(1), 78–81.

Dué, R. T. (1993). The Productivity Paradox. *Information Systems Management*, 10(1), p. 68.

Dué, R. T. (1994). The Productivity Paradox Revisited. *Information Systems Management*, 11(1), p. 74.

Dunegan, K., Duchon, D., & Barton, S. (1992). Affect, risk, and decision criticality: replication and extension in a business setting. *Organizational Behaviour and Human Decision Processes*. 53(3), 335–351.

Dyer, J. H. (1996). Specialized supplier networks as a source of competitive advantage: evidence from the auto industry. *Strategic Management Journal*, 17, 271–291

Dyson, R.G., & Thanassoulis, E. (1988). Reducing Weight Flexibility in Data Envelopment Analysis, *Journal of the Operational Research Society*, 39(6), 563–576.

Earl, M. (Ed.) (1988). *Information management: the strategic dimension*. Oxford, England: Clarendon Press.

Earl, M.J. (1993). Experiences in strategic information systems planning, *MIS Quarterly*, 17 (1) March, 1–24.

Ebers, M., & Ganter, H. (1991). Strategic applications of integrated information systems. Chapter 9 in E. Sutherland, & Y. Morieux (Eds.). *Business strategy and information technology*, 131–146. London: Routledge.

Egelhoff, W. (1982). Strategy and structure in multinational corporations: an information processing approach. Administrative Science Quarterly, 27, 435–458.

Egelhoff, W. (1991). Information–processing theory and the multinational enterprise. *Journal of International Business Studies*, Third quarter, 341–368.

Elam, J.J., & Leidner, D.G. (1995). EIS adoption, use, and impact: The executive perspective. *Decision Support Systems*, 14(2), 89–103.

Elbert, B., & Martyna, B. (1993). *Client/Server Computing*. Boston: Artech House.

Ellis, R.W., Jones, M.C., & Arnett K,P, (1994). Local Area Network Adoption: An Empirical Assessment. *Information Resources Management Journal*, 7(4), 20–29.

Emery, J. (1971). *Cost/Benefit Analysis of Information Systems*. Chicago, IL: The Society for Management Information Systems.

Emery, J. (1973). Cost benefit analysis of information systems. SMIS Workshop, No.1.

Emmelhainz, M.A. (1990). *Electronic Data Interchange: A Total Management Guide*. New York: Van Nostrand Reinhold.

Engemann, K., Filev, D., & R. Yager. (1996). Modelling decision making using immediate probabilities. *International Journal of General Systems*. 24(3), 281–294.

Engemann, K., Miller, H., & R. Yager. (1996). Decision making with belief structures: an application in risk management. *International Journal of Uncertainty, Fuzziness and Knowledge-Based Systems.* 4(1), 1–25.

Engemann, K., Miller, H., & R. Yager. (1995). Decision making using the weighted median applied to risk management. Proceedings of the Third International Symposium on Uncertainty Modeling and Analysis and the Annual Conference of North American Fuzzy Information Processing Society, 9–13.

Engemann, K., & Miller, H. (1992). Operations risk management at a major bank. *Interfaces.* 22(6), 140–149.

Engemann, K., Miller, H., & Yager, R. (1994). A decision making model under uncertainty applied to managing risk. *Uncertainty Modeling and Analysis: Theory and Application,* (ed. Ayyub and Gupta). Machine Intelligence and Pattern Recognition Series. North–Holland, Amsterdam.

Estabrooks, M. (1995). *Electronic Technology, Corporate Strategy, and World Transformation.* Quorum Books.

Ettlie, J.E. (1986). Implementing Manufacturing Technologies: Lessons from Experience in *Managing Technological Innovation,* D. D. David & Associates, Eds., San Francisco: Jossey–Bass, 72–104.

Ettlie, J.E., Bridges, W.P., & O'Keefe, R.D. (1984). Organizational Strategy and Structural Differences for radical versus Incremental Innovation. *Management Science,* 30 (6), 682–695.

Evans, J.S. (1991). Strategic flexibility for high technology maneuvers: A conceptual framework. *Journal of Management Studies,* 28 (1), 69–89.

Fafchamps, D. (1994). Organizational factors and reuse. *IEEE Software,* 31–41, September.

Fagerberg, J. (1994). Technology and international differences in growth rates. *Journal of Economic Literature,* 32, September:1147–1175.

Faier, J. (1995). The Truth About Multimedia: What It Is, Where It's At, Where It's Going. *Multimedia Today.* 3(1), 25–28.

Falk, J.E., & Palocsay, S.W. (1992). Optimizing the Sum of Linear Fractional Functions, in *Recent Advances in Global Optimization,* C.A. Floudas and P.M. Pardalos (eds.).

Fama, E.F., & Miller, M.H. (1972). *The Theory of Finance.* Hindsdale, IL: Dryden Press.

Farbey, B., Land, F., & Target, D. (1993). *How to Assess Your IT Investment,* Oxford: Butterworth Heinemann.

Farr, M.J., & Psotka, J. (1992). eds. *Intelligent Instruction by Computer.* New York: Taylor and Francis.

Farrell, J. (1994). A Practical Guide For Implementing Reengineering. *Planning Review,* 22, Mar./Apr., 40–45.

Federal Computer Week (1993). Business Process Reengineering, September 20, 1–27.

Feher, A., & Towell, E.R. (1996). Business Use of the Internet. *Internet Research,* 7:3.

Ferrentino, A. (1994). SNAP: The use of reusable templates to improve software productivity and quality. Template Software, Inc.

Feigenbaum, A.V. (1983). *Total Quality Control.* New York: McGraw–Hill.

Fenrich, P. (1997). *Practical Guidelines for Creating Instructional Multimedia Applications.* Ft. Worth: Dryden Press.

Fincham, R., Fleck, J., Proctor, R., Scarbrough, H., Tierney, M., & Williams, R. (1994). *Expertise and Innovation: Information Technology Strategies in the Financial Services Sector.* Oxford: Clarendon Press.

Fites, M., Kratz, P., & Brebner, A. (1989). *Control and Security of Computer Information Systems.* Computer Science Press.

Fonash, P. (1993). Metrics for reusable software code components, Ph.D. Dissertation. George Mason University.

Ford, J.C. (1994). Evaluating investment in IT. *Management Accounting*, Dec., 24–36.

Fortune, Time Inc. Magazines, 1992.

Frakes, W. (1992). *Software reuse empirical studies.* Virginia Polytechnic Institute and State University, Department of Computer Science, 11 October.

Frakes, W., & Riddle, W. (1993). Instituting and maturing a practical reuse program. *International Perspectives in Software Engineering*, 18–26, Summer 2nd Quarterly.

Frakes, W., & Isoda, S. (1994). Success factors of systematic reuse. *IEEE Software*, 15–19, September.

Frakes, W., & Fox, C. (1994). Sixteen questions about software reuse. Software Engineering Guide Draft Paper, 1–25, November 1994b.

Frakes, W., & Fox, C. (1994). Quality improvement using a software reuse failure modes model. Software Engineering Guild Draft Paper, 1–13, November 1994c.

Frakes, W., & Fox, C. (1995). Sixteen questions about software reuse. *Communications of the ACM*, 75–87 and 112, Vol. 38, No. 6, June 1995.

Framel, J.E. (1993). Information Value Management. *Journal of Systems Management* December, 16–41.

Freedman, D. (1991). The Myth of Strategic I.S. CIO, July 42–48.

Fuerst, W.L., & Cheney, P.H. (1982). Factors affecting the perceived utilization of computer-based decision support systems in the oil industry. *Decision Sciences, 13*(4), 554-569.

Gacek, C. et al. (1994). Focus workshop on software architectures: issue paper. USC Center for Software Engineering Paper, 1 April.

Gagne, R.M., & Briggs, L.J. (1992). *Principles of Instructional Design.* Fourth edition. New York: Harcourt Brace Jovanovich.

Galbraith, J.R. (1973). *Designing complex organizations.* Reading, MA: Addison–Wesley.

Galbraith, J.R. (1994). *Competing with flexible lateral organizations* (2nd ed.). Reading, MA: Addison Wesley Publishing Co.

Galbraith, J.R. (1977). *Organization design.* Reading, MA: Addison–Wesley.

Galbraith, J.R., & Kazanjian, R.K. (1986). *Strategy implementation: Structure, systems, and process.* St. Paul, MN: West Publishing Company.

Galbraith, J., & Nathanson, D. (1978). *Strategy implementation: the role of structure and process.* St. Paul, MN: West Publishing Co.

Ganger, R. (1990). Computer based training works. *Personnel Journal.* 69:9, 84.

Gardelin, P., & Barrows, R. (1996). Interviews, Information Technology, Coors Brewery. Golden, CO. January to June.

Garud, R., & Nayyar, P.R.(1994). Transformative capacity: continual structuring by intertemporal technology transfer. *Strategic Management Journal,* 15, 365–385.

Gates, W.H. III. (1995). *The Road Ahead.* New York: Viking Press.

Geishecker, M. (1996). New Technologies Supports ABC. *Management Accounting,* 42–48.

Gerwin, D. (1993). Manufacturing flexibility: a strategic perspective. *Management Science,* 39(4), 395–410.

Ghoshal, S., & Nohria, N. (1989). Internal differentiation within multinational corporations. *Strategic Management Journal,* 10, 323–337.

Gibbs, W. (1994). Software's chronic crisis. *Scientific American,* 86–95, September.

Gibson, B., & Nolan, R.L. (1994). Managing the fourth stages of EDP growth. *Harvard Business Review,* January/February, 76–88.

Giladi, R., Lipovetsky, S., & Tishler, A. (1993). Evaluation and Approximation of Large Systems Using Multi–Dimensional Eigenvector Analysis: An Application to MIS. Proceedings of the Second International Conference on Systems Science and Systems Engineering, August 24–27, Beijing, China, 44–48.

Gilster, P. (1995). *The New Internet Navigator.* John Wiley & Sons, Inc.

Ginther, W. Group Executive Vice President (1996). Technology & Operations Group, Crestar Bank. Personal communication. February 1.

Ginzberg, M.J. (1978). Redesign of managerial tasks: A requisite for successful support systems. *MIS Quarterly,* 2(1), 39-52.

Ginzberg, M.J. (1979). A study of the implementation process. *TIMS Studies in the Management Sciences,* 13, 85-102.

Gleckman, H. (1993). The Technology Payoff. *Business Week,* Special Report, June 14.

Gnadt, J. (1995–1996). Manager of Training and Development for Oppenheimer Funds.Personal Interviews and Education and OFS Training Documentation. Denver, CO. September, 1995 to June, 1996.

Goldenson, D.R., & Herbsleb, J.D. (1995). After the appraisal: A systematic survey of process improvement, its benefits, and factors that influence success. *Technical Report CMU/SEI–95–TR–009.*

Goodhue, D. (1986). IS Attitudes: Toward Theoretical and Definitional Clarity. In Proceedings of the Seventh International Conference on Information Systems, 181-194.

Goodhue, D.L., Kirsch, L.J., Quillard, J.A., & Wybo, M.D. (1992). Strategic Data Planning: Lessons from the Field, *MIS Quarterly,* 16 (1) March, 11–34.

Goodman, P., Lerch, F.J., & Mukhopadhyay, T. (1994). Individual and organizational productivity: linkages and processes. In D. H. Harris, (Ed.), *Organizational Linkages: Understanding the Productivity Paradox.* National Research Council, 54–73). Washington, DC: National Academy Press.

Gordon, R.J. (1989). Comments made at panel 12: Information Technology and the Productivity Paradox. In the Proceedings of the Tenth International Conference on Information Systems, Boston, Massachusetts.

Govindarajan, V. (1988). A contingency approach to strategic implementation at the business unit level: integrating administrative mechanisms with strategy. *Academy of Management Journal,* 31(4), 828–853.

Gow, K. (1991). Faster Tech Change means Organization Chart must adjust. *Software Magazine,* 36–38.

Grabowski, M., & Lee, S. (1993). Linking Information Systems Applications Portfolios and Organizational Strategy in *Strategic Information Technology Managegment: Perspectives on Organizational Growth and Competitive Advantage,* R.D. Banker, R.J. Kauffman and M.A. Mahmood (eds.), Idea Group Publishing, Harrisburg, PA, 33–54.

Grady, R. (1992). *Practical software metrics for project management and process improvement.* Englewood Cliffs: Prentice–Hall.

Gray, D.A. (1994). Under Fire: Lessons From the Front, *OR/MS Today,* 21 (5), 18–23.

Greene, W.H. (1990). *Econometric Analysis,* Macmillan Publishing Co.

Gremillion, L., & Pyburn, P. (1985). Justifying Decision Support and Office Automation Systems. *Journal of Management Information Systems,* 2, 1, 5-17.

Griss, M. (1993). Software reuse: from library to factory. *IBM Systems Journal,* Vol 32, No 4, 548–566.

Gronroos, C. (1982). *Strategic management and marketing in the service sector.* Helsingfors, Finland: Swedish School of Economics and Business Administration.

Grover, V. (1993). An empirically derived model for the adoption of customer–based interorganizational systems. *Decision Sciences,* 24(3), 603–640.

Grover, V., & Goslar, M. (1993). The Initiation, Adoption, and Implementation of Telecommunications Technologies in U. S. Organizations. *Journal of Management Information Systems,* 10(1), 141–163.

Grover, V., Goslar, M. & Segars, A. (1995). Adopters of Telecommunications Initiatives: A Profile Progressive U.S. Corporations. *International Journal of Information Management,* 15(1), 33–46.

Guha, S., Kettinger, W.J., & Teng, J.T.C. (1993). Business Process Reengineering:

Building A Comprehensive Methodology. *Information Systems Management*, 10, 13–22.

Gupta, A.K., & Govindarajan, V. (1991). Knowledge flows and the structure of control within multinational corporations. *Academy of Management Review*, 16(4), 768–792.

Gurbaxani, V., & Whang, S. (1991). The Impacts of Information Technology on Organizations and Markets. *Communications of the ACM*, 34 (1), 59–73.

Hackos, J. (1994). *Managing Your Documentation Projects*. New York: John Wiley and Sons.

Haeckel, S.H. (1995). Adaptive enterprise design: the sense and respond model. *Planning Review*, May–June, 6–13, 42.

Haeckel, S.H., & Nolan, R.L. (1993). Managing by wire. *Harvard Business Review*, September–October, 122–132.

Hage, J., & Aiken, M. (1967). Relationship of Centralization to other structural properties. *Administrative Science Quarterly*, 12, 72–92.

Hagström, P. (1991). The "wired" MNC: the role of information systems for structural change in complex organizations. A Dissertation for the Doctor's Degree in Business Administration, Stockholm, Sweden: Institute of International Business, Stockholm School of Economics.

Haley, B.J., & Watson, H.J. (1996). Using lotus notes in executive information systems. *Information Strategy: The Executive's Journal*, 12(3), 45–51.

Hall, B. (1995). Return on Investment and Multimedia Training. White Paper for Multimedia Training Newsletter. Sunnyvale, CA.

Hambrick, D. C. (1982). Environmental scanning and organizational strategy. *Strategic Management Journal*, 3, 159–174.

Hamel, G., & Prahalad, C. K. (1996). Research notes and communication: competing in the new economy: managing out of bounds. *Strategic Management Journal*, 17, 237–242.

Hamilton, S., & Chervany, N.L. (1981). Evaluating System Effectiveness–Part I: Comparing Evaluation Approaches. *MIS Quarterly*, 5(3), 55–69.

Hammer, M. (1990). Reengineering Work: Don't Automate, Obliterate. *Harvard Business Review*, 68, 104–12.

Hammer, M. (1994). Reengineering Is Not Hocus–Pocus. *Across the Board*, 31, 45–47.

Hammer, M. (1996). Implementing Reengineering: Strategies and Techniques, Center for Reengineering Leadership, Cambridge, MA.

Hammer, M., & Champy, J. (1994). *Reengineering the corporation: A manifesto for business revolution.* New York: Harper Business.

Hammer, M., & Champy, J. (1993). *Business Process Reengineering: A Manifesto for Business Revolution,* New York: Harper Business.

Hammer, M., & Mangurian, G.E. (1987). The Changing Value of Communications Technology. *Sloan Management Review*, 28(2), 65–71.

Hamilton, S., & Chervany, N.L. (1981). Evaluating System Effectiveness–Part I: Comparing Evaluation Approaches. *MIS Quarterly*, 5(3), 55–69.

Hammond, J. (1993). Quick response in retail/manufacturing channels. Chapter 8 in S. Bradley et al. (Eds.). *Globalization, technology and competition: the fusion of computers and telecommunications in the 1990s.* Boston: Harvard Business School Press.

Hancock, L., & Wingert, P. et al. (1995, Feb. 27). The Haves and the Have–Nots *Newsweek.* February 27, 50–53.

Harrigan, K. R. (1980). The effect of exit barriers on strategic flexibility. *Strategic Management Journal*, 1(2), 165–76.

Harrigan, K. R. (1985). *Strategic flexibility: A management guide for changing times.* Lexington, MA: Heath.

Harris, D. H. & Committee on Human Factors. (Eds.). (1994). *Organizational Linkages: Understanding the Productivity Paradox.* Washington D.C.: National Academy Press.

Harris, S.E., & Katz, J.L. (1989). Predicting Organizational Performance Using Information Technology Managerial control Ratios. *Proceedings of the Twenty Second Hawaiian International Conference on Systems Science*, Honolulu, Hawaii.

Harris, S.E., & Katz, J.L. (1988). *Capital Investment in Information Technology: Does it Make a Difference?* Life Office Management Association, Atlanta, Georgia.

Harris, S.E., & Katz, J.L. (1988). Profitability and Information Capital Intensity in the Insurance Industry. In Proceedings of the Twenty-First Annual Hawaii Conference on Systems Sciences, Applications Track, 4, 124-130.

Harris, S. E., & Katz, J. L. (1991). Organizational Performance and Information Technology Investment Intensity in the Insurance Industry. *Organization Science*, 2 (3), 263–295.

Harris, S.E., & Katz, J.L. (1991). Firm Size and the Information Technology Investment Intensity of Life Insurers. *MIS Quarterly* (15:3), 333–344.

Hatten, K. J., Schendel, D. E., & Cooper, A. C. (1978). A strategic model of the U.S. brewing industry, 1952–1971. *Journal of Industrial Economics.* 26(2), 97–113.

Hedlund, G., & Rolander, D. (1990). Action in heterarchies: new approaches to managing the MNC. In C. Bartlett, Y. Doz, & G. Hedlund (Eds.), *Managing the global firm* (pp. 15–46). Routledge, London.

Heineman, G. T., Botsford, J. E., Caldiera, G., & Kaiser, G. D. (1994). Emerging technologies that support a software process life cycle. *IBM Systems Journal*, 33, 501–529.

Henderson, J., & Curley, K. C. as cited by Carlson, W.M. & McNurlin, B.C. (1992). Do You Measure Up?. *Computerworld.* December 7, 95–98.

Henderson, J.C., & Venkatraman, N. (1994). Strategic alignment: a model for organizational transformation via information technology. Chapter 9 in T. Allen & M. Scott Morton (Eds.), *Information technology and the corporation of the 1990s: research studies*, 202–220. New York: Oxford University Press.

Henderson, R. & Cockburn, I. (1994). Measuring competence? Exploring firm effects in pharmaceutical research. *Strategic Management Journal*, 15, 63–84.

Henderson, R. M., & Clark, K. B. (1990). Architectural innovation: the reconfiguration of existing product technologies and the failure of established firms. *Administrative Science Quarterly*, 35, 9–30.

Hennart, J.F., & Park, Y.R. (1994). Location, governance, and strategic determinants of Japanese manufacturing investments in the United States. *Strategic Management Journal*, 15, 419–436.

Henry, J., Rossman, A., & Snyder, J. (1995). Quantitative evaluation of software process improvement. *Journal of Systems & Software*, 28, 169–177.

Hepworth, M. (1990). *Geography of the information economy*. New York: The Guilford Press.

Herbsleb, J., Carleton, A., Rozum, J., Siegel, J., & Zubrow, D. (1994). Benefits of CMM–based software process improvement: Initial results. *Technical report CMU/SEI–94–TR–13*.

Hersch, A. (1993). Where's the return on process improvement? *IEEE Software*, (July) 12.

Herscheim, R., & Smithson, H. (1988). A Critical Analysis of Information Systems Evaluation. In N Bjorn–Anderson and G. Davis (Eds.) *Information Systems Assessment: Issues and Challenges*. North–Holland, Amsterdam, Netherlands.

Hill, C., Hitt, M., & Hoskisson, R. (1992). Cooperative versus competitive structures in related and unrelated diversified firms. *Organization Science*, 3(4), November, 501–521.

Hilton, R. (1979). The Determinants of Cost Information Value: An Illustrative Analysis. *Journal of Accounting Research*, 17, 411-435.

Hilton, R. (1981). The Determinants of Information Value: Synthesizing Some General Results. *Management Science*, 27, 57-64.

Hinson, J. (1995). Vice president, Federal Express. Keynote address presentation given at IFORS SPC–3, Santa Monica, California (January).

Hitt, L., & Brynjolfsson, E. (1996). Productivity, Business Profitability, and Consumer Surplus: Three Different Measures of Information Technology Value. *MIS Quarterly*, 20(2), 121–142.

Hitt, L., & Brynolfsson, E. (1994). The Three Facets of IT Value: Theory and Evidence. In J. I. DeGross, S. L. Huff, & M. C. Munro (Editors). *Proceedings of the Fifteenth International Conference on Information Systems*, Vancouver, Canada, 263–276.

Hoel, P. (1954). *Introduction to Mathematical Statistics*. New York: John Wiley and Sons.

Hofer, C. W., Murray, E. W., Jr., Charan, R., & Pitts, R. A. (1984). *Strategic management: A casebook in policy and planning*. St. Paul, MN: West Publishing Company.

Hofer, C. W., & Schendel, D. (1978). *Strategy formulation: Analytical concepts*. St. Paul, MN: West Publishing Company.

Hoffer, J.A., & Straub, D.W. (1989). The 9 to 5 underground: Are you policing computer crime? *Sloan Management Review*. 30(4), 35–43.

Hogarth, R. (1980). *Judgment and Choice: The Psychology of Decision.* New York: Wiley.

Hogue, J., & Watson, H. (1983). Management's Role in the Approval and Administration of Decision Support Systems. *MIS Quarterly,* 7, 2, 15-26.

Holak, S. L., & Lehmann, D. R. (1990). Purchase intentions and the Dimensions of Innovation: An Exploratory Model. *Journal of Product Innovation Management,* 7 (1), 59–73.

Holland, C. P., Lockett, G., Richard, J.M., & Blackman, I. (1994). Evolution of a Global Cash Management System. *Sloan Management Review,* 35 (1), 37–47.

Horngren, C. Foster, G., & Datar, S. (1994). *Cost Accounting: A Managerial Emphasis,* Prentice–Hall.

Horngren, C. T., & Sundem, G. I. (1987). *Introduction to Management Accounting,* 3rd ed., Prentice Hall, Hemel Hempstead.

Houdeshel, G., & Watson, H. J. (1987). The management information and decision support (MIDS) system at Lockheed-Georgia. *MIS Quarterly,* 10(5), 127-40.

Housel, T.J., Bell, A.H., & Kanevshy, V. (1993). Calculating the Benefits of Reengineering at Pacific Bell. In *Reengineering Blueprint for the Future: A Comprehensive Report,* 664–678. Chicago: International Eng. Consortium.

Howard, T. (1995). *Global Expansion in the Information Age.* Van Nostrand Reinhold.

Huber, G. (1990). A theory of the effects of advanced information technologies on organizational design, intelligence, and decision making. *Academy of Management Review,* 15(1), 47–71.

Hufnagel, E. (1994). The Hidden Costs of Client/Server. *InformationWeek (Client/Server Supplement),* 22–28.

Hughes, C., & Gibson, M. (1991). Students as Surrogates for Managers in a Decision-Making Environment: An Experimental Study. *Journal of Management Information Systems,* 8, 2, 153-166.

Humphrey, W.S. (1989). *Managing the Software Process.* Reading, MA: Addison–Wesley.

Iacovou, C.L., Benbasat, I., & Dexter, A.S. (1995) Electronic Data Interchange and Small Organizations: Adoption and Impact of Technology. *MIS Quarterly* 19(4): 465–485.

Ian, M. (1989). Computing matters: Making it work to best effect. *Management Today,* January, 100 110.

Iivari, J. (1987). User Information Satisfaction (UIS) Reconsidered: An Information System as the Antecedent of UIS. In Proceedings of the Eighth International Conference on Information Systems, 57-73.

Ives, B., & Learmonth, G.P. (1984). The Information System as a Competitive Weapon. *Communications of the ACM,* 27(12), 1193–1194.

Ives, B., & Olson, M. (1984). User involvement and MIS success: A review of research. *Management Science,* 30(5), 586-603.

Ives, B., Olson, M., & Baroudi, J. (1983). The Measurement of User Information Satisfaction. *Communications of the ACM,* 26, 785-793.

Jander, M. (1994). Performance management keeps check on client–server systems. *Data Communications,* 23(8), 63–71.

Janz, D.B., Prakash, C.A., & Frolick, M. (1997). Fast Cycle Systems Development: The Link Between Work Group Characteristics and Systems Development Performance. *Cycle Time Research,* Vol. 3, No. 1, (forthcoming)

Jarvenpaa, S., Dickson, G., & DeSanctis, G. (1985). Methodological Issues in Experimental IS Research: Experiences and Recommendations. *MIS Quarterly,* 9, 141-156.

Jauch, L. R., & Kraft, K. L. (1986). Strategic management of uncertainty. *Academy of Management Review,* 11(4), 777–790.

Jensen, M., & Meckling, W. (1976). Theory of the Firm: Managerial Behavior, Agency Costs and Capital Structure. *Journal of Financial Econmics,* 3, October, 305–360.

Joint Logistics Commanders Joint Group on Systems Engineering (1995). *Software Reengineering Assessment Handbook.* Fort Belvoir, Virginia: Author. http://www.stsc.hill.af.mil/~red/index.html.

Jones, C. (1994). Globalization of software supply and demand. *IEEE software,* November, 17–24.

Jones, C. B. (1995). What Differentiates Leaders from Laggards. *Application Development Trends,* January, 27–31.

Jones, C.V. (1996). *Visualization and Optimization.* Boston: Kluwer Academic Publishers.

Jones, D. C. (1993). Reengineered Companies Must Keep Eye On Customers. *National Underwriter (Life & Health/Financial Services,* 97(6), 2.

Jones, J., & Mcleod, R. (1986). The structure of executive information systems: An exploratory analysis. *Decision Sciences,* 17, 220-49.

Jonscher, C. (1983). Information Resources and Economic Productivity. *Information Economics and Policy,* 1, 13–35.

Jonscher, C. (1994). An economic study of the information technology revolution. Chapter 1, in T. Allen & M. Scott Morton (Eds.) *Information technology and the corporation of the 1990s: research studies,* 5–42. New York: Oxford University Press.

Joos, R. (1994). Software reuse at Motorola. *IEEE Software,* 42–47, September.

Jurison, J. (1995). Defining and Measuring Productivity. In Paul Gray and Jaak Jurison, *Productivity in the Office and the Factory.* Danvers, MA: Boyd & Fraser.

Kabanoff, B., Waldersee, R., & Cohen, M. (1995). Espoused values and organizational change themes. *Academy of Management Journal,* 38(4), 1075–1104.

Kahneman, D., & A. Tversky. (1979). Prospect theory: an analysis of decisions under risk. *Econometrica.* 47(2), 263–291.

Kambil, A., & Short, J. (1994). Electronic integration and business network redesign: a roles–linkage perspective. *Journal of Management Information Systems,* 10(4), 59–83.

Kanter, J. (1970). *Management Guide to Computer System Selection and Use.* London:

Prentice–Hall.

Kaplan, R. (1986). Must CIM be justified by faith alone? *Harvard Business Review*, 64, 2, 87-95.

Kaplan, R. & Norton, D. (1992). Balanced Scorecard: Measures That Drive Performance. *Harvard Business Review*, 70(1), 71–79.

Katz, A.I. (1993). Measuring Technology's Business Value: Organizations seek to prove IT benefits. *Information Systems Management*, Winter: 33–39.

Kaufman, P.J. (1995). *Smarter trading: Improving performance in changing markets*, New York: McGraw–Hill.

Kauffman, R.J. & Kriebel, C.H. (1988). Identifying Business Value Linkages for Information Technology: An Exploratory Application to Treasury Workstations. Graduate School of Business Administration, New York University, Working Paper CRIS #182, GBA #88-47.

Kauffman, R.J., & Kriebel, C.H. (1988). Measuring and Modeling the Business Value of IT, in *Measuring Business Value of Information Technologies*, ICIT Research Study Team (2nd ed.), ICIT Press, Washington, DC, 93–120.

Kauffman, R. J., & Weill, P. (1989). An Evaluative Framework for Research on the Performance Effects of Information Technology Investment. In J. I. DeGross, J. C. Henderson, & B. R. Konsynski (Editors), *Proceedings of the Tenth International Conference on Information Systems*, Boston, Massachusetts, 377–388.

Keen, P.G.W. (1992). Positioning the IS Platform. *Modern Office Technology*, September, 12–14.

Keen, P.G.W. (1980). MIS Research: Reference Disciplines and a Cumulative Tradition. In *Proceedings of the First International Conference on Information Systems*, 9-18.

Keen, P.G.W. (1982). Accounting for Information Use: An Assessment of Relevant Research. In Proceedings of the Third International Conference on Information Systems, 199-218.

Keen, P.G.W. (1975). Computer-Based Decision Aids: The Evaluation Problem. *Sloan Management Review*, 16, 3, 17-29.

Keen, P.G.W. (1981). Value Analysis: Justifying Decision Support Systems. *MIS Quarterly*, 5(1), 1–15.

Keen, P.G.W. (1988) *Competing in Time. Using Telecommunications for Competitive Advantage*, New York: HarperBusiness.

Keen, P. G. W. (1991). *Shaping the Future: Business Design through Information Technology*, Boston, MA: Harvard Business School Press.

Keen, P.G.W., & Cummins, J.M. (1994). *Networks in Action. Business Choices and Telecommunications Decisions*, Belmont, CA: Wadsworth Publishing.

Keeney, R., & Raiffa, H. (1976). *Decisions with Multiple Objectives*. New York: John Wiley & Sons.

Keil, M. (1995). Pulling the plug: Software project management and the problem of project escalation. *MIS Quarterly*, Vol. 19, No. 4, Dec.

Keith, R.B. Jr. (1994). MIS + TQM = QIS. *Quality Progress*, 27 (4), (April), 29–31.

Kekre, S., & Mukhopadhyay, T. (1992). Impact of Electronic Data Interchange Technology on Quality Improvement and Inventory Reduction Programs: A Field Study. *International Journal of Production Economics*, 28: 265–282.

Keller, J.A. III (1990). Effective Float Management. *Business Credit*, April: 14-16.

Kelley, M.E. (1994). Productivity and Information Technology: The Elusive Connection, *Management Science*, 40 (11), 1406–1425.

Kemna, A. (1993). Case studies in real options. *Financial Management*, 22(3), 259–270.

Kendall, K.E., & Kendall, J.E. (1992). *Systems Analysis and Design*. Englewood Cliffs: Prentice–Hall.

Kester, W.C. (1984). Today's options for tomorrow's growth. *Harvard Business Review*. March/April, 153–160.

Kettinger, W.J., Grover, V., Guha, S., & Segars, A.H. (1994). Strategic information systems revisited: A study in sustainability and performance, *MIS Quarterly*, 18 (1), (March), 31–58.

Kettinger, W.J., Grover, V., & Segars, A.H. (Winter 1995). Do strategic systems really pay off?. *Information Systems Management*. 12(1), 35–43.

King, J.L., & Schrems, E.L. (1978). Cost–Benefit Analysis in Information Systems Development and Operation. *ACM Computing Surveys*, 10(1), 19–34.

King, J. (1995). No time for training throws IS off track. *Computerworld*, August 14.

King, R. (1994). Magic Formula. *The Wall Street Journal*, November 14, R10–R18.

King, W., Grover, V. & Hufnagel , E. (1989). Using information and information technology for sustainable competitive advantage: some empirical evidence. *Information and Management*, 17, 87–93.

King, W.R., & Premkumar, G. (1989). Key Issues in Telecommunications Planning. *Information and Management*, 17(5), 255–265.

King, W. R., & Rodriguez, J. (1981). Participative design of strategic decision support systems. *Management Science*, 26(6), 717-726.

King, W.R., & Sabherwal, R. (1992). The Factors Affecting Strategic Information Systems Applications. *Information and Management*, 23(4), 217–235.

King, W.R., & Teo, T. (1994). Facilitators and Inhibitors for the Strategic Use of Information Technology. *Information and Management*, 27(2), 71–87.

Klammer, T. (1994). *Managing Strategic and Capitol Investment Decisions*. New York: Irwin.

Kleijnen, J. (1980). Bayesian Information Economics: An Evaluation. *Interfaces*, 10, 3, 93-97.

Kleijnen, J. (1980) *Computers and Profits*. Reading, MA: Addison-Wesley.

Kliewer, H. (1993l). Enabling Learning through Multimedia. *OS/2 Professional*, March/ April, 70–74.

Kogut, P., & Wallnau (1994). Software architecture and reuse: senses and trends. Tutorial for Tri–Ada Conference, 7 November.

Komaki, J. (1977) Alternative Evaluation Strategies in Work Settings: Reversal and Multiple–Baseline Designs. *Journal of Organizational Behavior Management* 1: 53–77.

Konsynski, B. R. (1993). A Perspective on the "Case Study Approach" in Evaluating Business Value of Information Technology. In Banker et al. (eds) *Strategic Information Management: Perspectives on Organizational Growth and Competitive Advantage*. Harrisburg, PA: Idea Group Publishing.

Kotha, S., & Nair, A. (1995). Strategy and environment as determinants of performance: evidence from the Japanese machine tool industry. *Strategic Management Journal*, 16, 497–518.

Kraemer, L., Gurbaxani, V., Mooney, J., Dunkle, D., & Vitalari, N. (1994). The Business Value of Information Technology in *Corporations*. *I/S Intercorporate Measurement Program Report*, CSC Consulting and Center for Research on Information Technology and Organizations, University of California, Irvine.

Kraus Organization. (1994). *Beyond the Basics of Reengineering: Survival Tactics for the '90s* Quality Resources/The Kraus Organization Industrial Engineering and Management Press, Institute of Industrial Engineers, Norcross, Georgia.

Kraut, R., Dumais, S., & Koch, S. (1989). Computerization, productivity, and quality of work-life. *Communications of the ACM, 32*(2), 220-38.

Kriebel, C. H. (1989). Understanding the Strategic Investment in Information Technology. In K. C. Laudon & J. A. Turner (Editors). *Information Technology and Management Strategy*, 106–118. Englewood Cliffs, N.J.: Prentice–Hall.

Krohe, J. Jr. (1993). The Productivity Pit. *Across the Board*, October, 16–21.

Kumar, R. (1995). An options view of investments in expansion–flexible manufacturing systems. *The International Journal of Production Economics*, 38, 281–291.

Kumar, R., & Crook, C. (1997). Using EDI for competitive advantage: the case of the textile industry. *Cases in the Management of Information Technology*. Harrisburg, PA: Idea Group Publishing.

LaBay, D. G., & Kinnear, T. C. (1981). Exploring the consumer decision process in the adoption of solar energy systems. *Journal of Consumer Research*, 8(3), 271–278.

Lacity, M.C., Willcocks, L.P., & Feeny, D.F. (1996). The value of selective IT sourcing. *Sloan Management Review*, Spring, 13–25.

Lamos, J. (1996). Program Manager, COMET Distance Learning Program. UCAR. Interviews November 1995 to July 1996.

Lamos, J. (1995). Production of a Multimedia Curriculum: The Experience of the Cooperative Program for Operational Meteorology, Education and Training (COMET). *Proceedings of the IconAuthor User Conference*. Nashua, New Hampshire.

Landauer, T.K. (1995). *The Trouble with Computers: Usefulness, Usability and Productivity*. Cambridge, MA: MIT Press.

Larson, C., & Lafasto, F.M.J.. (1989). *TeamWork: What Must Go Right/What Can Go Wrong.* Newbury Park, CA: Sage Publications.

Law, A.M., & Kelton, W.D. (1982). *Simulation Modeling and Analysis.* New York: McGraw–Hill Book Co.

Lawless, M.W., & Finch, L. (1989). Choice and determinism: a test of Hrebiniak and Joyce's framework on strategy–environment fit. *Strategic Management Journal*, 10, 351–365.

Lawlis, P., Flowe, R., & Thordahl, J. (1995). A corelational study of the CMM and software development performance. *Crosstalk*, September, 21–25.

Lawrence, P.R., & Lorsch, J. W. (1967). *Organization and Environment: Managing Differentiation and Integration.* Boston, MA: Division of Research, Graduate School of Business Administration, Harvard University.

Lay, P.M.Q. (1985). Beware of the Cost/Benefit Model for IS Project Evaluation. *Journal of Systems Management*, 36(6), 30–35.

Layard, R., & Glaister, S. (eds.). (1994). Cost Benefit Analysis. New York: Cambridge University Press.

Learned, E. P., Christensen, C. R., Andrews, K. R., & Guth, W. D. (1965). *Business policy: text and cases.* Homewood, IL: Irwin.

Leary, J. (1994). Information architecture notions, Briefing slides presented to Defense Simulation and Modeling Office meeting, 19 October.

Lee, S., & Leifer, R. P. (1992). A framework for linking the structure of information systems with organizational requirements for information sharing. *Journal of Management Information Systems*, 8(4), 27–44.

Leth, S. A. (1994). Critical Success Factors For Reengineering Business Processes. *National Productivity Review*, 13, 557–68.

Lichtenburg, F.R. (1993). The Output Contributions of Computer Equipment and Personnel: A Firm–Level Analysis. International Workshop on The Productivity of Information Technology Investments, Organized by the National Science Foundation, the Organization for Economic Cooperation and Development, and the Massachusetts Institute of Technology, Charleston, SC, November 11–13.

Lile, A.E. (1993). Client/Server Architecture. *Journal of Systems Management*, 44(12), 26–27.

Lim, W. (1994). Effects of reuse on quality, productivity, and economics. *IEEE Software*, Vol. 11, No. 5, pp. 23–30, September.

Lincoln, T. (1986). Do Computer Systems Really Pay-off? *Information & Management*, 11, 25-34.

Lipovetsky, S., & Tishler, A. (1994). Linear Methods in Multimode Data Analysis for Decision Making. *Computers & Operations Research*, 21, 169–183.

Lippman, S. A., & Rumelt, R. P. (1982). Uncertain imitability: an analysis of interfirm differences in efficiency under competition. *The Bell Journal of Economics*, 13, 418–438.

Loch, K.D., Carr, H.H., & Warkentin, M.E. (1992). Threats to information systems: today's reality, yesterday's understanding. *MIS Quarterly.* 16(2), 173–186.

Lockamy A., & Cox, J.F. (1994). *Reengineering Performance Measures: How to Align Systems to Improve Processes, Products, and Profits.* Burr Ridge, Ill: Irwin Professional Publishers.

Loh, L., & Venkatraman, N. (1992). Diffusion of Information Technology Outsourcing: Influence Sources and the Kodak Effect. *Information Systems Research* (3:4), December, 334–358.

Loral Federal Systems (1994). Air Force/STARS demonstration project experience report. *ARPA Report,* 25 July.

Lorange, P., Scott Morton, M. F., & Ghosal, S. (1986). *Strategic control.* St. Paul, MN: West Publishing Company.

Lovejoy, J. (1990). Companies Grow with Proper Cash Flow. *Business Credit,* April: 10-12.

Loveman, G.W. (1988). An Assessment of the Productivity Impact of Information Technologies. Sloan School of Management, Massachusetts Institute of Technology, Management in the 1990's Working Paper No. 88-154.

Loveman, G. W. (1990). *An assessment of the productivity impact of information technologies.* Cambridge, MA: MIT, Sloan School of Management.

Loveman, G.W. (1994). An Assessment of the Productivity Impact of Information Technologies, in T. J. Allen and M.S. Scott Morton (eds.), *Information Technology and the Corporation of the 1990s: Research Studies,* Cambridge, MA: MIT Press.

Loveman, G. W. (1986). *The productivity of information technology capital: an economic analysis.* Cambridge, MA: MIT, Sloan School of Management.

Loveman, G. W. (1994). Assessing the Productivity Impact of Information Technologies. In T. J Allen & M. S. Scott–Morton (editors), *Information Technology and the Corporation of the 1990s.* New York: Oxford University Press.

Lucas, H. C., Jr. (1982). *Information systems concepts for management.* New York: McGraw-Hill Book Co.

Lucas, H. C., Jr. (1981a). *Implementation: The key to successful information systems.* New York: Columbia University Press.

Lucas, H. C., Jr. (1081b). *The analysis, design and implementation of information systems.* New York: McGraw-Hill.

Lucas, H. C., Jr. (1996). *The T–form organization: using technology to design organizations for the 21ˢᵗ century.* San Francisco, CA : Jossey–Bass Publishers.

Lucas, H.C., Jr., (1975). The Use of An Accounting Information System: Action and Organization Performance, *The Accounting Review* (50:4), 735–746.

Lucas, H.C., Jr., (1993). The Business Value of Information Technology: A Historical Perspective and Thoughts for Future Research, in *Strategic Information Technology Management: Perspectives on Organizational Growth and Competitive Advantage,* R.D. Banker, R.J. Kauffman and M.A. Mahmood (eds.), Harrisburg, PA: Idea Group Publishing, 359–374.

Lucas, H.C., & Baroudi, J. (1994). The role of information technology in organization design. *Journal of Management Information Systems*, 10(4), 9–23.

Lucas, H.C., Berndt, D.J. & Truman, G. (1996). A Reengineering Framework for Evaluating A Financial Imaging System. *Communications of the ACM*, 39(5), 86–96.

Lucas, H. C., Jr., Ginzberg, M. J., & Schultz, R. L. (1990). *Information system implementation: Testing a structural model.* Norwood, N.J.: Ablex Publishing Corporation.

Lucas, H.C., Weill, P. & Cox, S. (1993). The Big–Bang–for–Your–Buck Theory. *Journal of Business Strategy*, 14(4), 46–51.

MacDonald, K. H. (1991). The strategic alignment process. Appendix E in M. Scott Morton (Ed.), *The corporation of the 1990s: information technology and organizational transformation,* 310–322. New York: Oxford University Press.

Madansky, A. (1988). *Prescriptions for Working Statisticians.* New York: Springer–Verlag.

Madnick, S. (1991). The information technology platform. Chapter 2 in M. Scott Morton (Ed.), *The corporation of the 1990s: information technology and organizational transformation,* 27–60. New York: Oxford University Press.

Mahmood, M.A. (1994). Evaluating Organizational Efficiency Resulting from Information Technology Investment: An Application of Data Envelopment Analysis. *Journal of Information Systems.* 4, 93–115.

Mahmood, M.A. (1993). Introduction to Perspectives on Investments in New Information Technologies. In Banker et al. (eds). *Strategic Information Management: Perspectives on Organizational Growth and Competitive Advantage.* Harrisburg, PA: Idea Group Publishing.

Mahmood, M.A. (1995). Managing information as a strategic resource: A new approach to help achieve competitive advantage. *Information Resources Management Journal*, 8 (2), 3–4.

Mahmood, M.A. (1993). Associating organizational strategic performance with information technology investment: An exploratory research, *European Journal of Information Systems*, 2 (3), 185–200.

Mahmood, M.A., & Mann G.J. (1991). Measuring the Impact of Information Technology on Organizational Strategic Performance: A Key Ratios Approach. *Proceedings of the 24th Annual Hawaii International Conference on System Sciences,* Kauaii, Hawaii, January, 251–258.

Mahmood, M.A., & Mann, G.A. (1993). Measuring the Organization Impact of Information Technology Investment: An Exploratory Study. *Journal of Management Information Systems*, 10(1), 97–122.

Mahmood, M.A., & Medewitz, J.N. (1985). Impact of design methods on decision support systems success: An empirical assessment. *Information and Management*, 9(3), 137–151.

Mahmood, M.A., Pettingell, K., & Shaskevich. (1996). Measuring productivity of software projects: A data envelopment analysis approach. *Decision Sciences*, 27(1):57–80.

Mahmood, M.A., & Soon, S.K. (1991). A Comprehensive Model for Measuring the Potential Impact of Information Technology on Organizational Strategic Variables, *Decision Sciences*, 22 (4), 869–897.

Maleki, R. A. (1991). *Flexible manufacturing systems: The technology and management.* New York: Prentice Hall.

Malone, T. W. (1987). Modeling Coordination in Organizations and Markets. *Management Science*, 33 (10), 1317–1332.

Malone, T. W., Yates, J., & Benjamin, R. I. (1987). Electronic markets and electronic hierarchies. *Communications of the ACM*, 30, 484–497.

Malone, T., Yates, J., & Benjamin, R. (1994). Electronic markets and electronic hierarchies. Chapter 3, in T. Allen & M. Scott Morton (Eds.). *Information technology and the corporation of the 1990s: research studies*, 61–83. New York: Oxford University Press.

Mangaliso, M. (1995). The strategic usefulness of management information as perceived by middle managers. *Journal of Management*, 21(2), 231–250.

March, J., & Shapira, Z. (1987). Managerial perspectives on risk and risk taking. *Management Science*. 33(11) 1404–1418.

Marino, V. (1996). Corporate Downsizing Continues at Full Speed. *The Denver Post*. January 4, 3c.

Markus, M.L. (1983). Power, Politics and MIS Implementation. *Communications of the ACM*, 26(6), 430–444.

Markus, M.L. (1987). Towards a "Critical Mass" Theory of Interactive Media: Universal Access, Interdependence and Diffusion. *Communication Research*. 14, 491–511.

Markus, M.L., & Robey, D. (1988). Information Technology and Organizational Change: Causal Structures in Theory and Research. *Management Science*, 34:5, 583–598.

Markus, M. L., & Soh, C. (1993). Banking on Information Technology: Converting IT Spending into Firm Performance. Chapter 19 in R. Banker, et al. (Eds.). Strategic Information Technology *Management: Perspectives on Organizational Growth and Competitive Advantage*, 375–403. Harrisburg, PA: Idea Group Publishing.

Marold, K.A. (1994). Constituent Elements of the Electronic Noetic, Ph.D. dissertation. University of Denver.

Marold, K.A., & Larsen, G. (1990). *The Internet and Beyond*. Danvers, MA: International Thompson Publishing.

Marschak, J. (1968). Economics of Inquiring, Communicating, Deciding. American Economic Review, 58, 2, 1-18.

Marschak, J. (1971). Economics of Information Systems. *Journal of the American Statistical Association*, 66, 192-219.

Marshall, J.F. (1989). *Futures and Options Contracting*, South–Western Publishing Company.

Martin, M.P., & Trumbly, J.E. (1986). Measuring Performance of Automated Systems. *Journal of Systems Management*, 37(2), 7–17.

Martin, R. (1994). The premise and the promise. *Journal of Systems Management*, 45(1), 26–27.

Mason, D., & Turner, M. (1995). A Time For Change. *Communications Week*, issue 583, 31–32.

Mathewson, G.F., & Winter, R.A. (1984). An Economic Theory of Vertical Restraints. *Rand Journal of Economics* 15:1, Spring, 27–38.

Mathieson, K., & Wharton, T.J. (1993). Are information systems a barrier to total quality management? *Journal of Systems Management*, 44 (9), (September), 34–38.

Matlin, G. (1982). What is the Value of Investment in Information Systems? In R. Goldberg & H. Lorin (Eds.). *The Economics of Information Processing*, Vol. 1, 187–195. New York: John Wiley & Sons Inc.

McAndrews, J. (1993). Network Business Value Externalities. In R. Banker, R. Kauffman & M. Mahmood (Eds.). *Strategic Information Technology Management*, 151–160. Harrisburg, PA: Idea Group Publishing.

McAuliffe, T. P., & Shamlin, C. S. (1992). *Critical information network: The next generation of executive information systems*. Wilmington, MA: ZBR Publications.

McCabe, T. (1976) A Complexity Measure. *IEEE Transactions on Software Engineering* December, SE–2(4):308–320.

McCain, R. (1992). Introduction to reuse technology and application, slides – Defense Systems Management College, 24 September.

McDonald, K. H. (1991). The value process model. In M. S. Scott Morton (Ed.), *The corporation of the 1990s*, 299–309. New York: Oxford University Press.

McFarlan, F. W. (1984). Information technology changes the way you compete. *Harvard Business Review*, 62, May–June, 98–103.

McFarlan, F. W. (1981). Portfolio approach to information systems. *Harvard Business Review*, Sept.–Oct., 142–151.

McFarlan, F.W., & McKenney, J.L. (1983). *Corporate Information Systems Management: The Issues Facing Senior Executives*. Richard D. Irwin, Inc.

McGaughey, R., Snyder, C., & Carr, H. (1994). Implementing Information Technology for Competitive Advantage: Risk Management Issues. Information and Management, 26(5), 273–280.

McKeen, J.D., Smith, H.A., Agrawal, P.C., & Smyth, D.R. (1990). The Investment Information Technology: 1977 – 1989. *Proceedings of the Administrative Sciences Association of Canada*, Vol. 11, No. 4, 128–139..

McKeen, J.D., & Smith, H.A. (1991). The Value of Information Technology: A Resource View. *Proceedings of the Twelfth Annual International Conference on Information Systems*, New York, NY, December, 41–52.

McKeen, J.D., & Smith, H.A. (1993). Linking IT Investment with IT Usage. *Proceedings of the 26th Annual Hawaii International Conference on System Sciences* (3), Maui, Hawaii, January, 620–629.

McKeen, J. D., & Smith, H. A. (1993). The Relationship Between Information Technology Use and Organizational Performance, Chapter 20 in R. Banker, R. Kauffman, & M. Mahmood (Eds.). *Strategic Information Technology Management: Perspectives on Organizational Growth and Competitive Advantage,* 405–444. Harrisburg, PA: Idea Group Publishing.

McKeen, J.D., & Smith, H.A. (1993). How Does Information Technology Affect Business Value? — A Reassessment and Research Propositions. *The Canadian Journal of Administrative Sciences,* 10:3, September, 229–240.

Meekings, A. (1995). Unlocking The Potential Of Performance Measurement: A Practical Implementation Guide. *Public Money and Management,* 15(4), 5–12.

Mellers, B., & Chang, S. (1994). Representations of risk judgments. *Organizational Behaviour and Human Decision Processes.* 57(2), 167–184.

Melone, N. (1990). A Theoretical Assessment of the User-Satisfaction Construct in Information Systems Research. *Management Science,* 36, 76–91.

Mendelson, H. (1988). *The Economics of Information Systems Management,* Draft.

Menkus, B. (1991). Control is fundamental to successful information security. *Computers and Security.* 10(4), 293–297.

Meredith, J.R., & Hill, M.M. (1987). Justifying New Manufacturing Systems: A Managerial Approach. *Sloan Management Review,* 28(4), 49–61.

Merkhofer, M.W. (1987). *Decision Analysis and Social Risk Management: A Comparative Evaluation of Cost–benefit Analysis, Decision Analysis, and Other Formal Risk Analysis Approaches.* Boston: Kluwer Academic Publishers.

Messina, F, & Singh, S.K. (1995). Executive information systems: Not for executives anymore!!!. *Management Accounting,* July, 60–63.

Meyer, A.D., & Goes, J.B. (1988). Organizational Assimilation of Innovations: A Multi-Level Contextual Analysis. *Academy of Management Journal,* 31(4), 897–923.

Meyer, N.D., & Boone, M.E. (1987). *The Information Edge.* New York: McGraw–Hill Book Co.

Miles, R.E., & Snow, C.C. (1978). *Organizational strategy, structure, and process.* New York: McGraw–Hill.

Miller, D. (1986). Configurations of strategy and structure: toward a synthesis. *Strategic Management Journal,* 7, 233–240.

Miller, D. (1987). The structural and environmental correlates of business strategy. *Strategic Management Journal,* 8, 55–76.

Miller, D. (1988). Relating Porter's business strategies to environment and structure: analysis and performance implications. *Academy of Management Journal,* 31(2), June, 280–308.

Miller, D., & Friesen, P. H. (1982). Innovation in conservative and entrepreneurial firms: two models of strategic momentum. *Strategic Management Journal,* 7, 1–25.

Miller, D., & Friesen, P. H. (1983). Strategy–making and environment: the third link. *Strategic Management Journal,* 4, 221–235.

Miller, D., & Shamsie, J. (1995). A contingent application of the resource–based view of the firm: the Hollywood film studios from 1936 to 1965. In D. Moore (Ed.). Academy of Management Best Papers Proceedings 1995, 55th Annual Meeting, Vancouver, British Columbia, Canada, August 6–9, 57–61.

Miller, G. (1974). The Magical Number Seven, Plus or Minus Two. *The Psychological Review.* 63, 81–97.

Miller, H., & Engemann, K. (1992). Decision making in a crisis: information, process and values. *International Journal of Value Based Management.* 5(2), 11–42.

Miller, H., & Engemann, K. (1996). A methodology for managing information–based risk. *Information Resources Management Journal.* 9(2), 17–24.

Miller, H., & Engemann, K. (1993). A simulation approach to managing risk for money transfer telecommunications lines. *Proceedings of the Twenty–second Annual Meeting of the Northeast Decision Sciences Institute.* Philadelphia, PA, 81–83.

Miller, J., & Doyle, B. (1987). Measuring the Effectiveness of Computer-Based Information Systems in the Financial Services Sector. *MIS Quarterly,* 11, 1, 107-124.

Mintzberg, H. (1979). *The structuring of organizations.* Englewood Cliffs, NJ: Prentice Hall.

Mintzberg, H. (1983). *Structure in fives: designing effective organizations.* Englewood Cliffs, NJ: Prentice Hall.

Moad, J. (1993). New Rules, New Ratings As IS Reengineers. *Datamation,* November 1, 85–87

Moad, J. (1994). IS rises to the competitiveness challenge. *Datamation,* (January 7), 16-18.

Monnoyer, M., & Philippe, J. (1991). Using Minitel to enrich the service. In E.Sutherland & Y. Morieux (Eds.). *Business strategy and information technology,* 175–185. London: Routledge.

Mooney, G. J., Gurbaxani, V., & Kraemer, L. K. (1995). A Process Oriented Framework for Assessing the Business Value of Information Technology. In the *Proceedings of the Sixteenth Conference on Information Systems,* Amsterdam, 17–29.

Moore, G.C., & Benbasat, I. (1991). Development of an Instrument to Measure the Perceptions of Adopting an Information Technology Innovation. *Information Systems Research,* 2 (2), 193–222.

Morhado, E. M., Reinhard, N., & Watson, R. T. (1995). Extending the Analysis of Key Issues in Information Technology Management. In J. D. Gross, Gad Ariav, Cynthia Beath, Rof Hoyer, & Chris Kemerer (editors). *Proceedings of the Sixteenth International Conference on Information Systems,* Amsterdam, 13–16.

Morrison, D.G. (1979). Purchase Intentions and Purchase Behavior. *Journal of Marketing,* 43 (1), 65–74.

Mukhopadhyay, T., & Cooper, R. (1993). A Microeconomic Production Assessment of the Business Value of Management Information Systems: The Case of Inventory Control. *Journal of Management Information Systems,* 10, 33–55.

Mukhopadhyay, T., Kekre, S., & Kalathur, S. (1995). Business Value of Information Technology: A Study of Electronic Data Interchange. *MIS Quarterly*, 19(2), 137–156.

Myers, K. (1993). *Total Contingency Planning for Disasters: Managing Risks — Minimizing Loss — Ensuring Business Continuity.* New York. Wiley.

Myers, S. (1977). Determinant of corporate borrowing. *Journal of Financial Economics*, No.5, 147–75.

Myers, S.C., ed. (1976). *Modern Developments in Financial Management.* Hinsdale, IL: Dryden Press.

NACHA (1993). *Corporate Financial EDI User Guide.* Herdon, VI: Bankers EDI Council, National Automated Clearing House Association.

Naisbitt, J. (1982). *Megatrends: Ten New Directions Transforming our Lives.* New York: Warner Books.

NASA–GB–001–95 (1996). *Software Engineering Program: Software Process Improvement Guidebook.* National Aeronautics and Space Administration, Washington, DC.

Nash, K.S. (1995). Oracle, Sybase embrace multimedia databases. *Computerworld*, January 9.

Nass, C., & Steuer, J. (1993). Voices, Boxes, and Sources of Messages: Computers and Social Actors. *Human Communication Research.* 19(4), 504–527.

National Research Council. (1991). *Computers at Risk.* Washington, DC: National Academy Press.

National Research Council. (1994). *Information technology in the service society: a twenty-first century lever.* Washington, DC: National Academy Press.

Nault, B.R., Wolfe R., & Dexter, A.S. (1997). Electronic Communication Innovations: Addressing Adoption Resistance. Forthcoming in *IEEE Transactions on Engineering Management.*

Negroponte, N. (1995). Being Digital. New York: Alfred Knopf.

Nejmeh, B. A. (1995). Process cost and value analysis. *Communications of the ACM*, (38)6:19–24.

Neo, B.S. (1988). Factors Facilitating the Use of Information Technology for Competitive Advantage: An Exploratory Study. *Information and Management*, 15(3), 191–201.

Neter, J., Wasserman, W., & Kutner, M.H. (1985). *Applied Linear Statistical Models* Homewood, IL: Richard D. Irwin, Inc.

Nickerson, J. (1993). Client/server chaos yields valuable lessons. *Network World*, 10(21), 41, 44.

Niederman, F., Brancheau, J.C., & Wetherbe, J.C. (1991). Information systems management issues for the 1990's. *MIS Quarterly.* 15(4), 475–495.

Nohria, N., & Garcia–Pont, C. (1991). Global strategic linkages and industry structure. *Strategic Management Journal*, 12, 105–124.

Nohria, N., & Ghoshal, S. (1994). Differentiated fit and shared values: alternatives for managing headquarters–subsidiary relations. *Strategic Management Journal*, 15, 491–502.

Nolan, R. L., & Gibson C. F. (1974). Managing the Four Stages of EDP Growth. *Harvard Business Review*, January/February, 76.

North, H.Q., & Pyke, D.L. (1969). Probes of the Technological Future. Harvard Business Review, 47(3), 68–82.

Nunnally, J. C. (1978). *Psychometric theory*. New York: McGraw Hill.

O'Callaghan, R., Kauffman, P.J., & Konsynski, B.R. (1992). Adoption Correlates andShare Effects of Electronic Data Interchange Systems in Marketing Channels. *Journal of Marketing*, 56 (2), 45–56.

O'Connor, J. et al. (1994). Reuse in command–and–control systems. *IEEE Software*, 70–79, September.

O'Hagan, M. (1990). Using maximum entropy–ordered weighted averaging to construct a fuzzy neuron. Proceedings of the 24th Annual IEEE Asilomar Conference on Signals, Systems and Computers. Pacific Grove, CA. 618–623.

OECD. (1992). *Information Networks and New Technologies: Opportunities and Policy Implications for the 1990s*, Paris, OECD.

Oman, R.C., & Ayers, T. (1988). Productivity and Benefit–Cost Analysis for Information Technology Decisions. *Information Management Review* (3:3), Winter, 31–41.

Orlikowski, W. J., & Robey, D. (1991). Information technology and the structuring of organizations. *Information Systems Research*, 2(2), 143–169.

Osborn, R. N., & Baughn, C.C. (1990). Forms of interorganizational governance for multinational alliances. *Academy of Management Journal*, 33(3), 503–519.

Ostlund, L. E. (1974). Perceived innovation attributes as Predictors of Innovativeness. *Journal of Consumer Research*, 1(2), 23–29.

Packer, M.B. (1982). *Measuring Productivity in R & D Groups*. The MIT Report X, no. 11, November.

Paller, A., & Laska, R. (1990). *The EIS book: Information Systems for top managers*. Homewood, IL: Business One Irwin.

Palvia, P., Perkins, J.A., & Zeltmann, S.M. (1992). The PRISM System: A Key to Organizational Effectiveness at Federal Express Corporation, *MIS Quarterly*, 16 (3) September, 277–292.

Panepinto, J. (1993). Client/Server Breakdown. *Computerworld*, 107–110.

Parnisto, J. (1995). Assessment of the Impacts of BPR and Information Technology Use on Team Communication. In Varun Grover and William Kettinger, *Business Process Change: Reengineering Concepts, Methods, and Technologies*. Harrisburg, PA: Idea Group Publishing.

Panko, R.R. (1982). Spending on Office Systems: A Provisional Estimate. *Office: Technology and People* (1:1), September, 177–194.

Panko, R.R. (1991). Is the Office Productivity Stagnant? *MIS Quarterly* 15, no. 2., 191–

203.

Parasuraman, A., Berry, L.L., & Zeithaml., V.A (1993). More on improving the measurement of service quality. *Journal of Retailing, 69*(1), 140–147.

Parasuraman, A., Berry, L.L., & Zeithaml., V.A (1991). Refinement and reassessment of the SERVQUAL scale. *Journal of Retailing, 67*(4), 420–450.

Parasuraman, A., Zeithaml, V.A. & Berry, L.L. (1988). SERVQUAL: A multiple-item scale for measuring consumer perceptions of service quality. *Journal of Retailing, 64*(1), 12-40.

Parasuraman, A., Zeithaml, V.A. & Berry, L.L. (1985). A conceptual model of service quality and its implications for future research. *Journal of Marketing, 49*(Fall), 41-50.

Parent, M., & Chan, Y. (1990). Paradigm Found: The Application of Organizational Economics to MIS. Proceedings of the Administrative Sciences Association of Canada (15:4), June.

Parker, D.B. (1981). *Computer Security Management.* Reston: Reston Publishing Company.

Parker, M. M. (1996). *Strategic Transformation and Information Technology.* Prentice Hall.

Parker, M.M., & Benson, R.J. (1989). Enterprisewide Information Economics: Latest Concepts. *The Journal of Information Systems Management, 6*(4), 7–13.

Parker, M.J., & Benson, R.J. (1987). Information Economics: An Introduction. *Datamation, 33*(23), 86–96.

Parker, M.M., & Benson, R.J. (1988). *Information Economics: Linking Business Performance to Information Technology.* Englewood Cliffs, NJ: Prentice–Hall, Inc.

Parnas, D. (1976). On the design and development of program families. *IEEE Transactions on Software Engineering,* Vol SE–2, pp. 1–9.

Parsons, D.J., Golieb, C.C., & Denny, M. (1990). Productivity and Computers in Canadian Banking. Working Paper #9012. Department of Economics, University of Toronto, Canada.

Pastore, R. (1992). Justifying Technology: Many Happy Returns. *CIO, 5*(14), 66–74.

Pate–Cornell, M. E. (1984). Fault trees vs. event trees in reliability analysis. *Risk Analysis 4*(3), 177–186.

Paulk, M.C. (1993). Capability maturity model, version 1.1. *IEEE Software,* 10, 18–27.

Paulk, M.C., Weber, C.V., Garcia, S.M., & Chrissis, M.B. (1993). Key Practices of the Capability Maturity Model, Version 1.1, *CMU/SEI–93–TR–25.* Software Engineering Institute, Carnegie Mellon University, Pittsburgh, PA.

Paulk, M.C. (1995). How ISO 9001 Compares With The CMM. *IEEE Software,* January, 74–83.

Pentland, B.T. (1989). Use and Productivity in Personal Computing: An Empirical Test. *Proceedings of the Tenth International Conference on Information Systems,* Boston, MA, 211–222.

Peteraf, M.A. (1993). The cornerstones of competitive advantage: a resource–based view. *Strategic Management Journal,* 14, 179–191.

Pettypool, M.D. (1989). An Examination of Some Mathematical Programming Approaches to Productivity Ratio Estimation. Unpublished Doctoral Dissertation, Department of Management, Southern Illinois University, Carbondale, Illinois 62901–4627.

Pfeffer J., & Nowak, P. (1976). Joint ventures and interorganizational interdependence. *Administrative Science Quarterly,* 21, September, 398–418.

Pfleeger, C. (1989). *Security in Computing.* Prentice Hall.

PIMS Program (1984). *Management Productivity and Information technology.* The Strategic Planning Institute, Cambridge, MA.

Pine, B. J., II. (1993). *Mass customization.* Boston, MA: Harvard Business School Press.

Pitt, L. F., & Watson, R. T. (1995). Longitudinal study of service quality in information systems: A case study. *Proceedings of the Fifteenth International Conference of Information Systems,* Vancouver, B.C.

Popkin, J. (1993). Measurement Problems in Quantifying Information Technology's Contribution to Productivity. International Workshop on The Productivity of Information Technology Investments, Organized by the National Science Foundation, the Organization for Economic Cooperation and Development, and the Massachusetts Institute of Technology, Charleston, SC, November 11–13.

Porat, M. (1977). *The Information Economy: Definition and Measurement.* Washington, DC: U.S. Department of Commerce, Office of Telecommunications.

Porter, M. (1991). Towards a dynamic theory of strategy. *Strategic Management Journal,* 12, 95–117.

Porter, M. (1985). *Competitive strategy.* New York: Free Press.

Porter, M. (1986). *Competition in global industries.* Boston: Harvard Business School Press.

Porter, M.E. (1985). *Competitive Advantage: Creating And Sustaining Superior Performance.* New York: Free Press.

Porter, M.E. (1983). The Technological Dimension of Competitive Strategy. *Research on Technological Innovation, Management and Policy,* 1, 1–33.

Porter, M.E., & Millar, V.E. (1985). How Information Gives You Competitive Advantage. *Harvard Business Review,* 63(4), 149–160.

Powell, D. (1994). IT's Real Payoff. *Computing Canada* (20:2), Special Report, January 19.

Powell, P. (1992). Information Technology Evaluation: Is It Different? *Journal of the Operational Research Society,* 43(1), 29–42.

Prahalad, C.K., & Hamel, G. (1990). The core competence of the corporation. *Harvard Business Review,* May–June, 71–91.

Prakash, C.A. (1995). Distributed Information Technology Governance: An Organizational–Economic Perspective. In the *Proceedings of the Sixteenth Conference on Information Systems, Amsterdam, 358.*

Prakash, C. A. (1996). Cycle Time Reduction: The Role of Interorganizational Information Systems. Unpublished Ph.D. dissertation. The University of Memphis.

Prakash, C.A., Janz, D.B., & Wetherbe, J. (1996). Client/Server Technology Adoption in Organizations: An Innovation Diffusion Approach. *Proceedings of the Second Americas Conference on Information Systems, Phoeniz, AZ.*

Premkumar, G., & King, W.R. (1994). Organizational characteristics and information systems planning: An empirical study. *Information Systems Research,* 5 (2), (June), 75–109.

Prescott, J. E. (1986). Environments as moderators of the relationship between strategy and performance. *Academy of Management Journal,* 29(2), 329–346.

Press, S.J. (1972). *Applied Multivariate Analysis,* Holt, Rinehart and Winston, Inc.

Price, J.L., & Mueller, C.W. (1986). *Handbook of Organizational Measurement.* Cambridge, MA: Ballinger Publishing.

Quesada, I., & Grossman, I.E. (1995). A Global Optimization Algorithm for Linear Fractional and Bilinear Programs. *Journal of Global Optimization,* 6, 39–76.

Radcliffe, R. C. (1982). *Investment: Concepts, Analysis, Strategy.* Glenview, IL: Scott, Foreman and Co.

Raffish, N. (1991). How Much Does that Product Really Cost? *Management Accounting,* 36–39.

Raiffa, Howard. (1968). *Decision Analysis: Introductory Lectures on Choices Under Uncertainty.* New York: Random House.

Rainer, R., Snyder, C. & Carr, H. (1991). Risk Analysis for Information Technology. *Journal of Management Information Systems,* 8(1), 129–147.

Rainer, R. J., & Watson, H.J. (1995). The keys to executive information system success. *Journal of Management Information Systems, 12*(2), 83–98.

Rao, C.R. (1973). *Linear Statistical Inference and It's Application,* John Wiley and Sons.

Rawles, R. (1994). Multimedia is the message in computer-based training. *MacWEEK.* October 31.

Raymond, I. (1987). Validating and applying user satisfaction as a measure of MIS success in small business. *Information and Management, 12,* 173-179.

Renkema, Theo, J. W. (1995). Information infrastructure: value of money ? The role and evaluation of investments in the information infrastructure. *Proceedings of the 13th Annual Int. Conf. of the AoM, Vol 13, No. 1, 152–161.*

Research–Technology Management. (1996). *Few Firms Measure Technology Payback,* 39(4), 5–6.

Reich, B.H., & Benbasat, I. (1990). An Empirical Investigation of Factors Influencing the

Success of Customer-Oriented Strategic Systems. *Information Systems Research* 1(3): 325-349.

Reisman, S. (1994.) *Multimedia Computing: Preparing for the 21st Century.* Harrisburg, PA: Idea Group Publishing.

Resnick, R., & Taylor, D. (1995). *The Internet Business Guide.* Sams.net Publishing.

Rifkin, G. (1992). What–if software for manufacturers. *The New York Times,* October 18.

Ritvo, R., Litwin, A., & Butler, L. (eds) (1995). *Managing in the Age of Change.* New York: Irwin Professional Publishing.

Roach, S.S. (1987). America's Technology Dilemma: A Profile of the Information Economy. *Special Economic Study,* Morgan Stanley.

Roach, S.S. (1984). Productivity, Investment, and the Information Economy. *Economic Perspectives,* March 14, 1-14, Morgan Stanley & Co.

Roach, S.S. (1984). *The Industrialization of the Information Economy. Special Economic Study,* June 15, Morgan Stanley & Co.

Roach, S.S. (1987). Technology and the Service Sector: America's Hidden Competitive Challenge. Special Economic Study, September 25, Morgan Stanley & Co.

Roach, S. S. (1991). Services under siege– the restructuring imperative. *Harvard Business Review,* September/October, 82–92.

Roach, S. S. (1989). The Case of the Missing Technology Payback. Tenth International Conference on Information Systems, Boston, MA.

Roach, S. S. (1989). America's White–Collar Productivity Dilemma. *Manufacturing Engineering,* August, 104.

Roach, S.S. (1994). A Resounding May Be. *CIO.* Feb., pp. 35–37.

Robinson, D.G. (1985). Justifying Information Systems: Use Business Change Instead of ROI. *Information Strategy,* 21(1), 44–46.

Rockart, J.F. (1979). Chief Executives Define Their Own Data Needs. *Harvard Business Review,* 57:2, 81–93.

Rockart, J. F., & DeLong, D. W. (1988). *Executive support systems.* Homewood, IL: Dow Jones-Irwin.

Rockart, J. F., & Short, J. E. (1991). The networked organization and the management of interdependence. Chapter 7 in M. Scott Morton (Ed.), *The corporation of the 1990s: information technology and organizational transformation,* 189–219). New York: Oxford University Press.

Rockart, J.F., & Treacy, M. (1982). The CEO Goes On Line. *Harvard Business Review,* 60:1, 82–88.

Rogers, & Shoemaker, F.JF. (1971). *Communication of innovations,* New York: FreePress.

Rogers, E.M. (1983). *Diffusion of Innovations.* New York: Free Press.

Roll, Y., Cook, W., & Golany, B. (1991). Controlling Factor Weights in Data Envelopment

Analysis, *IIE Transactions*, 23(1), 2–9.

Roper–Lowe, G.C., & Sharp, J.A. (1990). The Analytic Hierarchy Process and its Applications to an Information Technology Decision. *Journal of the Operational Research Society*, 41(1), 49–59.

Rothschild, M. (1993). The Coming Productivity Surge. *Forbes.* 151. 17–18.

Rozum, J. (1993). Concepts on measuring the benefits of software process improvements. Technical report CMU/SEI–93–TR–09.

Rumelt, R., Schendel, D., & Teece, D. (1991). Strategic management and economics. *Strategic Management Journal*, 12, 5–29.

Rumelt, R., Schendel, D. & Teece, D. (Eds.) (1994). *Fundamental issues in strategy.* Boston, MA: Harvard Business School Press.

Rushinek, A., & Rushinek, S. F. (1986). What makes users happy? *Communications of the ACM, 29*(7), 594-598.

Saaty, T. L. (1980). *The Analytical Hierarchy Process.* New York: McGraw–Hill.

Sabherwal, R., & King, W.R. (1992). Decision Processes for Developing Strategic Applications of Information Systems: A Contingency Approach. *Decision Sciences*, 23(4), 917–943.

Saiedian, H., & Kuzara, R. (1995). SEI Capability Maturity Model's Impact on Contractors. *IEEE Computer*, January, 16–26.

Sanchez, R. (1993). Strategic flexibility, firm organization, and managerial work in dynamic markets: a strategic–options perspective. *Advances in Strategic Management*, 9, 251–291.

Sappington, D.E.M. (1991). Incentives in Principal–Agent Relationships. *Journal of Economic Perspectives* (5:2), Spring, 45–66.

SAS/IML Software, *Usage and Reference*, Version 6, First Edition (1990). SAS Institute, Inc., Cary, NC 27513.

Sasser, W. E., Olsen, R. P., & Wychoff, D. D. (1978). *Management of service operations: Text and cases.* Boston, MA: Allyn and Bacon.

Sassone, P. (1988). A survey of cost-benefit methodologies for information systems. *Project Appraisal*, 3, 73-84.

Sassone, P., & Schaffer, W. (1978). *Cost-Benefit Analysis: A Handbook.* New York: Academic Press.

Saunders, C.S., & Jones, J.W. (1992). Measuring Performance of the Information Systems Function, *Journal of Management Systems*, Spring, Vol 8, No. 4, 63–82.

Saverline, D., Project Manager, Virginia Department of Transportation. Personal conversation, July 23, 1996.

Saxon, J.L. (1995). Staff Services Manager, California DMV. Vendor selection at the California DMV. Presentation to the advisory committee, College of Engineering, University of California, Riverside, June.

Schell, G.P. (1986). Establishing the value of information systems. *Interfaces.* 16(3), May–June, 82–89

Schendel, D. E. (1985). Strategic management and strategic marketing: what's strategic about either one? In H. Thomas & D. Gardner (Ed.), *Strategic marketing and management,* 41–63. New York: John Wiley and Sons, Ltd.

Schneider, S., & Lopes, L. (1986). Reflection in preferences under risk: who and when may suggest why. *Journal of Experimental Psychology: Human Perception and Performance.* 12(4), 535–548.

Schonberger, R. J. (1994). Human Resource Management Lessons From A Decade of Total Quality Management and Reengineering. *California Management Review.* 36. 109–23.

Schultheis, & Bock, D.. (1994). Benefits and barriers to client/server computing. *Journal of Systems Management,* 12–14.

Schumpeter, J. (1947). The creative response in economic history. *Journal of Economic History,* 7, November, 149–159.

Scott Morton, M. S. (1991). Introduction. Chapter 1 in M. Scott Morton (Ed.), *The corporation of the 1990s: information technology and organizational transformation,* 3–23. New York: Oxford University Press.

Scott Morton, M.S. (1991). *The Corporations of the 1990s: Information Technology and Organizational Transformation.* New York: Oxford University Press.

Scupski, S. (1994). Don't get reengineered away, *Datamation* 40 (17) (Sep.)

Segev, E. (1995). *Corporate Strategy. Portfolio Models.* London: Boyd and Fraser.

Selznick, P. (1957). *Leadership in administration: a sociological interpretation.* New York: Harper & Row.

Semich, J.W. (1994). Here's How to Quantify IT Investment Benefits. *Datamation,* 40(1), 45–48.

Senn, J.A. (1978). *Information Systems in Management.* New York: Wadsworth Publishing.

Serafeimidis, V. (1996). Information Technology Investment Evaluation: Rationale, Concepts and Facilitation. In *Proceedings of the 1996 IRMA International Conference, Washington, DC.* 183–191.

Sethi, A. K., & Sethi, S. P. (1990). Flexibility in manufacturing: A survey. *The International Journal of Flexible Manufacturing Systems,* 2, 289–328.

Sethi, V., & King, W. (1994). Development of measures to assess the extent to which an information technology application provides competitive advantage. *Management Science,* 40(12), 1601–1627.

Shafer, G. (1976). *Mathematical Theory of Evidence.* Princeton, NJ: Princeton University Press.

Shank, R. (1995). Learning and Multimedia Software. Presentation for CASI (Colorado Advanced Software Institute. US West Advanced Technologies Lab. Boulder, CO. April 12.

Sharda, R., Barr, S., & McDonnell, J. (1988). Decision Support System Effectiveness: A Review and an Empirical Test. *Management Science*, 34, 139-159.

Sharpe, W.F. (1969). *The Economics of Computers*. New York: Columbia University Press.

Sheppard, J. (1991). IT Investment Decisions, a UK Perspective. Chapter 7 in E. Sutherland & Y. Morieux (Eds.), *Business strategy and information technology*, 85–108. London: Routledge.

Sherer, S.A. (1992). *Software Failure Risk: Measurement and Management*. New York: Plenum Press.

Sherman, R.L. (1992). Distributed systems security. *Computers and Security*. 11(1), 24–28.

Shoval, P., & Lugasi, Y. (1988). Computer Systems Selection: The Graphical Cost–Benefit Approach. *Information and Management*, 15(3), 163–172.

Siha, S. (1993). A decision model for selecting mutually exclusive alternative technologies. *Computers and Enging*, Vol. 24, No. 3, 459–475.

Simmons, P. (1996). Quality Payoffs: Determining Business Value. *IEEE Software*, January 25–32.

Simon, H.A. (1965). *The Shape of Automation for Men and Management*. New York: Harper & Row.

Simon, H.A. (1990). Information technologies and organizations. *The Accounting Review*. 65(3), 658–667.

Simon, J.L. (1969). *Basic Research Methods in Social Science*. New York: Random House.

Simon, J.L., & Bruce, P. (1993). Probability and Statistics with Resampling Stats and Mathematica. *The Mathematica Journal*, 3(7), 48–55.

Simpson, D. (1994). CIO Survey Reveals Five–Fold Gain in C/S. *Client/Server Today*, 36–38.

Singh, S.K., Watson, R.T., & Watson, H.J. (1995). Technology, task, people, and structure: An analysis of their interdependencies in context of an executive information system. *Journal of Decision Systems*, 3(4), 359–383.

Sitkin, S., & Pablo, A. (1992). Reconceptualizing the determinants of risk behavior. *Academy of Management Review*. 17(1), 9–38.

Slovic, P. (1972). From Shakespeare to Simon: Speculations – and some evidence – about man's ability to process information. *Oregon Research Institute Monograph*, Vol. 12, No. 12.

Smith, H.A., & McKeen, J.D. (1991). How Does Information Technology Affect Business Value? A Reassessment and Research Proposition. Twenty–fourth Hawaii Conference on Systems Science, Kauai, Hawaii.

Smith, P. (1995). Performance Indicators and Outcome in the Public Sector. *Public Money and Management*, 15(4), 13–16.

Smith, P., & Gueugerich, S., (1994). *Client/Server Computing*, Sams Publishing.

Smith, S., & Cusumano, M. (1993). Beyond the Software Factory: A Comparison of "Classic" and PC Software Developers. Working Paper WP#3607-93/BPS (September). Massachusetts Institute of Technology Sloan School.

Software Productivity Consortium (SPC) (1993). *Reuse Adoption Guidebook.* SPC-92051-CMC, Ver 02.00.05, November.

Sokol, P.K. (1989). *EDI: The Competitive Edge.* New York: McGraw-Hill.

Sommerville, I. (1996). Software Engineering, 5th Edition. New York: Addison-Wesley.

Son, Y.K. (1990). A Performance Measurement Method Which Remedies the "Productivity Paradox.?" *Production and Inventory Management Journal,* 31(2), 38-43.

Sonnemann, R. (1995). Exploratory study of software reuse success factors, Ph.D. Dissertation, George Mason University, Spring.

Srinivasan, A. (1985). Alternative Measures of System Effectiveness: Associations and Implications. *MIS Quarterly,* 9, 243-253.

Srinivasan, A., & Davis, J. (1987). A reassessment of implementation process models. *Interfaces, 17*(3), 64-71.

Srinivasan, K., Kekre, S., & Mukhopadhyay, T. (1994). Impact of Electronic Interchange Technology on JIT Shipments. *Management Science* 40(10): 1291-1304.

Staringer, W. (1994). Constructing applications from reusable components. *IEEE Software,* 61-68, September.

Staw, B., Sandelands, L., & Dutton, J.. (1981). Threat-rigidity effects in organizational behaviour: a multilevel analysis. *Administrative Science Quarterly.* 26(4), 501-524.

Steger, H. (1995). End-User's dream, an IS Manager's Nightmare. *Computing Canada,* 21 (5), s34.

Stewart, T.A. (1993). Reengineering the hot new managing tool. *Fortune,* August 23, 40-48.

Strassmann, P.A. (1984). Value-added Productivity Measurement: Concepts and Results. *EDP Analyzer,* June, 13-14.

Strassmann, P.A. (1987). *Information Payoff.* New York: MacMillan.

Strassmann, P.A. (1985). *Information Payoff: The Transformation of Work in the Electronic Age.* New York: The Free Press.

Strassman, P.A. (1990). *The business value of computers: an executive's guide.* New Canaan, CT: Information Economics Press.

Straussman, P. A., Berger, P., Swanson, B. E., Kriebel, C. H., & Kauffman, R. J. (1988). *Measuring the business value of information technologies.* Washington, DC: ICIT Press.

Straub, D.A., & Collins, R.W. (1990). Key information liability issues facing managers: Software piracy, proprietary databases and individual rights to privacy. *MIS Quarterly.* 14(2), 143-156.

Sullivan, G. (1996). Describing and Evaluating Processes CASE: Ford Motor Company

BPR. http://nerv.nede.ufl.edu/~gsulliv/ch03/html.

Sullivan-Trainor, M. (1993). Behind every great CIO is a savvy chief executive. *Computerworld*, September 13, 18-19.

Sullivan, W. (1986). Models IEs can use to include strategic, non–monetary factors in automation decisions. *Indust. Engng*, Vol. 18, 42–50.

Symons, V. J. (1991). Impacts of Information Systems: Four Perspectives. *Information & Software Technology*, 33 (3), 181–190.

Swanson, E. (1988). Business Value as Justificatory Argument. In ICIT Research Study Team # 2, *Measuring Business Value of Information Technologies*. Washington D.C.: ICIT Press.

Swanson, E. B. (1994). Information systems innovation among organizations. *Management Science*, 40(9), 1069–1092.

Tait, P., & Vessey, I. (1988). The effect of user involvement on system success: A contingency approach. *MIS Quarterly, 12*(1), 91-108.

Takeuchi, K., Yanai H., & Mukherjee, B.N. (1985). *The Foundation of Multivariate Analysis*, Wiley Eastern.

Tan, J. J., & Litschert, R. J. (1994). Environment–strategy relationship and its performance implications: an empirical study of the Chinese electronics industry. *Strategic Management Journal*, 15, 1–20.

Tapscott, D. (1996). *The digital economy: Promise and peril in the age of networked intelligence*. New York: McGraw-Hill.

Tapscott, D., & Caston, A. (1993). *Paradigm Shift: The New Promise of Information Technology*. McGraw–Hill.

Tatum, T., & Aiken, P. (1996). Applying a Redesign Comparison Framework – A Case Study. *Reverse Engineering Newsletter*, Committee on Reverse Engineering Technical Council on Software Engineering IEEE Computer Society (Fall 1996 publication).

Tatum, T., & Aiken, P. (1996). Measuring and Assessing IT Investment in Reengineering: A Case Dilemma. Proceedings of the 5th Reenginering Forum, IEEE Publishing Services, St. Louis, MO, June 27–28.

Teece, D. J., Pisano, G., & Shuen, A. (1992). Dynamic capabilities and strategic management. Working Paper, University of California at Berkeley.

Teo, H.H., Tan, Bernard C.Y., & Wei, K.K. (1995). Innovation Diffusion Theory as a Predictor of Adoption Intention for Financial EDI. In the Proceedings of the Sixteenth Conference on Information Systems, Amsterdam, 155–165.

Thierauf, R. J. (1991). Executive information systems: A guide for senior management and MIS professionals. New York: Quorum Books.

Thompson, J. (1967). *Organizations in action*. New York: McGraw–Hill.

Tirso, J., & Gregorious, H. (1993). Management of reuse at IBM. *IBM Systems Journal*, Vol 32, No 4, 612–615.

Tishler, A., & Lipovetsky, S. (1993). A Lot of Data with Little Theory: A Possible Solution

Based on Canonical and Partial Canonical Correlations with an Application to Management Information Systems. Israel Institute of Business Research, Working Paper No. 32/93, Faculty of Management, Tel Aviv University.

Tishler, A., Lipovetsky, S., & Giladi, R. (1994). Information Systems (IS) Attributes and the Performance of Firms: A Multivariate Analysis/Israel Institute of Business Research, Working Paper No. 47/93 (revised), Faculty of Management, Tel Aviv University.

Tom, P.L. (1987). *Managing Information As A Corporate Resource.* Glenview: Scott Foresman.

Tornatzky, & Klein, K.J. (1982). Innovation characteristics and innovation adoption–implementation: A meta–analysis of findings. *IEEE transactions on engineering management*, 29(1), 28–45.

Tracz, W., 'Software reuse: motivators and inhibitors,' Stanford University paper presented at the Workshop on Future Directions in *Computer Architecture and Software*, 5–8 May 1986.

Tracz, W. (1989). Where does reuse start? Transcript – keynote address for the Reuse in Practice Workshop sponsored by IDA, SEI, and SIGAda at Software Engineering Institute, 11–13 July.

Tracz, W. (1994). Domain–specific software architecture frequently asked questions. *ACM SIGSOFT Software Engineering Notes*, Vol 19, No 2, 52–56, April.

Treacy, M. (1981). Toward a Behaviorally Grounded Theory of Information Value. In Proceedings of the Second International Conference on Information Systems, 247-257.

Trice, A.W., & Treacy, M.E. (1986). Utilization as a Dependent Variable in MIS Research. In *Proceedings of the Seventh International Conference on Information Systems*, 227-239.

Trigeorgis, L. (1995). *Real options in capital investment: Models, strategies, and applications.* Westport, Connecticut: Praeger.

Troutt, M.D. (1995). A Maximum Decisional Efficiency Estimation Principle. *Management Science*, 41(1), 76–82.

Troutt, M.D., Rai, A., & Zhang, A. (1996). The Potential Use of DEA for Credit Applicant Acceptance Systems. *Computers & Operations Research.* 23(4), 405–408.

Troutt, M.D., Rai, A., & Tadisina, S.K. (1995). Aggregating Multiple Expert Clasification Data for Linear Scoring Models Using the MDE Principle. To appear, *Decision Support Systems.*

Troutt, M.D., Zhang, A., Tadisina, S.K., & Rai, A. (1996). Total Factor Productivity/Efficiency Ratio Fitting as an Alternative to Regression and Canonical Correlation Models for Performance Data. Working paper, under publication review, Management Department, Southern Illinois University, Carbondale, IL 62901-4627.

Troutt, M.D., & Gribbin, D.W. (1996). Estimating Best Practice Unit and Marginal Costs. Working paper, under publication review, Management Department, Southern Illinois University, Carbondale, IL 62901-4627.

Troy, R. (1994). Software reuse: making the concept work. Engineering Software, Special Editorial Supplement, 16–20, 13 June.

Turban E., McLean, E., & Wetherbe, J. (1996). *Information technology for management:*

improving quality and productivity. New York: John Wiley and Sons.

Turkle, S. (1984). *The Second Self: Computers and the Human Spirit.* New York: Simon and Shuster.

Turner, J. (1985). Organizational performance, size and the use of data processing resources, working paper, #58, Center for Research in Information Systems, New York University, New York.

Turner, M. (1994). Coaxing Cooperation. *Network World,* 11:2, 21–22.

Turner, M. (1995a). Deal Underscored Need for Users to Get Serious About Internet Services. *Network World,* 12:32, 32.

Turner, M. (1995b). Low Priorities but High Hopes for the Internet. *Business Communications Review,* 25:11, 29–32.

Turner, M. (1995c). Is the Internet Fit for Business? *Business Communications Review,* 25.

Turney, P.B.B. (1989). Using Activity Based Costing to Achieve Manufacturing Excellence. *Journal of Cost Management,* 23–31.

Tushman, M., & Nadler, D. (1978). Information processing as an integrating concept in organizational design. *Academy of Management Review,* July, 613–624.

Tyran, C. K., Dennis, A. R., Vogel, D. R , & Nunnamaker, J. F. (1992). The application of electronic meeting technology to support strategic management. *MIS Quarterly, 16*(3), 313-334.

Unisys Corporation. (1994). Army STARS demonstration project experience report. *ARPA Report,* 25 August.

U. S. National Research Council (1993).

Van den Hoven, J. (1996). Executive support systems & decision making. *Journal of Systems Management,* 47(2), 48–55.

Van Dyke, B. F., & Newton, J.M. (1972). Computer–assisted Instruction: Performance and Attitudes. *Journal of Educational Research,* 65(7), 291–293.

Van Horn, R. (1973). Empirical Studies of Management Information Systems. *Data Base,* 5, 2, 172-180.

van Loggerenberg, B.J., & Cucchiaro, S. (1981). Productivity Measurement and the Bottom Line. *National Productivity Review,* Winter, 87–99.

Van Kirk, D. (1994). What is Client/Server Computing, Anyway? *Infoworld,* 12(2),104.

Vaughn, L. (1994). *Client/Server Design and Implementation,* McGraw–Hill.

Venkatraman, N. (1994). IT–Enabled Business Transformation: From Automation to Business Scope Redefinition. *Sloan Management Review,* 35(2), 73–87.

Venkatraman, N. (1991). IT–induced business reconfiguration. Chapter 5 in M. Scott Morton (Ed.), *The corporation of the 1990s: information technology and organizational transformation,* 122–158). New York: Oxford University Press.

Venkatraman, N., & Ramanujam, V. (1987). Planning system success: A conceptualization and an operational model. *Management Science, 33*(6), 687-705.

Venkatraman, N., & Zaheer, A. (1990). Electronic Integration and Strategic Advantage: A Quasi–Experimental Study in the Insurance Industry. *Information Systems Research,* 1(4), 377–393.

Vitale, M.R., Ives, B., & Beath, C.M. (1986). Linking Information Technology and Corporate Strategy: An Organizational View. In L. Maggi, R. Zmud, & J. Wetherbe (Editors). Proceedings of the Seventh International Conference on Information Systems, San Diego, California, 265–276.

Vlek, C., & Stallen, P. (1980). Rational and personal aspects of risk. *Acta Psychologica.* 45(1–3), 273–300.

Volonino, L., & Watson, H. J. (1991). The strategic business objectives method for guiding executive information systems development. *Journal of Management Information Systems, 7*(3), 27-39.

Vygotsky, L. (1987). Thinking and Speech: Problems of General Psychology, Vol I. Translated by Morris Minick. River and Carton, Eds. New York: Plenum Press.

Wagner, M. (1995). Business execs fault IS info gap. *Computerworld.* 29(44) 28.

Wang, E.T.G., & Seidmann, A. (1995). Electronic data interchange: competitive externalities and strategic implementation policies. *Management Science,* 41(3), 401–418.

Ward, J.A. (1996). Measurement Management What You Measure Is What You Get. *Information Systems Management,* 13, 59–61.

Wasmund, M. (1993). Implementing critical success factors in software reuse. *IBM Systems Journal,* Vol 32, No 4, 595–611.

Watson, H. J., & Frolick, M. N. (1993). Determining information requirements for an EIS. *MIS Quarterly, 17*(3), 255-269.

Watson, H. J., & Glover, H. (1990). Common and avoidable causes of EIS failure. *Computerworld,* December 4, 90-91.

Watson, H. J., Harp, C. G., Kelly, G. G., & O'Hara, M. T. (1996). Including soft information in your EIS. *Information Systems Management, 13*(3), 66–77.

Watson, H. J., Rainer, R. K., & Koh, C. (1991). Executive information systems: A framework for development and a survey of current practices. *MIS Quarterly,* 13-30.

Watson, H.J., Watson, R.T., Singh, S.K., & Holmes, D. (1995). A Field Survey of EIS Developmental Practices. *Decision Support Systems,* 14, 171–184.

Weber, M. (1947). *The Theory of Social and Economic Organization.* New York: The Free Press. Translated by A.M. Henderson and T. Parsons.

Wecker, S. (1979) Computer Network Architectures, *IEEE Computer, 12*(9), 58–72.

Weil, U. (1988). Making computers pay their way. *Institutional Investor,* (UK) 18–19.

Weill, P. (1992). The Relationship Between Investment in Information Technology and Firm Performance: A Study of the Valve Manufacturing Industry. *Information Systems*

Research, 3(4), 307–333.

Weill, P. (1988). The Relationship Between Investment in Information Technology and Firm Performance in the Manufacturing Sector. Unpublished Ph.D. Thesis, Stern School of Business, New York University.

Weill, P. (1990). *Do Computers Really Pay Off?* Washington, D.C.: ICIT Press.

Weill, P. (1990). Strategic Investment in Information Technology: An Empirical Study. *Information Age,* 12(3), 141–147.

Weill, P. (1993). The Role and Value of Information Technology Infrastructure: Some Empirical Observations in *Strategic Information Technology Managegment: Perspectives on Organizational Growth and Competitive Advantage,* R.D. Banker, R.J. Kauffman and M.A. Mahmood (eds.), Harrisburg, PA: Idea Group Publishing, 547–572.

Weill, P, & Olson, M. (1989). Managing Investment in Information Technology: Mini Case Examples and Implications. *MIS Quarterly,* 13(1), 3–17.

Weiner, M. *et al.* (1970). *An Evaluation of 1968-1969 New York City Computer–assisted Instruction Project in Elementary Arithmetic.* City University of New York. New York.

Wernerfelt, B. (1984). A resource based view of the firm. *Strategic Management Journal,* 5, 171–180.

Wernerfelt, B., & Karnani, A. (1987). Research notes and communications: competitive strategy under uncertainty. *Strategic Management Journal,* 8, 187–194.

Wernerfelt, B., & Karnani, A. (1987). Competitive Strategy Under Uncertainty. *Strategic Management Journal,* 8, 187–194.

West, L.A. (1994). Researching the costs of information systems. *Journal of Management Information Systems.* 11(2), 75–107.

West, L.A. Jr., & Courtney, J.F. (1994). Does IO economics really make the case for investments in IT: A rejoinder, *Decision Sciences,* 25 (3), (May–June), 477–479.

Westland, J. C. (1993). The Marginal Analysis of Strategic Investments in Information Technology, In Banker et al. (eds) *Strategic Information Management: Perspectives on Organizational Growth and Competitive Advantage,* Harrisburg, PA: Idea Group Publishing.

Wetherbe, J. (1993). Four–Stage Model of MIS Planning Concepts, Techniques and Implementation. In Banker et al. (eds) *Strategic Information Management: Perspectives on Organizational Growth and Competitive Advantage.* Harrisburg, PA: Idea Group Publishing.

Who's Using Multimedia? (1994). *New Media.* 4(10), 48–58.

Williamson, M. (1994). High-tech training. *Byte,* December.

Williamson, O.E. (1975). *Markets and Hierarchies: Analysis and Antitrust Implications.* New York: The Free Press.

Williamson, O.E. (1992). Markets, hierarchies, and the modern corporation: An unfolding perspective. *Journal of Economic Behavior and Organizations* (17), 335–352.

Willinger, M., & Zuscovitch, E. (1988).Towards the economics of information–intensive production systems: The case of advanced materials. In R. Dosi et al. (Ed.), *Technical change and economic theory*, 239–255. Maastricht Economic Research Institute on Innovation and Technology, International Federation of Institutes for Advanced Study. London, England: Pinter Publishers.

Wilson, B., & Lowry, M. (1996). An Evaluation of the COMET Distant Learning Program. University of Colorado at Denver.

Wilson, D.D. (1988). Assessing IT performance: What the experts say, MIT working Paper on the 90s Project: SS–050. Cambridge, MA: MIT.

Wilson, D.D. (1993). Assessing the Impact of Information Technology on Organizational Performance. In R. D. Banker, R. J., Kauffman, & M. A., Mahmood (Editors). *Strategic Information Technology Management: Perspectives on Organizational Growth and Competitive Advantage*, 471–514. Harrisburg, Pennsylvania: Idea Group Publishing.

Wilson, D.D. (1993). IT Investment and its Productivity Effects: An Organizational Sociologist's Perspective on Directions for Future Research. International Workshop on The Productivity of Information Technology Investments, Organized by the National Science Foundation, the Organization for Economic Cooperation and Development, and the Massachusetts Institute of Technology, Charleston, SC, November 11–13.

Wiseman, C. (1988). *Strategic Information Systems*. Homewood, IL: Irwin.

Withey, J. (1993). Implementing model based software engineering in your organization: an approach to domain engineering. Technical report, CMU/SEI–93–TR, November.

Woo, C.Y.Y., & Cooper, A.C. (1981). Strategies of effective low share businesses. *Strategic Management Journal*, 2, 301–318.
Wood, C.C. (1990). How many information security staff people should you have? *Computers and Security*. 9(5), 395–402.

Wrigley, C.D. (1991). Research on EDI: Present and Future, Proceedings of the 4th EDI Electronic Data Interchange Conference -- EDI: Business Strategy for 90s (Moderna Organizacija Kranj): 353-367.

Yager, R. (1992). Decision making under Dempster–Shafer uncertainties. *International Journal of General Systems*. 20; 233–245.

Yager, R. (1995). *Fusion of Ordinal Information Using Weighted Median Aggregation; Technical Report #MII–1520*. Iona College. New Rochelle, NY.

Yager, R., Engemann, K., & Filev, D. (1995). On the concept of immediate probabilities. *International Journal of Intelligent Systems*, 10(4), 374–397.

Yan, T.K. (1992). Capital budgeting in information system development. *Information and Management*, Vol. 23, 345- 357.

Yates, J., & Benjamin, R. I. (1991). The past and present as a window on the future. Chapter 3 in M. Scott Morton (Ed.), *The corporation of the 1990s: information technology and organizational transformation*, 61–92). New York: Oxford University Press.

Yeh, H. (1993). *Software process quality*. New York: McGraw–Hill.

Yourdon, E. (1994). Client/Server catch–up. *Computerworld*, 28(36), 100.

Yourdon, E., & Constantine, L. (1986). *Structured Design: Fundamentals of a Discipline of Computer Program and System Design*. Englewood Cliffs, NJ: Yourdon Press.

Zaltman, D., & Holbek, J. (1973). *Innovations and Organizations.* New York: Wiley and Sons.

Zammuto, R. F. (1982). *Assessing organizational effectiveness: Systems change, adoption and strategy.* Albany, NY: State University of New York Press.

Zeithaml, V. A., Parasuraman, A., & Berry, L. L. (1990). *Delivering quality service: Balancing customer perceptions and expectations.* New York: Free Press.

Zeithaml, V. A., Berry, L. L, & Parasuraman, A. (1993). The nature and determinants of customer expectations of service. *Journal of the Academy of Marketing Science, 21*(1), 1–12.

Zimmerman, W. (Ed.) (1988). American Banker 1988 Managing Technology Survey. The Impact on the Bottom Line. New York: Thompson Publishing.

Zmud, R.W. (1978). An Empirical Investigation of The Dimensionality of the Concept of Information. *Decision Sciences,* 9, 2, 187-195.

Zmud, R. W. (1979). Individual differences and MIS success: A review of the empirical literature. *Management Science, 25*(10), 966-979.

Zuboff, S. (1988). *In the Age of the Smart Machine.* New York: Basic Books.

Zubrow, D., & Hayes, W. (1995). Moving On Up: Data and Experience Doing CMM–Based Process Improvement. Technical Report CMU/SEI–95–TR–008. (August). Software Engineering Institute, Carnegie Mellon University.

Authors

EDITORS

Mo Adam Mahmood is Professor of Information Systems and Ellis and Susan Mayfield Professor in Business Administration at the University of Texas at El Paso. He received his Ph.D. in Management Information Systems from Texas Tech University. His research interests include information technology in support of superior organizational strategic and economic performance, group decision support systems, software engineering, and the utilization of information technology for national and international competitiveness. Dr. Mahmood has published in *MIS Quarterly, Journal of Management Information Systems, Decision Sciences, European Journal of Information Systems, Expert Systems with Applications, INFOR — Canadian Journal of Operation Research and Information Processing, Information and Management, Journal of Computer–Based Instruction, Information Resources Management Journal, Journal of Systems Management, Data Base, International Journal of Policy and Management*, and others. He has also edited and published a book in the information technology investment and performance area. He is currently serving as the Editor of the *Journal of End User Computing*. He had also served or is serving as a guest editor, an associate editor, a member of the editorial review board, or a referee for a number of information systems journals. In addition, he has presented research papers, served as both a reviewer and discussant, and chaired sessions and tracks, and participated on program committees of several regional, national, and international conferences.

Edward J. Szewczak is a professor and Chair of the MCIS Department at Canisius College in Buffalo, New York. He received a Ph.D. in MIS from the University of Pittsburgh in 1985. His information systems research has been published in *Data Base, European Journal of Operational Research, Information & Management, Information Resources Management Journal, Journal of Management Systems, Journal of Microcomputer Systems Management, Journal of MIS, Omega*, and *Simulation & Games* as well as in a number of readings texts and scholarly conference proceedings. He has also co–edited two books of readings entitled *Management Impacts of Information Technology: Perspectives on Organizational Change and Growth* (1991) and *The Human Side of Information Technology Management* (1996) published by Idea Group Publishing of Harrisburg, PA. He is currently an associate editor of the *Information Resources Management Journal*.

CHAPTER AUTHORS

Niv Ahituv is the Marko and Lucie Chaoul Chair for Research in Information Evaluation in Tel Aviv University, Israel. From 1989 to 1994 he served as the Dean of the Faculty of Management—The Leon Recanati Graduate School of Business Administration in Tel Aviv University. He managed the Information Systems Department at the Bank of Israel from 1969–1975. In addition to his academic activities, he also consults to management of large organizations in the area of information systems policy and strategic planning. He is a member of the Intergovernmental Information Technology Committee of UNESCO. He has published books and numerous articles which have appeared in various leading academic journals. He is the coauthor of *Principles of Information Systems for Management,* a widely used textbook (four editions). Professor Ahituv's main areas of interest are information economics and information system strategy, management and development. He holds degrees of B.Sc. in Mathematics, an M.B.A., and M.Sc. and Ph.D. in Information Systems.

Peter Aiken is a research director with the Virginia Commonwealth University School of Business – Information Systems Research Institute in Richmond, Virginia. Dr. Aiken has consulted with a number of organizations. Additional major project experience and publications have been in the areas of systems integration and engineering, software engineering, strategic planning, decision support systems, and project management. Current interests include research into links between process and systems reengineering. His e–mail address is phaiken@vcu.edu.

Asokan Anandarajan is currently an assistant professor of Accounting and Finance in the School of Industrial Management at the New Jersey Institute of Technology. He has a Ph.D. from Drexel University, and an M.B.A. and M.Phil from Cranfield University, U.K. He also received an Executive Diploma in Business Administration from the University of Ceylon, Sri Lanka, and is an associate member of the Chartered Institute of Management Accountants, London, U.K. Dr. Anandarajan has published in *Accounting Horizons, Auditing: A Journal of Practice and Theory, Journal of Commercial Lending,* and the *International Journal of Physical Distribution Management.*

Murugan Anandarajan is an assistant professor of Information Systems in the College of Business and Administration at St. Joseph's University, Philadelphia. He received his Ph.D. in Management Information Systems from Drexel University. He holds an M.B.A. and M.S. in Accounting. He is an associate member of the Chartered Institute of Management Accountants, London, U.K. Dr. Anandarajan has articles forthcoming in *Computers and Operation Research,* and the *International Journal of Computer Information Systems.*

Marielle Bergeron is an assistant professor in the Faculty of Business Administration at the Université Laval in Quebec. She received her doctorate in management information systems from the University of British Columbia, her master of computer science from the Concordia University, and her bachelor of business administration from the Hautes Études Commerciales of Montreal. She has been a member of the Canadian Institute of Chartered Accountants since 1980. Professor Bergeron has been a multidisciplinary professional in the accounting and IS fields for more than a decade. As a senior MIS consultant, she has conducted several opportunity and feasibility studies, as well as strategic planning, project management, system modeling and quality insurance mandates for a wide variety of public and private organizations. Her current research interests, in addition to electronic data interchange, include the impact of IT on organizational performance and strategic information systems.

Jack D. Callon joined the MIS faculty in the College of Business at San Jose State University in September 1987. This followed his retirement from IBM after 28 years of service that included assignments in the United States, Japan and Germany. His background includes eighteen years of IBM marketing management. He received his M.B.A. in Management and B.S. in Accounting from Indiana University. After graduating from college, he spent three years in the U.S. Air Force and then joined IBM in Long Beach, California. His IBM assignments included Marketing Representative and Manufacturing Industry Marketing Representative in Los Angeles; Asia Pacific Area Manufacturing Industry Marketing Manager in Tokyo, Japan; Manufacturing Industry Center Manager in Munich, Germany; Manufacturing Industry Education Manager in San Jose; Marketing Manager and Regional Marketing Manager in San Francisco; Manager of Marketing in the General Products Division Special Business Unit and Information Systems Consultant in the Customer Executive Education Program in San Jose, CA. His research and consulting interests have concentrated on management issues as they relate to information systems use within an organization. He is the author of a textbook published in 1996 by McGraw–Hill entitled *Competitive Advantage Through Information Technology*.

Chrys de Almeida is an assistant professor in the Department of Mathematics, Computing and Information Systems at St. Francis Xavier University in Antigonish, Nova Scotia. He teaches information systems. His current research and professional interests are multimedia, collaborative systems, knowledge–based systems, telecommunications, and organizational impact of information technology. Professor de Almeida obtained his Ph.D. in Management Information Systems and an M.B.A. in Finance from the University of Florida, Gainesville, Florida. He has a B.Sc. in Electrical Engineering from the University of Moratuwa, Sri Lanka. He has worked for several years as an engineer in the radio and television broadcasting industry and was also an adjunct faculty member in the Graduate School of Business Administration and Entrepreneurship at the Open University of Florida.

Albert S. Dexter is a professor in the Faculty of Commerce and Business Administration of the University of British Columbia, where he has taught since 1971. He has served as an expert witness for the Supreme Court of British Columbia on issues of economics and of software copyright infringement. He has been a director of the British Columbia Systems Corporation, a Crown Corporation, which provided information technology and telecommunications services to various ministries and other agencies of the province. He has consulted on issues relating to Income Tax Credits and computing software in the Canadian context for more than a decade. Professor Dexter has been working with Electronic Data Interchange for several years, and has led a Strategic Social Sciences Council of Canada Grant investigating the impact of EDI and competitive advance in Canada. Professor Dexter's research has appeared in such journals as the *Accounting Review, Journal of Accounting Research, Communications of the ACM, Journal of Money, Credit and Banking, INFOR, MIS Quarterly, Management Science,* and *Marketing Science.* He is an Associate Editor for *INFOR.* His current research interests in addition to EDI include: IT and competitive advantage, the impact of IT in medical care systems, software copyright, and the impact of IT on organizational form.

Kurt J. Engemann is a professor of Management Science and Systems in the Hagan School of Business at Iona College in New Rochelle, New York.. He received his Ph.D. in Operations Research from New York University. Dr. Engemann's main areas of interest are computer–based modeling and data analysis, simulation, optimization, and decision support systems. His consulting and research concentrates on the development of models and information systems to support executives within the functional areas of business.

Susan A.R. Garrod is a doctoral candidate in Strategic Management at the Krannert Graduate School of Management of Purdue University and an associate professor in the Department of Electrical Engineering Technology at Purdue, where she has taught telecommunications courses as a member of the faculty since 1986. With this background, she brings a unique and in–depth technological perspective to her research regarding the strategic aspects of information technologies and telecommunications. She is a member of the Institute of Electrical and Electronics Engineers (IEEE) and the Pacific Telecommunications Council, and she has actively served in the North American ISDN Users' Forum. She was awarded two faculty fellowships with NASA Lewis Research Center, where she worked on application development for the Advanced Communications Technology Satellite (ACTS) program. Her engineering background and experience with telecommunications enables her to examine the details of competitive applications of telecommunications and information technology. This expertise provides a unique market and technological perspective that is invaluable for analyzing a firm's information strategy and its contributions to the firm's competitive advantage.

Rick Gibson is an assistant professor at the American University in the

Department of Computer Science and Information Systems in Washington, D.C. He completed his Ph.D. in Information Systems at the University of Maryland in 1992. His research has been focused on international computing with a particular focus on software development by offshore companies that are now competing heavily with U.S. based firms. In his consulting work during the past year, he has been helping major telecommunications companies by evaluating the software process maturity of their software vendors. Dr. Gibson has over 15 years of software engineering experience, with a background that includes system development using both structured and object–oriented software development methodologies. He is certified by the Software Engineering Institute to conduct software capability evaluations.

Elizabeth Kennick is a Software Process Engineer for Morgan Stanley's Global Information Technology Group, concentrating on the implementation and continuous improvement of project management processes for software development. She is a founder of CitySPIN, the newly formed Software Process Improvement Network for New York City. Sponsored by Morgan Stanley and Merrill Lynch, CitySPIN is a leadership forum for the free and open exchange of software process improvement ideas and experience, with a practical focus on the Software Capability Maturity Model promulgated by the Software Engineering Institute at Carnegie–Mellon University. Liz has an M.S. in Information Systems/Operations Analysis from the University of Maryland, Baltimore County (UMBC), a B.A. in English, and an A.A. in Education. She is certified as a Novell NetWare Engineer and has applied for certification as a Project Management Professional by the Project Management Institute. Her most recent speaking engagement was at Project World in Washington, D.C., in August 1996, where she spoke on communications management for global software development projects.

Ram L. Kumar is an assistant professor in the Information & Operations Management Department at the Belk College of Business Administration, the University of North Carolina, Charlotte. He received his B.Tech and Post Graduate diploma in Management (M.B.A.) degrees from the Indian Institute of Technology, Madras, and Indian Institute of Management, Bangalore, respectively. He has worked for five years in information systems development and management. He received his Ph.D. from the University of Maryland in 1993, where he was the recipient of the Frank T. Paine Award for Academic Merit. His research interests include management of investments in technology, security and control in information systems, and the interface between MIS and Operations Management. His research has appeared in *Computers & Operations Research, International Journal of Production Economics, Journal of MIS, Journal of Systems Management,* edited books, and several conference proceedings. His research has been funded by organizations such as the U.S. Department of Commerce, the Maryland Industrial Partnerships Scheme, and BarclaysAmerican. He is a member of AIS, DSI, and INFORMS.

Stan Lipovetsky holds an M.Sc. In Theoretical Physics and a Ph.D. in Mathematical Methods in Economics from Moscow University. He is affiliated with the Faculty of Management at Tel Aviv University. His primary areas of research are multivariate statistics, multiple criteria decision making, econometrics, microeconomics, and management information systems. Presently he is located in New York, USA, e–mail 102170.2625@compuserve.com.

Ray Maghroori is an associate dean at the Anderson Graduate School of Management at the University of California, Riverside. He is the co–author of three books and numerous articles. Dr. Maghroori teaches in the area of business government relations and conducts research in the field of leadership. He has served on the board of directors of financial institutions, health care organizations and engineering firms.

Kathryn A. Marold is a professor in the Computer Information Systems and Management Science Department of Metropolitan State College in Denver, Colorado. She teaches multimedia and visual programming systems, and has authored numerous text books on microcomputer literacy and computer mediated communication. Dr. Marold's special research interests include the cognitive changes that occur within the electronic environment, the move from a text–based to electronic culture, and the impact of computer interfaces upon the end user.

James D. McKeen is a professor of MIS at the School of Business, Queen's University, Kingston, Canada. He received his Ph.D. in MIS from the University of Minnesota. His research interests include the design and implementation of application systems and strategies for selecting application systems in organizations. Most recently, he is involved in a large program of research to determine the value of information technology. He has published articles on related topics in the *MIS Quarterly, the Journal of Systems and Software, Information and Management, Communications of the ACM, Computers and Education, OMEGA,* and *Database,* and has recently published on textbook with Heather A. Smith entitled *Management Challenges in IS: Successful Strategies and Appropriate Actions.* Prior to joining the academic world, Dr. McKeen worked as a programmer, a systems analyst, and as a consultant. He convenes two quarterly forums for IT managers – the CIO Brief and the IT Management Forum.

Holmes E. Miller is an associate professor of Business at Muhlenberg College in Allentown, PA. He holds a Ph.D. from Northwestern University. Prior to joining Muhlenberg, he worked for several Fortune 500 companies in the chemical and financial services industries. His current research interests include decision making under risk, quality, and service sector operations management. He has published in *Operation Research, Socio–economic Planning Sciences,* and *Interfaces.*

Kathleen K. Molnar is an assistant professor at St. Norbert College. She earned a Ph.D. in MIS at Oklahoma State University in May 1997. Her background is interdisciplinary including a B.S. in Natural Science from Xavier University and an M.B.A. from the University of Wisconsin–Oshkosh. She has over ten years of commercial experience spanning programming, systems analysis, consulting, and directing a computer department. She has published in the *International Journal of Human–Computer Studies and the Journal of Information Technology* and has presented papers at the Decision Sciences Institute Conferences and the Americas Conferences on Information Systems. Her current research interests are telecommunications investments, the Internet and human–computer interaction.

Michael Parent is an assistant professor of MIS at the Richard Ivey School of Business at The University of Western Ontario, London, Canada. He received his Ph.D. in MIS and Marketing and M.B.A. from Queen's University. His research interests include the application of group support systems to multi–organizational groups, the use of IT in marketing management and strategy development, telecommunications, and the emerging popularity of the Internet and Intranets. Most recently, he has been involved in a research program to determine the relevance and utility of group support technology to strategy development by multifirm alliances. Prior to joining the academic world, he worked for over ten years in public and private sector organizations in Canada and abroad, specializing in marketing management, new product development, and technology transfer. His last position was as Director of the peripheral products division for the Canadian arm of a Japanese multinational firm.

Amarnath C. Prakash has over ten years of consulting experience in the area of Management Information Systems. He was a Manager (Systems Consulting) at Digital Equipment Corporation and a Senior Consultant at Royal Dutch/ Shell Oil and has consulted with various Fortune 500 companies such as Digital Equipment, Royal Dutch/Shell Oil, FedEx, HP, and TI in the areas of information systems analysis and design, interorganizational information systems, emerging technologies such as Client/Server Technology, Electronic Commerce, and Internet, and IS Management. He has over 30 leading publications in various IS journals such as *Information Systems Management, Journal of International Information Management, Cycle Time Research,* and numerous international and national conferences. Dr. Prakash is currently an assistant professor of MIS at the College of Business Administration at Texas Tech University, Lubbock, Texas.

Arun Rai is an associate professor in the Department of Decision Sciences at Georgia State University. His research interests include management of systems delivery processes, diffusion and infusion of information technologies, strategic alliances in the IT industry, an integration of information systems and management science for decisionmaking. He has published articles on these subjects in several journals including: *Communications of the*

ACM, *Journal of Management Information Systems, Decision Sciences, Decision Support Systems, European Journal of Information Systems, Computers & Operations Research, OMEGA, Long Range Planning,* and others. He is associate editor of *MIS Quarterly* and *Information Resources Management Journal,* and president of the Diffusion Interest Group on Information Technology.

David C. Rine received the Ph.D. in 1970 from the University of Iowa in the Mathematical Sciences Division with a dissertation in theoretical computer science. He has been in the computing field for over 30 years, working primarily with universities, but researching, consulting, and software and information systems developing in software for businesses and government agencies as well. He joined George Mason University in June 1985 and was the founding chair of the Department of Computer Science, as well as co–developer of the School of Information Technology and Engineering. He is presently a professor of Computer Science and Information Systems and Software Systems Engineering and senior researcher in the Center for Software Systems Engineering (CSSE) where he guides bachelors, masters, and doctoral level graduate students in the area of software engineering and information systems design. In the CSSE, he has been researching and teaching in the areas of object–oriented development, software maintenance–reuse–domain engineering, software engineering, information systems, and software development metrics environments. Within the span of his career in computing, he has published over 170 papers in the general areas of theoretical computer science, logic design (including multiple–valued logic and fuzzy logic), information systems, computational sciences, computer applications, computer education, software quality, and software engineering.

Erik Rolland is an assistant professor of Management Information Systems at the A. Gary Anderson Graduate School of Management, University of California, Riverside. Dr. Rolland's research interests include modeling for reasoning and decision making, the interface between computer science and management science, and organizational impacts of new technology. He is the author and co–author of numerous articles on information technology and modeling. His industry experience includes consulting and software engineering with major national and international companies. His Ph.D. is from Ohio State University.

Ramesh Sharda is the Conoco/DuPont Professor of Management of Technology and a professor of Management Science and Information Systems in the College of Business Administration at the Oklahoma State University. Currently, he also serves as the Interim Director of the M.S. in Telecommunications Management Program. He received his B.Eng. Degree from the University of Udaipur, M.S. from the Ohio State University and an M.B.A. and Ph.D. from the University of Wisconsin–Madison. He is the founding editor of Interactive Transactions of OR/MS. He is also a member of the editorial board of the *IJCIO,* the computer science editor of *OR/MS Today*, and an associate editor of the *ORSA Journal on Computing*. Ramesh has co–edited three books and is also the editor for a Kluwer book series in Computer Science/Operations Research Interfaces. His research interests are in optimization applications on desktop computers, information systems support for new product development, neural networks, business uses of the Internet, and policy analysis.

Sanjay Singh holds a Ph.D. in MIS from The University of Georgia. He is currently an assistant professor at The University of Alabama at Birmingham. He has published articles in journals like *Decision Support Systems, Database, Informatics & Telematics, Information Technology & People, Journal of Decision Systems, Management Accounting,* and *Radiology Management.* His research interests are electronic commerce; strategic, cultural, and legal issues of global and healthcare information systems. Having lectured and taught in eight countries, Dr. Singh is actively involved in setting up business education programs in the areas of international management and global information technology. He is involved in public policy formulation by serving on the Communication and Infrastructure Committee of the States of the Gulf of Mexico Accord, formed for the rapid implementation of NAFTA. Dr. Singh has also provided extensive consulting services to Fortune 500 companies in the areas of strategic management and information systems.

Heather A. Smith is a research associate at the School of Business, Queen's University. She has an M.A. from Queen's University and has worked in and researched business and non–profit organizations for over 20 years. Her interests include: the impact of I/T on organizations, identification of best management practices, and effective management of I/T. She is a founder and facilitator of the Queen's IT Management Forums and a research associate with the SIM Advanced Practices Council. Ms. Smith has published articles in *The Journal of Information Technology Management, The Canadian Journal of Administrative Studies, Information and Management, Strategic Information Technology Management: Perspectives on Organizational Growth and Competitive Advantage,* and *Business Process Change: Reengineering Concepts and Methods.* She is co–author with Yolande Chan of the *SIM Practitioner's Guide to I.S. Performance Measurement* and with J.D. McKeen of *Managing Information Systems: Strategies for Action.*

Robert Michael Sonnemann is an officer in the United States Air Force (USAF). He received his Bachelor of Science in Business Administration with a major in Management Information Systems from the University of Arizona, Tucson, Arizona, in 1979. He has a Master of Public Administration, Master of Business Administration and Master of Science in Computer Science. He received his Ph.D. from George Mason University in 1995 in the area of Software Systems Engineering. Throughout his 17 years in the USAF, he has worked in the areas of modeling and simulation, Ada software engineering, software and logistics testing, and software reuse. He was recently a Visiting

Scientist at the Software Engineering Institute, Carnegie–Mellon University, in 1993–95. He was certified Level III in Communication and Computers under the Acquisition Development Program, Defense Acquisition University, in 1995. He is currently working on enterprise–level domain specific architectures and software reuse with the USAF.

Cheickna Sylla received his M.S. and Ph.D. in Industrial Engineering from the State University of New York at Buffalo, New York. He is currently an associate professor in the School of Industrial Management at the New Jersey Institute of Technology. His research interests include quality assurance, decision support systems, and the modeling of training systems, etc. He published articles in *European Journal of Operational Research, IEEE Transactions on Engineering Management, Decision Sciences, Computers and Industrial Engineering, Human Factors*, etc. He is a member of ORSA and TIMS, IIE, APICS, ASQC and Human Factors Society.

Suresh (Reddy) K. Tadisina is an associate professor with the Department of Management, Southern Illinois University, Carbondale, Illinois. He holds a B.Eng. (Mech.) and an M.B.A. from Osmania University in India, and an M.B.A. and Ph.D. in Quantitative Analysis and Operations Management from the University of Cincinnati. He has published in *Computers & Operations Research, Decision Support Systems, IIE Transactions, Journal of Applied Business Research, Journal of the Operational Research Society, Mathematical and Computer Modeling, OMEGA, Malaysian Journal of Management Science, Project Management Journal* among others. His research interests include decision support/expert systems, mathematical programming in statistics, multicriteria decision making, operations strategy, and R&D management.

Tim Tatum is a staff member of the Virginia Commonwealth University Information Systems Research Institute in Richmond, Virginia. He has consulted with a number of organizations including the Virginia Department of Transportation. Additional project experience and publications have been in the areas of systems integration and engineering. Current interests include research into links between process and systems reengineering. His e–mail address is jtatum@vcu.edu.

Asher Tishler received his B.A. in Economics and Statistics from the Hebrew University, Israel, and his Ph.D. in Economics from the University of Pennsylvania. He is currently at the Faculty of Management at Tel Aviv University, Israel. His primary areas of research are applied microeconomics, econometrics, multivariate statistics and energy economics. His publications have appeared in the *Journal of Econometrics, Journal of Applied Econometrics, Review of Economics and Statistics, Energy Journal, Journal of the American Statistical Society, European Economic Review, Operations Research, Management Science*, and *Journal of Optimization Theory and Applications*.

Elizabeth R. Towell is an assistant professor in the Operations Management and Information Systems Department at Northern Illinois University. She received her Ph.D. in Management Information Systems from the University of Wisconsin at Milwaukee in 1993. She teaches courses in Operating Systems and Database Management Systems. Her publications include articles in the *Journal of Database Management, Internet Research, the Journal of Computer Information Systems, the Journal of Global Information Management and Interface*, the *Computer Education Quarterly*. She has conducted panel discussions, seminars, and training sessions on client–server technologies and the Internet for students, faculty, and community groups as well as for corporations such as Walgreens and McDonald's.

Marvin D. Troutt is the Rehn Research Professor of Management at Southern Illinois University, Carbondale, Illinois. His Ph.D. is in Mathematical Statistics from the University of Illinois at Chicago. He has worked as an actuary and also in higher education information systems. He has published articles in several journals including: *Management Science, Operations Research, INTERFACES, Decision Support Systems, Journal of the Operational Research Society, Computers & Operations Research, OMEGA, Operations Research Letters, Mathematical Programming, Naval Research Logistics*, and *European Journal of Operational Research*. He is an associate editor of *Decision Sciences* and recently served as the Visiting Fellow in the Applied Mathematics Department at the Hong Kong Polytechnic University.

William E. Wehrs is an associate professor of Management in the Management Department at the University of Wisconsin–LaCrosse. Professor Wehrs has maintained a long standing research interest in the area of information technology evaluation—especially economic evaluation. In addition to a master's degree in Management Information Systems, he also holds a Ph.D. in Economics.

H. Joseph Wen is an assistant professor of Information Systems at New Jersey Institute of Technology. He has published several papers in international academic journals. His area of expertise is multimedia decision support systems design (DSS), client/server systems, geographical information systems (GIS), and applying information technology in production management and transportation management. He currently conducted research projects for the New Jersey Department of Transportation (NJDOT), the National Center for Transportation and Industrial Productivity (NCTIP), and the New Jersey Transportation Planning Authority (NJTPA).

Aimao Zhang is a candidate for the Doctorate in Business Administration at Southern Illinois University at Carbondale, Illinois. Her interests include computing related to decision support, operations research, and rule induction for expert systems.

Index